MODERN WESTERN CIVILIZATION

MODERN WESTERN CIVILIZATION

JAMES R. CHRISTOPHER

GEORGE G. WITTET

Toronto
OXFORD UNIVERSITY PRESS

Oxford University Press
70 Wynford Drive, Don Mills, Ontario M3C 1J9

http://www.oupcan.com

Oxford New York Athens Auckland Bangkok Bogotá
Buenos Aires Calcutta Cape Town Chennai Dar es Salaam
Delhi Florence Hong Kong Istanbul Karachi Kuala Lumpur
Madrid Melbourne Mexico City Mumbai Nairobi Paris
São Paulo Singapore Taipei Tokyo Toronto Warsaw

and associated companies in
Berlin Ibadan

Canadian Cataloguing in Publication Data

Christopher, James, R., 1951–
Modern Western civilization

Includes bibliographical references.
ISBN 0-19-540661-3

1. Civilization, Occidental – History.
2. Civilization, Occidental – History – Sources.
3. Civilization, Modern. 4. Civilization, Modern – Sources.
5. History, Modern. 6. History, Modern – Sources.
I. Wittet, George Graham, 1951– . II. Title.

CB245.C48 1991 909'.09821 C90-095318-7

Senior Editor: Geraldine Kikuta
Project Editor: Loralee Case
Assistant Editor: Christine Anderson
Design Manager: Marie Bartholomew
Production Manager: Joanna Gertler
Cartography: Susan Calverly
Photo Editor: Natalie Pavlenko Lomago
Compositor: Q Composition Inc.

Printed and bound in Canada by The Bryant Press

6 7 8 9 BP 82 81 00

Contents

ACKNOWLEDGEMENTS

A book like this is the product of a lifetime of experiences and the influence of outstanding teacher colleagues. We have been extremely fortunate to have worked with talented professionals and we express our thanks to them.

We would also like to thank John Lord of the History Department at Stephen Leacock Collegiate Institute and Cam Coulter of The Woodlands Secondary School for their valuable reviews and comments on the manuscript.

Finally, we would like to thank our wives, Wendy Christopher and Anne Wittet, and our children, Brett, Brandon, and Mary-Kate Christopher and Jeremy Wittet, for their patience throughout this project. Their support has made this book possible.

Jack Bush, Night Spin *(acrylic on canvas, 1976).*
Reproduced by permission of the Estate of Jack Bush. Copyright 1990. Canadian artist Jack Bush's (1909–1977) painting evolved from figuration in the early years to abstraction in his mature paintings. Bush was known particularly for his use of colour. In his earlier works, these colours were often vibrant and intense. In his later paintings, however, he turned to softer colours presented across the canvas in an incredible array of hues. The artist died in January 1977.

The Origins of Modern Western Civilization

The continent of Europe in 1500 gave no indication that it was on the verge of global domination. After the collapse of the Roman Empire in the fifth century, Western Europe had split into a myriad of small political and economic units. During the medieval period, from approximately 450 to 1450, Western Europe had developed a culture that combined old Roman laws and traditions, Germanic practices, and Christian beliefs. During much of this time, society was organized into small, personal estates which were dominated by overlords who guaranteed physical security and social stability. This *feudal system*, which was characteristic of most of Europe, concentrated on local concerns and maintaining a subsistence economy.

By the eleventh century, pressures created by an increasing population and decreasing land productivity had led to severe economic problems. Small landowners were no longer able to support their families; tax revenues were falling; and squabbles were erupting as growing numbers of the landed aristocracy fought over the limited available land. These pressures were relieved to some extent by the Crusades, Western Europe's first imperialist venture since the fall of Rome. The Crusades were a series of military expeditions carried out between 1096 and 1272 by the Christian states of Western Europe against the Turkish Muslims, who had conquered the Middle East and were threatening the Christian Byzantine Empire. Although the battles of the Crusades were by and large military failures, they provided an outlet for large segments of the unemployed and restless population and thus produced some relief for the problems of overcrowding and economic uncertainty in Europe. As a result, the standard of living improved for those who stayed behind. Perhaps even more importantly, however, the Crusades re-established contact with the remnants of classical civilization. As the European armies passed through Constantinople, they became reacquainted with many of the ideas and products of the Far and Middle East. These contacts would have a lasting effect on European civilization.

With the reopening of direct contact between the two regions, the Crusades sparked an increase in east-west trade, especially through the Italian city-states of Venice, Florence, Genoa, Pisa, and Milan. As trade grew between Europe and the Orient, the ruling classes of medieval society became more dependent upon the new luxury goods they were receiving from abroad. When trade routes were closed down again with the fall of Constantinople to the Turks in 1453, this dependence encouraged the European ruling classes to look for alternative sea routes to re-establish contact, thus sparking an era of overseas expansion.

The Crusades, however, marked more than a political or economic turning point in European society. The initial call to arms had been made by the spiritual leader of Europe, the Pope. In a generally decentralized world, one institution had emerged to unify most of the continent: the Roman Catholic church. In the vacuum left by the collapse of the political order of the Romans in the West, the Church had developed into the centre of law and commerce as well as of religion. Western Europe was referred to as Christendom, and there is no question that in early modern Europe no individual exercised more power than the Pope. Not only were the papal authorities theologians, but they tended to act as lawyers, diplomats, and economic advisors as well. While by 1500 papal power had decreased from its peak during medieval times, the Roman Catholic church was still the predominant force as modern Western civilization began to emerge.

The other significant development in the early modern period was the growth of cities. Although they played an important role in classical times, cities had declined during the Middle Ages as people had come to depend on local agriculture for their survival. As living conditions became more secure, however, there was a gradual regrowth in urban population. Increasing trade created a need for new markets and production centres. New crafts resulted in the growth of a skilled working class. Overseas commerce expanded the need for ports and transportation facilities. Although the population of the average town was about 5000 during this period, more prominent cities, such as Milan and Venice, boasted over 100 000 residents. Perhaps the best indicator of urban growth in Europe was Paris. Its population of 100 000 in 1200 had more than doubled by 1300, and had topped half a million by 1650.

The growth in cities meant the emergence of a new merchant class. More wealthy and independent than the peasant farmers, and not as powerful as the landed aristocracy, these new merchants were called the middle class, or *bourgeoisie*. Eventually they would come to dominate the course of Western civilization. Their appetite for new raw materials and expanded markets would be responsible for the drive for overseas exploration and settlement. It is not surprising, therefore, that the most prominent merchant classes appeared in cities such as Amsterdam, Paris, and London.

By 1500, Europe was on the verge of an economic explosion called the Commercial Revolution. The population had reached 65 million and would rise to 90 million a century later. The work force was increasing, and along with it the production of goods. When the east-west trade route was closed in 1453, European merchants looked westward in search of new routes to wealth. The world they faced, however, was not a vulnerable one waiting to fall prey to their advances. In fact, Western civilization was at a comparative disadvantage when measured against its Middle and Far Eastern competitors in 1500.

First, Europe was strategically vulnerable. It had no central authority, which meant invaders could conquer small sections of the continent piecemeal with no strong opposition; southeastern Europe was especially vulnerable to this type of attack, as the Ottoman Turks would prove over the next 150 years. In addition, northern Europe was icebound much of the year, there were no natural barriers between the Europeans and attackers from the eastern plains, and the west and south had long, easily accessible coastlines.

Second, Europe was technologically and culturally backward compared to the great Asian civilizations such as China. In the fields of art, music, mathematics, engineering, industry, and navigation, Western civilization lagged far behind their accomplishments. Many of Europe's scientific achievements were borrowed from the Islamic world.

So why did Europe emerge and expand to dominate the world? It is critical to note that at the moment when Western civilization was beginning to mature in Europe and was looking to expand beyond the continent, many of the other great powers, such as the Ottoman Empire, Northern India, and Ming China, had reached their peaks or were already in decline. European civilization, on the other hand, was vital and growing. Historian Paul Kennedy, in his book *The Rise and Fall of the Great Powers*, claims that Europe had a unique dynamic that was driven by new economic and technological advances. In fact, many of Europe's "disadvantages" actually proved to be strengths. The political fragmentation created a decentralized and highly competitive environment. While there was no central authority to encourage development, there was none to suppress it either. The resulting progress might have been uneven, but it was fast paced. Small political units also meant that no nation was self-sufficient. Trade in both staple and luxury goods led to the development of a sophisticated system of international trade, banking, and commerce. In addition, ships capable of conducting year-round trade in the stormy north Atlantic soon proved their worth on global expeditions.

Finally, like the world of the late twentieth century, the international political competition of the 1500s led to an escalating arms race. European nations, striving to outdo one another, soon outstripped the rest of the world. As a result, modern Western civilization began to spread beyond the boundaries of Europe, carried by the most efficient and well-armed armies and navies on the globe.

THE STUDY OF MODERN WESTERN CIVILIZATION

At first glance, the study of five centuries of Western civilization seems to be a monumental undertaking. It requires students to become familiar with the interrelationships among political, social, economic, and cultural forces in a wide variety of places and time periods. In order to facilitate our study, this book will examine the history of modern Western civilization in terms of five basic themes.

The Individual and the Community

This theme examines the relationship between the rights of the individual and the demands and powers of the state. We will consider such topics as political theories and philosophies, human rights, and dissent and revolution.

Humanity and Nature

This theme considers not only the interrelationship between humankind and the global environment, but the changing attitudes toward the world as reflected in art, music, science, and society.

Economy and Technology

No study of Western civilization would be complete without an in-depth look at the major economic trends and technological developments of the past 500 years. Topics to be considered include the Industrial Revolution, international trade and trading blocs, economic theories, and post-industrial technological change.

Values

Human values and beliefs are critical to understanding past events. Why did certain events happen? How have the experiences of the past shaped the contemporary ethical values of Western civilization? These are some of the values questions we will consider.

The Arts and Society

This theme will examine the arts (including the visual arts, music, drama, architecture, and literature) as a reflection of social values and a shaper of social trends.

It is difficult to travel into the past without taking our contemporary ideas along with us. We tend to examine past events, people, and ideas with the benefit of hindsight rather than from the perspective of the people living at the time. As a result, students of history often make the mistake of assuming that the actual outcome of events was either obvious or inevitable. This is often a critical error. Every historical investigation should begin with an attempt to transplant oneself into the physical and mental setting of the participants. It is only when we come to understand not only *how* people thought and acted but *why* they did so that we can begin to apply the more sophisticated tools of historical analysis to events.

It is therefore necessary for us to take a candid and unrestricted view of the past. This is often difficult. Evidence can be fragmented and contradictory. Winners tend to preserve the records of their ideas and deeds more completely than losers; the attitudes of men tend to be recorded more often than those of women; the viewpoints of racial and linguistic minorities are often not heard at all.

In this book, each chapter is divided into two distinct sections. The first half examines a particular historical period, theme, or concept. Information, ideas, and analyses are provided from the perspective of our own twentieth-century Canadian society. The second half of each chapter allows the participants in events to speak to us in their own words. These primary sources provide us with a direct window on the past. The ideas expressed are either those that were in fashion at the time or the opinions of subsequent generations of historians.

We may find many of the ideas and actions of past societies alien or even repugnant to us today. Attitudes toward various racial and religious groups and women often reflect a point of view that is no longer acceptable in our day and age. So why do we include these ideas in this book? We hope the answer is obvious. It does a disservice to whitewash the past. To understand why people acted as they did, we must first understand how they thought. As a result, many of the primary sources reflect a variety of viewpoints or *biases*. Part of your task will be to uncover these biases and to deal with them in their historical contexts. The first half of each chapter is designed to provide the analytical background to do this, but you should also ask yourself the following questions when you are considering the primary source materials.

1. Who is speaking? What is her/his background? What is her/his point of view?
2. Why was the document written? Is it a personal diary or does it have an intended audience with certain demands or expectations?
3. What contradictory viewpoints are presented? How do their arguments compare?
4. What is the historical background of the document? Is it being written in a time of crisis or during a period of stability?
5. What were the prevailing social, political, and economic attitudes at the time the document was written? How might these have affected the point of view being expressed?

It is easy for us to sit in judgment on the past. After years or decades of further experience, even novice historians may find themselves in a position to see through the biases of participants in historical events. That is why it is important to recognize biases as well as their historical contexts. The result will be a more complete and intellectually mature understanding of the past.

Louis XIV founded the Observatory in 1667. Here the members of the Academy of Sciences were presented to the king.

PART ONE

From Enlightenment to Revolution, 1638 to 1815

During the seventeenth and eighteenth centuries, philosophers, scientists, artists, and many members of the educated middle and upper classes believed that they were living in an Age of Enlightenment. This was characterized by a scientific revolution that changed humanity's relationship with the natural universe, questioned the political principles that formed the basis of the absolutist state, re-evaluated traditional religious values and beliefs, and ultimately revolted against the established order.

An outgrowth of the medieval period, absolute rule characterized many European states. Often the system was supported by the hierarchical structure of the established church. As scientists began to identify natural laws and systems within nature, many of the church's traditional assumptions and beliefs were called into question. In addition, the scientific method was applied to government. Philosophers began to ask fundamental questions, such as What was life like in the "state of nature" before there were governments? What is the purpose of government? What should be the relationship between the state and its citizens? And what are the natural rights of all people?

Many people concluded that government was no longer fulfilling its intended role and called for changes to the system and a restructuring of government based upon natural law. Two Western nations revolted against the existing order and attempted to put the ideas of the Enlightenment into practice. In the British Thirteen Colonies of North America, Enlightenment ideals were incorporated into a Declaration of Independence from colonial rule. The new United States of America became the first Western nation to apply the writings of the philosophers to the practical realities of government. In the second instance, the slow application of new ideas under Louis XVI in France did not keep pace with the demands of its citizens. The result was the violent overthrow of the existing order and a quarter of a century of upheaval for all of Western civilization.

In art, this rejection of the excesses of aristocratic life found expression in the neoclassicist movement. Harkening back to the ideal beauty of ancient Athens and the simple values of republican Rome, this return to classical lines and motifs paralleled the social goals of revolutionary Europe. Like Rome, republican France would eventually fall prey to its own imperial ambitions, and the conquests of Napoleon Bonaparte would spread the ideas of nationalism and liberalism across the continent.

	POLITICS	PHILOSOPHY/LEARNING	ART	SCIENCE/TECHNOLOGY
1600	1603 Coronation of James I of England 1610 Henry IV of France assassinated; succeeded by Louis XIII		1600 Shakespeare, *Hamlet* 1601 Caravaggio, *Conversion of St. Paul* 1605 Cervantes, *Don Quixote* Shakespeare, *King Lear, Macbeth* 1607 Monteverdi, *Orfeo* 1614 Rubens, *Descent from the Cross*	1600 Gilbert, *De Magnete* 1609 Kepler, *The New Astronomy* 1610 Galileo, *Sidereal Messenger* 1620 Bacon, *Novum Organum*
1620	1625 James I of England succeeded by Charles I 1637 Ferdinand III becomes Holy Roman Emperor		1623 Mansart, St. Marie de la Visitation 1624 Poussin, *Rape of the Sabine Women* 1631 Lemercier, Chateau Richelieu 1639 da Cortona, *Allegory of Divine Providence and Barberini Power*	1628 Harvey, *On the Movement of the Heart and Blood* 1632 Galileo, *Dialogue on Two World Systems* 1637 Descartes, *Discourse on Method*
1640	1642 English Civil War begins 1643 Louis XIII succeeded by Louis XIV 1646 English Civil War ends 1649 Charles I of England beheaded 1654 Coronation of Louis XIV	1651 Hobbes, *Leviathan*	1642 Rembrandt, *The Night Watch* 1643 Corneille, *Polyeucte* 1644 Bernini, Cornaro Chapel 1652 Bernini, *Vision of the Ecstasy of St. Theresa* 1656 Velasquez, *Las Meninas*	1643 Torricelli invents the barometer 1652 von Guericke invents the air pump
1660	1661 Coronation of Charles II of England 1665 Charles II of Spain succeeds Philip IV	1675 Spinoza, *Ethics*	1661 Versailles begun 1666 Molière, *Le Misanthrope* 1667 Milton, *Paradise Lost* Racine, *Andromaque* 1675 Von Ruisdael, *The Jewish Cemetery* Wren begins St. Paul's Cathedral Wychereley, *The Country Wife*	1661 Boyle, *The Sceptical Chemist* 1665 Hooke, *Micrographia*
1680	1685 Charles II of England succeeded by James II 1688 James II flees to France 1689 William of Orange assumes English throne	1690 Locke, *Two Treatises of Civil Government*	1681 Dryden, "Absolom and Achitophel" 1691 Purcell, *The Fairy Queen* 1695 Congreve, *Love for Love*	1687 Newton, *The Mathematical Principles of Natural Philosophy*
1700	1701 King Frederick I becomes first King of Prussia			

Time lines are based on Bernard Grun, *The Timetables of History* (New York: Simon and Schuster, 1963, 1975); Isaac Asimov, *Asimov's Chronology of Science and Discovery* (New York: Harper and Row, 1989); and Alexander Hellemans and Bryan Bunch, *The Timetables of Science* (New York: Simon and Schuster, 1988).

	POLITICS	PHILOSOPHY/LEARNING	ART	SCIENCE/TECHNOLOGY
1700	1702 William II succeeded by Queen Anne 1713 Peace of Utrecht Frederick William I of Prussia succeeds Frederick I 1715 Louis XV succeeds Louis XIV		1711 *The Spectator* begun by Addison and Steele 1717 Watteau, *Embarkation for the Isle of Cythera* Handel, *Water Music* 1719 Defoe, *Robinson Crusoe*	1714 Fahrenheit introduces his temperature scale 1717 Inoculation against smallpox begins in England
1720	1721 Peter I proclaimed King of all the Russias	1733 Voltaire, *Philosophical Letters on the English*	1720 Boffrand and Neumann, The Residenz 1722 Bach, *The Well-Tempered Clavier* 1726 Swift, *Gulliver's Travels* 1733 Pope, *Essay on Man* 1735 Hogarth, *The Rake's Progress*	1733 Kay invents the flying shuttle loom 1735 Linneas, *System Naturae* 1738 Excavation of Herculaneum begun
1740	1740 Marie Theresa assumes power in Austria; Frederick II assumes power in Prussia 1745 Charles VII, Holy Roman Emperor 1746 Ferdinand VI assumes power in Spain	1748 Hume, *Philosophical Essays Concerning Human Understanding* Montesquieu, *The Spirit of the Laws* 1751 French *Encyclopédie* begins publication (ends 1772)	1741 Handel, *The Messiah* 1742 Boucher, *Diana after her Bath* 1749 Fielding, *History of Tom Jones* 1751 Voltaire, *The Age of Louis XIV* 1757 Soufflot, "The Pantheon"	1745 von Kliest invents the capacitor (Leyden jar) 1752 Franklin invents the lightning conductor
1760	1760 George III assumes power in England 1762 Catherine II of Russia succeeds Peter III 1763 Peace of Paris 1774 Louis XVI succeeds Louis XV 1776 American Declaration of Independence	1763 Voltaire, "Treatise on Tolerance" 1767 de Nemours, *Physiocracy* 1776 Smith, *An Inquiry into the Nature and Causes of the Wealth of Nations*	1761 Rousseau, *Nouvelle Héloïse* 1766 Goldsmith, *The Vicar of Wakefield* Fragonard, *The Swing* 1770 Gainsborough, *The Blue Boy* 1774 Goethe, *The Sorrows of Werther* 1776 Gibbon, *Decline and Fall of the Roman Empire* 1779 Lessing, *Nathan the Wise*	1761 Avenbrugger, *Inventum Novum* 1767 Priestley, *The History and Present State of Electricity* 1775 Watt perfects the steam engine
1780	1783 Britain recognizes U.S. independence 1788 Estates-General called for May 1789 U.S. Constitution comes into force 1789 Meeting of Estates-General Tennis Court Oath	1781 Kant, *Critique of Pure Reason* 1783 Mendelssohn, *Jerusalem* 1788 Lemprière, *Classical Dictionary* 1789 Sieyes, *What is the Third Estate?* Bentham, *Introduction to the Principles of Morals and Legislation*	1781 Mozart, *Idomeneo* 1783 David, *Grief of Andromanche* 1785 David, *Oath of the Horatii* 1786 Mozart, *The Marriage of Figaro* 1787 Mozart, *Don Giovanni* 1789 Blake, *Songs of Innocence*	1781 Discovery of Uranus 1785 Salsano develops seismograph 1789 Jussien, *Genera plantarum* Galvani conducts experiments on muscular contraction

	POLITICS	PHILOSOPHY/LEARNING	ART	SCIENCE/TECHNOLOGY
1780	1789 Formation of the National Assembly Fall of the Bastille Abolition of feudalism Declaration of the Rights of Man and of Citizens			
1790	1790 Louis XVI accepts the constitution Civil Constitution of the Clergy 1791 Louis's flight to Varennes 1792 Legislative Assembly suspended Royal family imprisoned Trial of Louis XVI 1793 Louis XVI executed Committee of Public Safety established Reign of Terror begins Marat murdered Marie Antoinette executed First coalition formed against France 1794 Terror ends 1795 The Directory Napoleon appointed commander-in-chief in Italy 1797 Peace of Campo Formio 1798 French proclaim Roman republic Napoleon's Egyptian campaign Nelson defeats French fleet at Abukir Bay 1799 Napoleon leaves Egypt Austria declares war on France	1790 Burke, *Reflections on the Revolution in France* 1791 Paine, *The Rights of Man* 1792 Young, *Travels in France* Wollstonecraft, *Vindication of the Rights of Woman* 1793 Fichte, *Contribution to the Correction of the Public's Judgement Regarding the French Revolution* 1794 Paine, *The Age of Reason* 1798 Malthus, *Essay on the Principle of Population* 1799 Herder, *Metacritique of the Critique of Pure Reason*	1790 Mozart, *Cosi fan tutte* 1791 Langhans, Brandenburg Gate 1793 David, *The Murder of Marat* 1794 Blake, *Songs of Experience* 1796 Goya, *Los Caprichos* 1797 Coleridge, *Kubla Khan* Haydn, *Emperor Quartet* 1798 Wordsworth and Coleridge, *Lyrical Ballads* 1799 David, *Rape of the Sabine Women* Beethoven, Symphony No. 1 Haydn, *The Creation* (oratorio)	1790 Lavoisier, *Table of Thirty-one Chemical Elements* 1794 Legendre, *Elements of Geometrie* 1796 Vaccination against smallpox begins 1798 Senefelder invents lithography
1800	1800 Napoleon, First Consul 1802 Napoleon First Consul for life 1803 Louisiana Purchase 1804 Duc d'Enghien executed Napoleon proclaimed emperor 1805 Battle of Austerlitz	1802 Bentham, *Civil and Penal Legislation* 1804 Brown, *Inquiry into the Relation of Cause and Effect*	1800 Mme de Staël, *On Literature* 1802 Canova, Sculpture of Napoleon Bonaparte Beethoven, Symphony No. 2 1804 Schiller, *Wilhelm Tell* Beethoven, *Eroica*	1800 Volta invents first battery 1802 Dalton introduces atomic theory into chemistry

	POLITICS	PHILOSOPHY/LEARNING	ART	SCIENCE/TECHNOLOGY
1800	1806 Battles of Jena and Auerstadt Berlin Decree begins the Continental Blockade Confederation of the Rhine founded 1807 Battle of Eylau Battle of Friedland Treaty of Tilsit 1808 France occupies Rome, invades Spain Rebellion in Madrid Napoleon abolishes the Inquisition in Spain and Italy 1809 Napoleon annexes Papal States Pope Pius VII taken prisoner Metternich becomes chief minister of Austria	1806 Fichte, *The Way Towards the Blessed Life* 1807 Hufeland, *New Foundations of Political Economy* 1809 Ricardo, *The High Price of Bullion*	1807 David, *Coronation of Napoleon* 1808 Goethe, *Faust*, Part I Beethoven, *Pastoral Symphony* Goya, *Execution of the Citizens of Madrid*	1807 Bell, *System of Comparative Survery* 1808 Guy-Lussac, *The Combination of Gases*
1810	1810 Napoleon annexes Holland 1812 Napoleon's Russian campaign U.S. declares war on Britain 1813 "Battle of the Nations" at Leipzig French expelled from Holland 1814 Napoleon abdicates, exiled to Elba Louis XVIII assumes French throne Congress of Vienna begins Treaty of Ghent ends War of 1812 1815 Napoleon returns to France Louis XVIII flees Napoleon defeated at Waterloo Napoleon banished to St. Helena Second Peace of Paris	1812 Hegel, *Die objektive Logik* 1813 Owen, *A New View of Society* 1814 Chateaubriand, *De Buonaparte et les Bourbons* 1815 Malthus, *An Inquiry into the Nature and Progress of Rent* Ricardo, *The Influence of a Low Price of Corn on the Profits of Stocks*	1810 Mme de Staël, *De l'Allemagne* Goya, *The Disasters of War* 1812 Grimm, *Fairy Tales* 1813 Austen, *Pride and Prejudice* 1814 Goya, *The Second of May, 1808* *The Third of May, 1808* Ingres, *L'Odalisque* 1815 Canova, *The Three Graces*	1812 Davy, *Elements of Chemical Philosophy* 1814 Berzelius, *Theory of Chemical Proportions* 1815 Lamarck, *Histoire naturelle des animaux*

CHAPTER ONE

Absolutism in the Age of Reason

THE INDIVIDUAL AND THE COMMUNITY: THE EMERGENCE OF ABSOLUTISM

Modern Western civilization is the product of the cultural legacies of the ancient and medieval past. Our languages, laws, religions, art, architecture, science, and philosophy all bear the unmistakable stamp of these influences. Yet Western civilization is more than the reinterpretation of cultural legacies. The sixteenth and seventeenth centuries saw rapid revolutionary changes that dramatically altered Western civilization and the world.

The fundamental characteristics of modern Western civilization emerged in the sixteenth and seventeenth centuries. Society was becoming more secular in its orientation and people were placing greater faith and trust in science than in religion. The philosophy and practices of capitalism awaited only the Industrial Revolution to reach maturity. The centralized, democratic, parliamentary governments that today characterize Western society were evolving in the developing nation-states, where the forces of nationalism were being slowly forged by language and other cultural traits.

During this period, philosophers, scientists, artists, and the educated middle and upper classes believed that they were living in a new era, an "Age of Enlightenment." As new ideas challenged the accepted norms of the old order, Western society began to move toward a period of violent upheaval and change.

The medieval past was not abandoned overnight. In fact, the transition to the modern world began during the Renaissance and continued until the French Revolution. During this period, many parts of Europe underwent a process of political consolidation. Gradually, through marriage, inheritance, or force, small feudal kingdoms began to coalesce into large nation-states ruled by a member of a single family—an *absolute monarch*.

Absolute monarchs ruled by divine right. James I of England (1566–1625), in a speech before Parliament in 1610, argued that "Kings are not only God's lieutenants upon earth and sit upon God's throne" but they "exercise a manner or resemblance of divine power on earth." (See readings.) Absolute monarchs possessed unfettered power, unhindered by a constitution or any other agency. They dominated all other political and social institutions, including the Church and the aristocracy. As a result, not only the land but also the people of a country were considered to be the personal property of the ruler. The person of the monarch came to symbolize the embodiment of the nation-state.

L'état c'est moi: Absolutism in France

The epitome of the absolute monarch was Louis XIV (1638–1715) of France. His reign, the longest in French history, saw a degree of centralized control hitherto unknown in Europe.

Louis is said to have proclaimed "L'état, c'est moi"—"I am the state." Whether or not this is true, he clearly believed in the concept. In the sixty-one years of his reign, Louis never called upon the Estates-General, the representative body of the three estates in France, to participate in the government. All of Louis's decisions were final, and parliament was not permitted to interfere with their implementation. Under Louis, the members of the French nobility were reduced to courtiers, shorn of power but not of privilege, while the growing bourgeoisie remained content to live under the rule of a monarch.

The key to Louis's power lay in his administrative machinery. His bureaucracy was led by six ministers—the chancellor (who was in charge of the justice system), the controller-general of finance, and four secretaries of state. Under this central ministry were thirty-four royal *intendants* who administered provinces in the king's name. In theory, municipal leaders came under the direct control of these *intendants*. In reality, however, in an age before rapid transportation and communication, local authorities were too far from the centre of power, resulting in little effective royal administration at that level.

Louis's administration was highly dependent upon competent ministers. One of the greatest of these was Jean-Baptiste Colbert (1619–1683), who was controller-general of finance for over twenty years. Colbert reformed the chaotic system of taxation by suppressing many of the abuses of collection and making taxation more uniform throughout the country. He reorganized industry and commerce by encouraging industrial development, regulating quality, granting monopolies, and revising the tariff system. To implement these *mercantilist* policies, he expanded the navy and encouraged the building of merchant vessels. Colbert's reforms doubled revenue within ten years, but the conflicting aims of Colbert and Louis blunted many of the minister's initiatives. While Colbert wanted to use the increased revenue to further the country's economic development, Louis used it to wage wars against France's European neighbours and to increase the splendours of his court.

Louis XIV was the centre of attention at Versailles. This painting shows him having breakfast with playwright Molière, surrounded by servants and courtiers.

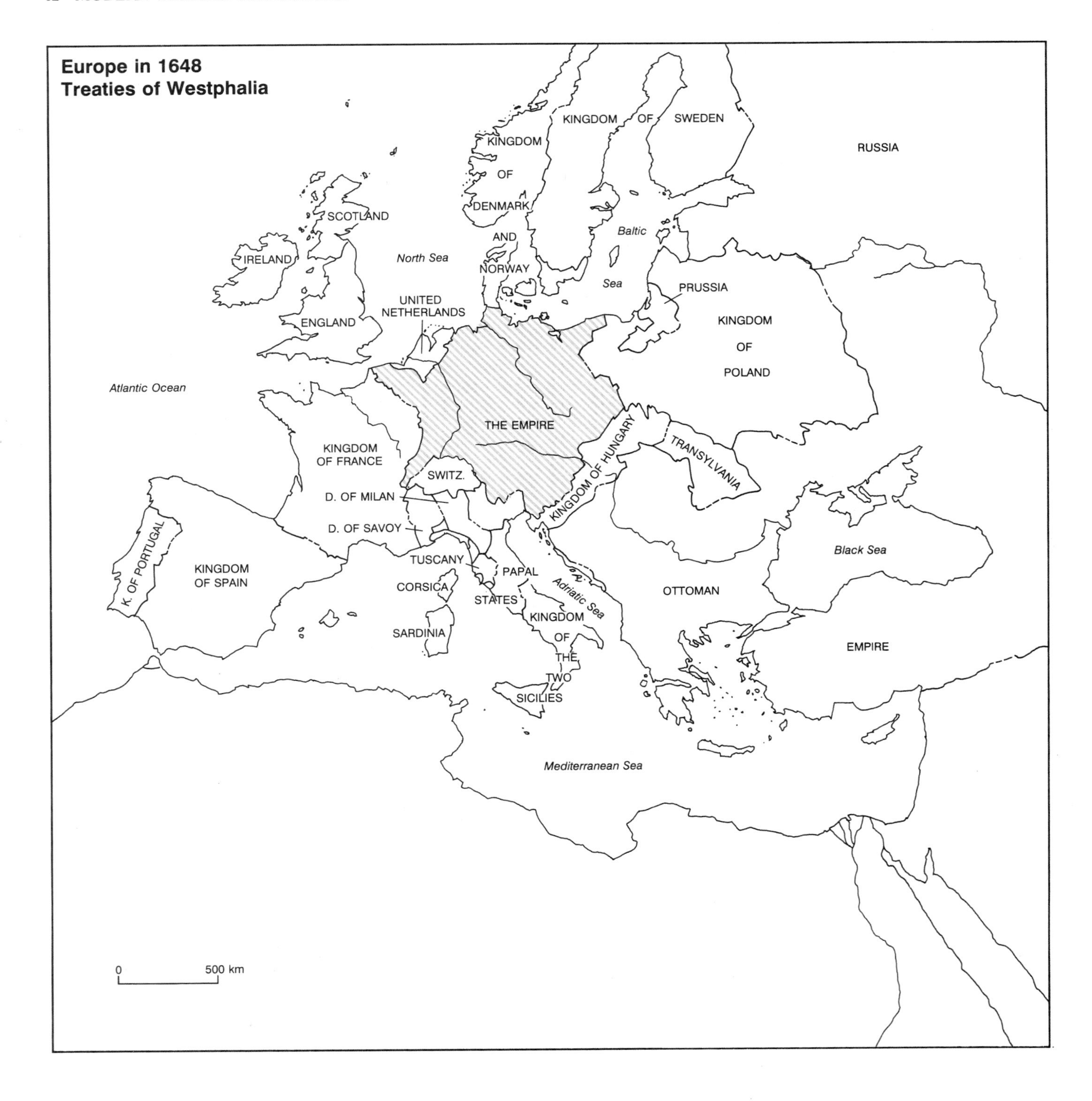
Europe in 1648
Treaties of Westphalia
KINGDOM OF SWEDEN
RUSSIA
KINGDOM OF DENMARK AND NORWAY
SCOTLAND
IRELAND
North Sea
Baltic Sea
PRUSSIA
UNITED NETHERLANDS
ENGLAND
KINGDOM OF POLAND
Atlantic Ocean
THE EMPIRE
KINGDOM OF FRANCE
TRANSYLVANIA
SWITZ.
KINGDOM OF HUNGARY
D. OF MILAN
D. OF SAVOY
K. OF PORTUGAL
KINGDOM OF SPAIN
TUSCANY
PAPAL STATES
CORSICA
Adriatic Sea
Black Sea
OTTOMAN EMPIRE
SARDINIA
KINGDOM OF THE TWO SICILIES
Mediterranean Sea
0
500 km

LOUIS DE ROUVROY,
The Duke of Saint-Simon

The Duke of Saint-Simon (1675–1755) was a descendant of a noble French family that traced its roots to the Dark Ages and the court of the powerful ruler Charlemagne. A musketeer in the service of Louis XIV, Saint-Simon later became a regular attendant of the court at Versailles. As an independent noble, his life at court "allowed him to observe in intimate fashion the behaviour of the several hundred courtiers with their jealousies, ambitions, and acceptance of personal abasement in the search for royal favours." A natural enemy of centralized power, Saint-Simon eventually fell out of favour with the king and was isolated from the mainstream of political decision-making.

In 1694, Saint-Simon began to keep the notes that would eventually evolve into his *Memoirs*. (See readings.) Written primarily between 1740 and 1750, his work is a scathing attack on life in Louis's court. Although some of Saint-Simon's observations were based more on rumour than fact, his accounts nonetheless provide a fascinating insider's view of the personalities and intrigues that characterized life at Versailles.

Louis XIV took very special care to be well informed about everything that was going on . . . in public and in private. . . . He had an infinity of spies . . . of every kind. Some were ignorant of the fact that their relations went all the way to him, others knew it. . . .

But the cruelest of all the ways by which the king was kept informed, and it was many years before this was realized, and many never did realize it . . . was by opening letters. . . .

It is impossible to understand how promptly and efficiently this was done. The king saw extracts from every letter . . . which the chiefs of the postal service . . . judged should reach him.

A word of criticism of the king or the government, a bit of sarcasm could ruin one forever.

Foreign Policy under the Sun King

Under Louis, France's external policies were directed toward extending the country's frontiers to the "natural boundaries" of ancient Gaul: the Rhine, the Alps, and the Pyrenees. These expansionist policies were implemented at the expense of Holland, Germany, Italy, and Spain and led to four costly wars: the War of Devolution (1667–1668), the Dutch War (1672–1678), the War of the League of Augsburg (1688–1697), and the War of the Spanish Succession (1701–1714). Although the wars enlarged France's territory and provided it with more strategic boundaries, the half-century of conflict united most of Europe against the French nation. The expense of the wars and the neglect of the navy and colonial empire during this period were to haunt Louis's successors. (See the Seven Years' War on page 16.)

Louis also used his increased tax revenue to create the most magnificent court in all of Europe. Until 1682, the French court had been nomadic; after that, it was permanently centred 20 km southwest of Paris at Versailles. Louis spared no expense in building the Palace of Versailles, calling upon the greatest artists in Europe to contribute their talents to the glory of *Le Roi Soleil*—"the Sun King."

To secure royal favour, once powerful aristocrats had to spend much of their time living at or near the court. Louis provided lavish entertainment for his guests, who competed for the privilege of attending him. As a result, Versailles became the playground for displaced nobility and housed 10 000 semipermanent guests. The court attracted writers, artists, sculptors, and musicians. The royal patronage of Louis XIV encouraged the most brilliant cultural era in French history. During Louis's reign, France became the envy of all of Europe and the model for imitation. Even the French language was adopted extensively by the European upper classes. (See readings.)

Upon his death in 1715, however, Louis XIV left a divided legacy. He had increased the borders of France, but at the expense of creating enemies throughout Europe. He had encouraged the arts, but in doing so had spent vast sums of money that ultimately crippled the treasury. His policies were directed toward increasing the glories of himself and the nation, but they largely ignored the people of France. His death marked a resurgence of the political power of the nobility, which produced conflict for his successors and led to the French Revolution.

THE COURT OF LOUIS XIV

Louis XIV's bedchamber illustrated the baroque union of the arts. Interior decoration, furnishings, painting, and culture all combined to celebrate the glory of the Sun King.

More than any other ruler of his day, Louis XIV understood the importance of using theatre and ritual to create the illusion that he had supernatural powers. With the extravagant palace at Versailles serving as a kind of stage, Louis and the thousands of people making up his court performed their daily activities like actors and actresses in a play. "Those who imagine that these are merely matters of ceremony," wrote the king, "are gravely mistaken."

The Sun King began the "performance" with his morning rise from bed. Like the first scene of a day-long play, *courtiers*, or nobles from the court, competed for the privilege of attending the king as he rolled from his luxurious bed and dressed in his royal garb. Nobles then followed Louis through the rest of his day, becoming both audience and performers.

After a morning of work, the king made his afternoon entrance, gathering nobles to accompany him in some outdoor activity. Often, this scene took Louis and his courtiers to the forests and meadows outside the palace, where he rode a favorite horse and hunted deer.

Walking on the grounds of Versailles also occupied many of Louis's afternoons. With members of the court struggling to keep up with him, Louis walked briskly by the thousands of fountains and many formal gardens around the grounds. He stopped only to listen to music played by small orchestras set up at various points.

In the evening, the entertainment moved inside, with the king playing billiards for about an hour every night. The evening usually continued with music and dancing and ended with a closing scene much like the opening, with members of the court attending the king as he prepared for bed.

To bring variety to his "theatre," Louis staged lavish events called *divertissements*, which lasted up to three weeks. During a *divertissement*, daytime entertainment included performances of the latest works by the greatest French playwrights, as well as mock battles. The days usually ended with boating on the canals and lakes around Versailles, accompanied by music and magnificent fireworks displays. Evening entertainment consisted of grand balls, where hundreds of guests danced to the music of court composer Jean-Baptiste Lully.

The Sun King's elaborate staging of court life created an atmosphere that surrounded him with what seemed to others like supernatural powers. Drawn into this atmosphere, aristocrats largely became what the Sun King wished—planets revolving around him.

From Peter N. Stearns, Donald R. Schwartz, and Barry K. Beyer, *World History: Traditions and New Directions* (Menlo Park, CA: Addison-Wesley Publishing Company, 1990), p. 383.

THE EMERGENCE OF THE STATE ECONOMY

As the nation-state developed, the monarchy became increasingly involved in the economy. Taxes supported a standing army and paid for the construction of roads, canals, and bridges and the clearing of land and the draining of marshes. A national currency was instituted, standardized weights and measures were introduced, and internal barriers to commerce, such as tolls, were reduced or eliminated. Government involvement in the economy grew substantially as a result of expanding markets, colonization, and the Commercial Revolution. By the seventeenth century, there was an acceptance of government participation in and regulation of economic affairs.

The Development of Mercantilism

The belief that national prosperity was linked to international trade was the essence of *mercantilism*. Mercantile theorists such as Thomas Mun (1571–1641) believed that the means of increasing a nation's wealth was "by Forraign Trade, wherin wee must observe this rule; to sell more to strangers than we consume of theirs in value." (See readings.)

In the early seventeenth century, the most successful commercial expansion was carried out by the Dutch. By mid-century they controlled New Amsterdam (New York), the northeast coast of Brazil, and the Cape of Good Hope in South Africa. Their merchant marine was second to none. In 1669, French finance minister Colbert estimated that of the 20 000 vessels plying the maritime trade in Europe, between 15 000 and 16 000 were Dutch.

Both the French and the English tried to cut into this near monopoly with a series of protectionist regulatory policies. Government subsidies were provided to established industries, such as woollens in England and paper and textiles in France. New industries, such as French silks, were established with government assistance. But the success of domestic mercantilist policies was dependent upon the establishment and exploitation of overseas colonies.

Under mercantilism, colonies existed for the sole economic benefit of the home country. Government regulations, such as the English Navigation Acts of 1651, 1663, and 1670, closed colonial ports to foreign commerce. Raw materials from the colonies fueled domestic industry, while the colonies provided a ready market for finished goods. All exports to and imports from the colonies were restricted to ships of the home country.

As the colonies prospered and expanded, their importance became even greater. England and France had established competing colonies in North America, the Caribbean, and India. Their rivalry for commercial supremacy led to a series of conflicts, which reached their peak during the Seven Years' War (1756–1763). By 1763 the English had won, controlling both North America and India.

The Decline of Mercantilism

At the same time that the French colonial empire was declining, the mercantile system in France was likewise beginning to crumble. Mercantilism had evolved as a series of short-term responses to economic crises. But taxes and government regulations were stifling merchants and industrialists. What started as a strategy to stimulate growth through directing trade and development was now restricting its further progress. A group of French economists known as the *physiocrats* called for the liberalization of government policies.

The physiocrats took their name from the title of a book by Dupont de Nemours (1739–1817) entitled *Physiocracy, or the Natural Constitution of That Form of Government Most Advantageous to the Human Race*, published in 1767. Physiocrats such as de Nemours, François Quesnay (1694–1774), and Jean Vincent, Sieur de Gournay (1712–1759) believed that economics was governed by natural laws and that any legislative limitations on economic affairs was a violation of those laws. Government, they believed, should restrict itself to the protection of life, liberty, and property. The term *laissez-faire* ("leave alone") was used to describe this economic theory. The physiocrats' ideas corresponded to the limitations on absolute power advocated by the *philosophes*; in fact, the physiocrats were prominent contributors to the *Encyclopedia*. (See chapter 2.) Some of their ideas were put into practice under Anne Robert Jacques Turgot (1727–1781), the finance minister under Louis XVI.

Adam Smith

English merchants, particularly those in the Thirteen Colonies, were also chafing under the burdens of the mercantile system. Their demands for economic liberty were echoed by the Scottish economist Adam Smith (1723–1790). Smith's influential work, *An Inquiry into the Nature and Causes of the Wealth of Nations* (1776), was the most significant economic work of the eighteenth century. In it Smith argued that

THE SEVEN YEARS' WAR

The Seven Years' War was typical of the conflicts between the Great Powers during this period. The past seventy-five years had seen no fewer than three world wars. In each case, France and Britain, the rising colonial powers, had found themselves on opposite sides of a global conflict.

In North America, there were clashes between American and French settlers in the Ohio River Valley and upper New England over territorial rights. On the Indian subcontinent, the French and British battled for supremacy in colonial trade. The colonies were of critical importance to the balance of power in Europe. Colonies fostered trade, and trade led to sea power. France and Britain were competing for control on these fronts. This imperial struggle came to a climax in the Seven Years' War.

Fighting broke out in India and North America more than two years before the formal declaration of war in Europe. The battles in the colonies could have escalated into broader conflicts had war in the European theatre not diverted military attentions. War in Europe broke out in August 1756 when Frederick II of Prussia invaded Saxony. Frederick believed there was an international conspiracy on the part of Saxony, Austria, and France to destroy Prussian power. He considered the attack on Saxony a pre-emptive strike. Unfortunately, however, the Prussian invasion created the very alliance Frederick had feared. France and Austria joined in an alliance dedicated to the destruction of Prussia. They were eventually joined by Sweden, Russia, and the smaller German states.

While events unfolded in Europe, Britain formulated its own plan. In 1757, William Pitt the Elder (1708–1778) became prime minister. His primary concerns were the North American colonies and he saw the European conflict as a way to divert French resources and attention from the colonial struggle. He therefore provided huge financial subsidies to the Prussian war effort; in fact, Britain invested as much capital in aid of Prussia as Prussia did itself.

Ultimately, Britain was victorious over France in every conflict. In 1759, British General James Wolfe (1727–1759) decisively defeated France under the command of Marshall Louis Joseph de Montcalm (1712–1759) on the Plains of Abraham, effectively eliminating the French empire in North America. But Pitt's colonial vision extended beyond the St. Lawrence Valley and the Great Lakes Basin. British forces battled the French for control of the French West Indies. As the British fleet increased its hold over the region, French colonial trade plummeted from 30 million *livres* in 1755 to 4 million in 1760.

On the Indian subcontinent, British forces defeated the French at the Battle of Plassey (1757), opening the way for the eventual conquest of Bengal. In 1761, the French base at Pondicherry fell, leaving the region under British control.

The Seven Years' War finally came to an end in February 1763. Under the Treaty of Paris, France renounced to Britain its claims in North America and India. Six days later, the European conflict ended with the Treaty of Hubertusberg, with no significant changes in the prewar borders. But the years of conflict had changed the power base in the colonies. France was no longer a great colonial power; now Britain reigned supreme. Never had any European nation experienced such a complete worldwide military victory. For the next 180 years, until the Second World War, Britain would retain its status as the world's foremost power.

mercantilism was based on a mistaken theory of value. Wealth was not created by a favourable balance of trade, as the mercantilists maintained, nor was it based on land, as the physiocrats advocated. Smith believed that labour gave goods value and that to create more wealth free trade and competition had to be encouraged. He believed that the role of government should be restricted and that the marketplace should be governed by the "invisible hand" of supply and demand. As he wrote, "Every man, as long as he does not violate the laws of justice, is left perfectly free to pursue his own interest his own way, and to bring both his own industry and capital into competition with those of any other man. . . ." This was not to say that Smith advocated the abolition of the state. Instead, he perceived a different role for it: to provide national security, a system of justice, and public works and institutions.

The Wealth of Nations brought economics into the mainstream of Enlightenment thought and established modern economics theory. It was readily embraced by the new industrial order as its theoretical foundation. As a plea for liberty, it supported the revolutionary movements in the British colonies. Smith's economic philosophy would be the basis of the free enterprise system that would be the cornerstone of the newly created United States of America.

THE ARTS AND SOCIETY IN THE AGE OF ABSOLUTISM

Art is a mirror of the times, reflecting the values, goals, and ideas of a society in a particular period. As a result, it is an invaluable record of the lifestyle and people, particularly when written records are scarce. It is through the arts that we can experience rather than observe history.

The art of the seventeenth and eighteenth centuries was filled with the conflicts, aspirations, and discoveries of the era. Baroque art and architecture illustrate how art and religious or political statements can reinforce one another. During this period, censorship by the church and state required that ideas that were critical of the status quo be indirectly presented. As a result, art in the age of absolutism became a valuable historical resource.

One of the most significant aspects of the seventeenth and eighteenth centuries was the democratization and popularization of the arts. The rise of the middle class produced a new market for artists. As patronage waned in the eighteenth century, the subject and manner of presentation was shaped to fit middle-class tastes. Public theatres, opera houses, and museums all served to diffuse culture beyond the restrictive circle of the aristocracy.

The growth of literacy in the eighteenth century made possible the spread of magazines and popular literature. As the reading public increased, the visual arts were replaced by the written word as the principal means of conveying ideas. The reduced cost and availability of literature meant ideas spread farther and faster than ever before. In addition, the cosmopolitan nature of European society allowed ideas to move freely across borders, a process that would be accelerated during and after the French Revolution.

Painting and Sculpture

The Baroque Style

The dominant style in the visual arts from 1600 to 1750 was *baroque*. Originally the term was used to describe art that was absurd or grotesque, and until the nineteenth century baroque art was thought of in that way. Now it delineates the stylistic period between mannerism and rococo.

Baroque art uses naturalism and unity. It is characterized by a concern for balance and wholeness and an emphasis on light and emotion to achieve dramatic effect. Strong contrasts, such as light against dark and diagonals against curves, contribute to the overall grand effect. Its powerful presentation made it an appropriate vehicle for the propaganda of church and state. In fact, it is sometimes called the "style of absolutism."

The baroque style originated in Italy around 1585 and is generally divided into three periods: Early (from 1585), High (from 1625), and Late (from 1675 to 1715). The style soon became international, spreading to Flanders, Holland, and Spain and, to a lesser degree, England, Germany, Austria, and France. The leading baroque painter in Italy was Pietro da Cortona (1596–1669), whose masterpieces included *The Rape of the Sabines* (1630) and *Allegory of Divine Providence and Barberini Power* (1633–1639), which graces the ceiling of the Barberini palace in Bologna. In sculpture, the work of Giovanni Bernini (1598–1680), particularly *David* (1623) and *Vision of the Ecstasy of St. Theresa* (1647–1652), overshadows that of all others in the field. In the Cornaro Chapel, of which *Vision* is but a part, Bernini fused sculpture and architecture to achieve a spiritual effect, which was the epitome of Counter-Reformation Catholicism. The work of the Italian architect Francesco Borromini (1599–1667) continued this emphasis.

In northern Europe, the school was dominated by the Flemish artist Peter Paul Rubens (1577–1640). Rubens studied in Italy from 1600 to 1608 and is credited with spreading the baroque style outside of Italy. He had many influential commissions, such as *The Descent from the Cross* (1614) intended for the Antwerp Cathedral; a series of twenty-four paintings entitled *The Life of Marie de Medicis* (1622–1625) for the Luxembourg Palace in Paris; and the *Apotheosis of James I* (1629–1634) for the ceiling of the King's Banqueting House in London. He died in 1640 while painting a series of 112 paintings for Philip IV of Spain.

The greatest religious artist of the Protestant north was the Dutch painter Rembrandt van Rijn (1606–1669). Rembrandt was profoundly religious and in later life became a follower of the Mennonites, a radical Protestant sect. His most famous works are *The Anatomy Lesson of Dr. Tulp* (1632), *The Descent from the Cross* (1633), and *The Night Watch* (1642; see colour plates). Rembrandt had many pupils who disseminated his style throughout northern Europe. So faithfully did they mimic his work that in 1990 research revealed that a majority of the paintings attributed to the great artist were not his work at all, but that of his students.

REMBRANDT VAN RIJN

One of the great masters, Rembrandt never achieved the financial success that he longed for. To support his own career, he took in students. His teaching was strictly a money-making proposition; he did not see his role as that of mentor to some aspiring talent. He charged the steep sum of 100 guilders per student annually, which meant that many of his students were the children of the rich, but not necessarily very talented. Like all masters, however, if Rembrandt approved of one of his student's works he signed his own name to it, sold it, and kept the money for himself.

By 1637, Rembrandt had established quite a large teaching practice. To accommodate his students he rented a warehouse. In effect, Rembrandt had established his own "art factory." He had several full-time assistants, many of whom were of considerable talent themselves. The assistants tried to copy the masterful works of Rembrandt, and many of their works were signed and claimed by Rembrandt as his own, too. This practice created confusion for later scholars who tried to determine which paintings credited to Rembrandt were actually his. Even today authorities are still discovering that paintings long believed to have been Rembrandt masterpieces were indeed painted by someone else.

In Spain, the leading artist of the baroque style was Diego Rodriguez de Silva y Velazquez (1599–1660). He is particularly renowned for his portraits and is still considered one of the finest of all portrait painters. His portrait of Pope Innocent X (1650) is one of the greatest portraits in existence.

Other Artistic Styles

Although baroque was the dominant style throughout the first half of the seventeenth century, many artists, particularly those in England and France, remained uninfluenced by it. In England, the most influential artist in the early seventeenth century was an associate of Rubens, Anthony van Dyck (1599–1641), who used the baroque style to enhance the portraits of his patrons. Dyck, however, was the exception. The first British-born artist to achieve international influence was William Hogarth (1697–1764), the creator of British painting. Hogarth was the first great comic-history painter and is best known for his satiric engravings of contemporary life; *The Rake's Progress* (1735), *Marriage à la Mode* (1743), and *An Election* (1754) are three of his better known works. Portraiture was the dominant art form in England during the period. Sir Joshua Reynolds's (1723–1792) *Nelly O'Brien* (1760–1762) and Thomas Gainsborough's (1727–1788) *The Blue Boy* (1779) are two of the best known examples of this genre.

Under Louis XIV, France replaced Rome as the world centre of the visual arts. The primary focus was the Palace of Versailles, which combined all the arts—architecture, landscape, painting, sculpture, furniture, and metal work—in a union glorifying the Sun King. Initially this "style of Louis XIV" moved away from the baroque school, drawing its inspiration from classical art and architecture. Even so, this classical revival did not escape the influence of the baroque school; as a result, by the seventeenth century a distinct French style had emerged.

The artist most closely associated with Louis XIV's brand of classicism was Nicolas Poussin (1593–1665), the greatest French painter of the century and the first to achieve international fame. His paintings tended to stress biblical and mythological themes, and his symmetry of composition became the standard in the Sun King's court.

After the death of Louis XIV, French art moved closer to the baroque style with the development of rococo, the "style of Louis XV." Colourful, fragile, and pastoral, the dreamlike quality of rococo contrasted with the more spartan norms of classicism. This decorative style was most closely associated with the lifestyle of the French aristocracy and frequently depicted trivial subject matter. Its greatest painters were Jean Antoine Watteau (1684–1721), who invested his pictures with vibrant colours, François Boucher (1703–1770), who painted historical, mythological, and landscape works, and Jean-Honoré Fragonard (1732–1806), who used light-hearted spontaneity in his amorous scenes and rustic landscapes. By the middle of the eighteenth century, however, popular rejection of the excesses of aristocratic life resulted in a re-emergence of the classical style.

The Emergence of Neoclassicism

The period from 1750 to 1820 was dominated by a return to classical forms. Early in the century, Italian well diggers discovered artifacts that were to lead archeologists to the full-scale excavations of the lost Roman cities of Pompeii and Herculaneum. Their discoveries led to a renewed interest in the classical world, and classical Greek ideals once again became the artistic standard for Western civilization. German art critic Johann Winckelmann commented in 1755 in his *Thoughts on the Imitation of Greek Art in Painting and Sculpture*:

> To those who know and study the works of the Greeks, their masterpieces reveal not only nature in its greatest beauty, but something more than that; namely, certain ideal beauties of nature which, as an old commentator of Plato teaches us, exist only in the intellect. (See readings.)

A study of the painting and sculpture of the period reveals a number of common characteristics: a level of harmony and unity; a belief in universal norms and standards; and a reflection of ideal values rather than eccentric or petty ones. (For more on neoclassical art, see chapter 3.)

Architecture

The development of architecture followed a pattern similar to that of the visual arts. Feeling stifled by the norms of the Renaissance, the architects of the baroque period rejected what they saw as a stagnant standardization. Under this baroque influence, straight lines gradually became curved lines and restraint was abandoned for more elaborate ornamentation. Baroque architects were more interested in effect than form. This led to an orchestration of all the arts—architecture, landscape, sculpture, painting, and interior design—to produce the desired effect, most frequently one of awe.

Italy, particularly Rome, offers several good examples of the Baroque style of architecture. Francesco Borromini's (1559–1667) baroque palace and church designs were based on geometric modules and had tremendous influence in Italy and northern Europe. One of his most notable works is S. Carlo alle Quattro Fontane in Rome (1634). Gianlorenzo Bernini's (1598–1680) design for the square of St. Peter's (1662–1664) is considered a masterpiece of baroque style.

The Spread of the Baroque Style

The success of baroque architecture made Italian architects in demand. They were commissioned for works abroad and this spread the baroque style. Foreign architects also came to study in Italy; upon returning to their native countries they re-expessed baroque in their own national architectural styles. In this fashion baroque gradually spread from Italy throughout Europe. In Austria, Fischer von Erlach (1656–1723), Lukas von Hildebrandt (1668–1745), and Jakob Prandtauer (1702–1736) spread the baroque style. In Karlskirche (1716–1737), the Church of St. Charles Borromeo in Vienna, von Erlach combined elements of Italian baroque with attributes from ancient Roman architecture. The unusually wide façade incorporates the portico of the Pantheon and a pair of triumphal columns modeled after the Column of Trajan. The Belvedere Palace (1721–1722) designed by von Hildebrandt for Prince Eugene in Vienna

Johann Lucas von Hildebrandt designed the Belvedere Palace in Vienna to serve as the summer residence of Prince Eugene of Savoy.

is actually a complex of two palaces, the Upper and Lower Belvedere, which face each other linked by terraced gardens and pools that reflect the palace's façade. The monastery at Melk is Prandtauer's masterpiece and is one of the greatest examples of baroque architecture in Austria. The location of the abbey, high on the crest of a promontory overlooking the Danube River, contributes to the striking design.

In Germany, the Residenz (1719–1744) in Wurzburg, designed by Gabriel-Germain Boffrand (1667–1753) and Balthasar Neumann (1687–1753), is thought to be the penultimate baroque palace, second only to Versailles.

In France, the Italian baroque style was modified to suit the tastes of Louis XIV. This produced a style known as baroque classicism. The greatest architects of this style were Jacques Lemercier (1585–1654), François Mansart (1598–1667), and Louis Le Vau (1612–1670). Lemercier worked on the Louvre and designed the Palais-Cardinal in Paris (begun in 1633 and now known as the Palais-Royal) for Cardinal Richelieu. His italianate dome for the chapel at the Sorbonne (1635–1642) is one of the best ecclesiastical examples of baroque classicism. The church of St. Marie de la Visitation (1632–1634) and the chateau at Blois (1635) are the best known examples of Mansart's work. The proportions and his design for the chateau have been much copied, most notably in the chateau built for René de Longueil in Paris (1642–1648), one of the finest examples of the French architecture of this period. Le Vau also worked on the Louvre and some of the early stages of Versailles. He is probably best known for the chateau of Vaux-le-Vicomte, built for Nicholas Fouquet. It is said that Louis XIV was so envious of Vaux-le-Vicomte that he imprisoned Fouquet for life and commissioned Le Vau to design the palace of Versailles.

Versailles is the greatest example of baroque architecture, and is the symbol of the age. Begun in 1661, it was completed in 1708, although both Louis XV and Louis XVI added to it, particularly the residential wing. The principal architects were Le Vau and Jules Hardouin-Mansart (1646–1708). The palace was both a residence and the seat of government and contained royal apartments and government offices. The centrepiece of the palace was the spectacular Hall of Mirrors, which would become the symbolic centre stage of Europe over the next two centuries.

The formal gardens, designed by André le Nôtre (1613–1700), contained fountains, statues, terraces, and arbors that illustrated Louis's dominion over his surroundings. The grounds included minor buildings, such as the Grand Trianon, the Petit Trianon, and Marie Antoinette's Hamlet, where the queen escaped the rigours of court etiquette by masquerading as a shepherdess. The estimated cost of $100 million to build Versailles was a severe strain on the French treasury and is cited by some historians as one of the causes of the French Revolution.

The palace at Versailles, built primarily by Le Vau and Hardouin-Mansart, became the ideal for baroque palaces. Some copies of Versailles include the Belvedere Palace in Austria, the Residenz in Germany, and Blenheim Palace in England.

From Baroque to Neoclassicism

Even before the death of Louis XIV there was a reaction against the grand scale and spectacle of baroque classicism. Under Louis XV, architecture became more functional. Spaces were designed for specific uses. Buildings were reduced in scale and became more intimate. Emphasis was shifted from the public to the private. This shift explains why rococo is a style of interior decoration, reflecting the desire for luxury, intimacy, and the indulgence of pleasure. Rococo architecture was primarily a French and German style and, as in painting and sculpture, it rapidly deteriorated into decadence.

As with the visual arts, neoclassicism came to dominate architecture by the mid-eighteenth century. The movement was stimulated by the enthusiasm for archeological knowledge brought on by the excavations at Herculaneum and Pompeii. The result was an explosion in the imitation of classicism. Neoclassicism emphasized a return to the pure forms of Greek and Roman architecture. Designs were solid, severe, and rigid. Classical forms were used for structure rather than ornamentation.

Perhaps the centrepiece of neoclassic architecture is the Pantheon (1764) in Paris. Designed as a church by Jacques Soufflot (1713–1780), it was dedicated to the memory of the country's great citizens during the French Revolution. Today it is a public building. In Berlin, Karl Friedrich von Schinkel's (1781–1841) Royal Theatre (1818–1821) and Old Museum (1822–1830) were the culmination of the revival of Greek architecture.

The grandeur of Greece and Rome was recalled in monumental architecture throughout the Western world, including the Arc de Triomphe (1806) in Paris, designed by Pierre Fontaine (1762–1853), and the Brandenburg Gate (1788–1791) in Berlin, designed by Carl G. Langhans (1732–1808).

The return to classicism was particularly influential in the United States (although it was called the federal style there). The monumental Roman temples dominated the design of public buildings, such as the Capitol in Washington, D.C., begun in 1793, and residential homes, such as Thomas Jefferson's Monticello (1770–1775). The revival was less evident in England, however, primarily because England had not adopted the baroque style of architecture but had continued in the classical renaissance tradition. St. Paul's Cathedral (1675–1711), built by Christopher Wren (1632–1723), is the best example of English architecture during this period.

The rejection of the decadence of baroque and rococo by the rising middle class in the late eighteenth century was paralleled by new political ideas. This challenge not only to the art and architecture of absolutism but to its fundamental principles marked the end of an era.

The U.S. Capitol building in Washington, D.C., designed by William Thornton, illustrates the federal style, as neoclassicism was called in the United States.

St. Paul's Cathedral in London was designed by Sir Christopher Wren. The west façade is shown here.

Literature

The literary standards of Western civilization in the late twentieth century owe a great deal to the authors and playwrights of the seventeenth and eighteenth centuries. Popular drama, novels, political and social satires, even science fiction and fantasy, have their modern roots in this period.

English Literature

During the seventeenth century, English literature tended to reflect the tastes of the monarch or ruling party. William Shakespeare (1564–1616) dominated the English literary scene, writing 154 sonnets and 40 plays. Considered by many to be the greatest playwright of all time, he is the most frequently quoted writer in the world. His plays have been performed continuously since the first production, of *Henry IV*, in 1590.

Shakespeare avoided current political topics by basing his plays in classical settings (*A Midsummer Night's Dream* [1595–1596], *Timon of Athens* [1607–1608]), on historical accounts (*Macbeth* [1605–1606], *King Lear* [1605–1606]), or among foreign societies (*The Merchant of Venice* [1596–1597], *The Taming of the Shrew* [1593–1594], *Othello* [1604–1605]). When his plays reflected more recent English history (*Richard III* [1592–1593], *Henry VIII* [1612–1613]) they tended to reinforce the self-image of the ruling Tudor house. Shakespeare's works cover the complete spectrum, from complex comedies such as *Twelfth Night* (1601–1602) and *As You Like It* (1599–1600), to highly theatrical historical plays such as *Henry IV* (1591–1592), to the great tragedies *Hamlet* (1600–1601), *Othello*, *King Lear*, and *Macbeth*. His plays are timeless studies of the human character and thus retain their significance to this day.

Along with Shakespeare, John Milton (1608–1674) is considered one of the greatest poets in the English language. His greatest works—"Paradise Lost" (1662–1667, 1674) and "Paradise Regained" (1671) and "Samson Agonistes" (1671)—epitomized the austerity, moral seriousness, and strict piety of the Puritan tradition and are the exact opposite of the characteristic genre of the restoration, the comedy of manners. The sexual innuendoes, sexual infidelity, and loose morals of the dramas of William Wycherely (1640–1716) and William Congreve (1670–1729) in Wycherely's *The Country Wife* (1675) and *The Plain Dealer* (1677) and Congreve's *The Way of the World* (1700) reflect the light-hearted lack of morals evident in the Stuart Court after the restoration.

On the other hand, a group of social critics was beginning to reflect dissatisfaction with social norms. The poet and playwright John Dryden (1631–1700) wrote stinging personal attacks on and parodies about political and literary rivals. Immensely popular and widely read during his day, his attacks have little meaning in the twentieth century, although his clear, forceful prose is impressive even three centuries later.

Alexander Pope (1688–1744) was the acknowledged master of satirical verse. *The Dunciad* (1728) and the *Epistle to Dr. Arbuthnot* (1735) are the best examples of his wit and use of ridicule and invective. He also wrote moral and philosophical poems, such as the "Essay on Man" (1733), which reflected the values of the period, although his attitude toward women would not be accepted today:

> Nothing so true as what you once let fall;
> 'Most women have no character at all,'
> Matter too soft a lasting mark to bear
> And best distinguished by black, brown or fair.

Neverthess, he effectively summed up the period in heroic couplet in his "Essay on Man" (1733).

> All Nature is but Art unknown to thee;
> All chance direction which thou canst not see;
> All discord harmony not understood;
> All partial evil, universal good:
> And spite of Pride in erring Reason's spite,
> One truth is clear, *Whatever is, is right.*

Pope was the first English poet of the period to enjoy contemporary fame on the continent. This was particularly true in Germany, where his use of heroic couplet was frequently imitated.

Jonathan Swift (1667–1745) was the foremost satirist of his day. Born in Ireland, he wrote numerous books criticizing Britain's treatment of his native country. His best known work, however, is *Gulliver's Travels* (1726). It is perhaps the greatest indictment of politics, diplomacy, war, human folly, and vice ever written, yet its fantastic tale of travels in wonderland appeals to all ages. Other writers of the day were alienated by Swift's coarse and bitter manner. However, critical interest in his clever satire has been revived in the twentieth century.

Other influential writers were the essayists and dramatists Joseph Addison (1672–1719) and Sir Richard Steele (1672–1729). The two are inseparably linked as the co-founders of *The Spectator* (1711–1712). The essays they wrote for this journal influenced the manners, morals, and literature of the time. Addison was particularly well known for his simple, unornamented prose, which signaled the end of seventeenth-century mannerisms and eccentricities.

Perhaps the greatest gift English literature bequeathed modern civilization was the introduction of the novel in the eighteenth century. Daniel Defoe (1659–1731) developed the modern form of the novel with *Robinson Crusoe* (1719) using vivid narrative combined with realistic detail. The first English novel with an English setting is credited to Samuel Richardson (1689–1762), who wrote *Pamela*, or *Virtue Unrewarded*, in 1740. The genre of the novel reached maturity in 1749 with *The History of Tom Jones* by Henry Fielding (1702–1754). *Tom Jones* presents a vivid look at London society in the eighteenth century through the exploits of the story's highly sexed hero. Fielding attempted "to laugh mankind out of their follies and vices." His work made a significant contribution to the development of the English novel.

Other significant British writers were Laurence Sterne (1713–1768), whose novel, *Tristram Shandy* (1759–1767), parodied the conventions of the still new novel; Tobias Smollett (1721–1771), whose most famous work, *Humphrey Clinker* (1771), was characterized by fast-moving narrative and humorous caricature; and Oliver Goldsmith (1728–1774), who wrote the most widely read English novel of the eighteenth century, *The Vicar of Wakefield* (1766).

Literature on the Continent

In France, three playwrights dominated the seventeenth-century theatre. Pierre Corneille (1606–1684) was renowned for his tragedies, particularly *Médée* (1635) and *Le Cid* (1637). His characters were often torn between duty and passion. Corneille was the leader of classical French tragedy until he was eclipsed by Jean Racine (1639–1699). Racine was one of the greatest literary figures of the period and is credited with perfecting disciplined seventeenth-century tragedy. A common theme in most of his work is the blind folly of human passion. His best-known works include *Andromaque* (1667), *Aphigémie* (1674), *Phèdre* (1677), and *Athalie* (1691).

It was during this period, however, that the art of French comedy was perfected by the most popular writer of the era, Molière (1622–1673). Molière had a profound understanding of the absurdity of human nature and was a genius at blending the intellectual with the comical. The most famous of his works are *Le Tartuffe* (1664), *Don Juan* (1665), *Le Misanthrope* (1666), *Le Bourgeois Gentilhomme* (1670), and *Le Malade imaginaire* (1673).

In prose, Voltaire (1694–1778) and Jean-Jacques Rousseau (1712–1778) criticized society and demanded change. A prolific writer, Voltaire used wit and satire to publicize the political philosophers he supported. A relentless opponent of France's royal autocracy and aristocratic privileges and of the Roman Catholic church, Voltaire found himself persecuted in his own country. As a result, he spent much of his life outside of France. (See page 44.) Rousseau was best known for his philosophical discourses (see pages 44–45), but he also used novels such as *Nouvelle Héloïse* (1760) and *Émile* (1762) to portray the new liberal society he envisioned.

The political chaos in Germany meant that little literature of distinction was produced there until the eighteenth century. A distinctive German national literature, liberated from the French classical school, began to develop with the work of Gotthold Ephraim Lessing (1729–1781). His greatest dramatic works, *Emilia Galotti* (1772) and *Miss Sara Sampson* (1755), were both tragedies, the latter the first significant domestic tragedy in German. *Nathan the Wise* (1779) was a nationalist plea for religious tolerance in divided Germany.

German literature attained international recognition with the works of the romantics Christoph Friederich von Schiller (1759–1805) and Johann Wolfgang von Goethe (1749–1832). Schiller's plays, such as *The Robbers* (1781), *Intrigue and Love* (1784), and *Mary Stuart* (1800), dealt with the problems of freedom and responsibility. Goethe's dramas closely related to events in his own life. He is most celebrated for his greatest work, *Faust* (1808–1832). A close friend of Schiller's, Goethe emerged as the major force in creating a national German literature.

Academic Literature

The period also saw the re-emergence of the academic study of history as a means of understanding society. Two significant works of the period came from Voltaire, who wrote *The Age of Louis XIV* (1756), and Edward Gibbon (1737–1794), who wrote *The Decline and Fall of the Roman Empire* (1776). Gibbon's lucid analysis of the reasons behind the decline and collapse of classical civilization was intended as a lesson to his own era. Gibbon saw history as cyclical, with periods of cultural achievement followed by periods of corruption and darkness. As we will discuss in the next chapter, Gibbon saw himself living in an age of reason and enlightenment and saw the gradual progress of human civilization as a reason for optimism.

MOLIÈRE (1622–1673)

The great playwright and master of comedy known as Molière was born Jean-Baptiste Poquelin in 1622. Trained as a lawyer, Molière abandoned law in favour of a theatrical career. He founded an acting company and began writing his own comedies and farces.

When Molière joined the theatre, the stage was a dubious profession and comedy an artificial genre. However, Molière's work invested comedy with a new dimension and brought dignity and authority to comic theatre in France. Comedy was elevated to a highly developed and powerful form of artistic expression.

The first indication of Molière's genius was in *Les Précieuses ridicules* (1659), in which he ridiculed the oddities, follies, and vices of French society. This was the first of a succession of such intellectual comedies. All of these plays balanced low comedy with high wit.

Molière was an astute observer of contemporary manners and types. As a result, many of his greatest plays were comedies of character. But although he ridiculed both customs and people, he did so without malice. There was, in fact, always compassion and understanding, for the truth beneath the high spirits of his works always lay close to tragedy. Through humour, Molière tried to alleviate some of life's despair.

In Louis XIV's France, engaging in political dissent frequently resulted in imprisonment or even death. Molière used his comedies as his means of social criticism. In spite of his plays' popularity, however, he was not free from conflict with the state. *Le Tartuffe* was banned when it first appeared because of its negative view of French society. Unruffled, Molière proceeded to write a fourth and fifth act to the play.

The banning of *Le Tartuffe* gave the play—and its writer—greater fame throughout Europe. Rumours about the play circulated throughout the continent and flamed the fires of curiosity. It was impossible to stop the play's distribution. Handwritten copies were distributed throughout France and the rest of Europe. The state had only succeeded in heightening interest in the play rather than quelling it.

Molière's plays provide considerable insight into life in seventeenth-century France. They are a window on the values, customs, and traditions of that era of absolutism. Their value as works of art is also evidenced by the many successful productions in the twentieth century.

Music

During the seventeenth century music shifted in subject from religious to secular; in tone from polyphonic (two or more lines of melody) to monophonic (a single line of melody); and in orchestration from choral to instrumental. As in the visual arts, the baroque style was dominant. Baroque music was written to express states of the soul, such as rage, excitement, and heroism. The style, instruments, melody, rhythm, harmony, and texture of the music were all incorporated into an expression of emotional feelings.

Baroque music originated in Italy and spread to Germany and throughout Europe. But its most influential musicians were the Italians and the Germans. The greatest musical genius of early baroque music was the Italian master Claudio Monteverdi (1567–1643). His work was a transition from the renaissance to the baroque, incorporating the old into the new. His genius at combining melody and harmony makes his music appealing even to contemporary twentieth-century audiences. His greatest achievement was the development of opera, a form of music combining orchestra, chorus, solo voice, poetry, drama, and set design into a unified expression. The first opera, *Orfeo*, was written by Monteverdi in 1607. Opera was one of the earliest forms of secular music and was tremendously popular throughout Europe.

Antonio Vivaldi (1678–1741) was a conductor, composer, and teacher at the Conservatory of the Pieta in Venice. His most popular music was the *concerto* (a form of instrumental music for festive services), of which there are approximately

450 still in existence. He was an important figure in the transition of music from the late baroque to the early classical style.

Vivaldi influenced many composers, particularly Johann Sebastian Bach (1685–1750), a German-born composer who mastered all of the musical forms of the period, with the exception of opera. Bach blended the characteristics of both Italian and German music, but his style was uniquely his own. As a devout Lutheran, his music had religious purpose and he faithfully presented his biblical messages. Bach is perhaps best known for his preludes and fugues, such as *The Well-Tempered Clavier* (1722) and the unfinished *Art of Fugue* (1751), and for toccatas, such as the *Toccata and Fugue in D Minor* (c. 1708). Bach also wrote many masses and choral pieces. After his death in 1750, his music suffered a period of neglect before being revived in the nineteenth century.

Although born in Germany, George Frederic Handel (1685–1759) settled in London in 1712. His music differed from Bach's in that he had a natural feeling for the dramatic and personal. While his work emphasized melody and harmony, he was in touch with all of the latest styles and developments. Works such as *Water Music* (1715–1717) and *Royal Fireworks Music* (1749), composed for the British royal family, were among his most popular. But his greatest achievements were in opera and oratorios. The oratorio *Messiah* (1741), famous for its "Hallelujah Chorus," is perhaps his most renowned work. Handel's work was so influential in England that it dominated music in that country for the next 150 years.

From Baroque to Classicism

The unity and logic of baroque music had been intended to represent one "state of the soul," or a theme. Around 1750, a new style of music employing many, at times contrasting, themes began to evolve. *Classical music* reflected not the work of classical civilization but the values of classicism. Musical styles were characterized by melodies with accompaniment and clear structures and forms. During the classical period, the piano replaced the harpsichord as the most popular keyboard instrument. The greatest classical composers—Franz Joseph Haydn (1732–1809), Wolfgang Amadeus Mozart (1756–1791), and Ludwig van Beethoven (1770–1827)—can be considered among the greatest composers of all time.

Haydn was a prolific composer, writing over one hundred symphonies, sixty-eight string quartets, and twenty operas. The perfected classical style of the late eighteenth century owed much to Haydn's symphonies, in particular the *London* symphonies. His oratorios, with their expansive choruses, were also extremely popular with the musical public. Haydn was a friend and great admirer of Mozart and eventually became a teacher of Beethoven.

Mozart was a musical genius, both playing and composing from early childhood. Before dying in poverty at the age of thirty-five, he had composed a total of 626 works. Haydn said of Mozart, "He is the greatest composer known to me either in person or by name." His operas *The Marriage of Figaro* (1786), *Don Giovanni* (1787), and *The Magic Flute* (1791), illustrate his great genius and are considered among the finest ever written. His symphonies, piano sonatas, and chamber music all represent the highest musical achievement of the classical period. His early death was a tragedy for music, for his later works appeared to be evolving in a direction no composer has subsequently been able to follow.

Beethoven's music spanned the classical and romantic periods. His early works were in the classic tradition of Haydn and Mozart, but his later works moved beyond their legacy. During his middle period he composed *Piano Concerto No. 5* (1809) and *Violin Concerto* (1806) despite increasing deafness. By the time he produced his *Ninth Symphony* (1824), which many critics regard as the greatest symphony ever composed, he was totally deaf. The personal emotion that characterized his later works marked the transition from classicism to romanticism.

RETROSPECTIVE

The seventeenth and early eighteenth centuries saw the flowering of Western civilization on the European continent. With the centralization of political control and the emergence of a strong state economy, more resources and attention were devoted to the arts.

At the same time, the visual arts, music, drama, and prose provided a vehicle for social commentary that was otherwise suppressed in absolutist regimes. By the middle of the eighteenth century, however, the social and political undercurrents had broken to the surface and significant challenges began to oppose the prevailing social order. At first scientific and philosophical, by the end of the eighteenth century these forces would bring the absolutist world of Louis XIV and his successors to a violent end.

JAMES I:
The Divine Right of Kings (1609)

James I became king of England upon the death of Elizabeth I. A member of the Stuart family, James was the son of Mary, Queen of Scots, and had sat as James VI of Scotland before being asked to take the English throne. James's predecessors, the Tudors, had centred their power around monarch worship. Appealing not to force but to the love of their subjects, the Tudors had managed to maintain their power through the most turbulent and expansive period in English history. To a great extent, the Tudor monarchy provided a national symbol in a period of the emergence of the nation-state. James I attempted to translate this emotion into a doctrine based not upon popular support, but divine right. In this excerpt, James comments on the nature of monarchy and its relationship to God.

From N. Sheffe and W. Fisher (eds.), *A Sourcebook for Modern History*, (Toronto: McGraw-Hill, 1964), pp. 10–11.

The state of monarchy is the supremest thing upon earth; for kings are not only God's lieutenants upon earth, and sit upon God's throne, but even by God himself are they called gods. There be three principal similitudes that illustrate the state of monarchy; one taken out of the word of God; and the other out of the grounds of policy and philosophy. In the Scriptures kings are called gods, and so their power after a certain relation compared to the divine power. Kings are also compared to fathers of families; for a king is truly *Parens patriae*, the politique father of his people. And lastly, kings are compared to the head of this microcosm of the body of man.

Kings are justly called gods, for they exercise a manner or resemblance of divine power upon earth; for if you will consider the attributes to God, you shall see how they agree in the person of a king. God hath power to create or destroy, make or unmake at his pleasure, to give life or send death, to judge all and to be judged nor accountable to none; to raise low things and to make high things low at his pleasure, and to God are both soul and body due. And the like power have kings: they make and unmake their subjects, they have power of raising and casting down, of life and of death, judges over all their subjects and in all causes and yet accountable to none but God only. They have power to exalt low things and abase high things, and make of their subjects like men at the chess, a pawn to take a bishop or a knight, and to cry up and down any of their subjects, as they do their money. And to the king is due both the affection of the soul and the service of the body of his subjects. . . .

---

1. To what three things does James I compare kings?

2. What examples does James cite to prove that kings have the power of God on earth?

3. Use James's arguments to account for the description of the court of Louis XIV by Saint-Simon.

SAINT-SIMON:
The Court of the Sun King (1700)

Without doubt the symbol of the age of absolutism was Louis XIV. If he did not actually say "L'état, c'est moi," his life certainly indicated that he believed it.

The Duke of Saint-Simon provided an insider's view of the functioning of Louis's court. Saint-Simon was not an unbiased observer, but many of his views are corroborated by other contemporary sources.

Louis XIV was made for a brilliant court. In the midst of other men, his figure, his courage, his grace, his beauty, his grand mien, even the tone of his voice and the majestic and natural charm of all his person, distinguished him till his death as the King Bee. . . .

Intellect, education, nobility of sentiment, and high principle in others, became objects of suspicion to him, and soon of hatred. The more he advanced in years the more this sentiment was confirmed in him. He wished to reign by himself. His jealousy on this point unceasingly became weakness. . . .

The superior ability of his early ministers and early generals soon wearied him. He liked nobody to be in any way superior to him. Thus he chose his ministers, not for their knowledge, but for their ignorance; not for their capacity, but for their want of it. . . . This vanity, this unmeasured and unreasonable love of admiration, was his ruin. . . . Suppleness, meanness, an admiring, dependent, cringing manner—above all, an air of nothingness—were the sole means of pleasing him. . . .

Thus we see this monarch grand, rich, conquering, the arbiter of Europe; feared and admired as long as the ministers and captains existed who really deserved the name. When they were no more, the machine kept moving some time by impulsion, and from their influence. But soon afterwards we saw beneath the surface; faults and errors were multiplied and decay came on in giant strides.

From *The Memoirs of the Duke of Saint-Simon on the Reign of Louis XIV*, in Brian Tierney, *et al*, *Great Issues in Western Civilization*, (New York: Random House, 1976), pp. 25–27.

---

1. How does Saint-Simon account for the gradual decline in the quality of Louis's ministers and generals?

2. To what extent does his description of Louis's practices provide a fundamental critique of absolutism?

3. Based upon your knowledge of Saint-Simon, discuss what bias he may have brought to the writing of this account.

THOMAS MUN:
England's Treasure by Foreign Trade (1630)

Thomas Mun was a successful merchant. In 1615, he joined the East India Company and acted as a "public relations" expert. Mun believed that trade was the best way to increase national wealth and that money was only valuable when exchanged for goods and services. He believed that world-wide production and trade would yield more wealth than was possible through local production and consumption. His book English Treasure by Foreign Trade *is one of the most important books on mercantile theory.*

From Wallace E. Adams, *et al*, (eds.), *The Western World*, Vol. 1, (New York: Dodd, Mead & Co., 1970), pp. 542–545.

Although a Kingdom may be enriched by gifts received, or by purchase taken from some other Nations, yet these are things uncertain and of small consideration when they happen. The ordinary means therefore to encrease our wealth and treasure is by *Forraign Trade*, wherein wee must observe this rule; to sell more to strangers yearly than wee consume of theirs in value. . . .

The revenue or Stock of a Kingdom by which it is provided of forraign wares is either *Natural* or *Artificial*. The Natural wealth is so much only as can be spared from our own use and necessities to be exported unto strangers. The Artificial consists of our manufactures and industrious trading with forraign commodities, concerning which I will set down such particulars as may serve for the cause we have in hand.

1. First, although this Realm be already exceedingly rich by nature, yet might it be much encreased by laying the waste grounds (which are infinite) into such employments as should no way hinder the present revenues of other manured lands, but hereby to supply our selves and prevent the importations of Hemp, Flax, Cordage, Tobacco, and divers other things which now we fetch from strangers to our great impoverishing.
2. We may likewise diminish our importations, if we would soberly refrain from excessive consumption of forraign wares in our diet and rayment . . . by enforcing the observation of such good laws as are strictly practised in other Countries against such excesses; where likewise by commanding their own manufactures to be used, they prevent the coming in of others, without prohibition, or offence to strangers in their mutual commerce. . . .
4. The value of our exportations likewise may be much advanced when we perform it our selves in our own Ships, for then we get only not the price of our wares as they are worth here, but also the Merchants gains, the charges of entrance, and fraight to carry them beyond the seas. . . .

5. The frugal expending likewise of our own natural wealth might advance much yearly to be exported unto strangers; and if in our rayment we will be prodigal, yet let this be done with our own materials and manufactures, as Cloth, Lace, Imbroderies, Cutworks and the like, where the excess of the rich may be employed by the poor, whose labours notwithstanding of this kind, would be more profitable for the Commonwealth, if they were done to the use of strangers.
7. A Staple or Magazin for forraign Corn, Indico, Spices, Raw-silks, Cotton wool or any other commodity whatsoever, to be imported will encrease Shipping, Trade, Treasure, and the Kings customes, by exporting them again where need shall require, which course of Trading, hath been the chief means to raise *Venice*, *Genoa*, the *low-Countreys*, with some others; and for such purpose *England* stands most commodiously, wanting nothing to this performance but our own diligence and endeavour.
8. Also wee ought to esteem and cherish those trades which we have in remote and far Countreys, for besides the encrease of Shipping and Mariners thereby, the wares also sent thither and receiv'd from thence are far more profitable unto the kingdom than have our trades neer at hand . . .
9. Lastly, in all things we must endeavour to make the most we can of our own, whether it be *Natural* or *Artificial*; And foreasmuch as the people which live by Arts are far more in number than those who are masters of the fruits, we ought the more carefully to maintain those endeavours of the multitude, in whom doth consist the greatest strength and riches both of King and Kingdom: for where the people are many, and the arts good, there the traffique must be great, and the Countrey rich. . . .

---

1. What economic role did Mun attribute to foreign trade and the acquisition of colonies?

2. (a) List Mun's recommendations.
(b) What restrictions would be needed to put Mun's recommendations in place?

3. What groups in society would benefit from these restrictions? What groups would be harmed? Explain why in each case.

ADAM SMITH: An Inquiry into the Nature and Causes of the Wealth of Nations (1776)

In The Wealth of Nations, *Adam Smith, a Scottish political economist, attacked mercantilism, arguing that greater gains could be secured through competitive trade and exchange. The following is the conclusion of his arguments against the mercantile system.*

Consumption is the sole end and purpose of all production; and the interest of the producer ought to be attended to, only so far as it may be necessary for promoting that of the consumer. The maxim is so perfectly self-evident, that it would be absurd to attempt to prove it. But in the mercantile system, the interest of the consumer is almost constantly sacrificed to that of the producer; and it seems to consider production, and not consumption, as the ultimate end and object of all industry and commerce.

In the restraints upon the importation of all foreign commodities which can come into competition with those of our own growth, or manufacture, the interest of the home-consumer is evidently sacrificed to that of the producer. It is altogether for the benefit of the latter, that the former is obliged to pay that enhancement of

From Adam Smith, *The Wealth of Nations*, edited by Edwin Cannan, (New York: Random House, 1937), pp. 625–626.

*Commercial Treaty concluded between Britain and Portugal, 1703.

price which this monopoly almost always occasions.

It is altogether for the benefit of the producer that bounties are granted upon the exportation of some of his productions. The home-consumer is obliged to pay, first, the tax which is necessary for paying the bounty, and secondly, the still greater tax which necessarily arises from the enhancement of the price of the commodity in the home market. By the famous treaty of commerce with Portugal,* the consumer is prevented by high duties from purchasing of a neighbouring country, a commodity which our own climate does not produce, but is obliged to purchase it of a distant country, though it is acknowledged, that the commodity of the distant country is of a worse quality than that of the near one. The home-consumer is obliged to submit to this inconveniency, in order that the producer may import into that distant country some of his productions upon more advantageous terms than he would otherwise have been allowed to do. The consumer, too, is obliged to pay, whatever enhancement in the price of those very productions, this forced exportation may occasion in the home market.

But in the system of laws which has been established for the management of our American and West Indian colonies, the interest of the home-consumer has been sacrificed to that of the producer with a more extravagant profusion than in all other commercial regulations. A great empire has been established for the sole purpose of raising up a nation of customers who should be obliged to buy from the shops of our different producers, all the goods with which these could supply them. For the sake of that little enhancement of price which this monopoly might afford our producers, the home-consumers have been burdened with the whole expense of maintaining and defending the empire. For this purpose, and for this purpose only, in the last two wars, more than two hundred millions have been spent, and a new debt of more than a hundred and seventy millions has been contracted over and above all that had been expended for the same purpose in former wars. The interest of this debt alone is not only greater than the whole extraordinary profit, which, it ever could be pretended, was made by the monopoly of the colony trade, but than the whole value of that trade, or than the whole value of the goods, which at an average have been annually exported to the colonies.

It cannot be very difficult to determine who have been the contrivers of this whole mercantile system; not the consumers, we may believe, whose interest has been entirely neglected; but the producers, whose interest has been so carefully attended to; and among this latter class our merchants and manufacturers have been the principal architects. In the mercantile regulations . . . the interest of our manufacturers has been most peculiarly attended to; and the interest, not so much of the consumers, as that of some other sets of producers, has been sacrificed to it.

---

1. (a) What advantages do producers gain from the mercantile system?
(b) What disadvantages do consumers suffer from the mercantile system?

2. (a) If Smith's emphasis on the consumer was adopted by the British government, what changes would have to take place?
(b) What would be the possible impact of these changes on producers? On consumers?

JOHANN WINCKELMANN: Thoughts on the Imitation of Greek Art in Painting and Sculpture (1755)

Johann Winckelmann was a German art historian and critic. He was a strong proponent of the idea of patterning "modern" art after the standards set up in classical Greece. His challenge for the artists of the day was "to take the ancients for models. . .to become great, yes, unsurpassable if we can. As someone has said of Homer; he who learns to admire him, learns to understand him; the same is true of the art works of the ancients, especially the Greeks." The following is from his Thoughts on the Imitation of Greek Art in Painting and Sculpture.

From Elizabeth Holt (ed.), *A Documentary History of Art*, Vol. II, (Garden City, New York: Doubleday Anchor Books, 1958) pp. 338–351.

The imitation of natural beauty either focuses upon a single model or it collects data from many models and combines them. The first produces a faithful copy, a portrait; it leads to the shapes and figures of Dutch art. The second, however, leads to universal beauty and its ideal images, and this is the path taken by the Greeks. But there is a difference between them and us: even assuming that the Greeks did not have more beautiful bodies than we do, they could form these ideal images because they were able to observe the beautiful in nature every day; we have this opportunity only on rare occasions, and rarely does it conform to the wishes of the artist. . . .

I believe that imitating the Greeks can teach us to become wise more quickly, since in their works we find not only the essence of whatever is beautiful throughout nature but also the extent to which even the highest form of natural beauty can be wisely and boldly transcended. Following the Greeks will teach us assurance in conceiving and designing works of art, since they have marked for us the utmost limits of human and divine beauty.

When the artist starts from this basis, when his hand and mind are guided by Greek principles, then he is on the safe road to the true imitation of nature. The ancient concepts of the unity and perfection of nature will clarify our concepts of nature in its diversity. The artist will discover the beauty of nature and combine it with beauty in the absolute; the constant presence of the noble forms of Greek art will help him to find his own rules.

1. Write a précis of Winckelmann's argument for the value of following the Greek example.

2. Select a neoclassical work of art from the period. Identify the artist, the year completed, and subject matter. Write a 100-word analysis of the characteristics of the painting or sculpture that would classify it as neoclassical.

MOLIÈRE: Le Tartuffe (1669)

Many contemporary critics of Le Tartuffe *claimed that Molière had satirized religion in his play. In fact, these feelings were so strong that the play was initially banned for five years. In reality, however,* Le Tartuffe *is an attack not only on religion but on the religious hypocrisy of the age.*

The title character, Tartuffe, is a seventeenth-century con artist who has convinced Mme Pernelle and her son Orgon that he is a holy man. In the first scene, Mme Pernelle tries to convince her grandson, Damis, that Tartuffe is a good man.

Damis: Your man Tartuffe is full of holy speeches . . .
Mme P: And practices precisely what he preaches,
He's a fine man, and should be listened to,
I will not hear him mocked by fools like you.
Damis: Good God! Do you expect me to submit,
To the tyranny of that carping hypocrite?
Must we forgo all joys and satisfactions
Because that bigot censures all our actions? . . .
Mme P: Well, mark my words, your souls would fare far better,
If you obeyed his precepts to the letter.
Dorine: You see him as a saint. I'm far less awed;
In fact, I see right through him. He's a fraud. . . .
Mme P: I tell you that you're blest to have Tartuffe
Dwelling, as my son's guest, beneath this roof;
That Heaven has sent him to forestall its wrath

By leading you, once more, to the true path;
That all he reprehends is reprehensible,
And that you'd better heed him and be sensible.
These visits, balls, and parties in which you revel
Are nothing but inventions of the Devil. . . .

Dorine: Doesn't it seem to you a trifle grim,
To give a girl to a man like him?
When two are ill-suited, can't you see
What the sad consequence is bound to be?
A young girl's virtue is imperilled, Sir,
When such a marriage is imposed on her;
For if one's bridegroom isn't to one's taste,
It's hardly an inducement to be chaste,
And many a man with horns upon his brow
Has made his wife the thing that she is now.
It's hard to be a faithful wife, in short,
To certain husbands of a certain sort,
And he who gives his daughter to a man she hates,
Must answer for her sins at Heaven's gates,
Think, Sir, before you play so risky a role. . . .
(*Aside*) They'll make a lovely pair.
If I were she, no man would marry me
Against my inclination, and go scot-free.
He'd learn, before the wedding day was over,
How readily a wife can find a lover. . . .
(*Later to Mariane*): Well have you lost your tongue, girl?
Must I play
Your part, and say the lines you ought to say?
Faced with a fate so hideous and absurd,
Can you not utter one dissenting word?

In Act 2 it is revealed that Orgon has promised the hand of his daughter Mariane in marriage to Tartuffe. Dorinne, Mariane's maid, criticizes him, and later pleads to Mariane to stand up for herself.

Mariane: What good would it do? A father's power is great.

Dorine: Resist him now, or it will be too late. . . .
Tell him one cannot love at a father's whim;
That you shall marry for yourself not him;
That since it's you who are to be the bride,
It's you, not he, who must be satisfied;
And that if his Tartuffe is so sublime,
He's free to marry him at any time.

---

1. What social values are illustrated by these excerpts?

2. Based upon what you have read, how do you think Molière felt about the issues raised here?

3. Read the play. With a group of students select a scene that you feel illustrates the social values of the period, the comedic nature of the play, and Molière's political viewpoint. Assign parts to each student and perform the scene.

WILLIAM CONGREVE:
Love for Love (1695)

William Congreve was only ten years old at the time of the Stuart Restoration. Even though his work appeared later than the other playwrights with whom he is associated, Congreve's plays are excellent examples of the Restoration-style comedies so popular during the period. If Restoration comedy has been characterized as sometimes realistic, sometimes satirical, and sometimes merely escapist, then Love for Love *may be safely placed in the last category.*

In Love for Love *the protagonist, Valentine, tries a variety of schemes to win the love of Angelica. None works. Angelica, for her part, sees through her suitor's plans but is attracted to him for his basic goodness, generosity, and faithfulness. In the closing scene of the play, Valentine tells the truth and as a result Angelica accepts him willingly.*

From William Congreve, *Love for Love*, in G. Salgado, *Three Restoration Comedies*, (Hammondsworth, UK: Penguin Books, 1968), pp. 360–363.

Valentine: I have been disappointed of my only hope, and he that loses hope may part with any thing. I never valued fortune but as it was subservient to my pleasure, and my only pleasure was to please this lady. I have made many vain attempts, and find at last that nothing but my ruin can effect it. . . .

Angelica: (*to Valentine*): Had I the world to give you, it could not make me worthy of so generous and faithful a passion. Here's my hand, my heart was always yours, and struggled very hard to make this utmost trial of your virtue. . . .

I have done dissembling now, Valentine, and if that coldness which I have always worn before you should turn to an extreme fondness, you must not suspect it.

Valentine: I'll prevent that suspicion, for I intend to dote on at that immoderate rate, that your fondness shall never distinguish itself enough to be taken notice of. If ever you seem to love too much, it must be only when I can't love enough.

Angelica: Have a care of large promises; you know you are apt to run more in debt than you are able to pay.

Valentine: Therefore I yield my body as your prisoner, and make your best on't.

Scandal: . . . Well, madam, you have done exemplary justice, in punishing an inhumane father and rewarding a faithful lover. But there is a third good work, which I, in particular, must thank you for. I was an infidel to your sex, and you have converted me. For now I am convinced that all women are not like fortune, blind in bestowing favours, either on those who do not merit, or who do not want 'em.

Angelica: 'Tis an unreasonable accusation that you lay upon our sex. You tax us with injustice, only to cover your own want of merit. You would all have the reward of love, but few have the constancy to stay till it becomes your due. Men are generally hypocrites and infidels. They pretend to worship, but have neither zeal or faith. How few, like Valentine, would persevere even unto martyrdom, and sacrifice their interest to their constancy. In admiring me you misplace the novelty.

The miracle today is that we find
A lover true, not that a woman's kind.

---

1. Rewrite this scene from *Love for Love* in modern English.

2. What social values are being illustrated here? To what extent is there a "feminist" ending to the play?

3. Compare the ideas behind *Le Tartuffe* and *Love for Love*. Based on additional research, determine whether there were common themes running through comedy during this period.

JONATHAN SWIFT:
A Modest Proposal (1730)

Jonathan Swift is best known as the author of Gulliver's Travels. *In this account, written between 1725 and 1730, Swift uses the fictional travels of a ship's surgeon, Lemuel Gulliver, to pass satiric judgment on the government and social customs of England.*

Swift, a staunch Irish nationalist, became disenchanted with English rule and by the 1720s was working for Irish independence. In one anonymous pamphlet, he called for a boycott of English goods and proclaimed "Burn everything that comes from England except the coal." The printer who put out the pamphlet was tried for sedition, but no Irish jury would convict him. Swift continued to write tracts in favour of independence, until in 1730 he published his most biting attack on British policy.

A government suggestion that Ireland's overpopulation problem be solved by allowing the king of France to conscript Irish citizens or that young people be sent to Australia prompted Swift to write his "Modest Proposal" to solve the overpopulation problem.

From Jonathan Swift, "A Modest Proposal . . . ," in Annette T. Rubinstein, *The Great Tradition in English Literature: From Shakespeare to Shaw*, Vol. 1, (New York: Modern Reader Paperbacks, 1953), pp. 242–246.

A Modest Proposal for Preventing the Children of Poor People in Ireland from Being a Burden to their parents or country, and for making them beneficial to the Public

It is a melancholy object to those who walk through this great town or travel in the country, when they see the streets, the roads, and cabin doors, crowded with beggars of the female sex, followed by three, four, or six children, all in rags and importuning every passenger for alms. These mothers, instead of being able to work for their honest livelihood, are forced to employ all their time in strolling to beg sustenance for their helpless infants: who as they grow up either turn thieves for want of work, or leave their dear native country to fight for the pretender in Spain, or sell themselves to the Barbados.

I think it is agreed by all parties that this prodigious number of children in the arms, or on the backs, or at the heels of their mothers, and frequently of their fathers, is in the present deplorable state of the kingdom a very great additional grievance; and, therefore, whoever could find out a fair, cheap, and easy method of making these children sound, useful members of the commonwealth, would deserve so well of the public as to have his statue set up for a preserver of the nation. . . .

I shall now therefore humbly propose my own thoughts, which I hope will not be liable to the least objection. I have been assured by a very knowing American of my acquaintance in London, that a young healthy child well nursed is at a year old a most delicious, nourishing, and wholesome food, whether stewed, roasted, baked, or boiled; and I make no doubt that it will equally serve in a fricassee or a ragout. I do therefore humbly offer it to public consideration that of the 120 000 children already computed, 20 000 may be reserved from breed, whereof only one-fourth part to be males; which is more than we allow to sheep, black cattle or swine; and my reason is, that these children are seldom the fruits of marriage, a circumstance not much regarded by our savages, therefore one male will be sufficient to serve four females. That the remaining 100 000 may, at a year old, be offered in sale to the persons of quality and fortune throughout the kindom; always advising the mother to let them suck plentifully in the last month, so as to render them plump and fat for a good table.

A child will make two dishes at an entertainment of friends; and when the family dines alone, the fore or hind quarter will make a reasonable dish, and seasoned with a little pepper or salt will be very good boiled on the fourth day especially in winter.

I have reckoned upon a medium that a child just born will weight 12 pounds, and in a solar year, if tolerably nursed, will increase to 28 pounds.

I grant this food will be somewhat dear, and therefore very proper for landlords, who, as they have already devoured most of the parents, seem to have the best title to the children. . . .

I profess, in the sincerity of my heart, that I have not the least personal interest in endeavouring to promote this necessary work, having no other motive than the public good of my country, by advancing our trade, providing for infants, relieving the poor, and giving some pleasure to the rich. I have no children by which I can propose to get a single penny; the youngest being nine years old, and my wife past child-bearing.

---

1. Write a response to Swift's "modest proposal" from the point of view of (a) a government official who, taking it at face value, is charged with trying to explain why it would not be appropriate, or (b) an Irish nationalist echoing the sentiments of the satire.

ANALYSIS AND APPLICATION

1. Write a defence of the theory of absolutism.

2. With your friends, create a "play within a play" docu-drama set in the Bourbon court.
  (a) Have a theatrical troupe perform excerpts from a Molière play, such as *Le Bourgeois Gentilhomme*, for the king and his courtiers.
  (b) Based upon a reading of Saint-Simon and other contemporary observers, depict the audience's response to the performance.

3. Using available resources, create a photo essay about one of the following:
  (a) life in Louis XIV's court;
  (b) a comparison of baroque and neoclassical art or architecture;
  (c) the life of the peasantry in pre-revolutionary France.

NOTE: Your essay might take the form of a slide show to be presented in class.

4. Evaluate the mercantile system as a means of creating wealth. In your view, what would be the impact upon such a system as the economies of the colonies matured?

5. Research the life of Jonathan Swift. Comment on the role of the artist as revolutionary.

6. Write a biographical profile of a classical composer, including an annotated list of his/her major works.

CHAPTER TWO

The Age of Reason: The Enlightenment to 1789

THE ORIGINS OF THE ENLIGHTENMENT

The Europe of the absolute monarch was living on borrowed time in the seventeenth and eighteenth centuries. In spite of the suppression of dissent, new forces were building up strength that would soon sweep the ancien régime from power. The first stage of this revolution, however, was not political or social; it was intellectual. Against the test of reason, absolutism could not prevail.

An explosion of new ideas emanated from Europe beginning in the late sixteenth century. Revolutionary ideas in science provided a new window on the physical world. Astronomers, physicists, and chemists shattered many of the commonly held beliefs of the Middle Ages.

As research uncovered the existence of natural laws governing the physical universe, it seemed only logical to search for the same basic tenets governing human behaviour, society, and government. The result was a generation of philosophers who would challenge the existing order by applying the test of reason to old prejudices. This new view of the world would usher in an *Age of Enlightenment* which would give birth to the modern world. Western thought would never be the same again.

The Revolution in Scientific Thought

Prior to the *Scientific Revolution* of the seventeenth and eighteenth centuries, exploration into the world of nature and the heavens was considered the purview of classical authority or religious teaching. To the leaders of the Roman Catholic church, the *geocentric* (earth-centred) theories of Ptolemy of Alexandria and the scientific views of Aristotle provided a sufficient corollary to the teachings of the Bible.

The following passage, taken from a tenth-century Anglo-Saxon document, gives a typical account of Biblical astronomy.

> On the second day, God made the heaven. It is visible, but can never be closely examined, since it is so high, the clouds are so thick, and our eyes are so weak. Heaven surrounds the whole world and turns about the world faster than any mill wheel. It is as deep under the earth as above. It is round and studded with stars.
>
> Truly the sun follows God's commands, going above the earth by day and below the earth by night. The sun is forever running around the earth, and so it shines under the earth at night as it does above our heads by day. The sun is very large. From what the books say, it is as broad as the entire earth. Yet it appears to be very small, since it is very far away. The farther anything is from us the smaller it appears. The moon and all of the stars receive their light from the great sun. The sun is typical of our saviour, Jesus Christ, who is the sun of righteousness. Good Christians are like the stars. They shine because Christ has let his light fall upon them.

Adapted excerpt from *The Shaping of Western Society* by John M. Good.

Modern science evolved during the seventeenth and eighteenth centuries. The same spirit that drove people to reject the guidance and authority of priests and to seek revelation in the Scriptures during the Reformation influenced them to reject medieval concepts and interpret nature for themselves. The "natural philosophers" observed, experimented with, and tested theories. Increasingly, mathematics was used to verify and quantify new discoveries. The invention of the printing press and the expansion of the reading public allowed scientists to share their knowledge.

In the first half of the seventeenth century, scientists invented the telescope, the microscope, the barometer, the thermometer, and the pendulum clock. These new means of measuring and observing natural phenomena resulted in new discoveries in physics, medicine, biology, and chemistry. But it was astronomy that was the first science in the modern sense, and it became the model for the sciences that followed.

Astronomy

Medieval Europe subscribed to the theory of the geocentric universe. This model was first formulated by Ptolemy, an Alexandrian, in the second century A.D. In his work *Almagest*, Ptolemy hypothesized that the earth was an immovable sphere at the centre of the universe and that the heavens revolved around the earth in fixed, transparent spheres. Each of these spheres in turn contained a heavenly body that moved around the earth in a circular orbit, east to west. The celestial spheres contained the seven known "planets"—the moon, Mercury, Venus, the sun, Mars, Jupiter, and Saturn—and the "Stellatum," or fixed stars. To make this model correspond with celestial observations, Ptolemy added epicycles to the spheres to explain the apparent shift in the position of the planets. His theory, with slight modifications, lasted over 1300 years.

The Ptolemaic model enjoyed such longevity because it was formulated in mathematical terms and could be supported by observation. But it was also supported by theology. Numerous biblical references lent support to the theory of the geocentric universe. The model also fit theological logic: as the home of God's greatest creation, the earth must be the centre of the universe. Because of this, the Roman Catholic church became the greatest popularizer and protector of the Ptolemaic universe. But even the support of the Catholic church could not stop people from questioning the validity of this theory.

The Copernican Revolution

Nicolaus Copernicus (1473–1543), in his work *On the Revolution of the Celestial Orbs* (1543), overturned the geocentric theory with his *heliocentric* theory, which placed the sun at the centre of the universe. (See readings.) This theory, however, was not self-evident. Copernicus's supporting arguments were primarily mathematical, not observational, and so his theory was not widely accepted in the sixteenth century. He also retained the circular orbit of the Ptolemaic universe, so predictions using his system were no more accurate than those of the geocentric universe. More accurate

---

GALILEO GALILEI

On 21 June 1633, Galileo Galilei stood before the Inquisition for a formal interrogation into his scientific theories. After he was found guilty of heresy, he was held over until the next day for sentencing. On June 22nd Galileo was forced to publicly recant his theories about Copernicanism.

I, Galileo . . . aged seventy years . . . have been pronounced by the Holy Office to be vehemently suspected of heresy, that is to say, of having held and believed that the sun is the centre of the world and immovable and that the Earth is not the centre and moves . . . with sincere heart and unfeigned faith I abjure, curse, and detest the aforesaid errors and heresies. . . .

But while Galileo was forced to publicly recant his work, in private his disgust with the Church was evident. In notes he had written in his own copy of the Dialogue, *he said:*

. . . And who can doubt that it will lead to the worst disorders when minds created free by God are compelled to submit slavishly to an outside will? When we are told to deny our senses and subject them to the whim of others? When people of whatsoever competence are made judges over experts and are granted authority to treat them as they please? These are the novelties which are apt to bring about the ruin of commonwealths and the subversion of the state.

From Colin A. Ronan, *Galileo*, (London: Weidenfeld and Nicolson, 1974), pp. 220–221.

and detailed observations and new discoveries were required before the Copernican system gained ground against the Ptolemaic universe.

The work of Copernicus was expanded by Tycho Brahe (1546–1601). But although Brahe supplied the observations needed to substantiate the heliocentric universe, the astronomer himself did not believe in the Copernican theory. Instead, he developed a short-lived compromise between the Ptolemaic and the Copernican systems: his universe retained the earth at its centre, with the moon and the sun in orbit around the earth, but the other planets orbited around the sun.

When Brahe died he bequeathed his substantial collection of astronomical observations to his assistant, Johannes Kepler (1571–1630). Using Brahe's observations of Mars, Kepler eventually disproved both Brahe's and Copernicus's theories. In *The New Astronomy* (1609), he proved conclusively that Mars orbited the sun elliptically. This discovery greatly improved the Copernican system. Later discoveries in astronomy, such as those made by Galileo Galilei (1564–1642), further substantiated the heliocentric theory.

Galileo, considered the founder of modern experimental science, used the newly discovered telescope to make astronomical observations that disproved the Ptolemaic universe. These were published in his book *Sidereal Messenger* (1610), which also drew attention to the wonders of the telescope. (See readings.) Galileo was so successful in supporting the Copernican theory that he was summoned before the Inquisition in 1615 and forced to renounce his findings. In 1616, *Sidereal Messenger* was placed on the *Index of Prohibited Books*. However, this did not stop Galileo from continuing his research and in 1632 he published his *Dialogue on the Two Chief World Systems—Ptolemaic and Copernican*. In this literary and scientific masterpiece, Galileo disseminated the Copernican theory to the common people. This again made him

The 1632 trial of Galileo Galilei by the Inquisition was depicted by Robert-Fleury. Galileo remained under house arrest until his death in 1642.

SIR ISAAC NEWTON

Isaac Newton was born on Christmas Day, 1642. He was raised by his elderly grandmother after the death of his father and the remarriage of his mother. As a youth, his greatest aptitude was in building mechanical toys such as watermills and waterclocks.

His formal education began at the King's School, a grammar school at Grantham. At the age of eighteen he entered Trinity College, Cambridge. The college was closed the following year, in 1662, because of the plague. Newton spent the next eighteen months at his home in Woolsthorpe, during which time he discovered the binomial theorem, differential calculus, and the theory of universal gravitation. He elaborated on this latter discovery in *The Mathematical Principles of Natural Philosophy*.

Newton's interests were not limited to mathematics. He conducted a number of experiments into the nature of light. One of the best known used a prism to break sunlight into the colour spectrum of white light. This and other findings were later published in *Opticks* (1704). He also improved the design of the telescope by using a concave mirror as a reflector to give a clearer image.

Newton held a number of public positions during his lifetime. He was a Fellow of Cambridge University and served as a Member of Parliament for the university for thirteen months beginning in 1689. He was Master of the Mint, a position which gave him an income of £1400 per annum, a considerable sum that gave him financial security. In 1703, he was elected president of the Royal Society and became the patriarch of English science. Two years later, Newton was knighted by Queen Anne, the greatest honour a grateful nation could bestow on the world's greatest living scientist.

Newton took ill on 3 March 1727 and died on March 20th at the age of eighty-five. A monument erected above his grave in Westminister Abbey bears the following inscription:

Here Lies

SIR ISAAC NEWTON, KNIGHT,

Who by a vigour of mind, almost supernatural,
First demonstrated
The motions and figures of the Planets,
The Paths of the Comets, and the
Tides of the Ocean.
He diligently investigated
The different refrangibilities of the Rays of Light,
And the properties of the Colours to which
they give rise.
An Assiduous, Sagacious, and Faithful Interpreter
of Nature, Antiquity, and the Holy Scriptures,
He asserted in his Philosophy the Majesty of
God, and exhibited in his Conduct the
simplicity of the Gospel.
Let Mortals rejoice that there has existed
such and so great

AN ORNAMENT OF THE HUMAN RACE.
Born 25 Dec., 1642; Died 20 March 1727.

a target of the Inquisition. In 1633, he was again forced to recant and was condemned for heresy and detained for the remaining nine years of his life. (See readings.)

Despite his belief in the Copernican theory, or perhaps because of it, Galileo never rejected the idea that the orbits of the planets were circular, even though this contradicted the findings of Kepler. The final piece to this puzzle was not uncovered until Sir Isaac Newton (1642–1727) discovered universal gravitation.

Newton's discovery of the laws of gravity unified Copernicus's heliocentric universe, Kepler's elliptical orbits, and Galileo's study of falling bodies into a single theory of universal gravitation. His great work, *The Mathematical Principles of Natural Philosophy* (1687), demonstrated that the moon stayed in its orbit around the earth and the planets orbited around the sun because of the centrifugal force created by gravitational pull. Newton further established the link between gravitation and the action of falling bodies, which Galileo failed to make. Newton's work had an enormous impact on the scientific community and his three laws of motion formed the basis of all further work in the field. His ideas were revised only in the twentieth century.

The publication of Newton's *Principles* was the theoretical proof of the Copernican theory. All that remained was to secure definite proof that the earth did move, a fact that was confirmed by James Bradley and Samuel Molyneux in an experiment to detect the shift of nearer stars against the background of more distant ones, conducted in 1729.

THE REVOLUTION SPREADS

Physics

Galileo laid the foundation for modern physics with his discoveries in the motion of falling bodies, the oscillation of the pendulum, the theories of mechanical action, and the cohesive power of solids. However, many other people contributed to the study of physics, with discoveries in the fields of optics, heat, electricity, and magnetism.

In optics, the invention of the telescope and the microscope paved the way for discoveries in other sciences, such as biology and astronomy. The most important theoretical advances were in the nature of light. Many notable scientists were involved in this research, including Kepler, Descartes, Snell, Hooke, Huygens, and Newton. In the early seventeenth century, Willebrord Snel (1591–1626) discovered the *sine law*, which explained the angle of refraction as light passed through one transparent medium into another. Although Newton provided the first satisfactory explanation of colour, observing the spectrum of white light (red, orange, yellow, green, blue, indigo, and violet) refracted through a prism, he mistakenly thought that light was a stream of particles. His work was so influential that his particle theory of light dominated scientific thought until the eighteenth century.

The seventeenth and eighteenth centuries also saw the invention of the thermometer and the development of the Fahrenheit (named after Daniel Fahrenheit) and the Celsius (named after Anders Celsius) scales. Although both systems of measurement were used interchangeably, the thermometer brought a previously unknown level of accuracy to experimental observations. Joseph Black (1728–1799) discovered that different bodies had different capacities for heat, a discovery that had immediate practical use in the steam engine.

William Gilbert (1540–1603) uncovered the new sciences of electricity and magnetism in his work *De Magnete* (1600). Gilbert, an English physician, laid down the theories of magnetism and coined the terms *electric force* and *magnetic pole*. In the 1750s, Benjamin Franklin (1706–1790) proved that lightning and electricity were identical by flying a kite in a thunderstorm and drawing sparks from a key on the kite's string. This laid the theoretical foundation for the only practical result of studies in electricity in the eighteenth century, the lightning rod. Most discoveries, such as Alessandro Volta's (1745–1827) discovery of the electric battery, provided little immediate practical value but gave the nineteenth century the necessary tools for new dimensions in research in electricity.

Mathematics

Mathematics became the universal language of science in the seventeenth and eighteenth centuries. Increasingly, qualitative assessments were rejected in favour of quantitative explanation and verification. This was partly because of the success of mathematical deductions and partly because of new and powerful developments in the science of mathematics, including decimals, logarithms, geometry, and mathematical probability. These innovations culminated in the simultaneous development of differential calculus by Newton and Gottfried Leibnitz (1646–1716). During the eighteenth century, mathematicians consolidated and extended the discoveries of the seventeenth century. The Swiss mathematician Leonhard Euler (1707–1786) developed calculus of variations and differential geometry, which made mathematics more accessible to every branch of the physical sciences. The greatest mathematician of the age was reputed to be French astronomer-mathematician Joseph-Louis Lagrange (1736–1813). Lagrange replaced Euler at the Prussian court of Frederich II after Euler resigned his position to join the royal court at St. Petersburg. Lagrange's influential *Analytical Mechanics* (1788) established mechanics as a branch of mathematical analysis. Late in the century, Gaspard Monge (1746–1818) contributed to a resurgence in geometry with the publication of his *Descriptive Geometry* (1799). Monge had originally developed descriptive geometry (geometry in three dimensions, the basis for mechanical drawing today) in 1763, but it remained a French military secret until 1795.

The Scientific Method

William Gilbert dedicated *De Magnete* to those "who looked for knowledge not in books but in themselves." The practitioners of the new science focused on experimentation rather than belief. Medieval scientists consulted the works of Aristotle to determine what he had written on a subject and then deduced what he would have written about something new. The scientific method evolved through the experimentation and evaluation of people like Copernicus, Brahe, Kepler, and especially Galileo and Newton. It was the work of Francis Bacon (1561–1626) and René Descartes (1596–1650), however, that formulated and defined the modern scientific method.

In *Novum Organum* (1620), Bacon criticized the contemporary methods of discovering knowledge. Distrustful of mathematics and deductive logic, Bacon relied on observation and experimentation. Instead of starting with assumed principles and proceeding through logical deduction, as medieval scientists had done, Bacon built from the particular to the general. He believed that scientific discoveries had to be made through induction—that is, through a process of reasoning from experimental data, to hypotheses and general laws, and finally to scientific principles.

By contrast, Descartes was a mathematical philosopher who tried to formulate a different approach to science. Like Bacon, he objected to past and current methods of obtaining scientific knowledge, but he rejected Bacon's empiricism in favour of rationalism and deduction. For Descartes, one of the basic problems in medieval reasoning was that it was based upon faulty assumptions. In his *Discourse on Method* (1637), he reduced problem solving to four rules:

1. Never accept anything as truth that is not self-evident or indisputable. (I think, therefore I am.)
2. Break the problem into as many small parts as possible.
3. Move from the simplest component to the most complex.
4. Review the work to be sure that it is complete; omit nothing.

He followed this method to show that all of nature functioned as a machine, governed by universal mathematical rules. His work was so influential that it became known as the Cartesian Revolution.

In spite of their contradictory methods, both Bacon and Descartes made profound contributions to the Scientific Revolution. Bacon's demand for concrete, empirical evidence resulted in new rigour in experimentation and observation. The accumulation of "new" data gave great impetus to the formulation of revolutionary hypotheses about the natural world. On the other hand, Descartes's reliance on deductive reasoning reintroduced rational thought into a discipline that had long been dominated by the rationalizations of scientists trying to reconcile their observations with classical theories.

From opposite directions, the scientist and the mathematician gave birth to a new Age of Reason in Western civilization. These principles were soon applied to all fields of scientific investigation.

Medicine

Medieval medical practitioners had believed that diseases were caused by imbalances in the *four humours*, the body fluids (blood, phlegm, choler, and melancholy) that supposedly determined one's physical and mental health. Barbers were responsible for both minor and major surgery; their most frequent response to disease was *blood-letting*, a procedure intended to put the humours back in balance. Surgery in the seventeenth and eighteenth centuries was crude by today's standards. Post-surgical shock killed many patients, and the absence of anesthesia and an effective means of fighting infection caused considerable pain and suffering.

By the seventeenth century, medical scientists were beginning to build upon the advances of renaissance researchers such as Paracelsus, Vesalius, and Paré, ushering in a new era in internal medicine. William Harvey (1578–1657), an English physician, discovered the primary circulation of blood. In *On the Movement of the Heart and Blood* (1628), he showed that the heart acted as a pump, circulating blood through the arteries and veins, thereby overthrowing the traditional view that blood was stationary. This discovery was an important step toward understanding how the human body functioned.

Diagnostic medicine also made significant advances during the period. Following Thomas Sydenham's (1624–1689) recognition of the importance of symptoms in treating diseases, Stephen Hales (1679–1761) became the first person to measure blood pressure by inserting a tube into a blood vessel and measuring the blood that rose in the tube. Leopold Auenbregger (1722–1809) discovered that tapping the chest could determine congestion, while René Laennac's (1781–1826) discovery of the stethoscope provided early diagnosis of heart and chest ailments.

Chemistry

It was during the Scientific Revolution that alchemy gave way to modern chemistry. Robert Boyle (1627–1691) gave birth to this new era by applying the methods of inductive science to chemistry. He discovered the relationship (known as Boyle's Law) between the pressure and volume of a gas. In 1661, he published *The Sceptical Chemist*, which challenged the old theories of Aristotle and defined chemical elements. However, it was over 100 years before the modern classification system was born.

Most of the new developments in chemistry involved combustion and respiration. Henry Cavendish (1731–1810) discovered hydrogen gas. Joseph Priestley (1733–1804) discovered "dephlogisticated air"—that is, oxygen. In the eighteenth century, Antoine-Laurent Lavoisier (1743–1794), building on the work of Priestley and Cavendish, discovered that water was made up of oxygen and hydrogen. Together with other French scientists, Lavoisier reorganized all of the chemical terminology in a work called *Method of Chemical Nomenclature* (1787). In 1789, he published the first modern chemistry textbook, *Elements of Chemistry*.

Biology

There were few advancements in the theory of biological science. However, the invention of the microscope did revolutionize the processes of observation and description. Although early microscopes suffered from *chromatic abberation* (images that were surrounded by coloured fringes), early microscopists, such as Anton Van Leeuwenhoek (1632–1723), made elaborate drawings of blood corpuscles, bacteria, and other organisms. Robert Hooke's (1635–1703) *Micrographia* (1665) was the first great work devoted to microscopy.

New classification systems were developed for plants and animals during this period. The most notable contributor was Linnaeus (1707–1778), who developed the *binomial*, or two-name system—one name for the *genus*, or common characteristic, and the other for the species. It was Linnaeus who coined the term *Homo sapiens* to describe our own species.

The Impact of the Scientific Revolution

The Scientific Revolution was not confined to isolated discoveries in obscure laboratories, nor was it simply characterized by a small group of scientists exchanging ideas. In fact, the changes in scientific thought began to affect every part of society.

Science was important for economics and trade, so governments became involved. The French National Observatory at Paris (1671) and the British Observatory at Greenwich (1676) were established to make astronomical observations to enable mariners to find longitude while at sea. Government interest, of course, was purely utilitarian. It was meant to assist in the navigation of overseas trading vessels. The problem was of such importance that in 1714 the British government established the Board of Longitude. Prizes were offered for effective methods of finding longitude at sea. Accurate navigation required precise time measurements. The problem was finally solved in 1764 when John Harrison produced a chronometer with such accuracy that it lost only fifteen seconds in five months.

The practical effects of the Scientific Revolution were many and varied. New discoveries in mathematics were used in surveying, navigation, map-making, and gunnery. New astronomical tables, coupled with the invention of the chronometer, improved navigation. Studies into the specific heat of metals enabled improvements to be made to the steam engine.

But it was the psychological impact of the Scientific Revolution that was the most profound. No longer was humankind the centre of the universe. Science undermined the Christian view of the world, even though scientists did not attack the Church directly. To many scientists, including Kepler, Descartes, and Newton, every scientific discovery was yet further proof of the perfect wisdom of God's creation. But by reducing the physical world to a series of mathematical laws, scientists turned attention away from religious studies and toward a more secular society.

This conflict between science and religion reached epic

proportions during the Scientific Revolution. The Roman Catholic church's defence of the Aristotelian philosophy in the face of the ever-growing number of scientific discoveries seriously weakened its position. The persecution of Galileo did nothing to stop the onslaught of scientific knowledge, nor did the *Index of Prohibited Books* in its attempts to censor scientific (and other) publications. Ultimately, science and reason were victorious, despite the vigorous efforts of the Inquisition.

By the end of the seventeenth century, miracles were becoming unthinkable and biblical prophecies unacceptable. The decline of theology created a loss of confidence and security for some, but for most educated people the scientific discoveries had positive results. Belief in witchcraft declined and superstitions were ridiculed. The waning faith in the wisdom of the ancients destroyed the belief that the Golden Age was past. It was replaced by a new attitude toward people, nature, and the universe. A new faith in the human capacity for progress through reason opened the floodgates, and the scientific method was applied to the study of society, religion, and politics.

Of course, the old customs and ideas held sway among the masses. The ideas of the Scientific Revolution were too complex for all but the educated few to grasp. It was left to the philosophers to create a world view based on science, not religion, by simplifying and popularizing the ideas of the Scientific Revolution.

THE INDIVIDUAL AND THE COMMUNITY IN THE AGE OF REASON

By the end of the seventeenth century, many of the scientific and intellectual assumptions inherited from the classical world and reinforced by the Roman Catholic church had been replaced by the new ideas generated by the scientific method. The scientists had proved that humanity had the ability to uncover the laws that governed nature. Almost immediately, critics of the existing social and political order embraced the same method of research in their fields. The logic was simple: if universal laws existed in the natural world, then similar "truths" must apply to the human condition. To many, therefore, the next challenge was obvious: discover the laws that regulate the relationship between the individual and the community.

The Debate over Absolutism

During the last half of the seventeenth and the first half of the eighteenth centuries, European writers debated the relative merits of absolutist rule. These arguments outlining human knowledge appeared in many different forms, from pamphlets, periodicals, and news sheets to books and encyclopedias. This new "political science" adopted the methods of its physical counterparts. Soon deductive reasoning and careful observation became the norm in the study of human political society.

Hobbes

At the beginning of the Age of Reason, absolutist rule was in fashion and several scientific defences of strong government were published. English political philosopher Thomas Hobbes (1588–1679) was repulsed by the disorder and violence of the civil war that wracked his country in the middle of the century. He argued that a strong government was necessary to protect people from themselves. In his book *Leviathan* (1651), he claimed that "during the time that men live without a common power to keep them all in awe, they are in that condition which is called war; and such a war, as is of every man, against every man."

Hobbes called this condition the "state of nature" in which life would be "solitary, poor, nasty, brutish, and short." He believed the state of nature was a violent world that existed when individuals had to depend on their own strengths and resources to survive. Under such conditions it was impossible to develop other aspects of society. The development of industry, art, trade, science, and literature could be possible only under established law, order, and social control. And this could be accomplished only under the strong leadership of an absolute ruler (the "leviathan"). But because people are motivated by their own selfish interests, they must enter into a contract with this absolute ruler in which they surrender their freedom and accept his or her total power. In return, the ruler ensures peace and security for the masses.

The exaggerated tales of torture, massacre, and cannibalism in other lands, which were being circulated throughout Europe by overseas explorers, further convinced Hobbes and his followers of the truth of his ideas. In addition, the social stability and artistic accomplishments of Louis XIV's France seemed to be living proof of the validity of his theories. It would take a half century before a new school of thought would emerge to challenge Hobbes's views of the world.

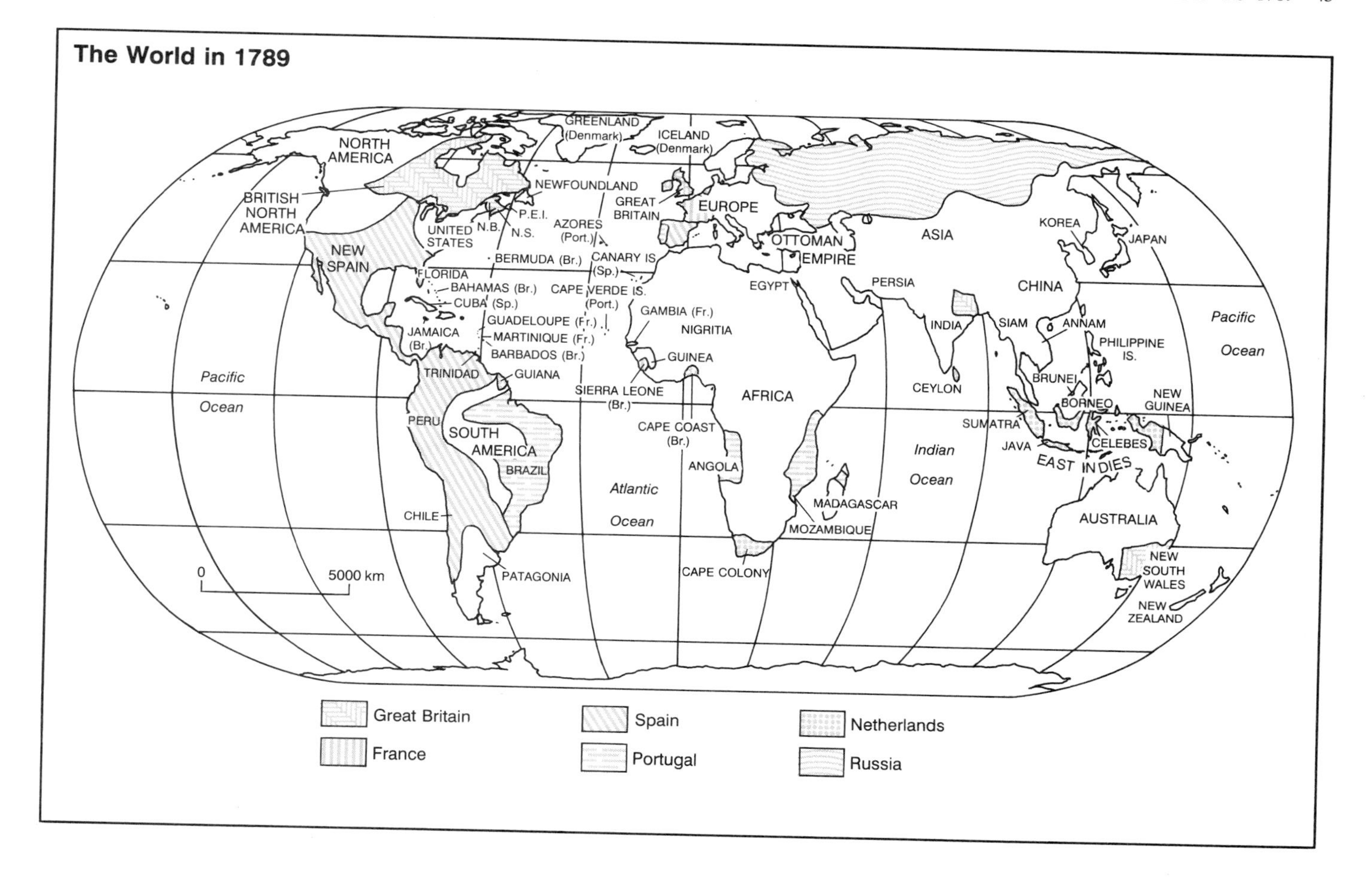

Locke

John Locke (1632–1704) supported the Glorious Revolution of 1688 in Great Britain, which brought William III (1650–1702) to the throne. Unlike his Stuart predecessors, William was invited to become monarch under the terms of a Bill of Rights that limited his powers. For Locke, this type of social contract, with clear expectations and limitations on the powers of the monarch, was preferable to the carte blanche of Thomas Hobbes. Like Hobbes, however, Locke believed that government was based on a contract between the people and their ruler. But Locke had a much different interpretation of human nature, which gave him an entirely different view of the human capacity to reason.

Locke believed that people were reasonable by nature and that they had certain natural rights—life, liberty, and property. In order to preserve these rights, people banded together to form a government based on a compact among equals. *Consent* therefore became the basis of political power; power came from the people, and so government was subject to their joint decisions. If the government broke the compact, then the citizens had the right to rebel against the government.

Locke's political philosophy was expressed in his *Two Treatises of Government* (1690), published two years after the British parliamentary revolution of 1688. (See readings.) He was, in fact, justifying the overthrow of James II (1633–1701) and defending the Bill of Rights, which set up the limited monarchy of William III and established Parliament as a significant political force in English government. Locke's writings provided a new prestige for constitutional principles, a fact that was not lost to the European continent and the English colonies in North America.

Enlightenment Thought in Europe

Montesquieu

Charles Louis de Secondat, the Baron de Montesquieu (1689–1755), was a French aristocrat credited with founding the modern historical method. His *Spirit of the Laws* (1748) was an empirical investigation of all aspects of social science written with a detachment uncommon in the eighteenth century. (See readings.) His principal contribution to political science was the hypothesis that political liberty could best be preserved through a balance of powers and a system of checks and balances.

Montesquieu looked to England as an example of good government. He believed the strength of the English system was in the separation of legislative, executive, and judiciary powers. Each branch provided checks on the others, thereby protecting political liberty by preventing absolute control by any one branch. Although Montesquieu's analysis of the English constitution has been attacked by subsequent writers as inadequate and inaccurate, he brought the English constitution to the attention of the continent and his ideas had a significant impact on the American Constitution.

Voltaire

Like Montesquieu, Voltaire (born François-Marie Arouet, 1694–1778) admired England. His *Letters on the English* (1733) popularized the ideas of Bacon and Locke, while his *Elements of the Philosophy of Newton* (1738) publicized Newton's natural philosophy. Throughout his writings Voltaire advocated freedom of thought and tolerance. He once wrote to an opponent: "I disapprove of what you say, but I will defend to the death your right to say it."

Voltaire attacked the Roman Catholic church as a bastion of prejudice, superstition, intolerance, and injustice. Without question, he was the most famous social critic in eighteenth-century France. Unlike many of his contemporaries, his main weapon was not reason and scientific investigation but subtle sarcasm and ridicule. In his writings he advocated rule by reason and justice. He contended that the ideal ruler need not be democratically elected, but could even be a hereditary monarch as long as that monarch was "enlightened" in her or his approach. For Voltaire, this meant a ruler who guaranteed individual rights and ruled the nation for the common good. His ideas were studied by Catherine the Great of Russia (1729–1796) and he was a personal friend of Frederick the Great of Prussia (1712–1786). The Bourbon family of France, however, paid him little attention.

Rousseau

Swiss philosopher Jean-Jacques Rousseau (1712–1778) rejected Voltaire's enlightened despotism in favour of democracy. He outlined his justification of democracy in *The Social Contract* (1762).

Like Locke, Rousseau believed that government derived its authority from the consent of the governed through a contract. But Locke's contract was a political compact between the ruler and the ruled; Rousseau's contract was a social and political contract among the people to preserve the common good. Governments, whether they were kings or elected officials, were merely representatives of the people and could be replaced if they failed to keep their part of the contract. Decisions were made democratically through the expression of the general will of the people. Anyone who refused to obey would be compelled to do so.

Although Rousseau's *Social Contract* was not widely read at the time, the rallying cry of the French Revolution—Liberty, Equality, and Fraternity—was taken from its pages.

Jean-Jacques Rousseau, the most radical of the philosophes, *was an inspiration to the French revolutionaries.*

(See readings.) Many of Rousseau's ideas were implemented in the *Declaration of the Rights of Man* (1789).

Rousseau's greatest influence on his contemporaries was through his novels *Nouvelle Héloïse* (1760) and *Émile* (1762). In both of these works, Rousseau criticized the artificiality of aristocratic life and advocated the concept of the "noble savage"—a person unencumbered and uncontaminated by civilization. Rousseau's popularity was attested to by the spectacle of Marie Antoinette (1755–1793), queen of France, masquerading as a shepherdess in a rustic setting built especially for her on the grounds of Versailles. Here the queen and her attendants could escape the confines and rigid ceremony of the court and return to a simpler, idealized past. But while the queen was playing with the philosopher's ideas, much more serious forces would soon put them into effect with a vengeance. (See chapter 3.)

The Philosophes

Montesquieu, Voltaire, and Rousseau were the most influential political writers of the Enlightenment. Their ideas were popularized throughout France and Europe by a group of writers known as the *philosophes*. The centre of the movement was in the salons of Paris, where the *philosophes* found a ready audience for their ideas.

The ideas of the *philosophes* found expression in the *Encyclopedia of Classified Dictionary of the Sciences, Arts and Trades*, a multivolume compendium of the scholarship and thought of the time, edited by Denis Diderot (1713–1784) and Jean le Rond d'Alembert (1717–1783). The intent of the *Encyclopedia*, according to Diderot, was "to gather together the knowledge scattered over the face of the earth, to set forth its general plan to the men with whom we live, and to transmit it to the men who will come after us." Its subversive nature was soon realized by the authorities, who disliked its criticisms of religion and the Establishment. The *Encyclopedia* was banned by royal decree in 1759, but still sold thousands of copies in France and translated editions throughout Europe. It had a profound influence on the political, social, and cultural trends of the time.

The *philosophes*' attack on privilege struck at the roots of absolutism. They continued the traditions of the Scientific Revolution by questioning tradition and dogma. By advocating natural law, natural rights, and equality, they created discontent among the bourgeoisie and enlightened them to other political and religious possibilities, thereby preparing the way for the French Revolution.

THE ENCYCLOPEDIA

This copper engraving from the Encyclopedia *depicted slavery in the West Indies.*

One of the greatest literary achievements of the eighteenth century was the publication of the *Encyclopedia*. The French *philosophes* Denis Diderot and Jean le Rond d'Alembert edited thirty-five volumes containing contributions from 160 of the greatest writers, philosophers, and scientists of the era. The *Encyclopedia* was a comprehensive review of the arts and sciences of the day. It featured articles on literature, religion, government, science, and technology and proclaimed a new philosophy of humanism. It took over twenty years to complete the project. The first volume was published in 1751; the final volume appeared in 1772.

Beautifully drawn illustrations accompanied the articles in the *Encyclopedia*. These helped to explain such things as astronomy, technology, exploration, and wildlife. But while many people used the *Encyclopedia* as a reference work, this was not its major purpose. Diderot was a progressive scholar who wanted to change the thinking of his day and improve society through reason. By educating the public about the wonders of modern science, he hoped to eliminate intolerance and superstition.

The *Encyclopedia's* critical view of religion drew opposition from the Church. A decree in 1752 suppressed the first volumes; in 1759 the entire *Encyclopedia* was placed on the *Index of Prohibited Books*. Nevertheless, it continued to circulate and made a significant contribution to the spirit of the Enlightenment.

THE IMPACT OF THE ENLIGHTENMENT: PHASE 1

Although the Enlightenment tradition in Western society frequently traces its roots to the French Revolution, many of the ideas of the *philosophes* were first applied elsewhere. In response to the criticisms about absolutism, some monarchs implemented reforms and established a new rule of *enlightened despotism*. Elsewhere, however, people openly rejected the old order and replaced it with a popular government based upon the ideals of the Enlightenment philosophers.

Enlightened Despotism

With the exception of France and England, almost every country in Europe was ruled by enlightened despots in the eighteenth century. Charles III of Spain and the Netherlands, Joseph I of Portugal, Gustavus III of Sweden, and Charles Emmanuel of Sardinia all regarded themselves as enlightened monarchs, or at least employed advisors who pursued enlightened policies.

Enlightened despotism was rational, reformist, and absolute. It marked the transition from the divine right of monarchies to the modern secular state. Enlightened monarchs claimed no mandate from heaven, and in fact accelerated the separation of church and state. Although unwilling to accept constitutional restraints on or limitations to their absolute power, they promoted religious tolerance, reformed the legal systems, and improved the machinery of government. However, the reigns of the three most famous enlightened despots—Frederick II (1712–1786) of Prussia, Joseph II (1741–1790) of Austria, and Catherine the Great (1762–1796) of Russia—illustrated the gap between Enlightenment philosophy and practice.

Frederick II of Prussia was the prototype of the enlightened despot. He was a poet, a musician, and a composer. Voltaire was an admirer and correspondent of Frederick's and even lived at Frederick's court for several years. At the time of his death, Frederick was admired throughout Europe and was imitated by many enlightened despots, particularly Joseph II.

Frederick inherited the throne and an efficient, centralized government from his father, Frederick William I, in 1740. During his reign he initiated a state-sponsored education program, encouraged the arts and sciences, and promoted religious tolerance. The legal system was clarified and codified and the practice of torturing prisoners to obtain confessions was banned. To improve the economy, Frederick built roads, canals, and bridges, cleared forests, encouraged new industries, developed mines, founded a state bank, and stabilized prices. To improve agriculture, he encouraged the use of modern technical innovations and the raising of new crops. But while Frederick may have seemed "enlightened," his policies were largely self-serving. He wanted to centralize power within the state and obtain a stronger position of authority for Prussia within Europe. He followed the reforms of the *philosophes* only insofar as they helped him to achieve these goals.

Joseph II of Austria was perhaps the best intentioned of all the enlightened despots. During his ten-year reign, from 1780 to 1790, he attempted to reorganize and centralize the government, to bring the church under state control, to create a state educational system, and to encourage industry. But the speed and comprehensiveness of his reforms promoted opposition and revolt at every turn. Despite this, however, he did improve the legal system, education, and government administration. He abolished serfdom and promoted religious tolerance and justice for all.

The monarch with the weakest claim to the title of enlightened despot was Catherine the Great of Russia. Catherine continued the Westernization of Russia originated by Peter I (1672–1725). She improved the machinery of government, codified the laws, promoted religious tolerance, and encouraged education. However, few of these reforms reached the poorest—and most populous—segment of Russian society, the peasants. The continuation of serfdom prevented any real improvements in the lives of the majority of the population.

The Legacy of Enlightened Despotism

The rule of the enlightened despots is generally viewed as the application of enlightenment philosophy to government. However, many of the policies of these monarchs were the logical continuation of the policies of their predecessors, and as such they predate many of the enlightened ideas of the period. If these monarchs cloaked their programs in the rhetoric of the Enlightenment, it was to place their policies into the popular mainstream of political philosophy. They used Enlightenment philosophy only when it coincided with their own aims. They advocated religious tolerance, for example, only because it coincided with their desire to reduce the influence of religion in their countries. Tolerance allowed them to reduce religious strife and promote the separation of church and state.

CATHERINE THE GREAT

Catherine the Great was born a German princess, Sophia of Anhalt-Zerbst. In 1745, she married the future Russian czar, Peter III, a cruel and feeble-minded man. Catherine became thoroughly Russian and was popular with powerful groups that opposed her husband. Within months of ascending the throne in 1762, a group of conspirators, headed by Catherine's lover, Grigori Orlov, deposed Peter. Catherine was proclaimed the czarina of Russia and Peter was murdered, possibly by Orlov himself.

Catherine was intelligent and ambitious. She wrote plays, edited a satirical journal, and read the literature of the Enlightenment. She fancied herself as an intellectual and corresponded regularly with such Enlightenment philosophers as Voltaire and Diderot. She also knew the importance of twentieth-century-style public relations. She wanted leaders in the West to view her and Russia in high regard, thus her considerable correspondence with influential people of the West. Her strategy met with some success. Voltaire called her "the benefactress of Europe," while Diderot described her as having "the soul of Brutus and the charms of Cleopatra."

Although theoretically a supporter of Enlightenment thought, Catherine's actions usually served to maintain the status quo. Although she may have had some sympathies toward the working class, her position as a foreigner on the throne of Russia depended on the good will of the nobility. Her supporters were rewarded with huge grants of government land; these grants included the hundreds of thousands of state peasants who worked the land. Peasants became privately owned serfs who could be bought and sold just like any other commodity. Catherine did establish a commission between 1765 and 1774 to codify the laws, but while the commission may have curbed some of the worst abuses, it did nothing to change the fundamentals of Russian law.

When revolution in France broke out, Catherine began to hate the French as much as she had loved them before. She referred to the revolution as France's "abominable bonfire" and proposed burning the books—and symbolically the ideas—of the Enlightenment.

Many of the reforms of the enlightened monarchs did not last. The achievements in religious tolerance were largely lost under their successors. The conservative reaction to Joseph II's reforms forced his successor, Leopold II, to rescind most of Joseph's decrees. King Frederick William II of Prussia abolished religious tolerance and re-established censorship.

Many of the reforms of the enlightened monarchs were merely the first steps on a long path toward enlightened ideals. The modernization and codification of laws still retained class distinctions. Society remained highly stratified, with position largely determined by birth. In Russia under the rule of Catherine the Great, the control of the peasants by the nobility actually increased.

In politics and economics, the policies of the despots were contrary to enlightenment ideals. Frederick, Catherine, and Joseph were all determined to strengthen the state at the expense of the local assemblies. This centralization of power whittled away at the influence of the Prussian and Austrian *Stande* and the Russian *Zemskii sobor*. In economics, the enlightened despots were dedicated mercantilists. Government programs were intended to reduce dependence on imports and strengthen domestic production. Government interference increased as they tried to control the state economy.

Enlightenment ideas were largely developed by Western Europeans, particularly the French. Yet enlightened despotism was strongest in Central and Eastern Europe. Neither France nor England pursued enlightened despotism. Under Louis XV the centralization of France's government, initiated by Louis XIV, began a reversal as local parliaments and the nobility reasserted their influence. In England, George III's attempts to increase royal power met with failure, resulting in the loss of the Thirteen Colonies in North America and increases in the powers of Parliament. By the end of George III's reign, mercantilist views were beginning to give way to *laissez-faire* policies.

Enlightened despotism marked the last phase of the powerful monarchies in most of the nations of Europe. Reform from above had run its course, even before the French Revolution began. By arguing against the need for reform, the monarchs had weakened their ability to resist pressure for further change. This conflict between conservatism and reform was to dominate nineteenth-century politics.

The American Revolution

The first large-scale impact of Enlightenment ideas was not in the Old World at all but in the New World. The first assault on the traditional political, social, and economic system occurred in England's Thirteen Colonies.

The Origins of Revolution

The origins of the American Revolution (1775–1783) lay in the struggle between England and its American colonies over increases in taxation, which resulted from the Seven Years' War (1756–1763). The campaign had caused the English national debt to double. Parliament sought increased tax revenues from the colonies to cover at least part of the cost of their administration and defence. The first attempt to increase revenue was the Stamp Act (1765), which introduced a tax in the form of stamps that had to be affixed to colonial papers such as newspapers and legal documents. Opposition in the colonies was intense and immediate. Revisions to the Sugar Act in 1764 had already prompted James Otis of Boston to attack "taxation without representation" in his *Rights of the British Colonies*. This now became the rallying cry of the American colonists. Colonial ports were closed to English ships. This prompted the opposition of English merchants, who also demanded the repeal of the Stamp Act.

The Declaratory Act of 1766, however, left no question about the English government's position on taxation without representation. It reiterated the right of the crown and Parliament to pass laws governing the colonies. In 1767, the Townsend Acts levied duties on colonial imports of paint, lead, glass, and tea. These were subsequently repealed (with the exception of the tax on tea) in 1770.

In 1773, the Tea Act led to the famous Boston Tea Party. In retaliation, Britain passed the Coercive Acts in 1774 (called the Intolerable Acts in the colonies). This led to the calling of the First Continental Congress, which passed the Declaration of Rights and Resolves condemning imperial policy in the colonies and proclaiming the rights of the colonists.

The Declaration of Independence

The phrase "life, liberty, and property" would be the key to the Declaration of Independence passed by the Second Continental Congress on 4 July 1776. The declaration, often attributed to Thomas Jefferson (1743–1826), borrowed considerably from the writings of Locke and Rousseau.

Well-educated and wealthy, the leaders of the American Revolution were representatives of the new rising middle class in Western civilization who subscribed to the anti-aristocratic views of the *philosophes*.

But while these liberal democratic leaders subscribed to the philosophy of "life, liberty, and property," they believed it should apply to only one segment of the population—white males. The rights of women, black slaves, Native peoples, and indentured servants were ignored. Some women, however, were not willing to quietly accept their exclusion from the new liberal democracy. Abigail Adams (1744–1818), wife of the second U.S. president John Adams (1735–1826), called on her husband to extend the new democratic rights to women. In March 1776, she wrote to him while he was attending the Continental Congress in Philadelphia that:

> . . . in the new code of laws which I suppose it will be necessary to make, I desire you would remember the ladies and be more generous and favorable to them than your ancestors. Do not put such unlimited power in the hands of the husbands. . . . If particular care and attention is not paid to the ladies, we are determined to foment a rebellion, and will not hold ourselves bound by any laws in which we have no voice or representation.
>
> From Miriam Schneir (ed.), *Feminism: The Essential Historical Writings* (New York: Random House, 1972), pp. 3–4.

Unfortunately, however, John Adams, Benjamin Franklin, Thomas Jefferson, and others who contributed to the Declaration of Independence did not seriously consider Adams's demands. In a letter in May 1776, Adams pointed out the irony of her husband's position that "whilst you are proclaiming peace and good-will to men, emancipating all nations, you insist upon retaining an absolute power over wives."

The Constitution

The American Revolution had actually begun a year before the Declaration of Independence, in April 1775 at Lexington and Concord. It was to continue until the Peace of Paris in 1783. During this time the Thirteen Colonies united under the Articles of Confederation (1777). This preliminary constitution vested most of the legislative and executive power in the individual state governments. However, the weak central government was unable to solve the economic, political, and diplomatic problems facing the fledgling nation. As a result, a constitutional convention was held in Philadelphia in 1787.

The Constitution, which resulted from the convention, was a compromise between states' rights and the need for a stronger central government. Opponents argued that the Constitution was created to serve the interests of the wealthy and privileged classes at the expense of the ordinary people. This criticism was partially answered by the first ten amendments to the Constitution—the Bill of Rights—which guaranteed trial by jury, due process of law, the right of assembly, and the freedom of speech, press, and religion. The Constitution demonstrated that the ideas of the Enlightenment could be implemented into society. Written constitutions became a means of social progress.

Setting the Stage in France

Louis XVI had sent troops and a naval squadron to support the American rebels against his old enemy, England. Hoping for a share of the spoils, he received instead an increased national debt and a returning armed contingent of trained revolutionaries.

If the American colonists were justified in revolting against the English, the overburdened French Third Estate had even more right to rebel. The American declaration of human rights against a tyrannical government and their demands for a new social contract would soon be echoed in France.

RETROSPECTIVE

The aim of the Enlightenment was perhaps best expressed in Immanuel Kant's (1724–1804) *What Is Enlightenment?* (1784): "Enlightenment is the liberation of man from his self-caused state of minority. Minority is the incapacity of using one's understanding without the direction of another. This state of minority is self-caused when its source lies not in a lack of understanding but in a lack of determination and courage to use it without the assistance of another. *Sapere aude!* Dare to use your own understanding! is thus the motto of the Enlightenment." This confidence in reason produced a revolution in thinking that had as its aim the perfection of humankind. Ultimately, however, this perfection required reform, which was resisted by the dominant economic and political forces. The conflict between the status quo and the reformers led the revolution in thinking into the realm of politics.

NICOLAUS COPERNICUS:
The Heliocentric Theory (1530)

Nicolaus Copernicus was born in Poland and studied Ptolemaic astronomy at the University of Krakow. His heliocentric theory, which was probably devised around 1530, was not published until shortly before he died in 1543. It stated that the sun was the centre of a planetary system, with a number of smaller planets, including the earth, orbiting around it. Far from being the stationary centre of the universe, the earth was merely a spaceship traveling at great speed. Copernicus feared that the Roman Catholic church would react against his revolutionary theories and he was right. On the Revolution of the Celestial Orbs *was placed on the* Index of Prohibited Books *in 1616, where it remained until 1835.*

From Norman Sheffe and William E. Fisher (eds.), *A Sourcebook for Modern History* (Toronto: McGraw-Hill, 1964), pp. 3–5.

Our ancestors assumed, I observe, a large number of celestial spheres for this reason especially, to explain the apparent motion of the planets by the principle of regularity. For they thought it altogether absurd that a heavenly body, which is a perfect sphere, should not always move uniformly. They saw that by connecting and combining regular motions in various ways they could make any body appear to move to any position.

Callippus and Eudoxus, who endeavored to solve the problem by the use of concentric spheres, were unable to account for all the planetary movements; they had to explain not merely the apparent revolutions of the planets but also the fact that these bodies appear to us sometimes to mount higher in the heavens, sometimes to descend; and this is incompatible with the principle of concentricity. Therefore it seemed better to employ eccentrics and epicycles, a system which most scholars finally accepted.

Yet the planetary theories of Ptolemy and most other astronomers, although consistent with the numerical data, seemed likewise to present no small difficulty. For these theories were not adequate unless certain equants were also conceived; it then appeared that a planet moved with uniform velocity neither on its deferent nor about the center of its epicycle. Hence a system of this sort seemed neither sufficiently absolute nor sufficiently pleasing to the mind.

Having become aware of these defects, I often considered whether there could perhaps be found a more reasonable arrangement of circles, from which every apparent inequality would be derived and in which everything would move uniformly about its proper center, as the rule of absolute motion requires. After I had addressed myself to this very difficult and almost insoluble problem, the suggestion at length came to me how it could be solved with fewer and much simpler constructions than were formerly used, if some assumptions (which are called axioms) were granted me. They follow in this order.

ASSUMPTIONS

1. There is no one center of all the celestial circles or spheres.

2. The center of the earth is not the center of the universe, but only of gravity and of the lunar sphere.

3. All the spheres revolve about the sun as their mid-point, and therefore the sun is the center of the universe. . . .

4. The ratio of the earth's distance from the sun to the height of the firmament is so much smaller than the ratio of the earth's radius to its distance from the sun that the distance from the earth to the sun is imperceptible in comparison with the height of the firmament.

5. Whatever motion appears in the firmament arises not from any motion of the firmament, but from the earth's motion. The earth together with its circumjacent elements performs a complete rotation on its fixed poles in a daily motion, while the firmament and highest heaven abide unchanged.

6. What appear to us as motions of the sun arise not from its motion but from the motion of the earth and our sphere, with which we revolve about the sun like any other planet. The earth has, then, more than one motion.

7. The apparent retrograde and direct motion of the planets arises not from their motion but from the earth's. The motion of the earth alone, therefore, suffices to explain so many apparent inequalities in the heavens.

Having set forth these assumptions, I shall endeavor briefly to show how uniformity of the motions can be saved in a systematic way. However, I have thought it well, for the sake of brevity, to omit from this sketch mathematical demonstrations, reserving these for my larger work. But in the explanation of the circles I shall set down here the lengths of the radii; and from these the reader who is not unacquainted with mathematics will readily perceive how closely this arrangement of circles agrees with the numerical data and observations.

Accordingly, let no one suppose that I have gratuitously asserted, with the Pythagoreans, the motion of the earth; strong proof will be found in my exposition of the circles. For the principal arguments by which the natural philosophers attempt to establish the immobility of the earth rest for the most part on the appearances; it is particularly such arguments that collapse here, since I treat the earth's immobility as due to an appearance.

---

1. (a) Summarize the geocentric theory of the universe.
(b) What data was used to support this theory?

2. (a) Summarize the heliocentric theory of the universe.
(b) What data was used to support this theory?

GALILEO GALILEI: Letter to the Grand Duchess Christina (1615)

Galileo's observations about the moons of Jupiter, as outlined in Sidereal Messenger, *found critics among scientists and theologians. Only ten years earlier, Italian philosopher Giordano Bruno (1549–1600) had concluded that there was no limit to or centre of the universe; that there was an infinite number of universes;*

Some years ago, as Your Serene Highness well knows, I discovered in the heavens many things that had not been seen before our own age. The novelty of these things, as well as some consequences which followed from them in contradiction to the physical notions commonly held among academic philosophers, stirred up against me no small number of professors—as if I had placed these things in the sky with my own hands in order to upset nature and overturn the sciences. They seemed to forget that the increase of known truths stimulates the investigation, establishment, and growth of the arts; not their diminution or destruction.

Showing a greater fondness for their own opinions than for truth, they sought to deny and disprove the new things which, if they had cared to look for themselves, their own senses would have demonstrated to them. To this end they hurled various charges and published numerous writings filled with vain arguments, and

and that stars, planets, and comets moved independently through space. He was convicted of heresy and burned at the stake by the Holy Inquisition of the Roman Catholic church.

Galileo was concerned that his observations would bring him under suspicion as well. In 1615, he wrote a letter to the mother of his patron, the Grand Duchess Christina. In it, he outlined his belief that his observations were consistent with the Scriptures.

From Stillman Drake (ed.), *Discoveries and Opinions of Galileo*, (New York: Doubleday Anchor Books, 1957), pp. 173–216.

they made the grave mistake of sprinkling these with passages taken from places in the Bible which were ill suited to their purposes. . . .

Possibly because they are disturbed by the known truth of other propositions of mine which differ from those commonly held, and therefore mistrusting their defense so long as they confine themselves to the field of philosophy, these men have resolved to fabricate a shield for their fallacies out of the mantle of pretended religion and the authority of the Bible. These they apply, with little judgment, to the refutation of arguments that they do not understand and have not listened to.

First they have endeavoured to spread the opinion that such propositions in general are contrary to the Bible and are consequently damnable and heretical. . . .

Hence they have no trouble in finding men who would preach the damnability and heresy of the new doctrine from their very pulpits with unwonted confidence, thus doing impious and inconsiderate injury not only to that doctrine and its followers but to all mathematics and mathematicians in general. . . . They know, too, that offical condemnation would not only suppress the two propositions which I have mentioned, but would render damnable all other astronomical and physical statements and observations that have any necessary relation or connection with these. . . .

I do not believe that the same God who has endowed us with senses, reason, and intellect has intended to forgo their use and by some other means to give us knowledge which we can attain by them. He would not require us to deny sense and reason in physical matters which are set before our eyes and minds by direct experience or necessary demonstrations. . . .

If in order to banish the opinion in questions from the world it were sufficient to stop the mouth of a single man—as perhaps those men persuade themselves who, measuring the minds of others by their own, think it impossible that this doctrine should be able to continue to find adherents—then it would be very easily done. But things stand otherwise. To carry out such a decision it would be necessary not only to prohibit the book of Copernicus and the writings of other authors who follow the same opinion, but to ban the whole science of astronomy. Furthermore, it would be necessary to forbid men to look at the heavens, in order that they might see . . . many other sensory observations which can never be reconciled with the Ptolemaic system in any way.

---

1. What tactics does Galileo say that his opponents have used against him?

2. What basic philosophic proof does Galileo give to show God's acceptance of scientific investigation?

3. Explain in your own words what Galileo meant when he claimed "The intention of the Holy Ghost is to teach how a person goes to heaven, not how heaven goes."

THOMAS HOBBES: Leviathan (1651)

Thomas Hobbes was a major English philosopher of the seventeenth century. His opinions were shaped by the English civil war. He wrote that his country was "boiling hot with questions concerning the rights of dominion and obedience due from subjects." Hobbes thought that he had the answer. He wrote Leviathan *to explain why absolutism was a political necessity.*

From Louis L. Snyder, *The Age of Reason* (Princeton, NJ: D. Van Nostrand Co., Inc., 1955), pp. 125–129.

Of the Causes, Generation, and Definition of a Commonwealth

The final cause, end, or design of men (who naturally love liberty, and dominion over others) in the introduction of that restraint upon themselves . . . is the foresight of their own preservation, and of a more contented life thereby; that is to say, of getting themselves out of that miserable condition of war, which is necessarily consequent to the natural passions of men, when there is no visible power to keep them in awe, and tie them by fear of punishment to the performance of their covenants.

For the laws of nature (as *justice*, *equity*, *modesty*, *mercy*, and [in sum] *doing to others, as we would be done to*) of themselves, without the terror of some power, to cause them to be observed, are contrary to our natural passions that carry up to partiality, pride, revenge, and the like. And covenants, without the sword, are but words, and of no strength to secure a man at all. . . .

. . . therefore it is no wonder if there be somewhat else required (besides covenant) to make their agreement constant and lasting; which is a common power, to keep them in awe, and to direct their action to the common benefit.

The only way to erect such a common power, as may be able to defeat them from the invasion of foreigners, and the injuries of one another . . . is, to confer all their power and strength upon one man, or upon one assembly of men, that may reduce all their wills, by plurality of voices, unto one will: which is as much as to say, to appoint one man, or assembly of men, to bear their persons; and everyone to own, and acknowledge himself to be author of whatsoever he that so beareth their person, shall act, or cause to be acted, in those things which concern the common peace and safety; and therein to submit their wills . . . and their judgments, to his judgment. This is more than consent, or concord; it is a real unity of them all, in one and the same person, made by covenant of every man with every man . . . as if every man should say to every man, *I authorize and give up my right of governing myself, to this man, or to this assembly of men, on this condition, that thou give up thy right to him, and authorize all his actions in like manner.*

This done, the multitude so united in one person, is called Commonwealth, in Latin *Civitas*. This is the generation of that great Leviathan, or rather (to speak more reverently) of that mortal God, to which we owe under the immortal God, our peace and defence. For by this authority, given him every particular man in the Commonwealth, he has the use of so much power and strength conferred on him, that by terror thereof, he is enabled to form the wills of them all, to peace at home, and mutual aid against their enemies abroad. And in him consists the essence of the Commonwealth; which (to define it) *is one person, of whose acts a great multitude, by mutual covenants one with another, have made themselves every one the author, to the end he may use the strength and means of them all, as he shall think expedient for their peace and common defence.*

And he that carries this person, is called *sovereign*, and said to have *sovereign power*; and every one besides his *subject*.

---

1. According to Hobbes, why is it necessary for people to form commonwealths?
2. What is the purpose of the commonwealth and how does it remain in power?

JOHN LOCKE:
Two Treatises of Civil Government (1690)

John Locke was an English philosopher, physician, and scientist. Originally a support of the Glorious Revolution (1688–1689), Locke called upon "the present King William to make good his title in the consent of the people." His concept of the social contract and natural rights had widespread popularity in the eighteenth century and was adopted to a great extent by the leaders of the American Revolution. Locke's writings were intended to refute two theories: the divine right of kings and Hobbes's theory of absolutism.

From Wallace E. Adams, *et al*, (eds.), *The Western World*, Vol. 1. (New York: Dodd, Mead & Co., 1970) pp. 499, 504, 508–509.

[Chapter II—Of the State of Nature]

To understand political power right, and derive it from its original, we must consider what state all men are naturally in, and that is, a state of perfect freedom to order their actions and dispose of their possessions and persons, as they think fit, within the bounds of the law of nature; without asking leave, or depending upon the will of another man.

A state also of equality, wherein all the power is reciprocal, no one having more than another; there being nothing more evident than that creatures of the same species and rank, promiscuously born to all the same advantages of nature, and the use of faculties, should also be equal one amongst another without subordination and subjection. . . .

[Chapter IX—Of the Ends of Political Society and Government]

If man in the state of nature be so free as has been said; if he be absolute lord of his own person and possessions, equal to the greatest, and subject to nobody, why will he part with his freedom, why will he give up this empire, and subject himself to the dominion and control of any other power? To which it is obvious to answer, that though in the state of nature he hath such a right, yet the enjoyment of it is uncertain, and constantly exposed to the invasion of others; for all being kings as much as he, every man his equal, and the greater part no strict observers of equity and justice, the enjoyment of the property he has in this state is very unsafe, very insecure. This makes him willing to quit a condition, which, however free, is full of fears and continual dangers: and it is not without reason that he seeks out, and is willing to join in society with others, who are already united, or have a mind to unite, for the mutual preservation of their lives, liberties, and estates, which I call by the general name property.

[Chapter XIX—Of the Dissolution of Government]

The reason why men enter into society is the preservation of their property; and the end why they choose and authorize a legislative is, that there may be laws made, and rules set, as guards and fences to the properties of all members of the society: for since it can never be supposed to be the will of the society that the legislative should have power to destroy that which every one designs to secure by entering into society, and for which the people submitted themselves to legislators of their own making; whenever the legislators endeavour to take away and destroy the property of the people, or to reduce them to slavery under arbitrary power, they put themselves into a state of war with the people, who are thereupon absolved from any further obedience, and are left to the common refuge, which God hath provided for all men, against force and violence. Whensoever therefore the legislative shall transgress this fundamental rule of society; and either by ambition, fear, folly, or corruption, endeavour to grasp themselves, or put into the hands of any other, an absolute power over the lives, liberties, and estates of the people; by this breach of trust they forfeit the power of the people, who have the right to resume original liberty, and, by the establishment of a new legislative, (such as they shall think fit) provide for their own safety and security, which is the end for which they are in society. What I have said here, concerning the legislative in general, holds true also concerning the supreme executor, who having a double trust put in him, both as part of the legislative, and the supreme execution of law, acts against both, when he goes about to set up his own arbitrary will as the law of the society.

---

1. According to Locke, what natural rights did people possess in the state of nature?

2. If people are naturally independent, why would they join together to form a government?

3. On what basis could the agreement between the governed and the governing be dissolved?

4. Working with a partner, assume the roles of Hobbes and Locke and debate your respective positions.

BARON DE MONTESQUIEU:
The Spirit of Laws (1748)

Charles-Louis de Secondat, Baron de Montesquieu, was an eighteenth-century political scientist who conducted a study of different forms and theories of government. He believed that there was no ideal form of government and that the characteristics of each nation dictated which style of government it should adopt. In spite of this, Montesquieu greatly admired the British form of government. Although he misunderstood the British system, his conclusions on checks and balances greatly influenced the Constitution of the United States.

From Wallace E. Adams, *et al* (eds.), *The Western World*, Vol. 2, (New York: Dodd, Mead and Co., 1970), pp. 26–27.

There is no word that admits of more various significations, and has made more varied impressions on the human mind, than that of Liberty. . . . It is true that in democracies the people seem to act as they please; but political liberty does not consist in an unlimited freedom. In governments, that is, in societies directed by laws, liberty can consist only in the power of doing what we ought to will, and in not being constrained to do what we ought not to will.

We must have continually present to our minds the difference between independence and liberty. Liberty is a right of doing whatever the laws permit, and if a citizen could do what they forbid he would be no longer possessed of liberty, because all his fellow citizens would have the same power.

Democratic and aristocratic states are not in their own nature free. Political liberty is to be found only in moderate governments; and even in these it is not always found. It is there only when there is no abuse of power. But constant experience shows us that every man invested with power is apt to abuse it, and to carry his authority as far as it will go. Is it not strange, though true, to say that virtue itself has no limits?

To prevent abuse, it is necessary from the very nature of things that power should be a check to power. A government may be so constituted, as no man shall be compelled to do things to which the law does not oblige him, nor forced to abstain from things which the law permits. . . .

In every government there are three sorts of power: the legislative; the executive in respect to things dependent on the law of nations; and the executive in regard to matters that depend on the civil law.

By virtue of the first, the prince or magistrate enacts temporary or perpetual laws, and amends or abrogates those that have been already enacted. By the second, he makes peace or war, sends or receives embassies, establishes the public security, and provides against invasions. By the third, he punishes criminals, or determines the disputes that arise between individuals. The latter we shall call the judiciary power, and the other simply the executive power of the state.

The political liberty of the subject is a tranquillity of mind arising from the opinion each person has of his safety. In order to have this liberty, it is requisite that government should be constituted as one man need not be afraid of another.

When the legislative and executive powers are united in the same person, or in the same body of magistrates, there can be no liberty; because apprehensions may arise, lest the same monarch or senate should enact tyrannical laws, to execute them in a tyrannical manner.

Again, there is no liberty if the judiciary power be not separated from the legislative and executive. Were it joined with the legislative, the life and liberty of the subject would be exposed to arbitrary control; for the judge might behave with violence and oppression.

There would be an end of everything, were the same man, or the same body, whether of the nobles or of the people, to exercise those three powers, that of enacting laws, that of executing the public resolutions, and of trying the causes of individuals. . . .

. . . in a country of liberty, every man who is supposed to be a free agent ought to be his own governor; the legislative power should reside in the whole body of the people. But since this is impossible in large states, and in small ones subject to many inconveniences, it is fit the people should transact by their representatives what they cannot transact themselves.

---

1. How did Montesquieu define political liberty?

2. What did he believe was essential to guarantee political liberty? Why was this necessary?

3. Outline the three branches of government and their respective responsibilities.

VOLTAIRE:
Philosophical Dictionary (1764)

Voltaire was one of the dominant writers of the eighteenth century and the leader of the French Enlightenment. He used his wit and biting satire to attack superstition and religious persecution. In his writings he

What is tolerance? It is the consequence of humanity. All of us are formed of frailty and error. Let us mutually pardon each other's folly. That is the first law of nature.

It is quite clear that the individual who persecutes a man, his brother, because he is not of the same opinion, is nothing more than a monster. That admits of no difficulty. But the Government! The Magistrates! The Princes! How do they treat those who have different worships from theirs? If they are powerful strangers, it is certain that a prince will make an alliance with them. François I, very Christian, will unite with Muslims against Charles V, very Catholic. François I will give *advocated rule by reason and justice. He contended that the ideal ruler need not be democratically elected but could even be a hereditary monarch as long as that monarch was "enlightened." The following is his essay on tolerance.*

From Louis L. Snyder, *The Age of Reason* (Princeton, NJ: D. Van Nostrand and Co., Inc., 1955), pp. 118–120.

The memory of Voltaire is honoured in Paris today.

money to the Lutherans of Germany to support them in their revolt against the emperor, but, in accordance with custom he will commence by having Lutherans burnt at home. He pays them in Saxony for political reasons, but in Paris he burns them for political reasons. But what will happen? Persecutions make proselytes? Soon France will be filled with new Protestants. At first they will let themselves be hanged, later it will come their turn to hang. There will be civil wars, then will come the Night of St. Bartholomew, then this corner of the world will be worse than all that the ancients and moderns ever told of hell.

Madmen, who have never been able to give worship to the God who made you! Miscreants, whom the examples of the Noachides, the learned Chinese, the Parseems, and all the sages, have never been able to lead! Monsters, who have the need of superstitions as crows' gizzards have need of carrion! You will have been told it already, and there remains nothing else to tell you—if you have two religions in your countries, they will cut each others's throats; if you have thirty religions, they will dwell in peace. Look at the great Turk. He governs Guebres, Banians, Greek Christians, Nestorians, Romans. The first who dare to stir up trouble would be impaled. Hence everyone is tranquil.

Of all religions, the Christian is no doubt the one which should inspire tolerance most, although to this point in history the Christians have been the most intolerant on men. The Christian Church is divided in its cradle, and was divided even in the persecutions which under the first emperors it sometimes endured. Often the martyr was regarded as apostate by his brethren, and the Carpocratian Christian expired beneath the sword of Roman executioners, excommunicated by the Edionite Christian, which in its turn was anathema to the Sabellian.

This terrible discord, which lasted for so many centuries, is a very striking lesson that we should pardon each other's errors. Discord is the great ill of mankind. Tolerance is the only remedy for it. . . .

Every sect, as one knows, is a ground of error; there are no sects of geometers, algebraists, arithmeticians, because all the propositions of geometry, algebra, and arithmetic are true. In every other science one may be deceived. What Thomist or Scotish theologian would dare say seriously that he is certain of his case?

If it were permitted to reason consistently in religious matters, it is clear that we all ought to become Jews, because Jesus Christ our Savior was born a Jew, lived a Jew, died a Jew, and because he said expressly that he was accomplishing and fulfilling the Jewish religion. But it is clearer still that we ought to be tolerant of one another, because we are all weak, inconsistent, liable to fickleness and error. Shall a reed laid low in the mud by the wind say to a fellow reed fallen in the opposite direction: "Crawl as I crawl, or I shall petition that you be torn up by the roots and burned!"

---

1. Why does Voltaire believe in tolerance?

2. (a) What country does Voltaire use to illustrate religious tolerance?
(b) Do you believe this is a good example? Why or why not?

JEAN-JACQUES ROUSSEAU:
The Social Contract (1762)

Jean-Jacques Rousseau was a citizen of Geneva who renounced his citizenship and lived most of his life in France. In The Social Contract *Rousseau sought to prove that all government was based on the consent of the governed. Before the French Revolution it became a manual for the revolutionary movement. Cited in court, and in the Constituent Assembly,* The Social Contract *was the most influential work of its age.*

From Wallace E. Adams, *et al*, (eds.), *The Western World*, Vol. 2, (New York: Dodd, Mead & Co., 1970), pp. 35, 36, 37, 38, 39.

I will suppose that men in the state of nature are arrived at that crisis when the strength of each individual is insufficient to overcome resistance of the obstacles to his preservation. This primitive state can therefore subsist no longer; and the human race would perish unless it changed its manner of life.

As men cannot create for themselves new forces, but merely unite and direct those which already exist, the only means they can employ for their preservation is to form by aggregation an assemblage of forces that may be able to overcome the resistance, to be put in motion as one body, and to act in concert.

This assemblage of forces must be produced by the concurrence of many; but as the force and liberty of each man are the chief instruments of his preservation, how can he engage them elsewhere without neglecting the care which is due himself? This difficulty, which leads directly to my subject, may be expressed in these words:

"Where shall we find a form of association which will defend and protect with the whole common force the person and the property of each associate, and by which every person, while uniting himself with all, shall obey only himself and remain as free as before?" Such is the fundamental problem of which the Social Contract gives the solution.

If . . . we exclude from the social compact all that is not essential, we shall find it reduced to the following terms: "Each of us places in common his person and all his power under the supreme direction of the general will; and as one body we receive each member as an indivisible part of the whole."

From that moment, instead of as many separate persons as there are contracting parties, this act of association produces a moral and collective body, comprising as many members as there are votes in the assembly, which from this act receives its unity, its common self, its life, and its will. . . .

. . . The body politic, or the Sovereign [authority], which derives its existence from the sacredness of the contract, can never bind itself, even towards outsiders, in anything that would derogate from the original act, such as alienating any portion of itself, or submitting to another Sovereign. To violate the contract by which it exists would be to annihilate itself; and that which is nothing can produce nothing.

In order . . . to prevent the social compact from becoming an empty formula, it tacitly comprehends the engagement, which alone can give effect to the others—that whoever refuses to obey the general will shall be compelled to it by the whole body: this in fact only forces him to be free; for this is the condition which, by giving each citizen to his country, guarantees his absolute personal independence, a condition which gives motion and effect to the political machine. This alone renders all civil engagements justifiable, and without it they would be absurd, tyrannical, and subject to the most enormous abuses.

. . . the general will alone can direct the forces of the State agreeably to the end of its institution, which is the common good; for if the clashing of private interests has rendered the establishing of societies necessary, the agreement of the same interests has made such establishments possible. It is what is common in these different interests that forms the social bond; and if there was not some point in which all unanimously centered, no society could exist. It is on the basis of this common interest alone that society must be governed.

I say, therefore, that sovereignty, being only the exercise of the general will, can never alienate itself, and that the Sovereign, which is only a collective being, cannot be represented but by itself: the *power* may be transmitted but not the *will*. . . .

---

1. Explain Rousseau's social contract in your own words.

2. One of the most controversial elements of this social contract is the idea that people can be forced to be free. Do you believe that anyone can be forced to be free? Why or why not?

3. Does *The Social Contract* give people the right to rebel against a government that does not follow the general will? Defend your answer with specific references to the document.

ANALYSIS AND APPLICATION

1. Outline how the scientific thought of the Enlightenment conflicted with existing institutions and traditional concepts.
2. Choose an invention or medical development that occurred during the period and examine how it changed medical practices.
3. Write a diary or journal entry for Galileo Galilei after he was forced to recant his belief in the Copernican system by the Inquisition.
4. Outline the relationship between the Protestant Reformation and the rise of science.
5. Trace the decline of religious influence from the Renaissance to 1789.
6. Compare and contrast the rule of an absolute monarch, such as Louis XIV or James I, with that of an enlightened monarch.
7. Analyse the relationship between Enlightenment philosophy and the Declaration of Independence and the U.S. Constitution.
8. Examine the role played by propaganda in the American Revolution.
9. Examine the limitations of the eighteenth-century value of freedom from the perspective of women and non-whites.
10. (a) Compare eighteenth-century values of freedom, the individual, and law with contemporary Canadian values.
    (b) How do Canadian values differ from other modern values? Why?

CHAPTER THREE

French Revolutionary Europe to 1815

FRANCE UNDER THE ANCIEN RÉGIME

In 1789, few people would have disputed that absolutism, as a system of government, worked. As British politician and essayist Edmund Burke (1729–1797) observed in his *Reflections on the Revolution in France* (see readings):

> Europe, undoubtedly, taken in a mass, was in a flourishing condition the day on which your revolution was completed. How much of that prosperous state was owing to the spirit of our old manners and opinions is not easy to say; but . . . we must presume that, on the whole, their operation was beneficial.

To some extent Burke was right. France was one of the most powerful states in Europe. While its colonial efforts overseas may have been second to the British, on the European continent itself its army was the dominant force. In the arts, literature, science, and philosophy, the French nation was an acknowledged leader; many people saw Paris as the cultural centre of the European world.

France's success appeared to be the result of the peace and internal stability that emerged from absolutism. However, much of this success was illusory. France's strength lay not in the organization and efficiency of the government, but in the inherent strengths of the nation itself. The country had a large, relatively homogeneous population that was able to support a powerful standing army and a permanent navy. In addition, the country was agriculturally self-sufficient. These characteristics should have freed France from any dependence on its allies or colonies.

The Growing Problems of Absolutism

By the time Louis XVI ascended the throne, internal instability and external weaknesses were apparent. Unlike the British, who had concentrated their resources on a powerful navy, or a landlocked continental power like Austria, which required only a powerful army, France had to maintain both a large army and navy. The responsibility for raising the considerable revenue required had traditionally been with local governments and agencies, which retained a large percentage of the taxes they collected for themselves, turning over what remained to the crown. Under this system, the monarchy received only a fraction of the tax revenue collected. It was not enough to maintain the armed forces and the quality of life at the court, and so successive monarchs had simply borrowed on the open market.

During times of prosperity this growing national debt was of little concern, but in periods of war or domestic crisis it became apparent that in spite of the wealth of the nation the government itself was bankrupt. Compounding the problem was the government's poor credit rating with Europe's bankers. Although Britain and France came out of the Seven Years' War with virtually identical national debts, France paid more than double the amount in interest payments.

In addition to the financial crisis, many other problems evolved out of absolutism. The most obvious of these was the system's basic inequality. The monarch outranked all the rest of society. Beneath the monarch were various levels of aristocracy who held rights and privileges that were denied to the middle and working classes. Nearly all aspects of life, including laws, taxes, education, government jobs, and military promotions, depended upon social class.

By 1789, the structure of the absolutist state in France had started to unravel. There was growing discontent with the inequalities of the system. The peasants were starving. The middle class was demanding a greater say in government. And Louis XVI was unable to resolve any of the nation's problems or to maintain the old order.

The plight of the French peasantry was recorded in 1787 by Arthur Young, a wealthy farming specialist from England, who was on a two-year tour of France. In a book entitled *Travels in France*, he recounted the horrible conditions he had observed. One town in Brittany was described as "one of the most brutal, filthy places that can be seen," with buildings in disrepair, the people dressed in dirty rags, and agricultural fields lying idle. Young blamed the impoverished conditions he encountered on the corruption of local officials and the oppressive taxes of the feudal system.

Conditions for women were particularly bad. Young recalled a meeting with a woman who complained about how few possessions she had—one cow, one horse, and a little land to support herself, her husband, and their seven children. In addition, they were required to pay rent to two different nobles. Young believed that peasant women worked even harder than men. He wrote: "This woman, at no great distance, might have been taken for sixty or seventy, her figure was so bent, and her face so furrowed and hardened by labour, but she said that she was only twenty-eight." The burden of child-bearing, which Young described as the "miserable labour of bringing a new race of slaves into the world," had stolen the beauty and youth of many young women. According to Young, the blame for the plight of the French peasants lay solely with the government.

What had gone wrong with the absolutist system of government in France? First, absolutism in the strictest sense was impossible in eighteenth-century France. Such a large nation could never be controlled by a single individual. But Louis XVI was the heir to—and the captive of—centuries of custom and tradition. He was confronted with not just the rigid structure established by Louis XIV, but with the deeper class divisions of French society as well.

The French Estates

France was socially and legally divided into three distinct classes, or *estates*. The First Estate comprised the Roman Catholic clergy. Traditionally, the church and state were mutually supportive hierarchies. Wealthy and powerful, the Church influenced all facets of life among the lower classes.

The Second Estate consisted of the hereditary aristocracy. In some cases these were the nobles of the sword, the descendants of the medieval lords who had played such significant roles in the history of the nation. Others were nobles of the robe, more recently elevated individuals who had come to dominate the growing government bureaucracy since the days of Louis XIV.

The Third Estate consisted of everyone else, almost 98 percent of the population. Its vast size made it the most disparate of the three groups, including in its ranks the peasantry of the feudal countryside, the growing urban working class, and the group of wealthy and influential professionals who were emerging as a new political and economic force challenging the government of the nation.

In theory, the three estates could meet and debate issues in a grand parliament called the *Estates-General*. Unlike its British counterpart, however, the Estates-General could be convened only at the king's request. At such times each estate would choose local deputies to travel to Paris or Versailles to debate the issues of the day. Of course, the process was all theoretical. In reality, no monarch had called upon the Estates-General in almost 175 years. Following its last meeting in 1615, it had remained an institution in name only.

THE COMING OF THE FRENCH REVOLUTION

During the seventeenth and eighteenth centuries, there had been considerable social mobility in France. The growth of the nobility of the "robe," the royally appointed civil servants of the regime, allowed wealthy merchants and professional members of the Third Estate to experience real social advancement. By the late 1770s, however, many of these opportunities had disappeared. Members of the first two estates tried to block attempts to reform the old system, fearing that their positions and privileges would be diminished. What started as resistance by the First and Second Estates to centralization under Louis XIV became a drive to reassert long-abandoned rights and privileges.

The Tax Crisis

As we have seen, Louis XVI's France was bankrupt. Not that the nation was not wealthy; it was. The problem lay in the monarch's inability to tax effectively all members of society in order to increase government revenues. A reform of the tax system was essential.

The first problem with taxation was the system of "tax farmers," which had been established in the eighteenth century. Individuals were contracted to collect the *aides*, or excise taxes, imposed by the court. They agreed to pay Versailles a certain amount of the tax they collected; in return, they could keep whatever money they received above this amount. The tax farmers were ruthless in their pursuit of revenue. By the late 1780s, over 70 percent of the peasants' income was being consumed by taxes, but only a small percentage of this ever found its way into the royal treasury.

The second problem was the tax exemptions granted by the king to the First and Second Estates. The nobility was exempt from paying any taxes, while the clergy was asked only to make voluntary contributions. Without the benefit of this source of revenue, it was difficult for the government to meet its financial needs. In addition, the favouritism toward the elite and the unfair burden placed on the poor served to heighten social tensions.

The tax crisis was compounded by drought in 1787 and 1788. The resulting crop failures caused crippling inflation of food prices. Grain dealers and even bakers were attacked by disgruntled citizens; there was rioting in the streets. Through it all, the government was bankrupt and powerless to act.

The Meeting of the Estates-General

In July 1788, Louis XVI called for a meeting of the Estates-General, to be held in Versailles in May 1789. Delegates were instructed to bring lists of grievances, or *cahiers*, from their own estates. These cahiers underlined the fundamental class divisions that existed in France. (See readings.)

Clearly the delegates had a wide range of goals and expectations. Before any of the grievances could be addressed, however, the fundamental question of how the voting would be conducted had to be resolved. The First and Second Estates were each allowed 300 delegates to the Estates-General. The Third Estate, representing the vast majority of the population, was allotted 600. Theoretically the Third Estate should have been able to command a majority in a general vote with the sympathies of a few open-minded nobles and clergy. However, even though the Third Estate had gained in importance by 1789, the rules that governed the Estates-General had been drawn up almost two centuries earlier. Traditionally the three estates met and voted separately. This meant that issues were decided not by the majority rule of the people but by the majority rule of the estates. Thus the First Estate and the Second Estate could outvote the Third Estate by two to one.

The delegates of the Third Estate wanted to change this system. But the other two estates refused. The resulting stalemate lasted five weeks. The frustrations of the Third Estate were summarized in a revolutionary pamphlet written by a lawyer/priest, Abbé Sieyes.

> The plan of this work is quite simple. We have three questions to consider:
>
> **1.** *What is the Third Estate?* Everything.
>
> **2.** *What has it been in the political order up to the present?* Nothing.
>
> **3.** *What does it demand?* To become something.
> . . . it is quite impossible that the body of the nation or even that any particular order should become free if the Third Estate is not free. Everyone who is privileged by law, in whatever manner, departs from the common order, is an exception to the common law and, consequently, does not belong to the Third Estate. We have said that a common law and a common representation are what make one nation . . .
>
> *What is the Third Estate?*
> It is like a strong and robust man whose arms are still in chains. If the privileged order were removed, the nation would not be something less but something more. So, what is the Third Estate? Everything, but an "everything" shackled and oppressed. What would it be without the privileged order? Everything, but an "everything" free and flourishing.

Sieyes's pamphlet stirred up revolutionary fervour among the delegates of the Third Estate. In mid-June the deputies declared themselves the "National Assembly" and invited the rest of the delegates to join them. On June 19th the First Estate, prompted by hundreds of parish priests who had more in common with the peasantry than with the high clergy of their own church, voted to join the Third Estate.

Fearing that a combined First and Third Estates would try to make radical changes to the system, Louis XVI responded by locking the delegates out of the assembly hall. But this failed to quell the dissidents. Far from turning away from the fight, the delegates gathered in an indoor tennis court in Paris, where they declared the Tennis Court Oath, which stated in part: "This Assembly shall . . . not separate, and [shall] reassemble whenever circumstances require, until the constitution of the kingdom is established and consolidated upon firm foundations." For many, this event marked the beginning of the French Revolution.

The Revolt of the Middle Classes

The ancien régime was unprepared for this middle-class revolt. For two weeks Louis XVI hesitated to take any action. His problems were compounded when he dismissed his most popular economic advisor, Jacques Necker (1732–1804). Necker was a Swiss banker who had been the one reformist in the king's inner circle. He had tried to enlighten Louis as to the serious state of France's finances and had urged him to revise his financial policies. Necker's dismissal signaled to the people that the king would not introduce reforms voluntarily. The discontent among the Third Estate grew and tensions mounted across the country.

On 14 July 1789, rumours spread that the king was marching an army on Paris. In response, the lower classes attacked the Bastille, the royal prison where they believed hundreds of prisoners were being held. (In fact, there were only seven.) Although the prison defence forces numbered ninety, they were no match for the mobs that stormed the fortress. The governor of the prison surrendered after assurances that there would be no further violence. He was then summarily executed, however, and his head severed and paraded on a pole through Paris.

David was commissioned in 1789 to portray the Tennis Court Oath. *However, he never got beyond preliminary sketches as by 1792 many of the deputies depicted here had fallen under suspicion in the new regime.*

THE STORMING OF THE BASTILLE

As a royal prison, the Bastille was more of a symbol than a fact. On 14 July 1789, it held only seven prisoners. The following is an eyewitness account by one of the peasants who joined in the storming of the Bastille.

Veteran soldiers innured to war have never performed greater prodigies of valor than this leaderless multitude of persons belonging to every class, workmen of all trades who, mostly ill-equipped and unused to arms, boldly affronted the fire from the ramparts and seemed to mock the thunderbolts the enemy hurled at them. . . .

The attackers, having demolished the first drawbridge and brought their guns into position against the second, could not fail to capture the fort. The Marquis de Launay (Governor of the Bastille) could doubtless have resisted the capture of the first bridge more vigorously, but this base agent of the despots . . . lost his head as soon as he saw himself hemmed in by the enraged people and hastened to take refuge behind his massive bastions. . . .

The drums were beat for a parley and the white flag was raised on the tower. . . . It was too late. The people, infuriated by the treachery of the Governor who had fired on their representatives, took these offers of peace for another trap and continued to advance, firing as they went up to the drawbridge leading to the interior of the fort. . . .

[those below had drawn up cannons.] They were just going to fire and the ranks of the crowd had already opened up to give passage to the cannonballs, when the enemy, seeing that we intended to demolish the big bridge, let down the small drawbridge on the left of the entrance to the fortress. In spite of the new danger arising from this manoeuvre, [several of the crowd] swarmed across it. . . .

About two minutes later one of the [soldiers] opened the gate behind the drawbridge and asked what we wanted. "The surrender of the Bastille," was the answer, on which he let us in. At the same time the besiegers lowered the great bridge, on which the brave Arne leapt while it was still in motion to prevent anyone from trying to raise it again. . . .

Those who came in first treated the conquered enemy humanely and embraced the staff officers to show there was no ill-feeling. But a few soldiers posted on the platforms and unaware that the fortress had surrendered discharged their muskets, whereupon the people, transformed with rage, threw themselves on the [soldiers] and used them with the utmost violence.

From G. Pernoud and S. Flaissier, *The French Revolution*, translated by Richard Graves Copyright 1961. Reprinted by permission of Martin Secker and Warburg Limited.

Although the Bastille itself was of little importance, its fall marked the beginning of a full-scale peasant uprising. Up until the storming of the Bastille, the challenge to the system had stemmed from a handful of middle-class deputies. Now throughout the country villagers revolted against their traditional masters and the collection of feudal dues and taxes ceased.

The *bourgeoisie* was quick to assume the leadership of the revolution. Recognizing that with peasant support they could exercise considerable power, on August 4th the National Assembly voted to abolish feudalism. The bourgeoisie were confident that they could use the peasants to achieve their own goals. The peasants, on the other hand, had tasted power. They would not willingly exchange one set of masters for another.

REVOLUTION: THE MODERATE PHASE, 1789 TO 1791

The new National Assembly produced two significant pieces of legislation during the first phase of the revolution. The first was the "Declaration of the Rights of Man and of Citizens" in October 1789. (See readings.) The declaration was a clear statement of the assembly's revolutionary goals and ideals and was intended to form the preamble to a constitution. It declared the "sacred" rights of citizens to be: equal rights; respect for liberty, property, security, and resistance to oppression; the sovereignty of the nation; political liberty; equal justice; government by Rousseau's General Will; freedom of speech; and participation in the government.

The Constitution

These principles were to be embodied in the second piece of legislation, the Constitution of 1791. It established a constitutional monarchy in which the king was the head of the executive branch, with veto power over the actions of the Legislative Assembly. The Legislative Assembly controlled the appointment and dismissal of ministers of the crown. This system of checks and balances was based upon an electoral system in which the general population voted for a college of electors, who in turn chose the members of the assembly. It was similar to the system adopted by the United States four years earlier.

The Constitution of 1791 declared that positions of responsibility were open to all citizens regardless of birth; that all citizens would be taxed equally according to their ability to pay; that the justice system would apply equally to everyone; and that freedom of expression, assembly, and religion would be guaranteed. But the right to vote was restricted to "active citizens"—French males of at least twenty-five years of age who paid in taxes "a direct contribution, at least equal to the value of three days' labour . . . (and was declared) not to be in a menial capacity; namely that of a servant receiving wages." This was, of course, rule by the upper middle class.

The new middle-class government of the National Assembly was more concerned with the principles of government than with the practicalities of human survival. But the peasants were starving. For them, the dramatic philosophic debates of the government only masked inaction on the social issues that stood at the heart of the revolution.

What actions that were taken by the government served only to benefit the middle class, while doing little to alleviate the impoverishment of the working class. For instance, to obtain financial resources, church lands were confiscated and sold. However, the sale of these lands served only to help middle-class land speculators; the peasants were simply exchanging one landlord for another. Perhaps most indicative of the decidedly bourgeois values of the assembly was the passage of the Chapelier Law in June 1791. This legislation virtually outlawed labour organizations and banned strikes. It was clear that this was not to be a working-class revolution.

After the constitution was passed in 1791, the National Assembly declared its work completed. But the revolution had produced few improvements in the lives of the lower classes. The fragile alliance between the conservative middle class and the peasants grew more tenuous as the peasants became more radical.

The Debate Over the Revolution

Outsiders agreed with the French middle class that the revolution was over. In *Reflections on the Revolution in France* (1790), the English politician Edmund Burke (1729–1797) launched an attack on the revolutionaries. He believed that society was held together by an intricate web of tradition and custom and that changing this too quickly would result in chaos. His analysis has been hailed as an excellent defence of the political philosophy of conservatism. By contrast, Thomas Paine (1737–1809) supported the revolution and was outraged by Burke's philosophy. In a brilliant expression of the ideas of liberalism, Paine rebutted Burke's analysis in the *Rights of Man* (1791–1792). (See readings.)

The debate between Burke and Paine sparked considerable interest and discussion. The argument, however, was over what most people believed to be a completed process. What they failed to realize was that the real revolution was just beginning.

REVOLUTION: THE RADICAL PHASE, 1791 TO 1795

A Constitutional Monarchy

The ambitions of the middle class to establish a new constitution with themselves at the centre of power were plagued with problems from the outset. Their goal was to create a constitutional monarchy, but Louis XVI was unwilling to rule under parliamentary control. The king tried to flee to Austria to raise an army of exiles and reconquer his kingdom. He was captured at Varennes, a French border station 32 km from the eastern frontier, and returned to Paris.

By attempting to flee the country, Louis XVI seriously weakened whatever loyalties the French people may have had toward him. Frances Moore, an employee in the British embassy in Paris, wrote:

> The more I consider the effects of the King's flight, the more I see reason to regret that rash measure. . . . [He] had acquired . . . the good will and confidence of the nation [but] by the fatal step of his evasion, he has laid the foundation of infinite misery to his country. He has irretrievably forfeited whatever hold he had of the confidence and affection of the people.

In spite of his opposition to constitutional monarchy, Louis XVI swore to uphold the new constitution when it was declared on September 14th. He did try to maintain some control by using his veto power to block legislation. This tactic slowed the pace of reform and proved frustrating to the new deputies in the assembly, although the wealthy bourgeoisie still remained satisfied with the state of their new government. With only 55 000 of France's 25 million people qualified to be active citizens under the constitution, they controlled the reins of power and believed that eventually they could bring the king under control. What they failed to realize was that they could not continue to deny security and prosperity to the working classes.

The delegates to the National Assembly had wanted to ensure that no one could accuse them of trying to secure personal power for themselves. To this end a clause was included in the constitution which forbade any present member of the assembly from running for office in the new government. (It is ironic that after 175 years, France finally had some experienced legislators but they were not allowed to serve.) Thus the National Assembly had provided the peasants with the means they would need to take control of the revolution.

Emerging Political Factions

Following the election, the new Legislative Assembly met in October 1791. Several new political factions had emerged among the 745 deputies. With no one faction in the majority, many groups competed to sway the uncommitted. On the right were the *Feuillants* (20 members), conservative monarchists who wanted to limit any further changes. On the left were two groups, the *Girondins* (250 members) and the *Jacobins* (30 members). The republican Girondins represented the propertied bourgeoisie and were supported by the rural peasants. They favoured the abolition of the monarchy and wanted the rights of citizens to be spread to all classes and eventually to all nations. They were challenged for control of the assembly by the Jacobins. The Jacobins were more radical than the Girondins and advocated a highly centralized republic. They used agitation and the press to influence the masses. Their power base was the relatively small urban working class and the Paris mob.

As these rival parties struggled for control, France was also threatened by external forces. Awakening to the dangers a revolutionary France posed to their own internal stability, neighbouring monarchies began to mobilize. The assembly, partly in defence of the revolution and partly to divert public attention from domestic problems, declared war on these enemies of the revolution in April 1792.

The Second Revolution

At this point, events began to overtake the more moderate elements of the revolution. By August, the obstructionism of Louis XVI had caused the king to be deposed and the first French Republic proclaimed. A National Convention was formed to create another constitution. This radical second revolution was more far-reaching than the first. The Girondins, who opposed the radical social reforms proposed by the Jacobins and their supporters, the *sans-culottes* (or urban working class), soon found themselves in the position of defending property and, to an extent, even the former king.

In January 1793, the convention held a show trial of Louis XVI. The king was accused of crimes against the French people and of treason by plotting with France's enemies to overthrow the government and the revolution. The verdict was inevitable: guilty. After heated debate, the convention decided by the narrow margin of 361 to 360 to execute the former monarch. As one Jacobin leader exclaimed: "The King must die so the nation can live." On 21 January 1793, Louis XVI became the first victim of the guillotine.

The Reign of Terror

Louis's death marked the ascension of the radical forces in the assembly. Conservative opponents were denounced as counterrevolutionaries. Soon the Jacobins, supported by the mobs in the street, had no rivals in the convention.

Robespierre

The leader of this new radical movement was a thirty-five-year-old lawyer named Maximilien de Robespierre (1758–1794). Robespierre, a follower of the principles of Rousseau, called for the establishment of a "republic of virtue." But virtue had a price. If people were not willing to adopt virtuous, self-sacrificing behaviour on their own, the state would force them to do so. Almost immediately the

THE EXECUTION OF LOUIS XVI

Louis XVI and Marie Antoinette were sentenced to death after a one-month trial by the National Convention. The sentence was carried out on 21 January 1793 at 10:22 a.m. The following account is by Abbé Edgeworth, who accompanied Louis to his place of execution. Edgeworth was an Irish catholic priest and the confessor of Madame Elizabeth, the king's sister.

The procession lasted almost two hours; the streets were lined with citizens, all armed, some with pikes and some with guns, and the carriage was surrounded by a body of troops, formed of the most desperate people of Paris. As another precaution, they had placed before the horses a number of drums, intended to drown any noise or murmur in favour of the King; but how could they be heard? Nobody appeared either at the doors or windows, and in the street nothing was to be seen, but armed citizens—citizens, all rushing towards the commission of a crime, which perhaps they detested in their hearts.

The carriage proceeded thus in silence to the Place de Louis XV, and stopped in the middle of a large space that had been left round the scaffold: this space was surrounded by cannon, and beyond, an armed multitude as far as the eye could reach. . . . As soon as the King had left the carriage, three guards surrounded him, and would have taken off his clothes, but he repulsed them with haughtiness: he undressed himself, untied his neckcloth, opened his shirt, and arranged it himself.

. . . a man on horseback . . . ordered the drums to beat. Many voices were at the same time heard encouraging the executioners. They seemed reanimated themselves, in seizing with violence the most virtuous of Kings, they dragged him under the axe of the guillotine, which with one stroke severed his head from his body. All this passed in a moment. The youngest of the guards, who seemed about eighteen, immediately seized the head, and shewed it to the people as he walked around the scaffold. . . . At first an awful silence prevailed; at length some cries of "Vive la République!" were heard. By degrees the voices multiplied, and in less than ten minutes this cry, a thousands time repeated, became the universal shout of the multitude, and every hat was in the air. . . .

From Daniel D. McGarry and Clarence L. Hohl, Jr., (eds.), *Sources of Western Civilization* (New York: Houghton Mifflin Co., 1963), pp. 237–239.

new republic introduced emergency measures to deal with the crises at home and abroad. (See readings.)

As the Jacobins tightened their iron grip on the nation, dissent was increasingly stifled. Soon "enemies" of the people were paraded to the guillotine and the trickle of victims

These severed heads of the kings of the Old Testament once graced statues in the façade of the Notre Dame Cathedral in Paris. Revolutionaries mistook the statues for the kings of France and decapitated them in a symbolic gesture after Louis XVI went to the guillotine. It was believed that the heads were destroyed, but they were uncovered during excavation in the Latin Quarter in 1977. Historians speculate that the heads were walled into the basement of the house that stood on the excavation site by a citizen who couldn't bear to see these art treasures destroyed. Today the heads are on display at the Cluny Museum in the Latin Quarter, Paris.

JACQUES-LOUIS DAVID

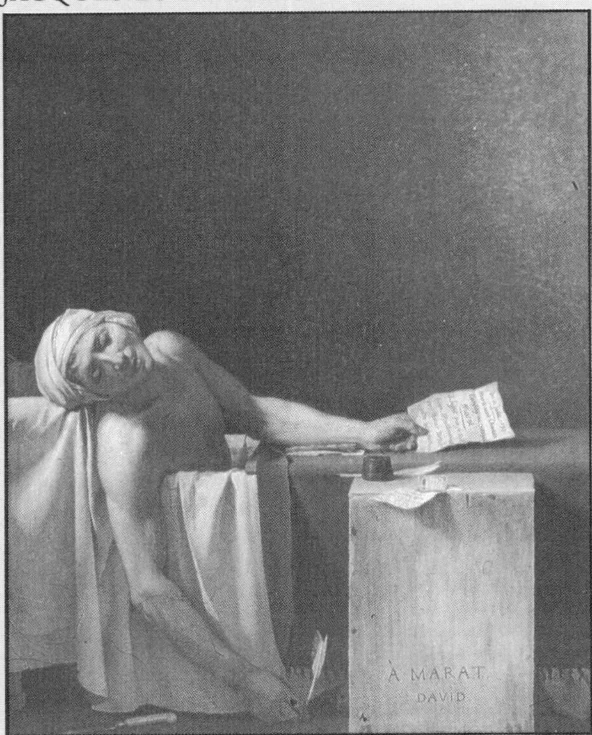

David's The Death of Marat *brought portraiture into the realm of universal tragedy.*

Jacques-Louis David (1748–1825) was born in Paris on 30 August 1748. His early training was in the studio of Joseph-Marie Vien, a history painter. He won the Prix de Rome in 1774 and enrolled in the Académie Royal de Peinture et de Sculpture in 1776. This scholarship allowed him to study in Italy, where he became interested in neoclassicism, a style that formally idealized the Greek and Roman period of antiquity and chose historical and mythological subject matter. David's *Oath of the Horatii* (1784) changed the course of painting and firmly established the neoclassical style in France. The painting depicts three sons swearing an oath to their father before they go to battle for their country. (See colour plates.) The virtues of self-sacrifice and devotion to duty were also reflected in David's *Death of Socrates* (1787) and *The Lictors Bringing Home to Brutus the Bodies of His Sons* (1789).

As the revolution progressed, David became increasingly involved in politics, becoming a deputy of the convention and voting in favour of the execution of Louis XVI. As a member of the Committee of Public Safety, he signed hundreds of warrants for the arrest of enemies of the revolution (a fact he later denied). As the leading French artist, David designed processions and monuments; recorded the revolution's history in the unfinished *Tennis Court Oath* (1791–1792); and glorified its martyrs with *The Death of Lepeletier* (1793), *The Death of Marat* (1793), and *The Death of Bara* (1794). During the Terror, David became the dictator of the arts and abolished the Académie.

After Robespierre's death, David was imprisoned for a short period, but rose to prominence once again and glorified the exploits of Napoleon with paintings such as *Napoleon Crossing the Alps* (1801), *The Coronation of Napoleon and Josephine* (1805–1807), and *Napoleon Distributing the Eagles* (1810). After the restoration of the Bourbons, all signatories of the death warrant of King Louis XVI, including David, were exiled. David died nine years later in 1825 in Brussels.

turned into a flood. From September 1793 until the following June, France bathed in the carnage of the "Reign of Terror." As almost 20 000 people met their death at the hands of their own government, countless more died on the fields of battle. For as the war escalated, so did Jacobin control.

The French republic was the first nation to mobilize its citizens fully for total war. Both men and property were conscripted. A new flag and a new anthem rallied the people around their country; they were expected to put the state ahead of themselves. Conformity was the order of the day. Nationalism was the new religion.

LA MARSEILLAISE

C.J. Rouget de Lisle composed "La Marseillaise" to inspire the revolutionary troops. It acquired its name because it was sung by troops from Marseilles as they marched into Paris in 1792.

Ye sons of France, awake to glory!
Hark! Hark! what myriads bid you rise!
Your children, wives, and grandsires hoary,—
Behold their tears and hear their cries!
Shall hateful tyrants, mischief breeding,
With hireling hosts, a ruffian band,
Affright and desolate the land,
While liberty and peace lie bleeding?

To arms! to arms! ye brave!
The avenging sword unsheathe!
March on! march on! all hearts resolved
On victory or death!

Now, now, the dangerous storm is rolling,
Which treacherous kings confederate raise;
The dogs of war, let loose, are howling,
And, lo! our fields and cities blaze.
And shall we basely view the ruin,
While lawless force, with guilty stride,
Spreads desolation far and wide,
With crimes and blood his hands imbruing?

To arms! to arms! ye brave!
The avenging sword unsheathe!
March on! march on! all hearts resolved
On victory or death!

With luxury and pride surrounded,
The bold insatiate despots dare—
Their thirst of gold and power unbounded—
To mete and vend the light and air.
Like beasts of burden would they load us,
Like gods would bid their slaves adore;
But man is man, and who is more?
Then shall they longer lash and goad us?

To arms! to arms! ye brave!
The avenging sword unsheathe!
March on! march on! all hearts resolved
On victory or death!

O Liberty, can man resign thee,
Once having felt thy generous flame?
Can dungeons, bolts, or bars confine thee,
Or whips thy noble spirit tame?
Too long the world has wept, bewailing,
That Falsehood's dagger tyrants wield;
But Freedom is our sword and shield,
And all their gifts are unavailing.

To arms! to arms! ye brave!
The avenging sword unsheathe!
March on! march on! all hearts resolved
On victory or death!

Although the tactics were extreme, they were effective. Driven by nationalism and revolutionary zeal, the citizen army was more than a match for its opponents. Their enemies were soon pushed back and the borders of France were secured. Without an external threat to national survival, the actions of the Jacobins no longer seemed justified. Extreme measures, such as the Law of 22 Prairial, eventually led to the overthrow of the regime. (See readings.) The Terror ended in June 1794 when Robespierre himself went to the guillotine.

CONSERVATIVE RESURGENCE, 1795 TO 1799

A moderate middle-class government emerged in the relative calm following the overthrow of the Jacobin tyranny. The new constitution established a stable bicameral legislature, the Council of Elders and the Council of Five Hundred, with an executive cabinet, or Directory.

At first it appeared that the new electoral system would be more democratic than the last. Voting rights were extended to all males over twenty-one who had lived in France for at least one year. The minimum tax restriction was eliminated, as was the provision forbidding servants to vote. However, following a nine-year period of grace, all voters would have to be able to read and write. With the high illiteracy rates of eighteenth-century France, this was yet another means of limiting control to a selected elite. Voting rights were restricted in other, less obvious, ways as well. Active citizens were not electing members to the new councils; instead they were choosing electors, who would then travel to Paris and pick deputies for the councils on the citizens' behalf. Electors had to be at least twenty-five and relatively wealthy. But even the electors could not become deputies; they had to be at least thirty, and in some cases forty, to be eligible for that office.

The Opposition

There was considerable opposition to the new constitution and at first it appeared that the government would be short-lived. Without the threat of the Terror not everyone was willing to obey government orders. Since the overthrow of the Jacobins, the National Convention had been struggling to maintain its authority. The people were still starving and repeatedly occupied the Convention Hall.

The new constitutional proposals aligned disgruntled royalists with the mob. These supporters of the king had hoped that a free election might allow them to regain power. In October 1795, rioting broke out and it seemed that the republic would be shaken by another civil war. Government forces were given little chance to maintain control, but the convention's army was led by a young artillery general who ordered his troops to fire point blank into the rebellious mob. Over 500 people were killed and the uprising was quelled. The new conservative republic was preserved by an officer named Napoleon Bonaparte.

NAPOLEON AND THE INSTITUTIONALIZATION OF REVOLUTION

Napoleon Bonaparte's (1769–1821) rise from obscurity to master of Europe is testimony both to his strategic brilliance and to his good fortune. The social, political, and military upheaval of the revolution created an ideal opportunity for an individual of Napoleon's talents. Although his military successes were short-lived, they guaranteed both the survival of social and political gains at home and the spread of revolutionary ideals across the continent.

Napoleon was born in Corsica. He became an officer in the French artillery in 1785. An active revolutionary, Napoleon advanced to become the youngest general in the revolutionary army after demonstrating his leadership in the siege of Toulon in 1793. Although he was imprisoned briefly as a Jacobin after Robespierre's execution, he was soon released and became a valuable asset to the Directory.

The army Napoleon inherited revolutionized warfare in the late eighteenth century. Soldiers were conscripted and for the first time the promotion of officers was based on merit rather than aristocratic birth. Massive troop concentrations and flexible tactics enabled decisive victories, making the French army the most powerful force on the continent. Building upon these advantages, Napoleon won France's greatest victory of the Revolutionary Wars by defeating Austria in a northern Italian campaign in 1796–1797. Acting independently of the government, he first established a new republic, the Cisalpine Republic, and then negotiated the transfer of the Austrian Netherlands to France in the Treaty of Campo Formio.

The Coup

While Napoleon's military victories were gaining him prominence in France, the reputation of the Directory was declining. By design, the executive branch of the government was weak and was therefore unable to effect the reforms demanded by the general population. There was unrest from the royalists on the right and from the early communists (the Conspiracy of Equals) on the left. Increasingly, the administration relied on the military to suppress dissent. By 1799 the government's hold on power was extremely tenuous.

Meanwhile, Napoleon was fighting in Egypt. Floundering in an unsuccessful campaign and blockaded by the British navy, he decided to abandon his troops and steal back to France for a political showdown with the Directory. His brother, Lucien, had joined a group of conspirators led by Abbé Sieyes who were planning a *coup d'état* to overthrow the government. Convinced that the weakness of the Directory was jeopardizing the gains of the revolution, some of the conspirators believed strong leadership was the key to consolidating the new order. The person they turned to for that leadership was Napoleon. Others, however, believed that Napoleon should act merely as a figurehead to ensure the popular support of the people and the army. They believed that once they had secured power, they could remove Napoleon from the leadership. It would turn out to be a gross miscalculation.

The coup was successful. As leader of a new triumvirate, Napoleon was named First Consul. A month later, a new constitution was created confirming his position for a term of ten years and giving him the power to control foreign affairs and the courts and to initiate all legislation. Legislative bodies were also established, but they had little real power. Once again, authority in France was centralized. This time, however, it was with popular approval. When Napoleon held a national plebiscite on his reforms early the next year, they were approved by a vote of over 3 million to 2000.

MADAME DE STAËL

Madame Germaine de Staël (1766–1817) was a novelist, essayist, historian, and playwright and one of the most influential women in Napoleonic France. Born Anne Louise Germaine Necker, she was the daughter of Jacques Necker, Louis XVI's minister of finance. She married Baron de Staël-Holstein (1749–1802), the Swedish ambassador to Paris, in 1786. Although the marriage was one of convenience (and was formally ended in 1798), it enabled her to establish a salon that became an intellectual and political centre in Paris. Her husband's diplomatic status also afforded her enough protection to remain in Paris throughout the revolutionary period, except for a year spent in England during the Terror.

Originally a supporter of General Bonaparte, de Staël remained true to the moderate liberal policies of her father, and eventually came to oppose Napoleon's rule as emperor. Her vocal opposition so irritated Napoleon that in 1803 he banished her to a distance of 64 km from Paris. She settled at Coppet, her father's estate near Geneva, Switzerland. Napoleon's agents continued to harass her and she fled to England, returning to Paris in 1814 after the fall of Napoleon, where she remained until her death in 1817.

De Staël's novels *Delphine* (1803) and *Corinne* (1807) are considered the first modern feminist psychological novels. Her work, *De l'Allemagne* (*On Germany*, 1810), introduced German culture to Europe and helped form the framework of French romanticism. Although her novels and plays are rarely read today, her liberal appraisal of the French Revolution, *Reflections on the Chief Events of the French Revolution* (1818), demonstrates her keen understanding of the events of her time.

Napoleon proclaimed himself emperor of France in 1804. For the next ten years he dominated France, and indeed most of western and central Europe, until he was forced to abdicate in 1814.

A PAINTING AS A PRIMARY SOURCE

This painting by David illustrates both the advantages and disadvantages of works of art as primary sources. As a neoclassical painter, David paid strict attention to detail. There are over 100 identifiable portraits in the painting and the costuming is exact. However, the scene does not depict the event as it actually occurred; changes were made by David, of his own volition, and in accordance with the wishes of Napoleon. David was fully aware of the historical importance of the event and painted himself and his family into the gallery. David also acceded to Napoleon's requests and painted Napoleon's mother into the scene (she was in Rome) and painted the Pope with his hands raised in blessing (something he refused to do). Works of art are valuable primary sources for students of history, but like any primary source, they must be used with caution and validated by other sources.

Under Napoleon, David's heroic paintings of the revolutionary period gave way to a new feeling for pageantry. This was illustrated in his Coronation of Napoleon *(1806).*

Napoleonic France

Once firmly established in power, Napoleon began reorganizing the state. Administrative procedures were streamlined; banking and coinage were centralized; the government budget was balanced. France's legal system, which consisted of revolutionary reforms as well as a wide range of feudal laws and customs, was modernized and rationalized. Finalized in 1804, the Napoleonic Code embodied many of the values of the revolution. It guaranteed as absolute rights freedom of expression and conscience; equality before the law; civil marriage and divorce; equal access to professions; and the security of property and its equal division among heirs. In addition, the new code confirmed the rights of citizenship and the complete abolition of the feudal system.

By modern standards the Napoleonic Code was conservative. Perhaps nowhere was this better demonstrated than in Napoleon's attitude toward women. This was reflected in the new educational system, which catered to the middle class in general and to men in particular. In Napoleon's France, women were required to be obedient housewives and mothers. In 1807, Napoleon wrote that, "What we ask of education is not that girls should think, but that they should believe." Such thinking was not uncommon at the beginning of the nineteenth century and Napoleon's reforms were seen as a model for the rest of Europe.

The Concordat

Another major reform of this period was the *Concordat* signed with Pope Pius VII. Under this agreement, the Roman Catholic church relinquished all claims to lands confiscated by the state during the revolution. It also gave up its power to collect tithes. The government, on the other hand, obtained the right to appoint bishops, but also assumed responsibility for paying the salaries of the clergy. Although distasteful to some revolutionary purists, Napoleon's bargain removed a powerful potential enemy and gained a number of rights and privileges for the French state.

The announcement of the *Concordat* was timed to coincide with the declaration of peace between France and Britain in the spring of 1802. Now both the clerical and antiwar opposition was silenced. Napoleon was the most popular leader in recent history. His popularity was confirmed later that year when he was named consul for life, and again two years later when he proclaimed himself hereditary emperor. Fifteen years after the outbreak of the revolution, absolutism was once again alive and well in France.

THE RISE AND FALL OF THE NAPOLEONIC EMPIRE

When Napoleon became First Consul, France was already at war with Britain, Austria, Russia, and Naples. The coalition began to crumble when Austria withdrew after military defeats in Italy and Germany. Britain carried on until the Treaty of Amiens (1802) established an uneasy truce.

The treaty brought peace to France for the first time in ten years. Napoleon used the fourteen-month period of peace that followed to consolidate his rule at home and in the colonies. Abroad he annexed Piedmont and extended French domination over Holland and Switzerland, reducing these countries to French dependencies. Alarmed by this strategic and economic threat, Britain resumed the conflict, blockading the ports of Toulon, Rochefort, and Brest, thereby cutting France off from its colonies. Napoleon countered by sending his armies to French ports along the English Channel in preparation for an invasion of England. When the French fleet was destroyed by Lord Nelson at the Battle of Trafalgar, the invasion became impossible.

Napoleon turned his attention to Britain's continental allies, defeating the combined forces of Alexander I (1777–1825) of Russia and Francis II (1768–1835) of Austria at Austerlitz in a brilliant battle. After the defeat, Russia withdrew from the coalition and Austria was forced to sign the Treaty of Pressburg. Napoleon now controlled all of Italy, Holland, and the south and west of Germany.

The next threat came from Germany, where the destruction of the Holy Roman Empire and the creation of the Confederation of the Rhine threatened Prussia. After defeating the Prussian army, Napoleon continued to move against the Russians. After the decisive victory at Freidland, Alexander I sued for peace.

Napoleon now governed France and the Netherlands directly as emperor. Spain, Italy, and the Confederation of the Rhine were satellite states controlled by Napoleon or his agents. Napoleon introduced the reforms of the French Revolution into these areas. Feudal and clerical rule were destroyed and serfdom was abolished. New laws based on the Napoleonic Code were introduced. But there was no real political liberty. The newly created governments were used to collect high taxes, which went directly to France. Conscription and confiscation of land increased discontent and fueled anti-French feelings, particularly in Prussia where smoldering nationalism awaited a chance for revenge.

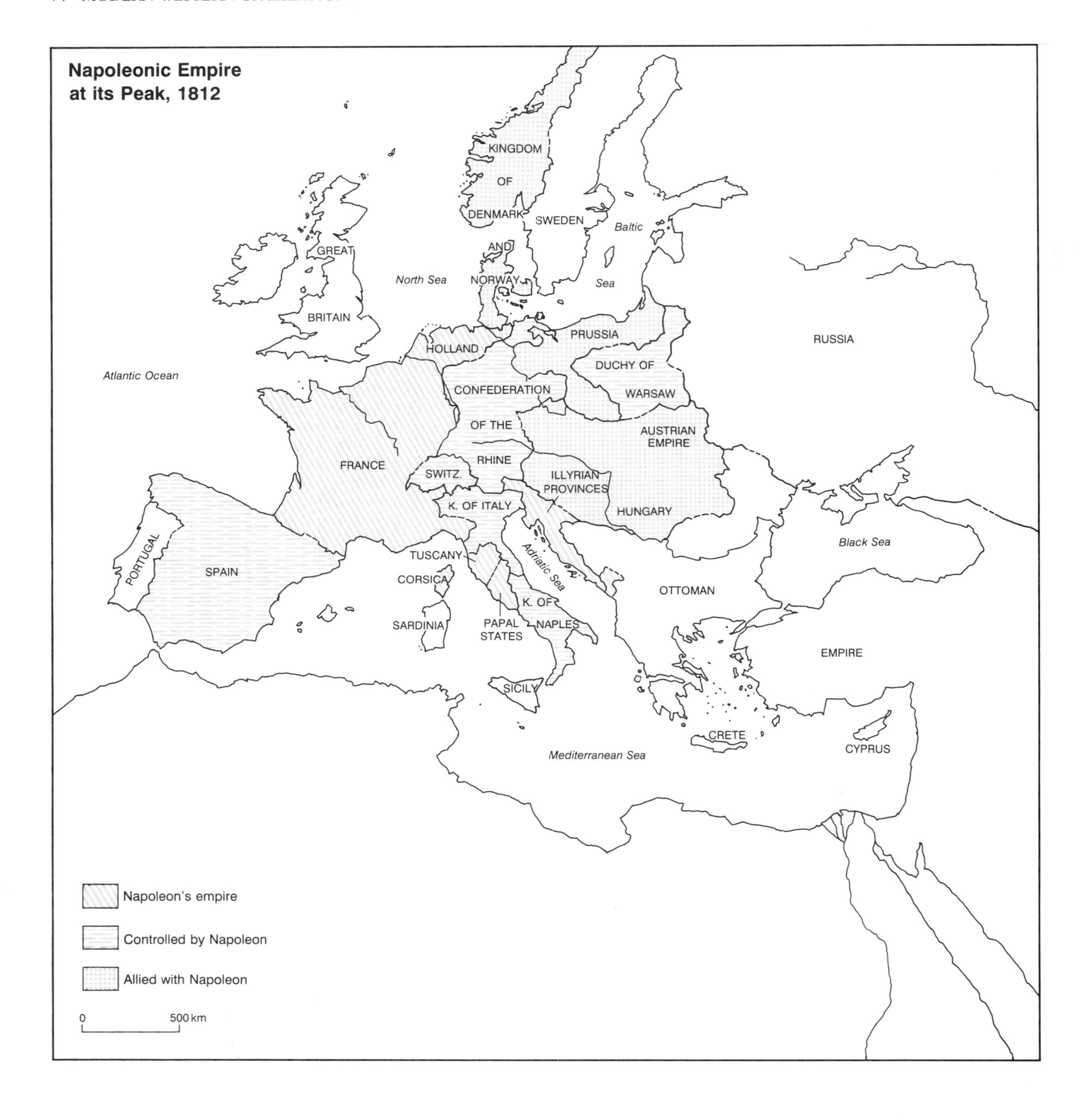
Napoleonic Empire
at its Peak, 1812
KINGDOM
OF
DENMARK
AND
NORWAY
SWEDEN
Baltic
Sea
North Sea
GREAT
BRITAIN
Atlantic Ocean
HOLLAND
PRUSSIA
RUSSIA
DUCHY OF
WARSAW
CONFEDERATION
OF THE
RHINE
AUSTRIAN
EMPIRE
FRANCE
SWITZ.
ILLYRIAN
PROVINCES
HUNGARY
K. OF ITALY
PORTUGAL
SPAIN
TUSCANY
CORSICA
Adriatic Sea
SARDINIA
PAPAL
STATES
K. OF
NAPLES
Black Sea
OTTOMAN
EMPIRE
SICILY
CRETE
CYPRUS
Mediterranean Sea
Napoleon's empire
Controlled by Napoleon
Allied with Napoleon
0
500 km

NAPOLEON'S GRAND DESIGN

The following excerpt from his Memoirs *is Napoleon's explanation of what he was trying to achieve in Europe.*

One of my favourite ideas was the fusion, the federation of the nations, which had been separated by revolutions and politics. There are in Europe more than 30 million French, 15 million Spaniards, as many Italians, and 30 million Germans. I wanted to unite them all into one strong, national body. . . . When this was done people could devote themselves to the realisation of the ideal, at present only a dream, of a higher civilisation. Then there would be . . . only one set of laws, one kind of opinion, one view, one interest, the interest of mankind. . . .

The fusion of the 30 million Frenchmen under one law had already taken place, that of the Spaniards being on the point of completion. . . . Because circumstances prevented the completion of the subjugation of the Spaniards, people now think they are impossible to subject. And yet it is a fact that, at the very moment when victory escaped me, the Cortes in Cadiz were in secret negotiations with me. Besides, Spain was not lost to me through her resistance, nor by means of England's help, but in consequence of my own mistakes, and the misfortunes which I met with, but especially because I was so careless as to remove myself and my whole power a thousand leagues from Spain. Had it not been for this mistake Spain would have been pacified in three or four years. Peace would have returned to the Peninsula, a new and happy period of intellectual and social freedom for the country would have begun, and, instead of hating me, the new-born nation would have blessed me. . . .

In Italy the fusion was almost completed. . . . Every day was bringing the fruits of unity, legislation, and the new flight in thought and feeling to maturity. The union of Piedmont, Parma, Tuscany, and the Papal States with France was only transitory, and had no other purpose than to facilitate the completion of the national education of the Italians, and to keep the whole under one's eye. . . .

The unification of Germany required more time. . . . It is incomprehensible to me that no German Prince up to the present has had the idea of unifying the whole. If Destiny had made me a German Prince, I would have rescued this nation from the storms of our days under one sceptre. . . .

This plan of bringing about a union of the nations—and it is the noblest, most courageous and highest-minded plan—was wrecked through my misfortune and fall . . . but it is not lost for all that. The start has been given, the force of circumstances will carry it out, and nothing can prevent it. In the first great general war that breaks out, the ruler who understands how to unite his interests with those of the common people, will see himself in a moment head of all Europe, and will then be able to do what he likes in this respect.

From *Memoirs of Napoleon*, compiled from his own writings by F.M. Kircheisen; translated by Frederick Collins (New York: Duffield and Co., 1929).

Napoleon's Quest for Naval Supremacy

Although Napoleon controlled the continent, the British controlled the seas. Napoleon endeavoured to gain power on the seas in 1806 by issuing the Berlin Decree, whereby all British trade and all British subjects were banned from the continent. This inaugurated the Continental System. To be effective, however, Napoleon had to control the east. To this end he seized Hanover and forced Prussia to join the boycott. As a result of the Treaty of Tilsit (1807), Russia too was forced to join the Continental System.

To round out the Continental System, Napoleon was determined to control Spain. He forced first King Charles IV (1748–1819) and then his son Ferdinand VII (1784–1833) to abdicate and proclaimed his brother, Joseph Bonaparte (1768–1844), king of Spain. But the Peninsular War proved that the French armies were not invincible. Spanish troops rallied against the French troops that had taken Madrid in July 1808 and forced them from the city. Napoleon led a new army of 200 000 back into Spain to regain the city in December. Although French troops occupied most of Spain and Portugal, a long and bitter guerrilla campaign developed. (It was immortalized by Francisco de Goya [1746–1828] in a series of engravings entitled *The Disasters of War* [1810–1813].) The Spaniards were aided by a British expeditionary force and they managed to keep the French troops in Spain busy. When Napoleon diverted troops to Germany in 1813, the Spanish and British armies took the offensive and drove French troops from the country.

Encouraged by Napoleon's difficulties in Spain and revolts in Holland, Switzerland, and Italy, the Austrians declared war on France. After a short campaign, however, they were resoundingly defeated at Wagram.

The Collapse of the Continental System

The two years of peace that followed the battle at Wagram were shattered when Alexander I, a hesitant ally of France since 1807, announced that Russia was withdrawing from the Continental System and resuming trade with Britain. Realizing that the withdrawal of Russia would destroy the system, Napoleon invaded Russia with a "Grand Army" of 600 000 that included contingents from twenty nations. Rather than confront Napoleon, the Russians fell back and adopted a "scorched earth" policy, depriving Napoleon's army of supplies. The drive to Moscow cost over 100 000 soldiers. When the Russians finally turned and fought, the indecisive battle of Borodino cost them 40 000 lives and Napoleon 30 000. The outcome—the French occupation of Moscow—was a hollow victory; the city was abandoned and in flames. Faced with a lack of supplies and the impossibility of wintering in Moscow, Napoleon began to retreat.

The French army suffered terribly in the long retreat from Moscow. Marquis de Caulaincourt, one of Napoleon's generals, described the retreat of the Grand Army:

> Cossacks kept up perpetual raids along the road, which they constantly crossed between one division and another—or even, when there was a gap, between one regiment and another. . . . Wherever there was no shooting to fear, wherever transport wagons were moving along in disorder or unarmed stragglers were making their way as best they could, the Cossacks improvised sudden attacks, killing and wounding, robbing all those whose lives they spared, and looting wagons and carriages when they came upon them.
>
> . . . The cold was so intense that bivouacking was no longer supportable. Bad luck for those who fell asleep by a campfire! . . . One constantly found men who, overcome by the cold, had been forced to drop out and had fallen to the ground, too weak or too numb to stand. . . . Once these poor wretches fell asleep, they were dead. If they resisted the craving for sleep, another passerby would help them along a little farther, thus prolonging their agony for a short while but not saving them; . . . What I have related about the effects of extreme cold and of this kind of death by freezing is based on what I saw happen to thousands of individuals. The road was covered with their corpses.
>
> From George Libaire (ed.), *With Napoleon in Russia, The Memoirs of General de Caulaincourt*, in Sydney Eisen and Maurice Filler (eds.), *The Human Adventure: Readings in World History* Vol. 1 (New York: Harcourt, Brace, and World, Inc., 1964), pp. 233–234.

The attacks and the severe winter reduced the army to less than 30 000. Napoleon abandoned his troops and rushed to Paris to quell internal dispute and raise a new army.

The Fall of Napoleon

The threat to Napoleon's empire was quick in coming. Prussia, Russia, and Austria joined forces and quickly had more than half a million troops in the field. Initially Napoleon was successful, winning victories at Lutzen, Bantzen, and Dresden. But his army was reduced to less than 60 000 after he was defeated at the Battle of the Nations at Leipzig. When Britain invaded southern France from Spain, the end came quickly.

The victorious allies entered Paris in March 1814 and forced the emperor to abdicate. The tired and dispirited French army agreed. Napoleon went into exile on the island of Elba in the Mediterranean. Meanwhile the allies met at Vienna to decide upon the restructuring of Europe after the collapse of the French empire. In France, a liberal, constitutional monarchy was restored under Louis XVIII (1755–1824). For many French citizens, however, it seemed that the revolution had been in vain. As a result, when Napoleon secretly landed at Cannes in March 1815 both the army and the citizenry rallied around him.

For 100 days Napoleon reigned supreme once again. But the days of glory were over. A combined force of British and Prussian troops, led by the Duke of Wellington, defeated the

Grand Army at Waterloo. Napoleon was once again sent into exile, this time under armed guard to the remote island of St. Helena in the South Atlantic. He died there in 1821.

RETROSPECTIVE

The turbulent period of the French Revolution completely upset the ancien régime in France. The domination of the king and the aristocracy was replaced first by a violent dictatorship and finally by a conservative republic of the middle class. The early alliance of the peasants and bourgeoisie against a system of privilege and unfair taxation collapsed with the disappearance of the common enemy, the king. After a period of peasant domination through Robespierre and the Terror, the middle class re-established itself under the Directory.

The Directory was a government of compromise and was able to rule more or less successfully for the next five years. By the end of the century, France had completed the transition from a fragmented and inefficient absolute monarchy to a stable, modern, centralized state.

What did sixteen years of Napoleonic rule accomplish? Outside of France, the political boundaries of the ancien régime had been smashed. Although the Great Powers would reassert themselves at the Congress of Vienna in 1815, the damage had been done. Napoleon's armies had carried the ideals of the French Revolution abroad. The seeds of liberal and national revolt had been planted and Europe would never be the same. At home, in spite of the dictatorial nature of his political regime, Napoleon had preserved the basic aims of the revolution. Even after his final defeat, the French people would not give up what they had struggled so long to gain. Although the monarchy was restored and the Bourbon family returned to the throne, there would be no return to the absolutist ideas of Louis XVI. The new king, Louis XVIII, would have to abide by the ideals of 1789.

ARTHUR YOUNG:
Travels in France (1789)

Arthur Young was an English farmer who traveled throughout France between 1787 and 1789 to study "the cultivation, wealth, resources, and national prosperity" of France. His Travels in France, *published between 1792 and 1794, was an immediate success and still provides a fascinating window on peasant life in prerevolutionary France.*

From Arthur Young, *Travels in France 1787, 1788, 1789*, in B. Tierney *et al*, *Great Issues in Western Civilization*, Vol. II, (New York: Random House, 1976), pp. 157–160.

Everybody is determined to pay no taxes, should the National Assembly so ordain. . . . The French soldiers will never fire on the people: but, if they should, it is better to be shot than starved. He gave me a frightful account of the misery of the people; whole families in the utmost distress; those that work have a pay insufficient to feed them—and many that find it difficult to get work at all. . . .

By the order of the magistrates no person is allowed to buy more than two bushels of wheat at a market, to prevent monopolizing. . . . Being here on a market day, I attended, and saw the wheat sold out under this regulation, with a party of dragoons drawn up before the market-cross to prevent violence. The people quarrel with the bakers, asserting the prices they demand for bread are beyond the proportion of wheat, and proceeding from words to scuffling, raise a riot, and then run away with bread and wheat for nothing . . . the consequence was, that neither farmers nor bakers would supply them till they were in danger of starving, and when they did come, prices under such circumstances must necessarily rise enormously, which aggravated the mischief, till troops became really necessary to give security to those who supplied the markets. . . .

This confirms what I have often heard remarked, that the deficit would not have produced the revolution but in concurrence with the price of bread. Does this not shew the infinite consequence of great cities to the liberty of mankind? Without Paris, I question whether the present revolution, which is fast working in France, could possibly have had an origin.

---

1. Describe the course of the French Revolution as a reflection of Young's comment that "the deficit would not have produced the revolution but in concurrence with the price of bread."

THE CAHIERS (1788–1789)

When Louis XVI announced in 1788 that the Estates-General would be called the following May, he requested that cahiers, or lists of grievances, be drawn up by delegates from each of the three estates. As a result, historians studying the period have an excellent resource outlining the concerns and political perceptions of the day. This excerpt is taken from the cahiers from each of the estates in the area of Dourdan, near Orléans.

From Micheal Creal, *The Dynamics of Revolution: France 1789–94* (Toronto: Macmillan of Canada, 1974), pp. 10–14.

(a) *Cahier* of the Clergy [first estate]

27 March 1789
His Majesty shall be humbly supplicated: . . .

—to preserve in its integrity the precious depository of the Catholic, Apostolic, and Roman religion, the most stable support of the fundamental laws of the State . . .
—to give consideration of the representations made by the last assembly of the clergy concerning the edict on non-Catholics, and not to permit any religion other than the Catholic to hold worship or give public instruction . . .
—since diversity of religious opinions in the schools for French youth is the greatest danger in the world, His Majesty shall be humbly supplicated also to order all necessary precautions lest there be admitted into any of the universities and academic societies of the kingdom any teacher or member who has not previously given proofs of the greatest ability and of his respectful devotion to the Catholic religion . . .
—we desire that in matters brought under deliberation in the Estates-General relative to all orders, voting be by head; but in those concerning more especially one of the three orders, we request that voting be by order.

(b) *Cahier* of the Nobles [second Estate]

29 March 1789
. . . the noble citizens of the bailliage of Dourdan request:
—That the legislative power reside collectively in the hands of the King and the united nation. . . .

Since the constitutional laws assure each and every one of his liberty, fortune, position, and property, the nobility requests:
—That every arbitrary order prejudicial to the liberty of citizens be abolished entirely;
—That individual liberty be assured and guaranteed, so that every citizen arrested may be placed in the prisons of the courts which are to take cognizance of his offence within twenty-four hours of the time of his arrest; that immediately upon his detention, he be permitted to choose a counsel . . .
—That liberty of the press be granted. . . .
—That no tax be established . . . without the concurrence of the legislative power . . .
—That all property, whoever be the owner, be inviolable and sacred . . .
—Finally, that ministers henceforth be responsible and accountable to the Estates-General. . . .
—The order of nobility desires further that the distinction of three orders in the Estates General be strengthened and regarded as inherent in the Constitution of the French monarchy, and that opinions be given therein only by order.

(c) *Cahier* of the Third Estate

29 March 1789
The order of the Third Estate . . . wishes:
—that all the orders, already united by duty and a common desire to contribute equally to the needs of the State, also deliberate in common concerning its needs . . .
—that no citizen lose his liberty except according to law . . .
—that the property of all citizens by inviolable . . .
—that every tax, direct or indirect, be granted only for a limited period of time. . . .
—that tax be borne equally, without distinction, by all classes of citizens.

---

1. Create a comparative chart outlining the demands cited by each of the estates.

2. Based upon the results of your chart, prepare a brief analysis of the areas of agreement and disagreement among the estates. What alliances may have been formed between pairs of estates?

DECLARATION OF THE RIGHTS OF MAN AND OF THE CITIZEN (1789)

The clearest statement of the aims of the French Revolution was decreed by the National Assembly on 27 August 1789. Thousands of copies of the document were printed and distributed by the National Assembly. The Declaration of the Rights of Man eventually became the preamble to the Constitution of 1791.

From Brian Tierney, *et al*, *Great Issues in Western Civilization* (New York: Random House, 1976), pp. 169–170.

The representatives of the French people, organized as a national assembly, believing that the ignorance, neglect or contempt of the rights of man are the sole causes of public calamities and of the corruption of governments, have determined to set forth in a solemn declaration the natural, inalienable and sacred rights of man. . . .

1. Men are born and remain free and equal in rights. . . .
2. The aim of all political association is the preservation of the natural and imprescriptible rights of man. These rights are liberty, property, security and resistance to oppression.
3. The principle of sovereignty resides essentially in the nation. . . .
4. Liberty consists in being able to do everything which injures no one else. . . .
5. Law can only prohibit such actions as are hurtful to society. . . .
6. Law is the expression of the general will. Every citizen has a right to participate personally or through his representative in its formation. . . .
9. . . . all persons are held innocent until they have been declared guilty. . . .
10. No one shall be disquieted on account of his opinions. . . .
11. The free communication of ideas and opinions is one of the most precious of the rights of man. . . .
13. A common contribution is essential for the maintenance of the public forces and for the cost of administration. This should be equitably distributed among all the citizens in proportion to their means. . . .

---

1. The authors of the declaration believed that it would be a standard against which the actions of governments could be measured. Using specific examples, judge the records of the Jacobins, the Directory, and Napoleon Bonaparte in terms of this standard.

2. Read a copy of the Canadian Charter of Rights and Freedoms. To what extent are the values embodied in the Declaration of the Rights of Man reflected in our own charter?

EDMUND BURKE:
Reflections on the Revolution in France (1790)

Edmund Burke was a British parliamentarian and the leading spokesperson for conservatives in England. Although he supported the colonial cause in the American Revolution, he opposed parliamentary reform at home, and strongly rejected the French course of action in 1789. Burke's conservative thesis called for evolutionary, not revolutionary, change in the development of government.

From Brian Tierney *et al*, *Great Issues in Western Civilization* (New York: Random House, 1976), pp. 171–177.

Dear Sir:

You are pleased to call again, and with some earnestness, for my thoughts on the late proceedings in France. . . .

The dislike I feel to revolutions, the signals for which have so often been given from pulpits; the spirit of change that is gone abroad; the total contempt which prevails with you, and may come to prevail with us, of all ancient institutions, when set in opposition to a present sense of convenience, or to the bent of a present inclination: all these considerations make it not unadvisable, in my opinion, to call back your attention to the true principles of our own domestic laws; that you, my French friend, should begin to know, and that we should continue to cherish them. We ought not, on either side of the water, to suffer ourselves to be imposed upon by the counterfeit waves which some persons, by a double fraud, export to you in illicit bottoms, as raw commodities of British growth though wholly alien to our soil, in order afterwards to smuggle them back again into this country, manufactured after the newest Paris fashion of an improved liberty.

You might, if you pleased, have profited of our example, and have given to your recovered freedom a correspondent dignity. Your privileges, though discontinued, were not lost to memory. Your constitution, it is true, whilst you were out of possession, suffered waste and dilapidation; but you possessed in some parts the walls, and in all the foundations of a noble and venerable castle. You might have repaired those walls; you might have built on those old foundations. Your constitution was suspended before it was perfected; but you had the elements of a constitution very nearly as good as could be wished. . . .

Those opposed and conflicting interests, which you considered as so great a blemish in your old and in our present constitution, interpose a salutary check to all precipitate resolutions. They render deliberation a matter not of choice, but of necessity; they make all change a subject of compromise, which naturally begets moderation . . . rendering all the headlong exertions of arbitrary power, in the few or in the many, forever impracticable. . . .

You had all these advantages in your ancient states; but you chose to act as if you had never been moulded into civil society, and had everything to begin anew. You began ill, because you began by despising every thing that belonged to you. . . . Respecting your forefathers, you would have been taught to respect yourselves. You would not have chosen to consider the French as a people of yesterday, as a nation of low-born servile wretches until the emancipating year of 1789. . . .

When ancient opinions and rules of life are taken away, the loss cannot possibly be estimated. From that moment we have no compass to govern us; nor can we know distinctly to what port we steer. Europe undoubtedly, taken in a mass, was in a flourishing condition the day on which your Revolution was completed. How much of that prosperous state was owing to the spirit of our old manners and opinions is not easy to say; but as such causes cannot be indifferent in their operation, we must presume, that, on the whole, their operation was beneficial.

1. Burke claimed that institutions must stand "the test of time" in order to prove their worth. How does he defend his point of view?

2. Do you agree with Burke's assessment of the ancien régime? Why or why not?

THOMAS PAINE: The Rights of Man (1791)

Thomas Paine played a key role in swaying public opinion during the American Revolution with the publication of Common Sense *in 1776. In 1791, he wrote* The Rights of Man *as a direct rebuttal to Burke. Reaction in England against his views was so strong that he was forced to flee to France, where he was elected to the National Convention. Although a staunch republican, Paine fought unsuccessfully for the life of Louis XVI and was subsequently imprisoned and threatened with execution under the rule of Robespierre.*

From Thomas Paine, *The Rights of Man*, edited by Henry Collins (Middlesex, UK: Penguin Books, 1969), pp. 63–69.

There never did, there never will, and there never can, exist a Parliament, or any description of men, or any generation of men in any country, possessed of the right or the power of binding and controuling [sic] posterity to the *end of time*, or of commanding for ever how the world shall be governed, or who shall govern it; and therefore, all such clauses, acts or declarations, by which the makes of them attempt to do what they have neither the right nor the power to do, nor the power to execute, are in themselves null and void. – Every age and generation must be as free to act for itself, *in all cases*, as the ages and generations which preceded it. The vanity and presumption of governing beyond the grave is the most ridiculous and insolent of all tyrannies. Man has no property in man; neither has any generation a property in the generations which are to follow. . . . It is the living, and not the dead, that are to be accommodated. When man ceases to be, his power and his wants cease with him; and having no longer any participation in the concerns of this world, he has no longer any authority in directing who shall be its governors, or how its government shall be organized, or how administered.

I am not contending for nor against any form of government, nor for nor against any party here or elsewhere. That which a whole Nation chooses to do, it has a right to do. Mr. Burke says, No. Where, then, does the right exist? I am contending for the rights of the living and against their being willed away, and controuled [sic] and contracted for, by the manuscript assumed authority of the dead; and Mr. Burke is contending for the authority of the dead over the rights and freedom of the living. . . .

The circumstances of the world are continually changing, and the opinions of men change also; and as government is for the living, and not for the dead, it is the living only that has any right in it. That which may be thought right and found convenient in one age may be thought wrong and found inconvenient in another. In such cases, Who is to decide, the living or the dead?

. . . It was not against Louis XVI, but against despotic principles of the government, that the nation revolted. These principles had not their origin in him, but in the original establishment, many centuries back; and they were become too deeply rooted to be removed . . . by anything short of a revolution.

---

1. Outline the arguments used by Paine in favour of the "right" of the living to govern themselves.

2. Why do you think that Paine claims that the revolution was not against Louis XVI?

3. Set up a two-person debate in which one person takes the role of Paine and the other the role of Burke. Each person should prepare a short précis of the ideas presented in her/his excerpt and prepare an argument on the resolution: *Revolution is justified*. After the debate, step out of role and discuss the issue.

MARY WOLLSTONECRAFT: A Vindication of the Rights of Woman (1792)

Mary Wollstonecraft (1759–1797) was an educator and writer who supported the progressive ideas of the philosophes. *During the French Revolution, Wollstonecraft lived in Paris, where she actively supported the revolutionary cause. In the first major feminist work of the period, she argued that women had the same ability to reason as men and compared the relationship of women with their husbands to the class system.*

From Rosemary Agonito, *A History of Ideas on Woman*, (New York: Perigee Books, 1977), pp. 147–158.

From the respect paid to property flow, as from a poisoned fountain, most of the evils and vices which render this world such a dreary scene to the contemplative mind. . . .

One class presses on another; for all are aiming to procure respect on account of their property: and property, once gained, will procure the respect due only to talents and virtue. . . .

There is a homely proverb, which speaks a shrewd truth, that whoever the devil finds idle he will employ. And what but habitual idleness can hereditary wealth and titles produce? For man is so constituted that he can only attain a proper use of his faculties by exercising them. . . .

It is vain to expect virtue from women till they are, in some degree, independent of men; nay, it is vain to expect that strength of natural affection, which would make them good wives and mothers. Whilst they are absolutely dependent on their husbands they will be cunning, mean, and selfish, and the men who can be gratified by the fawning fondness of spaniellike affection, have not much delicacy, for love is not to be bought. . . .

To illustrate my opinion, I need only observe, that when a woman is admired for her beauty, and suffers herself to be so far intoxicated by the admiration she receives, as to neglect to discharge the indispensible duty of a mother, she sins against herself by neglecting to cultivate an affection that would equally tend to make her useful and happy. . . .

The being who discharges the duties of its station is independent; and, speaking of women at large, their first duty is to themselves as rational creatures, and the next, in point of importance, as citizens, is that, which includes so many, of mother. . . . But, to render her really virtuous and useful, she must not, if she discharge her civil duties, want, individually, the protection of civil laws; she must not be dependent on her husband's bounty for her subsistence during his life, or support after his death—for how can a being be generous who has nothing of its own? or virtuous, who is not free? . . .

Would men but generously snap our chains, and be content with rational fellowship instead of slavish obedience, they would find us more observant daughters, more affectionate sisters, more faithful wives, more reasonable mothers—in a word, better citizens. We should then love them with true affection, because we should learn to respect ourselves; and the peace of mind of a worthy man would not be interrupted by the idle vanity of his wife, nor the babes sent to nestle in a strange bosom, having never found a home in their mother's.

1. What parallel does Wollstonecraft draw between women and the idle propertied class?

2. What does the author feel to be the true role of women in society?

3. To what extent do you agree with Wollstonecraft's contention that women must be financially independent to be free?

MAXIMILIEN DE ROBESPIERRE: The King Must Die! (1792)

Robespierre was a key figure in the trial of Louis XVI, speaking eleven times. In the following speech, delivered to the convention on 3 December 1792, Robespierre argued that it was essential for the preservation of the revolution that Louis XVI be executed. Louis was subsequently found guilty by the convention and condemned to death. He was guillotined on 21 January 1793.

From Guy Carleton Lee (ed.), *The World's Orators Comprising the Great Orations of the World's History* (New York: G.P. Putnam's Sons, 1900), pp. 99–111.

Louis was King: the Republic exists: the famous question which occupies you is decided by those words alone. Louis has been dethroned for his crimes; Louis denounced the French people as rebels; to chastise them, he summoned the armies of the tyrants, his brothers; but victory and the people have decided that he alone was a rebel: therefore, Louis cannot be judged; he is already judged. He is condemned, or the Revolution is not justified . . .

If Louis is absolved, if Louis can be presumed innocent, what does the Revolution become?

. . . You demand an exception to the death-penalty for him who alone can make it legitimate! Yes, the death-penalty is generally a crime, and for that reason only, according to the indestructible principles of nature, to be justified in the case where it is necessary for the safety of individuals or the social body. So, the public safety never makes use of it against ordinary offences, because society can always prevent these by other means, and can render the guilty incapable of injuring it. But with a King dethroned in the midst of a Revolution which is nothing less than cemented by the laws, a King whose name alone brings the scourge of war upon the agitated nation, neither prison or exile can render his existence indifferent to the public welfare; and this cruel exception to the ordinary laws avowed by justice can be imputed only to the nature of his crimes. I pronounce this fatal truth with regret—but Louis should die, because the country must live.

---

1. Précis Robespierre's arguments against (a) holding a trial for Louis and (b) preserving his life.

2. Imagine you are a royalist in revolutionary France. Write a rebuttal to Robespierre's arguments against a trial.

3. How did Robespierre's own actions during the Reign of Terror betray the sentiments expressed in this speech?

THE JACOBINS: Revolutionary Government (1793–1794)

Legislation passed by the National Convention under the Jacobins illustrated the control the government had over the nation. This first excerpt is from the formation of the Revolutionary Tribunal which was used to eliminate opposition.

. . . a Special Criminal Court shall be established at Paris to take cognizance of all counter-revolutionary activities, all attacks upon liberty, equality, unity, the indivisibility of the Republic, the internal and external security of the State, and all plots on behalf of the re-establishment of monarchy or any other authority hostile to the liberty, equality and the sovereignty of the people. . . .

Decision shall be executed without appeal. . . .

The Committee of Public Safety (created on 6 April 1793) was originally to act as a type of secretariat to the convention. Eventually, however, it became a government unto itself.

The Committee of Public Safety . . . shall debate in secret; it shall be responsible for supervising and accelerating the work of the administration . . . the decrees of which it may even suspend when it believes them contrary to the national interest. . . .

Under critical circumstances it is authorized to take measures of general defence, both internal and external; and orders signed by the majority of its deliberating members . . . shall be executed without delay.

The Law of 22 Prairial (10 June 1794 in the old calendar) placed the Revolutionary Tribunal under the control of the Committee of Public Safety. At the same time it broadened its powers in order to seek out and destroy all opposition to the Jacobins. It was the action that signaled that Robespierre had gone too far. He was overthrown and executed six weeks later.

The Revolutionary Tribunal is instituted to punish the enemies of the people.

The enemies of the people are those who seek to destroy public liberty, either by force or by cunning. The following are deemed to be enemies of the people:

those who have instigated the re-establishment of the monarchy,

. . . those who have betrayed the Republic in the command of places and armies,

. . . those who have deceived the people or the representatives of the people, in order to lead them into undertakings contrary to the interests of liberty,

. . . those who have disseminated false news in order to divide or disturb the people;

. . . and who by whatever appearances they assume, have made an attempt against the liberty, security and unity of the Republic.

The penalty provided for all offences under the jurisdiction of the Revolutionary Tribunal is death.

From Norman Sheffe and William Fisher, *A Sourcebook for Modern History* (Toronto: McGraw-Hill, 1964), pp. 44–47.

1. Using the Jacobin record as an example, comment on the assertion that government sometimes uses legislation to legitimize oppression.

2. Compare the law of the 22 Prairial with the actions taken against student protests in China in the spring and summer of 1989. To what extent did both governments use the same methods to suppress dissent?

THE CHARTER OF FRANCE (1814)

Louis XVIII accepted the throne of France in 1814. The restoration of the monarchy, however, could not return the nation to prerevolutionary days. Louis kept the bureaucracy and the financial and legal reforms that had been instituted by Napoleon. He granted the Charter of France, which recognized many of the gains of the revolution and placed limits on the nineteenth-century French monarchy.

We have voluntarily and by the free exercise of our royal authority granted . . . the Constitutional Charter as follows: . . . Articles:

1. The French are equal before the law, whatever may be their title or rank.

2. They contribute without distinction to the impositions of the State in proportion to their fortune. . . .

4. Their personal liberty is likewise granted. . . .

5. All may with equal liberty make profession of their religion. . . .

8. The French have the right to publish and cause their opinions to be printed. . . .

9. All property is inviolable. . . .

11. All investigation of opinions expressed or of votes cast previous to the Restoration is prohibited. . . .

13. The person of the King is inviolable and sacred. . . .

From Norman Sheffe and William Fisher, *A Sourcebook for Modern History* (Toronto: McGraw-Hill, 1964), pp. 63–64.

14. The King is the supreme head of the state. . . .
15. The legislative power is exercised jointly by the King, the Chamber of Peers, and the Chamber of Deputies. . . .
18. Every law must be discussed and passed freely by a majority of each of the two houses. . . .

---

1. In approximately 250 words, assess the Charter of France as a culmination of the original aims of the revolution. (NOTE: You may need to conduct further research into the charter.)

CHARLES DICKENS: A Tale of Two Cities (1859)

One of the most famous novels in the English language which uses the French Revolution as a backdrop was written by the Victorian novelist Charles Dickens. Dickens first thought of writing this novel while reading Thomas Carlyle's The French Revolution *(1837). His intent was to "add something to the popular and picturesque means of understanding that terrible time." Although* A Tale of Two Cities *is clearly a work of fiction, Dickens made every effort to make it historically accurate. In the preface he wrote: "Whenever any reference (however slight) is made here to the condition of the French people before or during the Revolution, it is truly made, on the faith of trustworthy witnesses." The following passage describes the fall of the Bastille.*

From Charles Dickens, *A Tale of Two Cities* (Toronto: Bantam Books, 1983), pp. 199–200.

"Come, then!" cried Defarge, in a resounding voice. "Patriots and friends, we are ready! The Bastille!"

With a roar that sounded as if all the breath in France had been shaped into the detested word, the living sea rose, wave on wave, depth on depth, and overflowed the city to that point. Alarm-bells ringing, drums beating, the sea raging and thundering on its new beach, the attack begun.

Deep ditches, double drawbridge, massive stone walls, eight great towers, cannon, muskets, fire and smoke. Through the fire and through the smoke—in the fire and in the smoke, for the sea cast him up against a cannon, and on the instant he became a cannonier—Defarge of the wine-shop worked like a manful soldier two fierce hours.

Deep ditch, single drawbridge, massive stone walls, eight great towers, cannon, muskets, fire and smoke. One drawbridge down! "Work, comrades all, work! Work, Jacques One, Jacques Two, Jacques One Thousand, Jacques Two Thousand, Jacques Five-and-Twenty Thousand; in the name of all the Angels or the Devils—which you prefer—work!" Thus Defarge of the wine shop, still at his gun, which had long grown hot.

"To me, women!" cried madame his wife. "What! We can kill as well as the men when the place is taken!" And to her, with a shrill thirsty cry, trooping women variously armed, but all armed alike in hunger and revenge.

Cannon, muskets, fire and smoke; but, still the deep ditch, the single drawbridge, the massive stone walls, and the eight great towers. Slight displacements of the raging sea, made by the falling wounded. Flashing weapons, blazing torches, smoking waggonloads of wet straw, hard work at neighbouring barricades in all directions, shrieks, volleys, execrations, bravery without stint, boom, smash and rattle, and the furious sounding of the living sea; but, still the deep ditch, and the single drawbridge, and the massive stone walls, and the eight great towers, and still Defarge of the wine shop at his gun, grown doubly hot by the service of Four fierce hours.

A white flag from within the fortress, and a parley—this dimly perceptible through the raging storm, nothing audible in it—suddenly the sea rose immeasurably wider and higher, and swept Defarge of the wine shop over the lowered drawbridge, past the massive stone outer walls, in among the eight great towers surrendered!

So resistless was the force of the ocean bearing him on, that even to draw his breath or turn his head was as impracticable as if he had been struggling in the surf in the South Sea, until he landed in the outer court-yard of the Bastille. There, against an angle of a wall, he made a struggle to look about him. Jacques Three was nearly at his side; Madame Defarge, still heading some of her women, was visible in the inner distance, and her knife was in her hand. Everywhere was tumult, exultation, deafening and maniacal bewilderment, astounding noise, yet furious dumbshow.

"The Prisoners!"

"The Records!"

"The secret cells!"

"The instruments of torture!"

"The Prisoners!"

Of all these cries, and ten thousand incoherencies, "The Prisoners!" was the cry most taken up by the sea that rushed in, as if there were an eternity of people, as well as of time and space.

---

1. Compare Dickens's recreation of the fall of the Bastille with the eyewitness account on page 64.

ANALYSIS AND APPLICATION

1. *The collapse of the ancien régime in France was not due so much to outside pressures as it was a result of internal weakness.*

Account for this statement with reference to the causes of events in France from 1789 to 1791.

2. Write a speech to the National Assembly or National Convention demanding a larger role for women in the affairs of the state.

3. Speaking on the occasion of the two hundredth anniversary of the French Revolution, Prime Minister Margaret Thatcher of Britain claimed that her country had accomplished as much without any of the bloodshed. Write a response to Thatcher's viewpoint with regard to the relative freedom in each nation by 1815.

4. With a classmate, stage a two-person debate between Edmund Burke and Thomas Paine. Rather than simply paralleling the arguments put forward in the readings, set your argument in 1815 and have the participants comment on the events of the previous twenty-five years.

At the end of your debate, step out of character and together consider whether or not the two debaters may have changed their original points of view in light of future events.

5. Write a brief interpretation of the writings of Rousseau from the viewpoint of Robespierre.

6. The Jacobins have been called the first modern "totalitarian state." Compare the tactics used by Robespierre and his followers with a twentieth-century totalitarian government.

7. *Napoleon, although a political dictator, effectively preserved the ideals and accomplishments of the French Revolution.*

Defend or refute this statement with reference to the social, legal, and religious reforms of the period and the degree of military security won by Napoleon's armies.

8. In chart form, trace the evolution of government in France from 1788 to 1815. Identify the type of government, its leadership, degree of popular involvement, and governing constitution.

PART TWO

Nationalism, Industrialism, and Romanticism, 1815 to 1880

The end of the French Revolutionary/Napoleonic era brought relative political stability to Western Europe. In spite of a conservative retrenchment in government, the era of peace that emerged after more than a century of conflict became a crucible for change.

The early nineteenth century saw a redefinition of the relationship between the citizen and the state. For many Europeans, the protection of the rights of the individual, prevalent in Enlightenment thought, could be guaranteed only by a strong and independent nation-state. These "new" nations would be based not upon the military conquests or inherited fiefdoms of the feudal past, but on a commonality of language, race, and culture. This new, vibrant nationalism would fuel the politics of the century and would spark revolutions in countries throughout the Western world.

Over the previous two centuries, Western civilization had become a dominant force in global affairs. This was accomplished primarily through its economic strength and technological innovation. This process, with its roots in the eighteenth century, exploded during the nineteenth century. The Industrial Revolution began in Britain and spread throughout the Western world. It transformed these societies from their rural-agricultural base to an urban-industrial one. While this rapid transformation improved the manufacturing process, it also caused considerable social upheaval.

The rapid industrialization of Western Europe and North America also propelled the countries of these regions to new heights of overseas expansion. The need of industrial society for new markets and inexpensive sources of raw materials fueled an imperialist drive unprecedented in the preceding two centuries. Western civilization extended its influence across the globe, to Asia, Africa, and South America. It was the start of a colonial empire that would not crumble until 150 years later.

If the Age of Reason culminated in the French Revolution, the generation that followed recognized that rational thought alone could not account for human behaviour. A new group of artists, writers, and social critics emerged to champion the emotional side of humanity. Called the romantics, these artists rejected the established rules and conventions of Western society and sought freedom in form and subject matter. The romanticists were inspired by the revolutions in France and the United States and supported the struggles for independence by other European nations. Their view of the world was to dominate the first half of the century.

	POLITICS	PHILOSOPHY/LEARNING	ART	SCIENCE/TECHNOLOGY
1815	1815 Second Peace of Paris (Congress of Vienna) Holy Alliance—Austria, Russia, and Prussia 1817 Sultan of Turkey grants partial autonomy to Serbia 1818 Chile proclaims independence from Spain France joins the Quadruple Alliance 1819 Carlsbad Decrees Peterloo Massacre (England) Bolivar declares the area encompassing Venezuela, Colombia, and Ecuador independent	1815 Malthus, *An Inquiry into the Nature and Progress of Rent* Ricardo, *The Influence of the Low Price of Corn on the Profits of Stock* 1816 Hegel, *The Science of Logic* 1817 Hegel, *Encyclopedia of the Philosophical Sciences* 1818 Dobrovsky, *History of the Czech Language*	1815 Canova, *Three Graces* Nash, Brighton Pavilion 1816 Rossini, *Barbière di Siviglia* 1817 P. Shelley, *The Revolt of Islam* 1818 M. Shelley, *Frankenstein* 1819 Gericault, *The Raft of the Medusa*	1815 U.S.S. *Fulton*, first steam warship 1816 Laennec invents stethoscope 1819 Laennec, *Treatise of Diagnosis by Listening to Sounds*
1820	1820 Nationalist revolt in Naples Revolution in Portugal and Spain 1821 Greek War of Independence begins Peru and Mexico gain independence 1822 Brazil gains independence from Portugal Turks massacre Greeks at Chios 1823 Monroe Doctrine 1824 Repeal of the Combinations Act in Britain allows trade unions 1825 Decembrist uprising in Russia Factory Act in Britain 1829 London Protocol guarantees territory of Greece	1820 Malthus, *Principles of Political Economy* 1821 Mill, *Elements of Political Economy* Catholic church removes ban on teaching Copernican system 1822 Saint-Simon, *Cathechisme des Industriels* Champollion translates the Rosetta Stone Galileo's *Dialogue on Two Chief World Systems* removed from the *Index of Prohibited Books* 1824 Ranke, *History of the Roman and Teutonic People, 1494–1514* 1828 Webster's *Dictionary* 1829 Milman, *History of the Jews* 1829 Guizot, *Histoire de la Civilisation en France*	1820 Shelley, *Prometheus Unbound* 1821 Constable, *Hay Wain* Mickiewicz, *Ballads and Romances* Weber, *Der Freischutz* 1822 de Vigny, *Poèmes* 1823 Stendhal, *Racine et Shakespeare* 1824 Delacroix, *Massacre at Chios* 1825 Manzoni, *I Promessi Sposi* Nash, Buckingham Palace 1827 Constable, *The Cornfield* 1828 Pushkin, *Oltava* 1829 Delacroix, *Sardanapalus*	1821 Faraday discovers electromagnetic rotation 1822 First iron railroad bridge Niepce produces the first photograph 1825 Opening of the first passenger railway line (Stockton-Darlington) Erie Canal opens 1826 First railway tunnel 1827 George Ohm formulates Ohm's Law
1830	1830 July Revolution in France 1831 French Foreign Legion created to subdue Algeria Poland declares independence; revolt suppressed by Russia 1832 First British Reform Bill passed 1832 Mazzini founds Young Italy	1830 Comte, *Cours de Philosophie positive* 1833 Michelet, *Histoire de France* 1834 Louis Braille devises system to read by touch 1835 Grimm, *German Mythology* 1836 Diez, *Grammar of the Romance Languages*	1830 Hugo, *Hernani* Berlioz, *Symphonie Fantastique* 1831 Delacroix, *The Barricade* 1833 Sand, *Lelia* 1834 Wilkins, National Gallery 1835 Gogol, *Dead Souls* Anderson, *Fairy Tales*	1830 Lyell, *The Principles of Geology* 1831 Faraday invents electric transformer Darwin joins the crew of the H.M.S. *Beagle*

	POLITICS	PHILOSOPHY/LEARNING	ART	SCIENCE/TECHNOLOGY
1830	1833 Prussia establishes the Zollevein British Factory Act passed 1837 Revolt of silk weavers in Lyon repressed Spanish Inquisition (begun in 13th century) suppressed 1835 Municipal Corporation Act in Great Britain 1836 People's Charter (Chartism) drawn up in Britain 1839 Belgian independence recognized by Holland Opium War begins in China	1837 Carlyle, *French Revolution* 1838 Arnold, *History of Rome* 1839 Blanc, *L'Organisation du travail* Ranke, *History of the Reformation in Germany*	1836 Arc de Triomphe completed 1837 Berlioz, *Requiem* 1838 Immermann, *Munchhausen* 1839 Chopin, 24 *Preludes* Turner, *Fighting Tremeraire*	1832 Morse invents telegraph Babbage conceives the analytical engine, the first computer 1834 McCormick invents the reaping machine 1836 Dreyse invents the needle gun 1838 First Atlantic crossing entirely by steam 1839 Goodyear vulcanizes rubber
1840	1842 Treaty of Nanking cedes Hong Kong to the British 1844 British Factory Act 1845 Irish potato famine (lasts 3 years) results in the death or emigration of 1.5 million people 1846 Repeal of British Corn Laws 1848 Revolutions in France, Hungary, Austria, Italy, and Prussia Liberia proclaims independence 1849 Failure of Frankfurt Assembly to secure unification Hungarian Diet proclaims independence	1840 Proudhoun, *Qu'est-ce-que la Propriété* 1841 List, *National System of Political Economy* Carlyle, *On Heroes, Hero-Worship and the Heroic in History* 1843 Carlyle, *Past and Present* 1844 Mill, *Unsettled Questions of Political Economy* 1845 Engels, *The Condition of the Working Classes in England* 1848 Marx and Engels, *The Communist Manifesto* Mill, *Principles of Political Economy*	1840 Barry, British Houses of Parliament 1841 Cooper, *The Deerslayer* Hoffman, *Deutschland, Deutschland uber Alles* 1842 Poe, *The Masque of the Red Death* 1843 Dickens, *A Christmas Carol* 1844 Verdi, *Hernani* Turner, *Rain, Steam and Speed* Heine, *Deutschland, ein Wintermarchen* 1845 Disraeli, *Sybil, or the Two Nations* Wagner, *Lohengrin* 1846 Liszt, *1st Hungarian Rhapsody* 1847 Brontë, *Wuthering Heights* 1848 Millet, *The Winnower* 1849 Dickens, *David Copperfield*	1842 Long uses ether as an anaesthetic Darwin writes a 35-page abstract of his theories of evolution 1845 McNaught's compound steam engine 1846 Discovery of the planet Neptune 1847 von Helmholtz, *On the Conservation of Energy*
1850	1850 Austro-Hungarian customs union Tai-Ping Rebellion begins in China 1851 Louis-Napoleon's coup d'état	1850 Spencer, *Social Studies*	1850 Paxton, Crystal Palace Courbet, *The Stonebreakers* 1851 Verdi, *Rigoletto*	1851 Great International Exhibition in London

	POLITICS	PHILOSOPHY/LEARNING	ART	SCIENCE/TECHNOLOGY
1850	1852 Beginning of second French Empire Cavour becomes prime minister of Piedmont 1854 Crimean War begins 1857 Sepoy Revolt in India 1858 Cavour secures the assistance of Napoleon III for Italian unification 1859 Peace of Villafranca grants Lombardy to Piedmont	1852 Ranke, *History of France* 1853 Mommsen, *History of Rome* 1854 Grimm, *German Dictionary* 1856 Spencer, *Principles of Psychology* de Tocqueville, *The Old Regime and the Revolution* 1858 Carey, *Principles of Social Science* 1859 Marx, *Criticism of Political Economy*	1852 Stowe, *Uncle Tom's Cabin* 1853 Verdi, *Il Trovatore, La Traviata* 1854 Liszt, *Les Preludes* 1855 Whitman, *Leaves of Grass* 1856 Flaubert, *Madame Bovary* 1857 Millet, *The Gleaners* 1859 Millet, *The Angelus* Wagner, *Tristan und Isolde*	1852 Otis develops the first safe passenger elevator 1853 Cayley founds the science of aerodynamics 1855 Koller makes tungsten steel Deville develops process for making aluminum Maury, *Physical Geography of the Sea* 1856 Bessemer converter Discovery of the Neanderthal 1858 Nightingale, *Notes on Matters Affecting the Health, Efficiency and Hospital Administration of the British Army* First Atlantic telegraph cable 1859 Lenoir invents first internal combustion engine Plante invents rechargeable storage battery Construction of Suez Canal begins
1860	1860 Parma, Modena, Tuscany, and Romagna annexed to Sardinia Garibaldi conquers the Kingdom of the Two Sicilies 1861 Kingdom of Sicily proclaimed U.S. Civil War begins 1862 Bismarck becomes prime minister of Prussia—"Blood and Iron speech" 1863 Lincoln issues Emancipation Proclamation 1864 Austria and Prussia declare war on Denmark over Schleswig and Holstein 1865 U.S. Civil War ends 1866 Seven Weeks' War War between Austria and Italy	1860 Bukhardt, *The Civilization of the Renaissance in Italy* 1861 Dahl, *Dictionary of the Living Russian Tongue* 1862 Spencer, *First Principles* 1863 Littre, *Dictionnaire de la langue française* 1864 Pope Pius IX, *Syllabus of Errors* 1867 Marx, *Das Kapital* 1869 Mill, *On the Subjection of Women*	1860 Eliot, *The Mill on the Floss* 1861 Dickens, *Great Expectations* 1862 Hugo, *Les Misérables* Turgenev, *Fathers and Sons* 1863 Berlioz, *les Troyens* 1864 Tolstoy, *War and Peace* 1865 Verne, *From the Earth to the Moon* 1866 Dostoyevsky, *Crime and Punishment* 1867 Strauss, *Blue Danube waltz* Verdi, *Don Carlos* 1868 Brahms, *A German Requiem* Wagner, *Die Meistersinger* 1869 Brahms, *Hungarian Dances* Flaubert, *L'Education Sentimentale*	1861 Siemens and Martins simultaneously invent open hearth process 1862 Gatling gun invented Pasteur publicizes the germ theory of disease 1863 Lyell, *Geological Evidence on the Antiquity of Man* 1865 Mendel publishes his theories of genetics 1866 Nobel invents dynamite 1869 First North American transcontinental railroad completed Suez Canal opens Mendeleyev develops the periodic table of elements

	POLITICS	PHILOSOPHY/LEARNING	ART	SCIENCE/TECHNOLOGY
1860	1867 Canada gains independence Formation of the North German Confederation Alaska purchased from Russia by the U.S. 1868 Prussia confiscates Hanover			
1870	1870 Franco-Prussian War Italian unification complete when the Italians seize Rome from the French 1871 William I proclaimed German Emperor at Versailles 1872 League of the Three Emperors (Germany, Russia, Austria-Hungary) 1875 Public Health Act (Great Britain) 1876 Korea becomes independent Serbia declares war on Turkey 1877 Russia declares war on Turkey 1878 Congress of Berlin; temporary settlement of the Balkan situation 1879 Alsace-Lorraine declared a part of Germany	1871 Wagner, *The Social Question* Taine, *History of English Literature* 1873 Spencer, *The Study of Sociology* Taine, *The Origins of Contemporary France* 1876 Taine, *The Old Regime* 1878 Treitschke begins racial anti-Semite movement in Germany Grove begins the *Dictionary of Music and Musicians* 1879 Spencer, *Principles of Ethics*	1870 Wagner, *Die Walküre* 1871 Verdi, *Aida* 1872 Whistler, *The Artist's Mother* 1874 Smetana, *My Fatherland* 1875 Bizet, *Carmen* 1876 Beyreuth opera house opens with the first complete performance of Wagner's *Ring des Nibelungen* 1878 Dvorak, *Three Slavonic Rhapsodies* Tchaikovsky, *Swan Lake* 1879 Tchaikovsky, *Eugen Onegin*	1870 Mont Cenis tunnel, first major railroad tunnel 1871 Darwin, *The Descent of Man* 1873 First streetcars 1878 Thomas and Gilchrist perfect "basic" process for steel production 1879 Siemens exhibits electric railway in Berlin

CHAPTER FOUR

Nationalism in Europe, 1815 to 1880

THE EMERGENCE OF THE MODERN NATION-STATE

Both romanticism and industrialization found their support in the nation-state. Romanticism tended to idealize the nation as the homeland of a common view of humanity. Industrialization depended upon centralized authority and commonality of purpose in order to develop. As a result, nationalism became the new "religion" of the age.

Nationalism is a potent ideological force. It can be used to unite people behind a common cause or to lead them to persecute others. Today we take the idea of nationalism for granted. But the concept of belonging to a particular nation (*nationality*) and the desire for the independence of that nation (*nationalism*) are relatively new phenomena.

People have long had a sense of cultural unity. That unity has been based on common language, religion, history, customs, manners, art, and folklore. Political nationalism began to develop when rulers extended these sentiments to developing nation-states. But it was not until the French Revolution that the fate of the individual came to be associated with the survival of the state. Identification of individual freedom with state freedom made nationalism a potent revolutionary force because it created the desire to make cultural nationalism a political reality.

Nationalism and the French Revolution

The modern French nation was born in 1789 with the Tennis Court Oath and the creation of the National Assembly. Prior to the French Revolution, the state's identity was closely intertwined with that of the king. During the revolution, however, patriotic festivals, masterminded by Jacques-Louis David (1748–1825), fostered a sense of fraternity and loyalty to the *state* rather than to an *estate*. Symbols of the new French nation flourished everywhere, from the new national flag, the tricolour, to a new national anthem, "La Marseillaise." French patriotic fervour also extended beyond the country's borders as the soldiers of the revolution fought back Austrian and Prussian invaders at Valmy.

Patriotism alone, however, can win battles, but not wars. To survive in the face of the Grand Alliance against the revolutionary regime, the nation had to muster all of its resources. On 23 August 1793, Bertrand Barere, a member of the National Convention and the Committee for Public Safety, announced a *levée en masse*, demanding that the citizens of France prepare themselves for battle.

> The young men shall go to battle; the married men shall forge arms and transport food supplies; the women shall make tents and uniforms, and shall serve in the hospitals; the children shall convert old cloth into surgical dressings; the old men shall proceed to the public squares, to stimulate the courage of the soldiers and to preach the unity of the Republic and the hatred of kings.

From Bertrand Barere, "Report on the Civil Requisitioning of Young Citizens for the Defense of Our Country," in John C. Rule, *et al* (eds.), *Critical Issues in History* (Boston: D.C. Heath and Co., 1967), p. 596.

By the end of the year France was a nation at arms. Within two years, its military victories had forced the anti-France coalition of Great Britain, Austria, Prussia, Spain, Savoy, and Holland to disintegrate.

The Spread of Nationalist Fervour

The nationalist fervour of the French troops spread to the enemy soldiers as well. At the beginning of the nineteenth century, Germans, Poles, and Italians, long dominated by foreign powers, welcomed Napoleon's armies as liberators. By creating the Confederation of the Rhine, the Cisalpine Republic, and the Duchy of Warsaw from his conquered territories, it appeared that Napoleon favoured self-determination for these nationalities. In reality, however, these new nations were little more than administrative structures. There was little room for non-French nationalism in Napoleon's Europe.

Eventually opposition to Napoleonic rule led to national crusades, such as the Great Patriotic War in Russia, the War of Liberation in Germany, and the Peninsular War in Spain. Ultimately, such resistance contributed to the decline of Napoleon's empire. In Germany and Italy, however, Napoleon's new administrative units disrupted the old political loyalties and played an important part in developing the concept of self-determination for Germans and Italians. Unfortunately, this idea was frustrated almost immediately by the conservative reaction of the victorious powers at the Congress of Vienna.

The Congress of Vienna, 1814 to 1815

Britain, Russia, Prussia, and Austria successfully joined forces to defeat Napoleon and his armies. In September 1814, the leadership of this powerful alliance gathered in Vienna to discuss the restoration of order to European society. Although officially labeled a diplomatic conference, it was in many ways more of a celebration. After almost twenty-five years of intermittent war, the continent was finally free of Napoleon and his crusading army. These leaders had weathered the revolutionary storm and now wanted to make certain that such turmoil could not erupt again.

As the Great Powers of the European continent, Britain, Russia, Prussia, and Austria believed themselves to be responsible for maintaining political stability in the future. It was their representatives, therefore, who were to make the key decisions in Vienna. Initially, France was excluded from the deliberations. However, the French foreign minister,

THE CARLSBAD DECREES

1. There shall be appointed for each university a special representative of the ruler of each state. . . .

This representative shall enforce strictly the existing laws and disciplinary regulations; he shall observe with care the attitude shown by the university instructors in their public lectures . . . and he shall . . . give beneficial direction to the teaching, keeping in view the future attitude of the students. Finally, he shall give unceasing attention to everything that may promote morality . . . among the students. . . .

2. The confederated governments mutually pledge themselves to eliminate from the universities or any other public educational institutions all instructors who shall have proved their unfitness . . . by abusing their legitimate influence over young minds, or by presenting harmful ideas hostile to public order or subverting existing governmental instructions. . . .

3. The laws that for some time have been directed against secret and unauthorized societies in the universities shall be strictly enforced. Such laws are applicable especially to . . . the society [that] implies the completely impermissible idea of permanent fellowship and constant intercommunication between the universities. . . .

The governments mutually agree that all individuals who shall be shown to have maintained their membership in secret or unauthorized associations, or shall have taken membership in such associations, shall not be eligible for any public office. . . . As long as this edict remains in force, no publication which appears daily or as a serial not exceeding twenty sheets of printed matter, shall be printed in any state of the Confederation without the prior knowledge and approval of the state officials.

From Louis L. Snyder, *Documents of German History* (New Brunswick, NJ: Rutgers University Press, 1958), pp. 158–159.

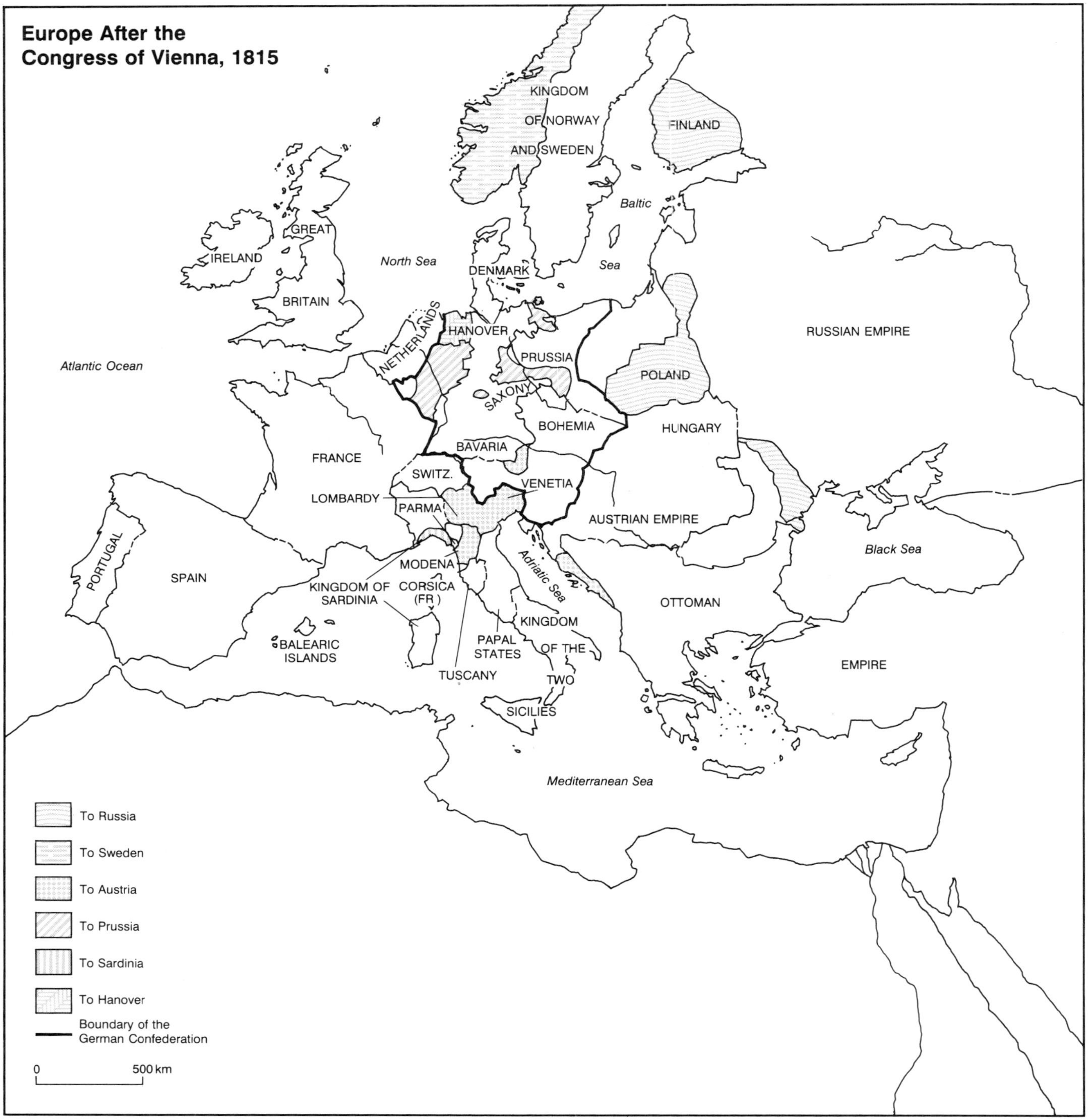

Europe After the Congress of Vienna, 1815

KINGDOM OF NORWAY AND SWEDEN
FINLAND
Baltic Sea
North Sea
GREAT BRITAIN
IRELAND
DENMARK
NETHERLANDS
HANOVER
PRUSSIA
SAXONY
POLAND
RUSSIAN EMPIRE
Atlantic Ocean
FRANCE
BAVARIA
BOHEMIA
HUNGARY
SWITZ.
VENETIA
LOMBARDY
PARMA
AUSTRIAN EMPIRE
PORTUGAL
SPAIN
MODENA
KINGDOM OF SARDINIA
CORSICA (FR.)
Adriatic Sea
Black Sea
OTTOMAN EMPIRE
KINGDOM OF THE TWO SICILIES
PAPAL STATES
TUSCANY
BALEARIC ISLANDS
Mediterranean Sea

To Russia
To Sweden
To Austria
To Prussia
To Sardinia
To Hanover
Boundary of the German Confederation

0 500 km

Charles Maurice de Talleyrand (1754–1838), successfully argued that France would have a more vested interest in supporting the new order in Europe if it had some participation in determining what that new order would be. As a result, France joined the other Great Powers at the bargaining table.

The first issues to be tackled by the Congress were the nature of the French indemnity and the restoration of the Bourbon monarchy. Then the leaders focused their attention on defusing the forces of liberalism and nationalism across Europe. To this end they decided that Germany and Italy should remain divided, that Poland should be partitioned between Prussia, Austria, and Russia, and that Belgium and Holland should be united under the Dutch monarchy.

The conservative leaders of Prussia, Russia, and Austria, however, felt that these measures alone were not enough. They equated nationalism with revolution. After the Congress of Vienna, they formed the Holy Alliance (1815) and embarked on a repressive campaign against both liberalism and nationalism. Four formal conferences of the Congress powers—Aix-la-Chapelle (1818), Troppau (1820), Laibach (1821), and Verona (1822)—were convened to deal with liberal and national revolts in Germany, Spain, Italy, Greece, and the Netherlands.

Although designed to maintain the status quo, the Congress system established in Vienna created the first real international approach to the preservation of peace in Europe. It ensured that an attack against any one member would constitute an attack against them all. In addition, the Great Powers agreed to meet periodically to discuss any outstanding issues. Originally this pact applied only to the wartime allies, but in 1818 it was expanded to include France. The truce that emerged from the Congress of Vienna would keep the continent in relative peace for the next century. Only when the Congress system broke down and was replaced by rival military alliances did major war once again break out on the continent.

THE BEGINNINGS OF NATIONALIST REVOLT

Germany

The first signs of nationalist revolt occurred in the German universities. A student fraternity called the *Burschenschaft* held a large rally in favour of national unity at Wartburg. Austrian chancellor Prince Klemens von Metternich (1773–1859) grasped the opportunity to arouse the fears of revolution among the members of the German *Diet*. He was thus able to manipulate them into supporting the suppression of such demonstrations of liberalism and nationalism. The Carlsbad Decrees, introduced in 1819, placed controls on the press and on education and forbade public meetings. The decrees effectively quashed agitation for national unity and self-determination in the German Confederation until 1848.

Spain

In 1820, revolution broke out in Spain, forcing Ferdinand VII (1784–1833) to adopt a liberal constitution. Although the revolt was suppressed by French troops in 1822 after the nations at the Congress of Verona agreed to help Ferdinand re-establish his rule, the relative ease of the Spanish rebellion inspired similar revolts in the Kingdom of the Two Sicilies, Milan and Sardinia. These were suppressed with brutal force by the Austrians, who were supported by Russia and Prussia at the Congress of Troppau. However, Metternich was unable to secure British and French support for a plan for collective security against revolution. In fact, many people in both those nations sympathized with the goals of the revolutionaries and were opposed to the extreme measures being used to control them. Finally, as a result of a disagreement over Spanish America, Britain withdrew from the Congress system.

Spain's colonies in the Americas had revolted against Spanish rule during the Napoleonic Wars and had established their independence. When Ferdinand VII tried to re-establish Spanish rule, the U.S. president, James Monroe (1758–1831), in June 1823 proclaimed his government's support for the former colonies and his opposition to any aggression on the part of Spain.

> With the governments who have declared their independence and maintained it, and whose independence we have, on great consideration and on just principles acknowledged, we could not view any interposition for the purpose of oppressing them, or controlling, in any other manner, their destiny, by any European power, in any other light than as the manifestation of an unfriendly disposition towards the United States.

This policy became known as the Monroe Doctrine; eventually it would form the cornerstone of American foreign policy in the Western Hemisphere. However, it would have been merely an idle threat had Monroe's support for the colonies not been strengthened by British objections to Spanish intervention. The British had increased their trade with the Spanish colonies significantly during the Napoleonic era and they did not want to see this commercial flow disrupted. Any attempt by Spain to suppress the revolt overseas would require a naval operation. Therefore, the opposition of the British, who dominated the seas, ensured that the Spanish colonies would maintain their independence.

Greece

The first successful national revolt on the European continent was in Greece. For several hundred years Greece had been part of the Ottoman Empire. (See readings.) The Greeks' long fight against Turkish oppression had aroused public support throughout Europe and had attracted many volunteers to their cause. Public pressure finally forced three Congress members—Great Britain, France, and Russia—to come to the aid of the Greek patriots. They demanded that Turkey accept an armistice, but the Turks refused. This led to a joint Anglo-French-Russian naval operation that defeated the Turkish fleet at Navarino Bay in 1827. Two years later the Turks acknowledged Greek independence in the Treaty of Adrianople.

NATIONALISM AND THE REVOLUTIONS OF 1830

Revolution and the Monarchy in France

The successful fight of the Greeks inspired the forces of liberalism and nationalism everywhere. In 1830, revolution in France sparked open revolt all across Europe.

THE ARTIST AS REVOLUTIONARY

Eugène Delacroix (1798–1863) was one of France's most prominent and influential artists. Often associated with romanticism, Delacroix is best known for his paintings depicting revolutionary sentiment. One of his most personal and passionate works, *The Massacre at Chios* (1824), portrayed an actual event in the Greek War of Independence. The acts of violence it depicted appealed to the viewer's sense of pity and horror.

The Massacre at Chios was followed in 1830 by *Liberty Leading the People*, which depicts the July Revolution in France in that year. Liberty was portrayed as a woman leading a variety of French citizens in revolt against the rule of Charles X. When the painting was finally exhibited in 1831, however, it created an outcry. The people were described as "rabble," while Liberty herself was called "a soiled and shameless woman of the streets." The painting was ostracized by the Second Republic and the Second Empire. It was not until the Third Republic that *Liberty Leading the People* was reinstated as an important work of art.

Eugène Delacroix's Massacre at Chios *was bitterly attacked as a rejection of French classicism. It is viewed by some as a manifesto of French romanticism.*

The Congress of Vienna had re-established the Bourbon monarchy in France under the terms of the Charter of 1814. Embodying many of the reforms of the revolutionary era, the charter created a limited constitutional monarchy. The new king, Louis XVIII, was Louis XVI's oldest surviving brother. (Louis XVII, the son of the former king, had died in 1795.) Louis recognized that the political clock could not be turned back to 1789. Thus during his reign (1814–1824) the bourgeoisie assumed an even greater role in government. Although political power was still restricted to the wealthy and propertied, there was a great deal of legal and social equality.

With Louis's death in 1824, however, his younger brother, King Charles X (1757–1836), assumed the throne. Increasingly, Charles moved toward reasserting the control of the ancien régime. He tried to dissolve parliament and disenfranchise the electorate. The middle class, however, would have none of this and they revolted. In 1830, Charles was forced to abdicate, fleeing into exile in Scotland. Louis Philippe (1773–1850), the Duc d'Orléans and a descendant of Louis XIV who had supported the revolution in 1789, was proclaimed king "by the grace of God, and the Will of the People."

VIVE LE DUC D'ORLÉANS

One Orleanist poster of 30 July 1830 expressed the view of most moderates.

> Charles X must not be allowed in Paris again:
> he has shed the blood of the people.
> A Republic would expose us to terrible dissension;
> it would embroil us with Europe.
> The Duke of Orleans is a prince devoted to the
> cause of the Revolution.
> The Duke of Orleans has never fought against us.
> The Duke of Orleans was at Jemappes.
> The Duke of Orleans has worn the republican
> colours under fire; he alone can wear them
> now; we do not want any other colours.
> The Duke of Orleans has made a statement;
> he accepts the Charter as we have always
> wanted it to be accepted.
> It is from the French people that he will hold
> his crown."

From R.W. Breach, *Documents and Descriptions in European History, 1815–1939*, (London: Oxford University Press, 1964), p. 5.

The Spread of Revolution

The success of revolution in France inspired liberal and national revolts in Italy, Germany, Poland, and Belgium. In Italy, the 1830 revolts led to new governments in Rome, Parma, and Modena. In Germany, revolts occurred in Brunswick, Hesse, Hanover, and Saxony. In Poland, the Polish *Diet* proclaimed its independence from Russia. By 1831, however, all of these revolts had been brutally suppressed by the ruling elites and liberals and nationalists were driven underground or into exile. Only in Belgium was nationalism triumphant.

The Congress of Vienna had united Belgium with Holland in the Kingdom of the Netherlands. The revolt in France in 1830 inspired the Belgians to demand a measure of self-control from the Dutch king, William I (1772–1843). When the king tried to suppress the movement by force, the Belgians proclaimed independence, formed a national assembly, and drafted a constitution. They were supported by Britain and France, which deterred Austria and Russia from suppressing the revolt. Finally, in 1839, the Dutch were forced to grant independence to the Belgians. This was formally guaranteed by the Great Powers at a conference in London later the same year.

Nationalism and the Revolutions of 1848

After the failure of revolution in 1830, nationalists in southern and central Europe went underground to avoid prosecution by the existing conservative regimes. United by a common enemy, each group had fundamentally different goals. While nationalists hoped to carve an independent homeland out of the empires and principalities of the region, liberals aspired to bring legal equality and liberal reforms to their regions. The resulting anti-government sentiment was enough to topple existing regimes in 1848, but it lacked the unity of purpose to construct anything lasting in their place.

In 1848, almost all of Europe erupted in revolt. Inspired by a new uprising in France, Germany, Italy, Hungary, and Austria saw the forces of liberalism and nationalism united in rebellion against the ruling governments in their attempts to establish constitutional self-rule.

France

In France, the monarchy of Louis Philippe had grown increasingly conservative with age. Always dominated by the wealthy middle class, the government paid little attention to the demands of the growing mass of industrial workers. Increasingly, political dissent was suppressed, until finally, in February 1848, the situation exploded. Frustrated with the inaction and resistance of the government, students and workers took to the streets. The barricades went up and, as in 1789, the army, most of whom were members of the working class themselves, joined the revolutionaries. One eyewitness recounted:

> The work of the insurrection went on with an extraordinary activity, in silence, and without any military force intervening to oppose it. Paris was filled with barricades . . . and soon the barricades were manned and guarded by their sentinels, and one saw, around sparkling braziers, groups of squatting men, casting bullets, and smoking their pipes peacefully, in this strange bivouac in the middle of the great city which was being tilled for the planting of freedom.
>
> From George Woodcock (ed.), *A Hundred Years of Revolution, 1848 and After* (London: Porcupine Press, 1948) pp. 161–162.

Faced with such opposition, Louis Philippe abdicated and the Second French Republic was proclaimed.

The success of the French revolt had a profound impact throughout Europe. Within a year liberal and national forces in Vienna, Berlin, Milan, and Venice had joined the revolutionary movements. At first these revolutions appeared to be successful, but it would soon be discovered that the success was illusory.

Austria

The greatest revolutionary gains were made in the Austrian Empire. In Hungary, Magyar nationalists, led by Louis Kossuth (1802–1894), proclaimed a free Hungary. (See readings.) The emperor signed a constitution and acknowledged the autonomous states of Hungary and Bohemia. In Bohemia, the Slavs organized the first Pan-Slav Congress. In Italy, rebels expelled the Austrian rulers of Milan and Venice. In Vienna itself, Metternich was driven into exile, while Ferdinand was forced to promise a liberal constitution.

The Collapse of the Revolutions

By the summer of 1848, it appeared that the face of Europe would be changed completely. Revolutionary forces held sway in every capital from Paris to Budapest. Soon, however, the coalitions of liberals and nationalists, students and workers, middle-class intellectuals and peasants, began to crumble. Once again, Paris led the way. A worker uprising was brutally suppressed by the army. Fearful of a return to the extremism of the Jacobin period, France looked for a leader who could bring stability. In December, Louis Napoleon (1808–1873), a nephew of the deposed emperor, was elected president of the republic. Within four years he had abolished the republic and had held a national plebiscite to ratify his declaration proclaiming himself Emperor Napoleon III. The Second Republic had become the Second Empire.

In Austria, a new young emperor, Franz Joseph (1830–1916), backed by the Russian Empire, led the army back to Vienna to restore order. Soon the nationalists throughout the empire were defeated and the Hapsburgs were once again in firm control.

The German states had elected a national assembly. From May 1848 on, it sat for almost a year drawing up a liberal-democratic constitution. While the intellectuals were debating, however, the traditional forces of conservatism were regaining power. By the time the constitution was drawn up in May 1849, the sovereigns were back in control in the German states. The national assembly was dissolved. It seemed that nothing had changed.

The year 1848 has been called the "turning point where Europe failed to turn." For many liberal and nationalist idealists, the immediate goal had been to overthrow the old regimes. Success left them without a clear plan on how to proceed, however, and in most cases the revolutionary alliances between classes and interest groups broke down with the defeat of their common enemy. For many central and southern Europeans, the failure of idealism was a bitter lesson. Future campaigns for national independence would adopt a more pragmatic approach. The idealism of the Frankfurt Assembly would be replaced in the next generation by the *realpolitik* of Otto von Bismarck (1815–1898).

Still, the revolutions of 1848 were not entirely unsuccessful. They had illustrated the strength of nationalism. The Hapsburg Empire had been able to survive only because of outside support. Within the next twenty-five years the emperor would be forced to recognize the independence of Germany and Italy and share his crown with Hungary.

NATIONALISM TRIUMPHANT: THE ITALIAN AND GERMAN EXPERIENCES, 1848 TO 1870

The Unification of Italy

Although a common religion, a common language, a common culture, and a common history had long favoured a united Italy, many factors worked against it. Italy had not been united since the fall of the Roman Empire. To some extent, many Italians saw their nationality in this larger European sense and a political consolidation of the Italian peninsula alone seemed to them to be a denial of their imperial heritage. As a result, Italy remained divided into small kingdoms and city-states. The rulers of these petty nations resisted unification because this would mean the loss of their personal power. In spite of this, however, the seeds of *risorgimento*—the vision of a united, independent Italy—had been sown by the political restructuring that took place under Napoleon.

The hopes of Italian nationalists were destroyed, however, when the Congress of Vienna placed much of Italy either under direct Austrian control (Savoy, Lombardy, and Venetia) or under rule by Austrian princes (Parma, Modena, and Tuscany). Only Rome and Piedmont were ruled by Italians. Unsuccessful revolts in 1820 and 1821 spurred the development of nationalist organizations such as the *Carbonari*. In 1830, revolts in Rome, Parma, and Modena brought temporary success. The lack of unity among the leadership and the lack of support by the lower classes, however, enabled the Austrians to suppress the uprisings quickly.

Mazzini

After the failure of the 1830 revolts, Giuseppe Mazzini (1805–1872) emerged as the philosophical leader of *risorgimento*. Mazzini was exiled by the Sardinian government for his revolutionary activities. While in exile he founded the *Giovine Italia* (Young Italy) movement, a secret revolutionary organization that took its inspiration from similar organizations in Poland, Switzerland, Germany, France, and Ireland. *Giovine Italia* sparked numerous rebellions in Italy, the most notable being in Genoa in 1834. This uprising led to the exile of one of the revolutionaries, Giuseppe Garibaldi (1807–1882), who was later to play a major role in the unification of Italy.

In 1848, revolts broke out across Italy and republics were established in Rome, Florence, and Venice. In Piedmont, the king granted a liberal constitution and declared war on Austria. Forces from Piedmont invaded Lombardy-Venetia and were joined in their fight by Italians in Tuscany and Naples. The Italian nationalists, however, were divided amongst themselves; this allowed Austria to reassert control in northern Italy. In Rome, where the political power of the Pope was challenged by nationalists, the old order was restored after France intervened. By the summer of 1849, the revolutions that had been ignited the previous year had been quelled.

As in 1830, the lack of unity among the nationalists had weakened their efforts in 1848. There were three distinct visions of a united Italy. Mazzini was a fervent republican. (See readings.) Vincenzo Gioberti (1801–1852), a Catholic priest, favoured a confederation under the Pope. And Count Camillo Benso di Cavour (1810–1861), the prime minister of Piedmont, supported a constitutional monarchy under Victor Emmanuel II (1820–1878), the king of Piedmont.

Unification of Italy, 1858-1870

Ultimately, Cavour and Garibaldi, who initially supported Mazzini and republicanism but realigned his position with that of Cavour after 1848, would succeed in unifying Italy.

Cavour

Not all of the gains of 1848 were lost after the revolutions were suppressed. In Piedmont, the liberal constitution was retained in 1849 and Cavour became the prime minister in 1852. His immediate goal was to unify northern Italy under the leadership of Piedmont. He entered the Crimean War (1854–1856) as an ally of Britain and France so that he could raise the question of Italian unity at the peace conference. In 1856, he defended Piedmont's participation in the conflict:

> We have gained two things: first, that the anomalous and unhappy condition of Italy has been proclaimed to Europe, not by demagogues or revolutionaries, excited journalists or party men, but by the representatives of the greatest nations in Europe; . . . The second is that these same powers have declared that, not only in the interests of Italy herself, but in the interests of Europe, a remedy must be found for the evils from which Italy is suffering.
>
> From A.J. Whyte, *The Political Life and Letters of Cavour, 1848–1861* (Oxford: Oxford University Press, 1930) p. 222.

In 1858, Cavour succeeded in securing the support of Napoleon III for a campaign against Austria. In return for this alliance, Cavour agreed to cede Nice and Savoy to his powerful neighbour. Piedmont provoked Austria into declaring war in 1859 by providing sanctuary for Austrian army deserters. Once Piedmont had its enemies engaged in battle it was quick to achieve victories. These military successes worried the French, however, and eventually Napoleon III abandoned the alliance and reached a compromise with the Austrians at Villafranca. Piedmont gained only Lombardy for its military efforts.

The successes in Piedmont led to a series of uprisings in central Italy. As a result, in 1860 local plebiscites in favour of unification led to the annexation by Piedmont of Parma, Modena, Tuscany, and the northernmost papal state, Romangna. Cavour's original goal for a northern Italian state was realized when the Kingdom of Northern Italy was declared. Unification of Italy was far from complete, however. In the north, Venetia remained under Austrian control. In central Italy, the Kingdom of Northern Italy was not recognized by the Pope, who controlled the papal states in that region. In southern Italy, the Kingdom of the Two Sicilies still maintained a separate existence. It would be here that the next step toward unification of Italy was to take place under the leadership of Giuseppe Garibaldi.

Garibaldi

After being sentenced to death for his part in an 1834 uprising in Genoa, Garibaldi had fled into exile. For twelve years he fought for Uruguayan independence in South America, but in 1848 he returned to Italy to help Mazzini establish the short-lived Republic of Rome. In 1860, Garibaldi organized a personal army of volunteers, called the "One Thousand," or the "Red Shirts." With this force he conquered Sicily and then crossed to the mainland and captured Naples. When Garibaldi's plans to march on Rome threatened to bring French intervention, Cavour sent an army into southern Italy. Carefully avoiding Rome, Cavour's army marched south to meet with Garibaldi. Cavour feared civil war, but Garibaldi was an idealist and an Italian nationalist first and foremost. Putting his personal ambitions aside, in November he peacefully turned over southern Italy to Victor Emmanuel II. In the meantime, Cavour annexed the papal states after plebiscites overwhelmingly supported unification with Piedmont.

In 1861, northern and southern Italy were united and the Kingdom of Italy (minus Venetia and the city of Rome) was proclaimed a parliamentary monarchy under Victor Emmanuel II. Cavour, who died in 1861, did not live to see Venetia (added in 1866 as a result of the Seven Weeks' War) and Rome (secured in 1870 when the French troops garrisoning the city were withdrawn during the Franco-Prussian War) complete Italian unification.

Although Italy was an independent, united country, problems remained. Italians in other areas, such as the Tirol, Dalmatia, Savoy, Nice, Corsica, and Malta, remained outside Italian jurisdiction and the loss of the papal states created tension between the church and state. Finally, centuries of separation had resulted in considerable disparity in social, political, and economic development between the northern and southern parts of the peninsula. Once nationalist enthusiasm died down, there still remained the monumental task of truly unifying the nation.

The Unification of Germany

Nationalism in Germany had been stimulated by Napoleon's conquest and had reached fever pitch in the War of Liberation against him. The 300 states of central Germany had been temporarily unified by Napoleon in the Confederation of the Rhine. Power was divided among the fifteen rulers of some of the larger states who had agreed to support him. This eliminated much of the petty bickering which had interfered with earlier attempts at national unity. After the fall of Napoleon, the Congress of Vienna redivided the confederation into thirty-nine states which were loosely associated as part of the new German Confederation, which also included such larger nations as Prussia and Austria. Each of the states retained self-rule, but Austria maintained dominance, holding the permanent presidency of the federal parliament. Only a few minor revolts in Brunswick, Hesse, Hanover, and Saxony in 1830 disturbed the political scene until 1848. Meanwhile, national unity was being fostered through closer economic ties between the German states.

The multiplicity of tariffs erected by the governments of the German Confederation seriously hampered industrial development. Prussia, the largest of the states, led a movement to establish a customs union. The union, called the *Zollverein*, adopted a trade policy that removed internal barriers and set established common tariffs against British and French manufactures. By 1840, over twenty German states belonged to the *Zollverein*. The Austrian Empire, however, because of its large non-German-speaking population, was excluded. Increasingly, Prussia was assuming the dominant leadership role over Austria within the confederation. In addition, the union's success increased support for national unity. As a result, news of the revolution in Paris in February 1848 sparked open revolt across Germany.

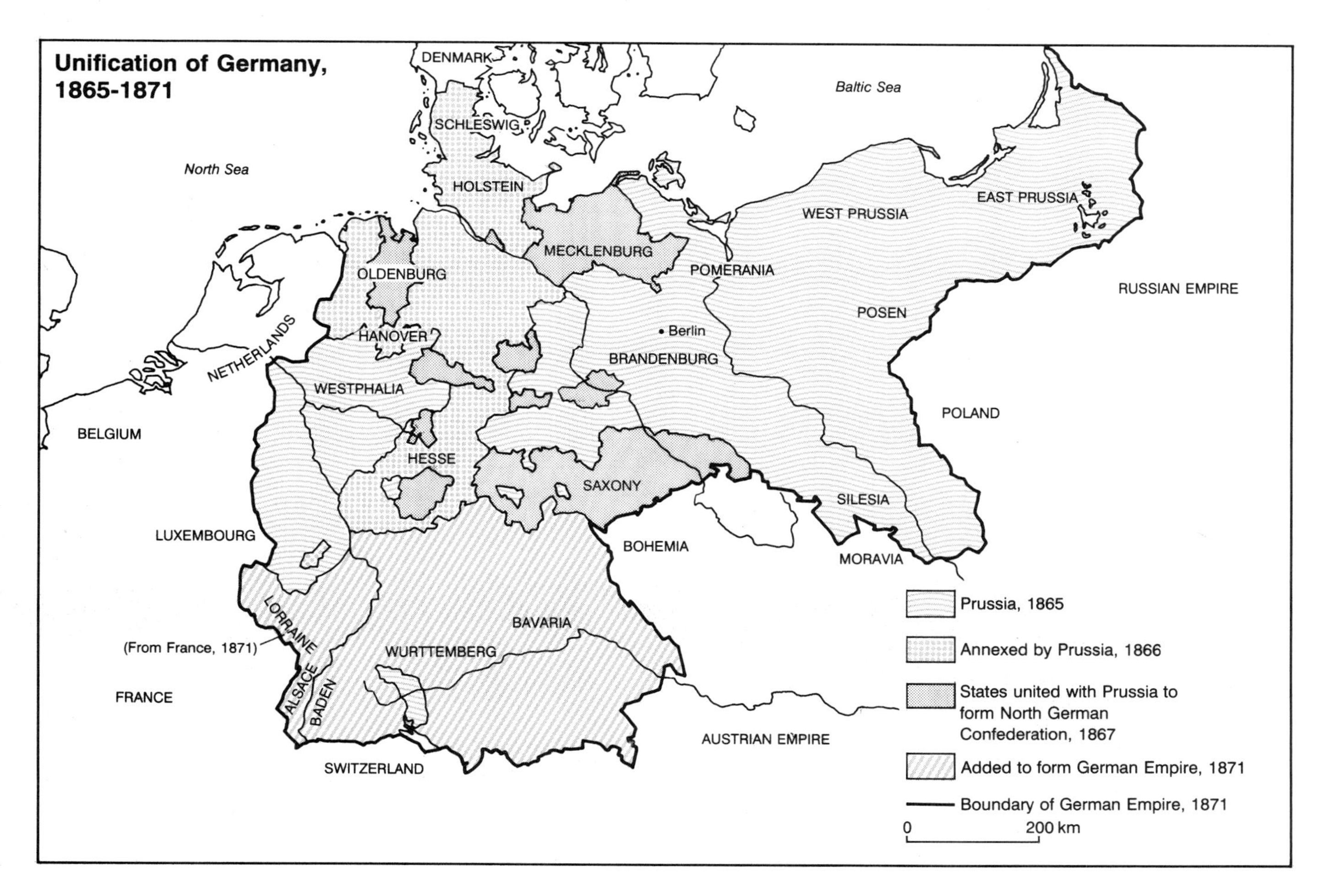

In the face of the German revolt, Frederick William IV (1795–1861) of Prussia promised to establish a liberal constitution. Fueled by this apparent success, the rebellions spread to other German states. In Bavaria, the king was forced to abdicate. In Frankfurt, liberals formed a national parliament and began to draft a constitution for a united Germany, with the king of Prussia as the constitutional monarch. Liberal and nationalist hopes were crushed, however, when Frederick William refused to accept such a crown and used Prussian troops to disperse the parliament. Inspired by Prussia's actions, other German princes reasserted their control and revolts were suppressed throughout Germany. It was clear that German unification would not be achieved through spontaneous revolt or liberal reform. Quite the contrary, the German people would be unified by "iron and blood." The architect of that unification would be Otto von Bismarck (1815–1898).

This rare photograph shows Bismarck, in the company of Prince Heinrich of Prussia, on his way to reconcile his differences with Kaiser Wilhelm II.

Bismarck

Bismarck was a member of the Prussian landowning aristocracy. He was not, strictly speaking, a nationalist, for the Germany he wished to create excluded the German Austrians. He was anti-parliamentary and anti-democratic. The failure of the rebellions of 1848 prompted him to comment ". . . not with speeches and majority decisions will the great problems of the day be decided—that was the great mistake of 1848 and 1849—but with iron and blood."

Bismarck was above all a Prussian, and his aim was to maintain Prussia as a great power by extending its control over the German Confederation. Aside from this, he was bound by no other principles; he was the classic practitioner of *realpolitik*—practical politics. This, then, was the individual who became chancellor of Prussia in 1862. Under his leadership German unification would take place only after three wars of aggression—in 1864 against Denmark, in 1866 against Austria, and in 1870 against France.

Bismarck's basic strategy of war was never to appear to be the aggressor. Instead he was a master at manoeuvring his opponents into declaring war and then crushing them in self-defence. This tactic was first applied in 1866. Prussia and Austria had wrested control of the duchies of Holstein and Schleswig away from Denmark in 1864. The resulting joint occupation of the region led to increased conflict between the two German "superpowers." Finally, in 1866, Prussia succeeded in provoking Austria into declaring war. The Prussian chancellor, however, had been waiting for this opportunity. Before the conflict escalated into war, he had ensured that Austria was diplomatically isolated without any allies outside Germany. Bismarck had secured Russian support when he helped that country quell a Polish revolt in 1863. Italy had joined the Prussian alliance in return for the promise of Venetia. And French neutrality had been obtained through vague promises about French expansion in the area of the Rhine. Within Germany itself, most of the German states favoured Austria, but when the Seven Weeks' War broke out in 1866, the speed of the Prussian victory prevented any effective joint action.

The Treaty of Prague formally ended the conflict between Prussia and Austria. Although it excluded Austria from German affairs, it was extremely generous in other areas. Austria was not required to pay any indemnity, nor did it lose any territory to Prussia (although Venetia was ceded to Italy). As a result of the treaty, the old German Confederation was dissolved. The twenty-two states north of the River Main were united into the North German Confederation, under Prussian domination. Technically, the remaining seventeen southern German states remained independent, but they quickly allied themselves with the new confederation. Before it would be able to bring the southern states completely into the fold, however, Prussia had to defeat the last opponent to German unification, France.

As he had with Austria, Bismarck had carefully isolated France from outside support. Napoleon III, feeling manipulated by the Prussians in the Seven Weeks' War, was further concerned when, in 1870, a cousin of King William I of Prussia was nominated for the throne of Spain. Fearing that France may be flanked by two powerful allied states, the French emperor asked the Prussian monarch to withdraw his support. William agreed, but would not give in to Napoleon's demands that he guarantee that his cousin's name would never be put forward again. The discussions took place in the resort town of Ems. William cabled an account of the exchange to Bismarck and left it to him to decide whether or not to release the story to the press. Bismarck decided to make the incident public, but he edited the exchange to make it appear that each had insulted the other. The resulting nationalist outcry in France led to a declaration of war in July 1870.

A half century earlier, it had taken the Grand Alliance to defeat the forces of Napoleon. This was 1870, however, and the French army was no match for the modern and well-equipped Prussian forces. The Franco-Prussian War lasted only six months. The result was a humiliating defeat for France. In the peace treaty that followed, France was forced to pay an indemnity of $1 billion and lost the territories of Alsace and Lorraine. In the wake of the victory, the southern German states united with the North German Confederation. On 18 January 1871 (the one hundred and eightieth anniversary of the creation of the Prussian kingdom), the German Empire was proclaimed in the Hall of Mirrors at Versailles.

The Hall of Mirrors, Versailles, witnessed many historical events, including the proclamation of the German Empire and the signing of the Treaty of Versailles.

The Results of Unification

The unification of Germany seriously altered the balance of power on the European continent. France had been overwhelmingly defeated. The Austrian Empire had been seriously weakened. It had lost its influence over Germany and Italy and had been forced to recognize Magyar national claims by creating the dual monarchy of Austria-Hungary. Only the newly unified Germany appeared vital enough to assume a leadership role, and once again it appeared that one country would dominate the continent.

To prevent a French war of revenge, Bismarck developed a system of diplomatic alliances designed to continue to isolate France. Austria and Russia joined with Germany in the League of the Three Emperors (1873–1878). Conflicts between Russia and Austria over the Balkans forced Bismarck to sign separate alliances with the two former allies: first the Dual Alliance with Austria in 1879 and later the secret Reinsurance Treaty with Russia in 1887. When Italy joined the Dual Alliance in 1881, one of the two alliances of the First World War was complete.

The wars of unification had developed the Prussian army to such an extent that it was the dominant military power in Europe. Equipped with the newest technology and bolstered by conscription, the German army had a profound influence on European affairs. Military preparedness became the object of every European government. The resulting arms race readied the future combatants for the First World War.

Tensions were also heightened as a result of Germany's determination to acquire an overseas empire. Although Bismarck at first resisted imperialist pressures, Germany soon secured colonies in Africa and the Pacific. Under Kaiser Wilhelm II (1859–1941), colonial expansion intensified as Germany tried to achieve its "place in the sun." This led to French-German conflict in North Africa and Anglo-German rivalry in the Middle East.

THE KULTURKAMPF (1871–1888)

In 1871, Otto von Bismarck embarked on a *kulturkampf*, or cultural struggle, to maintain unity in the new German Empire. Bismarck was concerned about the powerful influence of the Roman Catholic church on German unity. Pope Pius IX (1792–1878) had taken an increasingly aggressive position and in 1870 had redefined papal infallibility. In addition, German Catholics were sympathetic to the causes of other European Catholics, particularly the Catholic Poles within the empire. Bismarck was also concerned that German Catholics might unite under papal authority with their Catholic neighbours in Austria and France. To Bismarck, the power of the Catholic church was a threat to German nationalism.

To curb the influence of the Catholic church, on 8 July 1871 Bismarck abolished the special division for Catholic affairs in the Prussian Ministry for Public Worship and Education. The following year, on 4 July 1872, he succeeded in having the Reichstag pass a law dissolving the Jesuit order within the German Empire. Other anti-Catholic laws were passed by the Prussian minister for public worship and education, Adalbert Falk (1827–1900). The May Laws, passed in 1873, 1874, and 1875, gave the state the power to supervise education and appoint and discipline all clergy. Religious marriage ceremonies were banned, making civil marriages compulsory.

By 1876, the suppression of the Catholic church had reached the point where many bishops and priests had been imprisoned. The public, however, was becoming increasingly disturbed with the government's actions. Liberals were outraged by the infringement on basic liberties. Conservatives were concerned that similar action might be taken against the Lutheran church. With opposition to the *kulturkampf* growing, Bismarck had to find a way to retreat. His opportunity came when Leo XIII (1810–1903) became pope in 1878. The two men held direct negotiations which led to the gradual repeal of most of the anti-Catholic laws over the next decade.

NATIONALISM POST–1870

After 1870, nationalism began to play an increasingly abrasive role in European affairs. In Western Europe, where most of the struggles for national unity were complete, nations turned against each other and nationalist fever intensified hostilities. Overwhelming German national pride and the French desire for revenge poisoned Western European diplomatic affairs for decades. In Eastern and Central Europe, nationalism could succeed only by destroying the Austro-Hungarian and Ottoman empires. This struggle for national liberation in the region would eventually spark the First World War.

RETROSPECTIVE

In the first half of the nineteenth century, the forces of conservatism successfully resisted the forces of nationalism. Only in Greece and Belgium were nationalists successful. During the second half of the century, however, nationalism played a major role in international and national affairs. The successful unification of Italy and Germany seriously disrupted the balance of power in Europe and weakened the old empires. The Austrian Empire in particular was in serious trouble. Its multinational regions were clamouring for self-determination. The compromise with the Magyars that created the dual monarchy of Austria-Hungary served only to increase the demands of the other nationalities within the empire. Globally, other Western nations also experienced a radical growth in nationalist sentiment.

In the United States, nationalist forces in the southern states attempted to secede and form a separate confederacy. The government of the north, or Union, mobilized its forces and eventually crushed the rebellion after four bloody years of conflict. Nationalist uprisings in the Caribbean, Mexico, and South America led to the emergence of a wide variety of new republics during the period. In the north, the British North American colonies overcame their regional differences and united as the Dominion of Canada. As the century drew to a close, the new expansive nationalism of Western civilization would once again make itself felt on the global stage.

PRINCE KLEMENS VON METTERNICH:
Confession of Faith (1820)

Metternich has often been described as a brutal reactionary whose primary goal was to halt the progress of liberalism in Europe. In many ways, however, Metternich was a compassionate man who was trying to do what he felt was best for the people of his country. In this excerpt from a letter to Czar Alexander of Russia, he encourages him to suppress liberal revolts in his empire.

From "Memoirs of Prince Metternich," in Edwin Fenton (ed.), *32 Problems in World History*, (Glenview, IL: Scott, Foresman, and Co., 1969), pp. 136–138.

"Europe today," a famous writer said recently, "makes an intelligent man feel sad and a decent man feel horror." It would be difficult to describe the present situation in better words.

Kings have to wonder whether they will remain on their thrones; passions are released which aim at overthrowing everything that is respected as the basis of society; religion, public morality, laws, customs, rights, and duties are all being attacked. Most people are not taking part in these attacks and revolutions. Some are carried away by the flood of events but most wish simply to preserve things the way they were.

What is the cause of all these evils? How have they come about? Why are they so widespread? Can something be done about it? These are questions which every good man who loves peace and order should ask himself. Peace and order—these are really one and the same thing, which all men should be grateful for. . . .

. . . we must point out in particular the evil which is threatening to rob us of the real blessings and enjoyments of civilization. This evil may be described in one word—presumption, an overconfidence which comes from the rapid development of the human mind in so many directions. It is this which today leads so many men astray, because almost everybody suffers from it.

Religion, morality, legislation, economy, politics, administration, all have become the common property of every man. Knowledge seems to come by inspiration; experience has no value for our overconfident man; faith and trust is nothing to him. He puts in its place what he calls personal convictions and, to arrive at these convictions, eliminates all special study. Such application seems too petty for our modern men, who believe they are able to understand everything in a flash. Laws have no value for this modern man, simply because he has not personally had a part in making them and he is too self-important to approve of what "less gifted" men in generations before him had done. He himself is the source of power; why should he submit to things established by those who know less than he does? He may admit that certain laws were necessary in bygone, weaker days, but they are no longer suitable for an age of reason and vigor. He sees himself in a world of universal perfection, an idea which some Germans refer to in absurd terms as the Emancipation of the People! . . .

It is chiefly the middle classes which are infected with this "moral gangrene" and it is only among them that the real leaders of the movement are to be found. It can really have no attraction for the great mass of the people. They must spend too much of their lives working for a living to waste time on such dreams. The people know what is the happiest thing for them: this is to be able to count on the next day, for it is the next day which will repay them for the cares and sorrows of today. They wish simple laws which protect them and their families and their possessions and are afraid of anything which harms their jobs and makes their lives more difficult.

The dissatisfied classes are chiefly wealthy men who are looking out for their own advantage at the expense of changing the way things are. This includes officials and writers and lawyers and teachers. . . .

I am convinced our way of life can no longer be saved unless our governments act quickly and vigorously while they still are free to do this. . . .

There is a rule of behaviour common to individuals and to states which has been proven correct because it has been practised over the centuries and in everyday life. This rule declares that "man should not dream of changing things while emotionally excited about the matter; wisdom directs that at such moments we should limit ourselves to maintaining the status quo." . . .

There should exist a union between all governments to prevent the dissatisfied self-seekers from stirring up trouble in the various countries. Good citizens should have proper contempt for the meaningless words which these men use to stir up discontent. And, finally, there should be respect for change and new development along slow, peaceful paths. These ought to be the ideas of all great kings, and the world will be saved if they do something about them. It will be lost if they do not.

---

1. Account for Metternich's assessment of who is responsible for the unrest in Europe.

2. Outline Metternich's view of the goals of the average person. To what extent do you think his views are accurate?

3. Compare Metternich's "Confession" with his actions during this period. To what extent do his beliefs explain his tactics?

JOHANN GOTTLIEB FICHTE: Addresses to the German Nation (1808)

Early German nationalism was a rejection of the influence and occupation of France during the revolutionary period. Writers rejected the rationalism of the Enlightenment and called for freedom of emotion. Early writers such as Justus Moser (1720–1794) and F.G. Klopstock (1724–1803) celebrated ancient German customs and a love of country. Johann Gottfried von Herder (1744–1803) identified the German spirit within old folk tales and songs. His more humanistic ideas are in contrast to Johann Gottlieb Fichte (1762–1814), a German philosopher who delivered his "Addresses to the German Nation" during 1807–1808. Given as public orations in Berlin while the city was under the control of the Napoleonic army, Fichte's series of lectures were among the earliest manifestoes of German nationalism. The excerpts here are parts of the eighth of these lectures, "The People and the Fatherland."

From Guy Carleton Lee (ed.), *The World's Orators Comprising the Great Orations of the World's History* (New York: G.P. Putnam's Sons, 1900), pp. 177–182, 190–193, 195–201.

This then is the meaning of the word *a people*, taken in a higher sense and regarded from the standpoint of a spiritual world, namely: that whole body of men living together in society, reproducing themselves from themselves both physically and spiritually, which whole body stands together under certain special laws of the development of the divine part thereof. The participation in these special laws is that which in the eternal world, and therefore in the transitory world as well, unites this mass into a natural and homogeneous whole. The law itself can, in respect to its contents, be well comprehended as a whole, as we have apprehended it in the case of the Germans as a principal race or people; in many of its future determinations it can still further be comprehended through a consideration of the appearance of such a people; but it can never be understood by anyone who remains unconsciously under the law, although its existence may be clearly perceived. . . . This law determines and completes what has been called the national character of a people, namely, that law of the development of the original and divine. It is clear from this last consideration, that men who have hitherto described foreign lands do not all believe in their originality and their continued development, but merely in an unending circulation of apparent life, and by their faith these peoples become according to their faith, but in a higher sense are no people, and since they are not that in reality, they are quite unable to have a national character.

The belief of the noble-minded in the eternal continuance of his activity, even on this earth, is founded, accordingly, on the hope of the eternal continuance of the people from whom he has himself sprung, and of the distinctive character of that people according to that hidden law, without any mixing with, or deprivation by, anything foreign to it or any not belonging to the fulness of that law. This distinctive character is the eternal, to which he trusts the eternity of himself and his continued activity; it is the eternal order in which he places that in himself which is eternal; he must desire continuance, because it is his only means of deliverance, whereby the short span of his moral life may be prolonged to an eternal life. . . .

From all this it follows that the State, as a mere control of the human life as it advances in customary and peaceful course, is not that which is primary and existent for its own sake, but is merely a means for that higher purpose, the eternally, uniformly progressive development of the purely human in the nation; that is only the image and the love of this eternal progress, which shall in the quiet flow of time mould the higher ideas in the conduct of the State, and which, when the independence of the people is in danger, is alone able to save it. Among the Germans, amid whom as an original people this love of the fatherland was possible, and, as one who knew firmly believed, thus far has also been actual, this could so far with a high degree of confidence count upon the security of its most important affairs. As in the case of the Greeks in old time, so here in the case of the Germans the State and the nation were separated from each other, and each was presented for itself, the former in the various distinct German kingdoms and principalities, the latter visibly in the imperial union, and invisibly, not according to a written constitution but a fundamental law living in the hearts and minds of all, in a multitude of customs and institutions. As far as the German tongue was spoken, so far could every one upon whom the light dawned within that radius regard himself in a twofold aspect as a citizen: on account of his birthplace, to whose care he was first committed, and on account of the entire common fatherland of the German nation. It was permitted each one to obtain for himself over the entire surface of the fatherland that culture which had the greatest affinity with his spirit, or that field of work which was most appropriate to him, and his talent did not grow in its place as a tree grows, but it was permitted him to seek it. Whoever, by the direction which his education took, was estranged from his immediate surroundings, easily found acceptance elsewhere, found new friends in place of those whom he had lost, found time and leisure to explain himself more particularly, and perhaps to win to himself those who had been estranged and so unite the whole once more. No German prince has ever been able to compel his subjects to remain among the mountains and rivers where he rules, or to regard themselves as bound to the surface of the earth. A truth which might not be expressed in one place, might be expressed in another, in which place on the contrary those truths were forbidden which were allowed in the first region; and therefore, in spite of all the one-sidedness and narrow-mindedness of the various States, there was to be found in Germany, taken as a whole, the highest freedom of investigation and instruction ever possessed by a people, and the highest culture was, and everywhere remains, the result of the mutual action of the citizens of the German States, and this higher culture came gradually in this form to the vast multitude of the people also, so that it forthwith continued in the whole to educate itself by itself. This essential pledge of the continuance of a German nation detracts in no respect from any German who stands at the helm of the government; and although in respect to some original decisions have occurred, as has been thought, otherwise than as the higher German love of fatherland must wish, nevertheless the affairs of State have at least not been handled directly contrary to what has been desired; no one has been tempted to undermine that love, to exterminate it and to bring a contrary love in its place. . . .

These orations have attempted, by the only means remaining after others have been tried in vain, to prevent this annihilation of every noble action that may in the future arise among us, and this degradation of our entire nation. They have attempted to implant in your minds the deep and immovable foundations of the true and almighty love of the fatherland, in the conception of our nation as eternal and the people as citizens of our own eternity through the education of all hearts and minds.

---

1. "Fichte is trying to establish as philosophically true something that is politically false." Comment on this statement using specific references to the political situation in Germany in 1807–1808.

2. What distinction does Fichte make between Germany and the state?

3. Outline the elements of nationalism as explained by Fichte.

4. Debate the following statement: *Nationalism is the most destructive force ever unleashed on humanity.*

JOHANN GOTTFRIED VON HERDER: German Cultural Nationalism (1788)

Herder, a German philosopher, was greatly influenced by the French Revolution. He called the fall of the Bastille "the greatest event in human history since the Reformation." Although a supporter of the French Republic and its aims, Herder was a strong believer in German nationalism. He developed a concept of nationhood based on the "spirit of the people," or Volksgeist. *For Herder, Germany had a deep Gothic tradition different from that of "Roman" Europe. He tried to foster a national consciousness in Germany through the creation of a patriotic academy and continually referred to the days of the first Reich. Although Herder's ideas were given a sharper, more political edge by Fichte, he was nonetheless a significant contributor to the German cultural revolution of the period.*

From Johann Gottfried von Herder, "Plan for the First Patriotic Institute to Foster a Common Spirit in Germany," translated by Robert R. Ergang, in *Herder and the Foundations of German Nationalism* (New York: Columbia University Press, 1931) pp. 129–133.

Our language, whether it be considered as a learned or a political tool, deserves a center of union for the different provinces which might become the center for the development of this indispensable tool. Our nationality can boast that since the most ancient of times of which we know its language has remained unmixed with others, just as our people were not conquered by any other national group and in their wanderings carried their language into different parts of Europe. Hence it is just that this language not only be preserved as long as the nationality exists but that it also be clarified and strengthened just as the organization of the national group is strengthened. A purified language, regulated by definite rules, contributes incredibly much toward a set mode of thought. History shows that all the ruling peoples of the different periods of world history have ruled not with arms, but especially with reason, art and a highly developed language, often for thousands of years; nay, even after their political power had passed, the highly developed tool of their thoughts and organization remained as an example and sanctum for others. The Greek, Latin and Arabic languages are examples of this in the ancient and middle period; in the modern period, first the Spanish and then the French language have proved what advantages, nay, what a secret superiority a nationality whose language has become a dominant one may attain. Just it is, therefore, that the German language be the prevailing one at least within the confines of the nationality, that the German sovereigns understand it, speak it correctly and love it, that the German nobility and every cultured social group, spurred on by their example, endeavor to give it the elasticity and elegance which distinguishes the French language. This will come to pass when our purest book language seeks to become ever more the language of polite society and of every public discourse. To the present it has been far removed from such common use. It is a known fact that our book language, taken in the best sense of the word, is spoken hardly anywhere. Since the taste of our fatherland is anything but established and certain, every person of culture must welcome the establishment of a public institution which, without despotism, would promote the welfare of our fatherland. The exaggerated imitation of other nationalities of which we are accused would then be curbed and transformed into emulation which, with the united support of all, must produce good results.

These and other causes have moved several sovereigns of Germany to reflect upon the idea of establishing and supporting a German academy in which some and perhaps all of the German provinces are to be represented. . . .

Several lines of endeavor would be:

1. Language. The members of the academy will not only endeavor in their writings to give examples of the purity, strength and that unaffected simplicity which are most becoming to the character of our nationality; but they will also, each in his province, name and denote with due honor the writings which bear this stamp. The academy hopes thereby, and especially through its common efforts, to promote the dissemination of these writings. . . .

2. History of Germany. Although the learned men of our fatherland have applied much diligence to the elucidation of individual points and periods of German history, it is a matter of common opinion that, disregarding several of the important

newer works, we are far behind our neighbors in the study of the history of the individual provinces as well as the general history of Germany, at least in the fact that the patriotic study of this history is far from being a common interest of this nationality. And yet this study is indispensable for the creation of a common spirit. . . .

3. Everything that belongs to the active philosophy of national development and national happiness will be the ultimate and highest purpose of the academy; and nothing which might in any way contribute thereto be excluded. Every clear truth which decreases or puts an end to ruling prejudices and bad habits; every practical attempt and suggestion for the improvement of the education of rulers, the nobility, the peasants and the burghers; improvements in all public institutions in allotting justice, in the mutual relations of the classes, in the organization of churches and schools, in a rational political economy and human political wisdom, will become matters for consideration, deliberation and practical knowledge of the academy. It cannot be denied that in our fatherland prejudices and follies hold sway which in the neighboring lands are openly recognized as such. It cannot be denied that the division into many states, sects and religions has retarded the development of human reason in general, of the common prudence and reasonableness whose principles have long been the moral and political calculus in other countries. The members from the different provinces will at each meeting present an accurate report concerning the welfare of each province in behalf of the common welfare. The strong will inspire the weak, the experienced will teach the well-meaning and the different provinces and different religions will learn to know, tolerate and love one another.

---

1. Outline the reasons why Herder believes that language is the focus of nationality.

2. Outline the measures Herder suggests for the fostering of nationalism in Germany.

3. What forces were at work within Germany that hindered the development of a national consciousness?

4. What elements of romanticism are evident in Herder's writing?

GIUSEPPE MAZZINI:
Nationality: Some Ideas on a National Constitution (1835)

Giuseppe Mazzini (1805–1872) was a leading proponent of the ideas of nationalism in Europe. For Mazzini, the nation guaranteed individuals their basic rights as citizens. He believed that nation-states, created on the basis of self-determination, should be democratic and structured on the basis of liberal principles. In addition, how-

We often meet the word *nationality* in the pages of writers on politics, but they do not always mean the same thing by it. Like all words that stand for a *principle*, the word *nationality* has various meanings, depending on the place and time of the writer and his particular bias, whether *progressive* or *conservative*. During the middle ages *nationality* was a consequence of the warlike ideal and the general attempt to grow greater in land and riches at the expense of other peoples. Organized warfare was the prevailing condition. Obviously this is not what the nineteenth century means by *nationality*. To be sure, it has been defined in our own time as only passive self-interest by Casimir Perier, speaking in the French legislature. It is equally obvious that those who inscribe upon their banners the sacred word *Humanity* mean something wholly different by it; we may be sure that when, sooner or later, the Holy Alliance of the Peoples creates its own kind of *nationality*, it will rest upon *ever, he emphasized a more paternalistic responsibility of the state to its citizens in guaranteeing the right to work and the right to an education, as well as the basic tenets of liberal democracy. But while the nation protected rights it also demanded duties. The following is from the introduction of Mazzini's "Nationality: Some Ideas on a National Constitution," which appeared in the Swiss revolutionary journal* La Jeune Suisse *in 1835.*

different principles than those which presided over the Congresses of Westphalia and Vienna.

Since any system of ideas rests upon a definition of terms, let us attempt first of all to determine what we ourselves understand by *nationality*.

The essential characteristics of a nationality are common ideas, common principles and a common purpose. A nation is an association of all those who are brought together by language, by given geographical conditions or by the role assigned them by history, who acknowledge the same principles and who march together to the conquest of a single goal under the rule of a uniform body of law.

The *life* of a nation consists in harmonious activity (that is, the employment of all individual abilities and energies comprised within the association) towards this single goal.

Where there is no general uniform body of law, we find castes, privileges, inequality, and oppression. Where individual energies are stultified or left unorganized, we find inertia, immobility and obstacles in the way of progress. But where men do not acknowledge a common principle and all its consequences, where all do not share a common purpose, we find not a nation but only a crowd, a mass, a congeries which will fall apart in the very first crisis; it is a chance collection of men which chance events will dissolve sooner or later, and which will give way to anarchy.

To us these principles seem so self-evident, so much a part of the very nature of any association of men, that we see no need to prove them. The very history before our eyes teaches that whenever men lack ties of association and common purpose, nationality is just a meaningless word; it also teaches us that whenever a people does not live by the principles which gave it birth, it perishes.

Nationality depends for its very existence upon the sacredness within and beyond its frontiers.

If nationality is to be inviolable for all, friends and foes alike, it must be regarded inside the country as holy, like a religion, and outside a country as a grave mission. It is necessary too that the ideas arising within a country grow steadily, as part of the general law of Humanity which is the source of all nationality. It is necessary that these ideas be shown to other lands in their beauty and purity, free from any alien admixture, from any slavish fears, from any skeptical hesitancy, strong and active, embracing in their evolution every aspect and manifestation of the life of the nation. These ideas, a necessary component in the order of universal destiny, must retain their originality even as they enter harmoniously into mankind's general progress.

The people must be the *basis* of nationality; its logically derived and vigorously applied principles its *means*; the strength of all its *strength*; the improvement of the life of all and then happiness of the greatest possible number its *results*; and the accomplishment of the task assigned to it by God its *goal*.

This is what we mean by nationality.

---

1. List the characteristics of nationalism as outlined by Mazzini.

2. Outline the elements of liberalism expressed in Mazzini's essay. Contrast these ideas with those that stray from the concept of "pure liberalism."

LORD ACTON:
Nationality (1862)

Sir John Acton is perhaps best known for his maxim "Power tends to corrupt, absolute power corrupts absolutely." In actual fact this was the reworking of a speech given by William Pitt the Elder to the House of Lords in 1870. Lord Acton, diplomat, historian, and writer, felt that the nation-state was created for the good of its citizenry. "The ship exists for the sake of its passengers," was Acton's way of emphasizing this relationship. He saw great danger in the increase in "restrictive" nationalism in Europe. He felt that the emerging nation-states were intolerant of minority groups and more interested in purifying the citizenry than in serving it. It is interesting to consider his viewpoint when examining the nationalist policies of the Third Reich in the mid-twentieth century. The following is the conclusion to his analysis of the concept of nationality.

From Lord Acton, "Nationality," in *Home and Foreign Review*, Vol. 1 (July 1862), pp. 169–172, in John C. Rule, *et al*, *Critical Issues in History: 1648 to the Present* (Boston: D.C. Heath and Co., 1967), pp. 609–610.

. . . When different races inhabit the different territories of one Empire composed of several smaller States, it is of all possible combinations the most favourable to the establishment of a highly developed system of freedom. In Austria there are two circumstances which add to the difficulty of the problem, but also increase its importance. The several nationalities are at very unequal degrees of advancement, and there is no single nation which is so predominant as to overwhelm or absorb the others. These are the conditions necessary for the very highest degree of organisation which government is capable of receiving. They supply the greatest variety of intellectual resource; the perpetual incentive to progress which is afforded not merely by competition, but by the spectacle of a more advanced people; the most abundant elements of self-government, combined with the impossibility for the State to rule all by its own will; and the fullest security for the preservation of local customs and ancient rights. In such a country as this, liberty would achieve its most glorious results, while centralisation and absolutism would be destruction.

The problem presented to the government of Austria is higher than that which is solved in England, because of the necessity of admitting the national claims. The parliamentary system fails to provide for them, as it presupposes the unity of the people. Hence in those countries in which different races dwell together, it has not satisfied their desires, and is regarded as an imperfect form of freedom. It brings out more clearly than before the differences it does not recognise, and thus continues the work of the old absolutism, and appears as a new phase of centralisation. In those countries, therefore, the power of the imperial parliament must be limited as jealously as the power of the crown, and many of its functions must be discharged by provincial diets, and a descending series of local authorities.

The great importance of nationality in the State consists in the fact that it is the basis of political capacity. The character of a nation determines in great measure the form and vitality of the State. Certain political habits and ideas belong to particular nations, and they vary with the course of national history. A people just emerging from barbarism, a people effete from the excesses of a luxurious civilisation, cannot possess the means of governing itself; a people devoted to equality, or to absolute monarchy, is incapable of producing an aristocracy; a people averse to the institution of private property is without the first element of freedom. Each of these can be converted into efficient members of a free community only by the contact of a superior race, in whose power will lie the future prospects of the State. A system which ignores these things, and does not rely for its support on the character and aptitude of the people, does not intend that they should administer their own affairs, but that they should simply be obedient to the supreme command. The denial of nationality, therefore, implies the denial of political liberty.

The greatest adversary of the rights of nationality is the modern theory of nationality. By making the State and the nation commensurate with each other in theory, it reduces practically to a subject condition all other nationalities that may be within the boundary. It cannot admit them to an equality with the ruling nation which constitutes the State, because the State would then cease to be national, would be a contradiction to the principle of its existence. According, therefore, to the degree of humanity and civilisation in that dominant body which claims all the rights of community, the inferior races are exterminated, or reduced to servitude, or outlawed, or put in a condition of dependence.

If we take the establishment of liberty for the realisation of moral duties to be the end of civil society, we must conclude that those states are substantially the most perfect which, like the British and Austrian empires, include various distinct nationalities without oppressing them. Those in which no mixture of races has occurred are imperfect; and those in which its effects have disappeared are decrepit. A State which is incompetent to satisfy different races condemns itself; a State which labours to neutralize, to absorb, or to expel them, destroys its own vitality; a State which does not include them is destitute of the chief basis of self-government. The theory of nationality, therefore, is a retrograde step in history. It is the most advanced form of the revolution, and must retain its power to the end of the revolutionary period, of which it announces the approach. Its greatest historical importance depends on two chief causes.

First, it is a chimera. The settlement at which it aims is impossible. As it can never be satisfied and exhausted, and always continues to assert itself, it prevents the government from ever relapsing into the condition which provoked its rise. The danger is too threatening, and the power over men's minds too great, to allow any system to endure which justifies the resistance of nationality. It must contribute, therefore, to obtain that which in theory it condemns,—the liberty of different nationalities as members of one sovereign community. This is a service which no other force could accomplish; for it is a corrective alike of absolute monarchy, of democracy, and of constitutionalism, as well as of the centralisation which is common to all three. Neither the monarchical nor the revolutionary, nor the parliamentary system can do this; and all the ideas which have excited enthusiasm in past times are impotent for the purpose except nationality alone.

And secondly, the national theory marks the end of the revolutionary doctrine and its logical exhaustion. In proclaiming the supremacy of the rights of nationality, the system of democratic equality goes beyond its own extreme boundary, and falls into contradiction with itself. Between the democratic and national phase of the revolution, socialism had intervened, and had already carried the consequences of the principle to an absurdity.

Although, therefore, the theory of nationality is more absurd and more criminal than the theory of socialism, it has an important mission in the world, and marks the final conflict, and therefore the end, of two forces which are the worst enemies of civil freedom,—the absolute monarchy and the revolution.

---

1. Restate Acton's thesis in your own words.

2. List the arguments Acton uses to support his thesis.

3. In what ways do Acton's warnings about the dangers of nationalism foreshadow things to come?

4. In what ways could Acton's essay be used as a defence for imperialism?

THE GREEK PROCLAMATION OF INDEPENDENCE (1822)

In 1814, Greek patriots began to form secret societies for the overthrow of Turkish rule. For the next seven years there were a series of popular uprisings throughout the country, until in 1821 a true war of liberation was launched under the leadership of the Greek general Prince Alexander Ypsilanti (1792–1828). In order to attract international support, the National Congress, based in Epidauros, proclaimed the independence of the Greek people. It was effective not only in attracting volunteers to the Greek cause but also in enlisting the support of powers such as Britain, France, and Russia. The following is from the manifesto issued by the Greek National Assembly on 27 January 1822 during the first year of the Greek struggle for independence from the Turks.

From *British and Foreign State Papers*, Vol. IX (London: J. Harrison and Sons, 1829), pp. 629ff., in Hans Kohn, *Nationalism: Its Meaning and History* (New York: Van Nostrand Reinhold Co., 1965), pp. 116–118.

We, descendants of the wise and noble peoples of Hellas, we who are the contemporaries of the enlightened and civilized nations of Europe, we who behold the advantages which they enjoy under the protection of the impenetrable aegis of the law, find it no longer possible to suffer without cowardice and self-contempt the cruel yoke of the Ottoman power which has weighed upon us for more than four centuries,—a power which does not listen to reason and knows no other law than its own will, which orders and disposes everything despotically and according to its caprice. After this prolonged slavery we have determined to take arms to avenge ourselves and our country against a frightful tyranny, iniquitous in its very essence,—an unexampled despotism to which no other rule can be compared.

The war which we are carrying on against the Turk is not that of a faction or the result of sedition. It is not aimed at the advantage of any single part of the Greek people; it is a national war, a holy war, a war the object of which is to reconquer the rights of individual liberty, of property and honour,—rights which the civilized people of Europe, our neighbors, enjoy today; rights of which the cruel and unheard of tyranny of the Ottomans would deprive us—us alone—and the very memory of which would stifle in our hearts.

Are we, then, less reasonable than other peoples, that we remain deprived of these rights? Are we of a nature so degraded and abject that we should be viewed as unworthy to enjoy them, condemned to remain crushed under a perpetual slavery and subjected, like beasts of burden or mere automatons, to the absurd caprice of a cruel tyrant who, like an infamous brigand, has come from distant regions to invade our borders? Nature has deeply graven these rights in the hearts of all men; laws in harmony with nature have so completely consecrated them that neither three nor four centuries—nor thousands nor millions of centuries—can destroy them. Force and violence have been unable to restrict and paralyze them for a season, but force may once more resuscitate them in all the vigor which they formerly enjoyed during many centuries; nor have we ever ceased in Hellas to defend these rights by arms whenever opportunity offered.

Building upon the foundation of our natural rights, and desiring to assimilate ourselves to the rest of the Christians of Europe, our brethren, we have begun a war against the Turks, or rather, uniting all our isolated strength, we have formed ourselves into a single armed body, firmly resolved to attain our end, to govern ourselves by wise laws, or to be altogther annihilated, believing it to be unworthy of us, as descendants of the glorious peoples of Hellas, to live henceforth in a state of slavery fitted rather for unreasoning animals than for rational beings.

Ten months have elapsed since we began this national war; the all-powerful God has succored us; although we have not adequately prepared for so great an enterprise, our arms have everywhere been victorious, despite the powerful obstacles which we have encountered and still encounter everywhere. We have had to contend with a situation bristling with difficulties, and we are still engaged in our efforts to overcome them. It should not, therefore, appear astonishing that we were not able from the very first to proclaim our independence and take rank among the civilized peoples of the earth, marching forward side by side with them. It was impossible to occupy ourselves with our political existence before we had established our independence. We trust these reasons may justify, in the eyes of nations, our delay, as well as console us for the anarchy in which we have found ourselves. . . .

1. List the reasons the proclamation gives for the revolt.
2. Why would the Greeks feel the need to justify their national revolt?

THE HUNGARIAN DECLARATION OF INDEPENDENCE (1849)

In 1848, a new national government was established in Hungary. Initially allied with the Austrians, Hungary initiated such reforms as peasant emancipation and the abolition of aristocratic privilege. The imperial government in Vienna demanded the dissolution of the assembly and the recognition of the sovereignty of Emperor Franz Joseph. These demands were rejected and the following declaration of independence was delivered by liberal leader Louis Kossuth (1802–1894) on 14 April 1849 before the representatives of the short-lived Hungarian Republic.

From *Hungary and its Revolutions* (London, 1889), pp. 431–434, in Norman Sheffe and William E. Fisher (eds.), *A Sourcebook for Modern History* (New York: McGraw-Hill, 1964), pp. 72–74.

We, the legally constituted representatives of the Hungarian nation assembled in the *Diet*, do by these presents solemnly proclaim and maintain the inalienable natural rights of Hungary with all its dependencies, to occupy the position of an independent European State—that the House of Hapsburg Lorraine, as perjured in the sight of God and man, has forfeited its right to the Hungarian throne. At the same time, we feel ourselves bound in duty to make known the motives and reasons which have impelled us to this decision, that the civilized world may learn we have taken this step, not out of overweening confidence in our own wisdom, or out of revolutionary excitement, but that it is an act of the last necessity, adopted to preserve from destruction a nation persecuted to the limits of the most enduring patience.

Three hundred years have passed since the Hungarian nation, by free election, placed the House of Austria upon its throne, in accordance with stipulations made on both sides, and ratified by treaty. These three hundred years have been a period of uninterrupted suffering for the country.

The creator has blessed this land with all the elements of wealth and happiness. Its area of 100 000 square miles presents, in varied profusion, innumerable sources of prosperity. Its population numbering nearly fifteen millions feels the glow of youthful strength within its veins, and has shewn temper and docility which guarantee its proving at once the mainspring of civilization in Eastern Europe, and the guardian of that civilization when attacked. Never was a more grateful task appointed to a reigning dynasty by the dispensation of Divine Providence, than that which devolved upon the House of Hapsburg Lorraine. If nothing had been done to impede the development of the country, Hungary would now rank amongst the most prosperous of nations. It was only necessary to refrain from curtailing the moderate share of Constitutional liberty which the Hungarians united with rare fidelity to their Sovereigns, and cautiously maintained through the troubles of a thousand years, and the House of Hapsburg might long have counted this nation amongst the most faithful adherents to the throne.

But this Dynasty, which cannot point to a single ruler who has based his power on the freedom of the people, adopted, from generation to generation a course towards this nation which meets the name of perjury. . . .

Confiding in the justice of an eternal God, we in the face of the civilized world, in reliance upon the natural rights of the Hungarian nation and upon the power it has developed to maintain them, further impelled by that sense of duty which urges every nation to defend its own existence, do hereby declare and proclaim in the name of the nation, lawfully represented by us, as follows:—

1st. Hungary with Transylvania, as by law united, with its dependencies, are hereby declared to constitute a free independent Sovereign state. The territorial unity of this State is declared to be inviolable, and its territory to be indivisible.

2nd. The House of Hapsburg Lorraine, having by treachery, perjury, and levying war against the Hungarian nation, as well as by its outrageous violation of all compacts . . . is, as treacherous and perjured, for ever excluded from the throne of the United States of Hungary and Transylvania, and all their possessions and dependencies, and is hereby deprived of the style and title, as well as of the armorial bearings belonging to the Crown of Hungary, and declared to be banished for ever from the united countries, and their dependencies and possessions. They are therefore declared to be deposed, degraded, and banished for ever from the Hungarian territory.

3rd. The Hungarian nation, in the exercise of its rights and sovereign will, being determined to assume the position of a free and independent State amongst the nations of Europe, declares it to be its intention to establish and maintain friendly and neighbourly relations with those States with which it was formerly united under the same Sovereign, as well as to contract alliances with all other nations.

4th. The form of government to be adopted in future will be fixed by the *Diet* of the nation. . . .

---

1. Outline the reasons Kossuth gives for Hungarian independence.

2. Compare the Hungarian Declaration of Independence with the Greek Proclamation of Independence.

ANALYSIS AND APPLICATION

1. Defend or refute the following statement: *Imperialism is the natural outgrowth of aggressive nationalism.*

2. The German nationalist movement was based on the ideas of the Cultural Revolution of the late eighteenth century. Outline these ideas and account for their influence on the creation of a German national identity over the next 100 years.

3. Imagine you are a German living in Berlin in 1870. Write a letter to a friend living in France about your reaction to the Ems Dispatch.

4. (a) Debate the following resolution from Lord Acton's essay on nationalism: *The theory of nationality is a retrograde step in history.*

(b) Following the debate, write a paper explaining your point of view. Use evidence to support your position.

5. Write an editorial criticizing Austrian rule in Italy.

6. To what extent do you think the Greek and Hungarian declarations of independence were influenced by the American Declaration of Independence?

7. Using nineteenth-century Europe as your laboratory, identify the ways in which nationalism was influenced by geography, language, culture, and economics.

CHAPTER FIVE

The Industrial Revolution to 1880

BRITAIN AND THE INDUSTRIAL REVOLUTION

From 1760 to 1850, Britain experienced a period of remarkable change in industry and society. Machines replaced human labour; water and steam power were harnessed; and the use of coal, iron, and steel increased rapidly. The factory system replaced cottage industry and increased the production of goods. The movement of people from the farm to the factory accelerated, resulting in the rise of the bourgeoisie and the creation of the urban proletariat. Contemporaries coined the term *Industrial Revolution* to describe the startling changes that took place during this period.

Why did the Industrial Revolution originate in Britain? The country had several natural advantages: large quantities of coal and iron, navigable rivers, natural harbours, and a temperate climate. Medical advances resulted in higher birth rates and lower death rates; this produced a growing population as a pool of potential labour for developing industries and a large domestic market for the goods these industries produced. Private entrepreneurs provided the capital for industrialization, while improvements in agriculture, such as the introduction of fertilizers, crop rotation, and more sophisticated breeding practices, provided the food for the urban work force. Britain's foreign trade also spurred on the Industrial Revolution by providing access to raw materials and colonial markets. It also generated a considerable amount of the capital needed for industrial expansion. Lastly, Britain was free from invasion and domestic unrest throughout this period, which allowed the country to pursue its industrial course without interruption.

The Textile Industry

The first industry to undergo mechanization was textiles. Before the Industrial Revolution, the textile industry operated on the domestic system: a merchant furnished raw material to a craftworker, whose family carded and spun the wool to make yarn or thread, which was then woven on a loom to make cloth. When the cloth was finished and dyed, the merchant collected and sold the finished product. The process was slow and the amount of cloth produced was limited. Mechanization sped up the process and increased the output.

The first development in the mechanization of the textile industry was the flying shuttle, invented by John Kay in 1733. The shuttle allowed a weaver to weave a wider piece of cloth more easily and quickly. However, this meant that the processes of spinning and weaving were out of step: yarn could be woven into cloth faster than the yarn could be produced. This resulted in a chronic shortage of yarn. And so in 1768, James Hargreaves (1720–1778) invented the spinning jenny, which increased the output of thread eightfold.

Other inventions continued to improve the textile industry. Sir Richard Arkwright (1732–1792) pioneered mechanical cotton spinning in 1769 with the water frame, which harnessed water power and thereby increased cotton production. Samuel Crompton's (1723–1857) "mule" combined the features of Arkwright's water frame and Hargreave's spinning jenny into one machine and produced a finer thread for use in the manufacture of muslin. In 1785, Edmund Cartwright's (1743–1823) power loom increased cotton production and reduced costs at the same time. By 1820, cotton goods made up 46 percent of Britain's exports and British cottons were underselling native handmade calicoes in India.

The adoption of the water frame was the beginning of the transition from the workshop to the factory. Hargreave's spinning jenny had been hand operated and therefore could still be used in the domestic system. The water frame, on the other hand, had a much greater capacity and required water power. This meant the development of specialized mills near water that could be harnessed as a source of power. Since machines were now too large to be taken to the labour supply, the labour supply had to be brought to the machines. The adoption of the steam engine in the 1780s provided a continuous supply of power and meant factories could be located near raw materials and transportation centres. Some factories, particularly in the cotton industry, were extremely large, employing thousands of people (although these were the exception). However, some hand-loom operators continued to work in the textile industry until the 1850s.

The Iron Industry

The second industry to become mechanized was the iron industry. The steam engines and heavier machinery of the new industrial era required a higher grade of iron than had been made previously. Abraham Darby's (1678–1717) discovery of a technique for smelting iron ore with coke in 1709 had increased the quantity of iron, but until the steam engine was incorporated into the process (post–1775), furnaces could not generate a blast large enough to make the smelting of coke efficient. Henry Cort's (1740–1800) "puddling" process in 1784 removed the impurities in pig iron and produced the quality of iron mechanization required. The use of the steam engine in the smelting process and for rolling and hammering pig iron into shape increased the quality and quantity of wrought iron. Cheap and plentiful iron provided the tough industrial material needed for agricultural implements, building materials, military hardware, and industrial machinery. Britain soon became the world's leading producer of iron.

The expansion of the iron industry and the increased use of steam reinforced one another. Steam power was used in almost every phase of iron production, from the blast furnace to the rolling mill. The increased use of steam power substantially increased the production of iron while reducing the cost. Both the iron industry and steam power required coal as fuel. The development of railways in the nineteenth century tied coal, iron, and steam together to such an extent that they became the symbol of the age.

Transportation

The transportation system was improved with the development of roads and canals in the latter half of the eighteenth century. These improvements dramatically reduced the cost of movement of raw materials and finished products: the price of coal fell 50 percent after the completion of an 11 km canal from the collieries to Manchester. The development of railways further reduced costs.

The first successful railways were built in the 1820s. By 1850, when the railway boom had peaked, Britain had 9797 km of track. Railways provided cheap and fast transportation for raw materials and finished products. Support industries producing railway tools and machinery proliferated and a great deal of labour was put to work building railway bridges and tunnels. Railways were also an export industry and as the nineteenth century progressed, British capital, materials, and expertise were exported the world over.

By 1850, textiles, iron, and railways were fully industrialized operations. In the process, Britain had become the most industrialized country in the world. Over half of the British people lived in cities and worked in manufacturing. At the Great Exhibition of 1851, Britain stood alone as the "workshop of the world."

THE SOCIAL EFFECTS OF INDUSTRIALIZATION

The dislocation caused by the movement from the country to the city and the adaptation to the factory system created hardship and discontent for many people. Machines required constant attention, so punctuality and concentration on the job were important. Fines for lateness or spoiled work were common, as was the threat of dismissal. Factories were filled, mainly with women and children who worked long, hard hours at low wages. One reason for the low wages is that these were generally unskilled workers. Few women underwent technical training and unions restricted the number of women who could work in the more highly skilled jobs in the industrial sector.

WOMEN AND CHILDREN IN THE FACTORIES AND THE MINES

Women and children workers were often treated no better than animals in the early days of the Industrial Revolution.

The exploitation of women and children was one of the most deplorable features of the Industrial Revolution. These evils were investigated by the Sadler Committee in 1832 that was called to examine conditions in the textile industry. One witness was Joshua Drake.

You say that you had a child that went to the flax mills and she was between 14 and 15? Yes

Was she a healthy girl? She was very healthy when she went there.

Was it the dust that injured her health? Whether it was the dust, or being sometimes over-worked till she sweated and then chilling again, I cannot say. . . . She said that sometimes they were made to sweat a good deal, and that they starved, and then this dust choked her; but it was not above three or four days before it was very visible that this dust had an effect upon her, and she fell sick.

Did she suffer more from it than her companions? I do not know whether she did or not, but I think that of the four girls who were her comrades, three of them are dead. . . .

You say that she was beaten several times, did she ever say what she was beaten for? For some neglect . . . the overlooker knocked her down, and beat her, and I took her away; . . .

Why do you allow your children to go to those places where they are overworked? Necessity compels a man that has children to let them work.

From John Bowditch and Clement Ramsland (eds.), *Voices of the Industrial Revolution* (Ann Arbor: University of Michigan Press, 1961), pp. 82–83.

Lord Ashley's Mines Commission in 1842 investigated the working conditions in the mines, with an emphasis on child labour in the coal pits. Patience Kershaw was seventeen years old when she testified before the commission.

My father has been dead about a year; my mother is living and has ten children, five lads and five lasses; the oldest is about thirty, the youngest is four; three lasses go to mill; all the lads are colliers, two getters and three hurriers; one lives at home and does nothing. . . .

I never went to day school; I go to Sunday-school, but I cannot read or write; I go to pit at five o'clock in the morning and come out at five in the evening; I get my breakfast of porridge and milk first; I take my dinner with me, a cake, and eat it as I go; I do not stop or rest any time. . . .

I hurry the corves a mile and more under ground and back . . . sometimes they beat me, if I am not quick enough, with their hands; they strike me upon my back; the boys take liberties with me . . . I am the only girl in the pit; there are about 20 boys and 15 men; all the men are naked; I would rather work in mill than in coal-pit.

From John Bowditch and Clement Ramsland, (eds.), *Voices of the Industrial Revolution*, (Ann Arbor: University of Michigan Press, 1961), pp. 89–90.

These reports caused a public outcry against such terrible working conditions. An act passed in 1833 limited hours for women and children in textile factories, and one in 1842 prohibited employment in mines of all women and of boys under the age of thirteen.

Working Conditions

Working conditions were poor, industrial accidents were frequent, and health hazards were numerous. In 1844, Friedrich Engels (1820–1895) wrote: "The health of whole generations of workers is undermined, and they are racked with disease and infirmities." Each industry developed its own characteristic illnesses and deformities: miners developed consumption and suffered spinal deformities, for instance, while textile workers developed bronchial disorders.

Legislation began to set limits on the number of hours and conditions of work for women and children in the 1830s. The first effective Factory Act was passed in 1833. It restricted the number of working hours for children under thirteen to nine a day, with a maximum of forty-eight hours in a week, and children under eighteen to twelve hours a day, with a maximum of sixty-nine hours in a week. The act prohibited the employment of children under nine years of age. The Factory Act of 1847 established a ten-hour day for women and young people in the textile mills. In practice, this limited the hours of men in textile mills to ten hours as well. Later legislation extended the benefits to workers in other industries.

EMILY MARY OSBORNE

Emily Mary Osborne was typical of female artists of the industrial period. Often noted for domestic scenes of everyday life, their work has an underlying social message and gives keen insights into the values of the period. Osborne's painting Nameless and Friendless *is an excellent example of the value of studying such works.*

Nameless and Friendless was meant to be "read" rather than merely looked at, to arouse moral feeling rather than simple appreciation of its visual qualities. . . .

The heroine occupies the centre of the stage, emphasized by the sharp vertical of the shop window and the pallor of the prints behind her, as well as by the light falling on her face and hands. The pathos of her situation—social, financial, professional, and sexual—is clearly established by both the larger elements of the composition and the smaller details of her surroundings. That she is an unmarried orphan is indicated by her black dress and ringless left hand; that she is poor, by her worn-out clothes, unfashionable shawl, and shabby dripping umbrella; that her social position is low is brought out by the eloquent emptiness of the chair against which the umbrella is propped; had she been a wealthy lady client rather than a nameless and friendless woman painter, she would naturally have been sitting down rather than standing up. With downcast eyes and fingers twisting the strings of her packet, she awaits the verdict of the dealer. . . . At the same time, the skepticism or indifference of the dealer and his assistants is contrasted with the insolent, obviously sexual interest aroused in the two wealthy clients to the left, who, in the arrogant nonchalance of their poses and the flashy elegance of their dress . . . [are] ogling the vulnerable heroine [and] looking up from a print of a scantily clad dancing girl; obviously their interest in art, like their attention to the young artist, is motivated more by prurience than aesthetic concern. . . .

From *Women Artists 1550–1950* by Ann Sutherland Harris and Linda Nochlin.

Disraeli

Benjamin Disraeli (1804–1881), future prime minister of England, called attention to the growing rift between rich and poor in his novel, *Sybil, or The Two Nations.* In it, he claimed that the rich and the poor were:

> Two nations; between whom there is no intercourse and no sympathy; who are as ignorant of each other's habits, thoughts and feelings, as if they were . . . inhabitants of different planets. . . . They come forth: the mine delivers its gang and the pit its bondsmen. . . . The plain is covered with the swarming multitude . . . troops of youth, alas! of both sexes, though neither their raiment nor their language indicates the difference; all are clad in male attire; and oaths that men might shudder at issue from lips born to breathe words of sweetness. . . . But can we wonder at the hideous coarseness of their language, when we remember the savage rudeness of their lives? . . .
>
> From Dennis Sherman (ed.), *Western Civilization: Images and Interpretations* (New York: Alfred Knopf, 1983), pp. 148–149.

While his book was a nominal call for social reform, Disraeli actually considered the working class to be little better than animals. What he really advocated was for the peasantry to once again put its trust in the aristocracy, which he claimed would never abuse them in the way that the bourgeoisie had. Some critics have equated the social concerns of Disraeli and his aristocratic contemporaries as being similar to that of modern-day associations like the Society for the Prevention of Cruelty to Animals—that is, they viewed the peasants as helpless creatures who needed their protection.

Life outside the factory was not much better. Industrialization led to rapid urbanization, which produced unsanitary living conditions, overcrowding, and unparalleled squalor. In addition, the new social order contributed to the breakdown of traditional family life and authority. Engels commented: "In the working-men's dwellings of Manchester, no cleanliness, no convenience, and consequently no comfortable family life was possible; that in such dwellings only a physically degenerate race, robbed of all humanity, degraded, reduced morally and physically to beastiality, could feel comfortable at home."

Reforms in the 1830s provided elected councils in most of the larger municipalities in England and Wales. These councils passed by-laws to improve sanitation and establish police forces. By the 1850s, acts of Parliament had extended the power of the municipal councils to improve housing, clear slums, build sewers, and operate gas and water works. Gradual improvements in living conditions resulted from these reforms.

This cartoon graphically depicted the outcome of the poor working conditions in the sweat shops.

The Workers' Response

Some workers responded to the abhorrent living and working conditions with violence. A group of artisans known as the Luddites demanded a return to traditional methods of production. To make their point, they broke into factories and destroyed knitting frames. Violence also plagued some labour strikes and political protests. In 1819, soldiers charged a crowd listening to the radical orator Henry Hunt at St. Peter's Fields, killing eleven and wounding over 300 of the spectators. Violence continued throughout the 1820s.

Chartism

In the 1830s, violence also plagued the Chartist movement. Chartism was a working-class organization founded in the 1830s to express dissatisfaction with the Reform Bill of 1832. The movement derived its name from the "People's Charter," which demanded economic improvement for workers, social equality, and universal male suffrage without property qualifications. The government used repressive measures to suppress the Chartist movement, particularly after revolution broke out in France in 1848 and rapidly spread to the rest of Europe. In time, government policy changed; legislation helped the workers and the use of violence as a solution diminished. The real solutions to the problems created by industrialization, however, had to come from the workers themselves.

Individually, workers were powerless to improve their living and working conditions; collectively, however, they could force higher wages and better working conditions. Although the Anti-Combination Acts of 1799–1800 forbade workers from forming associations, secret unions were organized. These came into the open after the repeal of the Combination Acts in 1824 and were quickly joined by new unions.

This 1843 Punch *cartoon, entitled "Capital and Labour," was inspired by the report of a government commission on the horrible working conditions in the coal mines.*

Unionism

These first unions focused on skilled tradespeople who could afford to pay the higher dues required to support a national organization with full-time officials. By 1868, the most important unions were gathering at Trade Union Congresses to develop general policies for all members. In the 1880s, the poorly paid unskilled and semiskilled workers joined the movement, forming their own, more radical unions. By 1900, the total membership in British trade unions was over 2 million. Concern over the strength of the unions and fear of the radicalism of the unskilled unions led to further attacks on their legal position in the twentieth century.

Until the working class received the right to vote with the Reform Acts of 1867 and 1884, political solutions to the social and economic problems were largely unsuccessful. The Chartist movement failed because of government repression. Direct political involvement by the working class did not come until the end of the century with the formation of the first party to appeal to labour, the Independent Labour party (1893). The Labour party gradually increased its representation until it formed the government in 1924.

That is not to say that the standard of living remained the same for the working class during this period. A measure of the new industrial prosperity did trickle down to the workers. After remaining stationary during the 1850s, the average real wages of an English industrial worker rose by over 40 percent during the next fifteen years. In Germany, the average industrial wage doubled during the 1860s; at the Krupp Works workers earning 1.25 marks a day in 1850 were taking home 2.86 marks by 1869.

What did such increases mean to the working class? For most it meant the increased consumption of meat, sugar, beer, and imported goods such as tea, cocoa, and rice. It may also have meant better clothes, a nicer home, and perhaps even the occasional holiday. This gradual *embourgeoisement* of the industrial working class made it difficult for radical political ideas to find support.

THE SPREAD OF INDUSTRIALIZATION

The French revolutionary wars seriously hindered industrial development in continental Europe. The movement of armies across the continent, the heavy casualties, and the division of labour into industries that provided clothes, arms, and provisions for the military limited the industrial process and magnified Britain's early lead. Competition from cheap British imports, expensive technology, and high capital costs slowed development even after European disputes were settled at the Congress of Vienna in 1815.

To counter Britain's industrial lead, the other European governments became much more involved in the economy than had their British counterpart. Several countries recruited skilled craftworkers from foreign competitors, provided subsidies to industries, and protected infant industries with tariffs. Some sectors of the economy, such as mines, naval dockyards, armament factories, railways, and other public utilities where high capital costs were prohibitive to private entrepreneurs, were nationalized to promote development. Indirect government assistance in the form of lifting restrictions on the movement of labour and goods as well as providing stable currencies and central banking facilities also encouraged industrial development.

The first continental nation to undergo large-scale industrialization was Belgium. Like Britain, Belgium had large deposits of coal and iron. After gaining independence from Holland in 1839, the rapid development of a railway system allowed the country to exploit these resources. Soon Belgium was exporting coal and iron products to France and machinery to Holland and Germany. By 1880, France and Germany had surpassed Belgium in industrial development, but Belgium's early lead had given it a share of the market disproportionate to its size.

Industrialization in France

In France, revolutionary and Napoleonic reforms had abolished serfdom, created a central bank, and standardized weights and measures; however, industrial progress was slow during the Restoration. The railway boom of the 1830s illustrated the weakness of France's coal and iron industries as much of the demand for iron that was generated by the railways had to be met by imports. It was not until the 1850s, when improved methods of smelting ore were introduced and Louis Napoleon provided loans to manufacturers and encouraged the development of credit banks for industry, that France experienced an industrial boom. Industrial expansion slowed somewhat, however, after the loss of the immense iron ore reserves of Lorraine to Germany as a result of France's defeat in the Franco-Prussian War.

THE INDUSTRIALISTS

The Industrial Revolution was a period of great individual achievement. People with the right combination of inventive genius and entrepreneurial spirit were able to turn their ideas into successful business opportunities.

James Watt (1736–1819) was born in Greenock, Scotland, in 1736. The son of a master carpenter, Watt demonstrated a remarkable inventive facility. In 1763, he redesigned the engines used to pump water out of coal mines. Unfortunately, having the idea was one thing, but finding someone willing to invest in it was another. Finally, in 1774, Watt went into partnership with a toy manufacturer named Matthew Boulton (1728–1809). Boulton's toy factory near Birmingham was converted to produce the new engines. So successful was the design that by 1800 the new firm of Boulton and Watt had sold over 700 pumps and 300 newly designed rotary engines in Europe and North America. It proved to be the single most important innovation of the early Industrial Revolution.

Werner Siemens (1816–1892) began his career as a cadet in the Prussian army. The technical training he received there led him to develop new methods of electric telegraphy. Eventually, in partnership with an engineer named Halske, Siemens established an international reputation in the field of overland and submarine telegraph technology. Always searching for new products, at the age of sixty Siemens invented the electric dynamo. Four years later his firm perfected the first electric elevator, and within twelve months had built a factory for making electric lamps. Siemens retired after merging with his principal rival to form the giant German electric cartel A.E.G.

Alfred Krupp (1812–1877) took over his father's small steel business in Essen in 1826 at the age of fourteen. With the economic support provided by the German *Zollverein*, Krupp's business expanded rapidly. By the 1850s, the Krupp Works was a major supplier of steel springs, axles, and wheels for the expanding German rail network. Within a decade Krupp had also become the leading armaments manufacturer for the Prussian army and his cannons were the mainstay of the Prussian artillery during the successful battles of 1864, 1866, and 1871. By the time he died in 1887, Krupp had expanded the small business he had inherited, with its staff of seven, into an empire employing 70 000 workers.

Industrialization in Germany

German industrial development began with the opening of the Graf Beust mine in the Ruhr in 1841. Germany's strength lay not in the textile industry, which lagged far behind that of Great Britain, France, and Belgium, but in its coal and metallurgical industries. After the removal of internal tariff barriers and the expansion of the railway system in the 1840s and 1850s, the coal resources of Saxon, Silesia, and the Saar were developed. By 1880, Germany was producing more coal than the rest of continental Europe combined, although this was still less than half the production of Great Britain.

Prior to 1850, there were few coke furnaces producing pig iron outside of Silesia. The introduction of this process into the Ruhr in the late 1850s led to an annual increase in production of 8.5 percent between 1855 and 1870. Developments in high-grade steel led to a rapid expansion of the armament industry. By 1880, German production of iron and steel exceeded that of all continental countries and created significant competition for British industry. This was merely a portent of the future, however. The exploitation of the immense iron ore reserves of Lorraine meant that the greatest growth in the German heavy metal industry was yet to come.

Industrialization in Russia

In Russia, the scarcity of free labour hampered industrial development. Even after the emancipation of the serfs in 1861, Russia lacked an effective transportation system, a capital market, and a stable currency, all of which were prerequisites for an industrial upsurge. The groundwork for industrial expansion was not laid until the 1860s and 1870s. During this time the railway network increased from 1626 km to 22 865 km; over 350 joint stock commercial banks were formed; and the currency was gradually stabilized as the country adopted the gold standard. These developments, under the aggressive, competent leadership of Sergei Witte, the minister of finance from 1892 to 1903, led to massive industrial growth in the 1890s.

Industrialization Elsewhere in Europe

By 1880, little industrial development had taken place in Italy or the Austrian Empire. In Italy, the lack of coal and iron ore meant that much of the industrialization process would remain on hold until the twentieth century; the few developments that occurred were localized, primarily north of the Po River. In Austria-Hungary, the lack of developed resources restricted industrialization to the area around Vienna, but production was limited and was primarily for export.

In 1850, the industrialization of the continent was impressive in terms of the rapid advancements that had been made, but it was still backward, unprogressive, and inefficient when compared to British industry. Things had changed by 1880, however. The loss of monopoly meant Britain was losing its advantage. European competition, coupled with Britain's older and less efficient machinery, meant Britain was being undersold in many markets by its continental rivals.

THE THEORETICAL RESPONSE TO INDUSTRIALISM

Laissez faire

Laissez-faire economics began as a reaction to mercantilism and government intervention in the economy. The economic liberals who supported laissez faire believed that free competition, with no restrictions or regulations, would promote economic progress. This coincided with the philosophy of the new industrialists, who resented government interference in what they saw as their own business.

The father of classical economics, Adam Smith (1723–1790), argued in his *Inquiry into the Nature and Wealth of Nations* that individual and national prosperity were linked and that business, by pursuing its own advantage, inevitably advanced the prosperity of the nation. (See readings.) In so doing, the businessperson "as in many other cases, [was] led by an invisible hand to promote an end which was no part of his intention." Other classical economists, most notably Thomas Malthus (1766–1834) and David Ricardo (1773–1823), promoted the doctrine of laissez faire.

Malthus rejected the idea that industrialization had caused the poor conditions of the working class. In his *Essay Upon the Principles of Population* (1798), he argued that the natural rate of population growth increased geometrically while food production increased arithmetically. Thus population constantly increased beyond the means to sustain it. Since "no fancied equality, no agrarian regulations in their utmost intent, could remove the pressure from it for a single century," government intervention in the economy was pointless. (See readings.)

Ricardo argued that as wages rose workers had larger families; the resulting increase in population created unemployment, which in turn drove wages back down again. Therefore the widening gulf between rich and poor, growing unemployment, and human suffering was not the result of industrialization but the fault of the relentless forces of economic law. The poor themselves were responsible for their condition, and self-help was the only remedy for the problem.

Utopian Socialism

Liberal reformers fervently believed in the policy of laissez faire. But the failure of this system to eliminate the suffering of the proletariat led some liberals to adopt a more active role in government. They believed that government intervention was necessary to stop the abuses of industrialization. The primary means of achieving this was to reorganize society into ideal communities. The goal of an ideal society led to these early socialists being called *utopians* (from Sir Thomas More's *Utopia*). The most notable utopian socialists were Robert Owen (1771–1858), Claude Henri Saint-Simon (1760–1825), and François Marie Charles Fourier (1772–1837).

Robert Owen

Owen, a British factory owner, was appalled at the suffering created by the factory system. At New Lanark, he established a model factory community with reduced working hours, better working and living conditions, and worker participation in management and profits. (See readings.) Owen provided health care and education as well as payment for workers during periods of unemployment. Despite his successes, however, few industrialists followed Owen's lead. His attempt to create a model society in the United States at New Harmony, Indiana, failed. Yet Owen had a lasting impact in Britain, so much so that he is sometimes called the "father of English socialism."

Saint-Simon

Both Saint-Simon and Fourier believed that property corrupted people and that salvation could be gained through co-operative communities established with government funds. Saint-Simon believed these communities should be led by captains of industry representing the amalgamation of technological and scientific knowledge. These social engineers would lead communities in which inheritance was abolished so that each generation could rise on its own merits, without the obstacle of competition from inherited wealth. Public ownership of industry would provide the greatest good for the greatest number, and each person would be rewarded in terms of his or her labour. Saint-Simon's ideas did find some practical expression through the work of Louis Blanc (1811–1882), who organized workshops for the unemployed in Paris during the Revolution of 1848.

Fourier

Fourier envisioned ideal communities of approximately 1500 people with a variety of talents. There would be a system of common ownership and a formal system for the distribution of products, but a certain level of private property would be permitted. Labour would be organized for each task and labourers would choose the task they wanted to do so that they could avoid an activity that did not suit them. However, larger incomes would go to those who performed the most disagreeable tasks.

Although Fourier believed that his pilot projects would set an example that would eventually lead to a change in society at large, none of these communities was ever established in France. However, one community was set up in Massachusetts in the United States. The Brook Farm movement struggled for five years between 1842 and 1847 before admitting defeat and disbanding.

Scientific Socialism

Scientific socialism was fundamentally different from early utopian socialism. Utopian socialists believed in gradualism and leadership through example. They were parochial, rarely seeing beyond a national socialist state. Scientific socialism, on the other hand, was radical in its orientation. Its focus was best summed up by the rallying cry, "Workers of the world, unite!" (See readings.)

Marx

Karl Heinrich Marx (1818–1883), the father of scientific socialism, was a German-born scholar who was ejected from both Prussia and France for his radical views. His most significant writings were the revolutionary pamphlet *Manifesto of the Communist Party*, written in 1848 in collaboration with Friedrich Engels, and *Das Kapital* (1867–1881), one of the most influential books of all time. In these two works, Marx outlined the basic ideas of scientific socialism: the dialectic (a process of change involving conflict between ideas and/or groups); economic determinism; state ownership of the means of production; abolition of private property; surplus value; revolution; the dictatorship of the proletariat; and the achievement of a classless society. Marx

THE THEORY OF MARXISM

Karl Marx believed that history was like nature and so operated likewise: according to scientific laws. He disagreed with utopian socialism, which was based on morality and was dependent on the kindness of the rich to the poor. As long as capitalism survived and flourished, Marx believed that the workers would always be poor. The only resource was the violent overthrow of the capitalist system.

The Communist Manifesto (1848) was Marx's answer to the social evils of the industrial world. The manifesto urged workers to revolt against the capitalist system. The term *communism* was used to describe an ideal society in which property would be commonly owned and the necessities of life shared by all members of the community. As Marx and Engels wrote, "Let the ruling classes tremble at a communistic revolution. The proletarians have nothing to lose but their chains. They have a world to win."

Marx believed that two groups—those who controlled all the wealth, political power, and factors of production (the bourgeoisie) and those who did all the work (the proletariat)—historically had always been in conflict. He believed, however, that the real value of goods and services was the amount of labour used to produce them and that those who performed the labour should be paid its full value.

Marx felt the collapse of capitalism was inevitable. Competition would drive small companies out of business, thereby creating a growing number of the working class. As the number of capitalists declined, the workers would begin to develop greater class awareness and would realize that they would be better off if they were free from the oppression of the bourgeoisie.

After the revolution there would be a "dictatorship of the proletariat." Land and all the means of production would be controlled by the workers. Eventually everyone would be equal and the state would disappear. Since there would be only one class, there would be no class struggle. This final stage of socialism was called *communism*.

The Communist Manifesto shed new light on the economic forces of history and created an increased level of social awareness. What Marx underestimated, however, was capitalism's ability to change life for the better. Instead of more workers sinking deeper into poverty, as Marx envisioned, in the industrialized countries the workers received significant improvements in wages and working conditions. The formation of labour unions and political parties also helped to give the working class a greater voice in industry and society. Ultimately, Marxism was not embraced by the industrialized West. While communist revolutions were successful in Russia in 1917, the People's Republic of China in 1949, and in other smaller countries, they have failed to reach Marx's goals. Many of the people in these societies are now demanding change.

believed that the struggle between the bourgeoisie and the proletariat in the industrial age would result in the overthrow of the existing system. In the transition between the industrial state and a classless society, a ten-point plan for social reform would be implemented. This would shift control of economic resources from the bourgeoisie to the proletariat and would establish "common ownership of the means of production," or communism. As the dictatorship of the proletariat was established and the classless society achieved, the political infrastructure would wither away.

The appeal of scientific socialism led to the development of socialist parties throughout Europe. In 1864, the First International was formed to unite workers of the world to overthrow capitalism. Although internal disputes caused the First International to disband in 1873, the international socialist movement continued to spread. A Second International was formed in 1889 and continued until the First World War. (See chapter 7.)

THE RESULTS OF THE INDUSTRIAL REVOLUTION

Rapid urbanization and industrialization resulted in serious social problems. Overcrowded, unsanitary living environments and unsafe working conditions were the norm for much of the first half of the nineteenth century in England. By 1850, these problems were also evident in industrial and urban centres on the continent. Increasingly, governments found it necessary to become involved in the economy and to expand their role in health and welfare. Gradually urban conditions were improved with better sewer systems and higher housing standards. However, life expectancy for the proletariat still lagged behind that of the nation as a whole.

As the population and the economy shifted from rural-agricultural to urban-industrial, the power of the landed aristocracy dwindled. The middle class was the primary beneficiary of this shift and of the political reforms of the first half of the century.

However, the Industrial Revolution created a new class—the proletariat. Its members were poorly educated and were not given the same rights (such as the right to vote) as the rest of society. By 1880, trade unions and other labour organizations had developed a common consciousness. By the end of the century they had started to develop their own political agenda.

Economic Results

The economic results of the Industrial Revolution were far-reaching. The development of the factory system brought many changes in employment and production. Domestic industry decreased. Regular hours of work were established. Female and child labour decreased, eventually leaving the work place to be dominated by men. Increasingly, new products were developed for the consumer market; mass production eventually reduced their costs so that more people could afford them. Increased production and employment and improvements in health, education, and welfare raised the standard of living.

As trade expanded, the interdependence of economies grew. As this dependence increased, the "boom-bust" cycle, which had been apparent in domestic economies, created waves throughout the international economic community. Increased foreign trade also resulted in increased competition for markets and raw materials. Domestic industries demanded tariff protection from foreign industry. Increased foreign competition also led to the demand for protected markets abroad; a period of imperialistic expansion followed, which saw most of the world divided into economic spheres of influence by the turn of the century.

RETROSPECTIVE

The Industrial Revolution began in Great Britain in the mid-eighteenth century, spread to the European continent in the nineteenth century, and to the world in the twentieth century. In the process, it transformed the nature of Western civilization. Improvements in transportation and communication broke down the isolation of villages and small towns, accelerating the development of national culture. Political power shifted from the landowning aristocracy to the middle class. The middle class in turn was challenged by a new social class, the urban proletariat.

The spread of industrialization and the trend toward urbanization led to an increased role for the government in the economy, particularly on the European continent. Internationally, the disparity in industrial development between different countries resulted in shifts in the balance of power. As the search for raw materials and markets accelerated, so too did the development of the global village as Western civilization spread around the planet. The emerging nation-states of Europe, fueled by the power of the Industrial Revolution, would transform the face of the earth.

FLORENCE NIGHTINGALE

Florence Nightingale has often been depicted as an "angel of mercy," the tireless nurse who ran the military hospital at Scutari during the Crimean War. However, this one-sided view overlooks the essential contributions she made to medicine after the war.

As Nightingale had experienced first-hand in the Crimea, army hospitals were in a deplorable condition. Soldiers were poorly clothed and fed and generally suffered in squalor. Upon returning to England in 1856, Nightingale, whose fame was second only to that of Queen Victoria (1819–1910), decided to use her newly found influence to press for changes in the medical world. First she pressured the government into establishing a commission to investigate the state of military hospitals. The result was a series of reforms introduced between 1859 and 1861, including new ventilation, heating, lighting, and water systems for military hospitals; the creation of a commission to inspect and improve field hospitals; and the establishment of an army medical school. By 1861, these reforms had cut the mortality rate in British military hospitals in half.

Nightingale did not limit her reform movement to military hospitals, however. She also tackled the sorry state of medical care in industrial centres. Her *Notes on Hospitals* revolutionized hospital construction and management. And with the opening of the Nightingale Training School for Nurses in 1860 she became the founder of modern nursing.

To achieve her goals, Nightingale relied on political connections as well as the patronage of Queen Victoria and Prince Albert. Ultimately, she believed her work was part of God's plan. At one point she remarked that God moved in strange ways: "How inefficient I was in the Crimea, yet [God] has raised up from it trained nursing."

ADAM SMITH:
The Wealth of Nations (1776)

The spread of the factory system was given momentum by the dramatic successes of those manufacturers who were among the first to take advantage of it. In addition, the convincing arguments of economic theorists such as Adam Smith seemed to give a philosophic base for capitalism. In his monumental work The Wealth of Nations, *Smith discussed the "natural laws" that he believed regulated the economic system. Among the principles he addressed was the division of labour. In the following excerpt, Smith demonstrated the advantages of such an approach when applied to the production of the common pin.*

From Crane Brinton (ed.), *The Portable Age of Reason Reader*, (New York: Viking Press, 1956), pp. 186–188.

To take an example, therefore, from a very trifling manufacture, but one in which the division of labour had been very often taken notice of, the trade of the pinmaker; a workman not educated to this business (which the division of labour has rendered a distinct trade), nor acquainted with the use of machinery employed in it (to the invention of which the same division of labour has probably given occasion) could scarce, perhaps, with his utmost industry, make one pin in a day, and certainly could not make twenty. But in the way in which this business is now carried on, not only the whole work is a peculiar trade, but it is divided into a number of branches, of which the greater part are likewise peculiar trades. One man draws out the wire, another straights it, a third cuts it, a fourth points it, a fifth grinds it at the top for receiving the head; to make the head requires two or three distinct operations; to put it on is a peculiar business, to whiten the pins is another; it is even a trade by itself to put them into the paper; and the important business of making a pin is, in this manner, divided into about eighteen distinct operations, which in some manufactories are all performed by distinct hands, though in others the same man will sometimes perform two or three of them. I have seen a small manufactory of this kind where ten men only were employed, and where some of them consequently performed two or three distinct operations. But though they were very poor, and therefore but indifferently accommodated with the necessary machinery, they could when they exerted themselves make among them about twelve pounds of pins a day. There are in a pound upwards of four thousand pins of a middling size. Those ten persons, therefore, could make among them upwards of forty-eight thousand pins in a day. Each person, therefore, making a tenth part of forty-eight thousand pins might be considered as making four thousand eight hundred pins in a day. But if they had all wrought separately and independently, and without any of them having been educated to this peculiar business, they certainly could not each of them have made twenty, perhaps not one in a day; that is, certainly, not the two hundred and fortieth, perhaps not the four thousand eight hundredth part of what they are at present capable of performing, in consequence of a proper division and combination of their different operations.

---

1. In your own words, précis Smith's description of the process of pin making under the factory system.

2. Account for Smith's assertion that this process is potentially "four thousand eight hundred" times as efficient as individual hand labour.

3. What arguments might traditional craftspeople and artisans use against Smith?

THOMAS MALTHUS:
Essay on the Principle of Population as it Affects the Future Improvement of Society (1798)

Thomas Malthus was a member of the clergy and a classical economist who rejected the idea that industrialism was the cause of the impoverished condition of the working class. His "Essay on the Principle of Population" first appeared in 1798; it was revised and expanded in 1803. In it, Malthus rejected the optimism and humanitarianism characteristic of the Enlightenment tradition. He claimed that no society could exist in which happiness and prosperity were coincidental. His arguments became an excellent defence of the exploitation of the working class during the Industrial Revolution. Malthus's ideas were to have a profound influence on Charles Darwin later in the century.

From Richard Powers, *Readings in European Civilization Since 1500* (Boston: Houghton Mifflin, 1961), pp. 307–310.

I think I may fairly make two postula.

First, That food is necessary to the existence of man.

Second, That the passion between the sexes is necessary. . .

Assuming, then, my postula as granted, I say, that the power of population is indefinitely greater than the power in the earth to produce subsistence for man.

Population, when unchecked, increases in a geometrical ratio. Subsistence only increases in an arithmetical ratio. A slight acquaintance with numbers will show the immensity of the first power in comparison to the second.

By that law of nature which makes food necessary to the life of man, the effects of these two unequal powers must be kept equal.

This implies a strong and constantly operating check on population from the difficulty of subsistence. This difficulty must fall some where; and must necessarily be severely felt by a large portion of mankind.

Through the animal and vegetable kingdoms, nature has scattered the seeds of life abroad with the most profuse and liberal hand. She has been comparatively sparing in the room, and the nourishment necessary to rear them. The germs of existence contained in this spot of earth, with ample food, and ample room to expand it, would fill millions of worlds in the course of a few thousand years. Necessity, that imperious, all-pervading law of nature, restrains them within the prescribed bounds. The race of plants, and the race of animals, shrink under this great restrictive law. And the race of man cannot, by any efforts of reason, escape from it. Among the plants and animals its effects are waste of seed, sickness, and premature death. Among mankind, misery and vice. The former, misery, is an absolute necessary consequence of it. Vice is a highly probable consequence, and we therefore see it abundantly prevail; but it ought not, perhaps, to be called an absolutely necessary consequence. The ordeal of virtue is to resist all temptation to evil.

This natural inequality of the two powers of population, and of production in the earth, and that great law of nature which must constantly keep their effects equal, form the great difficulty that to me appears insurmountable in the way to perfectability of society. All other arguments are of slight and subordinate consideration of this. I see no way by which man can escape from the weight of this law which pervades all animated nature. No fancied equality, no agrarian regulations in their utmost extent, could remove the pressure of it even for a single century. And it appears, therefore, to be decisive against the possible existence of a society, all the members of which should live in ease, happiness, and comparative leisure; and feel no anxiety about providing the means of subsistence for themselves and families.

Consequently, if the premises are just, the argument is conclusive against the perfectability of mankind.

---

1. (a) State Malthus's thesis in your own words. What is its final outcome?
(b) Do you agree with this outcome? What other possibilities are there?

2. How do Malthus's beliefs about the "perfectability of society" differ from those of Enlightenment thinkers?

JEREMY BENTHAM:
A Manual of Political Economy (1789)

Jeremy Bentham was the most influential of the utilitarians. Human nature, he felt, was directed by two forces: pleasure and pain. Bentham's "standard of utility," therefore, was a judgment passed on laws. How much did a particular law increase pleasure and decrease pain? He took this a step further and said that all laws should provide "the greatest good for the greatest number." As a result he felt that government and every other social institution should be required to show its usefulness by increasing the well-being of individuals. Bentham believed that government should stay out of people's lives as much as possible. The following selection, from the introduction to A Manual of Political Economy, *represents the laissez-faire response to the Industrial Revolution.*

From Brian Tierney *et al*, *Great Issues in Western Civilization* (New York: Random House, 1976), pp. 381–382.

Political Economy is at once a *science* and an *art*. The value of the science has for its efficient cause and measure, its subserviency to the art.

According to the principle of utility in every branch of the art of legislation, the object or end in view should be the production of the maximum of happiness in a given time in the community in question.

In the instance of this branch of the art, the object or end in view should be the production of that maximum of happiness, in so far as this more general end is promoted by the production of the maximum wealth and the maximum of population.

The practical questions, therefore, are—How far the measures respectfully suggested by these two branches of the common end agree?—how far they differ, and which requires the preference?—how far the end in view is best promoted by individuals acting for themselves? and in what cases these ends may be best promoted by the hands of government? . . .

With the view of causing an increase to take place in the mass of national wealth, or with a view to increase of the means either of subsistence or enjoyment, without some special reason, the general rule is, that nothing ought to be done or attempted by government. The motto, or watchword of the government, on these occasions ought to be—*Be quiet*.

For this quietism there are two main reasons:—1. Generally speaking, any interference for this purpose on the part of the government is *needless*. The wealth of the whole community is composed of the wealth of the several individuals belonging to it taken together. But to increase his particular portion is, generally speaking, among the constant objects of each individual's exertions and care. Generally speaking, there is no one who is disposed with so much ardour and constancy to pursue it.

2. Generally speaking, it is moreover likely to be pernicious, viz. by being unconducive, or even obstructive, with reference to the attainment of the end in view. Each individual bestowing more time and attention upon the means of preserving and increasing his portion of wealth, than is or can be bestowed by government, is likely to take a more effectual course than what, in his instance and on his behalf, would be taken by government.

It is, moreover, universally and constantly pernicious in another way, by the restraint or constraint imposed on the free agency of the individual. Pain is the general concomitant of the sense of such restraint, wherever it is experienced.

Without being productive of such coercion, and thereby of such pain—in such a way more or less direct—more or less perceptible, with this or any other view, the interposition of government can hardly take place. If coercion be not applied to the very individual whose conduct is endeavoured to be made immediately subservient to this purpose, it is at any rate applied to others—indeed, to the whole community taken together.

In coercive measures, so called, it is only to the individual that the coercion is applied. In the case of measures of encouragement, the field of coercion is vastly more extensive. Encouragements are grants of money or money's worth, applied in some shape or other to this purpose. But for this, any more than any other purpose, money is not raised but by taxes, and taxes are the produce of coercive laws applied to the most coercive purpose.

This would not be the less true, though the individual pieces of money thus applied happened to come from a source which had not been fed by any such means. In all communities, by far the greatest share of the money disposed of by government being supplied by taxes, whether this or that particular portion of money be so applied, be supplied from that particular source, makes no sort of difference.

To estimate the good expected from the application of any particular mass of government money, compare it always with the mischief produced by the extraction of an equal sum of money by the most burthensome species of tax; since, by forebearing to make application of that sum of money by that tax, and thereby forebear imposing the mass of burden that results from it.

---

1. Briefly state Bentham's thesis and list the arguments he uses to support it.

2. Suppose a government decided to adopt Bentham's philosophy. Discuss the possible outcomes.

3. Decide which groups in society today would support Bentham's views and which ones would oppose them. List the reasons for your choices. Share your opinions in a class forum.

ENGELS AND URE: The Debate Over Industrialism

The fundamental debate over industrialization was not over its increased efficiency. Few economists argued with the views put forward by Adam Smith. Rather, the debate centred on whether or not the economic benefits of industrialization outweighed the social costs. In these two excerpts, arguments from both sides are presented. In the first, written in 1844, Friederich Engels describes the living conditions created by the Industrial Revolution. In the second, written in 1835, Andrew Ure defends the factory system in his Philosophy of Manufactures.

From Friedrich Engels, *The Condition of the Working Class in England in 1844*, in George L. Mosse *et al*, (eds.), *Europe in Review* (Chicago: Rand McNally, 1957), pp. 208–218.

Competition is the completest expression of the battle of all against all which rules in modern civil society. This battle, a battle for life, for existence, for everything, in case of need a battle of life and death, is fought not between the different classes of society only, but also between the individual members of these classes. Each is in the way of the other, and each seeks to crowd out all who are in his way, and to put himself in their place. . . .

Every great city has one or more slums where the working class is crowded together. True, poverty often dwells in hidden alleys close to the palaces of the rich; but, in general, a separate territory has been assigned to it, where, removed from the sight of the happier classes, it may struggle along as it can. . . . The streets are generally unpaved, rough, dirty, filled with vegetable and animal refuse, without sewers or gutters, but supplied with stagnant pools instead. . . .

The death rate is kept so high chiefly by the heavy mortality rate among young children in the working class . . . no one need wonder that in Manchester . . . more than fifty-seven percent of the children of the working class . . . die under five years of age. . . .

Next to intemperance in the enjoyment of intoxicating liquors, one of the principal faults of English workingmen is sexual licence. . . . The bourgeoisie has left the working class only these two pleasures, while imposing upon it a multitude of labours and hardships, and the consequence is that the workingmen, in order to get something from life, concentrate their whole energy upon these two enjoyments, carry them to excess, surrender to them in the most unbridled manner. . . . Thus the social order makes family life almost impossible for the worker.

From Andrew Ure, *Philosophy of Manufactures, 1835*, in George L. Mosse *et al*, (eds.), *Europe in Review* (Chicago: Rand McNally, 1957), pp. 208–218.

The blessings which physico-mechanical science has bestowed on society, and the means it has still in store for ameliorating the lot of mankind, have been too little dwelt upon. . . .

It seems established by a body of incontestable evidence that the wages of our factory work-people, if prudently spent, would enable them to live in a comfortable manner, and decidedly better than formerly, in consequence of the relative diminution in the price of food, fuel, lodgings and clothing. . . .

Nothing shows in a clearer point of view the credulity of mankind in general, and of the people of these islands in particular, than the ready faith which was given to the tales of cruelty exercised by proprietors of cotton-mills towards young children. The system of calumny somewhat resembles that brought by Pagans against the primitive Christians, of enticing children into their meetings in order to murder and devour them. . . .

I have visited many factories, both in Manchester and in the surrounding districts, during a period of several months, entering the spinning rooms unexpectedly, and often alone, at different times of the day, and I never saw a single instance of corporal chastisement inflicted on a child, nor indeed did I ever see children in ill-humor. They seemed to be always cheerful and alert, taking pleasure in the light play of their muscles—enjoying the mobility natural to their age.

---

1. Write a critique of either Engels or Ure's philosophy from the point of view of the other author.

2. Debate the following resolution: *The benefits of the Industrial Revolution were well worth the costs.*

SAMUEL SMILES: Self-Help (1859)

Samuel Smiles's (1812–1904) "Self-Help," which appeared in 1859, sold 20 000 copies that year and a further 130 000 over the next thirty years. It was followed by a series of works—"Thrift," "Character," and "Duty"—which formed a "catalogue" of English Victorian values. David Thomson, in his book England in

"Heaven helps those who help themselves" is a well-tried maxim, embodying in a small compass the results of vast experience. The spirit of self-help is the root of all genuine growth in the individual; and, exhibited in the lives of many, it constitutes the true source of national vigor and strength. Help from without is often enfeebling in its effects, but help from within invariably invigorates. Whatever is done for men or classes to a certain extent takes away the stimulus and necessity of doing for themselves; and where men are subjected to over-guidance and over-government, the inevitable tendency is to render them comparatively helpless.

Even the best institutions can give a man no active aid. Perhaps the utmost they can do is, to leave him free to develop himself and improve his individual condition. But in all times men have been prone to believe that their happiness and well-the Nineteenth Century, *wrote that: "This long series of smug lay sermons on the virtues of industry and honesty, connecting always the practice of such virtue with the reward of material prosperity, is the shoddiest side of the mentality of the time." Smiles's works reflected the guiding laissez-faire creed of the prosperous industrialists and financiers who dominated the British political scene.*

From Samuel Smiles, *Self-Help* (London: J. Murray, 1859), pp. 1–2, 232–234; in Gerald Walsh (ed.), *Industrialization and Society* (Toronto: McClelland and Stewart Ltd., 1969), pp. 91–93.

being were to be secured by means of institutions rather than by their own conduct. Hence the value of legislation as an agent in human advancement has always been greatly over-estimated. To constitute the millionth part of a Legislature, by voting for one or two men once in three or five years, however conscientiously this duty may be performed, can exercise but little active influence upon any man's life and character. Moreover, it is every day becoming more clearly understood that the function of Government is negative and restrictive, rather than positive and active; being resolved principally into protection—protection of life, liberty, and property. Hence the chief "reforms" of the last fifty years have consisted mainly in abolitions and disenactments. But there is no power of law that can make the idle man industrious, the thriftless provident, or the drunken sober; though every individual can be each and all of these if he will, by the exercise of his own free powers of action and self-denial. Indeed all experience serves to prove that the worth and strength of a State depend far less upon the form of its institutions than upon the character of its men. For the nation is only the aggregate of individual conditions, and civilization itself is but a question of personal improvement.

National progress is the sum of individual industry, energy, and uprightness, as national decay is of individual idleness, selfishness and vice. What we are accustomed to decry as great social evils, will, for the most part, be found to be only the outgrowth of our own perverted life; and though we may endeavour to cut them down and extirpate them by means of Law, they will only spring up again with luxuriance in some other form, unless the conditions of human life and character are radically improved. If this view be correct, then it follows that the highest patriotism and philanthropy consist, not so much in altering laws and modifying institutions, as in helping and stimulating men to elevate and improve themselves by their own free and independent action. . . .

There is no reason why the condition of the average workman in this country should not be a useful, honourable, respectable, and happy one. The whole body of the working classes might (with few exceptions) be as frugal, virtuous, well-informed and well-conditioned as many individuals of the same class have already made themselves. What some men are, all without difficulty might be. Employ the same means, and the same results will follow. That there should be a class of men who live by their daily labour in every state is the ordinance of God, and doubtless is a wise and righteous one; but that this class should be otherwise frugal, contented, intelligent, and happy, is not the design of Providence, but springs solely from the weakness, self-indulgence, and perverseness of man himself. The healthy spirit of self-help created amongst working people would more than any other measure serve to raise them as a class, and this, not by pulling down others, but by levelling them up to a higher and still advancing standard of religion, intelligence, and virtue.

---

1. Outline Smiles's thesis. What arguments does he use to support it?

2. Why is Smiles against government intervention?

3. Discuss how the following would respond to Smiles: the poor, the middle class, industrialists, socialists, and communists.

ROBERT OWEN:
Experimental Societies (1820)

Robert Owen was a highly successful British entrepreneur. By the time he was thirty, he had built an efficient textile business employing over 2000 people. Owen realized that it was pointless to upgrade machinery while the conditions of the operators continued to decline. Appalled by the factory conditions of the time, he improved working conditions, raised wages, reduced hours, built model housing, and provided free public education for the children of his workers. His experimental program at his mill complex at New Lanark, Scotland, was highly successful. In spite of this success, however, few of his contemporaries adopted his methods.

From Wallace E. Adams, *et al*, *The Western World*, Vol. 2 (Toronto: Dodd, Mead & Co., 1969), pp. 226–227.

Report to Lanark

Society, ever misled by closet theorists, has committed almost every kind of error in practice, and in no instance perhaps a greater, than in separating the workman from his food, and making his existence depend upon the labour and uncertain supplies of others, as is the case under our present manufacturing system; and it is a vulgar error to suppose that a single individual more can be supported by means of a system than without it; on the contrary, a whole population engaged in agriculture, with manufactures as an appendage, will, in a given district, support many more, and in a much higher degree of comfort, than the same district could do with its agricultural separate from its manufacturing population.

Improved arrangements for the working class will, in almost all cases, place the workingman in the midst of his food, which it will be beneficial for him to create as to consume.

Sufficient land, therefore, will be allotted to these cultivators, to enable them to raise an abundant supply of food and the necessaries of life for themselves, and as much additional agricultural produce as the public demands may require from such a portion of the population.

Under a well-devised arrangement for the working classes they will all procure for themselves the necessaries and comforts of life in so short a time, and so easily and pleasantly, that the occupation will be experienced to be little more than a recreation, sufficient to keep them in the best health and spirits for rational enjoyment of life.

An association, therefore, of 1200 persons, would require from 600 to 1800 statute acres, according as it may be intended to be more or less agricultural.

Thus, when it should be thought expedient that the chief surplus products should consist of manufactured commodities, the lesser quantity of land would be sufficient; if a large surplus from the produce of the soil were deemed desirable, the greater quantity would be allotted; and when the localities of the situation should render it expedient for the association to create an equal quantity of each, the medium quantity, or 1200 acres, would be best suitable.

It follows that land under the proposed system of husbandry would be divided into farms of from 150 to 3000 acres, but generally perhaps from 800 to 1500 acres. The division of land will be found productive of incalculable benefits in practice; it will give advantages, without any of the disadvantages of small and large farms.

The next head for consideration is . . . the arrangement for feeding, lodging, and clothing the population, and for training and educating the children.

It being always most convenient for the workman to reside near to his employment, the site for the dwellings of the cultivators will be chosen as near to the centre of the land, as water, proper levels, dry situation, etc., etc., may admit; and as courts, alleys, lanes, and streets create many unnecessary inconveniences, are injurious to health, and destructive to almost all natural comforts of human life, they will be excluded, and a disposition of the buildings free from these objections and greatly more economical will be adopted.

As it will afterwards appear that the food for the whole population can be provided better and cheaper under one general arrangement of cooking, and that the children can be better trained and educated together under the eye of their parents than under any other circumstances, a large square, or rather parallelogram, will be found to combine the greatest advantages in its form for the domestic arrangements of association.

This form, indeed, affords so many advantages for the comfort of human life, that if great ignorance respecting the means necessary to secure good conduct and happiness among the working classes had not prevailed in all ranks, it must long ago have become universal.

---

1. Summarize the reasons Owen gives for placing the worker in closer relation to the land.

2. (a) If Owen's ideas were to be implemented today, what legislation would be required?
(b) What would be the implications for a nation if Owen's ideas were adopted?

3. Who would oppose Owen's ideas? Why?

HENRI DE SAINT-SIMON: The Industrialists' Catechism (1823)

Saint-Simon is considered the father of utopian socialism. He believed that class conflict would develop between the two classes he identified as the producers (the industrialists) and the parasites (the bureaucrats).

From Wallace E. Adams, *et al*, *The Western World*, Vol. 2 (Toronto: Dodd, Mead & Co., 1969), pp. 222–223.

Q: What is an industrialist?
A: An industrialist is a man who works to produce or to put at the disposal of different members of society one or several material means which can satisfy their needs or physical appetites. Thus, a farmer who sows wheat, raises poultry or stock animals, is an industrialist; a wheelwright, a blacksmith, a locksmith, are all industrialists; a cobbler, a hatter, a linen maker, a draper, a sweater maker, each is equally an industrialist; a merchant, a printer, a sailor employed on merchant ships, are industrialists. All industrialists work in unity to produce and to provide for the members of society all material means to satisfy their needs and physical tastes, and they constitute three great classes which are known as cultivators, manufacturers, and merchants.
Q: What rank must these industrialists occupy in society?
A: The industrial class must occupy the first ranks in society because they are the most important of all, because they can surpass all the others and because no other can surpass them, because they subsist through proper functions by their personal toil. The other classes should work for the industrial class, for it is that class which has created the means by which the others obtain their existence. In a word, everything is done by industry; everything must be done for it.
Q: What rank does the industrial class currently hold in society?
A: The industrial class actually constitutes the lowest class in the present social order. The social organization presently accords greater considerations to the secondary workers, even to the idle, than to workers who perform the most useful functions.
Q: Why does the industrial class, which should occupy the first position, find itself placed at the bottom? Why are those who constitute, in fact, the first actually in the position of the last?
A: We shall explain such an anomaly in the following discussion of this catechism.
Q: What must the industrial class do in order to move from the lower position in

which they have been placed to the superior one which they should occupy?
A: We will explain in the catechism the manner in which that class must conduct itself in order to bring improvement to its social status.
Q: Then what is the nature of the task you must undertake? In a word, what are the purposes of the catechism?
A: We propose to indicate to the industrialists the means to render possible their well-being. We propose to teach them the general procedures which they should employ in order to realize their social importance.
Q: What means must be employed to attain such an objective?
A: In the first place we will give the industrialists a clear outline of their true social situation. We will make them see that it is a situation entirely substandard, and as a consequence very inferior to what it should be, even though they are the most capable and useful class in society. On the other hand, we will even trace for them the course which they must follow in order to bring themselves to the first rank of society. . . .
Q: You will preach, then, in the catechism, insurrection and revolt, because the classes which are currently invested with authority and special consideration will not renounce voluntarily the advantages which they enjoy?
A: Rather than preaching insurrection and revolution, we will present the only means of preventing the acts of violence which will menace society and from which it can not escape so long as the industrial authority continues to remain passive amid the factions which compete for power. The public tranquility can not remain stable as long as the most important industrialists are not charged with direction and administration of public property.
Q: Explain and tell us why the public tranquility will be disturbed if the leaders of the industrial class do not gain control of public property.
A: The reason is very simple. The general inclination of the immense majority of society is to be governed under the best possible consensus, to be governed as little as possible, to be governed by the most capable and talented men who guarantee public tranquility. The only means of satisfying, under these circumstances, the desires of the majority is to place the public fortunes under the direction of the industrialists, for it is the industrialists who are the most interested in maintaining the public order. They are the ones interested in maintaining public peace; they are the ones interested in economizing in public expenditures; they are, moreover, the ones most interested in limiting arbitrary authority. Finally, they are, of all the members of society, the ones who have proved to exhibit the greatest capacity for positive administration through the achievements in their own special fields of enterprise and special skills. . . .

---

1. What is Saint-Simon's definition of an industrialist? How does it differ from the modern definition?
2. (a) According to Saint-Simon, why should the industrialists govern society?
(b) How will they attain leadership?
3. Write an editorial responding to Saint-Simon's ideas from the point of view of (a) the upper classes, (b) the middle classes, or (c) the proletariat. Share your viewpoint with other members of the class.

MARX AND ENGELS:
The Communist Manifesto (1848)

The Communist Manifesto *remains one of the most influential political pamphlets ever written. The philosophy is based on the ideals of Gregor Hegel, who believed in the natural evolution of states to the point where the interests of the state and its citizens were one. The process of this evolution was called "the dialectic." The concept of the dialectic comes from the Greek, meaning "to reach conclusions through the clash of opposite elements." In Hegel's case, these opposite elements were the status quo, or "thesis," and a revolutionary challenge or the opposite of that thesis, the "antithesis." Emerging from this conflict would be a new combination of the two forces, called the "synthesis." This would form the new thesis or status quo and so the process would continue.*

From Karl Marx and Friedrich Engels, *The Communist Manifesto* (Middlesex, UK: Penguin Books, 1975), pp. 79–80, 95, 104–105, 120–121.

Bourgeois and Proletarians

The history of all hitherto existing society is the history of class struggles.

Freeman and slave, patrician and plebian, lord and serf, guild-master and journeyman, in a word, oppressor and oppressed, stood in constant opposition to one another, carried on an uninterrupted, now hidden, now open fight, a fight that each time ended, either in a revolutionary reconstitution of society at large, or in common ruin of the contending classes. . . .

The modern bourgeois society that has sprouted from the ruins of feudal society has not done away with class antagonisms. It has but established new classes, new conditions of oppression, new forms of struggle in place of the old ones.

Our epoch, the epoch of the bourgeoisie, possesses, however, this distinctive feature: it has simplified the class antagonisms into two great hostile camps, into two great classes directly facing each other: Bourgeoisie and Proletariat.

Proletarians and Communists

In what relation do the Communists stand to the proletarians as a whole?

The Communists do not form a separate party opposed to other working-class parties. . . .

The Communists are distinguished from the other working-class parties by this only: 1) In the national struggles of the proletarians of the different countries, they point out and bring to the front the common interests of the entire proletariat, independently of all nationality. 2) In the various stages of development which the struggle of the working class against the bourgeoisie has to pass through, they always and everywhere represent the interests of the movement as a whole. . . .

The immediate aim of the Communists is the same as that of all other proletarian parties: formation of the proletariat into a class, overthrow of the bourgeois supremacy, conquest of political power by the proletariat. . . .

The proletariat will use its political supremacy to wrest by degrees, all capital from the bourgeoisie, to centralize all instruments of production in the hands of the State, i.e., of the proletariat organized as a ruling class; and to increase the total of the productive forces as rapidly as possible.

Of course, in the beginning, this cannot be effected except by means of despotic inroads on the rights of property, and on the conditions of bourgeois production; by means of measures, therefore, which appear economically insufficient and untenable, but which, in the course of the movement, outstrip themselves, necessitate further inroads upon the old social order, and are unavoidable as a means of entirely revolutionizing the mode of production.

These measures will of course be different in different countries.

Nevertheless, in the most advanced countries, the following will be pretty generally applicable:

1. Abolition of property in land and application of all rents of land to public purposes.
2. A heavy progressive tax or graduated income tax.

3. Abolition of the right of inheritance.

4. Confiscation of all property of all emigrants and rebels.

5. Centralization of credit in the hands of the State. . . .

6. Centralization of the means of communication and transport in the hands of the State.

7. Extension of factories and instruments of production owned by the State; the bringing into cultivation of wastelands, and the improvement of the soil generally in accordance with a common plan.

8. Equal liability of all labour. Establishment of industrial armies, especially for agriculture.

9. Combination of all agriculture with manufacturing industries; gradual abolition of the distinction between town and country, by a more equable distribution of the population over the country.

10. Free education for all children in public schools. Abolition of children's factory labour in its present form. . . .

When, in the course of development, class distinctions have disappeared, and all production has been concentrated in the whole nation, the public power will lose its political nature. . . .

In place of the old bourgeois society, with its classes and class antagonisms, we shall have an association, in which the free development of each is the condition for the free development of all.

Position of the Communists in Relation to the Various Existing Opposition Parties

The Communists disdain to conceal their views and aims. They openly declare their ends can be attained only by the forcible overthrow of all existing social conditions. Let the ruling classes tremble at a Communistic revolution. The proletariats have nothing to lose but their chains. They have the world to win.

WORKERS OF THE WORLD, UNITE!

---

1. How did Marx interpret history?

2. Define the two classes into which society is divided.

3. What features distinguish communism from other proletariat parties?

4. Stage a two-person debate on the topic: *The Gorbachev revolution has restored Marxism to Europe*. In order to prepare for the debate, consider:

(a) the relationship between *glasnost* and Marx's theory of history;
(b) the aims of Marx's theories for social action; and
(c) the response of people and governments to the views of Marxism.

ANALYSIS AND APPLICATION

1. Defend or refute the following statement: *The Industrial Revolution should be called the Industrial Evolution.*

2. Investigate the impact of the Industrial Revolution on agricultural life in Great Britain.

3. Create an editorial cartoon that attacks the practice of child labour.

4. The problems of an urban society first began to manifest themselves in the nineteenth century. Choose one of the industrialized cities of Europe during this time and outline the urban problems it faced.

5. In chart form, compare and contrast the goals and methods of laissez-faire capitalists, utopian socialists, and scientific socialists.

6. Write a biographical profile of an entrepreneur of the early Industrial Revolution.

7. It has been said that imperialism was a result of the Industrial Revolution. Examine the relationship between imperialism and industrialization and prepare a report of your findings.

8. With the help of a librarian, choose a piece of literature that portrays the Industrial Revolution. Some suggestions include Charles Dickens's *Hard Times*; Émile Zola's *Germinal*; Benjamin Disraeli's *Sybil, or the Two Nations*; and George Gissing's *The Unclassed*. Read the book and report on how it depicted life during the Industrial Revolution. Share your findings in a class discussion.

9. Create a drama about the Industrial Revolution. Divide the class into three groups. Group 1 should be the proletariat or working class, Group 2 the bourgeoisie or middle class, and Group 3 the colonizers and colonials. With your group prepare a series of short, first-person vignettes. Your presentation should be no more than fifteen minutes and should be based on primary research.

   Choose one member of the class to act as the producer/director. This person should interrelate the material to form a cohesive forty-five minute production.

CHAPTER SIX

Romanticism, 1815 to 1848

THE NATURE OF ROMANTICISM

The political, social, and economic upheavals of post-Napoleonic Europe were to a great extent the product of international stability. Freed from the threat of war, Europeans had time to reassess the values and principles upon which their society was built. For many Western thinkers, it was clear that the rationalism of the Enlightenment had been a failure. Rather than producing a new Golden Age, as so many had envisioned, it unleashed twenty years of violent conflict as the ideals of the French Revolution were spread throughout Europe. The disillusionment with the vision of society that characterized the Age of Reason was evident in the revolutionary nature of the age. In addition, rejection of the old social order was reinforced by the social upheaval caused by the Industrial Revolution. In the arts, the result was the emergence of a new perception of humanity, *romanticism*.

It is almost impossible to make generalizations about romanticism. Its essence was the rejection of established rules and conventions. Although there were many inconsistencies within the movement itself, a common element was the refusal to accept the rigidity of neoclassical standards of form and expression. Instead, romanticism focused on the "intuitive and emotional dimensions of the individual."

Poets, writers, painters, and musicians cast off the rules of classicism and sought freedom in form and subject matter. Conservatism, authoritarianism, and moderation gave way to liberalism and excess. The movement drew inspiration from the American and French revolutions and the struggles for independence and national unity in Greece, Germany, Italy, and elsewhere. Although romanticism started in Britain and Germany at the turn of the century, it spread throughout Europe after 1815. The greatest flowering of the romantic spirit, however, was in the revolutionary era of 1830 to 1848.

The emphasis on feelings, imagination, and beauty has been a recurring theme in the arts. What distinguished the romantic movement from others in which artists rejected classicism was its intensity and extensiveness. Romanticism pervaded all art forms—literature, music, painting, sculpture, and architecture. It was diverse, encompassing utopian socialists and reactionaries, atheists and devout Christians. For some the central theme was nature; for others it was the Middle Ages; for still others it was exotic, faraway lands. Romanticism also flourished at different times. The German romantic movement, for instance, was largely finished before French romanticism even began.

ROMANTICISM IN LITERATURE

Elements of romanticism were evident in the latter half of the eighteenth century in the writings of Jean-Jacques Rousseau and in the German *Sturm und Drang* ("storm and stress") movement, which encompassed the work of Johann Wolfgang von Goethe (1749–1832) and Johann Friedrich von Schiller (1759–1805). These writers were not romantics but romanticism was fostered by their writings. Rousseau's *Nouvelle Héloïse* (1760) Goethe's *The Sorrows of Young Werther* (1774), and Schiller's *The Robber* (1781) exalted nature, feeling, and human individualism, the essence of romanticism. But it was the publication of Wordsworth and Coleridge's *Lyrical Ballads* in 1798 that heralded the beginning of romanticism.

CHARLES BAUDELAIRE:

What Is Romanticism?

The eclectic diversity of romanticism is explained in part by the fact that there was no clearly identifiable romantic style. In 1846, Charles Baudelaire (1821–1864), a poet and art critic, described romanticism as "precisely situated neither in choice of subjects nor in exact truth, but in mode of feeling." In other words, romantic artists sought to experience reality through feeling, imagination, instinct, and passion in ways that were uniquely their own.

Few people today will want to give a real and positive meaning to this word; yet will they dare to say that a generation has carried on a battle for several years for the sake of a flag that symbolizes nothing?

When one recalls the troubles of these recent times, one will realize that if few romantics remain, it is because few really discovered romanticism, even though all sought it sincerely and steadfastly.

Some applied themselves only to the choice of subjects; they had not the temperament for their subjects.—Others, still believing in a Catholic society, sought to reflect Catholicism in their works.—To call oneself a romantic and to look systematically to the past is to contradict oneself.—These, in the name of romanticism, blasphemed the Greeks and the Romans, but Romans and Greeks can be made romantic if one is romantic himself.—Truth in art and local color misled others. . . .

Romanticism is precisely located neither in the choice of subject nor in exact truth, but in the mode of feeling.

They looked for it outside themselves, and it is only to be found within.

For me, romanticism is the most recent, the most up-to-date, expression of the beautiful.

There are as many kinds of beauty as there are habitual ways of seeking happiness.

The philosophy of progress explains this clearly; thus, just as there have been as many ideals as there have been ways for conscientious people to understand morality, love, religion, etc., so romanticism will not consist in a final perfect formulation, but in a conception analogous to the moral philosophy of the time. . . .

From Joshua C. Taylor, *Nineteenth-Century Theories of Art* (Berkeley: University of California Press, 1987), pp. 221–222.

English Romanticism

Wordsworth and Coleridge

In the preface of the *Lyrical Ballads*, William Wordsworth (1770–1850) called for a new era in poetry. (See readings.) He rejected the poetic diction and subject matter of the classicists in favour of the language of commoners and nature as a source of inspiration. Great poetry, he said, could be written about simple subjects in a simple manner. The *Lyrical Ballads* were instrumental in reopening people's eyes to the beauty of nature and effectively started the English romantic movement. Included in the collection were many of Wordsworth's best short and lyrical poetry, such as *Lines Written a Few Miles above Tintern Abbey*, which expresses Wordsworth's love of nature and illustrates his use of simple language. Samuel Coleridge's (1772–1834) contributions include his best known poem, *The Rime of the Ancient Mariner* (1797–1798). Like his poems *Christabel* (1816) and the opium-induced poetic fragment *Kubla Khan* (1797), the dreamlike setting of the *Rime of the Ancient Mariner* represents another quality of romanticism: the use of exotic settings which were remote from the real universe. Coleridge's poetic creativity was short-lived and he turned to prose in his later years. His *Biographia Literaria* (1817) contains an explanation and defence of the aims of the English romantic movement.

The first generation of romantic poets—Wordsworth, Coleridge, Robert Southey (1774–1843), and William Blake (1757–1827)—revolted against the conventions of contemporary poetry. The second generation of romantic poets—Lord [George Gordon] Byron (1788–1824), John Keats (1795–1821), and Percy Bysshe Shelley (1792–1822)—revolted against English society itself and in the process they produced some of the most endearing poetry in the English language.

Byron, Shelley, and Keats

The symbol of English romanticism, at least on the European continent, was Lord Byron. Many of Byron's characters, such as the hero of *The Corsair* (1814), were swashbuckling brigands. He frequently portrayed defiant, melancholy young men in his poetry and it was this type of character that he was most closely associated with in his personal life as well. While he became the toast of London society after the publication of *Childe Harold's Pilgrimage* in 1812, scandals in his personal life forced him to flee England after his marriage was dissolved in 1815. He spent most of his remaining life in Italy, where he became interested in the cause of Greek independence. It was also in Italy that Byron wrote some of his best poetry. His masterpiece, "Don Juan" (1819–1824), is a record of his moods, thoughts, feelings, and opinions of people and events. The hero, a Spanish rake, is a thinly disguised version of Byron himself. Byron died in Greece from brain fever on 19 April 1824 while fighting alongside the Greeks for their independence from the Turks. Both Byron and the Greek struggle for independence fueled romanticism on the continent.

Shelley was the most idealistic of the romantic poets. Many of his poems were prompted by political events, such as "The Mask of Anarchy" (1819), which was inspired by the Peterloo Massacre. Other poems championed liberal causes, such as the "Revolt of Islam" (1818) which advocated women's rights and the emancipation of women. Like Byron, Shelley fled England to Italy, where he too wrote some of his best known poems, such as the "Ode to the West Wind" (1822). (See readings.) His creativity was cut short when he drowned in the Gulf of Spezia after his boat capsized in a storm.

Keats was perhaps the most talented of the English romantic poets. Most of his poetry dealt with Greek mythology or medieval themes and represented the climax of the English romantic tradition. His "Ode on a Grecian Urn," "Ode to Melancholy," and "Ode to a Nightingale," all published in 1820, examined the transient nature of youth, beauty, and life. (See readings.) Keats died of tuberculosis the following year.

Literary Criticism

The interests and attitudes of romanticism seemed more conducive to poetry than prose, and there is nothing in romantic prose that equals romantic poetry. However, the insightful and sensitive literary criticisms of Coleridge, William Hazlitt (1788–1830), and Charles Lamb (1775–1834) raised this genre to a new level. Coleridge's *Lectures on Shakespeare* (1808) and Hazlitt's *The Characters of Shakespeare's Plays* (1825) helped to create a new understanding of Shakespeare's creative genius. Hazlitt was also known for his studies of contemporary poets, such as *Lectures on the English Poets* (1818), which brought the work of many poets to the attention of the reading public. Charles Lamb carried on the tradition of the informal essay, which had been initiated by Addison and Steele. He wrote much of his work under the pen name "Elia" for the *London Magazine*. He also collaborated with his sister on the children's classic, *Tales from Shakespeare* (1807).

The Novel

Although the gothic horror novels, such as Anne Radcliffe's (1764–1823) *Romance of the Forest* (1791) and Mary Shelley's (1797–1851) *Frankenstein* (1818), were typical of the novels that studied the darker side of human nature, the best representations of the English romantic novel were the historical novels of Sir Walter Scott (1771–1832). Scott established the form of the historical novel. His works, such as *The Bride of Lammermoor* (1819) and *Ivanhoe* (1819), were extremely influential on the continent, particularly in France where his style was frequently copied.

French Romanticism

In France, the leader of the romantic movement was Victor Hugo (1802–1885), prolific poet, novelist, and dramatist.

Hugo was one of the greatest writers of nineteenth-century France. Originally a royalist under Louis XVIII, he rejected the extremism of Charles X and was a staunch supporter of Louis Philippe in his early years as king. Eventually, the July monarchy became too conservative for Hugo and he increasingly identified with the plight of the peasantry and the working class. A republican by 1848, Hugo left France after the coup that put Napoleon III on the throne.

From 1851 to 1870, Hugo lived in exile, first in Brussels and then later on the channel islands of Jersey and Guernsey where he wrote the violent satire against Napoleon, *Les Châtiments* (1853). He returned to France after the fall of the Second Empire and became a senator in the Third Republic.

As the leader of the French romantic movement, Hugo brought new freedom to French poetry. His many works include the spiritual collections *Les Orientales* (1829) and *Les Contemplations* (1856). The production of his play *Hernani* (1830) inaugurated the romantic age in French drama. The classical rules of construction were abandoned in favour of a mixture of tragedy and comedy. A new extravagant, emotional spirit prevailed. The play actually caused a riot between supporters of classicism and romanticism.

Today Hugo is best known for his historical novels *The Hunchback of Notre Dame* (1831) and *Les Misérables* (1862). The central characters of these novels—the hunchback Quasimodo and the convict Jean Valjean—are social outcasts who rise above the world around them. They illustrate how Hugo used his novels as platforms for his political and social ideas. In *Les Misérables*, for example, Hugo focused on the dislocation and disenfranchisement of the ordinary individual during the period 1830 to 1848. His bitterness against the regime of Napoleon III is reflected in his depiction of the sacrifice of revolutionary idealism on the barricades of Paris.

In spite of his great literary achievements, national recognition came to him only in the last years of his life. When he died in 1885, he was a revered national figure and was buried in the Pantheon in Paris.

George Sand (1804–1876) was another key figure of French romanticism. Born Amandine-Aurore Dupin in Paris in 1804, she married Baron Dudevant, but at the age of twenty-seven she left him to seek an independent literary life in Paris. There she fell in love with Jules Sandeau, a young writer. Together they wrote several articles and a novel under the name of "J. Sand." When Dupin published her first novel, *Indiana*, in 1831, she adopted what was to become her permanent pseudonym, George Sand.

Sand's early novels—*Indiana, Valentine* (1832), and *Lélia* (1834)—are all romantic novels portraying women's struggles against conventional morals. In the early 1840s, she wrote novels such as *Counsuelo* (1842–1843) and *Le Péché de Monsieur Antoine (1847)*, which sympathized with the lower classes. She also wrote idyllic works of rustic life, such as *La mare au diable* (1846) and *François le champi* (1850).

After the revolution of 1848, Sand returned to romance with novels such as *La Petite Fadette* (1849) and *Les Maîtres sonneurs* (1852). Throughout her work she demanded equality in love and equality before the law for women. But she never advocated political equality.

Sand's personal life was the subject of some of her work as well. *Elle et lui* (1859) is a fictionalized account of her affair with Alfred de Musset; *Un hiver à Majorque* (1841) describes an unhappy episode during her passionate liaison with Frédéric Chopin. Her autobiography, *Histoire de ma vie*, provides interesting reading about many of the leading characters

George Sand was well known for her love affairs as well as for her novels.

GEORGE SAND: Indiana

When George Sand abandoned her husband at the age of twenty-seven, she also abandoned the social conventions of the day. Sand rebelled against the social mores that kept women subservient to men and believed that unless society was totally transformed "from top to bottom" there could be no happiness for women in marriage or love. Many of her popular novels explored this theme of women bound to a life of unhappiness through marriage. In Indiana, the young wife asserts her independence from the domination of her husband.

"Will you condescend to tell me, madam," said he, "where you spent this morning, and perhaps, last night?" . . .

"No, sir!" she answered, "my intention is not to tell you."

Delmare turned pale with surprise and anger. "Indeed!" said he in a trembling voice, "do you hope to hide it from me?"

"I do not care about it;" she resumed in an icy tone, "if I refuse to answer you, it is only for form. I wish to convince you, that you have no right to address me that question."

"I have not the right! Who is master here, you or I? Who wears a petticoat, and ought to spin on a distaff? Do you pretend to take the beard from my chin? It would well become you."

"I know that I am a slave, and you are my lord. The law of this country has made you my master. You can bind my body, tie my hands, govern my actions: you are the strongest, and society adds to your power; but with my will, sir, you can do nothing. God alone can restrain it and curb it. Seek then a law, a dungeon, an instrument of torture, by which you can hold it, it as if you wished to grasp the air, and seize vacancy."

"Be silent, foolish and impertinent creature! Your romantic phrases annoy me."

"You may impose silence upon me, but you cannot prevent me from thinking."

"Miserable pride! haughty worm! you abuse the pity that is felt for you! But you will see that this proud spirit can be conquered without much trouble."

"I do not advise you to try. Your repose will suffer, and it will add nothing to your manly dignity. . . . You used violence in keeping me in my chamber. I escaped by my window to show you, that reigning over a woman's will is exercising an imaginary sway; I passed some hours out of your dominion; I have been breathing the air of liberty, to show you that you are not morally my master, and that I depend upon myself alone on this earth. In walking, I reflected that I owed it alike to duty and to conscience, to return to your protection. I did so freely. . . ."

"I pity your mental derangement," said the Colonel, shrugging his shoulder.

From Miriam Schneir (ed.), *Feminism: The Essential Historical Writings* (New York: Random House, 1972), pp. 26–27.

of French romanticism, including Victor Hugo, Gustave Flaubert, and Eugène Delacroix, with whom she was friends. Her work provides valuable insight into the values and attitudes of French society during the period.

As a novelist and dramatist, Alexandre Dumas (1802–1870) was extremely popular in nineteenth-century France. He was a pioneer of romantic theatre, producing historical plays such as *Henry III et sa cour* (1829) and *Anthony* (1831). Even more popular were the historical novels for which he is best known today, *The Three Musketeers* (1844) and *The Count of Monte Cristo* (1845).

Other authors, such as Stendhal (pen name of Marie Henri Beyle, 1783–1842), used romantic plots and subjects but portrayed them in a realistic fashion. Honoré de Balzac (1799–1850) was a romantic in ideology and imagination, but his socio-economic observations of life (*La Comédie Humaine* [1834–1842] and *Les Paysans* [1844]) were written with great realism.

German Romanticism

In Germany, the philosophical and critical basis for romanticism was established in the writing of Wilhelm Heinrich Wackenroder (1773–1798), Ludwig Tieck (1773–1853), and Novalis (Friedrich von Hardenburg, 1772–1801). Wackenroder's *Outpourings of the Heart of an Art-Loving Monk* (1796) laid the theoretical foundations for German romanticism. His *Fantasies about Art* (1799) was published after his death from typhoid at the age of twenty-four. In it, he elevated music to the level of visual art and poetry as a means of expressing the sublime, a position which was subsequently justified by the creativity of romantic composers. Ludwig Tieck assisted Wackenroder in the preparation of *Outpourings*, helped August Wilhelm Schlegel (1767–1845) in his translations of the works of Shakespeare, and was the first editor of Novalis's work. Novalis's book of verse *Hymns of the Night* (1799) celebrated death as a means of being reunited with Sophie von Kuhn, his fiancée who had died of tuberculosis at the age of fifteen. The emotional sensitivity and darkness of his free verse had a substantial influence on subsequent German romantic poets.

The brothers August Wilhelm Schlegel and Friedrich Schlegel (1772–1829) helped to develop the future path of romanticism with their scholarship. August's lectures, *On Literature and Art* (Berlin, 1801–1802) and *On Dramatic Art and Literature* (Vienna, 1807–1808), were instrumental in formulating and publicizing the ideas of the romantics. Friedrich's *History of Ancient and Modern Literatures* (1815) also popularized the romantic aesthetic. Together, August and Friedrich published the quarterly periodical *Athenaum* (1798–1800), which spread the ideas of romanticism and published the writings of German romantics.

Heinrich Heine (1797–1856) spread the ideas of German romanticism beyond the borders of Germany. Heine had gone to Paris in 1831 after the revolt in that city, as many foreign romantics had. He lived there until his death. His *Romantic School* (1833–1835) and *On the History and Philosophy in Germany* (1834–1835) were critical of contemporary German culture and its recent historical past. (See readings.) His verse satire, *Germany, A Winter's Tale* (1844) attacked the reactionary feelings which were developing in Germany. This, and his connection with the Young Germany movement which protested against the old order through literature and politics, resulted in his books being banned in Germany.

Romanticism achieved its greatest distinction in Germany in the novel and the short story. Notable in this field were Goethe's *Wilhelm Meister* (1795–1796), a chief source of inspiration for German romantics such as Tieck. Tieck's *Franz Sternbald's Wanderings* (1798), which recounts the travels and adventures of a young artist, and his *History of Mr. William Lovell* (1795–1796), a novel that describes the moral self-destruction of a young intellectual, most clearly show the influence of Goethe. Among the best of his short stories is *Fair Eckbert* (1797), a tale of the supernatural.

Romanticism Elsewhere

Romanticism also influenced literature in other countries. In Russia, Alexander Pushkin (1799–1837) wrote romantic poems, such as *Ruslan and Lyudmila* (1820), based on traditional Russian folk tales. In Poland, Adam Mickiewicz (1798–1855) glorified the Polish countryside in his first collection of poems, *Ballads and Romances* (1821). In Italy, Alessandro Manzoni wrote his historical novel *I Promessi Sposi (The Betrothed*, 1825), considered the greatest Italian novel of the century. In the United States, the poetry and prose of Edgar Allan Poe (1809–1849), such as "The Raven" (1845) and *The Pit and the Pendulum* (1843), portrayed some of the darker themes of romanticism.

ROMANTICISM IN THE VISUAL ARTS

Painting

In France, early signs of romanticism were evident in the art of neoclassical artists. Jacques-Louis David (1748–1825), the greatest of these artists, adhered to the tenets of classical form and composition, but his subjects were decidedly romantic. Jean Auguste Dominique Ingres (1780–1867), a student of David, although a classical painter, explored exotic, oriental subjects in his paintings *La Grande Odalisque* (1814) and *The Turkish Bath* (1859–1863).

Théodore Géricault (1791–1824) was a forerunner of the romantic movement and later came to associate himself with the romantic cry for revolution. He produced the first great masterpiece of French romanticism, *The Raft of the Medusa* (1818–1819). Although the painting is realistic in detail, the use of light and the psychological, political, and philosophical intent of the painting are romantic. (See colour plates.)

Géricault's death in 1824 coincided with the rise of Eugène Delacroix (1798–1863) as the genius of French romantic painters. Delacroix's depiction of an episode in the Greek War of Independence, *The Massacre at Chios* (1824), established him as the leader of the romantic school. His *Liberty Leading the People* (1830), inspired by the 1830 revolution in

France, resulted in his being awarded the Legion of Honour by the new French government. His real impact upon the movement, however, was in the nature of the emotive subject matter he chose for his work. Delacroix's paintings are full of the exotic and the oriental, the medieval and the classical. He looked to poetry, not reality, for his inspiration.

In England, the trend toward romanticism could be seen in the work of John Henry Fuseli (1741–1825) and William Blake (1757–1827). Fuseli was a Swiss-born painter who sought most of his inspiration from literary subjects, particularly Shakespeare, Dante, and Milton. Like his friend Blake, Fuseli enjoyed the fantastic and exotic; his popular painting, *The Nightmare* (1781), borders on the macabre. Blake's most characteristic works were the illustrations of his own poems, as well as the works of Milton and Dante. Both Blake and Fuseli made extensive use of symbolism as they tried to achieve a fusion of the arts in their work, blending poetry and drama, painting and illustration, to achieve an effect that was romantic in intent and inspiration. It was this feature that kept them outside of the mainstream of English romantic painting.

The greatest of all English romantic painters were John Constable (1776–1837) and William Turner (1775–1851). Constable's love of nature was apparent in his many landscapes. In his masterpiece, *The Hay Wain* (1821), he applied a radical modularism to transform a commonplace landscape into an in-depth visual analysis. (See colour plates.) Increasingly, however, his style developed into a more generalized view of nature, replacing observation with expression. Turner's masterpiece, *Rain, Steam and Speed* (1844), introduced the machine into the landscape. Turner disregarded all conventional principles of art. Many of his paintings were a riot of colour and light. His later works anticipated the impressionist style.

In Germany, the greatest master of the romantic school was Caspar David Friedrich (1774–1840). Unlike many of the romantics, Friedrich saw nature as a hostile force. Many of his paintings, such as *The Monk and the Sea* (1808–1809) and *The Sea of Ice* (1823–1824), depict humans and their achievements as insignificant against the power and majesty of nature.

The greatest Spanish painter of the period was Francisco

(Left) *Blake's* Songs of Innocence and Experience *(1789) was a good example of illuminated painting.* (Right) *This was one of several versions Fuseli painted of* The Nightmare.

Friedrich's The Monk and the Sea *(1808-1809) was one of many paintings in which he depicted the insignificance of humanity in the face of nature.*

Goya y Lucientes (1746–1828). Goya's work displayed elements of romanticism in his choice of subject, in his pictorial technique, and in his emphasis on the unconscious mind. Some of his greatest works were his etchings *The Caprices* (1796) and *The Disasters of War* (1810), both of which were psychological examinations of the foibles of humanity and indictments of war. Some of his work (*Man Walking Among the Ghosts, The Sleep of Reason*, and *Scenes of Cannibalism*, for instance) border on the macabre. His best-known paintings were *The Second of May 1808* and *The Third of May 1808* (1814–1815), both indictments of the peninsular campaign of the French Revolutionary War.

The End of Romanticism

The great age of romantic painting was over by 1850. The emphasis on feeling and imagination led some critics to believe that romantics merely wished to escape from reality. The escapism of romanticism was eventually replaced in the mid-nineteenth century by a move to a more realistic depiction of society. The realist school portrayed the social problems, industrial strife, strikes, unemployment, poverty, slums, disease, and vice created by urbanization and industrialization. As violent a reaction to romanticism as the former had been to neoclassicism before it, realism would remain the dominant trend until the 1890s. (See chapter 7.)

Sculpture

It is more difficult to arrive at a definition of romantic sculpture than it is for romantic literature or painting. The focus of sculpture during most of the period was the human body. Although sculptors looked to antiquity for the ideal human form, they expressed sensitivity and feeling in their interpretations of the classical. This resulted in a new, idealized interpretation of Greek culture, an interpretation that was expressed in terms of contemporary life. The emphasis on classical form means that most of the sculptors of the age were considered to be neoclassical sculptors. However, in theme and subject matter many of the sculptors are closely related to the romantic movement. The dominant sculptors of the period were François Rudé (1784–1855), Antonio Canova (1757–1822), John Tobias Sergel (1740–1814), and Bertel Thorwaldsen (1768–1844).

François Rudé was a supporter of Napoleon. After Napoleon's fall from power in 1814, Rudé was forced into exile. There he was appointed sculptor for the Court of the Netherlands. He returned to France in 1828 and produced one of the greatest masterpieces of French romantic sculpture, *Departure of the Volunteers* (also known as *La Marseillaise*, 1833–1836). The visual representation of the fiery patriotism of the French national anthem adorns the Arc de Triomphe in Paris.

The Italian sculptor Antonio Canova (1757–1822) was one of the most popular sculptors of the late eighteenth and early nineteenth centuries. At one time he rejected offers by Emperor Franz II, Catherine the Great, and Napoleon to be their court sculptor. He completed over 168 works, including *Cupid and Psyche* (1787) and the tombs of popes Clement XII and Clement XIV. Canova was strongly influenced by classical proportion and simplicity and frequently used Greek statues as a source of inspiration.

John Tobias Sergel (1740–1814), a German-born Scandinavian, was one of the most influential Swedish sculptors of the eighteenth century. Like Canova, he studied the works of antiquity for inspiration; he was also influenced by Henri Fuseli's romantic imagination, as was evidenced by the sculpture *The Faun* (1774). Sergel became the official sculptor of the Swedish court in 1779.

Although Bertel Thorwaldsen was a Dane, he accomplished his greatest works in Rome, where he lived from 1796 until 1838. He readily accepted commissions in Germany, Poland, Austria, Denmark, Russia, and England. One of his greatest masterpieces was the tomb of Pope Pius VII (1823). His statues were so popular that copies of his work were made almost immediately. Thorwaldsen's contemporaries regarded his sculptures as perfect reincarnations of antiquity, but most twentieth-century critics feel that his work, although visually impressive, is lacking in emotion.

The patriotism of the French national anthem is depicted in Rude's sculpture La Marseillaise.

Antonio Canova's Cupid and Psyche *(1792) was one of his many works with a mythological subject.*

Architecture

The renewed interest in the Middle Ages led to a revival of gothic architecture; architects copied medieval castles, cathedrals, and town halls. Gothic architecture was characterized by the use of the ribbed vault, the pointed arch, and the flying buttress. These architectural elements allowed the construction of taller buildings and larger window openings, which encouraged the development and use of stained glass. By the nineteenth century, architecture erected in the style of the Middle Ages was termed *gothic revival*. Although this gothic revival took place in most European countries, it was in England and Germany that it held the greatest sway.

Horace Walpole (1717–1797) was credited with re-establishing the gothic style in England with the design of his country house, Strawberry Hill (1743). The style became so popular that railway stations, hotels, and many private homes were built in the gothic style or had gothic ornamentation. The best example is the British Houses of Parliament (1840–1860), designed by Sir Charles Barry (1795–1860). Other examples include the Assize Courts building (1859–1864) and the Manchester City Hall (1869–1877) by Alfred Waterhouse and the London Law Courts (1868) by George Edmund Street (1824–1881). The gothic style was also popular in church design; George Gilbert Scott's (1811–1878) Martyr's Memorial (1841) in Oxford is perhaps the best example.

The gothic style was almost as popular in Germany as it was in England. The restoration of the Cologne Cathedral, based on medieval sketches, firmly established the gothic revival in that country. The greatest German architect of the first quarter of the nineteenth century was Karl Friedrich Schinkel (1781–1841), who designed Babelsberg Castle (1834) in the neo-gothic style. Some of the most spectacular buildings in the German-speaking nations built in the nineteenth century—the town halls of Vienna (1872) and Munich (1874) and the Houses of Parliament in Budapest (begun 1885)—were built in the gothic style.

(Left) *The Cologne Cathedral is the largest gothic church in northern Europe and remains the most impressive architectural feature of the city of Cologne.*
(Above right) *The design of Strawberry Hill by Horace Walpole was credited with re-establishing the gothic style in England.*
(Below right) *The design of the British Houses of Parliament was Sir Charles Barry's masterpiece.*

ROMANTICISM IN MUSIC

If romanticism aspired to transcend the immediate present and to emphasize freedom, movement, and passion, then music was perhaps the most romantic of the arts. Romanticism in music embraced fantasy and emotion, sometimes at the expense of musical structure. Early romanticism represented a departure from classicism. Poetry was introduced to the symphonic form. Program music blended poetic, descriptive, and even narrative subject matter by means of imaginative suggestion. Instrumental music became a vehicle for the expression of thoughts that could not be put into words.

Another change that took place during the period was in the nature of the musical audience. Classical composers often created their work for performance in front of a very specific, small, cultured, and socially homogeneous audience. The romantics, on the other hand, composed for posterity, "for some imaginable, ideal audience which, they hoped, would some day understand and appreciate them. . . . The artist was a 'genius' who wrote under 'inspiration,' a prophet even though his message might be rejected."

From Donald J. Grout, *A History of Western Music* (New York: W.W. Norton and Company, 1973), p. 370.

The Emergence of Romanticism

Haydn's *Creation* (1798) and *Seasons* (1800), Mozart's *Don Giovanni* (1787) and *Magic Flute* (1791), and Beethoven's *Fifth* (1807) and *Ninth* (1823) symphonies are often cited as the immediate sources of musical romanticism. Haydn brought a focus upon nature; Mozart, the preoccupation with the inner self; and Beethoven, the passion of the assault on the concept of the "ideal." However, it was not until the work of Franz Schubert (1797–1828) that romanticism began to emerge in music.

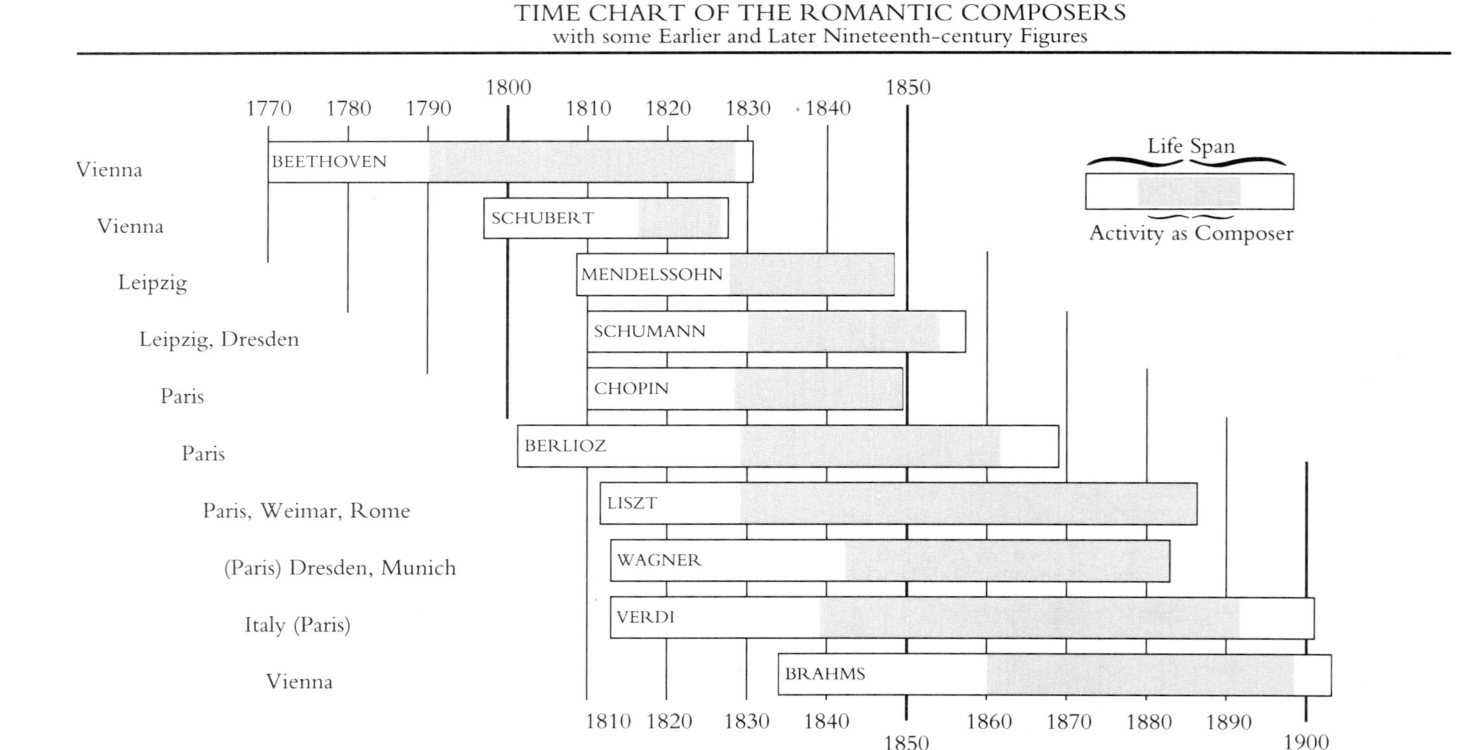

H. W. Janson and Joseph Kerman, *A History of Art and Music,* Published by Harry N. Abrams, Inc., New York

THE CULT OF INDIVIDUAL GENIUS

Ludwig van Beethoven's (1770–1827) career bridged the classical and romantic periods. In technique, Beethoven remained true to classical tenets, but he was heroic in conception and used music as a means of self-expression, an essential element of romanticism. Whether or not the incident which Beethoven relates to his friend, Bettina Bretano, actually occurred, it represents a key element of romanticism: the cult of individual genius.

–Toplitz, August 15, 1813

My good and very dear friend,

Kings and princes can turn out as many professors and privy councillors as they please, grant titles and ribbons, but they cannot produce great men, minds that rise above the human herd and whose task it is to make themselves, for which they must be regarded with respect. When two men like Goethe and myself walk together, these great lords must be shown what we hold to be great. Yesterday, as we were walking back, we met all the Imperial family . . . and Goethe let go my arm to get out of their way onto the side of the road. No good arguing with him, it was impossible to make him take another step ahead. For myself, I pulled my hat down over my eyes and bore down on to the very centre of the company, hands crossed behind my back! Princes and courtiers parted and stood aside, the Archduke Rudolph took off his hat to me, the Empress was the first to salute me; their lordships know me. I saw, to my great amusement, the procession pass before Goethe: he stood there by the roadside, hat in hand, bowing deeply; then I told him off good and proper, allowing no excuses, and I taxed him with all his sins. . . .

Your very loyal friend and your dear brother,
Beethoven.

From Eugene Weber (ed.), *Paths to the Present: Aspects of European Thought from Romanticism to Existentialism* (New York: Dodd, Mead and Co., Inc., 1960), pp. 123–124.

Although Schubert was largely unappreciated during his own time, today he is considered a genius of melody. His lyrics and harmony were romantic in nature, although he retained strong links to the classical tradition. Included among the more than 600 songs he composed are "Die Schöne Müllerin" (1823) and "Ave Maria" (1825).

Schubert was succeeded by Robert Schumann (1810–1856). A pure romantic, Schumann focused on the musical duet as a technique for expression. Works such as *Mondnacht* (1840) and *Die beiden Grenadiere* (1840) are outstanding examples of this genre. Prior to 1840, all of Schumann's work had been designed exclusively for piano, such as *Fantasia in C Major Op. 17* (1836) and a set of symphonic variations entitled *Symphonic Etudes* (1834). Among his later work, he published the *Album for the Young* (1848) made up of pieces for children to play.

Schumann usually wrote the music before he thought of the title, preferring to let the composition form itself. More than any other composer, Schumann's music embodies the depths, contradictions, and tensions of the romantic spirit and has been described in turns as being "ardent and dreamy," "vehement and visionary," and "whimsical and learned."

Music historians consider Karl Maria von Weber's (1786–1826) opera *Der Freischütz* (1820) to be the definitive work that established German romantic opera. His operas *Euryanthe* (1823) and *Oberon* (1826) used supernatural elements in their plots, and in all of his operas nature played an essential role. Weber also composed cantatas, masses, and works for the piano.

The Second Generation of Romantic Composers

Felix Mendelssohn (1809–1847), together with Schumann and Wagner, was part of the second generation of German romantic composers. Mendelssohn began his career as a composer at the age of seventeen when he wrote an overture for *A Midsummer Night's Dream* (1826). He was credited with rediscovering the music of Bach when he performed the *Saint Matthew Passion* in Berlin in 1829. Perhaps his best-known works were his chamber music (the two *Sonatas for Cello and Piano, String Quartets*, and *Octet*) and his dramatic music (*Walpargisnacht, St. Paul*, and *Elijah*).

Richard Wagner (1813–1883) was one of the most influential composers of the nineteenth century. His greatest work was *The Ring of the Nibelungen*, based on legends from German mythology, which comprises four operas—*Das*

Rheingold (1853–1854); *Die Walküre* (1854–1856); *Siegfried* (1856–1869); and *Götterdammerung* (1869–1874). The work was first performed in its entirety in 1876 at Bayreuth in a theatre built to Wagner's specifications. Wagner's romanticism was evident in his use of Nordic and German mythology, his musical technique, and his creation of music-drama. His use of *leitmotive* (representative themes associated with the ideas of the drama) for musical development revolutionized opera. His other major compositions include *The Flying Dutchman* (1841), *Tannhauser* (1845), *Lohengrin* (1845), *Tristan und Isolde* (1859), and *Die Meistersinger von Nürnberg* (1868).

Hector Berlioz (1803–1869) was one of the greatest of the romantic musicians. Berlioz wrote symphonies (*Symphone fantastique* [1830]); religious music (*Requiem* [1835] and *Te Deum* [1849]); music for the stage (*Waverly* [1827] and *Rob Roy* [1832]); and operas (*Cellini* [1838], *Les Troyens* [1863], and *Romeo and Juliet* [1839]). His works frequently required unprecedented orchestration (such as four kettledrums in his *Symphone fantastique*) and huge choruses (he once used 900 singers in a performance of *Te Deum*). Although these occasions frequently led to ridicule by many of his critics and contemporaries, his *Treatise on Modern Instrumentation and Orchestration* (1844) developed the modern concept of the symphony orchestra and was extremely influential.

Gioacchino Rossini (1792–1868) was one of the leading figures of Italian romanticism. His comic operas *The Italian Girl in Algiers* (1813) and *The Barber of Seville* (1816) were his best known works. His debt to literature was evident in the operas *Otello* (1816) and *La Donna del Lago* (1819). Rossini's last opera, *William Tell* (1829), was a masterpiece of grand opera and enjoyed immense success at the Paris Opera House.

Giuseppe Verdi's (1813–1901) operas *Rigoletto* (1851), *La Traviata* (1853), and *Il Trovatore* (1853) are three of the world's best lyric operas. Like many of the romantics, Verdi was inspired by Shakespeare; the librettos for three operas, *Macbeth* (1847), *Otello* (1887) and *Falstaff* (1893), were based on his plays. Many of Verdi's early operas contained choruses that were thinly disguised appeals to Italian nationalism, which made him immensely popular with Italian patriots. Verdi, along with Wagner, dominated opera during the latter half of the nineteenth century and was one of the greatest Italian composers.

The Hungarian Franz Liszt (1811–1886) was one of the most brilliant composers of the romantic era. He wrote over 1200 compositions, including over 400 solo works for the piano. Basing his piano style on that of Frederic Chopin (1810–1849), Liszt took it even further, adding new effects, lyrical melodic qualities, and harmonic innovations. A considerable proportion of Liszt's piano music consisted of arrangements of the symphonic work of earlier composers, such as Berlioz and Beethoven. At the same time, however, he produced a wide range of compositions based on national folk music. Chief among these are his famous nineteen *Hungarian Rhapsodies* (1856). Like many other nineteenth-century composers, however, Liszt did not really understand genuine Hungarian folk tunes but based his work instead on gypsy music.

The variety of Liszt's work is evident in his many short, separately published piano pieces and in several collections of tone pictures, of which the principal ones are the three-part work *Années de pèlerinage* (1850–1877), *Consolations* (1850), and *Harmonies poétiques et religieuses* (1852). These collections help to dispel the myth that the composer was concerned only with spectacular effects. In some of Liszt's later works, he experimented with harmonies that anticipated late nineteenth-century developments in impressionism.

In spite of his outstanding work for piano, Liszt is probably best known for his *Faust Symphony* (1854), which he dedicated to Berlioz. In this work, the composer combined a grandiose program with music of great inspiration, substance, and passion. Its monumental form is justified by the scope and power of the ideas it generates. Liszt was a great influence on the composers of his day, including his son-in-law Richard Wagner.

The Polish composer Frédéric Chopin wrote almost exclusively for the solo piano and is regarded as one of the greatest composers for that instrument. The music is highly melodic and lyrical and was important in the development of piano technique. He composed two concertos and three sonatas for the piano, but he is best known for short ballads, waltzes, and preludes. Chopin's music also reflected his Polish nationalism. Although he lived in Paris after 1831, his works—particularly the mazurkas, waltzes, and polonaises—were strongly influenced by Polish folklore. Chopin was friends with many other romantics, including Heine, Mickiewicz, and Delacroix. His love affair with the female author George Sand was infamous. He died of tuberculosis in 1849.

The romantic era produced some of the most enduring music of all time. Romantic composers broke down the

This painting by Josef Danhauser (1840) depicts Franz Liszt at the piano, with Madame d'Agoult kneeling beside him. Seated are Alfred de Musset and George Sand. Standing in the background are Victor Hugo, Niccolo Paganini, and Gioacchino Rossini. (Detail)

barriers between the arts, combining poetry, drama, and music to achieve an emotional whole. Instrumental music assumed a pre-eminent role. Most of the operas performed today were composed during this period. The ability of music to "express the unexpressible" made it first among the romantic arts.

ROMANTICISM AND POLITICAL MOVEMENTS

Although romanticism was primarily a theory of the arts, it had much in common with national movements. In Germany, Novalis, Schlegel, and Arndt were spokespersons for the struggle for national unity, as were Leopardi in Italy and Mickiewicz in Poland. Greece's struggle against Turkish oppression inspired Delacroix to paint *Greece Expiring under the Ruins of Missolonghi (1822)* and *The Massacre at Chios* (1822–1824) and Hugo to write *Les Orientales* (1829); Byron supported the Greek struggle with his money, and ultimately with his life. In Poland, Hungary, and Italy, romanticism inspired and united people to revolt against foreign control and to establish their own governments. But it was the search for cultural and national identity in Germany that forged the strongest link between nationalism and romanticism.

Romantic writers were nonconformists, politically as well as creatively. As the revolutionary ideals of justice, liberty, and equality were sacrificed to conservatism, romantics became revolutionaries. The goals of liberalism—individual liberty and freedom, equality before the law, and the participation of the people in government—became part of the romantic quest. Byron and Shelley were ardent champions of political liberty; Pushkin participated in the Decembrist Movement, the only significant liberal revolt in Russia in the nineteenth century; Hugo supported the 1848 revolt in France.

Cultural Nationalism

One of the cornerstones of romanticism was cultural nationalism. It had its strongest and earliest expression in Germany. Herder's concept of *volksgeist* (national character), developed in his *Ideas on the Philosophy of the History of Mankind* (1784), became a national crusade under Napoleon's rule. Herder believed that true culture must arise from the common people—the *volk*. The vernacular language and folk tradition of the peasant was superior to that of the French-speaking, cosmopolitan German aristocracy. Folklore became a major source of inspiration for poets, novelists, and scholars. Friedrich Ludwig Jahn (1778–1852), who founded the national gymnasium (high school) movement, and Achim von Arnim (1781–1831), one of the leaders of the Younger School of Romanticism, gave great impetus to this movement in Germany.

Cultural nationalism soon spread beyond the borders of Germany into the general movement of romanticism, particularly in countries struggling to achieve national unity. (See chapter 4.) This led to the formation of historical societies and the publication of national histories and collections of folklore, songs, dances, and dictionaries.

The period 1830 to 1848 was the heyday of romanticism, especially of romantic revolutionaries. The failure of the 1848 revolts to produce long-term results extinguished the emotional spark of both liberalism and romanticism. Liberalism gave way to *realpolitik,* romanticism to realism. Although artists continued to examine the emotional and the subjective, the desire to escape dwindled as the century progressed. Realism became the dominant artistic trend as subjective exploration gave way to realistic action.

RETROSPECTIVE

The romantic artist, like the political revolutionary, rebelled against tradition and authority. Poets, writers, painters, and musicians reacted against the rules of classicism and sought freedom in form and subject matter. For the romantic, imagination was more important than reason, colour more important than construction. Romantic artists wanted the audience or reader to participate in an experience, to feel rather than to think.

The romantic world was a world in flux. Romanticism took Western civilization from the confines of the imperial court to the open seas and the wonders of the far reaches of the world. It took the certainty and permanence of the Age of Reason and tossed it aside for the desire to change and explore. In every sense, the world of the romantics was the bridge between the Age of Enlightenment and our own.

WILLIAM WORDSWORTH: Lyrical Ballads (1798)

The publication of the Lyrical Ballads *ushered in a new age in English poetry. Over the course of the eighteenth century, the diction of poetry and prose had become increasingly diverse. Wordsworth believed that poetry, like prose, should use the language and phrasing of real life rather than the elevated poetic diction that had become common. Although the poems contained in the* Lyrical Ballads *were initially the subject of ridicule because of their language and simplicity, they have become very popular. The preface to* Lyrical Ballads *contains Wordsworth's philosophy of poetry and is considered by many to be the manifesto of romanticism.*

The principal object, then, proposed in these Poems was to choose incidents and situations from common life, and to relate or describe them, throughout, as far as possible in a selection of language really used by men, and at the same time, to throw over them a certain colouring of imagination, whereby ordinary things should be presented to the mind in an unusual aspect; and further, and above all, to make these incidents and situations interesting by tracing in them, truly though not ostentatiously, the primary laws of nature: chiefly, as far as regards the manner in which we associate ideas in a state of excitement. Humble and rustic life was generally chosen, because, in that condition, the essential passions of the heart find a better soil in which they can attain their maturity, are less under restraint, and speak a plainer and more emphatic language; because in that condition of life our elementary feelings coexist in a state of greater simplicity, and, consequently, may be more accurately contemplated, and more forcibly communicated; because the manners of rural life germinate from those elementary feelings, and, from the necessary character of rural occupations, are more easily comprehended, and are more durable; and, lastly, because in that condition the passions of men are incorporated with the beautiful and permanent forms of nature. The language, too, of these men has been adopted (purified indeed from what appear to be its real defects, from all lasting and rational causes of dislike or disgust) because such

William Wordsworth, "Observations Prefixed to *Lyrical Ballads*," in M. Schorer, J. Miles, and G. McKenzie (eds.), *Criticism: The Foundations of Modern Literary Judgement* (New York: Harcourt, Brace and World, Inc., 1948, 1958), pp. 31–35, 39.

men hourly communicate with the best objects from which the best part of language is originally derived; and because, from their rank in society and the sameness and narrow circle of their intercourse, being less under the influence of social vanity, they convey their feelings and notions in simple and unelaborated expressions. Accordingly, such a language, arising out of repeated experience and regular feelings, is a more permanent, and far more philosophical language, than that which is frequently substituted for it by Poets . . .

Taking up the subject, then, upon general grounds, let me ask, what is meant by the word Poet? What is a Poet? To whom does he address himself? And what language is to be expected from him?—He is a man speaking to men: a man, it is true, endowed with more lively sensibility, more enthusiasm and tenderness, who who has a greater knowledge of human nature, and a more comprehensive soul, than are supposed to be common among, mankind; a man pleased with his own passions and volitions, and who rejoices more than other men in the spirit of life that is in him; delighting to contemplate similar volitions and passions as manifested in the goings-on of the Universe, and habitually impelled to create them where he does not find them. To these qualities he has added a disposition to be affected more than other men by absent things as if they were present; an ability of conjuring up in himself passions, which are indeed far from being the same as those produced by real events, yet (especially in those parts of the general sympathy which are pleasing and delightful) do more nearly resemble the passions produced by real events, than any which, from the motions of their own minds merely, other men are accustomed to feel in themselves:—whence, and from practice, he has acquired a greater readiness and power in expressing what he thinks and feels, and especially those thoughts and feelings which, by his own choice, or from the structure of his mind, arise in him without immediate external excitement.

. . . poetry is the spontaneous overflow of powerful feelings: it takes its origin from emotion recollected in tranquillity: the emotion is contemplated till, by a species of reaction, the tranquillity gradually disappears, and an emotion, kindred to that which was before the subject of contemplation, is gradually produced, and does itself actually exist in the mind. In this mood successful composition generally begins, and in a mood similar to this it is carried on; but the emotion, of whatever kind, and in whatever degree, from various causes, is qualified by various pleasures, so that in describing any passions whatsoever, which are voluntarily described, the mind will, upon the whole, be in a state of enjoyment. If Nature be thus cautious to preserve in a state of enjoyment a being so employed, the Poet ought to profit by the lesson held forth to him, and ought especially to take care, that, whatever passions he communicates to his Reader, those passions, if his Reader's mind be sound and vigorous, should always be accompanied with an overbalance of pleasure.

---

1. (a) What is the preferred subject and language of Wordsworth's poetry?
(b) List the reasons that Wordsworth gives for his choice.

2. What did Wordsworth believe to be the role of the poet?

3. Describe the creative process outlined by Wordsworth.

WILLIAM WORDSWORTH:
"Tintern Abbey" (1798)

Romantic poets discarded the neoclassic principles of reason, propriety, and simplicity in favour of individualism, intuition, and a love of nature. Wordsworth's works glorified nature. He described poetry as "the spontaneous overflow of powerful feelings." "Tintern Abbey" expresses the feeling of unity between people and nature.

From Desmond Pacey, *Our Literary Heritage*, 2nd ed. (Toronto: McGraw-Hill Ryerson Ltd., 1982), pp. 240–243.

Lines Composed a Few Miles Above Tintern Abbey on Revisiting the Banks of the Wye during a Tour, July 13, 1798

Five years have past; five summers, with the length
Of five long winters! and again I hear
These waters, rolling from their mountain-springs
With a soft inland murmur.—Once again
Do I behold these steep and lofty cliffs,
That on a wild secluded scene impress
Thoughts of more deep seclusion; and connect
The landscape with the quiet of the sky.
The day is come when I again repose
Here, under this dark sycamore, and view
These plots of cottage-ground, these orchard-tufts,
Which at this season, with their unripe fruits,
Are clad in one green hue, and lose themselves
'Mid groves and copses. Once again I see
These hedge-rows, hardly hedge-rows, little lines
Of sportive wood run wild: these pastoral farms,
Green to the very door; and wreaths of smoke
Sent up, in silence, from among the trees!
With some uncertain notice, as might seem
Of vagrant dwellers in the houseless woods,
Or of some Hermit's cave, where by his fire
The Hermit sits alone.
These beauteous forms,
Through a long absence, have not been to me
As in a landscape to a blind man's eye:
But oft, in lonely rooms, and 'mid the din
Of towns and cities, I have owed to them,
In hours of weariness, sensations sweet,
Felt in the blood, and felt along the heart;
And passing even into my purer mind,
With tranquil restoration:—feelings too
Of unremembered pleasure: such, perhaps,
As have no slight or trivial influence
On that best portion of a good man's life,
His little, nameless, unremembered, acts
Of kindness and of love. Nor less, I trust,
To them I may have owed another gift,
Of aspect more sublime; that blessed mood,
In which the burthen of the mystery,
In which the heavy and the weary weight
Of all this unintelligible world,
Is lightened:—that serene and blessed mood,
In which the affections gently lead us on,—
Until, the breath of this corporeal frame
And even the motion of our human blood
Almost suspended, we are laid asleep
In body, and become a living soul:
While with an eye made quiet by the power
Of harmony, and the deep power of joy,
We see into the life of things.
If this
Be but a vain belief, yet, oh! how oft—
In darkness and amid the many shapes
Of joyless daylight; when the fretful stir
Unprofitable, and the fever of the world,
Have hung upon the beatings of my heart—
How oft, in spirit, have I turned to thee,
O sylvan Wye! thou wanderer thro' the woods,
How often has my spirit turned to thee!
And now, with gleams of half-extinguished thought,
With many recognitions dim and faint,
And somewhat of a sad perplexity,
The picture of the mind revives again:
While here I stand, not only with the sense
Of present pleasure, but with pleasing thoughts
That in this moment there is life and food
For future years. And so I dare to hope,
Though changed, no doubt, from what I was when first
I came among these hills; when like a roe
I bounded o'er the mountains, by the sides
Of the deep rivers, and the lonely streams,
Wherever nature led: more like a man

Flying from something that he dreads, than one
Who sought the thing he loved. For nature then
(The coarser pleasures of my boyish days
And their glad animal movements all gone by)
To me was all in all.—I cannot paint
What then I was. The sounding cataract
Haunted me like a passion: the tall rock,
The mountain, and the deep and the gloomy wood,
Their colours and their forms, were then to me
An appetite; a feeling and a love,
That had no need of a remoter charm,
By thought supplied, not any interest
Unborrowed from the eye.—That time is past,
And all its aching joys are now no more,
And all its dizzy raptures. Not for this
Faint I, nor mourn nor murmur; other gifts
Have followed; for such loss, I would believe,
Abundant recompense. For I have learned
To look on nature, not as in the hour
Of thoughtless youth; but hearing oftentimes
The still sad music of humanity,
Nor harsh grating, though of ample power
To chasten and subdue.—And I have felt
A presence that disturbs me with the joy
Of elevated thoughts; a sense sublime
Of something far more deeply interfused,
Whose dwelling is the light of setting suns,
And the round ocean and the living air,
And the blue sky, and in the mind of man:
A motion and a spirit, that impels
All thinking things. All objects of all thought,
And rolls through all things. Therfore I am still
A lover of the meadows and the woods
And mountains; and of all that we behold
From this green earth; of all the mighty world
Of eye, and ear,—both what they half create,
And what perceive; well pleased to recognise
In nature and the language of the sense
The anchor of my purest thoughts, the nurse,
The guide, the guardian of my heart, and soul
Of all my mortal being.

Nor perchance,
If I were not thus taught, should I the more
Suffer my genial spirits to decay:
For thou art with me here upon the banks
Of this fair river; thou my dearest Friend,
My dear, dear Friend, and in thy voice I catch
The language of my former heart, and read
My former pleasures in the shooting lights
Of thy wild eyes. Oh! yet a little while
May I behold in thee what I was once,
My dear, dear Sister! and this prayer I make,
Knowing that Nature never did betray
The heart that loved her; 'tis her privilege,
Through all the years of this our life, to lead
From joy to joy: for she can so inform
The mind that is within us, so impress
With quietness and beauty, and so feed
With lofty thoughts, that neither evil tongues,
Rash judgements, nor the sneers of selfish men,
Nor greetings where no kindness is, nor all
The dreary intercourse of daily life,
Shall e'er prevail against us, or disturb
Our cheerful faith, that all which we behold
Is full of blessings. Therefore let the moon
Shine on thee in thy solitary walk;
And let the misty mountain-winds be free
To blow against thee: and, in after years,
When these wild ecstasies shall be matured
Into a sober pleasure; when thy mind
Shall be a mansion for all lovely forms,
Thy memory be as a dwelling-place
For all sweet sounds and harmonies; oh! then,
If solitude, or fear, or pain, or grief,
Should be thy portion, with what healing thoughts
Of tender joy wilt thou remember me,
And these my exhortations! Nor, perchance—
If I should be where I no more can hear
Thy voice, nor catch from thy wild eyes these gleams
Of past existence—wilt thou then forget
That on the banks of this delightful stream
We stood together; and that I, so long
A worshipper of Nature, hither came
Unwearied in that service: rather say
With warmer love—oh! with far deeper zeal
Of holier love. Nor wilt thou then forget,
That after many wanderings, many years
Of absence, these steep woods and lofty cliffs,
And this green pastoral landscape, were to me
More dear, both for themselves and for thy sake!

1798

1. What connection is there between the mood of the poet and nature? Give examples.

2. "Wordsworth is a classic example of the romantic idealist who lost his idealism." Account for this statement with reference to the poet's later work. For comparison, you could examine his ideas on slavery as expressed in the *Prelude* in the 1790s with his writing in defense of compensation for slave owners in 1840.

3. Wordsworth's work after 1810 has been assessed as "the most dismal anticlimax of which the history of literature holds record." Defend or refute this statement.

William Wordsworth was one of the leading romantic poets and was poet laureate of England from 1843 to 1850.

SAMUEL TAYLOR COLERIDGE: "Kubla Khan" (1797)

Romanticism has often been characterized as delving into the realm of the supernatural. The romantic artist often tried to tap into the fantastic world of dreams. The unfinished poem "Kubla Khan," based on an opium-induced dream Coleridge had, illustrates another major characteristic of romantic poetry: the love of the mysterious and the exotic.

From Desmond Pacey (ed.), *Our Literary Heritage*, 2nd ed. (Toronto: McGraw-Hill Ryerson Ltd., 1982), pp. 249–251.

Kubla Khan
Or, A Vision in a Dream

In Xanadu did Kubla Khan
A stately pleasure-dome decree:
Where Alph, the sacred river, ran
Through caverns measureless to man
Down to a sunless sea.
So twice five miles of fertile ground
With walls and towers were girded round:
And there were gardens bright and sinuous rills
Where blossomed many an incense-bearing tree;
And here were forests ancient as the hills,
Enfolding sunny spots of greenery.

But oh! that deep romantic chasm which slanted
Down the green hill athwart a cedarn cover!
A savage place! as holy and enchanted
As e'er beneath a waning moon was haunted
By woman wailing for her demon-lover!
And from this chasm, with ceaseless turmoil seething.
As if this earth in fast thick pants were breathing,
A mighty fountain momently was forced:
Amid whose swift half-intermitted burst
Huge fragments vaulted like rebounding hail,
Or chaffy grain beneath the thresher's flail:

And 'mid these dancing rocks at once and ever
It flung up momently the sacred river.
Five miles meandering with a mazy motion
Through wood and dale the sacred river ran,
Then reached the caverns measureless to man,
And sank in tumult to a lifeless ocean:
And 'mid this tumult Kubla heard from far
Ancestral voices prophesying war!

The shadow of the dome of pleasure
Floated midway on the waves;
Where was heard the mingled measure
From the fountain and the caves.
It was a miracle of rare device,
A sunny pleasure-dome with caves of ice!

A damsel with a dulcimer
In a vision once I saw:
It was an Abyssinian maid,
And on her dulcimer she played,
Singing of Mount Abora.
Could I revive within me
Her symphony and song,
To such a deep delight 'twould win me,
That with music loud and long,
I would build that dome in air,
That sunny dome! those caves of ice!
And all who heard should see them there,
And all should cry, Beware! Beware!
His flashing eyes, his floating hair!
Weave a circle round him thrice,
And close your eyes with holy dread,
For he on honey-dew hath fed,
And drunk the milk of Paradise.

---

1. How does Coleridge's style and subject matter differ from that of his friend and fellow contributor to the *Lyrical Ballads*, Wordsworth?

2. (a) List the characteristics of romanticism.
(b) Select two or three of the images created by Coleridge in "Kubla Khan." Explain why each could be characterized as romantic.

3. The last ten lines of the poem describe an inspired romantic. Apply this view to one of Coleridge's darker works, such as "The Rime of the Ancient Mariner."

JOHN KEATS:
"Ode on a Grecian Urn" (1820)

Keats was one of the most talented of the English romantic poets. His "Ode to a Nightingale," "Ode to Autumn," "Ode to Melancholy," "Ode to Psyche," and "Ode on a Grecian Urn" are considered his greatest works.

From Desmond Pacey, *Our Literary Heritage*, 2nd ed. (Toronto: McGraw-Hill Ryerson Ltd., 1982), pp. 310–311.

I

Thou still unravish'd bride of quietness,
Thou foster-child of silence and slow time,
Sylvan historian, who canst thus express
A flowery tale more sweetly than our rhyme:
What leaf-fring'd legend haunts about thy shape
Of deities or mortals, or of both,
In Tempe or the dales of Arcady?
What men or gods are these? What maidens loth?
What mad pursuit? What struggle to escape?
What pipes and timbrels? What wild ecstasy?

II

Heard melodies are sweet, but those unheard
Are sweeter; therefore, ye soft pipes, play on;
Not to the sensual ear, but, more endear'd,
Pipe to the spirit ditties of no tone:
Fair youth, beneath the trees, thou canst not leave
Thy song, nor ever can those trees be bare;
Bold Lover, never, never canst thou kiss,
Though winning near the goal—yet, do not grieve;
She cannot fade, though thou hast not thy bliss,
For ever wilt thou love, and she be fair!

III

Ah, happy, happy boughs! that cannot shed
Your leaves, nor ever bid the Spring adieu;
And, happy melodist, unwearied,
For ever piping songs for ever new;
More happy love! more happy, happy love!
For ever warm and still to be enjoy'd,
For ever panting, and for ever young;
All breathing human passion far above,
That leaves a heart high-sorrowful and cloy'd,
A burning forehead, and a parching tongue.

IV

Who are these coming to the sacrifice?
To what green altar, O mysterious priest,
Lead'st thou that heifer lowing at the skies,
And all her silken flanks with garlands drest?

What little town by river or sea shore,
   Or mountain-built with peaceful citadel,
      Is emptied of this folk, this pious morn?
And, little town, thy streets for evermore
   Will silent be; and not a soul to tell
      Why thou art desolate, can e'er return.

V
O Attic shape! Fair attitude! with brede
   Of marble men and maidens overwrought,
With forest branches and the trodden weed;
   Thou, silent form, dost tease us out of thought
As doth eternity: Cold Pastoral!
   When old age shall this generation waste,
      Thou shalt remain, in midst of other woe
Than ours, a friend to man, to whom thou say'st,
   'Beauty is truth, truth beauty,'—that is all
   Ye know on earth, and all ye need to know.

---

1. What characteristics of romanticism are evident in the poem?

2. *Keats early death at the age of twenty-six saved him from losing his dreams like many of his contemporaries.*

Account for this statement with reference to Keats's radicalism and his categorization as the "last of the great romantic poets," even though he was the first among them to die.

PERCY BYSSHE SHELLEY: "Ode to the West Wind" (1822)

Percy Bysshe Shelley was one of the most highly regarded of the romantic poets. His intellect, originality, and powerful lyrics earned him high praise. "Ode to the West Wind" is one of his best-known works. It was published after his death in a boating accident in 1822.

From Desmond Pacey, *Our Literary Heritage*, 2nd. ed. (Toronto: McGraw-Hill Ryerson Ltd., 1982), pp. 292–294.

I
O Wild West Wind, thou breath of Autumn's being,
Thou, from whose unseen presence the leaves dead
Are driven, like ghosts from an enchanter fleeing,

Yellow, and black, and pale, and hectic red,
Pestilence-stricken multitudes: O thou,
Who chariotest to their dark wintery bed

The winged seeds, where they lie cold and low,
Each like a corpse within its grave, until
Thine azure sister of the Spring shall blow

Her clarion o'er the dreaming earth, and fill
(Driving sweet buds like flocks to feed in air)
With living hues and odours plain and hill:

Wild Spirit, which art moving everywhere;
Destroyer and preserver; hear, O, hear!

II
Thou on whose stream, 'mid the steep sky's commotion,
Loose clouds like earth's decaying leaves are shed,
Shook from the tangled boughs of Heaven and Ocean,

Angels of rain and lightning: there are spread
On the blue surface of thine aery surge,
Like the bright hair uplifted from the head

Of some fierce Maenad, even from the dim verge
Of the horizon to the zenith's height,
The locks of the approaching storm. Thou dirge

Of the dying year, to which this closing night
Will be the dome of a vast sepulchre,
Vaulted with all thy congregated might

Of vapours, from whose solid atmosphere
Black rain, and fire, and hail will burst: O, hear!

III
Thou who dist waken from his summer dreams
The blue Mediterranean, where he lay,
Lulled by the coil of his crystalline streams,

Beside a pumice isle in Baiae's bay,
And saw in sleep old palaces and towers
Quivering within the wave's intenser day,

All overgrown with azure moss and flowers
So sweet, the sense faints picturing them! Thou
For whose path the Atlantic's level powers

Cleave themselves into chasms, while far below
The sea-blooms and the oozy woods which wear
The sapless foliage of the ocean, know

Thy voice, and suddenly grow gray with fear,
And tremble and despoil themselves: O, hear!

IV
If I were a dead leaf thou mightest bear;
If I were a swift cloud to fly with thee;
A wave to pant beneath thy power, and share

The impulse of thy strength, only less free
Than thou, O uncontrollable! If even
I were as in my boyhood, and could be

The comrade of thy wanderings over Heaven,
As then, when to outstrip thy skiey speed
Scarce seemed a vision; I would ne'er have striven

As thus with thee in prayer in my sore need.
Oh, lift me as a wave, a leaf, a cloud!
I fall upon the thorns of life! I bleed!

A heavy weight of hours has chained and bowed
One too like thee: tameless, and swift, and proud.

V
Make me thy lyre, even as the forest is:
What if my leaves are falling like its own!
The tumult of thy mighty harmonies

Will take from both a deep, autumnal tone,
Sweet though in sadness. Be thou, Spirit fierce,
My spirit! Be thou me, impetuous one!

Drive my dead thoughts over the universe
Like withered leaves to quicken a new birth!
And, by the incantation of this verse,

Scatter, as from an unextinguished hearth
Ashes and sparks, my words among mankind!
Be through my lips to unawakened earth

The trumpet of a prophecy! O, Wind,
If Winter comes, can Spring be far behind?

1. What is the mood of the poet? How is the mood conveyed to the reader?

2. "Ode to the West Wind" must be read on more than one level. Not only is the author describing an autumn storm, but he is also referring to the process of revolutionary change. Reread the poem and explain its allusion to the forces of revolution and reaction that dominated the political climate of Europe during the period.

3. In chart form, outline to what extent each of the four poems in this chapter complies with the requirements of romantic poetry outlined in the preface to the *Lyrical Ballads*.

HEINRICH HEINE:
German Romanticism (1836)

Heinrich Heine was a German poet, critic, and journalist. A great lyric poet and one of the most brilliant minds of the nineteenth century, Heine's prose was often bitterly satirical and offered a sharply perceptive commentary on his times. The following selection is taken from The Romantic School. *At the time, Heine was being attacked by socialists, radicals, and conservatives for his sympathy toward France. This essay responded to his critics.*

Why Did the Germans Take to the Romantic School?

The political conditions in Germany were then especially favorable to the Christian Old-German movement. "Poverty teaches us to pray," says the proverb, and as a matter of fact, never was Germany in greater distress; hence people were more inclined to prayer, religion, and Christianity. There are no people more devoted to their princes than the Germans. What grieved them even more deeply than the sad condition to which their country had been reduced by war and foreign domination was the melancholy sight of their vanquished princes grovelling at the feet of Napoleon. The whole country resembled those faithful old servants of great houses we often see on the stage, who feel the humiliations of their masters more profoundly than the masters themselves; who secretly weep bitter tears when the family plate is to be sold, and even buy aristocratic wax-tapers with their own savings, so that the plebian tallow candles may not be seen on the gentlefolk's tables.

This general depression found relief in religion, and there arose a pietistic surrender to the will of God, from whom alone help could be expected. For indeed, what other help could avail against Napoleon? No longer was reliance placed on earthly armies. All eyes turned expectantly toward heaven.

We could have made our peace with Napoleon. But our princes, though they were hopeful that God would free them, thought that the united strength of the people could also be of great help. With this in view, they sought to arouse a feeling of solidarity among them, and even the most eminent personages now spoke of a German nation, of a common German Fatherland, of the union of Christian-German races, of a united Germany. We were commanded to become patriots—and patriots we became; for we do as our princes command.

But one must not confuse the term patriotism as here used with what it implies for the French. The patriotism of the Frenchman consists of the fact that his heart is warmed by it; as a result, it expands, spreads, and with its love no longer embraces only his next of kin, but also all of France, the land of civilization. The patriotism of the German, on the other hand, makes his heart narrower, so that it contracts like leather in the cold—he hates whatever is foreign, and does not wish to be a citizen of the world, or of Europe, but only a cabined and cribbed German. Hence that idealized churlishness which was erected into a system by Herr Jahn, and thus commenced that shabby, crude, unwashed opposition to that holiest and most glorious sentiment ever felt in Germany—that humanitarianism, that universal brotherhood of man, that cosmopolitanism to which our great spirits, Lessing, Herder, Schiller, Goethe, Jean Paul and all the learned men of Germany, did homage.

What happened soon thereafter in Germany is too well known. When God, snow, and the Cossacks destroyed the best of Napoleon's forces, we Germans received the all-highest order to liberate ourselves from the foreign yoke; we became enflamed with manly rage at the servitude we had so long endured; and we were filled with an inspiration drawn from the good tunes and bad lines of Korner's songs, and we won our freedom. For we do as our princes command.

At the moment we were preparing for this struggle, a school of thought, most inimical to all that was French and glorifying all that was German in art and life, naturally prospered. The Romantic School then worked hand in hand with the efforts of the governments and secret societies, and A. W. von Schlegel conspired against Racine with the same end in view as Minister Stein against Napoleon. The Romantic School followed the current of the time—that is, the current which was reverting to its source. When at last German patriotism and German nationalism triumphed, the German-Christian Romantic School also triumphed with equal decisiveness, and "Neo-German-Religious-Patriotic Art" as well. Napoleon, that great classicist—as classical as Alexander and Caesar—succumbed, and Messrs. August Wilhelm von Schlegel and Friedrich Schlegel, the little Romantics, as romantic as Tom Thumb and Puss-in-Boots, were victorious. But here too as everywhere else reaction followed on the heels of excess. Just as spiritual Christianity represented a reaction against the brutal sway of the materialism of Imperial Rome; as the renewed love of joyous Greek art and learning was a reaction against Christian spiritualism which degenerated into imbecile asceticism; as the reawakening of medieval romance was a reaction against the prosaic imitation of ancient, classical art—so we now witness a recoil against the restoration of Catholic-Feudal thought and that knighthood and priesthood which had been preached in word and image under the most amazing forms. When the highly praised models—the masters of the Middle Ages—were extolled and admired, their excellence was attributed to the fact that they believed in the subjects they were portraying. It was said that in their artless simplicity they were capable of greater achievements than their successors who lacked faith, although they possessed more advanced techniques;—and that it was this very faith which had wrought miracles in their souls. And indeed, how else could one explain the glories of Fra Angelico da Fiesole or the poetry of Brother Ottfried? Hence it followed that those artists who took art seriously, and hoped to reproduce the divine distortions of these wonder-paintings, and the saintly awkwardness of those wonder-poems—in short, to capture the ineffable mysticism of the ancient works of art—decided to repair to the same Hippocrene from which the old masters have drawn their miraculous inspiration. They made pilgrimmages to Rome, where the vicar of Christ was to strengthen consumptive German art with the milk of the she-ass. They betook themselves to the bosom of the only soul-saving Roman Catholic Apostolic Church. Many of the adherents of the Romantic School needed no formal conversion. Herr Gorres and Herr Klemens Brentano, for example, were born Catholics, and they merely renounced their former free thinking. Others like Friedrich Schlegel, Herr Ludwig Tieck, Novalis, Werner, Schutz, Carove, Adam Muller, etc., had been brought up in the Protestant Church—and their conversion to Catholicism required a public declaration. Here I have only named the writers; the number of painters who abjured their evangelical faith in droves—and along with it, reason—was much greater.

When the German world saw these young people waiting in line for tickets of admission to the Roman Catholic Church, and again crowding into the old prisonhouse of the spirit, from which their fathers had with so much labor succeeded in delivering themselves, they shook their heads with concern. But when they discovered that the propaganda of priests and Junkers which had conspired against the religious and political freedom of Europe had a hand in this game too, and that it was really Jesuitism which was enticing German youth to destruction with the dulcet notes of romance—like the Pied Piper of Hamelin—then great disaffection and burning indignation took hold of the friends of Protestantism and of freedom of thought.

I have mentioned freedom of thought and Protestantism in one breath; and I hope that even though I belong in Germany to the Protestant Church, I shall not be charged with partisanship in her favor. Without partiality I have classed freedom of thought and Protestantism; for there is, in very fact, a friendly relation between them in Germany. They are closely allied, like mother and daughter. Though we may reproach the Protestant Church with many instances of frightful narrowness, we must still grant, to her immortal credit, that she allowed free inquiry into the Christian religion, and liberated our mind from the yoke of authority, so that bold investigation could take root, and learning and science develop independently. German philosophy, though it would at the present time rank itself by the side of, even above, the Protestant Church—is nevertheless always her daughter; and as such, obliged to retain an indulgent reverence for her mother—and the interests of her family require alliance between them when both are threatened by a common enemy, Jesuitism. All friends of free thought and Protestantism, sceptics and believers, rose at once against the restorers of Catholicism, and, it goes without saying, that the liberals too, who were interested in defending bourgeois political freedom than philosophy or Protestantism, made common cause with them. In Germany, the liberals have always been at the same time professors of philosophy and theologians, and they always fight for the ideas of freedom, no matter that it takes a purely political, philosophical, or theological form.

---

1. According to Heine, why did the Germans take to the romantic school?

2. What differences does Heine outline between German and French nationalism?

3. According to Heine, why did the Germans reject romanticism?

4. Write a speech by Heine to be given to the National Assembly in Frankfurt in 1848. In it have Heine address the issue of the narrow-minded or restrictive patriotism sweeping Germany in the mid-nineteenth century.

VICTOR HUGO: Romanticism and Liberalism (1830)

Victor Hugo was a poet, novelist, dramatist, and the leader of the romantic movement in France. He played an active role in politics and lived in exile under the rule of Napoleon III, becoming a national hero under the Third Republic. In the preface to his play Hernani *(1830), Hugo outlined the relationship between liberalism in art and politics.*

Some weeks ago the author of this play wrote these words about a poet who died before his time:

In his hour of literary strife and storm, whom shall we pity—the dying or those who still fight? It is surely sad to see a poet who leaves us at the age of twenty, a lyre shattered, a future that will not be. But should we not also give sleep its due? Why may not they have their rest too, those upon whom calumny and insult, hatred, envy, secret intrigues and foul treason are ceaselessly heaped; the loyal men against whom disloyal war is raged; the dedicated men who wish only to give their country one more freedom—the freedom of art and the intellect; the toiling men who peaceably perform the tasks which conscience assigns them, but who are on the one hand the prey of the vile schemes of censors and policemen and on the other only too frequently the victims of the ingratitude of the very people for whom they toil? Have they no right to turn envious eyes now and then upon those who have already fallen and rest now in the tomb? *"Invideo,"* said Luther in the cemetery at Worms, *"invideo, quia quiescunt."**

Yet what does it matter? Be of good heart, you who are young! Harsh as our present may be made, the future will be good. In the final analysis, romanticism (to which so many false definitions have been given) is, considered as a combatant, nothing but *liberalism* in literature. That is its true definition. Almost all right-thinking people—and their number is great—already understand the truth of this definition, and soon liberalism in literature will have no less popularity than liberalism in politics: for the work is already far advanced. Freedom in art, freedom in society—these are the double goals toward which all consistent and logical minds should march in single step; these are the double banners around which rally all the youth, who today are so strong and so patient (a very few excepted, and even these will be enlightened); and then, with this youth and at its head, will come the elite of the generation which came before us, all those wise old men who recognized after a first moment of mistrust and inquiry that the deeds of their sons were the consequence of their own deeds and that freedom of literature is the daughter of political freedom. In vain will the Ultras of every species, classicists and monarchists, lend each other aid in the endeavour to rebuild the Old Regime in its entirety, in society and literature. Their whole shaky edifice will topple under the blows of every advance made by the country, every development of intellectual life, every gain of liberty. Their reactionary endeavors will serve a purpose after all is done. In revolutions every change results in progress. It is one of the merits of truth and freedom that they are served equally by what is done for them and against them. Now we have witnessed all the great accomplishments of our fathers and leave the old social order behind: it is possible that we shall not also leave the old form of poetry behind? For a new people—a new art. Although they will admire the literature of Louis XIV, which benfitted his monarchy so well, France—the France of our own day, the nineteenth century, which received its freedom from Mirabeau and its power from Napoleon—will be able to produce its own individual and national literature.—*Letter to the Publishers of M. Dovalle.*

May the author of this play be pardoned for quoting himself. His weak words

* "I envy those who are at rest."

Victor Hugo was the most important of the French romantic writers.

are not such as to engrave themselves on men's memories and so he must repeat them often. In any case, it may well be fitting at this moment to place before his readers the two pages I have just transcribed. Not that this play of mine can deserve in any way the fine name of *new art* or *new poetry*; far from it. But it's as true that the principle of freedom in literature has made a step forward, that progress has been made not in the field of art—this play is too slight a thing—but in the public, and that at least in one respect some portion of the predictions which I have ventured has come true.

There was certainly some danger in changing one's audience in this way, in risking upon the stage trial efforts which hitherto had been entrusted only to paper, *which puts up with no matter what;* the book-reading public is quite different from the playgoing public and there was reason to fear that the latter would reject what the former had accepted. This has not happened. The principle of literary freedom, which the public which reads and thinks has already understood, has also been adopted with equal completeness by the immense crowd which thirsts for pure artistic experience and nightly floods the theatres of Paris. The people's voice, loud and strong like the voice of God, proclaims that henceforth poetry shall bear the same device as politics: TOLERANCE AND FREEDOM!

Now the poet may come, for he has a public!

And the public desires freedom in its proper form, harmonized with order in the state and with art in its literature. Freedom has a wisdom of its own, without which it is not complete. It is well that D'Aubignac's old rule book of dramatic art should perish along with Cuja's old book of customary law; it is still better that a people's literature should succeed a court literature; but it is best that an inner purpose should be at work within all these innovations. Let freedom do what it wills, but let it do it well. In literature as in society, we need neither ceremonials nor anarchy but laws, neither red-heeled aristocrats nor red-capped revolutionaries.

This is what the public wants, and rightly. As for us, in deference to that public which has so indulgently welcomed a trial effort which deserved so little indulgence, we now offer it this play as it has been staged. The day may come to publish it as it was first conceived by the author, indicating and discussing the changes required by the stage. Such critical details may not be without their interest and their lessons, but today they would look like minutiae. Freedom of art has been accepted and the principal question is decided: why tarry on secondary problems? In any event, we shall return to them some day, and we shall also discuss then in great detail, in order to destroy it by argument and fact, that censorship of the stage which is the sole obstacle to freedom of the theatre now that the public is not an obstacle. At our own risk and peril (because we are dedicated to art and its works), we shall attempt to depict the myriad misdeeds of this petty inquisition of the intellect, which, like that other Holy Office, possesses its secret judges, its masked executioners, its tortures, mutilations and penalties of death. We shall rip off, if we can, the swaddling clothes in which the police have shamefully swathed the theatre even today, in the nineteenth century.

Now my duty is only to express gratitude and thanks. From the bottom of his heart the author of this play expresses his gratitude and thanks to the public. The public has given this work generous protection against numerous enmities, not because the play displays talent but because it is dedicated to honesty and liberty, to which the public is also dedicated. Thanks be then to the public, and to that mighty generation of our youth which has given aid and favor to the work of a young man who has the same sincerity and independence as they! It is for them above all that he works, because the applause of this elite of intelligent, logical and consistent youth, true liberals in literature as in politics—a noble generation which does not balk at opening its eyes wide to look upon truth and to receive light from either side—would be very great glory indeed.

---

1. Outline the characteristics of liberalism in the arts.

2. Why does Hugo direct his comments to the young generation?

3. What reasons did Hugo have for feeling optimistic in 1830? Was his optimism justified? Why or why not?

ANALYSIS AND APPLICATION

1. Write a biographical profile of an artist of the romantic period. Include an annotated list of his or her major works.

2. Choose a romantic painting and write a poem or short story that captures the "feeling" of the painting.

3. Defend or refute the statement: *Romantic architecture was incapable of new invention.*

4. A love of nature was one of the central themes of romanticism. Examine the change in the feeling for nature that was evident in English romantic painting.

5. The romantic era was one of the greatest eras of poetry. Compare and contrast English, French, and German romantic poetry.

6. Defend or refute the statement: *Of all the arts, that which lends itself least to romantic expression is sculpture.* Use evidence to support your position.

7. Richard Wagner believed that opera represented a fusion of equally important contributions of poetic language, vocal and instrumental music, dance, acting, and stage design. Show how the Festival House at Beyreuth designed by Wagner fits into this concept of *Gesamtkunstwerk.*

8. Consider the present age. Discuss whether you consider it to be romantic or realistic.

9. Was romanticism a cause of nationalism? Discuss.

Théodore Géricault
(1791–1824) The Raft of the Medusa, *1818–1819.*

The inspiration for this work was an actual event—the Medusa, *a French government vessel, foundered off the coast of Africa. Only a handful of the crew survived after many days of hardship on a makeshift raft. In an attempt to ensure authenticity, Géricault had a scale model of the raft constructed and invited survivors to pose for him. The romantic style enabled him to depict the heroic drama of the event as well as the sense of survival in humanity pitted against the power of nature.*

Musée du Louvre, Paris © R.M.N.

John Constable
(1776–1837) The Hay Wain, *1821.*

Constable used a phrase from Wordsworth—"One brief moment caught from fleeting time"—to describe what he hoped to accomplish with his art. His intense feeling for nature is evident in all his landscapes, particularly this view of a friend's house on the Stour, near Flatford Mill, England. The painting made such an impression on Delacroix when it was exhibited at the Paris salon in 1824 that he repainted the background of his painting The Massacre at Chios *using Constable's techniques.*

Eugène Delacroix
(1798–1863)
Liberty Leading the People,
1830.

This painting celebrates the 1830 uprising that deposed Charles X and put Louis-Philippe, the "republican king," in power. The allegorical figure of Liberty leads a surge of ordinary citizens over the barricades in a revolt to regain their rights. Delacroix painted himself into the painting as the respectable student in the top hat on Liberty's right.

Musée du Louvre, Paris © R.M.N.

Gustave Courbet
(1817–1877)
The Stone Breakers, *1849.*

Courbet's work was a reaction against the romantic emphasis on feeling and imagination. The artist must, he said, rely on his own direct experience. Courbet's realism, as well as his social and political leanings, are evident in his depiction of two men—one too old, one too young—whom he had met on the road to Ornans. Rather than idealize his subjects, Courbet painted them at their back-breaking labour.

Staatlichen Kunstsammlungen
Dresden, Reinhold, Leipzig-Mölkau

Edgar Degas
(1834–1917)
L'Absinthe, *1876.*

Degas painted these two lonely people off centre to suggest a space larger than he shows in the painting. The two people, who seem preoccupied with their own thoughts, are Marcellin Desboutin, a painter, and the actress Ellen André. They posed for this painting in the Nouvelle-Athenes Café in Paris, which was popular with impressionist painters. The title comes from absinthe, a liqueur so potent that it was outlawed.

Musée d'Orsay, Paris

Rembrandt van Rijn
(1606–1669) The Night Watch, *1642.*

In his most famous work, Rembrandt used the baroque techniques of chiaroscuro *(the use of light and shade), dramatic composition, and movement to elevate the traditional Dutch civic portrait to new heights. In this group portrait, the individuals are subordinate to the actions of the group. The title* The Night Watch *is a nickname which came into popular use around 1800 when the painting had become so dark with dirt and discoloured varnish that it looked like a night scene. (Its proper title is* The Corporalship of Captain Banning Cocq's Civic Guards.*) Originally the painting depicted thirty-four people, but three disappeared in the eighteenth century when the painting was cut off to make it fit into the town hall.*

Rijksmuseum – Stiching, Amsterdam

Antoine Watteau
(1684–1721) The Embarkation for Cythera, *1717.*

This rococo work was Watteau's enrolment picture for the Academy in Paris. Because The Embarkation for Cythera *did not fit into any of the established categories, the category of* fêtes galantes, *or paintings showing lovers in pastoral settings, was created. The painting depicts a group of courtiers and their ladies preparing to depart for the mythical island of Cythera, the island of love. The painting was inspired by a contemporary play and introduced a new style of art. Watteau rejected the formality and restraint of classicism in favour of the more playful rococo style.*

Jean Honoré Fragonard ►
(1732–1806) The Swing, *1766.*

Although Fragonard engaged in a variety of different painting styles throughout his career, he is best known for the lighthearted spontaneity of his amorous scenes. The Swing *captures the sophistication and frivolity of the rococo style which was popular with the French aristocracy of the mid-eighteenth century. The flirtatious scene was commissioned by the Baron de St. Julien, who asked Fragonard to paint his mistress on a swing.*

Jacques-Louis David
(1748–1825)
The Oath of the Horatii, *1784.*

The simplicity and severity of the poses and the bare space, clear lighting, and sober colours of this painting are a radical departure from the rococo style. David's treatment of the Roman virtues of self-sacrifice and civic duty coincided with the prevailing philosophical and social outlook in France just prior to the French Revolution. The work was seen as a criticism of the ancien régime and was heralded as the manifesto of neoclassicism.

Francisco de Goya y Lucientes
(1746–1828) The Third of May 1808, *1814.*

This painting commemorates the 1808 uprising by the citizens of Madrid against the French occupation forces during the Napoleonic Wars. The painting is strikingly modern and marks a turning point in the history of modern art. Goya's intent was to portray the victims of war, not the heroics of the battlefield. The soldiers in the painting are faceless and emotionless; the focus of attention is on the defiance, hatred, and terror of the martyred victims.

Henri Matisse
(1869–1954) The Red Studio, *1911.*

Matisse was the central figure of fauvism, *a style which experimented with colour and the effects of distortion. Matisse rejected the traditional use of colour in favour of a bold, sometimes violent, contrast of tones. Fauvism was the first of the avant-garde movements in art in the twentieth century.*

Oil on canvas, 181 × 219.1 cm. Collection, The Museum of Modern Art, New York. Mrs. Simon Guggenheim Fund.

Marcel Duchamp
(1887–1969)
Nude Descending a Staircase, *1912.*

This work is the climax of Duchamp's cubist period and is one of the most famous twentieth-century works of art. The painting superimposes five successive images of movement to achieve an effect similar to multiple-exposure photography. The painting caused a scandal when it was exhibited at the Armory Show in New York in 1913. One critic called it an "explosion in a tile works."

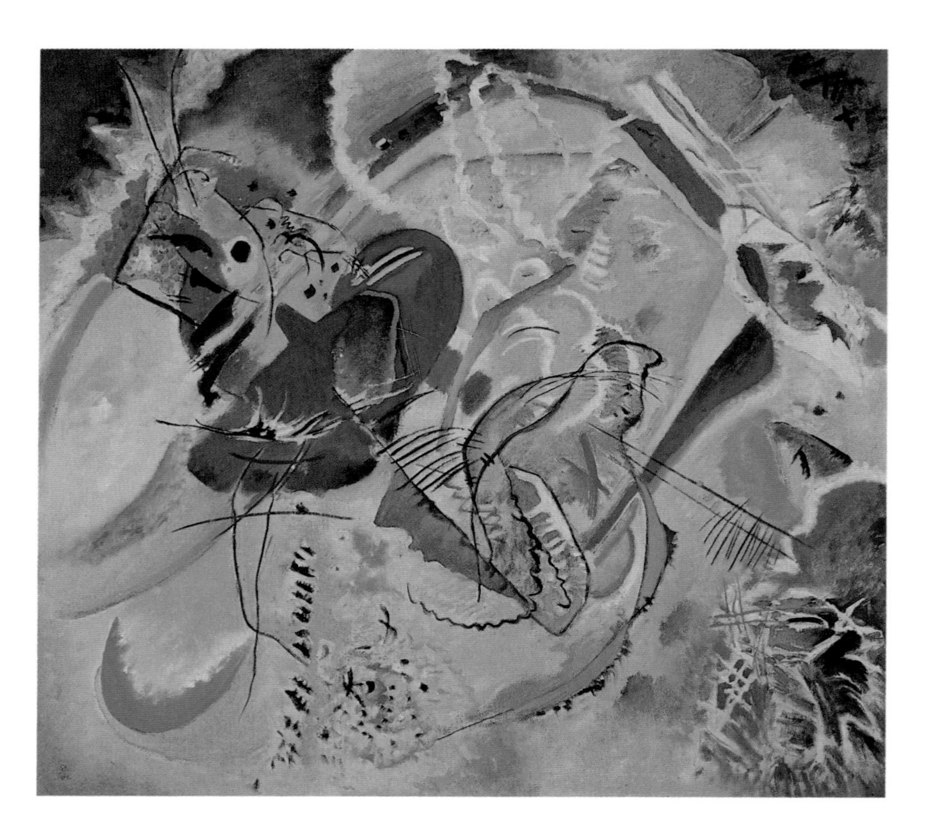

Wassily Kandinsky
(1866–1944) Improvisation 35, *1914.*

Kandinsky was one of the most influential artists of his generation and was the founder of abstract expressionism. *He developed two groups of works:* compositions—*arrangements of geometric shapes which were consciously planned and ordered—and* improvisations *such as the one shown here—paintings that were shaped by the subconscious rather than by preconceived themes. This painting illustrates Kandinsky's belief that colour is the basis for the expression of emotions in visual art. The title was intended to call music to mind.*

Öffentliche Kunstsammlung Basel Kunstmuseum. Colorphoto Hans Hinz. © Wassily Kandinsky 1991/ VIS*ART Copyright Inc.

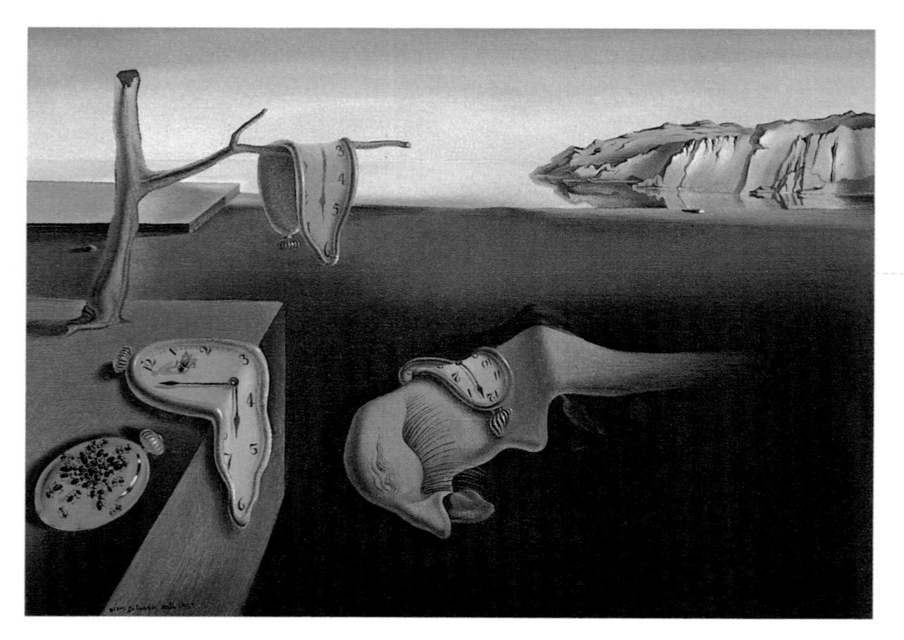

Salvadore Dali
(1904–1989) The Persistence of Memory, *1931.*

Dali once said of his paintings: "I register without choice and with all possible exactitude the dictates of my subconscious, my dreams, the manifestation of that obscure world discovered by Freud." In perhaps his most famous work, Dali sought to express the inner workings of the mind through an allegorical dream landscape in which unrelated and unrealistic images are combined with disturbingly realistic objects.

Oil on canvas, 24.1 × 33 cm. Collection, The Museum of Modern Art, New York. Given anonymously.

Pierre August Renoir
(1841–1919)
Le Moulin de la Galette, *1876.*

This is one of the paintings in which Renoir depicted the pastimes of lower and middle class Parisians under the Third Republic. The painting is an impressionist masterpiece and illustrates a new approach in technique. La Galette was an open-air dance hall popular with working class people, students, and artists. Renoir painted the canvas over a number of weeks entirely on the spot.

Musée d'Orsay, Paris

Georges Seurat
(1859–1891)
A Sunday Afternoon on the Island of La Grande-Jatte, *1884–1886.*

Although displayed at the last impressionist exhibition in 1886, La Grande-Jatte *was the spearhead of a new movement,* neoimpressionism. *Seurat was a painter-theoretician who developed his technique by applying new scientific theories on colour to his paintings. His technique of* pointillism—*a method of applying paint in isolated dots of pure colour—was the hallmark of this style.* La Grande-Jatte *created a scandal when it was exhibited and the majority of artists and critics ridiculed the new technique.*

Oil on canvas, 207.6 × 308 cm. Helen Birch Bartlett Memorial Collection, 1926. 224 photograph

Paul Cézanne
(1839–1906) Mont Sainte-Victoire, *1885–1887.*

Unlike the rest of the impressionists, Cézanne was more interested in structure than the effects of light. Like Monet, he painted the same subject many times. This painting is one of approximately sixty that he did depicting Mont Sainte-Victoire and the surrounding landscape. The painting is a good illustration of the impressionist technique of creating depth through gradations of colour rather than perspective. This technique gives a simultaneous perception of flatness and depth.

Four by Five/Superstock

Vincent Van Gogh
(1853–1890) The Starry Night, *1889.*

Van Gogh's work reflects the second reaction to impressionism: expressionism. *In* The Starry Night *everything seems to be in motion; only the church offers any feeling of stability as Van Gogh transforms the sky as we see it into a vision entirely his own. The painting was executed between attacks of hallucination while Van Gogh was in the asylum at Saint Remy. His expressive use of colour had a profound effect on the painters who followed him.*

Oil on canvas, 73.7 × 92.1 cm. Collection, The Museum of Modern Art, New York. Acquired through the Lillie P. Bliss Bequest.

Claude Monet
(1840–1926)
Rouen Cathedral, West Façade, Sunlight, *1894.*

Monet painted a series of twenty-six views of the Rouen Cathedral. With scientific precision, he depicted the movement of light over the cathedral from the same point of view, but at different times of the day and in different climatic conditions. He used the gothic façade of the cathedral more as a moderator of light than as a subject.

National Gallery of Art, Washington. Chester Dale Collection. Canvas 1.002 m × 0.660 m.

Pablo Picasso ►
(1881–1973)
Les Demoiselles D'Avignon, *1907.*

This work is really a chronicle of the development of cubism. Although not a fully resolved cubist composition, it illustrates the abstraction of natural objects, the use of multiple viewpoints, the lack of depth, and the severe composition that became the hallmarks of the style. Cubism was perhaps the most important of the avant-garde movements of the twentieth century.

Oil on canvas, 243.9 × 233.7 cm. Collection, The Museum of Modern Art, New York. Acquired through the Lillie P. Bliss Bequest. © Pablo Picasso 1991/ VIS*ART Copyright Inc.

PART THREE

From Optimism to Destruction, 1848 to 1918

To the industrializing world of the mid-nineteenth century, nothing seemed impossible. New technologies, expanding markets, and growing middle-class power convinced most societies of Western civilization that nothing lay in the way of continued progress and global enlightenment. By 1918, however, that optimistic world view lay in ruins.

As Western society rapidly transformed itself from a rural base to an urban one, new problems and issues arose for governments to face. In the eighteenth century, it was the middle class that had demanded its political say in the running of the nation; in the nineteenth century, it would be the workers and other disenfranchised groups, such as women and blacks, who would begin to demand equal rights.

A new generation of political philosophers appeared in the mid-1800s and, like their Enlightenment predecessors, they called into question many of the existing values and systems. New questions were raised: What role should government play in the economy? Why should the rights to vote and hold public office be restricted by wealth, race, or sex? How may wealth be more equitably distributed among all members of society? And what should be the nature of the relationship between the individual and the state and between sovereign states with one another?

By the end of the century, new forces emerged to challenge the existing order. The ideas of writers such as Karl Marx, Charles Darwin, Friedrich Nietzsche, and Sigmund Freud challenged many of the traditionally held beliefs about society, humanity, and political rights and freedoms. New political movements, such as Marxism, anarchism, and liberalism, appeared as oppressed national and economic groups struggled for equality.

In the arts, the firm hand of the *salon* was shaken by the new "wild beasts" of the artistic community. The romantic depiction of society was cast aside. In its place were new impressions and expressions that criticized the evils of the new urban-industrial society and set the tone for the century to come.

Prior to 1914, the existing social and political order, though under attack, was able to maintain a relative air of stability and had resisted change. The First World War ended that, however. Four years of bloody—and many would argue senseless—conflict left the traditions of Western civilization in ruins and a generation buried in the debris. Western society had been challenged and had collapsed under the strain.

	POLITICS	PHILOSOPHY/LEARNING	ART	SCIENCE/TECHNOLOGY
1848	1848 Revolutions in France, Austria, Hungary, Italy, and Prussia	1848 Marx and Engels, *The Communist Manifesto* Mill, *Principles of Political Economy*		
1850	1851 Coup d'état of Louis Napoleon 1854 Crimean War begins 1857 Emancipation of serfs begins in Russia	1852 Ranke, *History of France* 1857 Spencer, "On Social Evolution" 1859 Marx, *Critique of Political Economy* Mill, *Essay on Liberty*	1850 Paxton, Crystal Palace 1851 Verdi, *Rigoletto* 1854 Thoreau, *Walden* 1855 Berlioz, *Te Deum* 1857 Beaudelaire, *Les Fleurs du mal* 1859 Dickens, *A Tale of Two Cities*	1852 Spencer first uses the term "evolution" in *The Development Hypothesis* 1856 Bessemer converter 1857 Pasteur's studies on fermentation 1859 Darwin, *On the Origin of Species by Natural Selection*
1860	1861 U.S. Civil War begins 1862 Bismarck becomes Prussian prime minister 1863 Lincoln issues Emancipation Proclamation 1864 Danish War 1865 End of U.S. Civil War 1866 Austro-Prussian War 1867 Austria-Hungary created by the *Ausgleich* (compromise) British North America Act creates the Dominion of Canada	1860 Mill, *Considerations on Representative Government* 1862 Spencer, *First Principles* 1863 Mill, Utilitarianism 1864 *Syllabus Errorum* issued by Pope Pius IX 1867 Marx, *Das Kapital*, Vol. 1 1869 Mill, *On the Subjection of Women*	1861 Eliot, *Silas Marner* 1862 Turgenev, *Fathers and Sons* 1863 Berlioz, *Les Troyens* 1864 Tolstoy, *War and Peace* 1865 Wagner, *Tristan und Isolde* 1867 Strauss, *The Blue Danube* 1868 Dostoevsky, *The Idiot* Wagner, *Die Meistersinger* Tchaikovsky, Symphony #1 1869 Wagner, *Rheingold*	1862 Gatling gun invented 1863 Martins and Siemens open-hearth furnace 1864 Pasteur invents "pasteurization" 1865 Lister initiates antiseptic surgery 1866 Nobel invents dynamite 1868 Darwin, *The Variation of Animals and Plants under Domestication* 1869 Galton, *Hereditary Genius*
1870	1870 Franco-Prussian War 1871 Proclamation of the German Empire 1872 League of the Three Emperors 1878 Congress of Berlin 1879 Dual Alliance	1873 Spencer, *The Study of Sociology* 1879 Spencer, *Principles of Ethics*	1870 Wagner, *Die Walkure* 1872 Whistler, *The Artist's Mother* 1873 Tolstoy, *Anna Karenina* 1874 First Impressionist exhibition 1875 Bizet, *Carmen* 1877 Zola, *L'Assommoir*	1871 Darwin, *The Descent of Man* 1873 First colour photographs 1876 Bell invents telephone 1877 Edison invents phonograph 1879 First electric tram
1880	1882 Triple Alliance (Italy, Austria, Germany) 1885 Berlin Conference on Africa 1887 Reinsurance Treaty 1888 William II becomes Kaiser	1882 Bakunin, *God and the State* 1883 Nietzsche, *Thus Spake Zarathustra* 1884 Spencer, *The Man Versus the State* 1885 Marx, *Das Kapital* (posthumously) 1889 Huxley, *Agnosticism*	1880 Dostoevsky, *The Brothers Karamazov* Zola, *The Experimental Novel* 1885 Zola, *Germinal* Van Gogh, *The Potato Eaters* 1886 Seurat, *Sunday Afternoon on the Grande Jatte* 1887 Verdi, *Otello* 1889 Eiffel Tower	1880 First practical electric light 1882 Maxim machine gun invented 1884 First practical steam engine 1885 Pasteur develops rabies vaccine 1888 Eastman perfects Kodak box camera

	POLITICS	PHILOSOPHY/LEARNING	ART	SCIENCE/TECHNOLOGY
1890	1890 Bismarck dismissed by William II 1891 Young Turk Movement founded 1894 Dreyfus convicted in France Franco-Russian alliance 1898 Spanish-American war begins 1899 Boer War begins	1890 Frazer, *The Golden Bough* Mahan, *The Influence of Sea Power Upon History* 1896 Nobel prizes established 1897 Mahan, *Interest of America in Sea Power* 1898 Zola, "J'Accuse"	1891 Hardy, *Tess of the D'Urbervilles* 1892 Tchaikovsky, *The Nutcracker* 1894 Kipling, *The Jungle Book* 1895 Wells, *The Time Machine* 1896 Strauss, *Also Sprach Zarathustra* 1897 Rousseau, *Sleeping Gypsy*	1890 Discovery of antitoxins 1891 Wireless telegraphy begins 1892 Diesel engine developed 1893 Ford builds his first car 1895 Roentgen discovers X-rays Marconi invents radio telegraphy 1897 Thomson discovers electron 1898 Dysentery bacillus discovered 1899 Rutherford discovers alpha and beta rays
1900	1900 Boxer rebellions in China 1901 Cuba becomes a protectorate of the United States 1902 United States acquires control of Panama Canal 1904 Russo-Japanese War begins Entente Cordiale 1905 Tangier Crisis 1907 Triple Entente Peace Conference at The Hague	1900 Freud, *The Interpretation of Dreams* 1902 Hobson, *Imperialism* 1904 Weber, *The Protestant Ethic and the Spirit of Capitalism*	1901 Mann, *Buddenbrooks* 1903 Shaw, *Man and Superman* 1904 Chekhov, *The Cherry Orchard* Puccini, *Madame Butterfly* 1905 Marinetti, *Futurist Manifesto* 1907 Rousseau, *The Snake Charmer* 1909 Wright, Robie House	1900 First Zepplin flight 1901 Planck develops quantum theory 1903 Wright brothers flight 1904 Construction of Panama Canal begins 1905 Einstein, Special Theory of Relativity 1906 *H.M.S. Dreadnought* launched
1910	1910 Portugal becomes a republic 1911 Agadir crisis 1912 War in the Balkans 1914 World War I begins 1917 Revolution in Russia United States enters the war 1918 Wilson's Fourteen Points End of World War I Treaty of Versailles	1910 Angell, *The Great Illusion* 1912 Jung, *The Theory of Psychoanalysis* 1914 Russell, *Our Knowledge of the External World* 1916 Dickinson, *The European Anarchy* 1917 Jung, *Psychology of the Unconscious* 1918 Spengler, *Decline of the West*	1910 Stravinsky, *The Firebird* 1911 Schoenberg, *Manual of Harmony* 1912 Picasso, *The Violin* 1913 Lawrence, *Sons and Lovers*	1910 Curie, *Treatise on Radiography* 1913 Bohr's theory of atomic structure 1915 Einstein's general theory of relativity 1916 Refrigeration of blood for transfusions begins

CHAPTER SEVEN

Nineteenth-century Ideas and Perceptions of Reality

PHILOSOPHY

The destruction of the old social order through the political and economic revolutions of the late eighteenth and early nineteenth centuries created an intellectual vacuum into which new ideas and social theories rushed to fill. Liberalism, which appeared dead in 1815, was revived by the theories of Jeremy Bentham and John Stuart Mill as utilitarianism provided the basis for the reform movement in Great Britain. On the continent, anarchism, a violent offspring of socialism, took the liberal belief in the goodness of humanity to the extreme.

Science responded to the Industrial Revolution with discoveries that sought to explain the new technology. However, it was not physics and chemistry that provided the breakthrough in the shaping of ninteenth-century perceptions of reality; it was biology.

In the arts, particularly literature and painting, criticism turned toward the evils and abuses created by industrialization and urbanization and thereby helped to shape nineteenth-century perceptions of reality.

The Utilitarians

The philosophy of utilitarianism had its origins in England with a group of so-called "philosophical radicals." Rather than create abstract philosophical theories, the utilitarians combined philosophy, economics, and politics to formulate theories that would lead to the betterment of humankind. Utilitarian philosophy sought to measure the value of laws and institutions based on their usefulness, in contributing to the greatest happiness of the greatest number. If laws and institutions did not contribute to the general happiness, then they should be changed in a peaceful and orderly manner.

Jeremy Bentham

The most famous of the early utilitarians was Jeremy Bentham (1748–1832). Bentham formulated his theories in 1789 in his *Introduction to the Principles of Morals and Legislation*. In it, he outlined a utilitarian morality based on *hedonism*—that is, that pleasure is the primary good in life and pain the primary evil. Bentham believed that securing "the greatest happiness for the greatest number" should be the theoretical justification for all laws and that the value of every social and political institution and law should have to be proven based on the contribution it made to human happiness and to the decrease of human misery.

Bentham determined that the ultimate measure of happiness was money. A lack of money brought misery, but a lot of money could provide at least some happiness. He did not, however, advocate unlimited wealth. Rather, he believed that there should be a limit on the amount of money an individual could acquire and that when an individual's wealth exceeded that limit the surplus should be divided among the poor to help them attain their own level of happiness. This philosophy of equality of wealth made Bentham's ideas popular with socialists, even though Bentham himself felt that the state should stay out of economic affairs. Nevertheless, his ideas were quickly picked up by social activists. (See readings.)

Bentham was more than a social critic and philosopher, however. He exercised a decisive influence over nineteenth-century British thought, particularly in the area of political reform. Bentham and other reformists were instrumental in bringing about legislation to remove controls on labour organizations, end religious discrimination, extend free public education, expand voting rights, improve public sanitation, and establish the Reform Bill of 1832. (See readings.) Bentham was also an inspiration to the next generation of English reformers. Perhaps his most famous disciple was the foremost English political thinker of the nineteenth century, John Stuart Mill.

John Stuart Mill

Although John Stuart Mill (1806–1873) is most often associated with the philosophy of liberalism, he also had a great impact on utilitarian thought. Like Bentham, the purpose of Mill's writing was to bring about social reform; however, he believed that reform was possible only if it was based on a logical social theory. For Mill, utilitarianism was that theory.

Unlike many of his contemporaries, John Stuart Mill believed that men and women should have the right to vote and equal access to education.

Bentham had been a friend of John Stuart Mill's father, James (1773–1836), himself a famous British philosopher and collaborator on Bentham's early theory of ethics. The younger Mill was unquestionably influenced by the earlier utilitarian writer; after reading Bentham for the first time at the age of fifteen, Mill vowed to be a reformer for life.

Mill's views were not always the same as Bentham's, however. Like Bentham, Mill believed in the utilitarian philosophy of the greatest happiness for the greatest number. However, he differed in his conclusions about the nature of happiness. He insisted that certain kinds of pleasures, such as those of the intellect, were more important than other kinds. In his essay "Utilitarianism" (1863), he argued that the quantity of pleasure produced was not an adequate measure of its value. For Mill, human liberty meant more than simply the freedom to satisfy one's desires. He believed that laws should be designed to enable individuals to maximize their abilities and skills. He also refined Bentham's theories to respond to critics who claimed that utilitarianism was a selfish philosophy. Mill argued that since utilitarians sought the maximum amount of pleasure for the greatest number of people, they were indeed unselfish.

But although Mill was a prominent utilitarian, he was more renowned for his defence of another school of thought, *liberalism*.

Liberalism

The concept of liberalism found its intellectual roots in the writings of such authors as Locke and Montesquieu. For liberals in the eighteenth and nineteenth centuries, social and political progress was based on a number of characteristics: freedom of the individual, protected by basic constitutional and human rights, including freedom of speech, freedom of the press, and equality before the law; a government based upon a constitution with clearly delineated powers, rights, and responsibilities; political participation by some portion of the citizenry (usually defined by sex, age, and property qualifications) through elections; and a laissez-faire free market economy.

Perhaps the most famous expression of the liberal ideas of the mid-nineteenth century came from John Stuart Mill. In his essay "On Liberty" (1859), Mill defended the concept of individual freedom, but emphasized the need for government to protect these rights. (See readings.) He argued for the importance of individuality and claimed that self-protection was the only valid reason for interfering with another person's freedom. His ideas had a great impact on political thought. This was perhaps best illustrated by the debate they generated over majority and minority rights in the United States. Within two years of the publication of "On Liberty," two opposing views of the nature of the political rights embodied in the American Constitution had emerged. The outcome of the dispute was the American Civil War. The following excerpts are from two speeches from this era. The first is from the first inaugural address by President Abraham Lincoln (1809–1865) in 1861; the second is from the president of the Confederate States of America, Jefferson Davis (1808–1889). Although their views on the rights of the majority and the minority are similar, their perception of events is quite different.

> If by the mere force of numbers a majority should deprive a minority of any clearly written constitutional right, it might in a moral point of view justify revolution; it certainly would if such a right were a vital one. But such is not our case. All the vital rights of minorities and of individuals are so plainly assured to them by affirmations and negations, guarantees and prohibitions, in the Constitution that controversies never arise concerning them. But . . . no foresight can anticipate nor any document of reasonable length contain express provisions for all possible questions. . . .
>
> From questions of this class spring all our constitutional controversies, and we divide upon them into majorities and minorities. If the minority will not acquiesce, the majority must, or the government must cease. . . . If a minority in such case will secede rather than acquiesce, they make a precedent which in turn will divide and ruin them, for a minority of their own will secede from them whenever a majority refuses to be controlled by such minority. . . .
>
> Plainly the central idea of secession is the essence of anarchy. A majority held in restraint by constitutional checks and limitations, and always changing easily with deliberate changes of popular opinions and sentiments, is the only true sovereign of a free people.

From Abraham Lincoln, "Message to Congress," 4 July 1861, in Richard Hofstadter (ed.), *Great Issues in American History* (New York: Vintage Books, 1958), pp. 402–405.

> Strange, indeed it must appear to the impartial observer, but it is none the less true that . . . [the Constitution] proved unavailing to prevent the rise and growth in the Northern States of a political school which has persistently claimed that the government thus formed was not a compact between States, but was in effect a national government, set up above and over the States. An organization created by the States to secure the blessings of liberty and independence against foreign aggression, has been gradually perverted into a machine for their control in their domestic affairs. The creature has been exalted above its creators. . . .
>
> With interests of such overwhelming magnitude imperiled, the people of the Southern States were driven by the conduct of the North to the adoption of some course of action to avert the danger with which they were openly menaced. With this view the Legislatures of the several States invited the people to select delegates to conventions to be held for the purpose of determining for themselves what measures were best adapted to meet so alarming a crisis in their history. Here it may be proper to observe that from a period as early as 1798 there had existed in all of the States of the Union a party almost uninterruptedly in the majority based upon the creed that each State was, in the last resort, the sole judge as well of its wrongs as of the mode and measure of redress. . . .
>
> In the exercise of a right so ancient, so well-established, and so necessary for self-preservation, the people of the Confederate States, in their conventions determined that the wrongs which they had suffered and the evils with which they were menaced required that they should revoke the delegation of powers to the Federal Government. . . . They consequently passed ordinances resuming all their rights as sovereign and independent States and dissolved their connection with the other States of the Union.
>
> Having done this, they proceeded to form a new compact among themselves by new articles of confederation, which have been ratified by the conventions of the several States with an approach to unanimity far exceeding that . . . of 1787.

From Jefferson Davis, "Message to the Confederate Congress," 29 April 1861, in Richard Hofstadter (ed.), *Great Issues in American History* (New York: Vintage Books, 1958), pp. 397–401.

Both Lincoln and Davis wanted to prevent tyranny and protect the rights of the individual. Yet each believed that the other's interpretation of these rights was wrong. The problem for liberals in the nineteenth century was to determine which rights should be protected and which ones should not.

Equal Rights

Feminism was a vital aspect of the Enlightenment doctrine of natural rights. The movement for equal rights for women was a logical extension of the general adoption of political democracy in Europe and North America. But in practice, individual rights belonged to a select group—white males.

SUSAN B. ANTHONY

In 1851, Susan B. Anthony (1820–1906) joined Elizabeth Cady Stanton and Lucretia Mott in the movement to gain women's suffrage. Anthony was a tireless advocate of the abolition of slavery and the enfranchisement of women. However, following the Civil War, she opposed the enfranchisement of freed black male slaves while women's voting rights were still excluded. In response to the government's decision, in 1872 Anthony and fifty other women registered to vote in Rochester, New York. On election day, Anthony cast her ballot and was later arrested for voting illegally.

On 17 June 1873, the case of the *United States of America v. Susan B. Anthony* came to trial. Anthony's defence was that the voting laws defined "citizen" as all *persons* born or naturalized in the United States, making her eligible to vote. The judge, however, ruled the law inapplicable and directed the all-male jury to find Anthony guilty. Before being sentenced, Anthony attacked the verdict.

> . . . I have many things to say; for in your ordered verdict of guilty you have trampled under foot every vital principle of our government. My natural rights, my civil rights, my political rights, my judicial rights, are all alike ignored. Robbed of the fundamental privilege of citizenship, I am degraded from the status of a citizen to that of a subject; and not only myself individually but all of my sex are, by your honor's verdict, doomed to political subjection under this so-called republican form of government. . . .
>
> Your denial of my citizen's right to vote, is the denial of my right of consent as one of the governed, the denial of my right of representation as one of the taxed, the denial of my right to a trial by a jury of my peers as an offender against law; therefore, the denial of my sacred right to life, liberty, [and] property. . . .

From Miriam Schneir (ed.),
Feminism: The Essential Historical Writings
(New York: Random House, 1972), p. 134.

For most nineteenth-century liberals, democratic politics and social freedom were products of race and sex.

The United States

The women's suffrage movement first took hold in the United States. Women's groups had long supported the abolitionists' cause to free black slaves. It was at the World's Anti-Slavery Convention in London in 1840 that the women's reform movement was stung into action when all female delegates were barred from the convention solely on the basis of sex. Two prominent women activists, Elizabeth Cady Stanton (1815–1902) and Lucretia Mott (1793–1880), set out to improve women's lot.

In 1848, a women's rights convention was held in Seneca Falls, New York. Stanton, Mott, and others drew up the Seneca Falls Declaration of Sentiments and Resolutions, using the American Declaration of Independence as their model. While the people of Europe were demanding that their nations adopt the liberal democratic principles embodied in the American declaration, the women of the United States were demanding that their country honour the principle of justice and equality for all.

Britain

Women's suffrage did not gain a foothold in Britain until later in the century. Although John Stuart Mill had always advocated equal rights and social equality for women, it was not until he was elected to parliament in 1865 that the women's movement received a political voice. Mill provoked the first parliamentary debate on votes for women in 1867 and argued eloquently not only for the enfranchisement of women but for their full social equality. In 1869, he published *The Subjection of Women*, one of the most significant essays on feminism. (See readings.)

Mill believed that the difference between men and women were shaped by the environment rather than by nature. Women were a subject class, in bondage much like black slaves. The difference, however, was that women were not forced slaves but were moulded by subtle but persuasive social conditioning into willing servants of men. Mill advocated that complete social change was necessary to ensure the equality of women. He was joined by women reformists such as his wife Harriet Taylor (1807–1858), who is credited with considerable input into his work.

Anarchism

One element in the climate of rebellion against conservatism was *anarchism*, which advocated the abolition of all laws and government. The theoretical basis of *anarchism* was provided by the French socialist writer Pierre-Joseph Proudhon (1809–1865). In his *What Is Property?*(1840), Proudhon declared himself an anarchist. He answered the title question by declaring that property was in fact theft, and since the state protected private property, the state must be destroyed.

Anarchists were deeply concerned with the plight of the peasants. They believed that all systems of government ultimately suppressed the poor; therefore, in order for the poor to be free there should be no system of government.

Mikhail Bakunin

The popularity of anarchism was largely because of the revolutionary agitator Mikhail Bakunin (1814–1876). Bakunin believed that people were basically good and that government had corrupted that natural quality. He saw government "as an inevitable negation and annihilation of all liberty." He summarized the objectives of the anarchists' philosophy:

> In a word, we reject all legislation, all authority, all privileged, licensed, official and legal influence, even though arising from universal suffrage, convinced that it can turn only to the advantage of a dominant minority of exploiters against the interests of the immense majority in subjection to them.
>
> From Michael Curtis (ed.), *The Great Political Theories*, Vol. 2 (New York: Avon, 1981), pp. 356–357.

Bakunin was one of Marx's greatest intellectual rivals. He opposed Marx's philosophy, claiming that when the proletariat took power they would be merely another form of authority over the peasants.

> One may ask then: if the proletariat is to be the ruling class, over whom will it rule? The answer is that there will remain another proletariat which will be subjected to this new domination, this new State. It may be, for example, the peasant "rabble," which, as we know, does not stand in great favour with the Marxists. . . .
>
> What does it mean a proletariat raised into a ruling class? Will the proletariat as a whole be at the head of the government? . . .
>
> This dilemma is solved very simply in the Marxist theory. By the people's government they mean the gov-

erning of the people by means of a small number of representatives elected by the people. Universal suffrage—the right of the whole people to elect its so-called representatives and rulers of the State—this is the last word of the Marxists as well as of the democratic school. . . .

Thus, from whatever angle we approach the problem, we arrive at the same sorry result: the rule of great masses by a small privileged minority. But, the Marxists say, this minority will consist of workers. Yes, indeed, of *ex-workers*, who once they become rulers or representatives of the people, cease to be workers and begin to look down upon the toiling people. From that time on they represent not the people but themselves and their own claims to govern the people. Those who doubt this know precious little about human nature.

From Marvin Perry, *et al* (eds.), *Sources of the Western Tradition*, Vol. 2 (Boston: Houghton Mifflin Co., 1987), p. 167.

Bakunin believed that the state should be replaced by relationships based on contracts and voluntary associations. Local associations would join with regional associations. Eventually the entire state would be joined in a free federation in which all would have equal rights and equal privileges, including the right of secession. Bakunin outlined his philosophy in *God and the State* (1882), in which he recognized natural law alone as consistent with liberty.

Nihilism

Nihilism was closely associated with anarchism, particularly in the popular mind. Like anarchism, it revolted against the established social order and rejected all forms of authority, including family authority. The term was popularized by Ivan Turgenev's novel *Fathers and Sons* (1862), which used the conflict between generations as its central theme. (See readings.) Nihilism rapidly degenerated into a justification of violence, however. By the 1890s, nihilists emphasized the "insurrectionary deed" as a means of inspiring mass revolt that would overthrow the state. It was this element of anarchism, emphasizing individual terrorism, that was responsible for the assassinations of Czar Alexander II of Russia (1881), President Carnot of France (1894), Antonio Canovas del Castillo of Spain (1897), the Empress Elizabeth of Austria (1898), Umberto I of Italy (1900), and President McKinley of the United States (1901).

SCIENCE

During the mid-nineteenth century, important discoveries were made in the fields of chemistry, physics, and biology. Some of these had immediate practical applications in the lives of the general population. Others created a furor of controversy unheard of since the scientific revolution.

Charles Darwin

While social, political, and economic ideas were changing in the second half of the nineteenth century, so was scientific thought. The architect of this change was Charles Darwin (1809–1882). His ideas had a widespread impact on many aspects of society. In his most famous work, *On the Origin of Species by Means of Natural Selection, or the Preservation of the Favoured Races in the Struggle for Life* (1859), Darwin wrote:

> There is a grandeur in this view of life . . . having been originally breathed by the Creator into a few forms or into one; and that, whilst this planet has gone cycling on according to the fixed law of gravity, from so simple a beginning endless forms most beautiful and most wonderful have been, and are being, evolved.

His concept of evolution was certainly revolutionary, but his ideas did not emerge in a vacuum. For over half a century new ideas had been evolving in botany, biology, and geology. As a young man Darwin had been influenced by the ideas of Thomas Malthus (1766–1834) on the nature of population growth and those of Sir Charles Lyell (1797–1875) on geology. Therefore, in order to understand Darwin and his contributions to nineteenth-century thought, it is important to consider the ideas of these two theorists.

Malthus, in his *Essay on the Principle of Population*, described the gap between the widespread existence of humans, animals, and plants and the limited geographic areas that are suitable for supporting life. He raised important questions about population increase and natural control. Although Malthus was primarily concerned with economic issues, his ideas had a profound effect upon biologists such as Darwin. Lyell, on the other hand, was a geologist. From his studies of rock strata, he challenged the biblical notion of the earth's relatively recent creation. In the 1830s, he estimated that the earth was millions of years old, not 6000 years old as many theologians claimed.

It was into this world that Charles Darwin was born in Shrewsbury, England, on 12 February 1809. As a youth

Darwin developed a keen interest in walking in the woods and observing nature. By the age of eighteen, he had become quite an amateur naturalist. In January 1828, Darwin entered Christ's College at Cambridge University with the intention of becoming a member of the Anglican clergy. While there, he continued to pursue his study of nature, and in December 1831 he joined the crew of the HMS *Beagle* as a naturalist on a British government expedition to South America.

The evolutionary theories of Charles Darwin had a profound impact on the scientific and religious thought of his time.

The Voyage of the Beagle

The *Beagle* first journeyed down the east coast of South America, stopping at several ports of call. Darwin frequently went ashore, traveling inland to observe flora and fauna. He began to combine his interest in biology and botany with a growing interest in geology. His observations of shells and the remains of undersea life on the plains of Argentina, and again later in the Andes Mountains, convinced him of the validity of Lyell's geological theories.

During the summer of 1834, the *Beagle* began its voyage up the west coast of the South American continent. In September 1835, they arrived at the Galapagos Islands off the coast of Equador, where Darwin would discover the secrets of evolution that would shake the world. (See readings.)

Upon returning to England on 2 October 1836, Darwin began the painstaking work of cataloguing his specimens and researching and recording his findings. He published several short essays as well as his major work of the period, *The Voyage of the Beagle*, an account of his travels and observations. (See readings.)

As Darwin examined his discoveries, several questions began to puzzle him. Why were living species in an area so closely related to those that were extinct? Why did species living in slightly different environments have slightly different characteristics from one another? The answers, he believed, might be found in the breeding processes of domesticated animals.

> We cannot suppose that all the breeds were suddenly produced as perfect or as useful as we now see them. . . . The key is man's power of accumulative selection; nature gives successive variations, man adds them up in certain directions useful to him. In this sense he may be said to have made for himself useful breeds.

Darwin believed that nature operated in a similar fashion. He considered that there might be a few common ancestors, but that over time the influence of changing environments had caused these ancestors to adapt to meet new conditions. This ability to adapt distinguished "successful" (that is, surviving) species from "unsuccessful" (or extinct) ones. Darwin referred to this process as "natural selection." Through competition for resources in a difficult environment, only those species blessed by nature with the ability to adapt could compete successfully and prosper. Later this process would be called "survival of the fittest" and would take on a very different meaning.

Darwin's Theories

The core of Darwin's theories was contained in only two books, *Origin of Species* (1859) and *The Descent of Man* (1871). The more controversial of the two, *Origin of Species* sent the academic and theological world into a turmoil. First it rejected the biblical version of creation. Darwin claimed that people were descended "from a hairy, tailed quadruped, probably arboreal in its habits." Three centuries earlier, Copernicus and Galileo had removed the earth from the centre of the universe. Now Darwin had removed humankind from the centre of living creation. The world would never be the same again.

The second controversial aspect of Darwin's findings concerned the laws of evolution. Darwin identified three facts from his research: (1) that living creatures tended to increase rapidly in numbers if left unchecked (the theory of exponential population growth); (2) that variation exists within each species (that is, a species might have the same general characteristics, but there are differences between individuals); and (3) that children tend to inherit the dominant characteristics of their parents. In *Origin of Species*, he maintained:

(a) that a population grows until it approaches the limit of its resources;

(b) that in the resulting struggle for existence, individuals with traits that help them to overcome the adverse forces of the environment—famine, disease, a harsh climate, and the attacks of predators—are more likely to survive and produce offspring;

(c) that offspring tend to inherit favourable traits from their parents and pass them on to future generations;

(d) that individuals with traits that handicap them in the struggle against adverse forces are less likely to reach maturity and therefore less likely to produce offspring, and so their traits will tend to disappear from the population; and

(e) that over the course of many generations, this process, which preserves and strengthens some traits while it prunes away others, gradually transforms the species.

The evolutionary law of natural selection does not use labels such as "stronger" or "superior" to describe the survivors. The species that are able to adapt and survive simply live longer, and therefore have a better chance of having offspring. Obviously, if a species has only a few offspring, the odds of these descendants surviving to have offspring of their own decreases. Long lives mean large families, and large families mean the ability to pass on characteristics to the next generation. Some of these ideas are outlined in Darwin's introduction to *Origin of Species*. (See readings.)

THE BOOK THAT ALMOST WASN'T

Darwin developed his theory in 1838 after reading Malthus's *An Essay on the Principle of Population*. However, he did not commit his ideas to paper until 1842 when he wrote a thirty-five-page abstract outlining his theory. Two years later he expanded the essay to 230 pages. By 1858, this had become eleven chapters of a proposed four-volume work. And then fate intervened.

On 18 June 1858, Darwin received an essay entitled "On the Tendency of Varieties to Depart Indefinitely from the Original Type," written by Alfred Russel Wallace, a naturalist working in Malaya. Wallace requested that Darwin read the essay and forward it to Charles Lyell if he thought it worthwhile. Darwin was stunned; Wallace's paper contained the key elements of his theory. In a letter to Lyell he wrote, "I never saw a more striking coincidence. . . . " Darwin explained what happened next in the introduction to *Origin of Species*. "Sir C. Lyell and Dr. Hooker, who both knew of my work—the latter having read my sketch of 1844—honored me by thinking it advisable to publish . . some brief extracts from my manuscripts." At the urging of his friends, Darwin sent an abstract to his publisher. It was finally published 24 November 1859, two decades after Darwin first developed his theory.

The Debate over Evolution

Darwin's theories launched controversies that affected many aspects of Western civilization. The liveliest debate took place in the United States, where Darwin's ideas met with some fierce resistance. Fundamentalist religious leaders advocated a literal interpretation of the Bible and rejected as heresy the theory of evolution. They pressured hundreds of school boards into banning the teaching of evolution. In three American states—Tennessee, Arkansas, and Alabama—it became a crime to teach the theory of evolution.

The Scopes "Monkey" Trial

Opponents of this restriction on the freedom of expression retaliated by continuing to teach Darwin's theories. In 1925, a high school biology teacher named John T. Scopes was arrested in Dayton, Tennessee, for teaching evolution. The American Civil Liberties Union supplied the lawyers for his defence. The most notable of these was Clarence Darrow (1857–1938), the most famous trial lawyer of his day. On the fundamentalists' side was William Jennings Bryan (1860–1925), an unsuccessful former candidate for the American presidency and a brilliant orator.

The trial became a media sensation. The issue soon became not John Scopes and his teaching, but the truth of the theory of evolution itself. Newspapers and radio stations from around the world covered the proceedings. In a surprise tactic, Darrow put Bryan on the stand as an expert witness on the Bible. Bryan fumbled in his efforts to explain the inconsistencies between the literal statements in the Bible and the realities of natural science. In the end, however, Scopes was convicted of teaching evolution, although his conviction was later overturned on a technicality.

Fortunately, the fundamentalist opposition to the theory of evolution was in the minority. However, this did not prevent the debate from raging on. Even today, "scientific creationists" counter Darwin's theories with their own "proof." One such theory contends that the long period of time necessary for the evolutionary process has not been proven because the fossil record dates back only to the great flood (as recounted in the story of Noah and the ark). Its supporters claim that the various strata of remains simply reflect the order in which creatures drowned. The better swimmers lasted longer, and that is why human skeletons tend to be so close to the surface. These views, however, are held by the minority. Although pressure has been placed on education systems throughout the West to give scientific creationism equal emphasis with the theory of evolution, there is little chance of a return to the atmosphere of seventy years ago.

THE WHITE MAN'S BURDEN

The following poem, written by the English author Rudyard Kipling, is a telling expression of the application of social Darwinism to imperialist activities.

Take up the White Man's burden—
Send forth the best ye breed—
Go bind your sons to exile
To serve your captives' need;
To wait in heavy harness,
On fluttered folk and wild—
Your new-caught, sullen peoples,
Half-devil and half-child.

Take up the White Man's burden—
In patience to abide,
To veil the threat of terror
And check the show of pride;
By open speech and simple,
An hundred times made plain,
To seek another's profit,
And work another's gain.

Take up the White Man's burden—
The savage wars of peace—
Fill full the mouth of Famine
And bid the sickness cease;
And when your goal is nearest
The end for others sought
Watch Sloth and heathen Folly
Bring all your hopes to nought.
Take up the White Man's burden—
No tawdry rule of kings,
But toil of serf and sweeper—
The tale of common things.
The ports ye shall not enter,
The roads ye shall not tread,
Go make them with your living,
And mark them with your dead.

Take up the White Man's burden—
And reap his old reward:
The blame of those ye better,
The hate of those ye guard—
The cry of hosts ye humour
(Ah slowly!) toward the light:—
"Why brought ye us from bondage,
Our loved Egyptian night?"

Take up the White Man's burden—
Ye dare not stoop to less—
Nor call too loud on Freedom
To cloak your weariness;
By all ye cry or whisper,
By all ye leave or do,
The silent, sullen peoples
Shall weigh your Gods and you.

Take up the White Man's burden—
Have done with childish days—
The lightly proffered laurel,
The easy, ungrudged praise.
Comes now, to search your manhood
Through all your thankless years,
Cold, edged with dear-bought wisdom,
The judgment of your peers!

From Rudyard Kipling, "The White Man's Burden," in E. Fenton, *32 Problems in World History* (Glenview, IL: Scott, Foresman, 1969), pp. 173–174.

The Corollaries of Darwin's Thought

Herbert Spencer

Darwin's theories had considerable impact beyond the realms of science and religion. The application of his ideas to human society was called *social Darwinism*. The foremost proponent of this theory was Herbert Spencer (1820–1903), who applied Darwin's theories to society, politics, and economics. Spencer believed in the idea of survival of the fittest and that, as in the plant and animal world, in the human world the most capable rose to the top. He also believed that governments should not interfere in this natural social process. Businesses should be allowed to fail, people should be left to starve, and disease and death should be free to weed out the unfit. The principle of competition would ensure that the ablest would emerge as victors in the economic and social struggle. Spencer's ideas were popular in the free enterprise and individualistic society of the United States. In fact, the cutthroat industrial competition of the late nineteenth century was justified by this theory.

Social Darwinism

Social Darwinism also formed the "scientific" basis of racism. Nationalist feelings were running strong in the nineteenth century. The industrialized white societies of Europe and North America used social Darwinism to claim racial superiority over the people of the nonindustrialized (and to Western thinking, less advanced) countries. Using this standard, Europeans considered themselves "the fittest" and therefore destined to "survive" and rule.

Social Darwinism was also used as a defence for imperialism. Empire building was justified in terms of a global mission to civilize the "inferior" races, thereby giving them a greater chance for survival. In North America, this "mission" was evident in the treatment of Native peoples as Canadian and American governments offered them a choice between "civilization" and extermination. Europeans turned their attention to Africa and Asia, where they politically and economically subjugated the people of these once-independent nations. Religion also became a factor in imperialist expansion as Western society felt it necessary to spread Christianity around the globe. By the end of the century, Darwin's scientific view of an ever-changing world in which species adapted to new conditions in order to survive had been turned into a defence of a rigid social order and imperial expansion.

THE SOCIAL SCIENCES

Auguste Comte

While scientists such as Lyell, Malthus, and Darwin were examining the laws of the physical world, and philosophers such as Spencer were attempting to apply their social theories, others were taking yet another approach to the study of human behaviour. The French scientist and philosopher Auguste Comte (1798–1857) developed the philosophy of *positivism* in his *Cours de Philosophe Positive* (1830–1842). By "positive" Comte meant "scientific"—that is, all propositions had to be verifiable through scientific means. Positivism viewed science as a progressive force for social change.

Comte believed that the development of society passed through three stages: the Theological stage, in which humanity invented gods and spirits to explain the workings of the world; the Metaphysical stage, in which abstract ideas were used to explain why things happened; and the final *Positive* stage, in which everything is explained on the basis of scientific laws. Just as the physical world could be explained by the principles of science, so too could society. A study of human history would reveal the laws of human behaviour. Comte called this new study "sociology."

Comte believed that this new social science could be divided into two components: social statics and social dynamics. The former would examine the customs, institutions, and laws of a society, while the latter would deal with social change as a means of discovering the scientific laws of social development. By studying the history of society, Comte tried to establish social patterns and behaviour. He predicted that humanity would progress to the point where the world would live in peaceful harmony and co-operation.

One of Comte's critics was the German writer Max Weber (1864–1920). Weber acknowledged that Comte was right in using scientific methods to analyse "what is." But he did not believe that this method could be used to predict the future. That was beyond the realm of human ability, for it did not take into account free choice and spontaneous behaviour. A study of history, Weber argued, showed that humanity quite often did the unexpected, therefore unpredictability could be the only guiding "law." Weber's views foreshadowed the existentialist movement. Rejecting the concept of human development as a systematic progression, Weber saw the future as the product of random choice, and believed the social determinism of Comte was a betrayal of the liberal values of individual freedom.

THE ARTS

Around the middle of the nineteenth century, romanticism gradually gave way to a new spirit of realism. The rejection of romanticism was most deeply felt in literature and painting. Rather than escape the problems of the emerging urban-industrial society, socially conscious writers and painters turned a penetrating eye toward observation and critical evaluation of contemporary society. It is in these novels and paintings that the lives of ordinary men and women of the nineteenth century come vividly alive.

Realism in Literature

England

Literature in the nineteenth century increasingly reflected the scientific bias toward the accurate observation and assessment of society. Writers such as Charles Dickens (1812–1870), Thomas Hardy (1840–1928), and George Eliot (1819–1880) recorded in realistic detail the decline of the agrarian society and the emergence of the new urban-industrial state.

Dickens was extremely popular during his day and remains the most widely read English novelist. Works such as *Oliver Twist* (1838), *Nicholas Nickleby* (1839), and *A Christmas Carol* (1843) presented memorable comic characters while effectively attacking the social injustices of nineteenth-century England. In 1850, Dickens wrote *David Copperfield*, which was the most autobiographical of his books, and in 1861 *Great Expectations* was published, considered by many critics to be his greatest work.

Most of Hardy's works were pessimistic portrayals of life in his native Dorsetshire. He gained attention in 1874 with *Far From the Madding Crowd*. This novel was followed by *The Return of the Native* (1878), *The Mayor of Casterbridge* (1886), and *Tess of the d'Urbervilles* (1891). Criticism of the gloom and doom of his novels led Hardy to turn to poetry, where he continued to express his negative outlook.

George Eliot created realistic portrayals of the problems of the new middle class. Born Mary Anne Evans, Eliot began her writing career and assumed her pen name during the 1850s. Her first work, *Scenes of Clerical Life* (1858), was serialized in *Blackwood's Edinburgh Magazine. Adam Bede* (1859) established Eliot as one of Britain's leading novelists. She followed this success with *The Mill on the Floss* (1860), *Silas Marner* (1861), and her masterpiece *Middlemarch* (1871–1872), which depicted Victorian intellect and society. Eliot's works were highly intellectual and psychologically analysed the emotions and actions of her characters. She has been called the first modern English novelist.

English literature of the period dealt with average working people. As a result, reading became an increasingly popular form of entertainment, although the price kept books the preserve of the middle and upper classes. However, greater literacy in the urban working class and the appearance of inexpensive "penny pamphlets" and serialized novels in newspapers and magazines brought literature into every home. Because most of the authors of these serialized novels were paid by the installment, their books were usually quite lengthy and were filled with descriptive passages that provide the reader with a fascinating window on the era.

In the 1870s, George Eliot was considered by many to be the greatest living English novelist.

France

The realist movement began in France with Honoré de Balzac's (1799–1850) series of over ninety interlocking novels, *La Comédie humaine*. This vivid commentary on nineteenth-century French society focused on everyday life rather than the exotic locales that characterized the romantic novels of Alexandre Dumas (1802–1870), a popular French writer at the time. Realism continued to gain strength as a literary movement and came of age with the novels of Gustave Flaubert (1821–1880). Flaubert featured the provincial bourgeoisie in many of his works, which include *Madame Bovary* (1857), *Sentimental Education* (1869), and *The Temptation of St. Anthony* (1874). Flaubert was arrested and unsuccessfully tried for offences against public morals for his portrayal of female infidelity in the novel *Madame Bovary*.

The writings of Émile Zola (1840–1902) brought the art of the realistic novel to its peak. Zola believed that human society functioned like any scientific experiment. Participants in events were doomed to behave in a predetermined fashion as a result of "heredity, blood, and the nervous system." Therefore, human behaviour could be predicted. As Zola commented: " . . . if the experimental method leads to the understanding of physical life, it must also lead to the understanding of emotional and intellectual life."

"OH, IF EVER I PRODUCE A GOOD BOOK I'LL HAVE WORKED FOR IT!"

Gustave Flaubert is regarded as the greatest of the French realists. He spent five years (1852–1856) writing Madame Bovary, *which was published in installments by the* Revue de Paris *from 1 October to 15 December 1856. The following excerpts, from his letters to the poet Louise Colet, provide some insight into the emotional highs and lows and the exhaltation and frustration of creating such a literary masterpiece.*

February 1, 1852
[Croisset,] Saturday night,
Bad week. Work didn't go; I had reached a point where I didn't know what to say. It was all shadings and refinements; I was completely in the dark: it is very difficult to clarify by means of words what is still obscure in your thoughts. I made outlines, spoiled a lot of paper, floundered and fumbled. Now I shall perhaps find my way again. Oh, what a rascally thing style is! . . . I am doing no more than five or six pages a week.

Saturday night
[Croisset, April 24, 1852]
The day before yesterday I went to bed at five in the morning and yesterday at three. Since last Monday I have put everything else aside, and have done nothing all week but sweat over my *Bovary*, disgruntled at making such slow progress. . . . Since you last saw me I have written 25 pages in all (25 pages in six weeks). They were tough. . . . Sometimes, when I am empty, when words don't come, when I find I haven't written a single sentence after scribbling whole pages, I collapse on my couch and lie there dazed, bogged in a swamp of despair, hating myself and blaming myself for this demented pride which makes me pant after a chimera. A quarter of an hour later everything changes; my heart is pounding with joy. Last Wednesday I had to get up and fetch my handkerchief; tears were streaming down my face. I had been moved by my own writing; the emotion I had conceived, the phrase that rendered it, and the satisfaction of having found the phrase—all were causing me to experience the most exquisite pleasure.

Friday night, midnight
[Croisset, April 7, 1854]
By July or August I hope to tackle the denouement. What a struggle it has been! My God, what a struggle! Such drudgery! Such discouragement!

From John C. Cairns (ed.), *The Nineteenth Century: 1815–1914* (New York: The Free Press, 1965), pp. 101–109.

Zola believed that as the scientist put substances into contact with the environment and then simply watched the inevitable reactions, the "modern" scientific novelist operated in the same way. The writer brought together certain types of people, put them in a certain environment, and then allowed scientific rules to govern the social reaction. The result was the "experimental novel."

Zola set out to illustrate his theory in a series of twenty novels called *The Natural and Social History of a Family under the Second Empire*. Written between 1871 and 1893, these books traced the effects of heredity and environment on one family. Zola believed that this "physiological determinism" could be slightly modified by social position and occupation, but could never be escaped. Ultimately, the results of a character's actions were out of the author's control. He or she could not be held accountable, nor could he or she be accused of poor taste or bad judgment. Everything that happened did so of its own accord.

Zola's novels were interesting not just for their literary value but also as a perspective of life in the Second Empire. For example, *Germinal*, the thirteenth novel in the series, illustrated the wretched conditions of the working class and the clash between capital and labour. (See readings.)

Russia

Some of the most popular realist writers were the Russians Fyodor Dostoevsky (1821–1881), Ivan Turgenev (1818–1883), and Leo Tolstoy (1828–1910). Tolstoy was one of the greatest writers in the history of Western civilization. Two of his works, *War and Peace* (1869), an epic novel of the Napoleonic invasion, and *Anna Karenina* (1873), about a married woman's passion for a young officer, are classics. (See readings.) Tolstoy attacked the inequalities of contemporary European society and rejected many of the values of industrialization. He called for a return to self-sufficiency where each individual lived by the labour of her or his own hands. This "back to the land" philosophy struck a responsive chord with the young. When Tolstoy died in 1910, there was a massive student demonstration in his memory. So that his ideals would not die with him, his student admirers launched a series of protests against capital punishment, a cause for which Tolstoy had fought. When the government banned the students' actions, they staged a walkout strike against the universities that lasted an entire term. (See readings.)

Leo Tolstoy was an important ethical philosopher and religious reformer as well as a prominent novelist.

Realism in Painting

In painting, the term *realism* is usually restricted to the predominantly French movement that took place between 1848 and 1860. As in literature, realism in painting began as a reaction to romanticism. The principal painters were Honoré Daumier (1808–1879), Jean François Millet (1814–1875), and Gustave Courbet (1819–1877).

Gustave Courbet

The realist movement originated with Courbet's painting *The Stone Breakers* (1850), which his friend Proudhon called "the first socialist painting." The painting depicted a new subject in art, an old man and a boy absorbed in back-breaking labour. Courbet based his painting on what he actually saw: "Show me an angel," he said, "and I will paint

Jean François Millet devoted himself to the portrayal of peasant life, as seen here in The Gleaners *(1857). He emphasized the serious aspects of rural life, presenting an emotional statement about the toil of the peasants.*

it." His protests against the conventions of the day led to attacks from the Establishment. When his works failed to gain entry into the Paris Exposition of 1855, he held a private exhibition and publicized it by distributing a "manifesto of realism" explaining his artistic aims: "To reflect the manners, the ideas, and the appearance of my period; to be not only a painter but a man; in short to practice a living art." Courbet's sympathy for the poor extended into politics; his socialist beliefs led to trouble during the Paris Commune (1871) and he was forced to flee France.

Jean François Millet

Jean François Millet was also accused of having socialist leanings because of his choice of subjects—*The Quarriers* (1847), *The Baker* (1854), and *Man with a Hoe* (1858–1862). But for Millet his subjects came from a desire to paint scenes from peasant life as it really was rather than from any political ideology. His best-known paintings, *Angelus, Sower* (1858–1859) and *The Gleaners* (1857), portray the nobility of honest work and are among the best-known paintings of the nineteenth century.

Honoré Daumier's caricature of Emperor Louis-Philippe as Gargantua resulted in his imprisonment for six months.

Honoré Daumier

Although Honoré Daumier was also a painter, his fame is largely the result of his caricatures and lithographs. Daumier used biting satire to expose the foibles of contemporary bourgeois France. In 1832, he was imprisoned for six months for a caricature of Emperor Louis-Philippe as Gargantua, which was published in the liberal newspaper *La Caricature*. He also published social satires for numerous papers, the most notable of which was *Le Charivari*. Although some of Daumier's caricatures have subjects too narrow to appreciate outside of their contemporary context, many still bring smiles of recognition from today's audiences.

RETROSPECTIVE

The nineteenth century saw an explosion of new ideas in government, economics, social values, and scientific principles. The political philosophies of writers such as Bentham and Mill and the revolution in scientific and social thought sparked by the ideas of Darwin presented a direct challenge to prevailing views of society.

As the decades passed, many of the accepted norms of the previous generation were swept away in a spirit of scientific discovery. Artistic and social conventions were also being challenged. In the next generation they would disappear as well, until finally under the pressure of world war the political structure, so carefully crafted at the Congress of Vienna, would cease to exist.

JEREMY BENTHAM:
Constitutional Code for the Use of All Nations (1827–1830)

The ideological foundation for the reform movement in Britain was provided by Jeremy Bentham and the utilitarians. Bentham and his followers placed considerable faith in written constitutions, believing that the "greatest good for the greatest number" was most easily attained when the process of governing was determined by constitutional constraints. In this excerpt, Bentham combines this idea with an overview of utilitarianism.

When I say the greatest happiness of the whole community, ought to be the end or object of pursuit, in every branch of the law—of the political rule of action, and of the constitutional branch in particular, what is it that I express?—this and no more, namely that it is my wish, my desire, to see it taken for such, by those who, in the community in question, are actually in possession of the powers of government, taken for such, on the occasion of every arrangement made by them in the exercise of such their powers, so that their endeavours shall be, to render such their cause of action contributory to the obtainment of that same end. . . .

In saying, as above, the proper end of government is the greatest happiness of all, or, in case of competition, the greatest happiness of the greatest number, it seems to me that I should be making a declaration of peace and good-will to all men.

On the other hand, were I to say, the proper end of government is the greatest happiness of some one, naming him, or some few, naming them, it seems to me that I should be making a declaration of war against all men, with the exception of that one, or of those few. . . .

This being the basis on which all legislation and all morality rests, these few words written in hopes of clearing away all obscurity and ambiguity, all doubts and difficulties, will not, I hope, be regarded as misapplied, or applied in waste.

First Principles Enumerated

The right and proper end of government in every political community, is the greatest happiness of all the individuals of which it is composed, say, in other words, the greatest happiness of the greatest number. . . .

In general terms, the proof of this position may be referred to particular experience, as brought to view by the history of all nations . . .

For further proof, reference may be made to the general, indeed the all-comprehensive principle of human nature. The position which takes this fact for its subject, may be termed an axiom, and may be expressed in the words following.

In the general tenor of life, in every human breast, self-regarding interest is predominant over all other interests put together. More shortly thus,—Self-regard is predominant,—or thus,—Self-preference has place everywhere . . .

By the principle of self-preference, understand that propensity in human nature, by which, on the occasion of every act he exercises, every human being is led to pursue that line of conduct which, according to his view of the case, taken by him at the moment, will be in the highest degree contributory to his own greatest happiness, whatsoever be the effect of it, in relation to the happiness of other similar beings, any or all of them taken together. For the satisfaction of those who may doubt, reference may be made to the existence of the species as being of itself a proof, and that a conclusive one. For after exception made of the case of children not arrived at the age of which they are capable of going alone, or adults reduced by infirmity to a helpless state; take any two individuals, A and B, and suppose the whole care of the happiness of A confined to the breast of B, A himself not having any part in it, and this to be the case throughout, it will soon appear that, in this

Jeremy Bentham had considerable influence on the reform movement in Great Britain.

state of things, the species could not continue in existence, and that a few months, not to say weeks, or days, would suffice for the annihilation of it. . . .

Note that, if in the situation of ruler, the truth of this position, held good in no more than a bare majority, of the whole number of instances, it would suffice for every practical purpose, in the character of a round for all political arrangements, in the character of consideration, by which the location of the several portions of the aggregate mass of political power should be determined; for, in the way of induction, it is only by the greater, and not the lesser number of instances, that the general conclusion can reasonably be determined; in a word, mathematically speaking, the probability of a future contingent event, is in the direct ratio of the number of instances in which an event of the same sort has happened; it is in this direct ratio, and not in the inverse.

If such were the condition of human beings, that the happiness of no one being came in competition with that of any other,—that is to say, if the happiness of each, or of any one, could receive increase to an unlimited amount, without having the effect of producing decrease in the happiness of any other, then the above expressions might serve without limitation or explanation. But on every occasion, the happiness of every individual is liable to come into competition with the happiness of every other. If, for example, in a house containing two individuals for the space of a month, there be a supply of food barely sufficient to continue for that time; not merely the happiness of each, but the existence of each, stands in competition with, and is incompatible with the existence of the other.

Hence it is, that to serve for all occasions, instead of saying the greatest happiness of all, it becomes necessary to use the expression, the greatest happiness of the greatest number.

If, however, instead of the word happiness, the word interest is employed, the phrase universal interest may be employed as corresponding indifferently to the interest of the greatest number or to the interest of all. . . .

What, then, is the best form of government? . . . My opinion is, that so far as they go, the proposed arrangements which here follow would be in a higher degree conducive to it than any other could be, that could be proposed in a work which was not particularly adapted to the situation in any one country, to the exclusion of all others. . . .

In every community in which a constitutional code, generally acknowledged to be in force, is in existence, is any such branch of law as a constitutional branch, or any such thing as a constitution, really in existence.

In a community in which, as above, no such thing as a constitution is really to be found, things to each of which the name of a constitution is given, are to be found in endless multitudes. On each occasion, the thing designated by the phrase "the constitution," is a substitute for a constitution,—a substitute framed by the imagination of the person by whom this phrase is uttered, framed by him, and, of course, adapted to that which, in his mind, is the purpose of the moment, whatsoever that purpose be; in so far as the purpose is the promotion, the creation or preservation of an absolutely monarchical form of government, the constitution thus imagined and inverted by him is of the absolutely monarchical cast; in so far as that purpose is the promoting the creation or preservation of a limitedly monarchical form of government, it is of the limitedly monarchical cast; in so far as the purpose is the creation or preservation of a democratical form of government, it is of the democratic cast. . . .

Under a representative democracy, the constitutional branch of law has, for its actual end, the greatest happiness of the greatest number.

---

1. Outline Bentham's concept of utilitarianism.

2. In your own words, explain Bentham's view of self-preference and why he feels that the most society can hope for is the "greatest happiness for the greatest number."

3. *Under a representative democracy, the constitutional branch of law has, for its actual end, the greatest happiness of the greatest number.*

Explain this statement, with specific references to both Bentham's theory of utility and his belief in constitutional democracy.

JOHN STUART MILL: On Liberty (1859)

John Stuart Mill was the best-known exponent of liberalism in nineteenth-century Europe. For Mill and his contemporaries, it was important to meet the needs of society without sacrificing the rights of the individual. In his most famous essay, On Liberty, *he argued that "the sole end for which mankind is warranted, individually or collectively, in interfering with the liberty of action of any of their number, is self-protection."*

From John Stuart Mill, *On Liberty*, edited by Edwin Fenton, *Thirty-two Problems in World History* (Glenview, IL: Scott, Foresman and Company, 1969), pp. 141–145.

The object of this Essay is to assert one very simple principle, as entitled to govern absolutely the dealings of society with the individual in the way of compulsion and control, whether the means used be physical force in the form of legal penalties, or the moral coercion of public opinion. That principle is, that the sole end for which mankind are warranted, individually or collectively, in interfering with the liberty of action of any of their number, is self-protection. That the only purpose for which power can be rightfully exercised over any member of a civilized community, against his will, is to prevent harm to others. His own good, either physical or moral, is not a sufficient warrant. He cannot rightfully be compelled to do or forbear because it will be better for him to do so, because it will make him happier, because, in the opinions of others, to do so would be wise, or even right. These are good reasons for remonstrating with him, or reasoning with him, or persuading him, or entreating him, but not for compelling him, or visiting in with any evil in case he do otherwise. To justify that, the conduct from which it is desired to deter him, must be calculated to produce evil to some one else. The only part of the conduct of any one, for which he is amenable to society, is that which concerns others. In the part which merely concerns himself, his independence is, of right, absolute. Over himself, over his own body and mind, the individual is sovereign. . . .

But there is a sphere of action in which society, as distinguished from the individual, has, if any, only an indirect interest; comprehending all that portion of a person's life and conduct which affects only himself, or if it also affects others, only with their free, voluntary, and undeceived consent and participation. . . . This, then, is the appropriate region of human liberty. It compromises, first, the inward domain of consciousness; demanding liberty of conscience, in the most comprehensive sense; liberty of thought and feeling; absolute freedom of opinion and sentiment on all subjects, practical or speculative, scientific, moral or theological. The liberty of expressing and publishing opinions may seem to fall under a different principle, since it belongs to that part of the conduct of an individual which concerns other people; but, being almost of as much importance as the liberty of thought itself, and resting in great part on the same reasons, is practically inseparable from it. Secondly, the principle requires liberty of tastes and pursuits; of framing the plan of our life to suit as may follow; without impediment from our fellow creatures, so long as what we do does not harm them, even though they should think our conduct foolish, perverse, or wrong. Thirdly, from this liberty of each individual, follows the liberty, within the same limits, of combination among individuals, freedom to unite, for any purpose not involving harm to others: the persons combining being supposed to be of full age and not forced or deceived.

No society in which these liberties are not, on the whole, respected, is free, whatever may be its form of government; and none is completely free in which they do not exist absolute and unqualified. The only freedom which deserves the name, is that of pursuing our own good in our own way, so long as we do not attempt to deprive others of theirs, or impede their efforts to obtain it. Each is the proper guardian of his own health, whether bodily, or mental and spiritual. Mankind are greater gainers by suffering each other to live as seems good to themselves, than by compelling each to live as seems good to the rest.

Though this doctrine is anything but new, and, to some persons, may have the air of a truism, there is no doctrine which stands more directly opposed to the general tendency of existing opinion and practice. . . .

It will be convenient for the argument, if, instead of at once entering upon the general thesis, we confine ourselves in the first instance to a single branch of it . . . the Liberty of Thought.

. . . the mental well-being of mankind (on which all other well-being depends) [requires] freedom of opinion, and freedom of the expression of opinion, [this right rests] on four distinct grounds. . . .

First, if any opinion is compelled to silence, that opinion may, for aught we can certainly know, be true. To deny this is to assume our own infallibility.

Secondly, though the silenced opinion be an error, it may, and very commonly does, contain a portion of truth; and since the general or prevailing opinion on any subject is rarely or never the whole truth, it is only by the collision of adverse opinions that the remainder of the truth has any chance of being supplied.

Thirdly, even if the received opinion be not only true, but the whole truth; unless it is suffered to be, and actually is, vigorously and earnestly contested, it will, by most of those who receive it, be held in the manner of a prejudice, with little comprehension or feeling of its rational grounds. And not only this, but fourthly, the meaning of the doctrine itself will be in danger of being lost, or enfeebled, and deprived of its vital effect on the character and conduct; the dogma becoming a mere formal profession, inefficacious for good, but cumbering the ground, and preventing the growth of any real and heartfelt conviction, from reason or personal experience.

---

1. According to Mill, what are the fundamental rights of the individual?

2. How does Mill define liberty?

3. What dangers does Mill see in the extension of the powers of society over the individual?

DECLARATION OF SENTIMENTS AND RESOLUTIONS, SENECA FALLS (1848)

On 19 July 1848, 300 people gathered at the Wesleyan Chapel in Seneca Falls, New York, to consider "the social, civil, and religious conditions and rights of women" in the United States. Organized by Elizabeth Cady Stanton and Lucretia Mott, the assembly adopted twelve resolutions. The declaration that resulted, based on the American Declaration of Independence, is considered to be the most important document of the American women's movement in the nineteenth century.

From Miriam Schneir (ed.), *Feminism: The Essential Historical Writings* (New York: Random House, 1972), pp. 77–82.

. . . We hold these truths to be self-evident: that all men and women are created equal; that they are endowed by their Creator with certain inalienable rights; that among these are life, liberty, and the pursuit of happiness; that to secure these rights governments are instituted, deriving their just powers from the consent of the governed. Whenever any form of government becomes destructive of these ends, it is the right of those who suffer from it to refuse allegiance to it . . . Prudence, indeed, will dictate that governments long established should not be changed for light and transient causes; . . . But when a long train of abuses and usurpations . . . evinces a design to reduce them under absolute despotism, it is their duty to throw off such government, and to provide new guards for their future security. Such has been the patient sufferance of the women under this government, and such is now the necessity which constrains them to demand the equal station to which they are entitled.

The history of mankind is a history of repeated injuries and usurpations on the part of man toward woman, having in direct object the establishment of an absolute tyranny over her. To prove this, let facts be submitted to a candid world.

He has never permitted her to exercise her inalienable right to the elective franchise.

He has compelled her to submit to laws, in the formation of which she had no voice.

He has withheld from her rights which are given to the most ignorant and degraded men—both natives and foreigners. Having deprived her of this first right of a citizen, the elective franchise, thereby leaving her without representation in the halls of legislation, he has oppressed her on all sides.

He has made her, if married, in the eye of the law, civilly dead.

He has taken from her all right in property, even to the wages she earns.

He has made her, morally, an irresponsible being, as she can commit many crimes with impunity, provided they be done in the presence of her husband. In the covenant of marriage, she is compelled to promise obedience to her husband, he becoming, to all intents and purposes, her master . . .

He has so framed the laws of divorce, as to what shall be the proper causes, and in the case of separation, to whom the guardianship of the children shall be given, as to be wholly regardless of the happiness of women—the law, in all cases, going upon a false supposition of the supremacy of man, and giving all power into his hands.

After depriving her of all rights as a married woman, if single, and the owner of property, he has taxed her to support a government which recognizes her only when her property can be made profitable to it.

He has monopolized nearly all the profitable employments, and from those she is permitted to follow, she receives but a scanty remuneration. He closes against her all the avenues to wealth and distinction which he considers most honorable to himself. . . .

He has denied her the facilities for obtaining a thorough education, all colleges being closed against her. . . .

He has endeavored, in every way that he could, to destroy her confidence in her own powers, to lessen her self-respect, and to make her willing to lead a dependent and abject life.

Now, in view of this entire disfranchisement of one-half the people of this country, their social and religious degradation—in view of the unjust laws above mentioned, and because women do feel themselves aggrieved, oppressed, and fraudulently deprived of their most sacred rights, we insist that they have immediate admission to all the rights and privileges which belong to them as citizens of the United States. . . .

Resolutions

Resolved, That such laws as conflict, in any way, with the true and substantial happiness of woman, are contrary to the great precept of nature and of no validity. . . .

Resolved, That all laws which prevent woman from occupying such a station in society as her conscience shall dictate, or which place her in a position inferior to that of man, are contrary to the great precept of nature, and therefore of no force or authority.

Resolved, That woman is man's equal—was intended to be so by the Creator, and the highest good of the race demands that she should be recognized as such.

Resolved, That the women of this country ought to be enlightened in regard to the laws under which they live, that they may no longer publish their degradation by declaring themselves satisfied with their present position, nor their ignorance, by asserting that they have all the rights they want.

Resolved, That inasmuch as man, while claiming for himself intellectual superiority, does accord to woman moral superiority, it is pre-eminently his duty to encourage her to speak and teach, as she has an opportunity, in all religious assemblies.

Resolved, That the same amount of virtue, delicacy, and refinement of behavior that is required of woman in the social state, should also be required of man, and the same transgressions should be visited with equal severity on both man and woman.

Resolved, That the objection of indelicacy and impropriety, which is so often brought against woman when she addresses a public audience, comes with a very ill-grace from those who encourage, by their attendance, her appearance on the stage, in the concert, or in feats of the circus.

Resolved, That woman has too long rested satisfied in the circumscribed limits which corrupt customs and a perverted application of the Scriptures have marked out for her, and that it is time she should move in the enlarged sphere which her great Creator has assigned her.

Resolved, That it is the duty of the women of this country to secure to themselves their sacred right to the elective franchise.

Resolved, That the equality of human rights results necessarily from the fact of the identity of the race in capabilities and responsibilities.

Resolved, therefore, That, being invested by the Creator with the same capabilities, and the same consciousness of responsibility for their existence, it is demonstrably the right and duty of woman, equally with man, to promote every righteous cause by every righteous means; and especially in regard to the great subjects of morals and religion, it is evidently her right to participate with her brother in teaching them, both in private and in public. . . .

Resolved, That the speedy success of our cause depends upon the zealous and untiring efforts of both men and women, for the overthrow of the monopoly of the pulpit, and for the securing to woman an equal participation with men in the various trades, professions, and commerce.

---

1. In chart form, list the women's grievances in one column and their demands for the resolution of these grievances in a second column.

2. Conduct a community meeting that might have been held in North America in the mid-nineteenth century. Divide the class into two groups, those who support giving women the franchise and those who oppose it. Each group should prepare a list of arguments to defend their position, being sure to be historically accurate. Choose representatives to present each group's case.

JOHN STUART MILL:
The Subjection of Women (1869)

John Stuart Mill's The Subjection of Women *(1869) is one of the finest feminist works written in the nineteenth century. Written during the early years of the feminist movement in England, it provided an excellent theoretical argument for equality. Mill used both liberal and utilitarian arguments to present his case that women were deprived of both freedom and dignity. In the final analysis, he contended that the subjection of women through paternalism, bribery, and economic dependence was no better than slavery.*

From Rosemary Agonito (ed.), *History of Ideas on Woman* (New York: Putnam's Sons, 1977), pp. 225–237.

The object of this Essay is to explain as clearly as I am able, the grounds of an opinion which I have held from the very earliest period when I had formed any opinions at all on social or political matters, and which, instead of being weakened or modified, has been consistantly growing stronger by the progress of reflection and the experience of life. That the principle which regulates the existing social relations between the two sexes—the legal subordination of one sex to the other—is wrong in itself, and now one of the chief hindrances to human improvement; and that it ought to be replaced by a principle of perfect equality, admitting no power or privilege on the one side, nor disability on the other. . . .

The difficulty is that which exists in all cases in which there is a mass of feeling to be contended against. So long as an opinion is strongly rooted in the feelings, it gains rather than loses in stability by having a preponderating weight of argument against it. For if it were accepted as a result of argument, the refutation of the argument might shake the solidity of the conviction; but when it rests solely on feeling, the worse it fares in argumentative contest, the more persuaded its adherents are that their feeling must have some deeper ground, which the arguments do not reach; and while the feeling remains, it is always throwing up fresh intrenchments of argument to repair any breach in the old. . . .

In every respect the burden is hard on those who attack an almost universal opinion. They must be very fortunate as well as unusually capable if they obtain a hearing at all. They have more difficulty in obtaining a trial, than any other litigants have in getting a verdict. . . .

In the first place, the opinion in favour of the present system, which entirely subordinates the weaker sex to the stronger, rests upon theory only; for there never has been a trial made of any other; so the experience, in the sense in which it is vulgarly opposed to theory, cannot be pretended to have produced a verdict. And in the second place, the adoption of this system of inequality never was the result of deliberation, or forethought, or any social ideas, or any notion whatever of what conducted to the benefit of humanity or the good order of society. It arose simply from the fact that from the very earliest twilight of human society, every woman (owing to the value attached to her by men, combined with her inferiority in muscular strength) was found in a state of bondage to some man. Laws and systems of polity always begin by recognizing the relations they find already existing between individuals. They convert what was a mere physical fact into a legal right, give it the sanction of society, and principally aim at the substitution of public and organized means of asserting and protecting these rights, instead of the irregular and lawless conflict of physical strength. Those who had already been compelled to obedience became in this manner legally bound to it. . . .

And this, indeed, is what makes it strange to ordinary ears, to hear it asserted that the inequality of rights between men and women has no other source than the law of the strongest. That this statement should have the effect of a paradox is in some respects creditable to the progress of civilization, and the improvement of the moral sentiments of mankind. We now live . . . in a state in which the law of the strongest seems to be entirely abandoned as the regulating principle of the world's affairs: nobody professes it, and, as regards most of the relations between human beings, nobody is permitted to practise it. . . .

This being the ostensible state of things, people flatter themselves that the rule of mere force is ended; that the law of the strongest cannot be the reason of existence of anything which has remained in full operation down to the present time. . . .

The social subordination of women thus stands out an isolated fact in modern social institutions; a solitary breach of what has become their fundamental law; a single relic of an old world of thought and practice exploded in everything else, but retained in the one thing of most universal interest. . . . This entire discrepancy between one social fact and all those which accompany it, and the radical opposition between its nature and the progressive movement which is the boast of the modern world, and which has successively swept away everything else of an analogous character, surely affords, to a conscientious observer of human tendencies, serious matter for reflection.

---

1. Explain Mill's assertion that some cases have more trouble getting a trial than others have in securing a verdict.

2. Compare Mill's argument with regard to the "legitimization" of the subjection of women with Hobbes's view on the need for strong government.

3. What impact do you think Mill's arguments would have had upon liberals of his generation? Account for your point of view based upon his own argument.

CHARLES DARWIN: Origin of Species (1859)

Charles Darwin's Origin of Species *caused an international controversy when it was published in 1859. Before Darwin's theory of evolution, the general public believed in the biblical account of the divine creation of each species. Darwin hypothesized that all life slowly evolved from a common ancestral origin. In these excerpts, Darwin outlined the basis for his theories of the "struggle for existence" and "natural selection."*

From K. Korey, *The Essential Darwin* (Toronto: Little, Brown, 1984), pp. 26–38.

No one ought to feel surprise at much remaining as yet unexplained in regard to the origin of species and varieties, if he makes due allowance for our profound ignorance in regard to the mutual relations of all the beings which live around us. Who can explain why one species ranges widely and is very numerous, and why another allied species has a narrow range and is rare? Yet these relations are of the highest importance, for they determine the present welfare, and as I believe, the future success and modification of every inhabitant of this world. . . .

Although much remains obscure, I can entertain no doubt, after the most deliberate study and dispassionate judgment of which I am capable, that the view which most naturalists entertain, and which I formerly entertained—namely that each species has been independently created—is erroneous. . . .

Furthermore, I am convinced that Natural Selection has been the main but not exclusive means of modification . . .

Struggle for Existence

Before entering on the subject of this chapter, I must make a few preliminary remarks to show how the struggle for existence bears on Natural Selection. . . .

It may be asked how is it that varieties . . . become converted into good and distinct species, which in most cases obviously differ from each other far more than do the varieties of the same species? . . . All these results . . . follow inevitably from the struggle for life. Owing to this struggle for life, any variation, however slight and from whatever cause proceeding, if it be in any degree profitable to an individual of any species, in its infinitely complex relations to other organic beings and to external nature, will tend to the preservation of that individual, and will generally be inherited by its offspring. The offspring, also, will thus have a better chance of surviving, for, of the many individuals of any species which are periodically born, but a small number can survive. I have called this principle, by which each slight variation, if useful, is preserved, by the term of Natural Selection. . . .

We will now discuss in a little more detail the struggle for existence. . . . Nothing is easier than to admit in words the truth of the universal struggle for life, or more difficult—at least I have found it so—than constantly to bear this conclusion in mind. Yet unless it be thoroughly engrained in the mind, I am convinced that the whole economy of nature, with every fact on distribution, rarity, abundance, extinction, and variation will be dimly seen or misunderstood. . . .

I should premise that I use the term Struggle for Existence in a large and metaphorical sense, including dependence of one being on another, and including (which is more important) not only the life of the individual, but success in leaving progency. . . .

A struggle for existence inevitably follows from the high rate at which all organic beings tend to increase . . . as more individuals are produced than can possibly survive, there must in every case be a struggle for existence, either one individual with another of the same species, or with individuals of distinct species, or with the physical conditions of life. It is the doctrine of Malthus applied with manifold force to the whole animal and vegetable kingdoms; for in this case there can be no artificial increase of food, and no prudential restraint from marriage. Although some species may now be increasing, more or less rapidly, in numbers, all cannot do so, for the world would not hold them.

Natural Selection

How will the struggle for existence, discussed too briefly in the last chapter, act in regard to variation? Can the principle of selection, which we have seen is so potent in the hands of man, apply in nature? I think that we shall see that it can act most effectively. . . .

Can we doubt . . . that individuals having any advantage, however slight, over others, would have the best chance of surviving and procreating their kind? On the other hand, we may feel sure that any variation in the least degree injurious would be rigidly destroyed. This preservation of favourable variations and the rejection of injurious variations, I call Natural Selection. . . .

For as all the inhabitants of each country are struggling together with nicely balanced forces, extremely slight modifications in the structure or habits of one inhabitant would often give it an advantage over others; and still further modifications of the same kind would often still further increase the advantage. No country can be named in which all the native inhabitants are now so perfectly adapted to each other and to the physical conditions under which they live, that none of them could anyhow be improved; for in all countries, the natives have been so far conquered by their naturalized productions, that they have allowed foreigners to take firm possession of the land. And as foreigners have thus everywhere beat on some of the natives, we may safely conclude that the natives might have been modified with advantage, so to have resisted such intruders. . . .

It may be said that natural selection is daily and hourly scrutinizing, throughout the world, every variation, even the slightest, rejecting that which is bad, preserving and adding up all that is good; silently and insensibly working, whenever and wherever opportunity offers, at the improvement of each organic being in relation to its organic and inorganic conditions of life. We see nothing of these slow changes in progress, until the hand of time has marked the long lapse of ages, and then so imperfect is our view into long past geologic ages, that we only see that the forms of life are now different from what they formally were.

---

1. (a) Explain Darwin's concept of "the struggle for existence."
(b) How was Darwin's thinking influenced by Malthus?

2. Using an example from nature, outline the theory of natural selection.

3. Write a defence of imperialism based upon the scientific theories of Darwin.

SOCIAL DARWINISM

Darwin's ideas of natural selection and the struggle for existence were soon taken from the biological sphere and applied to social and political concerns. Darwin's theories gave a scientific justification to a growing body of thought on the organic nature of society. His views of specialization and adaptation had already been explored by Herbert Spencer. Spencer described the nature of social evolution in his 1857 essay "On Social Evolution."

From Herbert Spencer, *On Social Evolution: Selected Writings*, edited by J.D.Y. Peel (Chicago: University of Chicago Press, 1972).

Now, we propose in the first place to show, that this law of organic progress is the law of all progress. Whether it be the development of the Earth, in the development of life upon its surface, in the development of Society, of Government, of Manufactures, of Commerce, of Language, Literature, Science, Art, this same evolution of the simple into the complex, through successive differentiations, holds throughout. . . .

Consider the growth of an industrial organization. When, as must occasionally happen, some individual of a tribe displays unusual aptitude for making an article of general use, a weapon for instance, which was before made by each man for himself, there arises a tendency toward the differentiation of that individual into a maker of such weapons. . . .

He . . . having not only an unusual faculty, but an unusual liking, for making such weapons . . . is predisposed to fulfill these commissions on the offer of an adequate reward. . . . This first specialization of function, once commenced, tends to become more decided.

Social Darwinists saw "survival of the fittest" as a natural description of human affairs. For Theodore Roosevelt, the American people were a living embodiment of the success of the fittest. In this speech to an audience in Chicago in 1899, Roosevelt described the "duties" tied to these successes.

From Theodore Roosevelt, "The Strenuous Life," in Brian Tierney, *et al*, *Great Issues in Western Civilization* (New York: Random House, 1976), pp. 328–332.

In the last analysis a healthy state can exist only when the men and women who make it up lead clean, vigorous, healthy lives; when the children are so trained that they shall endeavour, not to shirk difficulties but to overcome them; not to seek ease, but to know how to wrest triumph from toil and risk. . . .

As it is with the individual, so it is with the nation. It is a base untruth to say that happy is the nation that has no history. Thrice happy is the nation that has a glorious history. Far better it is to dare mighty things, to win glorious triumphs, even though checkered by failure, than to take rank with those poor spirits who neither enjoy much nor suffer much, because they live in the gray twilight that knows not victory nor defeat. . . .

If we are to be a really great people, we must strive in good faith to play a great part in the world. We cannot avoid meeting great issues. All that we can determine for ourselves is whether we shall meet them well or ill . . .

The timid man, the lazy man, the man who distrusts his country, the over-civilized man, who has lost the great fighting, masterful virtues, the ignorant man, and the man of dull mind whose soul is incapable of feeling the mighty life that thrills stern men with empires in their brains—all these, of course, shrink from seeing the nation undertake its new duties; shrink from seeing us build a navy and an army adequate to our needs; shrink from seeing us do our share of the world's work, by bringing order out of chaos in the great, fair tropic islands from which the valor of our soldiers and sailors has driven the Spanish flag. . . .

In the West Indies and the Philippines alike we are confronted by most difficult problems. . . . Many of their people are utterly unfit for self-government, and show no signs of becoming fit. Others may in time become fit but at present can only take part in self-government under a wise supervision, at once firm and beneficent.

We have driven Spanish tyranny from the islands. If we now let it be replaced by savage anarchy, our work has been for harm and not for good. I have scant patience with those who fear to undertake the task of governing the Philippines, and those who openly avow that they fear to undertake it, or that they shrink from it because of the expense and trouble; but I have even scanter patience with those who make a pretence of humanitarianism to hide and cover their timidity, and who rant about "liberty" and the "consent of the governed," in order to excuse themselves for their unwillingness to play the part of men. Their doctrines, if carried out, would make it incumbent upon us to leave the Apaches of Arizona to work out their own salvation, and to decline to interfere in a single Indian reservation. Their doctrines condemn your forefathers and mine for ever having settled in the United States.

By the turn of the century, the scientific community had come to defend not only Darwin but the ideas of his successors. In these excerpts, British scientist Karl Pearson gave a strong defence of the "scientific" conclusions of social Darwinism. His comments provide an insight into the racist undercurrent of this philosophy.

From Karl Pearson, "The Scope and Importance to the State of the Science of National Eugenics," in B. Tierney, *et al*, (eds.), *Great Issues in Western Civilization*, (New York: Random House, 1976), pp. 333–338.

From the standpoint of science there are two questions we can, or rather, we must, ask. First: What, from the scientific standpoint, is the function of a nation? What part from the natural history aspect does the national organization play in the universal struggle for existence? And, secondly, What has science to tell us of the best methods of fitting the nation for its task?

. . . How many centuries, how many thousands of years, have the Kaffir or the Negro held large districts of Africa undisturbed by the white man? Yet their intertribal struggles have not yet produced a civilization in the least comparable with the Aryan. Educate and nurture them as you will, I do not believe that you will succeed in modifying the stock. History shows me one way, and one way only, in which a high state of civilizaton has been produced, namely, the struggle of race with race, and the survival of the physically and mentally fitter race. If you want to know whether the lower races of man can evolve a higher type, I fear the only course is to leave them to fight it out among themselves. . . .

If you bring the white man into contact with the black, you too often suspend the very process of natural selection on which the evolution of a higher type depends. You get superior and inferior races living on the same soil, and that coexistence is demoralizing for both. They naturally sink into the position of master and servant, if not admittedly or covertly into that of slave-owner and slave. Frequently they intercross and if the bad stock be raised, the good is lowered. Even in the case of the Eurasians, of whom I have met mentally and physically fine specimens, I have felt how much better they would have been had they been pure Asiatics or pure Europeans. Thus it comes about that when the struggle for existence between races is suspended, the solution of great problems may be unnaturally postponed; instead of the slow, stern processes of evolution, cataclysmal solutions are prepared for the future. . . .

Let us suppose we could prevent the white man, if we liked, from going to lands of which the agricultural and mineral resources are not worked to the full; then I should say a thousand times better for him that he should not go than that he should settle down and live alongside the inferior race. The only healthy alternative is that he should go and completely drive out the inferior race. That is practically what the white man has done in North America. We sometimes forget the light that chapter of history throws upon our more recent experiences. . . .

I venture to assert, then, that the struggle for existence between white and red man, painful and even terrible as it was in its details, has given us a good far outbalancing its immediate evil. In place of the red man, contributing practically nothing to the work and thought of the world, we have a great nation, mistress of many arts, and able with its youthful imagination and fresh untrammelled impulses, to contribute much to the common stock of civilized man.

Seven years later, Pearson spoke against the system of social welfare as "interfering with the process of Natural Selection."

The struggle of man against man, with its victory to the tougher and more crafty: the struggle of tribe against tribe, with its defeat for the less socially organized: the contest of nation with nation whether in trade or in war, with the mastery for the foreseeing nation, for the nation with the cleaner bill of health, the more united purpose of its classes, and the sounder intellectual equipment of its units: are not these only phases of the struggle for existence, the factors which have made for human progress, which have developed man from brute to sentient being? . . .

Are not the physique, the intellectuality, the morality of man, the product of the grim warfare between individual and individual, between society and society, and between humanity and nature, of which we even yet see no end?

---

1. Precis Spencer's argument. Outline the parallels between his view of human society and Darwin's description of the struggle for existence in the natural world.

2. (a) Summarize the argument Roosevelt makes to justify American imperialism in terms of Darwin's views.

(b) Using Roosevelt's speech as a background, write your own definition of the concept of social Darwinism.

3. (a) How does Pearson explain the "struggle for existence" in racial terms?

(b) Why does he dismiss peaceful co-existence among races as an error in judgment?

(c) Outline Pearson's social Darwinist argument against social welfare.

THE RESPONSE TO SOCIAL DARWINISM

Not everyone shared Roosevelt's or Pearson's outlook. In this first excerpt, David Ritchie argued that the discovery of the principle of natural selection gave people the right and power to interfere in the process. He rejected the laissez-faire approach to the "struggle for existence."

From David Ritchie, *Darwin in Politics*, in B. Tierney, *et al* (eds.), *Great Issues in Western Civilization* (New York: Random House, 1976), pp. 343–348.

Charles Darwin himself told us that it was Malthus' *Essay on Population* which suggested to him the theory of Natural Selection. The constant tendency of population to outrun the means of subsistence and the consequent struggle for existence were ideas that only needed to be extended from human beings to the whole realm of organic nature in order to explain why certain inherited variations become fixed as the characteristics of definite types or species. Thus an economic treatise suggested the answer to the great biological problem; and it is therefore fitting that the biological formulae should, in their turn, be applied to the explanation of social conditions. It is felt, rightly enough, that the problems of human society cannot be fairly studied, if we do not make use of all the light to be found in the scientific investigation of nature; and the conception of the struggle for existence comes back to the explanation of human society with all the added force of its triumph in the solution of the greatest question with which natural science has hitherto successfully dealt. Our sociologists look back with contempt on older phrases, such as "Social Contract" or "Natural Rights," and think that they have gained, not only a more accurate view of what is, but a rule available in practical ethics and politics. Evolution has become not merely a theory but a creed, not merely a conception by which to understand the universe, but a guide to direct us how to order our lives.

The phrase "struggle for existence," as it came from the pages of Malthus, had a dreary enough sound; but, when this struggle for existence is shown to lead to the "survival of the fittest," and when it is seen to be the explanation of all the marvellous adaptations and of all the beauty of the living things in the world, it seems to gain a force and even a sanctity which makes it a very formidable opponent to have to reckon with in any political or ethical controversy. It is easy to see how the evolutionary watch-word can be applied. In Malthus the idea of struggle for existence was a very uncomfortable one; but, when it comes back to economics after passing through biology, it makes a very comfortable doctrine indeed for all those who are quite satisfied with things as they are. The support of scientific opinion can be plausibly claimed for the defence of the inequalities in the social organism; these inequalities, it can be urged, are only part of what exist inevitably throughout the physical world. The creed of Liberty, Equality, Fraternity can be discarded as a metaphysical fiction of the unscientific eighteenth century. The aspirations of socialism can be put aside as the foolish denial of the everlasting economic competition which is sanctioned by nature as only one phase of the general struggle for existence. . . .

The evolutionist politician is more likely to adopt the view that in the interests of the race we ought to remove every artificial restriction on the operation of natural and sexual selection. . . .

If we are to remove every artificial restriction that hampers the struggle for existence, are we not going back to Rousseau's "State of Nature," the primitive, uncivilised, pre-social condition of mankind? . . . The "State of Nature" i.e. the unsocial state, is more correctly described by Hobbes as "the war against all."

Evolution was seen by some Christian groups to oppose the ideas of creation found in the Bible. This argument was made by William Jennings Bryan in his prosecution of the Scopes "monkey" trial in July 1925. His views were summarized in this account published just after his death later that same year.

From William Jennings Bryan, in *The World's Most Famous Court Trial* (Cincinnati: National Book Company, 1925), pp. 333–338.

Our fourth indictment against the evolutionary hypothesis is that, by paralyzing the hope of reform, it discourages those who labour for the improvement of man's condition. Every upward-looking man or woman seeks to lift the level upon which mankind stands, and they trust that they will see beneficent changes during the brief span of our lives. Evolution chills their enthusiasm by substituting eons for years. It obscures all beginnings in the mists of endless ages. It is represented as a cold and heartless process, beginning with time and ending in eternity, and acting so slowly that even the rocks cannot preserve a record of the imaginary changes through which it is credited with having carried an original germ of life that appeared some time from somewhere. Its only program for man is scientific breeding, a system under which a few supposedly superior intellects, self-appointed, would direct the mating and the movements of the mass of mankind—an impossible system. Evolution, disputing the miracle, and ignoring the spiritual in life, has no place in the regeneration of the individual. . . .

Our fifth indictment of the evolutionary hypothesis is that if taken seriously and made the basis of a philosophy of life, it would eliminate love and carry man back to a struggle of tooth and claw. . . .

Darwin speaks with approval of the savage custom of eliminating the weak, so that only the strong will survive, and complains that "we civilized men do our utmost to check the process of elimination." How inhuman such a doctrine as this! He thinks it injurious to "build asylums for the imbecile, the maimed and the sick, or to care for the poor." All of the sympathetic activities of civilized society are condemned because they enable "the weak members to propagate their kind." Then he drags mankind down to the level of the brute and compares the freedom given to man unfavorably with the restraint that we put on barnyard beasts.

Let us then, hear the conclusion of the whole matter. Science is a magnificent material force, but it is not a teacher of morals. It can perfect machinery, but it adds no moral restraints to protect society from the misuse of the machine. It can also build gigantic intellectual ships, but it constructs no moral rudders for the control of storm-tossed human vessels. It not only fails to supply the spiritual element needed, but some of its unproven hypotheses rob the ship of its compass and thus endanger its cargo.

---

1. What impact does Ritchie say that the "struggle for existence" has had upon political thought?

2. How does Bryan characterize the moral position of "evolutionists"?

3. Write a 500-word criticism of social Darwinism from the standpoint of one of these authors.

ÉMILE ZOLA
Germinal (1885)

Germinal was the thirteenth of a series of twenty novels chronicling the life of one French family. The novel stands alone, however, as a bleak and provocative picture of life in newly industrialized France. More than a political pamphlet, Germinal *captured the nature of humanity at its best and worst. In this excerpt, the central character, Etienne Lantier, is taking his leave of the mining town in which he has participated in a brutal and crippling strike. He describes the miners returning to work.*

From *Germinal* by Émile Zola, translated by Leonard Tancock (Penguin Classics, 1954),

Gradually the deserted roads filled with people, and silent pale-faced miners continually passed Etienne. . . .

Everywhere, in the morning mist, along the shadowy roads, the trampling herd could be seen, lines of men plodding along with their noses to the ground like cattle being driven to the slaughterhouse. They were shivering in their thin cotton clothes, their arms folded for warmth, shambling and hunched up so that the briquet, held between shirt and coat, looked like a deformity. But behind this mass return to work, those silent black shapes with never a smile or glance to the side, you could just sense jaws set in anger and hearts bursting with hatred. They had only knuckled under because compelled to by starvation. . . .

As Etienne reached Jean-Bart the pit was emerging from the shadows and the lanterns on the trestles were still burning in the growing daylight. . . .

The descent was about to begin, and men were coming up from the locker-room. He paused for a moment in the midst of the din and bustle. Rumbling tubs shook the sheet-iron flooring, drums were turning, unwinding cables to the accompaniment of shouting megaphones, the ringing of bells and the clatter of the signal hammer. Here once again was the monster gulping down his ration of human flesh, cages emerged and plunged down again into the abyss loaded with men, bolted down tirelessly by the insatiable giant. . . . He had to look away, he could not stand it.

1. Review Zola's theories of "the experimental novel." To what extent did he apply these theories in *Germinal*?

2. Zola was known as a social critic as much as a novelist. Defend or refute this thesis: *Zola's truly literary significance lies in his subject matter rather than his style.*

IVAN TURGENEV:
Fathers and Sons (1861)

The central theme of Turgenev's realist novel, Fathers and Sons, *is the confrontation of the old and young. Bazarov, a young medical researcher, describes himself as a "nihilist," meaning he accepts nothing without scientific proof. This caused a storm among readers and critics of the left and the right. In the first excerpt, Arkady tries to explain nihilism to his uncle Pavel Petrovich Kirsanov.*

From Ivan Turgenev, *Fathers and Sons* (Middlesex, UK: Penguin Books, 1986), pp. 94, 125–127.

"What is Bazarov?" Arkady smiled. "Would you like me, uncle, to tell you what he really is?"

"He's a nihilist."

"Eh?" inquired Nikolai Petrovitch, while Pavel Petrovitch lifted a knife in the air with a small piece of butter on its tip, and remained motionless.

"He's a nihilist," repeated Arkady.

"A nihilist," said Nikolai Petrovitch. "That's from the Latin, *nihil*, *nothing*, as far as I can judge; the word must mean a man who . . . who accepts nothing?"

"Say, 'who respects nothing,' " put in Pavel Petrovitch, and he set to work on the butter again.

"Who regards everything from the critical point of view," observed Arkady.

"Isn't that just the same thing?" inquired Pavel Petrovitch.

"No, it's not the same thing. A nihilist is a man who does not bow down before any authority, who does not take any principle on faith, whatever reverence that principal may be enshrined in."

"Well, and is that good?" interrupted Pavel Petrovitch.

"That depends, uncle. Some people it will do good to, but some people will suffer for it."

"Indeed. Well, I see it's not in our line. We are old-fashioned people; we imagine that without principles, taken as you say on faith, there's no taking a step, no breathing. *Vous avez changé tout cela*. God give you good health and the rank of a general, while we will be content to look on and admire, worthy . . . what was it?"

"Nihilists," Arkady said, speaking very distinctly.

"Yes. There used to be Hegelists, and now there are nihilists."

In this excerpt Bazarov and Pavel argue over nihilism.

"In the first place, we advocate nothing; that's not our way."

"What do you do, then?"

"I'll tell you what we do. Not long ago we used to say that our officials took bribes, that we had no roads, no commerce, no real justice . . ."

"Oh, I see, you are reformers—that's what that's called, I fancy. I too should agree to many of your reforms, but . . ."

"Then we suspected that talk, perpetual talk, and nothing but talk, about our social diseases, was not worth while, that it all led to nothing but superficiality and pedantry; we saw that our leading men, so-called advanced people and reformers, are no good; that we busy ourselves over foolery, talk rubbish about art, unconscious creativeness, parliamentarism, trial by jury, and the deuce knows what all; while, all the while, it's a question of getting bread to eat, while we're stifling under the grossest superstition, while all our enterprises come to grief, simply because there aren't honest men enough to carry them on, while the very emancipation our Government's busy upon will hardly come to any good, because peasants are glad to rob even themselves to get drunk at the gin-shop."

"Yes," interposed Pavel Petrovitch, "yes; you were convinced of all this, and decided not to undertake anything seriously, yourselves."

"We decided not to undertake anything," repeated Bazarov grimly. He suddenly felt vexed with himself for having, without reason, been so expansive before this gentleman.

"But to confine yourself to abuse?"

"To confine ourselves to abuse."

"And that is called nihilism?"

"And that's called nihilism," Bazarov repeated again, this time with peculiar rudeness.

Pavel Petrovitch puckered up his face a little. "So that's it!" he observed in a strangely composed voice. "Nihilism is to cure all our woes, and you, you are our heroes and saviours. But why do you abuse others, those reformers even? Don't you do as much talking as every one else?"

"Whatever faults we have, we do not err in the way," Bazarov muttered between his teeth.

"What, then? Do you act, or what? Are you preparing for action?"

"Bazarov made no answer. Something like a tremor passed over Pavel Petrovitch, but he at once regained control of himself.

"Hm! . . . Action, destruction . . ." he went on. "But how destroy without even knowing why?"

"We shall destroy, because we are a force," observed Arkady. Pavel Petrovitch looked at his nephew and laughed.

"Yes, a force is not to be called to account," said Arkady, drawing himself up.

"Unhappy boy!" wailed Pavel Petrovitch; he was positively incapable of maintaining his firm demeanour any longer. "If you could only realise what it is you are doing for your country. No; it's enough to try the patience of an angel! Force! There's no force in the savage Kalmuck, in the Mongolian; but what is it to us? What is precious to us is civilisation; yes, yes, sir, its fruits are precious to us. And don't tell me those fruits are worthless; the poorest dauber, *un barbouilleur*, the man who plays dance music for five farthings an evening, is of more use than you, because they are the representatives of civilisation, and not of brute Mongolian force! You fancy yourselves advanced people, and all the while you are only fit for the Kalmuck's hovel! Force! And recollect, you forcible gentlemen, that you're only four men and a half, and the other are millions, who won't let you trample their sacred traditions under foot, who will crush you and walk over you!"

"If we're crushed, serves us right," observed Bazarov. "But that's an open question. We are not so few as you suppose."

---

1. (a) Define nihilism as explained by Arkady and Bazarov.
(b) What appears to be Bazarov's motivation behind his beliefs?

2. What arguments against nihilism could you add to Pavel Petrovitch's?

3. Why would a novel that deals with the confrontation between the old and young cause so much controversy in Russia in the 1860s?

FYODOR DOSTOEVSKY:
Crime and Punishment (1866)

Fyodor Mikhailovich Dostoevsky was one of the greatest Russian writers of the second half of the nineteenth century. Following a four-month imprisonment in Siberia for sedition, Dostoevsky wrote Crime and Punishment *as a form of confession for his wrongs. In the novel, a young student in St. Petersburg kills and robs a moneylender in order to improve his own fortunes and that of his family. He commits the "perfect" crime from the highest of motives, but eventually his guilt overwhelms him and he confesses to the police. In this excerpt, the protagonist sits in prison and contemplates what he has done.*

He did not repent of his crime.

He could at least be angry with himself at his stupidity, as he used to be angry before at his absurd and stupid actions which had brought him to prison. . . .

"How," he thought—"how was my idea any more stupid than any other ideas or theories that have swarmed and clashed in the world since the world existed? One has only to look at the thing soberly, to take a broad view of it, a view free from any conventional prejudice, and then my idea will not seem at all so—strange. . . .

"Why does my action strike them as so hideous? . . . Is it because it was a crime? What does crime mean? My conscience is clear. No doubt I have committed a criminal offence, no doubt I violated the letter of the law and blood was shed. All right, execute me for the letter of the law and have done with it! Of course, in that case many of the benefactors of mankind, who seized power instead of inheriting it, should have been executed at the very start of their careers. But those men were successful and therefore I had no right to permit myself such a step."

It was that alone he considered to have been his crime: not having been successful in it having confessed it.

The thought that he had not killed himself at the time also tormented him. Why had he hesitated to throw himself into the river and preferred to go out to the

From *Crime and Punishment* by Fyodor Dostoevsky, translated by David Magarshack (Penguin Classics, 1951).

police and confess? Was the will to live really so powerful that it was difficult to overcome it?

. . . He kept worrying over the question, and was unable to understand that even when he had been contemplating suicide, he had perhaps been dimly aware of the great lie in himself and his convictions. He did not understand that the vague feeling could be the precursor of the complete break in his future life, of his future resurrection, his new view of life.

---

1. Comment on the prisoner's contention that many great individuals were basically successful criminals.

2. Discuss the contention that it is only the threat of punishment that makes people obey laws.

3. Outline the "change of heart" described in this passage.

LEO TOLSTOY:
War and Peace (1869)

*Tolstoy is remembered primarily as a novelist, although he wrote only three full-length novels—*War and Peace *(1869),* Anna Karenina *(1877), and* Resurrection *(1899). Most of his works (forty-five volumes in total) were short stories and nouvelles. His greatest work,* War and Peace, *is a portrayal of the Napoleonic invasion of Russia and is considered by many to be the greatest novel ever written. The following excerpt illustrates Tolstoy's fatalistic view of history.*

From Leo Tolstoy, *War and Peace*, in John Cournos (ed.), *A Treasury of Classic Russian Literature* (New York: Capricorn Books, 1943), pp. 374–377.

Many historians say that the French did not win the battle of Borodino because Napoleon had a cold, and that if he had not a cold the orders he gave before and during the battle would have been still more full of genius, and Russia would have been lost and the face of the world would have been changed. To historians who believe that Russia was shaped by the will of one man—Peter the Great—and that France from a republic became an empire and French armies went to Russia at the will of one man—Napoleon—to say that Russia remained a power because Napoleon had a cold on the twenty-fourth of August may seem logical and convincing.

It it had depended on Napoleon's will to fight or not to fight the Battle of Borodino, and if this or that other arrangement depended on his will, then evidently a cold affecting the manifestation of his will might have saved Russia, and consequently the valet who omitted to bring Napoleon his waterproof boots on the twenty-fourth would have been the saviour of Russia. Along that line of thought such a deduction is indubitable, as indubitable as the deduction Voltaire made in jest (without knowing what he was jesting at) when he saw that the Massacre of St. Bartholomew was due to Charles IX's stomach being deranged. But to men who do not admit that Russia was formed by the will of one man, Peter I, or that the French Empire was formed and the war with Russia begun at the will of one man, Napoleon, that argument seems not merely untrue and irrational, but contrary to all human reality. To the question of what causes historic events, another answer presents itself; namely, that the course of human events is predetermined from on high—depends on the coincidence of the wills of all who take part in the events, and that a Napoleon's influence on the course of these events is purely external and fictitious.

Strange as at first glance it may seem to suppose that the Massacre of St. Bartholomew was not due to Charles IX's will, though he gave the order for it and thought it was done as a result of that order; and strange as it may seem to suppose that the slaughter of eighty thousand men at Borodino was not due to

Napoleon's will, though he ordered the commencement and conduct of the battle and thought it was done because he ordered it—strange as these suppositions appear, yet human dignity—which tells me that each of us is, if not more, at least not less a man than the great Napoleon—demands the acceptance of that solution of the question, and historic investigation abundantly confirms it.

At the Battle of Borodino Napoleon shot at no one and killed no one. That was all done by the soldiers. Therefore it was not he who killed the people.

The French soldiers went to kill and be killed at the Battle of Borodino not because of Napoleon's orders, but by their own volition. The whole army—French, Italian, German, Polish, and Dutch—hungry, ragged, and weary of the campaign, felt at the sight of an army blocking their road to Moscow that the wine was drawn and must be drunk. Had Napoleon then forbidden them to fight the Russians, they would have killed him and have proceeded to fight the Russians because it was inevitable.

When they heard of Napoleon's proclamation offering them, as compensation for mutilation and death, the words of posterity about their having been in the battle before Moscow, they cried "*Vive l'Empereur!*" just as they had cried "*Vive l'Empereur!*" at the sight of the portrait of the boy piercing the terrestrial globe with a toy stick, and just as they would have cried "*Vive l'Empereur!*" at any nonsense that might be told to them. There was nothing left for them to do but cry "*Vive l'Empereur!*" and go to fight, in order to get food and rest as conquerors in Moscow. So it was not because of Napoleon's commands that they killed their fellow-men.

And it was not Napoleon who directed the course of the battle, for none of his orders were executed, and during the battle he did not know what was going on before him. So the way in which these people killed one another was not decided by Napoleon's will, but occurred independently of him, in accord with the will of hundreds of thousands of people who took part in the common action. It only seemed to Napoleon that it all took place by his will. And so the question whether he had not a cold has no more historic interest than the cold of the least of the transport soldiers.

Moreover, the assertion made by various writers that his cold was the cause of his dispositions not being as well planned as on former occasions and of his orders during the battle not being as good as previously, is quite baseless, which again shows that Napoleon's cold on the twenty-sixth of August was unimportant.

The dispositions cited above are not all worse, but are even better, than previous dispositions by which he had won victories. His pseudo-orders during the battle were also no worse than formerly, but much the same as usual. These dispositions and orders only seem worse than previous ones because the Battle of Borodino was the first Napoleon did not win. The profoundest and most excellent dispositions and orders seem very bad, and every learned militarist criticizes them with looks of importance, when they relate to a battle that has been lost, and the very worst dispositions and orders seem very good, and serious people fill whole volumes to demonstrate their merits, when they relate to a battle that has been won.

The dispositions drawn up by Weyrother for the Battle of Austerlitz were a model of perfection for that kind of composition, but still they were criticized—criticized for their very perfection, for their excessive minuteness.

Napoleon at the Battle of Borodino fulfilled his office as representative of authority as well as, and even better than, at other battles. He did nothing harmful to the progress of the battle, he inclined to the most reasonable opinions, he made no confusion, did not contradict himself, did not get frightened or run away from the field of battle, but with his great tact and military experience carried out his role of appearing to command, calmly and with dignity.

---

1. According to Tolstoy, why did the Battle of Borodino have to be fought?

2. What fault, if any, can you find in Tolstoy's logic?

3. Assume you are Napoleon. Write a letter to Tolstoy commenting on what you have read here.

ANALYSIS AND APPLICATION

1. Defend or refute the following statement: *John Stuart Mill was the nineteenth-century embodiment of the 'Enlightenment tradition' in Western civilization.*

2. Write a report about women's rights and the women's suffrage movement in nineteenth-century England.

3. Defend or refute the following statement: *The passage of liberal legislation was intended to deflect support away from the more radical demands of the socialists, anarchists, and communists.*

4. (a) With a group of students, re-enact a scene from the play *Inherit the Wind*, a fictional account of the Scopes "monkey" trial.
(b) In a class discussion, examine the beliefs held on both sides of the evolutionary debate.

5. Summarize Darwin's main ideas in *Origin of Species*. To what extent did they present a challenge to the traditional values of nineteenth-century Western society?

6. Darwin's views on adaptation and natural selection were soon twisted to become a justification of imperialism. Write an imperialist justification for British expansion into Africa from a social Darwinist viewpoint.

7. Review a book written by one of the realist novelists of the period, such as Dickens, Balzac, Eliot, Hardy, Flaubert, or Tolstoy. Write your review from the perspective of how the novel is a reflection of its times.

8. Compare and contrast the romantic painting *The Hay-Wain* in the colour plates with the realist painting *The Gleaners* on page 187. How had the approach to similar subject matter changed during this period.?

9. Examine *Gargantua* on page 188. Imagine that you are Daumier and defend the picture in a written plea to the citizens of France.

CHAPTER EIGHT

The Tradition Challenged: The Human Crisis, 1880 to 1918

THE POLITICAL CHALLENGE

The late nineteenth and early twentieth centuries saw the expansion of the petty rivalries and competition that had plagued the European nations for centuries. The burgeoning energy of industrial Europe was not restricted to nationalism, imperialism, and militarism, however. As the norms of political and social behaviour were being rewritten, so too were the traditions of the artistic and literary worlds. Western civilization emerged at the end of the Great War with few of its traditions and values intact.

Marxism

Despite Karl Marx's (1818–1883) clarion call of "Workers of the world, unite!" in 1848, the first real impetus to the development of international Marxism did not come until the formation of the International Workingmen's Association in London in 1864. Founded by Marx, among others, the organization was a diverse group, including in its ranks trade unionists, Marxists, socialists, and anarchists. The combination of reformist and radical movements led to conflict between the Marxists and the non-Marxists. Marx denounced the nonrevolutionary reformism of British labour leaders. His greatest conflict, however, was with anarchist Mikhail Bakunin. Bakunin repudiated all forms of government authority and favoured the destruction of the state, after which a new society based on human dignity and freedom could be built. (See chapter 7.)

Eventually the conflicts within the International led to the organization's demise. The democratic elements from England, Italy, and Switzerland broke from the movement in opposition to the violent uprising staged by the Paris Commune in 1871, which was supported by Marx. The organization finally collapsed in 1874.

Despite the failure of the First International, attempts to organize the working class continued on the national level throughout the 1870s and 1880s. Numerous Marxist parties, such as the German Social Democratic party, the Belgian Socialist party, and the Russian Social Democratic party, were formed. Marxism thereby entered the mainstream of European politics.

In 1889, on the centennial of the French Revolution, all of the Marxist parties came together in the Second International, where they elected a permanent executive. They continued to meet every three years, sharing Marxist ideas and co-ordinating their actions. In 1890, the executive established May 1st as the annual one-day strike known as May Day, which continues to be a major celebration in communist countries to the present day.

Marxist theory saw war as the means by which capitalist leaders divided the proletariat and kept it from turning against its natural enemy, the bourgeoisie. As a result, the Second International called for a general strike in 1912, declaring it to be a weapon with which to combat war and demonstrate for peace. When the First World War broke out in 1914, however, the Second International disintegrated. Its pleas for peace had fallen on ears deafened by nationalist passions and war hysteria. It would take the collapse of the Russian war effort in 1917 to give new life to the Marxist movement.

Revisionism

Sharp disagreements developed among socialists in the last quarter of the nineteenth century. Some Marxists continued to advocate violence and revolution, while others favoured a democratic process of change. Other socialists advocated gradualism and education, while others called for massive trade unionism. The most prominent theorist among the revisionists was the German Eduard Bernstein (1850–1932).

Revisionist Marxism

Bernstein was a member of the German Social Democratic party and the imperial parliament, or *Reichstag*. In his book *Evolutionary Socialism* (1899), Bernstein suggested that Marxists should reform their doctrines and tactics. (See readings.) He pointed out that the growing concentration of capital ownership and the increasing sharpness of the class war predicted by Marx were in fact not being realized. Instead of the growing impoverishment and revolution Marx had foreseen, the success of the trade union movement and an increase in overseas trade had meant there had been a general increase in the standard of living for workers. Bernstein therefore rejected violent revolution as outdated and called for Marxists to seek reforms through parliamentary methods.

Bernstein's philosophy was formally rejected by the Social Democratic party and later by the Second International. Other revisionist theories continued to be rejected by classical Marxists and eventually led to the split of the Russian Social Democratic party in 1903. The anti-revisionists were led by Vladimir Ilich Lenin (1870–1924) and came to be known as the Bolsheviks. (See chapter 10.)

Syndicalism

In France, the main thrust of revisionism was revolutionary syndicalism. *Syndicalism* (after the French *syndicat*, meaning "union") did not merely want better wages and working conditions but sought total social revolution. The trade union movement had been slow to develop in France. The lack of large industries and the legal impediments to organized labour that persisted until 1884 kept unionism extremely small. By the mid–1880s, however, *bourse du travail* (labour exchanges) had begun to appear throughout the nation. Originally a job "clearing house" where skilled and unskilled workers came seeking employment, the labour exchange soon became famous for discussions, meetings, and union organization. Thereafter the labour movement grew rapidly. However, it was marred by violence, such as the massacre of demonstrating workers at Fourmies in 1891.

Syndicalism became the major thrust of the French labour movement when its policies were adopted by the General Confederation of Labour formed in 1895. The movement saw the state and political parties as instruments of bourgeois oppression. Thus the natural organization for workers was the trade union and the natural means of revolution was the strike. If all industries and essential services were shut down by a general strike, capitalism would simply cease and the *syndicat* would become the supreme authority. Theorists of syndicalism, such as Georges Sorel (1847–1922), emphasized class warfare and advocated violence as a means of direct action to destroy capitalism. Under the Amiens Charter of 1906, the syndicalist leadership became absorbed by the French section of the Second International.

The Fabians

The most important force in British revisionism was the Fabian Society. This organization took its name from the Roman general Quintus Fabius Maximus, who sought to weaken his enemies through harassment rather than direct attack. Formed in 1883, the society included a number of the British intelligentsia, such as Sidney and Beatrice Webb (1859–1947; 1858–1943), H.G. Wells (1886–1946), and George Bernard Shaw (1856–1950).

The Fabians were gradualists. They felt that socialism was a logical development in social and economic evolution and saw their goals as a natural counterpart to the values of political democracy. They therefore stressed parliamentary methods and reform within existing institutions as a means of achieving their goals. (See readings.)

The Fabians made several important contributions to socialism in Britain. They spread socialist ideas throughout the intelligentsia and the leadership of the trade unions. The Webbs' research and critical analyses supported those who advocated social reform in the areas of wages, social insurance, and education. The Fabians were also a key element in the formation and leadership of the British Labour party founded in 1903.

Liberalism

The classical liberal economic creed of *laissez faire* had been declining throughout the second half of the nineteenth century. The combined pressures of industrialization and urbanization as well as the agitation of socialists and trade unionists increasingly required state intervention in the economy. But if liberal values had been eclipsed in the economic sphere, in the political arena it was quite a different matter.

By the turn of the century, liberalism had succeeded in creating and developing the liberal state and the agenda of classical liberalism—written constitutions with elected parliaments and constitutional guarantees of freedom. Voting rights continued to widen. On the eve of the First World War, only Hungary and Romania still maintained limited male suffrage.

The extension of the voting franchise forced liberals and conservatives alike to introduce social reforms. The first country to move in this direction was Germany, which adopted a number of state-sponsored social security programs in the 1880s in an attempt to counter the appeal of socialism. These included protection against sickness (1883) and accident (1884) as well as old-age pensions (1889). Belgium, the Netherlands, and the Scandinavian countries also passed social legislation before the turn of the century. Britain and France followed suit in the decade before the First World War. Political liberalism had in effect adopted part of the social and economic agenda of socialism. But it was only a beginning. The real emergence of the modern concepts of welfare capitalism and social democracy were still decades in the future.

The Suffragists

Although the movement to gain universal suffrage had developed momentum in the middle of the nineteenth century, by the 1900s little real progress had been made. By the turn of the century, however, the fight for equal rights had become an international battle. Suffragist organizations in the United States and Canada worked with those in Britain and Europe, sharing ideas and strategies. In 1904, they founded the International Woman Suffrage Alliance, which held biannual conventions in the capital cities of Europe up until the outbreak of the First World War.

The first European country to grant unrestricted suffrage was Finland in 1906. (New Zealand [1893] and Australia [1902] had already given women the vote.) With this victory, efforts in other contries escalated. In 1904, the Second International issued a directive to its member parties to campaign for universal suffrage. Norway joined Finland's ranks in 1913, but for many countries the question of voting rights for women took a back seat after war broke out in 1914.

In the United States, where the suffragist movement had been under way the longest, only four states had granted voting rights to women by 1896, and it would not be until 1910 that a fifth state (Washington) followed suit. Other states came on board fairly rapidly after that, however, and helped to set the stage for full enfranchisement on the federal level. In August 1920, the U.S. Constitution was amended and women across the country were given the right to vote.

In Canada, the fight for voting rights was originally ignited by temperance groups trying to ban the sale of alcohol and eliminate prostitution. It soon became apparent, however, that if women were to effect change, they had to have the vote. Suffragist organizations lobbied their provincial politicians throughout the latter part of the nineteenth century and the first decades of the twentieth. Their first breakthrough came in the Prairie provinces, which finally acceded to the women's demands in 1916; Ontario and British Columbia followed in 1917. The federal government granted limited franchise to women who were British subjects and who had a family member in the armed forces in 1917 and extended suffrage to all women in May 1918. Provincial voting rights were granted by Nova Scotia in 1918, New Brunswick in 1919, Prince Edward Island in 1922, Newfoundland in 1925, and Quebec in 1940.

In Britain, the first suffragist organization, the Women's Social and Political Union (WSPU), was not formed until 1903. Once women began to organize, however, they became

The women's rights movement in Britain resorted to more violent tactics than its North American counterparts. Suffragettes were arrested outside Buckingham Palace in May 1914.

an active force. Not content to make speeches and write editorials, the British women's movement took a more militant approach. Members interrupted cabinet meetings, held street demonstrations, and chained themselves to the fence surrounding the prime minister's residence. The women were frequently arrested and jailed, but even then they continued their protests with hunger strikes. The tactics of the WSPU caused a split in the organization. Those who opposed violence formed the Women's Freedom League in 1907 and embarked on a campaign of civil disobedience, which included tax protests and census boycotts. In 1914, the prime minister promised to introduce a woman's suffrage bill, but the onset of war delayed the legislation. In 1918, Britain granted suffrage to women over the age of thirty. The age restriction was later reduced to twenty-one.

Years in Which Universal Suffrage Was Introduced

New Zealand	1893	Canada	1918
Australia	1902	United States	1920
Finland	1906	Sweden	1921
Norway	1913	Spain	1931
Denmark	1915	France	1946
Soviet Union	1917	Switzerland	1971
Britain	1918		

DESPERATE TACTICS

The militancy of the British suffragist movement at times reached extreme proportions. In 1913, little headway was being made with the British government to gain the vote. Frustrated by their inaction, Emily Davison resorted to a desperate tactic. During the annual Derby, a world renowned horse race, she ran onto the track and threw herself under the horse owned by King George V. She was then trampled to death by the stampede of horses racing for the finish line. Hundreds of thousands of spectators, including the royal family, watched in horror and disbelief. The tragic episode received international publicity and focused sympathy and attention on the women's cause.

THE SOCIAL CHALLENGE

Sigmund Freud

One of the most significant developments in turn-of-the-century Europe was the growth of the science of psychology. The most notable pioneer and researcher in this field was Sigmund Freud (1856–1939). Freud, a Viennese doctor, was convinced that humans were not rational beings, but were dominated by the unconscious mind. He attempted to explain human behaviour in terms of natural sexual impulses and the restraints placed on these by social conventions. Like Darwin before him, however, Freud's theories could not be tested by traditional scientific methods. As a result, many of his contemporaries rejected his ideas. Religious leaders, for example, condemned Freud for his attitudes toward religion. In this excerpt, Freud dismisses organized religion as a form of illusion.

> It does not lie within the scope of this enquiry to estimate the value of religious doctrines as truth. It suffices that we have recognized them, psychologically considered, as illusions. . . .
>
> We say to ourselves; it would indeed be very nice if there was a God, who was both creator of the world and a benevolent providence, if there were a moral world order and a future life, but at the same time it is very odd that this is all just as we should wish it ourselves. And it would be odder still if our poor, ignorant, enslaved ancestors had succeeded in solving all these difficult riddles of the universe.
>
> From Sigmund Freud, *The Future of an Illusion*, translated by W.D. Roloson-Scott, (London: The Hogarth Press, 1957).

Freud's major works were *The Interpretation of Dreams* (1899) and *Three Essays on the Theory of Sexuality* (1905). Although *The Interpretation of Dreams* received little attention when it was written (it took eight years to sell out its first printing of 600 copies), a new age was beginning. Freud's views of the irrational mind were a direct challenge to the values of the Age of Reason which had prevailed in the West since the Enlightenment. The destruction of the existing social order as a result of the First World War would call the Enlightenment tradition into question and cause an increased interest in Freud's ideas within the European intellectual community.

Friedrich Nietzsche

Perhaps the greatest challenge to the prevailing ideas of progress came from the German philosopher Friedrich Nietzsche (1844–1900). Nietzsche was a strong critic of Western civilization, believing that it had lost its creativity, particularly in the late nineteenth century. He rejected the social values of the Enlightenment tradition and called for a new age of individual achievement.

For Nietzsche, the individual was paramount. He celebrated the individual values of strength, courage, pride, and resolution and rejected the common values of a mass society. Great achievements were the product of exceptional individuals; common society only led to an inferior culture.

Nietzsche blamed the absence of exceptional individuals during his own time on Christianity, democracy, socialism, and universal suffrage. He believed that the values of self-sacrifice inherent in Christianity undermined cultural development; that democracy and socialism, which treated all people equally, stifled individual creativity and genius; and that universal suffrage gave power to the masses. Therefore it was up to exceptional individuals to take leadership. He outlined his plan for a new generation of "supermen" who were "free from sentimental inhibitions and prepared . . . to use violence in the building of a new, nobler world" in *Thus Spake Zarathustra* (1883–1884).

In *The Will to Power* (1884–1888), Nietzsche again called for superior individuals to take control of the masses.

> It is necessary for *higher* men to declare war on the masses! In all directions mediocre people are joining hands in order to make themselves masters. Everything that pampers, that softens, and that brings the "people" or "woman" to the front, operates in favour of universal suffrage—that is to say, the dominion of *inferior* men. But we must make reprisals, and draw the whole state of affairs (which commenced in Europe with Christianity) to the light of day and to judgment.
>
> A teaching is needed which is strong enough to work in a *disciplinary* manner; it should operate in such a way as to strengthen the strong and to paralyse and smash up the world-weary.

Nietzsche's ideas shocked contemporary readers, many of whom thought he was insane. This evaluation seemed to be confirmed when he suffered a total mental breakdown in 1889 and remained deranged until his death in 1900. Despite this, however, it is clear that Nietzsche merely interpreted many of the ideas that were implied by the period and anticipated many aspects of twentieth-century thought and literature. He had a profound impact on most of the German philosophers, writers, and poets who were to follow him. His philosophy was subsequently interpreted to support fascism and anti-Semitism. His vision of a *Ubermensch* ("superman") would come back to haunt Europe a generation later. (See readings.)

SCIENCE AND TECHNOLOGY

The International Exposition

The showcase of the world in 1900 was the International Exposition in Paris. Like Expo '67 in Montreal and Expo '86 in Vancouver, the International Exposition boasted the ultimate in technological achievements of the day. Covering 140 ha in the centre of the city, it entertained over 50 million visitors between April and November.

France, the host country, boasted such technical wonders as the new *Metropolitain* (the subway) and a moving-sidewalk that circled the grounds. Industrial pavilions highlighted the state-of-the-art technology in engineering, metallurgy, chemicals, and textiles. The Russian pavilion duplicated a ride on the Trans Siberian Railroad, complete with moving scenery. The German pavilion was the most spectacular, boasting the largest dynamos, the tallest spire, and the brightest searchlights. So elegant and expensive was the restaurant that it was rumoured that Wilhelm II had ordered that only the finest china, silver, and glassware be used.

The Metropolitain *in Paris was first introduced during the International Exposition in 1900.*

Innovations in Technology

The Exposition demonstrated that the world was in love with technology. There were countless innovations during the period. In 1901, the Italian inventor Guglielmo Marconi (1874–1937) demonstrated the capabilities of wireless transmission as transatlantic messages arrived at Signal Hill in St. John's, Newfoundland. In 1903, the Wright brothers made their famous flight at Kitty Hawk, North Carolina. Their glider, equipped with a twelve-horsepower gasoline engine, flew for an unbelievable 40 m. Within two years, however, they had increased their range to 40 km. In 1908, the Wrights took their technology to Europe and introduced aircraft to France, Britain, and Italy. Their innovations were followed the next year by those of French aviator Louis Blériot (1872–1936), who flew the first airplane flight across the English Channel. Other developments included the telephone (1876), the phonograph (1877), the machine gun (1883), the automobile (1885), the electric elevator (1889), cast concrete (1907), synthetic rubber (1909), and the tank (1911).

Technological advances resulted in the emergence of a new literary form, science fiction. Jules Verne's (1828–1905) *Twenty Thousand Leagues Under the Sea* (1870), Ralph Bellamy's (1850–1898) *Looking Backward* (1888), and H.G. Wells's (1866–1946) *War of the Worlds* (1898) captured the imagination of the public and foreshadowed the incredible technological changes of the century to come.

The innovations in transportation and communication seemed to mark the beginning of what Canadian communications theorist Marshall McLuhan (1911–1980) would later call the "global village." It was clear, however, that the village would be a Western one. The new technology was a product of the Industrial Revolution and international competition. European innovation simply became one more weapon in the imperialist domination of the developing world. Western writers viewed the rapid growth in technology in different fashions and the debate over these changes raged throughout Western society. On one side were writers such as the American Henry Adams (1838–1918), who warned that the new technology had such uncontrollable power that it grabbed the individual and "flung him about as though he had hold of a live wire or a runaway automobile." On the other hand, the young Viennese writer Stefan Zweig (1881–1942) commented that innovation was advancing so quickly that "it seemed merely a matter of decades before the last vestiges of evil and violence would finally be conquered."

THE NOBEL PRIZE

The Nobel Prize was established by the will of Alfred Bernhard Nobel (1833–1896). Nobel was a Swedish chemist, engineer, and industrialist who made his fortune from the invention of dynamite and other explosives. Upon his death he left over $8 million to be invested, with the interest to be used to award those people who achieved the greatest accomplishments in physics, chemistry, medicine, and literature and the person who contributed the most to the cause of peace. (A sixth prize in economics was added in 1969, financed by the Swedish National Bank.) Nobel stipulated that the prizes for physics and chemistry were to be chosen by the Swedish Royal Academy of Science (which today also chooses the economics prize); medicine by the Royal Caroline Institute of Medicine; literature by the Swedish Academy in Stockholm; and peace by a committee chosen by the Norwegian parliament.

Each year the awarding bodies receive approximately 2000 recommendations. The prizes are presented annually in Stockholm (with the exception of the peace prize, which is presented in Oslo) on December 10th, the anniversary of Nobel's death. Each recipient receives a gold medal, a diploma, and a financial award. The first prizes were awarded in 1901. The recipients were:

- *Physics*: Wilhelm Konrad Roentgen (Germany; 1845–1923) for his discovery of X-rays.
- *Chemistry*: Jacobus Hendricus van't Hoff (Dutch; 1852–1911) for his discovery of the laws of chemical dynamics.
- *Medicine:* Emil Adolph von Behring (Germany; 1854–1917) for the development of serum therapy.
- *Literature:* René François Armand Prudhomme (France; 1839–1907) for poetic composition.
- *Peace:* Jean Henri Dunant (Switzerland; 1828–1910) founder of the International Committee of the Red Cross and the Geneva Convention, and Frédéric Passy (France; 1822–1912) founder of the first French peace society.

Scientific Developments

Science was also developing rapidly. In 1905, Albert Einstein (1879–1955) introduced his *theory of relativity*, which explained that motion, position, and time were all relative to the observer. To prove this, he used an example of a person standing at the side of a railroad track; that person would have a different view of the speed and position of a passing train than would a passenger on another train going in the opposite direction.

Einstein said that space can be measured only as the relation between things in an "otherwise empty universe." The stars we observe at night appear to be shining on us in the present, but what we are actually seeing is the way they looked thousands or even millions of years ago. What is real? In Einstein's theory, reality is subjective and depends upon the observer. Like Galileo, Einstein called into question the widely accepted values and beliefs of his time. Such ideas upset a civilization used to dealing in stability and permanence.

Albert Einstein was one of the world's greatest thinkers and the pre-eminent scientist of the twentieth century.

Another major breakthrough took place in Germany. In 1900, Max Planck (1858–1947) introduced his quantum theory of atomic structure. Building on scientific observations that had shown that atoms did not give off heat and light energy at a consistent rate at all temperatures, Planck surmised that such energy must be released in quanta, or bundles. Individual atoms were therefore quite unpredictable in their characteristics. This was another blow to the orderly universe of Sir Isaac Newton.

Planck's quantum theory demonstrated, even to the non-scientist, that Enlightenment views of natural law and universal constants were incorrect. This challenge to traditional beliefs in physics, spearheaded by Einstein and Planck, would lead to a new world view by succeeding generations of Western scientists and philosophers.

Advances in physics and technology were matched by rapid strides in the field of medicine. Although perhaps best known for his discovery that heat could destroy harmful micro-organisms, in the process now known as pasteurization, the French chemist Louis Pasteur (1822–1895) also helped combat diseases. He discovered that certain disease-causing micro-organisms, such as cholera and anthrax in animals and rabies in humans, could be weakened and the weakened culture used to vaccinate against the disease. By the end of the century, the bacilli which caused diptheria, plague, tetanus, and typhoid had all been discovered. Immunization against typhoid fever (1896) and diphtheria (1913) helped reduce those debilitating diseases among the military. The introduction of antiseptics in 1865 by Joseph Lister (1827–1912) succeeded in lowering dramatically the rate of post-surgical infections.

One of the most significant scientific developments of the period was the discovery of radium by Marie Curie (1867–1934) and her husband Pierre (1859–1906). They shared a Nobel Prize for their work in 1903. Following her husband's death, Marie Curie became the first woman to hold the chair of physics at the Sorbonne in Paris, and her continued research on radium led to her being awarded a second Nobel Prize in 1911.

THE ARTISTIC CHALLENGE

During the first half of the nineteenth century, realism was the dominant pattern in the arts. Artists such as Jean François Millet (1816–1875) and the cartoonist Honoré Daumier (1808–1879) created sympathetic portrayals of the peasants and working class. (See chapter 7.) By the latter part of the century, however, realism had been supplanted by a new movement. A growing number of artists began to reject the "photographic" depictions of the realists in favour of the romanticism of artists such as Constable, Delacroix, and Turner.

Impressionism

The realist movement of the 1870s and 1880s was based on a desire to capture the "facts" of a subject. Many realist artists subscribed to Pierre-Joseph Proudhon's (1809–1865) philosophy that people should be painted "in the sincerity of their natures and their habits, in their work, in the accident of their civic and domestic functions, with their present-day appearance, above all without pose." Realism, however, did not necessarily mean simply capturing a photograph-like image. For many artists it meant capturing the sense or mood of an idea. Edouard Manet (1832–1883) said, "One doesn't just paint a landscape, or a marine, or a figure study, but the

Impressionism received its name from the hostile reaction of the art critic Louis Leroy to Monet's Impression—Sunrise *(1872).*

impression of a moment in time." That impression represented the total reality of the subject. Although highly criticized at first, the impressionists soon revolutionized artistic expression.

The Salon System

During the Second Empire, the artistic world in France was dominated by the *salon system* in Paris. Hopeful artists presented their work in the official salon. If the salon accepted the work, it meant the beginning of a profitable career; rejection, on the other hand, often meant a continuing struggle in obscurity. Eventually many artists refused to accept the judgments of the conservative salon and began to look for other ways of exhibiting their work. The result was the emergence of a "refusal" exhibition displaying works rejected by the salon. However, this too had its shortcomings. The organizers quickly fell into the same trap of rejecting or approving works according to their own tastes. In addition, most members of the viewing (and buying) public saw the refusal works as second rate. So, in 1874, a new series of exhibitions began. Careful to include artists who had been both selected and rejected by the salon, the organizers exhibited artists who had turned their backs on convention in favour of a new form of artistic freedom.

Critics dubbed the group "impressionists" after the name of the most notable of the works displayed, Monet's *Impression–Sunrise* (1872). Critic Jules Castagnary further developed the concept with his observation that these new artists were "impressionists in the sense that they render not the landscape, but the sensation produced by the landscape." Nevertheless, impressionism was part of the wider naturalist movement. This was evident not only in the tone and subject matter of early impressionist paintings in Europe but in paintings in other parts of the world as well. Lucius O'Brien, first president of the Royal Canadian Academy of Art, gained international acclaim for his *Sunrise on the Saguenay* (1880) and firmly established the impressionist tradition in Canada. In the early twentieth century, Tom Thompson and later the Group of Seven applied these impressionist techniques to the Canadian landscape with overwhelming effect.

Over the next twelve years there were eight impressionist exhibitions (although only the third exhibit in 1877 actually used the term "impressionism"). At least fifty-eight artists displayed their work at one time or another, including Claude Monet (1840–1926), Auguste Renoir (1841–1919), Edgar Degas (1834–1917), Berthe Morisot (1841–1917), Mary Cassatt (1845–1926), and Camille Pissarro (1830–1903).

In the final analysis, however, impressionism was less an artistic style than a convenient label for a group of painters and sculptors who were determined to challenge the traditions of the contemporary art establishment. As a result, it was less a restraint and more of a springboard to further artistic exploration.

Post-impressionism

Many young artists who were trained in the impressionist school soon found themselves moving beyond their teachers. One such *post-impressionist* was Paul Cézanne (1839–1906). Cézanne felt that the impressionists' works had lost some of their simplicity and order of nature. He broke away from the mainstream of the movement in the late 1870s. He wanted to recreate order and establish patterns without returning to the formalized structures of the past. Renoir's casual impression in *Le Moulin de la Galette* (1876) and the deliberate arrangement of forms and colours in Cézanne's *Mont Sainte-Victoire* (1904) illustrate the contrast in styles. (See colour plates.) The latter was clearly meant to be a permanent interpretation of the subject, for in Cézanne's view the artist had to take the motif and attempt to capture both its image and its essence. The result would be an abstraction of the original that would be superficially different and yet essentially the same. Cézanne rejected the approach of many of his contemporaries. Although he retained a great deal of respect for Monet and Pissarro, he rejected the work of Paul Gauguin (1848–1903), on one extreme, as being simply decorative, and that of Edvard Munch (1863–1944), on the other, as being strictly symbolic.

Cézanne's progression away from the norm found a parallel in the work of the Dutch artist Vincent Van Gogh (1853–1890). Van Gogh was obsessed by the use of colour for its symbolic value as a means of expression rather than for the reproduction of visual appearances. He wrote, "Instead of trying to reproduce exactly what I have before my eyes, I use colour more arbitrarily so as to express myself more forcibly." He also broke with tradition with his technique of using broad, vigorous, and swirling brushstrokes.

Van Gogh carried the art movement from the optical realism of the impressionists to the more abstract use of form and colour. Many of his paintings, like *The Potato Eaters* (1885), expressed his humanitarian concern for peasants and workers. *Self-Portrait* (1888) depicted the artist after the emo-

VAN GOGH :

The Potato Eaters

In the following letter to his brother Theo, Vincent Van Gogh explains what he was trying to achieve in the painting The Potato Eaters *(1885).*

I have tried to emphasize that those people, eating their potatoes in the lamplight, have dug the earth with those very hands they put in the dish, and so it speaks of *manual labor*, and how they have honestly earned their food. . . .

All winter long I have had the threads of this tissue in my hands, and have searched for the ultimate pattern; and though it has become a tissue of rough, coarse aspect, nevertheless the threads have been chosen carefully and according to certain rules. And it might prove to be a real *peasant picture*. I know it is. But he who prefers to see the peasants in their Sunday-best may do as he likes. I personally am convinced I get better results by painting them in their roughness than by giving them a conventional charm.

I think a peasant girl is more beautiful than a lady, in her dusty, patched blue skirt and bodice, which get the most delicate hues from weather, wind and sun. But if she puts on a lady's dress, she loses her peculiar charm. A peasant is more real in his fustian clothes in the fields than when he goes to church on Sunday in a kind of dress coat.

In the same way it would be wrong, I think, to give a peasant picture a certain conventional smoothness. If a peasant picture smells of bacon, smoke, potato steam—all right, that's not unhealthy; if a stable smells of dung—all right, that belongs to a stable; if the field has an odour of ripe corn or potatoes or of guano or manure—that's healthy. . . .

Such pictures may *teach* them something. But to be perfumed is not what a peasant picture needs. . . .

Painting peasant life is a serious thing, and I should reproach myself if I did not try to make pictures which will rouse serious thoughts in those who think seriously about art and about life. . . .

. . . one must paint the peasant as being one of them, as feeling, thinking as they do.

Because one cannot help being the way one is. . . .

From *The Complete Letters of Vincent Van Gogh*. By permission of Little, Brown and Company in conjunction with New York Graphic Society Books.

tional crisis that led him to cut off part of his ear. *Starry Night* (1889) was painted while Van Gogh was in an asylum and the frenzied colours and brushwork illustrate his personal emotional tumult. In 1890, he committed suicide at the age of thirty-seven.

Expressionism

The revolt against traditional artistic expression was continued by a group of French painters. An art critic, shocked by their innovative techniques of bold brushwork, strong contrasts, and intense colours, called the group *Les Fauves* (wild beasts). Fauvist painters such as Henri Matisse (1869–1954), Georges Rouault (1871–1951), and Pierre-Albert Marquet (1875–1947) painted ordinary objects in the most extraordinary ways to express a feeling or mood. For the first time the viewers were expected to develop their own interpretation of the work. Matisse gave perhaps the best definition of their movement.

> Expression . . . does not consist of the passion mirrored upon a human face or betrayed by a violent gesture. The whole arrangement of my picture is expressive. The place occupied by the figures or objects, the empty spaces around them, the proportions, everything plays a part. Composition is the art of arranging, in a decorative manner, the various elements at the painter's disposal for the expression of his feelings.
>
> From Herbert Read, *A Concise History of Modern Painting* (New York: Oxford University Press, 1974), p. 38.

The accepted norms and artistic standards of earlier periods were gone. As a result, expressionism had to redefine its own standards. As one critic put it, expressionists were caught in the "existential dilemma. . . . Art had lost all its sanctions—its divine sanction in the service of God (for God was dead), its human sanction in the service of the community (for man had lost his chains)." Georges Seurat (1859-1891) dismissed past schools even more simply: "There are two ways of expressing things, one is to show them crudely [the realists], the other is to evoke them artistically."

In Germany, young painters adopted an even more radical departure from traditional artistic techniques. The colours were more intense, the technique was cruder, and the themes were more violent than the art world had seen before. These characteristics were the hallmark of expressionism. The most notable expressionist artists included Max Beckmann (1884–1950), James Ensor (1860–1949), Oskar Kokoschka (1886–1980), and Emile Nolde (1867–1956). Gradually some painters, like Wassily Kandinsky (1866–1944), eliminated recognizable forms altogether and created a totally nonobjective or abstract style.

Cubism

Abstraction in art gained prominence with the introduction of cubism. Cubism was originated by Pablo Picasso (1881–1973) and Georges Braque (1882–1963). It combined symbolic expression with geometric form to create a complicated and radical new art form. The most important influences on early cubism were the later paintings of Cézanne and African sculpture. These are evident in Picasso's geometric, transitional painting *Les Demoiselles d'Avignon* (1907). (See colour print.) The three left figures are depicted in the form of Spanish statuary, while the two right figures are clearly African; the faces of the central figures combine frontal views and profiles and the still life presents a logical rather than an optical perspective. The painting heralded the cubist style and is considered a landmark in the development of modern art.

Cubist paintings were conceptually realistic rather than optically so. The artists relied on intellectual vision to change the way an object was depicted and how it was perceived. Many contemporaries did not understand cubist art, however, and looked for some higher level of explanation. Picasso himself rejected attempts to revolutionize the movement.

> Cubism is . . . an art dealing primarily with forms, and when a form is realized it is there to live its own life. . . .
>
> Mathematics, trigonometry, chemistry, psychoanalysis, music, and what not have been related to cubism to give it an easier interpretation. All this has been pure literature, not to say nonsense, which brought bad results, blinding people with theories.
>
> Cubism has kept itself within the limits and limitations of painting, never pretending to go beyond it.
>
> From Robert Goldwater and Marco Treves, *Artists on Art* (New York: Pantheon Books, 1945), pp. 418–419.

As an artistic school, cubism was short-lived, but it succeeded in transforming the art world and challenged our perceptions of the meaning of art.

The techniques of cubism were well established by 1910 and were employed by another group of artists, the *futurists*, who celebrated the machine and urban living. (See readings.) Although the futurists professed to glorify war, the horrors of the First World War effectively killed the short-lived movement. Perhaps the best-known futurist painting is Marcel Duchamp's (1887–1968) *Nude Descending a Staircase*, No. 2 (1912), which combines the elements of cubism and futurism. (See colour print.)

The impressionists and post-impressionists rejected realistic expression in favour of the exploration of technique. Their challenge to tradition created a means of achieving increased emotional expression. This trend continued in expressionism, cubism, and futurism, which explored new techniques and avenues of expression. The rejection of tradition continued after the First World War with dadaism and its successor, surrealism. Abstraction would become the artistic norm for the rest of the century.

Women and Art

European society in the late nineteenth century was very restrictive for women aspiring to be professional artists. While dabbling in art as a hobby was considered an acceptable pastime for a lady, pursuing a career as an artist was considered subversive and even dangerous to the continued stability of society. For those women who chose to ignore the social attitudes of the day, however, there were still many institutional restraints to overcome. There was no free state education for women in fine arts; the École des Beaux Arts, the state art school, was opened to women only in 1897 after a long struggle by women artists. In addition, women's general education was markedly different from men's; the classical education considered essential for success in fine arts was not available to women.

Mary Cassatt was an American expatriate painter who lived primarily in Paris. She was best known for her studies of mothers and children, such as this painting, Girl Arranging Her Hair *(1886). Her delicate style reflected the refinement of Paris society during this time.*

Wealthy women artists trained at private academies or with private tutors. Nearly all women who wanted to become artists worked as copyists in the Louvre. Some women did succeed in achieving artistic recognition. Mary Cassatt (1845–1926), the only American to exhibit with the European impressionists, was renowned for the unique and intimate detail of her portraits. But frequently women's art was judged on the basis of gender. For instance, in praising the work of impressionist Berthe Morisot (1841–1895) a critic said: "Since it is not necessary to have a long training in draughtsmanship in the Academy in order to paint a copper pot, a candlestick, and a bunch of radishes, women succeed quite well in this type of domestic painting." Such explanations for the quality of the work of women artists undermined the significant contributions they made to the artistic movements of the era.

MUSIC

Post-romanticism

The varied styles of the late nineteenth century have often been grouped together as components of the post-romantic period. One of the great post-romantic composers was the Austrian composer and conductor Gustav Mahler (1860–1911). Mahler wrote nine symphonies, leaving a tenth unfinished at the time of his death. The best known of these are Symphony No. 8 (*Symphony of a Thousand*, 1907), Symphony No. 1 in D (*Titan*, 1888) and Symphony No. 5 in C sharp Minor (*The Giant*, 1902). Mahler was in great demand as a conductor and divided his time between composing and conducting. Because of the length and complexity of many of his compositions, they were not well received by contemporary audiences. In fact, his music was not usually included in an orchestra's repertoire until it experienced a revival in the 1950s.

Like Mahler, Richard Strauss (1864–1949) was a composer and conductor. His most important compositions were symphonic poems and operas. Symphonic poems tried to convey emotions and ideas translating the non-musical into music. The best known of Strauss's symphonic poems were *Don Juan* (1888), *Death and Transfiguration* (1889), *Thus Spake Zarathustra* (1896), *Don Quixote* (1897), and *A Hero's Life* (1898). The most familiar of these to today's audience is *Thus Spake Zarathustra* (inspired by Nietzsche), which was used in the soundtrack of the film *2001: A Space Odyssey*.

Strauss also wrote fifteen operas, the most popular of which were *Salome* (1905) and *Cavalier of the Rose* (1911).

The rise of national music that had been such a large part of the romantic tradition continued in the latter part of the nineteenth century. It was particularly strong in countries that lacked a fully developed musical tradition. Folk songs, native rhythms, and national history provided the inspiration for operas, songs, and symphonies. Among the best composers in this tradition were the Czech Antonin Dvorak (1841–1904), the Finn Jean Sibelius (1865–1965), and the Italian Giacomo Puccini (1858–1924). Arguably the best composer of the post-romantic tradition outside of Germany was the Russian Peter Ilyich Tchaikovsky (1840–1893).

Very few composers are more popular with today's audiences than Tchaikovsky. Much of his popularity is due to his music's tunefulness, brilliant orchestration, and theatrical exhibition of emotion. His individual style was characterized by melodic flair marked with brooding fatalism. His best known music is from ballets; *Swan Lake* (1876) is one of the most frequently performed ballets today, and the *Nutcracker Suite* (1892) is a traditional favourite among contemporary audiences. His symphonies—Symphony No. 6 (*Pathétique*, 1893) and the Piano Concerto in B flat minor (1875)—and his operas—*Eugin Onegin* (1879) and the *Queen of Spades*—are also popular and are still performed today.

Impressionism

Impressionism in music was a manifestation of the movement in painting and literature. Just as in the visual arts, musical impressionism attempted to portray the composer's sensory "impression" of a scene or event. Impressionist music did not seek to express feeling or to tell a story like romantic music; instead it evoked a mood, created an atmosphere. Like the impressionist painter, composers used subtleties and understatement. The composer's palette—melody, harmony, colour, and rhythm—was less forthright than the German romantic tradition that had dominated most of the nineteenth century. In music, impressionism was primarily a French movement. The leading composers were Claude Debussy (1862–1918) and Maurice Ravel (1875–1937).

The first recognizable use of impressionism in music was Debussy's *Prelude to the Afternoon of a Faun* (1894), which many critics mark as the beginning of twentieth-century music. The first of what was to be a three-part work, only the *Prelude* was ever completed. Considered the founder of impressionistic music, Debussy introduced important changes to traditional harmony. His music was soft and suggestive and highly original and was a bridge between romanticism and modern music.

The music of Maurice Ravel is sometimes called post-impressionist because he refused to reject formal classical form. Ravel's style featured brilliant orchestration and unusual harmonies. His impressionist work is best illustrated in his piano pieces *Miroirs* (1905) and *Gaspard de la nuit* (1908). Today's audience may be more familiar with Ravel's *Bolero* (1928) (originally a ballet score), which was used in the soundtrack of the film *10*.

RETROSPECTIVE

Increasing socialism and the spread of liberal democracy through universal suffrage forced substantial changes in the outlook of both liberal and conservative governments in the decades prior to the outbreak of the First World War. During this period government intervention was extended beyond economics into social legislation, a trend which was to continue after the war with the development of the welfare state.

As in the political sphere, profound changes took place in other aspects of Western civilization as well. The literary conventions of the previous generation continued to be supplanted by a new generation of writers who used the medium to comment on the state of society. The Industrial Revolution, which had gained full force by the middle of the nineteenth-century, resulted in rapid and astonishing changes in technology as each member of the European community strove to gain a technical advantage over its neighbours. In the visual arts, the challenge to tradition, first sparked by the impressionists, gave birth to a variety of new movements around the turn of the century.

By 1918, the world of nineteenth-century Europe was dead. The postwar generation, having rejected the values and norms of the previous generation, would spend the next two decades searching for new values and the means to express them.

GEORGE BERNARD SHAW: Report on the Fabian Policy (1896)

The Fabians rejected revolutionary Marxism, favouring instead a gradual parliamentary approach to achieve the eventual triumph of socialism. A number of prominent English intellectuals, such as Sidney and Beatrice Webb, H.G. Wells, and George Bernard Shaw, belonged to the society, which was a founding member of the English Labour party. In this excerpt, Shaw sets out the basic principles of the Fabian society.

From the *Report on Fabian Policy and Resolutions*, in George H. Knoles and Rixford K. Synder (eds.), *Readings in Western Civilization*, (Chicago: J.B. Lippincott Co., 1954), pp. 663–666.

I. The Mission of the Fabians

The object of the Fabian Society is to persuade the English people to make their political constitution thoroughly democratic and so to socialize their industries as to make the livelihood of the people entirely independent of private capitalism.

The Fabian Society endeavors to pursue its Socialist and Democratic objects with complete singleness of aim. For example:

It has no distinctive opinions on the Marriage Question, Religion, Art, abstract Economics, historic Evolution, Currency, or any other subject than its own special business of practical Democracy and Socialism.

It brings all the pressure and persuasion in its power to bear on existing forces, caring nothing by what name any party calls itself, or what principles, Socialist or other, it professes, but having regard solely to the tendency of its actions, supporting those which make for Socialism and Democracy, and opposing those which are reactionary.

It does not propose that the practical steps towards Social-Democracy should be carried out by itself, or by any other specially organized society or party.

It does not ask the English people to join the Fabian Society.

II. Fabian Electoral Tactics

The Fabian Society does not claim to be the people of England, or even the Socialist party, and therefore does not seek direct political representation by putting forward Fabian candidates at elections. But it loses no opportunity of influencing elections and inducing constituencies to select Socialists as their candidates. . . .

III. Fabian Toleration

The Fabian Society, far from holding aloof from other bodies, urges its members to lose no opportunity of joining them and permeating them with Fabian ideas as far as possible. Almost all organizations and movements contain elements making for Socialism, no matter how remote the sympathies and intentions of their founders may be from those of the Socialists. On the other hand, unintentionally reactionary proposals are constantly being brought forward in Socialist bodies. Fabians are therefore encouraged to join all other organizations, Socialist or non-Socialist, in which Fabian work can be done.

IV. Fabian Constitutionalism

The Fabian Society is perfectly constitutional in its attitude; and its methods are those usual in political life in England.

The Fabian Society accepts the conditions imposed on it by human nature and by the national character and political circumstances of the English people. It sympathizes with the ordinary citizen's desire for gradual, peaceful changes, as against revolution, conflict with the army and police, and martyrdom. It recognizes the fact that Social-Democracy is not the whole of the working-class program, and that every separate measure towards the socialization of industry will have to compete for precedence with numbers of other reforms. . . .

V. Fabian Democracy

Democracy, as understood by the Fabian Society, means simply the control of the administration by freely elected representatives of the people. . . .

Democracy, as understood by the Fabian Society, makes no political distinction between men and women.

VI. Fabian Compromise

The Fabian Society, having learnt from experience that Socialists cannot have their own way in everything any more than other people, recognizes that in a Democratic community Compromise is a necessary condition of political progress.

VII. Fabian Socialism

Socialism, as understood by the Fabian Society, means the organization and conduct of the necessary industries of the country, and the appropriation of all forms of economic rent of land and capital by the nation as a whole, through the most suitable public authorities, parochial, municipal, provincial, or central.

The Socialism advocated by the Fabian Society is State Socialism exclusively. . . . For example, the distinction made between State Socialism and Social-Democracy in Germany, where the municipalities and other local bodies are closed against the working classes, has no meaning in England. The difficulty in England is not to secure more political power for the people, but to persuade them to make any sensible use of the power they already have.

VIII. Fabian Individualism

The Fabian Society does not suggest that the State should monopolize industry as against private enterprise. . . . to complete the social organization by adding the resources of private activity and judgment to those of public routine, is . . . as highly valued by the Fabian Society as Freedom of Speech, Freedom of the Press, or any other article in the charter of popular liberties.

IX. Fabian Freedom of Thought

The Fabian Society strenuously maintains its freedom of thought and speech with regard to the errors of Socialist authors, economists, leaders, and parties, no less than to those of its opponents. For instance, it insists on the necessity of maintaining as critical an attitude towards Marx and Lassalle, some of whose views must by this time be discarded as erroneous or obsolete, as these eminent Socialists themselves maintained towards their predecessors, St. Simon and Robert Owen. . . .

XII. Fabian Natural Philosophy

The Fabian Society endeavours to rouse social compunction by making the public conscious of the evil condition of society under the present system. This it does by the collection and publication of authentic and impartial statistical tracts, compiled, not from the works of Socialists, but from official sources. The first volume of Karl Marx's *Das Kapital*, which contains an immense mass of carefully verified facts concerning modern capitalistic civilization, and practically nothing about Socialism, is probably the most successful propagandist work ever published. . . .

XIII. Fabian Repudiations

The Fabian Society discards such phrases as "the abolition of the wage system" . . . far from desiring to abolish wages, [the Society] wishes to secure them for everybody.

The Fabian Society resolutely opposes all pretensions to hamper the socialization of industry with equal wages, equal hours of labor, equal official status, or equal authority for everyone. Such conditions are not only impracticable, but imcompatible with the equality of subordination to the common interest which is fundamental in modern Socialism.

XIV. Finally

The Fabian Society does not put Socialism forward as a panacea for the ills of human society, but only for those produced by defective organization of industry and by a radically bad distribution of wealth.

---

1. What are the goals of the Fabian society?

2. What methods do the Fabians advocate to achieve their goals?

3. In chart form, outline how the Fabians differ from (a) utopian socialists and (b) Marxists.

EDUARD BERNSTEIN: Revisionist Marxism (1898)

One of the first attempts to revise Marx's philosophy was made by Eduard Bernstein. While in London in the late nineteenth century, Bernstein became friends with Friedrich Engels and became acquainted with a number of prominent Fabians. Increasingly, he became convinced of the need to revise Marx's philosophy. He outlined his views in a letter to the German Social Democratic party, which was meeting at Stuttgart in October 1898. Although his views were rejected at the meeting, he lived to see revisionism become the dominant philosophy of the party.

From Eduard Bernstein, *Evolutionary Socialism*, in Irving Howe (ed.), *Essential Works of Socialism* (New Haven, CT: Yale University Press, 1976), pp. 241–242, 244–245.

I set myself against the notion that we have to expect shortly a collapse of the bourgeois economy, and that social democracy should be induced by the prospect of such an imminent, great, social catastrophe to adapt its tactics to that assumption. That I maintain most emphatically.

The adherents of this theory of a catastrophe, base it especially on the conclusions of the *Communist Manifesto*. This is a mistake in every respect.

The theory which the *Communist Manifesto* sets forth of the evolution of modern society was correct as far as it characterised the general tendencies of that evolution. But it was mistaken in several special deductions, above all in the estimate of the time the evolution would take. The last has been unreservedly acknowledged by Friedrich Engels, the joint author with Marx of the *Manifesto*, in his preface to the *Class War in France*. But it is evident that if social evolution takes a much greater period of time than was assumed, it must also take upon itself *forms* and lead to forms that were not foreseen and could not be foreseen then.

Social conditions have not developed to such an acute opposition of things and classes as is depicted in the *Manifesto*. It is not only useless, it is the greatest folly to attempt to conceal this from ourselves. The number of members of the possessing classes is today not smaller but larger. The enormous increase of social wealth is not accompanied by a decreasing number of large capitalists but by an increasing number of capitalists of all degrees. The middle classes change their character but they do not disappear from the social scale.

The concentration in productive industry is not being accomplished even today in all its departments with equal thoroughness and at an equal rate. In a great many branches of production it certainly justifies the forecasts of the socialist critic of society; but in other branches it lags even today behind them. The process of concentration in agriculture proceeds still more slowly. Trade statistics show an extraordinarily elaborated graduation of enterprises in regard to size. No rung of the ladder is disappearing from it. The significant changes in the inner structure of these enterprises and their interrelationship cannot do away with this fact.

In all advanced countries we see the privileges of the capitalist bourgeoisie yielding step by step to democratic organisations. Under the influence of this, and driven by the movement of the working classes which is daily becoming stronger, a social reaction has set in against the exploiting tendencies of capital, a counteraction which, although it still proceeds timidly and feebly, yet does exist, and is always drawing more departments of economic life under its influence. Factory legislation, the democratising of local government, and the extension of its area of work, the freeing of trade unions and systems of co-operative trading from legal restrictions, the consideration of standard conditions of labour in the work undertaken by public authorities—all these characterise this phase of the evolution.

But the more the political organisations of modern nations are democratised the more the needs and opportunities of great political catastrophes are diminished. He who holds firmly to the castastrophic theory of evolution must, with all his power, withstand and hinder the evolution described above, which, indeed, the logical defenders of that theory formerly did. But is the conquest of political power by the proletariat simply to be by a political catastrophe? Is it to be the appropriation and utilisation of the power of the State by the proletariat exclusively against the whole nonproletarian world? . . .

No one has questioned the necessity for the working classes to gain the control of government. The point at issue is between the theory of a social cataclysm and the question whether with the given social development in Germany and the present advanced state of its working classes in the towns and the country, a sudden catastrophe would be desirable in the interest of the social democracy. I have denied it and deny it again, because in my judgment a greater security for lasting success lies in a steady advance than in the possibilities offered by a catastrophic crash.

And as I am firmly convinced that important periods in the development of nations cannot be leapt over I lay the greatest value on the next tasks of social democracy, on the struggle for the political rights of the working man, on the political activity of working men in town and country for the interests of their class, as well as on the work of the industrial organisation of the workers.

In this sense I wrote the sentence that the movement means everything for me and that what is *usually* called "the final aim of socialism" is nothing; and in this sense I write it down again today. Even if the word "usually" had not shown that the proposition was only to be understood conditionally, it was obvious that it *could* not express indifference concerning the final carrying out of socialist principles, but only indifference—or, as it would be better expressed, carelessness—as to the form of the final arrangement of things. I have at no time had an excessive interest in the future, beyond general principles; I have not been able to read to the end any picture of the future. My thoughts and efforts are concerned with the duties of the present and the nearest future, and I only busy myself with the perspectives beyond so far as they give me a line of conduct for suitable action now.

The conquest of political power by the working classes, the expropriation of capitalists, are no ends in themselves but only means for the accomplishment of certain aims and endeavours. As such they are demands in the program of social democracy and are not attacked by me. Nothing can be said beforehand as to the circumstances of their accomplishment; we can only fight for their realisation. But the conquest of political power necessitates the possession of political *rights*; and the most important problem of tactics which German social democracy has at the present time to solve, appears to me to be to devise the best ways for the extension of the political and economic rights of the German working classes.

---

1. (a) In what ways does revisionist Marxism differ from the *Communist Manifesto*?
(b) Why does Bernstein argue that change had become necessary?

2. Discuss how revisionist Marxism differs from the philosophy of the Fabians.

ÉMILE ZOLA:
J'accuse (1898)

In 1894, Captain Alfred Dreyfus was convicted of treason for passing military secrets to Germany. A Jew, Dreyfus's conviction was based on circumstantial evidence and appeared to be an anti-Semitic set-up. Even when new evidence surfaced that seemed to prove his innocence, the military court that had convicted him did nothing. The militaristic mood of the country kept the military General Staff safe from government intervention.

After a controversial court martial upheld the earlier verdict, Émile Zola published J'accuse, *in which he made an impassioned accusation of a cover-up on the part of the military. Zola was subsequently charged with libel. In the trial, the jury was told that if Zola was found innocent, the entire General Staff would resign, leaving France defenceless. Under such pressure, the jury found Zola guilty and sentenced him to a fine and a year's imprisonment. Zola fled the country.*

Public outrage at punishing Zola for exposing the Dreyfus affair forced the French government to remove the case from

. . . I accuse Lieutenant-Colonel du Paty de Clam of having been the diabolical worker of the judicial error, unconsciously, I would like to believe, and of having afterwards defended his unhappy work for three years, by the most irrelevant and blameworthy machinations.

I accuse General Mercier of being an accomplice, at the very least, by weakness of spirit, to one of the greatest inequities of the century.

I accuse General Billot of having had in his hands certain proofs of Dreyfus' innocence and of having suppressed them, of being guilty of the crime of betraying society and justice for a political objective and to save the compromised General Staff.

I accuse General de Boisdeffre and General Gonse of being accomplices in the same crime, one doubtless motivated by clerical passion, the other by the *esprit de corps* which makes the offices of War a Holy Ark, unassailable.

I accuse General Pellieux and Major Ravary of having conducted a wicked investigation; I mean by that an investigation of the most monstrous partiality, of which we have, in the latter's report, an imperishable monument of naive audacity.

I accuse the three handwriting experts, Messieurs Belhomme, Varinard, and Couard, of having made false and fraudulent reports, unless a medical examination finds them stricken by diseased views and judgments.

I accuse the War offices of having led an abominable press campaign, especially in the *Eclair* and in the *Echo de Paris*, to mislead public opinion and to conceal their blunder.

I accuse, finally, the first Court-Martial of having broken the law in condemning the accused on secret evidence, and I accuse the second Court-Martial of having concealed this illegality, on orders, and committing in turn the juridical crime of knowingly acquitting a guilty man.

In making these accusations, I am aware that I put myself under the jurisdiction of articles 30 and 31 of the press law of July 29, 1881 which punishes libel offenses. And I willingly expose myself to it.

military jurisdiction. The captain was pardoned in 1899. Zola then returned to Paris in triumph, where he died in 1902. At his funeral, he was honoured as a man who "for a moment . . . was the conscience of mankind."

From L. Derfler, *The Third French Republic*, 1870–1940, (Princeton, NJ: Van Nostrand, 1966), pp. 142–143.

As for the people whom I have accused, I do not know them; I have never seen them, I bear them no hatred or bitterness. They are only entities to me, examples of social malfeasance. And the act that I have accomplished here is only a revolutionary means to hasten the revelation of truth and justice.

I have only one passion, for enlightenment, in the name of humanity which has suffered so and which has a right to happiness. My enflamed protest is only the cry of my soul. Let someone therefore indict me at the court of assizes and let the investigation take place in full daylight!

I am waiting!

---

1. Based upon your knowledge of the Dreyfus case, Zola's comments, and the militaristic mood of France, create a brief hypothesis stating why Zola's accusations caused such a public outcry against him.

2. Zola's letter was published in the Paris newspaper *L'aurore* on 13 January 1898.
(a) Write an editorial for that newspaper in support of Zola.
(b) Write an editorial for either a pro-Zola or pro-military paper after Zola's trial.

SIGMUND FREUD: The Unconscious (1915)

Freud believed that neurotic behaviour was based on trauma buried in the unconscious mind. (Freud almost never used the term "subconscious"; nevertheless, it has entered the popular vocabulary of Freudian theories.) Freud had been arguing about the importance of the unconscious for twenty years when the following was published in Zeitschift *in 1915.*

From Peter Gay (ed.), *The Freud Reader* (New York: W.W. Norton and Co., 1989), pp. 573–577.

We have learnt from psycho-analysis that the essence of the process of repression lies, not in putting an end to, in annihilating, the idea which represents an instinct, but in preventing it from becoming conscious. When this happens we say of the idea that it is in a state of being "unconscious," and we can produce good evidence to show that even when it is unconscious it can produce effects, even including some which finally reach consciousness. Everything that is repressed must remain unconscious; but let us state at the very outset that the repressed does not cover everything that is unconscious. The unconscious has the wider compass: the repressed is a part of the unconscious.

How are we to arrive at a knowledge of the unconscious? It is of course only as something conscious that we know it, after it has undergone transformation or translation into something conscious. Psycho-analytic work shows us every day that translation of this kind is possible. In order that this should come about, the person under analysis must overcome certain resistances—the same resistances as those which, earlier, made the material concerned into something repressed by rejecting it from the conscious.

Justification for the Concept of the Unconscious

Our right to assume the existence of something mental that is unconscious and to employ that assumption for the purposes of scientific work is disputed in many quarters. To this we can rely that our assumption of the unconscious is *necessary* and *legitimate*, and that we possess numerous proofs of its existence.

It is *necessary* because the data of consciousness have a very large number of gaps in them; both in healthy and in sick people psychical acts often occur which can be explained only by presupposing other acts, of which, nevertheless, consciousness affords no evidence. These not only include parapraxes and dreams in healthy people, and everything described as a psychical symptom or an obsession in the sick; our most personal daily experience acquaints us with ideas that come into our head we do not know from where, and with intellectual conclusions arrived at we do not know how. All these conscious acts remain disconnected and unintelligible if we insist upon claiming that every mental act that occurs in us must also necessarily be experienced by us through consciousness; on the other hand, they fall into a demonstrable connection if we interpolate between them the unconscious acts which we have inferred. A gain in meaning is a perfectly justifiable ground for going beyond the limits of direct experience. When, in addition, it turns out that the assumption of there being an unconscious enables us to construct a successful procedure by which we can exert an effective influence upon the course of conscious processes, this success will have given us an incontrovertible proof of the existence of what we have assumed. This being so, we must adopt the position that to require that whatever goes on in the mind must also be known to consciousness is to make an untenable claim.

We can go further and argue, in support of there being an unconscious psychical state, that at any given moment consciousness includes only a small content, so that the greater part of what we call conscious knowledge must in any case be for very considerable periods of time in a state of latency, that is to say, of being psychically unconscious. When all our latent memories are taken into consideration it becomes totally incomprehensible how the existence of the unconscious can be denied. But here we encounter the objection that these latent recollections can no longer be described as psychical, but that they correspond to residues of somatic processes from which what is psychical can once more arise. The obvious answer to this is that a latent memory is, on the contrary, an unquestionable residuum of a *psychical* process. But it is more important to realize clearly that this objection is based on the equation—not, it is true, explicity stated but taken as axiomatic—of what is conscious with what is mental. This equation is either a *petitio principii* which begs the question whether everything that is psychical is also necessarily conscious; or else it is a matter of convention, of nomenclature. In this latter case it is, of course, like any other convention, not open to refutation. The question remains, however, whether the convention is so expedient that we are bound to adopt it. To this we may reply that the conventional equation of the psychical with the conscious is totally inexpedient. It disrupts psychical continuities, plunges us into the insoluble difficulties of psycho-physical parallelism, is open to the reproach that for no obvious reason it over-estimates the part played by consciousness, and that it forces us prematurely to abandon the field of psychological research without being able to offer us any compensation from other fields.

It is clear in any case that this question—whether the latent states of mental life, whose existence is undeniable, are to be conceived of as conscious mental states or as physical ones—threatens to resolve itself into a verbal dispute. We shall therefore be better advised to focus our attention on what we know with certainty of the nature of these debatable states. As far as their physical characteristics are concerned, they are totally inaccessible to us: no physiological concept or chemical process can give us any notion of their nature. On the other hand, we know for certain that they have abundant points of contact with conscious mental processes; with the help of a certain amount of work they can be transformed into, or replaced by, conscious mental processes, and all the categories which we employ to describe conscious mental acts, such as ideas, purposes, resolutions and so on, can be applied to them. Indeed, we are obliged to say of some of these latent states that the only respect in which they differ from conscious ones is precisely in the absence of consciousness. Thus we shall not hesitate to treat them as objects of psychological research, and to deal with them in the most intimate connection with conscious mental acts.

The stubborn denial of psychical character to latent mental acts is accounted for by the circumstance that most of the phenomena concerned have not been the subject of study outside psycho-analysis. Anyone who is ignorant of pathological facts, who regards the parapraxes of normal people as accidental, and who is content with the old saw that dreams are froth . . . has only to ignore a few more problems of the psychology of consciousness in order to spare himself any need to assume an unconscious mental activity. Incidentally, even before the time of psycho-analysis, hypnotic experiments, and especially post-hypnotic suggestion, had tangibly demonstrated the existence and mode of operation of the mental unconscious.

The assumption of an unconscious is, moreover, a perfectly *legitimate* one, inasmuch as in postulating it we are not departing a single step from our customary and generally accepted mode of thinking. Consciousness makes each of us aware only of his own state of mind; that other people, too, possess a consciousness is an inference which we draw by analogy from their observable utterances and actions, in order to make this behaviour of theirs intelligible to us. . . . This inference (or this identification) was formerly extended by the ego to other human beings, to animals, plants, inanimate objects and to the world at large, and proved serviceable so long as their similarity to the individual ego was overwhelmingly great; but it became more untrustworthy in proportion as the difference between the ego and these "others" widened. Today, our critical judgment is already in doubt on the question of consciousness in animals; we refuse to admit it in plants and we regard the assumption of its existence in inanimate matter as mysticism. But even where the original inclination to identification has withstood criticism—that is, when the "others" are our fellow-men—the assumption of a consciousness in them rests upon an inference and cannot share the immediate certainty which we have of our own consciousness.

Psycho-analysis demands nothing more than that we should apply this process of inference to ourselves also—a proceeding to which, it is true, we are not constitutionally inclined. If we do this, we must say: all the acts and manifestations which I notice in myself and do not know how to link up with the rest of my mental life must be judged as if they belonged to someone else: they are to be explained by a mental life ascribed to this other person. Furthermore, experience shows that we understand very well how to interpret in other people (that is, how to fit into their chain of mental events) the same acts which we refuse to acknowledge as being mental in ourselves. Here some special hindrance evidently deflects our investigations from our own self and prevents our obtaining a true knowledge of it.

This process of inference, when applied to oneself in spite of internal opposition, does not, however, lead to the disclosure of an unconscious; it leads logically to

This painting of Sigmund Freud, the father of psychoanalysis, hangs in his former Hampstead home.

the assumption of another, second consciousness which is united in one's self with the consciousness one knows. But at this point, certain criticisms may fairly be made. In the first place, a consciousness of which its own possessor knows nothing is something very different from a consciousness belonging to another person, and it is questionable whether such a consciousness, lacking, as it does, its most important characteristic, deserves any discussion at all. Those who have resisted the assumption of any unconscious *psychical* are not likely to be ready to exchange it for an unconscious *consciousness*. In the second place, analysis shows that the different latent mental processes inferred by us enjoy a high degree of mutual independence, as though they had no connection with one another, and knew nothing of one another. We must be prepared, if so, to assume the existence in us not only of a second consciousness, but of a third, fourth, perhaps of an unlimited number of states of consciousness, all unknown to us and to one another. In the third place—and this is the most weighty argument of all—we have to take into account the fact that analytic investigation reveals some of these latent processes as having characteristics and peculiarities which seem alien to us, or even incredible, and which run directly counter to the attributes of consciousness with which we are familiar. Thus we have grounds for modifying our inference about ourselves and saying that what is proved is not the existence of second consciousness in us, but the existence of psychical acts which lack consciousness. We shall also be right in rejecting the term "subconsciousness" as incorrect and misleading. The well-known cases of "*double conscience*" (splitting of consciousness) prove nothing against our view. We may most aptly describe them as cases of splitting of the mental activities into two groups, and say that the same consciousness turns to one or the other of these groups alternately.

In psycho-analysis there is no choice for us but to assert the mental processes are in themselves unconscious, and to liken the perception of them by means of consciousness to the perception of the external world by means of the sense-organs. We can even hope to gain fresh knowledge from the comparison. The psycho-analytic assumption of unconscious mental activity appears to us, on the other hand, as a further expansion of the primitive animism which caused us to see copies of our own consciousness all around us, and, on the other hand, as an extension of the corrections undertaken by Kant of our views on external perception. Just as Kant warned us not to overlook the fact that our perceptions are subjectively conditioned and must not be regarded as identical with what is perceived though unknowable, so psycho-analysis warns us not to equate perceptions by means of consciousness with the unconscious mental processes which are their object. Like the physical, the psychical is not necessarily in reality what it appears to us to be. We shall be glad to learn, however, that the correction of internal perception will turn out not to offer such great difficulties as the correction of external perception—that internal objects are less unknowable than the external world.

---

1. List the justifications Freud gives for the unconscious.

2. Outline the ways in which Freud's ideas were a challenge to traditional thought.

FRIEDRICH NIETZSCHE:
The Intellectual Challenge
(1883–1886)

Perhaps the most potent challenge to the prevailing ideas of progress came from the German philosopher Friedrich Nietzsche. He believed that Christianity, democracy, and socialism were undercutting the natural development of humanity by imposing morality on the Ubermensch *(literally, "the superior man"). For Nietzsche, great achievements were the product of exceptional individuals who freed themselves from the corruption of modern consciousness and created their own set of values. He described his ideal person in* Thus Spake Zarathustra.

From Friedrich Nietzsche, *Thus Spake Zarathustra*, in Michael Curtis (ed.), *The Great Political Theories*, Vol. 2 (New York: Avon Books, 1962), pp. 261–263.

The Superior Man

1

When I went among men for the first time, I committed the anchorit's folly, the great folly: I stood in the marketplace.

And when I talked to all, I talked to no one. In the evening, rope-dancers and corpses were my companions. I myself was almost a corpse.

But with the new morning, a new truth came to me. I learned to say, "What do I care for marketplace and rabble and rabble-noise and long rabble-ears!"

You superior men! Learn this from me: No one in the marketplace believes in superior men. If you must speak there, very well. But the rabble, squinting, will say, "We are all equal."

"You superior men," the rabble will squint, "there are no superior men. We are all equal; man is man; before God—we are all equal!"

Before God! but now this God is dead. And before the rabble we do not wish to be equal. You superior men, go away from the marketplace.

2

Before God! But now this God is dead. You superior men, this God was your greatest danger.

Only since he is in his grave, have you risen again. Only now comes the great noontide; only now the superior man will be—lord!

Did you understand this word, oh my brothers? You are shocked—are your hearts reeling? Do you see the abyss sprawling? Do you hear the hell-hound brawling?

Onward! Upward! You superior men! Only now the mountain of man's future screams in labor. God died: now we want—the Superman to live.

3

The most worried men today ask, "How can we preserve man?" But Zarathustra is the first and only one who asks, "How can we master man?"

The Superman is close to my heart; *he* is my first and only—*not* man. Not the nearest, not the poorest, not the greatest sufferer, not the best—

Oh my brothers, what I can love in man is that he is a transcending and a descending into the depths. In you, too, there is much to make me love and hope.

That you have contempt, you superior men, makes me hope. For those who have great contempt have great reverence.

That you despair is greatly to be honoured. For you have not learned to give in; you have not learned small clevernesses.

Today, you see, the small people have become lords; they all preach giving in and doing without, and cleverness and diligence and considerateness and the whole long etcetera of the small virtues.

Whatever is of female and servile origin, especially the rabble-hodge-podge—*they* now want to be lord over all human destiny! Oh nausea! Nausea! Nausea!

They now ask and peer and don't grow weary: "How can man be preserved best, longest, most pleasantly?" With that—they are lords of today.

Master these lords of today, oh my brothers! These small people—*they* are the greatest danger to the Superman!

Master the small virtues, you superior men, the small clevernesses, the grain-of-sand considerations, the ant-swarmings, the wretched creature-comforts, the "happiness of the greatest number!"

Despair rather than give in! Truly, I love you, you superior men, for not knowing how to live today. For that way you live best!

5

"Man is evil"—so the wisest men told me to console me. Ah, if it were only still true! For evil is man's best strength.

"Man must grow stronger in good and in evil"—that is my teaching. The worst is necessary for the Superman's best.

Suffering and taking sin upon himself might have been right for that preacher of small people. But I rejoice in great sin as my great *solace*.—

But such things are not said for long ears. Not every word belongs in every snout. These are delicate distant things—not made for sheeps' paws to paw at!

6

You superior men, do you think I exist to make good what you did badly? . . .

You have not suffered enough to suit me. For you have always suffered from yourselves—you have not yet suffered from *mankind*. You would be lying if you denied it. None of you suffers my sufferings.—

FRIEDRICH NIETZSCHE: Beyond Good and Evil (1886)

In Beyond Good and Evil, *Nietzsche outlined two types of morality: the master morality and the slave morality. The master morality lived in freedom and held others in subjection; the slave morality lived in slavery and subjection. It was the slave morality that fostered Christianity and promoted the principle of equality and democracy in an attempt to drag the superior individual down to his or her level.*

From Friedrich Nietzsche, *Beyond Good and Evil*, in Joseph P. Zaccano, Jr. (ed.), *Topics in Western Civilization* (Berkeley, CA: McCutchan Publishing Co., 1969), pp. 234–237.

In strolling through the many finer and coarser forms of morality which have hitherto prevailed or yet prevail on the earth, I found certain characteristics recurring regularly in connection with one another, until at last two fundamental types betrayed themselves to me, and a fundamental distinction was brought to light. There is *Master-morality* and *Slave-morality*. I would at once add, however, that in all higher and compound civilizations one finds attempts at the reconciliation of the two systems, while still oftener one finds their confusion and mutual misunderstanding; in fact, sometimes their close juxtaposition—even in the same man, in the same soul. The distinctions of moral worth have arisen either in a ruling caste, agreeably conscious of being distinct from the ruled; or among the ruled themselves, the slaves and dependents of all classes. In the first case, when it is the ruling caste that determines the conception "good," it is the exalted, proud disposition which is regarded as distinguishing and decisive as to the degree of rank. The noble type of man separates from himself those in whom the opposite of this is exalted, proud disposition displays itself—he despises them. (Let it be noted that in this first kind of morality the antithesis "good" and "bad" signifies practically the same as "noble" and "contemptible"; the antithesis "good" and "evil" has a different origin.) The despised ones are the cowards, the timid, the insignificant, those thinking merely of narrow utility, and moreover the distrustful with their constrained glances, the self-abasing, the dog-species of men who allow themselves to be misused, the mendacious flatterers and, above all, the liars—it is a fundamental belief of all aristocrats that the common people are deceitful; "we true ones," the nobility of ancient Greece called themselves.

It is obvious that the designations of moral worth everywhere were at first applied to *men*, and were only derivatively and at a later period applied to actions. It is a bad mistake, therefore, when historical moralists start with questions such as—"Why have sympathetic actions been praised?" The noble type of man regards *himself* as the determiner of worth, it is not necessary for him to be approved of, he passes the judgment—"What is injurious to me is injurious in itself;" he recognizes that it is he himself only that confers honour on things—he is a *creator of worth*, of values. The type of man in question honours whatever qualities he recognizes in himself: his morality is self-glorification. In the foreground there is the feeling of plenitude and power which seeks to overflow, the happiness of high tension, the consciousness of riches which would fain five and bestow; the noble man also helps the unfortunate, not (or scarcely) out of sympathy, but rather out of an impulse produced by the super-abundance of power. The noble man honours the powerful one in himself, and also him who has self-command, who knows how to speak and keep silence, who joyfully exercises strictness and severity over himself and reverences all that is strict and severe. "Wotan has put a hard heart in my breast" says the hero of an old Scandinavian saga: the idea is thus expressed right out of the heart of a proud viking. Such a type of man is in fact proud of not being made for sympathy; the hero of the saga therefore adds by way of warning: "He who has not had a hard heart when young, will never have a hard heart." The noble and brave who think thus are furthest removed from the morality which sees precisely in sympathy, in acting for the good of others, or in disinterestedness, the characteristic of morality; a belief in oneself, a pride in oneself, a fundamental hostility and irony with respect to "selflessness," belong as distinctly to the higher morality as do careless scorn and precaution in presence of sympathy and the "warm heart." It is powerful who *know* how to honour: it is their art, their domain, their invention. The profound reverence for age and tradition—all law rests on this double reverence—the belief and prejudice in favour of ancestor and unfavourable to newcomers, is typical of the morality of the powerful; and if, reversely, men of "modern ideas" believe almost instinctively in "progress" and "the future," and are more and more lacking in respect for the old, the ignoble origin of these "ideas" complacently betrays itself thereby.

The morality of the ruling class, however, is more especially foreign and irritating to the taste of the present day, owing to the sternness of the principle that one has only obligations to one's equals, that one may act toward beings of a lower rank, and towards all that is foreign to one, according to discretion, or as the heart desires, and in any case "beyond Good and Evil." It is here that sympathy and similar sentiments like to have a place. The capacity and obligation for prolonged gratitude and prolonged revenge—both only among equals—artfulness in retaliation, refinement of ideas in friendship, certain necessity to have enemies (as outlets for the passion of envy, quarrelsomeness, arrogance—in fact, in order to be a good friend): these are all typical characteristics of the noble morality, which, as we have indicated, is not the morality of "modern ideas," and on that account is at present difficult to realize, and also difficult to unearth and disclose.

Friedrich Nietzsche was one of the foremost critics of Western civilization in the late nineteenth century.

It is different with the second type of morality, Slave-morality. Supposing that the misused, the oppressed, the suffering, the enslaved, the weary and those uncertain of themselves should moralise, what will be the common element in their estimates of moral worth? Probably a pessimistic suspicion with regard to the whole situation of man will find expression, perhaps a condemnation of man together with disapproval the virtues of the powerful; he has a thorough skepticism and distrust, a *refinement* of distrust, of everything "good" that is there honoured; he would like to persuade himself that the very happiness there is not genuine. On the other hand, *those* qualities are brought into prominence and into the light which tend to alleviate the existence of sufferers; it is here that the kind helping hand, the warm heart, along with sympathy, patience, diligence, submissiveness and friendliness attain to honor; for these are the most useful qualities here, and almost the only expedients for supporting the burden of existence. Slave-morality is essentially the morality of utility. This is the seat of the origin of the celebrated antithesis "good" and "evil"; the notion of power and dangerousness is introduced into the evil, the ideas of dreadfulness, subtlety and strength, which do not admit of being despised. According to slave-morality, the "evil" man also excites fear; according to master-morality, it is precisely the "good" man who excites fear and seeks to excite it, while the "bad" man is regarded as the contemptible being. The contrast attains its maximum when, according to the logical consequences involved, a tinge of depreciation attaches itself to the "good" man of slave-morality; because in any case he has to be the *safe* man: he is good-natured, easily deceived, perhaps a little stupid, *un bonhomme*. Wherever slave-morality gets the upper hand, language shows a tendency to approximate the significations of the words "good" and "stupid."

A last fundamental distinction: the desire for *liberty*, the instinct for happiness, and the refinements of the feeling of freedom, belong as necessarily to the domain of slave-morals and slave-morality, as enthusiasm and art in reverence and devotion are the regular symptoms of an aristocratic mode of thinking and valuing.

---

1. Describe the attributes of Nietzsche's "superior man."

2. What is Nietzche's attitude toward women?

1. Define *master morality* and *slave morality*.

2. How would Nietzsche respond to the ideas of Marx? Darwin? Spencer? Bakunin?

3. *According to Neitzsche, society should be ruled not by the whims of the mob but rather through the inspired leadership of the exceptional individual.*

Based on your study of European history in the eighteenth and nineteenth centuries and your consideration of the historians' debate on the role of the individual, create and defend a thesis either supporting or rejecting Nietzsche's view of humanity. (NOTE: Your thesis defence should be between 500 and 750 words long and should include specific historical examples to support your position.)

HENRIK IBSEN:
A Doll's House (1879)

The Norwegian playwright Henrik Ibsen is sometimes called the "father of modern drama" because his plays established realism as the ruling principle of that genre. Ibsen's plays attacked the social problems of the day. In A Doll's House, *Ibsen criticized the parent-child relationship that existed between a husband and wife. The feminist ideas presented here provoked considerable controversy. The play is perhaps the best known drama about the role and rights of women.*

In A Doll's House, *Torvald and Nora Helmer have a conventional middle-class marriage. A crisis develops, however, when Nora is blackmailed because of a signature she forged in order to obtain money when her husband had been ill years before. When Torvald learns of the deceit, he reviles Nora and claims she is unfit to care for their children. Nora realizes that she has been nothing more than a child to her husband and she resolves to leave her home, her husband, and her children to educate herself about life.*

Helmer. You have loved me as a wife ought to love her husband. Only you had not sufficient knowledge to judge of the means you used. But do you suppose you are any the less dear to me, because you don't understand how to act on your own responsibility? No, no; only lean on me; I will advise you and direct you. I should not be a man if this womanly helplessness did not just give you a double attractiveness in my eyes. You must not think any more about the hard things I said in my first moment of consternation, when I thought everything was going to overwhelm me. I have forgiven you. Nora; I swear to you I have forgiven you.
Nora. Thank you for your forgiveness.
[*She goes out through the door to the right.*]
Helmer. No, don't go—. (*Looks in.*) What are you doing in there?
Nora. (*from within*). Taking off my fancy dress.
Helmer. (standing at the open door). Yes, do. Try and calm yourself, and make your mind easy again, my frightened little singing-bird. Be at rest, and feel secure; I have broad wings to shelter you under. (*Walks up and down by the door.*) How warm and cosy our home is, Nora. Here is shelter for you; here I will protect you like a hunted dove that I have saved from a hawk's claws; I will bring peace to your poor beating heart. It will come, little by little, Nora, believe me. Tomorrow morning you will look upon it all quite differently; soon everything will be just as it was before. Very soon you won't need me to assure you that I have forgiven you; you will yourself feel the certainty that I have done so. Can you suppose I should ever think of such a thing as repudiating you, or even reproaching you? You have no idea what a true man's heart is like, Nora. There is something so indescribably sweet and satisfying, to a man, in the knowledge that he has forgiven his wife—forgiven her freely, and with all his heart. It seems as if that had made her, as it were, doubly his own; he has given her a new life, so to speak; and she has in a way become both wife and child to him. So you shall be for me after this, my little scared, helpless darling. Have no anxiety about anything, Nora; only be frank and open with me, and I will serve as will and conscience both to you—. What is this? Not gone to bed? Have you changed your things?
Nora (*in everyday dress*). Yes, Torvald, I have changed my things now.
Helmer. But what for?—so late as this.
Nora. I shall not sleep to-night.
Helmer. But, my dear Nora—
Nora (*looking at her watch*). It is not so very late. Sit down here, Torvald. You and I have much to say to one another.
[*She sits down at one side of the table.*]
Helmer. Nora—what is this?—this cold, set face?
Nora. Sit down. It will take some time; I have a lot to talk over with you.
Helmer (*sits down at the opposite side of the table*). You alarm me, Nora—and I don't understand you.
Nora. No, that is just it. You don't understand me, and I have never understood you either—before to-night. No, you mustn't interrupt me. You must simply listen to what I say. Torvald, this is a settling of accounts.
Helmer. What do you mean by that?

Nora (*after a short silence*). Isn't there one thing that strikes you as strange in our sitting here like this?

Helmer. What is that?

Nora. We have been married now eight years. Does it not occur to you that this is the first time we two, you and I, husband and wife, have had a serious conversation?

Helmer. What do you mean by serious?

Nora. In all these eight years—longer than that—from the very beginning of our acquaintance, we have never exchanged a word on any serious subject.

Helmer. Was it likely that I would be continually and for ever telling you about worries that you could not help me to bear?

Nora. I am not speaking about business matters. I say that we have never sat down in earnest together to try and get at the bottom of anything.

Helmer. But, dearest Nora, would it have been any good to you?

Nora. That is just it; you have never understood me. I have been greatly wronged, Torvald—first by papa and then by you.

Helmer. What! By us two—by us two, who have loved you better than anyone else in the world?

Nora (*shaking her head*). You have never loved me. You have only thought it pleasant to be in love with me.

Helmer. Nora, what do I hear you saying?

Nora. It is perfectly true, Torvald. When I was at home with papa, he told me his opinion about everything, and so I had the same opinions; and if I differed from him I concealed the fact, because he would not have liked it. He called me his doll-child, and he played with me just as I used to play with my dolls. And when I came to live with you—

Helmer. What sort of an expression is that to use about our marriage?

Nora (*undisturbed*). I mean that I was simply transferred from papa's hands into yours. You arranged everything according to your own taste, and so I got the same tastes as you—or else I pretended to, I am really not quite sure which—I think sometimes the one and sometimes the other. When I look back on it, it seems to me as if I had been living here like a poor woman—just from hand to mouth. I have existed merely to perform tricks for you, Torvald. But you would have it so. You and papa have committed a great sin against me. It is your fault that I have made nothing of my life.

Helmer. How unreasonable and how ungrateful you are, Nora! Have you not been happy here?

Nora. No, I have never been happy. I thought I was, but it has never really been so.

Helmer. Not—not happy!

Nora. No, only merry. And you have always been so kind to me. But our home has been nothing but a playroom. I have been your doll-wife, just as at home I was a papa's doll-child; and here the children have been my dolls. I thought it great fun when you played with me, just as they thought it great fun when I played with them. That is what our marriage has been, Torvald.

Helmer. There is some truth in what you say—exaggerated and strained as your view of it is. But for the future it shall be different. Playtime shall be over, and lesson-time shall begin.
Nora. Whose lessons? Mine, or the children's?
Helmer. Both yours and the children's, my darling Nora.
Nora. Alas, Torvald, you are not the man to educate me into being a proper wife for you.
Helmer. And you can say that!
Nora. And I—how am I fitted to bring up the children?
Helmer. Nora!
Nora. Didn't you say so yourself a little while ago—that you dare not trust me to bring them up?
Helmer. In a moment of anger! Why do you pay any heed to that?
Nora. Indeed, you were perfectly right. I am not fit for the task. There is another task I must undertake first. I must try and educate myself—you are not the man to help me in that. I must do that for myself. And that is why I am going to leave you now.
Helmer (*springing up*). What do you say?
Nora. I must stand quite alone, if I am to understand myself and everything about me. It is for that reason that I cannot remain with you any longer.
Helmer. Nora! Nora!
Nora. I am going away from here now, at once. I am sure Christine will take me in for the night—
Helmer. You are out of your mind! I won't allow it! I forbid you!
Nora. It is no use forbidding me anything any longer. I will take with me what belongs to myself. I will take nothing from you, either now or later.
Helmer. What sort of madness is this!
Nora. To-morrow I shall go home—I mean, to my old home. It will be easiest for me to find something to do there.
Helmer. You blind, foolish woman!
Nora. I must try and get some sense, Torvald.
Helmer. To desert your home, your husband and your children! And you don't consider what people will say!
Nora. I cannot consider that at all. I only know that it is necessary for me.
Helmer. It's shocking. This is how you would neglect your most sacred duties.
Nora. What do you consider my most sacred duties?
Helmer. Do I need to tell you that? Are they not your duties to your husband and your children?
Nora. I have other duties just as sacred.
Helmer. That you have not. What duties could those be?
Nora. Duties to myself.
Helmer. Before all else, you are a wife and a mother.
Nora. I don't believe that any longer. I believe that before all else I am a reasonable human being, just as you are—or, at all events, that I must try and become one. I know quite well, Torvald, that most people would think you right, and that views

of that kind are to be found in books; but I can no longer content myself with what most people say, or with what is found in books. I must think over things for myself and get to understand them.

Helmer. Can you not understand your place in your own home? Have you not a reliable guide in such matters as that?—have you no religion?

Nora. I am afraid, Torvald, I do not exactly know what religion is.

Helmer. What are you saying?

Nora. I know nothing but what the clergyman said, when I went to be confirmed. He told us that religion was this, and that, and the other. When I am away from all this, and am alone, I will look into that matter too. I will see if what the clergyman said is true, or at all events if it is true for me.

Helmer. This is unheard of in a girl of your age! But if religion cannot lead you aright, let me try and awaken your conscience. I suppose you have some moral sense? Or—answer me—am I to think you have none?

Nora. I assure you, Torvald, that is not an easy question to answer. I really don't know. The thing perplexes me altogether. I only know that you and I look at it in quite a different light. I am learning, too, that the law is quite another thing from what I supposed; but I find it impossible to convince myself that the law is right. According to it a woman has no right to spare her old dying father, or to save her husband's life. I can't believe that.

Helmer. You talk like a child. You don't understand the conditions of the world in which you live.

Nora. No, I don't. But now I am going to try. I am going to see if I can make out who is right, the world or I.

Helmer. You are ill, Nora; you are delirious; I almost think you are out of your mind.

Nora. I have never felt my mind so clear and certain as tonight.

Helmer. And is it with a clear and certain mind that you forsake your husband and your children?

Nora. Yes, it is.

Helmer. Then there is only one possible explanation.

Nora. What is that?

Helmer. You do not love me any more.

Nora. No, that is just it.

Helmer. Nora!—and you can say that?

Nora. It gives me great pain, Torvald, for you have always been so kind to me, but I cannot help it. I do not love you any more.

Helmer (*regaining his composure*). Is that a clear and certain conviction too?

Nora. Yes, absolutely clear and certain. That is the reason why I will not stay here any longer.

Helmer. And can you tell me what I have done to forfeit your love?

Nora. Yes, indeed I can. It was tonight, when the wonderful thing did not happen; then I saw you were not the man I had thought you.

Helmer. Explain yourself better—I don't understand you.

Nora. I have waited so patiently for eight years; for, goodness knows, I knew very well that wonderful things don't happen every day. Then this horrible misfortune came upon me; and then I felt quite certain that the wonderful thing was going to happen at last. When Krogstad's letter was lying out there, never for a moment did I imagine that you would consent to accept this man's conditions. I was so absolutely certain that you would say to him: Publish the thing to the whole world. And when that was done—
Helmer. Yes, what them?—when I had exposed my wife to shame and disgrace?
Nora. When that was done, I was so absolutely certain, you would come forward and take everything upon yourself, and say: I am the guilty one.
Helmer. Nora—!
Nora. You mean that I would never have accepted such a sacrifice on your part? No, of course not. But what would my assurances have been worth against yours? That was the wonderful thing which I hoped for and feared; and it was to prevent that, that I wanted to kill myself.
Helmer. I would gladly work night and day for you. Nora—bear sorrow and want for your sake. But no man would sacrifice his honour for the one he loves.
Nora. It is a thing hundreds of thousands of women have done.
Helmer. Oh, you think and talk like a heedless child.
Nora. Maybe. But you neither think nor talk like the man I could bind myself to. As soon as your fear was over—and it was not fear for what threatened me, but for what might happen to you—when the whole thing was past, as far as you were concerned it was exactly as if nothing at all had happened. Exactly as before, I was your little skylark, your doll, which you would in future treat with doubly gentle care, because it was so brittle and fragile. (*Getting up.*) Torvald—it was then it dawned upon me that for eight years I had been living here with a strange man, and had borne him three children—. Oh, I can't bear to think of it! I could tear myself into little bits!
Helmer (*sadly*). I see, I see. An abyss has opened between us—there is no denying it. But, Nora, would it not be possible to fill it up?
Nora. As I am now, I am no wife for you.
Helmer. I have it in me to become a different man.
Nora. Perhaps—if your doll is taken away from you.
Helmer. But to part!—to part from you! No, no, Nora, I can't understand that idea.
Nora (*going out to the right*). That makes it all the more certain that it must be done. [*She comes back with her cloak and hat and a small bag which she puts on a chair by the table.*]
Helmer. Nora, Nora, not now! Wait till tomorrow.
Nora (*putting on her cloak*). I cannot spend the night in a strange man's room.
Helmer. But can't we live here like brother and sister—?
Nora (*putting on her hat*). You know very well that would not last long. (*Puts the shawl around her.*) Good-bye, Torvald. I won't see the little ones. I know they are in better hands than mine. As I am now, I can be of no use to them.
Helmer. But some day, Nora—some day?

Nora. How can I tell? I have no idea what is going to become of me.
Helmer. But you are my wife, whatever becomes of you.
Nora. Listen, Torvald. I have heard that when a wife deserts her husband's house, as I am doing now, he is legally freed from all obligations towards her. In any case I set you free from all your obligations. You are not to feel yourself bound in the slightest way, any more than I shall. There must be perfect freedom on both sides. See, here is your ring back. Give me mine.
Helmer. That too?
Nora. That too.
Helmer. Here it is.
Nora. That's right. Now it is all over. I have put the keys here. The maids know all about everything in the house—better than I do. Tomorrow, after I have left her, Christine will come here and pack my own things that I brought with me from home. I will have them sent after me.
Helmer. All over! All over!—Nora, shall you never think of me again?
Nora. I know I shall often think of you and the children and this house.
Helmer. May I write to you, Nora?
Nora. No—never. You must not do that.
Helmer. But at least let me send you—
Nora. Nothing—nothing—
Helmer. Let me help you if you are in want.
Nora. No. I can receive nothing from a stranger.
Helmer. Nora—can I never be anything more than a stranger to you?
Nora (*taking her bag*). Ah, Torvald, the most wonderful thing of all would have to happen.
Helmer. Tell me what that would be!
Nora. Both you and I would have to be so changed that—. Oh, Torvald, I don't believe any longer in wonderful things happening.
Helmer. But I will believe in it. Tell me! So changed that—?
Nora. That our life together would be a real wedlock. Good-bye.
[*She goes out through the hall.*]
Helmer (*sinks down on a chair at the door and buries his face in his hands*). Nora! Nora! (*Looks round, and rises.*) Empty. She is gone. (*A hope flashes across his mind.*) The most wonderful thing of all—?
(*The sound of a door shutting is heard from below.*)

---

1. What attitudes are revealed in Helmer's remarks to Nora?

2. (a) Whom does Nora blame for her ignorance and helplessness?
(b) In your opinion, is this a valid observation? Why or why not?

3. Discuss how Nora's view of her duty to herself conflicts with the contemporary view of a woman's duty.

4. Describe "real wedlock" from Nora's point of view.

ANALYSIS AND APPLICATION

1. In chart form, compare and contrast the goals and methods of revisionist Marxists, syndicalists, and the Fabians.

2. Compare syndicalism with the Polish Solidarity movement.

3. Compare and contrast the approaches to the nonrational adopted by Freud and Nietzsche.

4. Investigate how Nietzsche's ideas were adapted by fascists.

5. Create a pictoral essay illustrating the artistic developments of the period. Identify the artist, style, and significance of each painting chosen.

6. Select an individual from this period and pursue further research in order to create a profile of this person.

7. With a classmate, stage a two-person debate between Émile Zola and a member of the French High Command over the following resolution: *The good of the nation is more important than the rights of the individual.*

   At the conclusion of your debate, write a one-page, point-form summary of the arguments used by both sides.

8. Investigate the relationship between the struggle to enfranchise women and the emancipation of blacks in the nineteenth century in the United States.

9. Stage a scene from a play by George Bernard Shaw. Have the audience evaluate not the performance, but the social values depicted in the scene as a reflection of turn-of-the-century Europe.

10. In what way were traditions challenged during this period?

CHAPTER NINE

The Tradition Challenged: The Global Crisis, 1880 to 1918

THE NEW NATIONALISM AND THE EUROPEAN WORLD

The late nineteenth century was a time of rapid change in economic, scientific, and political thought. In spite of this, however, by 1880 the social structure of Europe was still much the same as it had been in 1815. But between 1880 and 1918 monumental changes were to take place in the areas of social policy, artistic pursuit, and political and economic expansion. Internationally, the relationship among nations was clouded by the emergence of the dominant forces of nationalism, imperialism, militarism, and military alliances. The pressures caused by social change and the tension-charged international climate were to result in a catastrophic clash on the battlefields of Europe in the First World War. The society that emerged from the ashes would be greatly changed.

Forces of Nationalism

The forces of nationalism had a firm grip on Europe by 1900. In some nations, such as the Russian Empire, the Austrian Empire, and the Ottoman Empire, where different national groups were bound together by an imperial government, nationalism was discouraged and suppressed. The governments of these empires realized that outbursts of nationalism would lead to the destruction of their states. This had to be avoided at all costs.

The Austro-Hungarian Empire faced the greatest threat of nationalist division from within. Twelve million German-speaking Austrians controlled a combined population of almost 9 million Czechs and Slovaks and millions of Poles and Italians. In the other "half" of the empire, the Hungarians, who had only recently been granted equal status with the Austrians, maintained an iron grip over more than 10 million Romanians, Slovaks, Serbs, and Croats. Sitting on the southern border of the empire, the independent Kingdom of Serbia was an example of the type of independent nation-state these nationalities wanted to form. The Russian Empire also posed a threat in the region because the czar saw himself as the leader of a new Pan-Slav movement that would liberate the Slavs from Austro-Hungarian domination and unite all of southeastern Europe.

In other countries, such as Great Britain, France, Italy, Germany, and the United States, nationalism was a force for unification and strength. In these nationally "pure" states, the sentiment of nationalism was a positive force for the establishment of collective goals and policies. Consequently these governments tended to reach outward rather than inward in their priorities.

In France, national sentiment focused on revenge. Prior to 1870, France had been the most powerful nation on the continent. In the Franco-Prussian War of 1870–1871, however, Germany had not only beaten France but had exacted a heavy toll from the loser. France was ordered to pay Germany a large indemnity and its two most valuable provinces, Alsace and Lorraine, were annexed by the new empire. In these conquered territories, the use of French was banned in official documents and the teaching of the language was discouraged in the schools. In the Place de la Concorde in Paris, a statue depicting Strasbourg, the principal city of Alsace, was draped in black from 1871 to 1918. National sentiment called for the restoration of the two "lost" provinces.

The New German Empire

Perhaps the most significant political event of the late nineteenth century was the emergence of the "new" German Empire. Forged together by Prussia through a series of foreign policy manoeuvres, its birth in 1871 marked a new reality in European power politics. The declaration of the Second Empire in the Hall of Mirrors at Versailles at the end of the Franco-Prussian War marked the attainment of a nationalist dream for many Germans. The next decades would be spent bringing glory to their newly constituted homeland. For the practical politicians of Germany, however, the present afforded much more substantial challenges.

Prince Otto von Bismarck (1815–1898) recognized that German security depended on maintaining a balance of power on the European continent. Although the German Empire had supplanted France as the dominant power, the basic power structure had not changed. No individual nation was strong enough to pursue an irresponsible course in its foreign policy. Over the next two decades, however, this collective stability would disappear.

THE EMERGENCE OF THE ALLIANCE SYSTEM

The Congress of Berlin

Following the Russo-Turkish War of 1877–1878, the weaknesses within the existing Congress system for resolving international disputes were apparent. The Russian Empire had defeated Turkey and in the process had "liberated" a great deal of the Balkan peninsula previously controlled by the Ottomans. The Russians created the buffer state of Bulgaria under their control and considered the reorganization of the rest of the former Turkish territory. Fearful of the emergence of a Russian hegemony in the region, Bismarck convened the Congress of Berlin in 1878 to settle the Balkan question. Russia was allowed to keep a small portion of territory on the Black Sea. But its desire to secure access to a warm-water port on the Mediterranean was frustrated by the recognition of the autonomous states of Romania, Serbia, and Montenegro. In compensation for the increase in Russian territory, Austria-Hungary was given the right to "occupy and administer" Bosnia and the British were given the island of Cyprus. Russia felt that it had won the war only to lose the peace.

The Move Toward Bilateral Alliances

The Congress of Berlin marked the end of the Congress system, which had more or less maintained the peace since 1815. Led by Germany, most nations began to move away from collective action and toward a more binding system of two-party alliances. In 1879, the Germans signed a secret protocol with Austria to form the Dual Alliance. Under its terms, Germany agreed to come to the defence of Austria if it were attacked by Italy, while the Austrians made the same commitment to Germany in the event it was attacked by France. Additional secret protocols were signed with Italy in 1882 to form the Triple Alliance and with Romania in 1883. Within eight years Bismarck had protected both his flanks. Under the Reinsurance Treaty with Russia in 1887, Moscow pledged neutrality in any French-German conflict, while Berlin made the same pledge in the case of a war between Russia and Austria. With Bismarck in charge, the German people had no fear of a two-front war.

Within two years of the signing of the Reinsurance Treaty, however, the face of German foreign policy had begun to change. Wilhelm II (1859–1941) became kaiser in 1889. He rejected Bismarck's conservative defence-oriented policies in favour of a more aggressive expansionist German role in international affairs. Bismarck was soon dismissed as chancellor and Wilhelm himself took charge.

One of the first acts of the young emperor was to cancel the Reinsurance Treaty in 1890. This threw Russia into the arms of the French, who concluded their own mutual defence pact, the Franco-Prussian Alliance, in 1894. Under its terms the two allies agreed to mobilize if any member of the Triple Alliance were to do so. In addition, each pledged to go to war if the other were attacked by Germany. As a further incentive during the negotiations, French capital was pledged to help the Russians develop their industrial and rail transportation systems.

Wilhelm's second major initiative, his *Weltpolitik*, had equally ominous ramifications for the German Empire. The kaiser's global ambitions threatened Great Britain, particularly as Germany embarked on an accelerated program of ship construction. British attempts to negotiate a limit on shipbuilding were rejected by the Germans and so it began to look for allies of its own. In 1904, Great Britain concluded the *Entente Cordiale* with France. Although primarily designed to settle outstanding colonial disputes, the entente was the first step toward a more substantial military commitment. Three years later, Great Britain signed an agreement with the Russian Empire resulting in the formation of the Triple Entente (1907). Now the lines had been drawn in Europe. The Great Powers were divided into two armed camps.

IMPERIALISM

The three decades following the Berlin Conference of 1884–1885 saw the rise and fall of the philosophy of imperialism in Europe. In the single generation spanning the 1880s to 1914, Europe's domination of the rest of the world was completed. The feeling of national and racial superiority fostered by imperialism would carry Europe on its crest until it all came crashing down in the First World War.

The New Empire Building

How did this new empire building differ from the old? First, it had little do with establishing colonies or transplanting surplus population. The new targets of empire tended to be densely populated areas that had experienced rapid Westernization through the expansion of the European industrial system. In actual fact, the European powers were politically and economically partitioning the entire world. The new colonies became sources of valuable raw materials and equally valuable markets for surplus European goods. The main target of this explosion of imperialism was Africa. At the Berlin Conference, the major powers agreed that any nation occupying a clearly defined coastal area on that continent would automatically gain rights on the adjacent interior as well. Thus there was an immediate scramble to obtain colonies in Africa. While Africa had been 95 percent independent prior to 1870, by 1900 the entire continent, with the exception of Abyssinia (Ethiopia), was under European control.

This movement to "Europeanize" the world was a natural extension of nationalism. Supported by economic interests and enforced by the military, European colonizers spread Western civilization around the world. The colonizers developed the infrastructures necessary to establish control. They built schools, rail lines, and hospitals. They dug harbours, established plantation agriculture, and opened mines. In the process, the indigenous people of these regions were either subjugated or eliminated. So successful was this Europeanization that by 1900 over 700 million European descendants lived outside of Europe. By 1914, Great Britain alone controlled over 20 percent of the earth's land surface.

Imperialism was not restricted to the European powers alone, however. Japan had industrialized in the late nineteenth century and it moved to expand its empire into Manchuria and Korea. This brought it into conflict with Russia. The Russo-Japanese war of 1904–1905 ended in victory for the Japanese and indicated that the Russian military was not as powerful as people had thought.

North American Imperialism

North Americans also subscribed to this new vision of the world. In 1898, the United States, after more than a century of focusing its attention on North America, suddenly took an interest in affairs in the Pacific. As a result of the Spanish-American War, the United States took control of the Philippines and Guam. That same year it annexed Hawaii. Those acquisitions, coupled with the takeover of Cuba and Puerto Rico, marked the emergence of the United States as a full-fledged imperialist power.

The Anglo-Saxon Alliance

For many North Americans this new imperialism was a natural extension of the continental expansion of the previous century. Theorists such as Josiah Strong, John Fiske, and John W. Burgess saw a new mission for the United States as part of a world unified and dominated by an Anglo-Saxon alliance. This was not a new idea. The British had already absorbed large portions of the globe into their empire. It was considered only natural that the United States should continue the process. But while their ideas were supported by the proponents of overseas expansion, these people were not actually imperialists. Rather, they were idealists who believed in the gradual spread of the English language, the Christian church, and democratic institutions. Although often quoted by imperialist politicians, they had little impact on popular thought.

Canada, too, had a role to play in this new imperialism. George Munro Grant (1835–1902), principal of Queen's University, saw Canada as the "living link" between the United States and Britain in this global mission. He

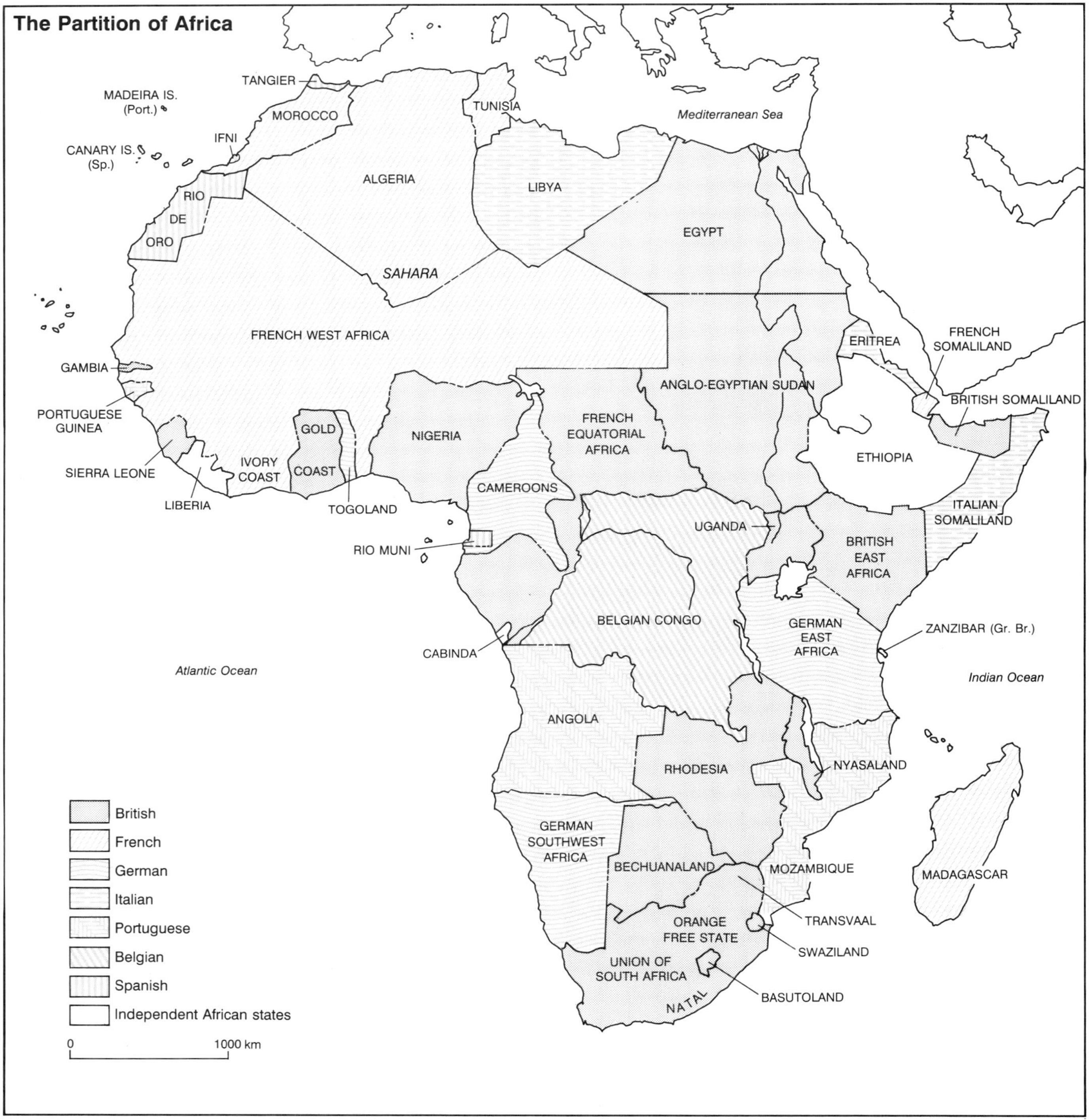

The Partition of Africa

TANGIER
MADEIRA IS. (Port.)
CANARY IS. (Sp.)
IFNI
MOROCCO
TUNISIA
Mediterranean Sea
ALGERIA
LIBYA
RIO DE ORO
EGYPT
SAHARA
FRENCH WEST AFRICA
ERITREA
FRENCH SOMALILAND
GAMBIA
ANGLO-EGYPTIAN SUDAN
BRITISH SOMALILAND
PORTUGUESE GUINEA
FRENCH EQUATORIAL AFRICA
GOLD COAST
NIGERIA
ETHIOPIA
SIERRA LEONE
IVORY COAST
LIBERIA
TOGOLAND
CAMEROONS
ITALIAN SOMALILAND
UGANDA
RIO MUNI
BRITISH EAST AFRICA
BELGIAN CONGO
GERMAN EAST AFRICA
ZANZIBAR (Gr. Br.)
CABINDA
Atlantic Ocean
Indian Ocean
ANGOLA
RHODESIA
NYASALAND
GERMAN SOUTHWEST AFRICA
BECHUANALAND
MOZAMBIQUE
MADAGASCAR
TRANSVAAL
ORANGE FREE STATE
SWAZILAND
UNION OF SOUTH AFRICA
NATAL
BASUTOLAND

British
French
German
Italian
Portuguese
Belgian
Spanish
Independent African states

0 1000 km

RESPONSES TO IMPERIALISM: INDIA AND CHINA

Imperialist expansion resulted not only in conflict between imperialists but conflict between indigenous peoples as well. The responses to imperialism were many and varied. In India, they were generally within the traditions of modern Western civilization. This first excerpt is from a speech by Dadabhai Naoroji, president of the Indian National Congress. Naoroji was a moderate nationalist who believed that education of the Indian people would eventually bring down the British.

The power that is now being raised by the spread of education, though yet slow and small, is one that in time, must for weal or woe, exercise great influence. In fact, it has already begun to do so. . . .

The voice of the power of the rising education is, no doubt, feeble at present. Like the infant, the present dissatisfaction is only crying at the pains it is suffering. Its notions have not taken any form or shape or course yet, but it is growing. Heaven only knows what it will grow to! If the present material and moral destruction of India continues, a great convulsion must inevitably arise by which either India will be more and more crushed under the iron heel of despotism and destruction, or may succeed in shattering the destroying hand and power.

A more radical viewpoint was expressed by Bal Gangadhar Tilak, an extreme nationalist. He advocated that the Indian people take more direct action in the form of a boycott.

We shall not give [the British] assistance to collect revenue and keep peace. We shall not assist them in fighting beyond the frontiers or outside of India with Indian blood and money. We shall not assist them in carrying on the administration of justice. We shall have our own courts, and when the time comes we shall not pay taxes. Can you do that by your united efforts? If you can, you are free from tomorrow. Some gentleman who spoke this evening referred to half a bread as against the whole bread. I say I want the whole bread, and that immediately. But I cannot get the whole, don't think that I have no patience.

I will take the half they give me and then try for the remainder. . . .

From Sydney Eisen and Maurice Filler (eds.), *The Human Adventure*, Vol. 2 (New York: Harcourt, Brace & World, 1964), pp. 66–68.

In China, the I-ho-ch'uan ("righteous harmony fists"), commonly called the Boxers, took a more violent course of action against foreigners. The Boxer Rebellion was originally directed at Roman Catholic missionaries and converted Chinese, but it grew into opposition to everything foreign. The following placard was distributed in Tientsin on 4 June 1900.

The Catholic and Protestant religions being insolent to the gods and extinguishing sanctity, rendering no obedience to Buddhism and enraging both Heaven and Earth, the rain clouds now no longer visit us; but 8 000 000 Spirit Soldiers will descend from Heaven and sweep the Empire clear of all foreigners. Then will the gentle showers once more water our lands: and, when the tread of soldiers and the clash of steel are heard, heralding woes to all our people, then the Buddhist's Patriotic League of Boxers will be able to protect the Empire and bring peace to all its people.

Hasten, then, to spread this doctrine far and wide; for, if you gain one adherent to the faith, your own person will be absolved from all future misfortunes. If you gain five adherents to the faith, your whole family will be absolved from all evils; and, if you gain ten adherents to the faith your whole village will be absolved from all calamities. Those who gain no adherents to the cause shall be decapitated; for, until all foreigners have been exterminated, the rain shall never visit us. . . .

From Louis L. Snyder (ed.), *The Imperialism Reader: Documents and Readings on Modern Expansionism* (Princeton, NJ: Van Nostrand Co., Inc., 1962), p. 324.

The Boxer Rebellion led to the deaths of 242 Westerners and several thousand Chinese converts. The Western governments responded by sending an Allied force to crush the rebellion.

expressed those same sentiments on behalf of the British Empire:

> We have a mission on earth. Our mission was to make this world the home of freedom, of justice, of peace, and to secure these ends the British Empire was the highest secular institution the world has ever known.

His sentiments were echoed by Sir George Robert Parkin (1846–1922), who stated in defence of British imperial influence, "I am one of those who believe that power and influence are not given to some nation without divine purpose."

Parkin and Grant were proponents of the concept of social Darwinism, whereby the "organism" of the state had to adapt to the changing "environment" of global power politics. The mission of the empire was to provide benign protection for the "weaker races" of Asia and Africa. (See chapter 7.)

The Expansion of American Sea Power

In his *Interest of America in Sea Power* (1897), naval historian Admiral Alfred Thayer Mahan (1840–1914) wrote that the commercial and military interests of the United States necessitated the expansion of American sea power. Mahan believed that the goal of overseas expansion should not be the acquisition of colonies but the development of markets. He advocated that the navy be rebuilt with modern battleships, that a canal be built across Central America, and that naval bases be established worldwide. His suggestions struck a responsive note. The decade of the 1890s had seen a general economic decline in the United States. Farm prices were at an all-time low and industrial production had run out of profitable markets. Over 75 percent of all American exports went to Europe, but there were other possibilities. At the end of the century, only 10 percent of U.S. foreign trade was with Latin America and less than 5 percent was with Asia. If these markets could be tapped, then renewed growth might be possible.

This economic argument, coupled with Mahan's vision of a strong global naval presence, began to provide a focus for policy-makers. As the nineteenth century drew to a close, the United States began to look beyond its borders once again. Canadians too read Mahan with interest. For some, his writings represented the telling argument for an integrated defence policy for the whole empire. For others, he was living proof of the direct link between imperialism and militarism in the modern world.

THE PRELUDE TO WAR

The Growth of Militarism

The emergence of continental power blocs and the rapid acquisition of overseas territories necessitated military expansion. This new militarism had two faces. Its more obvious characteristic was the emergence of a naval arms race. Between 1890 and 1914, Germany increased its spending on shipbuilding almost six times to over $1.3 million. Great Britain, already spending almost $700 000 a year in 1890, was forced to increase spending to almost $3 million a year by 1914 to counter this German growth.

Ironically, Britain undermined its own naval superiority. In 1906, the British launched the super-battleship, the HMS *Dreadnought*. Suddenly all other vessels were obsolete. Now the Germans could ignore Britain's advantage in other ships and concentrate on building dreadnoughts. Over the next eight years forty-six of the superships would be built, twenty-nine by Britain and seventeen by its rival. The drain on the economies of both nations was substantial. On a per capita basis, the dollars invested by Great Britain ($8.53) and Germany ($8.52) far outstripped land-based rivals such as Austria-Hungary ($3.48) and Russia ($2.58). Only France ($7.33), trying to maintain both a naval fleet and a large standing army, came close to matching military spending in Britain and Germany.

There was a second, hidden face to militarism. In each European nation the military exercised a great deal of political influence. In some countries, such as Germany and Russia, the connection was public. The emperor was seen as the leader of the armed forces and the high command formed an aristocratic power group within the country. In other nations, such as France, the military remained in the shadows. Its influence was felt through subtle political and economic pressure on the democratic leadership. In both cases, there was an ever-present danger that military concerns and priorities might take precedence over civilian ones. As tensions mounted in the first two decades of the twentieth century, this situation became more and more common.

The Europe that had emerged by the beginning of the second decade of the twentieth century had all the characteristics of an armed camp. Like the Cold War fifty years later, European nations were heavily armed and were surrounded with dependable allies. They wrapped themselves in the rhetoric of national and economic independence. With so many loaded cannons it would take only a spark to set things off.

The Balkan Spark

The face of southeastern Europe rapidly changed in the late nineteenth and early twentieth centuries. Following the Congress of Berlin in 1878, the Ottoman Empire (Turkey) continued to lose influence and control in the region. The resulting power vacuum led to increased interference by the region's powerful neighbours, Austria-Hungary, Italy, and Russia. In 1908, an internal uprising within the Ottoman Empire, led by the Young Turk party, resulted in revolts in many of the outlying provinces.

Following Bulgaria's declaration of independence, Austria annexed neighbouring Bosnia and Herzegovina, over Serbian objections. The Serbs had seen the two areas as natural additions to a larger Slavic state, giving them potential access to the Adriatic Sea. As a result, they mobilized their army against Austria. At the same time, the Russian Empire agitated for the opening of the Bosphorus and Dardanelle straits to its shipping. Britain saw this drive by the Russians for a warm-water port as a threat to its domination of the Mediterranean and therefore it opposed its ally's demands. As compensation, Britain backed the Russians in their support of Serbia against the Austrians. A secret treaty in 1909 finally preserved the status quo but did nothing to lessen tensions in the region.

Within three years there was conflict again. In 1912, Serbia, Bulgaria, Greece, and Montenegro formed the First Balkan League. In October of that year, they attacked Turkey and virtually took over all of its European territory. Once the war was won, however, the victors turned on each other. Serbia's demands to annex Albania were rebuffed (it became an independent nation the following year) and Bulgaria, in an attempt to expand westward, attacked Serbia.

The Second Balkan War saw a whole new configuration of alliances. Romania, Greece, and Montenegro, with the support of their former arch enemy, Turkey, backed Serbia against their old ally, Bulgaria. The final result was more confusion and tension.

Bulgaria lost Macedonia to Greece, which annexed that region and Crete in 1913. The offer to aid Bulgaria further alienated Austria-Hungary from Romania and Serbia. The independence of Albania completely frustrated Serbian ambitions and left that nation feeling bitter and betrayed. It is no wonder that by 1914 the Balkans were called the powder keg of Europe.

THE OUTBREAK OF WAR

By 1914, the European continent had divided into two power blocs. On one side, linked by secret agreements and protocols, stood the Triple Entente of Great Britain, France, and Russia. On the other side was the Triple Alliance of Germany, Austria-Hungary, and Italy. This balance of power was intended to keep the peace. Instead, it gave individual nations the security to take reckless action. The whole continent teetered on the brink of war; it would take only a small shove to push it over. That came in the small town of Sarajevo, Bosnia, in June 1914.

Archduke Franz Ferdinand (1863–1914), the heir to the throne of Austria, was shot by terrorists while driving through the town. The assassin, Gavrillo Princip, was a member of the Black Hand, an organization dedicated to the union of Bosnia with Serbia. Although there was no evidence of direct involvement in the assassination by the Serbian government, the Austrian government delivered an ultimatum to the Serbs on July 23rd. Among its demands was a time limit of forty-eight hours for the Serbs to agree to Austrian participation in a full-scale investigation of the incident. Although Serbia agreed to many of the other demands, it objected to this one as an encroachment upon its sovereignty. Austria-Hungary, buoyed by German guarantees of support, declared war on its small neighbour on July 28th.

Mobilization

Russia immediately began to mobilize in defence of its ally, Serbia. Meanwhile the Austrians were receiving mixed messages from their German allies. Chancellor Bethmann-Hollweg (1856–1921) was attempting to mediate the dispute between Austria and Serbia, but the German general staff was encouraging the Austrian military to mobilize. On 31 July 1914, Austria did begin to mobilize, and at the same time presented Russia with a twelve-hour ultimatum demanding that it discontinue its mobilization. Germany also asked France for a declaration of neutrality.

The Russian Empire ignored the Austro-Hungarian ultimatum. Consequently, the next day it found itself at war with both Germany and Austria-Hungary. Within two days, Germany had mobilized and declared war on France, which had announced that it would act "in accordance with its own interests."

The Schlieffen Plan

In the decades prior to the outbreak of war, Germany had devised a plan to deal with the eventuality of a two-front war

Europe Before the First World War

FINLAND
NORWAY
SWEDEN
Baltic Sea
GREAT BRITAIN
IRELAND
North Sea
DENMARK
RUSSIAN EMPIRE
NETH.
GERMAN EMPIRE
Atlantic Ocean
BELGIUM
LUX.
FRANCE
SWITZ.
AUSTRO-HUNGARIAN EMPIRE
ITALY
PORTUGAL
SPAIN
BOSNIA
Adriatic Sea
SERBIA
ROMANIA
Black Sea
BULGARIA
CORSICA
SARDINIA
ALBANIA
GREECE
OTTOMAN EMPIRE
SICILY
Mediterranean Sea

Triple Entente
Triple Alliance

0 500 km

THE ASSASSINATION OF ARCHDUKE FRANZ FERDINAND

The following eyewitness account of the assassination of the archduke and his wife was given by Borijove Jevtic, one of the conspirators involved in the incident. Although arrested, Jevtic was released because of lack of evidence.

The fateful morning dawned. Two hours before Franz Ferdinand arrived in Sarajevo, all the twenty-two conspirators were in their allotted positions, armed and ready. They were distributed five hundred yards apart over the whole route along which the Archduke must travel from the railroad station to the Town Hall.

When Franz Ferdinand and his retinue drove from the station they were allowed to pass the first two conspirators. The motor cars were driving too fast to make an attempt feasible and in the crowd were Serbians; throwing a grenade would have killed many innocent people.

When the car passed Gabrinovic, the compositor, he threw his grenade. It hit the side of the car, but Franz Ferdinand with presence of mind threw himself back and was uninjured. Several officers riding in his attendance were injured.

The cars sped to the Town Hall and the rest of the conspirators did not interfere with them. After the reception in the Town Hall, General Potiorek, the Austrian commander, pleaded with Franz Ferdinand to leave the city, as it was seething with rebellion. The Archduke was persuaded to drive the shortest way out of the city and to go quickly. . . .

The road to the manoeuvres was shaped like the letter V, making a sharp turn at the bridge over the river Nilgacka. Franz Ferdinand's car could go fast enough until it reached this spot, but here it was forced to slow down for the turn. Here Princip had taken his stand.

As the car came abreast he stepped forward from the curb, drew his automatic pistol from his coat, and fired two shots. The first struck the wife of the Archduke, the Archduchess Sofia, in the abdomen. . . . She died instantly.

The second bullet struck the Archduke close to the heart.

He uttered only one word, "Sofia"—a call to his stricken wife. Then his head fell back and he collapsed. He died almost instantly.

The officers seized Princip. They beat him over the head with the flat of their swords. They knocked him down, they kicked him, scraped the skin from his neck with the edges of their swords, tortured him, all but killed him.

Then he was taken to the Sarajevo jail. The next day he was transferred to the military prison and the roundup of his fellow conspirators proceeded, although he denied that he had worked with anyone. . . .

His only sign of regret was the statement that he was sorry he had killed the wife of the Archduke. He had aimed only at her husband and would have preferred that any other bullet should have struck General Potiorek.

From *The New York World*, 29 June 1924, in Sydney Eisen and Maurice Filler (eds.), *The Human Adventure: Readings in World History* (New York: Harcourt, Brace & World, 1964), pp. 116–117.

with Russia and France. The Schlieffen Plan was based upon a series of premises: (1) that Germany could not fight and win a two-front war; (2) that it would take Russia six weeks to mobilize its massive army to the point where it was ready to attack Germany; and (3) that Germany therefore had to ignore Russia, attack and defeat France in four to five weeks, and quickly move its forces to the eastern front. Thus when France refused to stay neutral and Russia began to mobilize in early August 1914, the Germans had no choice but to declare war on their western neighbours and to put the Schlieffen Plan into action.

Germany's basic strategy was a simple one. One arm of

the army would launch an attack toward Paris from a base in Alsace-Lorraine. While the French army engaged this thrust, a second wing of the German army would sweep through Belgium and northern France and come up against the enemy from behind. Caught between the two flanks of the German attack, the French would be crushed.

From the start, the Schlieffen Plan did not unfold the way the Germans had hoped. First Belgium refused to allow the German army free passage. The subsequent German invasion of Belgium, while an easy victory, sparked an unexpected British reaction. Under the Treaty of London (1838), Great Britain, France, Austria, Russia, and Prussia had guaranteed Belgian neutrality. This violation of that agreement gave the British government (who had not made public its secret commitments to the French and the Russians) a concrete reason to enter the war. In addition, the southern flank of the German army, instead of engaging the French and then drawing them back to expose them to a crushing attack from the north, was too strong and simply pushed their opponents back. As a result, rather than catching the French in a vise, both German flanks confronted their enemy just outside of Paris. In the "miracle" of the Marne, France regrouped and threw the invaders back. Now not strong enough to deliver the knock-out blow, the Germans dug in. By mid-August British forces, with troops from the rest of the British Empire, including Canada, had joined the French on the front lines. The long trench war had begun. Four long, bloody years of conflict lay ahead.

RESPONSIBILITY FOR THE WAR

Why did war erupt in August 1914? Basically it was a matter of mutual distrust and the mistaken belief that a limited, local war could be fought and won on the European continent. In addition, extreme nationalism, coupled with a militaristic mentality and supportive alliances, made most nations unwilling to compromise in seeking a peaceful solution. Austria-Hungary and Russia refused to give up the idea of a "supra-national" empire and Czar Nicholas and Emperor Franz Joseph both wanted to establish their own hegemony in the Balkans. Emergent nation-states, such as Bulgaria, Romania, and especially Serbia, vehemently resisted any encroachment on their national sovereignty. For their part, France and Germany, fearful of political and military isolation, allied themselves with the aggressive policies of their partners and failed to exercise any moderating influence upon their actions. And Britain, by not declaring itself clearly, gave mixed messages to the French (who expected its support) and the Germans (who expected it to remain neutral).

As the war dragged on, the belligerents used propaganda to boost morale on the home front. News from the front was controlled and censored and atrocities, real or invented, were well publicized. Posters were designed to instill confidence of victory or, as in the case of this 1917 anti-German poster by David Wilson, to foster hatred for the enemy.

PROPAGANDA

Propaganda was used by all the belligerents in the First World War, both for maintaining popular support for the war effort and for influencing foreign opinion. Atrocity stories, real and imagined, established German "war guilt" and did much to build the feelings of hatred and vindictiveness that surrounded the peace conference at Versailles.

Propaganda Leaflets

One common practice was to drop leaflets by plane or balloon into the trenches of the enemy. The hope was to demoralize opposing troops to the point of desertion. The excerpt below is from a French pamphlet aimed at German troops. It was supposed to be written by German prisoners of war.

Pass this along!

German War Comrades!

Think about this:

—Only greedy rulers want war. The people want peace, and work, and bread . . .

—No one wanted to fight Germany, no one opposed her desires for a "place in the sun."

—Stop fighting! Turn your cannons around! Come over to us. Shoot anyone who wants to hinder you from coming.

The following excerpt is from a British leaflet.

For what are you fighting, Michel?

They tell you that you are fighting for the Fatherland. Have you ever thought why you are fighting?

You are fighting to glorify Hindenburg, to enrich Krupp. You are struggling for the Kaiser, the Junkers and the militarists. . . .

They promise you victory and peace. You poor fools! It was promised your comrades for more than three years. They have indeed found peace, deep in the grave, but victory did not come!

This German pamphlet was dropped over American lines near the end of the war.

Never say die!

Don't die until you have to! . . .

Isn't it better anyhow to live than to die, no matter how "glorious" a cause? Isn't it better to live and come back to the old folks at home, than to rot in the shell holes and trenches of France?

If you surrender to us, we'll treat you fair enough. Why run any more chances than you have to? You might as well be a free boarder in Germany till the war is over.

The "Evolution" of News in Wartime

Basic news stories often did not carry enough of a propaganda message on their own. Copywriters and editorialists around the world embellished stories to make a point. The excerpts below illustrate how one incident—in this case the fall of Antwerp—was reported in papers throughout Europe.

THE FALL OF ANTWERP

November 1914

When the fall of Antwerp got known, the church bells were rung [in Germany].—*Kolnische Zeitung* (Berlin)

According to the *Kolnische Zeitung*, the clergy of Antwerp were compelled to right the church bells when the fortress was taken.—*Le Matin* (Paris)

According to what *Le Matin* has heard from Cologne, the Belgian priests who refused to ring the church bells when Antwerp was taken have been driven away from their old places.*The Times* (London)

According to what The *Times* has heard from Cologne via Paris, the unfortunate Belgian priests who refused to ring the church bells when Antwerp was taken have been sentenced to hard labour.—*Corrière della Sera* (Milan)

According to information to the *Corrière della Sera* from Cologne via London, it is confirmed that the barbaric conquerors of Antwerp punished the unfortunate Belgian priests for their heroic refusal to ring the church bells by hanging them as living clappers to the bells with their heads down.—*Le Matin* (Paris)

From Louis L. Snyder (ed.), *Historic Documents of World War I* (Princeton, NJ: Van Nostrand, 1958), pp. 134–135, 137–138.

Canadian soldiers captured German trenches at Vimy Ridge. Many people believe that the Canadian nationality was born on this battlefield.

THE GREAT WAR, 1914 TO 1918

The Western Front

After the sweeping invasions of the German troops in August 1914, the First World War settled into a brutal war of attrition. On the Western Front (northeastern France and Belgium), the opposing armies dug trenches and protected them with mines and barbed wire. Various attempts to break through enemy lines failed and for the next four years attack and counterattack saw little territory change hands while millions of people died. In the four-year battle to control the area around Verdun, for example, over 700 000 soldiers died without gaining any tangible tactical advantage. For those planning the campaigns, the harsh realities of battle often bore little resemblance to the military strategies they adopted. Troops were considered expendable and the carnage was without precedent.

New weapons of war added to the death toll. The machine gun killed thousands of soldiers. Poison gas was introduced by the Germans in 1915 and became an effective weapon used by both sides. Tanks and airplanes were dramatic additions to military arsenals, but they had little effect on the course of the war. Another new weapon, the submarine, had a decided effect on public opinion in the United States when unrestricted submarine warfare resulted in the loss of over 1000 lives—128 of whom were American—aboard the British ocean liner *Lusitania*. The attack heightened anti-German sentiment in the United States and helped draw that country into the war in 1917.

Patriotic songs such as "Over There" by George M. Cohan were popular during the war.

GAS ATTACK

On 22 April 1915, the Germans dropped chlorine gas over a 6 km stretch of the Allied lines at Ypres. This was a tactical surprise and the portion of the line held by French colonial troops collapsed immediately. Only the extraordinary heroism of small detachments of Canadian troops prevented the collapse of the entire front. The Germans failed to follow up on this devastating attack and within a few days Allied troops were equipped with functional respirators that allowed them to filter the gas.

Two Canadian soldiers take shelter in a trench on Vimy Ridge in April 1917.

New York Tribune, 27 April 1915

[*Boulogne, April 25*]—The gaseous vapour which the Germans used against the French divisions near Ypres last Thursday, contrary to the rules of The Hague Convention, introduces a new element into warfare. The attack of last Thursday evening was preceded by the rising of a cloud of vapour, greenish gray and iridescent. That vapour settled to the ground like a swamp mist and drifted toward the French trenches on a brisk wind. Its effect on the French was a violent nausea and faintness, followed by an utter collapse. It is believed that the Germans, who charged in behind the vapour, met no resistance at all, the French at their front being virtually paralysed.

Everything indicates long and thorough preparation for this attack. The work of sending out the vapour was done from the advanced German trenches. Men garbed in a dress resembling the harness of a diver and armed with retorts or generators about three feet high and connected with ordinary hose pipe turned the vapor loose towards the French lines. Some witnesses maintain that the Germans sprayed the earth before the trenches with a fluid which, being ignited, sent up the fumes. The German troops, who followed up this advantage with a direct attack, held inspirators in their mouths, thus preventing them from being overcome by the fumes.

In addition to this, the Germans appear to have fired ordinary explosive shells loaded with some chemical which had a paralyzing effect on all the men in the region of the explosion. Some chemical in the composition of those shells produced violent watering of the eyes, so that the men overcome by them were practically blinded for some hours.

The effect of the noxious trench gas seems to be slow in wearing away. The men come out of their nausea in a state of utter collapse. Some of the rescued have already died from the after effects. How many of the men left unconscious in the trenches when the French broke died from the fumes it is impossible to say, since those trenches were at once occupied by the Germans.

This new form of attack needs for success a favorable wind. Twice in the day that followed the Germans tried trench vapour on the Canadians, who made on the right of the French position a stand which will probably be remembered as one of the heroic episodes of this war. In both cases the wind was not favorable, and the Canadians managed to stick through it. The noxious, explosive bombs were, however, used continually against the Canadian forces and caused some losses.

The Eastern Front

In the east, the attacks by the Triple Alliance proved to be more successful. The Eastern Front was much larger than the Western Front and extended from the Baltic Sea to the Black Sea. Along this long line Russians and Serbs fought Germans, Austrians, and Turks. Although the Russians had the largest troop reserves, they were ill-equipped and were further hampered by poor communications and corrupt and inefficient leadership. After initial success in East Prussia, the Russians proved to be no match for the German army. The devastating losses at the front, coupled with discontent on the home front, led to the overthrow of the czar. A provisional government was subsequently overthrown when it tried to maintain the war effort. The new Bolshevik regime dropped out of the war in late 1917. (See chapter 10.) This permitted the Germans to concentrate on the Western Front.

The entry of the United States into the war in 1917 reinforced the Western Front with hundreds of thousands of fresh troops. When the Germans launched a final desperate offensive at the Marne in 1918, the Allied armies defeated the Germans and launched a counter-offensive that smashed through German lines and threatened Germany itself. Faced with a possible invasion, and with its citizens starving as a result of the naval blockade of its ports, Germany revolted. The kaiser was forced to flee the country. A provisional government signed harsh armistice demands to end the conflict.

WORLD WAR I CASUALTIES AND MOBILIZED FORCES

Countries	Total forces	Dead	Wounded	Prisoners and missing	Total casualties	Percentage of casualties in mobilized forces
Allies and Associated Powers:						
Russia	12 000 000	1 700 000	4 950 000	2 500 000	9 150 000	76.3
France	8 410 000	1 357 800	4 266 000	537 000	6 160 800	73.3
British Empire	8 904 467	908 371	2 090 212	191 652	3 190 235	35.8
Italy	5 615 000	650 000	947 000	600 000	2 197 000	39.1
United States	4 355 000	126 000	234 300	4 500	364 800	8.2
Japan	800 000	300	907	3	1 210	0.2
Romania	750 000	335 706	120 000	80 000	535 706	71.4
Serbia	707 343	45 000	133 148	152 958	331 106	46.8
Belgium	267 000	13 716	44 686	34 659	93 061	34.9
Greece	230 000	5 000	21 000	1 000	27 000	11.7
Portugal	100 000	7 222	13 751	12 318	33 291	33.3
Montenegro	50 000	3 000	10 000	7 000	20 000	40.0
TOTAL	42 188 810	5 152 115	12 831 004	4 121 090	22 104 209	52.3
Central Powers:						
Germany	11 000 000	1 773 700	4 216 058	1 152 800	7 142 558	64.9
Austria-Hungary	7 800 000	1 200 000	3 620 000	2 200 000	7 020 000	90.0
Turkey	2 850 000	325 000	400 000	250 000	975 000	34.2
Bulgaria	1 200 000	87 500	152 390	27 029	266 919	22.2
TOTAL	22 850 000	3 386 200	8 388 448	3 629 829	15 404 477	67.4
GRAND TOTAL	65 038 810	8 538 315	21 219 452	7 750 919	37 508 686	57.6

Figures from US War Department, February 1924.

Women and the War Effort

The First World War created another type of social upheaval in modern Western civilization. Women, like men, responded to their nation's call-to-arms and established refugee shelters and Red Cross first-aid stations. As more and more men were required to sustain the military effort, women began to serve as army cooks and drivers at base camps in Britain and France. By 1917, women were even serving in the armed forces in non-combatant roles. On the home front, women increased their role in agriculture and had the opportunity to work in industrial jobs that had generally been open only to men.

Before the war, women had worked outside the home. Traditionally, however, they had been confined to the roles of servants and nurses or labourers in textile mills. The war gave women the opportunity to drive buses on the homefront and ambulances on the battlefront. The relaxation of trade union restrictions on such things as apprenticeships greatly increased the number of women working in industry. Women took the new jobs that were rapidly becoming available in the munitions factories and by 1918 made up 60 percent of the work force in the British shell-making industry. In addition, they became skilled craftworkers, welding bombs, assembling airplanes, and building railway locomotives. They also filled positions in banks, business management, and government offices.

Some of these jobs were not new to women. What was new was the publicity the work received as newspapers drew attention to the role women were playing in the war effort. When the war ended, many women gave up their jobs, some willingly, others with regret. But the number of employed women remained higher than it had been before the war and it continued to increase throughout the 1920s. Women had come to realize that there were many new opportunities for them in the working world and men belatedly realized the important role women played in the economy.

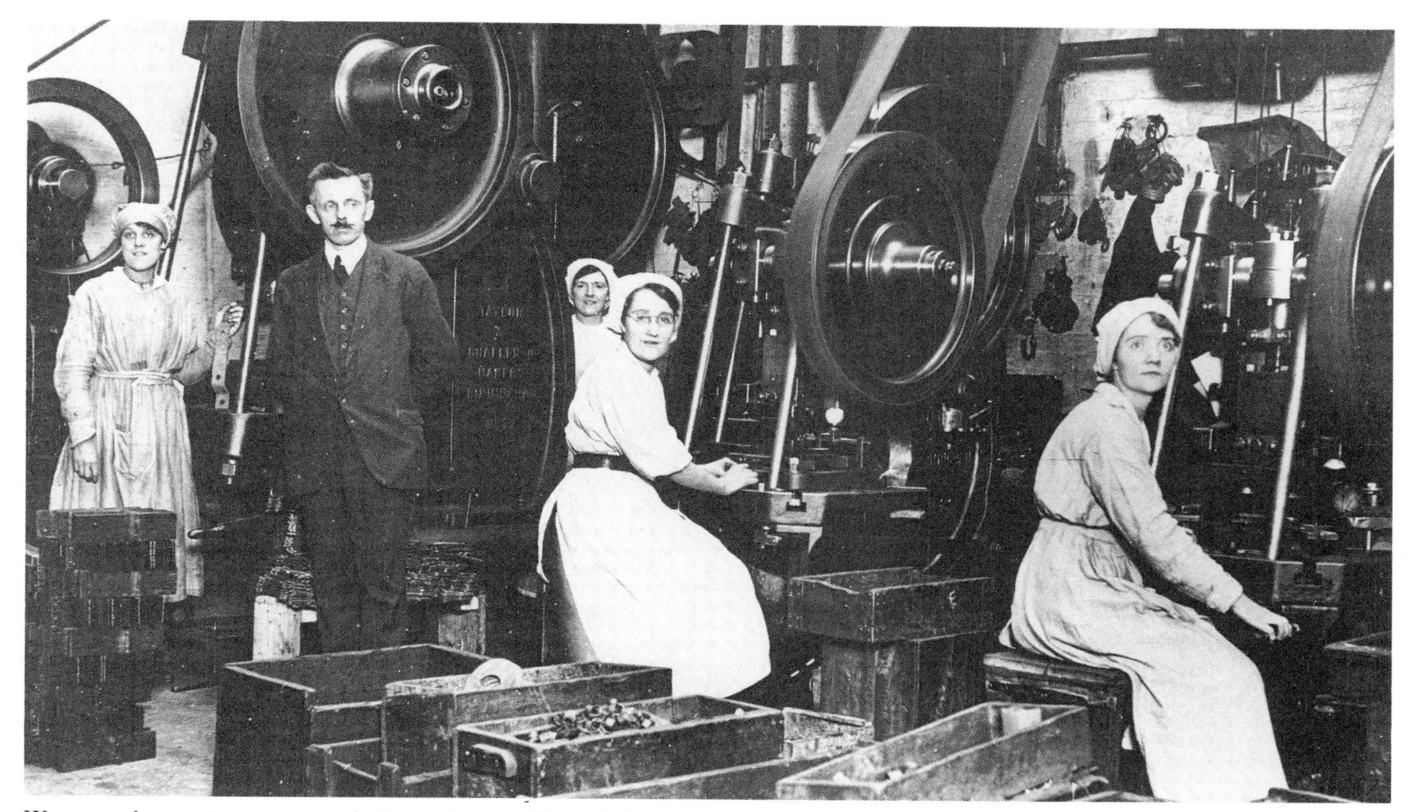

Women made many important contributions to the war effort, including working in munitions factories.

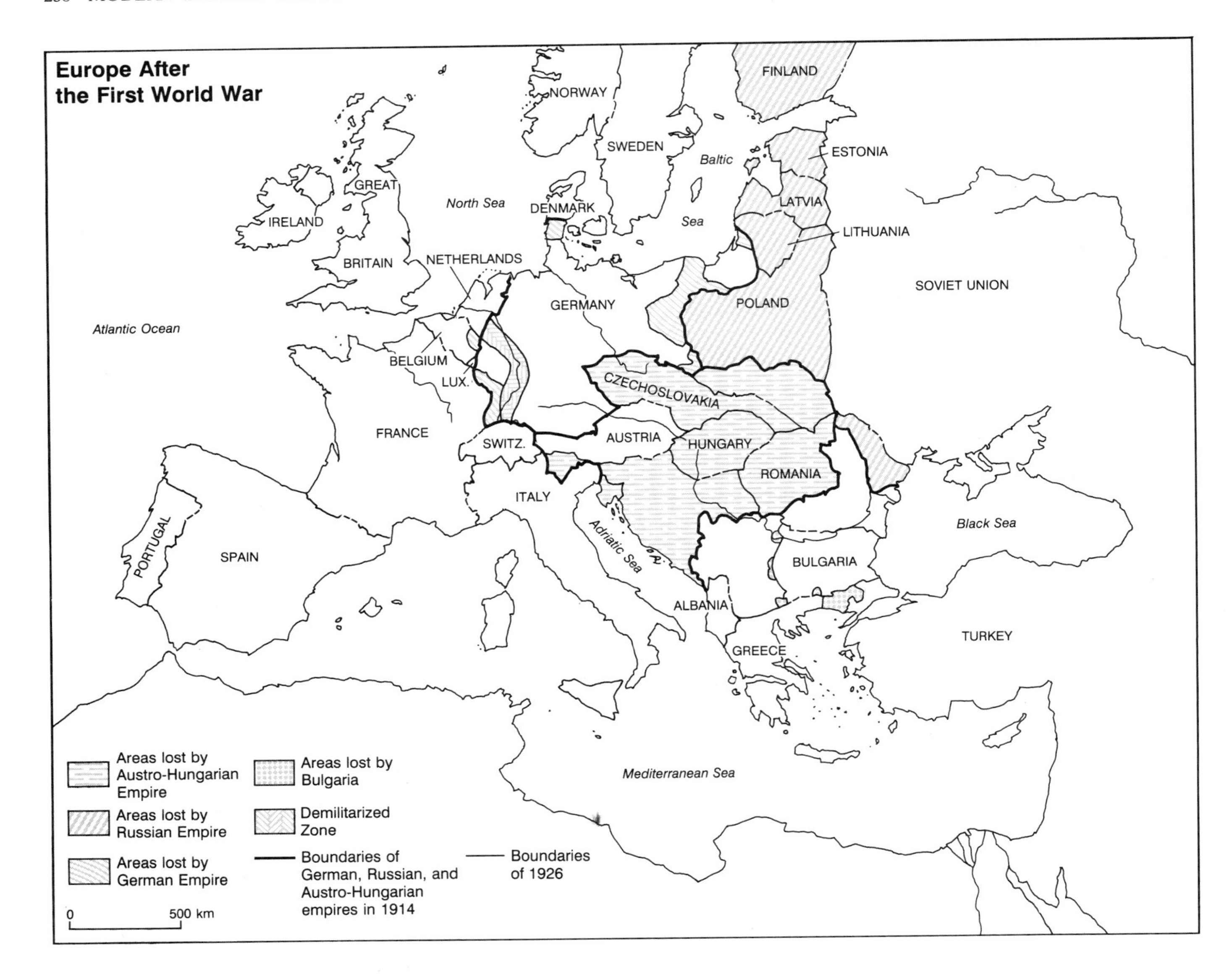

THE LOST PEACE

Woodrow Wilson and the Fourteen Points

In January 1917, prior to the entry of the United States into the war, American president Woodrow Wilson (1856–1924) had proposed that his country take part in a postwar League of Nations designed to maintain world peace. Consequently, the league became the cornerstone of his proposals for a just settlement following the war.

Addressing Congress early in 1918, the president outlined a program that would ensure that "the world [was] made fit and safe for every nation" and that would guarantee that each nation would be safe against "force and aggression." These proposals came to be known as the Fourteen Points. They proposed that once the war was over:

1. There would be no more secret international agreements;

2. There would be absolute freedom of the seas;
3. All trade barriers would be eliminated among nations;
4. There would be guaranteed mutual disarmament;
5. There would be fair distribution of colonies with considerations for the wishes of subject peoples;
6. All Russian territory would be evacuated by foreign troops to allow the Russian people to determine their own future;
7. Belgium would be evacuated and restored to its prewar independence;
8. The French provinces of Alsace and Lorraine would be returned to France;
9. The boundaries of Italy would be adjusted to include all Italians now living in neighbouring countries (meaning Austria-Hungary);
10. The various national groups of the Austro-Hungarian Empire would be free to develop their own nations;
11. Romania, Serbia, and Montenegro would be evacuated;
12. Turkey would be allowed to exist as an independent nation but all of its subject peoples would be freed;
13. An independent state of Poland would be created whose independence would be guaranteed by international agreement;
14. A general association of nations would be created to protect the political independence and territory of all states.

Wilson's ideas were applauded by progressive elements in North America and Europe. With his discussion of fair treatment of the enemy and an extension of welcome to a new, democratic Germany into his League of Nations, the president even received considerable support from the Central Powers as well as the Western Allies.

After the German defeat at the Second Battle of the Marne in August 1918, Germany's allies began to sue for peace—first Bulgaria, then Turkey, and then Austria-Hungary. This left southern Germany open to invasion. Morale at home disintegrated; mutinies in the armed forces and revolts in southern Germany led to the kaiser's abdication. The new government turned to Wilson to make good on his promises. But the Entente powers had a different view of things. Now that victory was at hand, Britain, France, and Italy (which had joined the Allied side after war had been declared) started to have second thoughts about Wilson's generous proposals. Britain objected to the proposal for freedom of the seas, and all three powers insisted upon their right to collect reparations from the losers. To preserve the rest of his plan, Wilson agreed. On those terms, the Allies invited the Germans to sign the surrender. On 11 November 1918, the war was over.

The Treaty of Versailles, 1919

Most European leaders saw Wilson as an idealistic amateur in international relations. The premier of France, Georges Clemenceau (1841–1929), threw up his hands in frustration with the president and his ideas: "I am sick of hearing about Wilson and his fourteen points; God Almighty was satisfied with only ten." In spite of such attitudes, however, there is no doubt about Wilson's influence on the final version of the treaty. It reflected a combination of his ideals and the practical political concerns of the other Allies.

The Treaty of Versailles addressed three basic concerns. The first was territorial concessions. Alsace-Lorraine was returned to France, and Germany had to demilitarize the Rhine Valley. The Germans also had to forfeit control and raw materials from the industrial region of the Saar Coal Basin to the victors. Other German concessions included the creation of a land corridor through German territory to give the new state of Poland access to the sea; the designation of the city of Danzig (modern Gdansk) as a "free city"; the loss of all overseas colonies; and the promise never to join with Austria again. The Austrian Empire was also dismembered. From the remnants, parts of Poland, Romania, and Yugoslavia and all of Czechoslovakia were formed.

Germany was also required to accept all of the blame for starting the war. Article 231 of the treaty stated:

> The Allied and Associated Governments affirm and Germany accepts the responsibility of Germany and her allies for causing all the loss and damage to which the Allied and Associated Governments and their nationals have been subjected as a consequence of the war subjected upon them by the aggression of Germany and her allies.

This "guilt clause" would have wide-reaching implications. It was obviously unfair to lay all of the blame upon the Germans, and this would be greatly resented in the years to come. (See readings.) In addition, Article 231 gave the Allies the excuse they needed to make the Germans pay for all damages. In 1921, these reparations would be set at a crippling $33 billion.

As for Wilson's League of Nations, it came into existence as planned but without the involvement of the United States.

Political in-fighting at home resulted in the rejection of the treaty by the American Senate. It was the final defeat for Wilson's ideals, and it gave notice of a growing mood of isolationism in the United States.

THE RESULTS OF THE FIRST WORLD WAR

In the postwar world, one of the driving forces of the nineteenth century triumphed while another collapsed. Nationalism, specifically the principle of self-determination, reshaped Eastern Europe, while liberalism, the aim of political reformers since the Enlightenment, perished in the attempt to sustain the war effort.

In Eastern Europe, the new states of Poland, Lithuania, Czechoslovakia, Estonia, Latvia, and Yugoslavia were created from the breakup of the Hapsburg, Romanov, and Hohenzollern empires. But the principle of self-determination was not extended to Germany or to the colonies of either the defeated or victorious powers. Minority problems soon arose in these areas as well as in Eastern Europe, where Hungarians were ruled by Romania and Yugoslavs by Italy.

Nearly all of the new states, as well as the defeated powers, were established as republics. This trend toward democratic and socialist republics was short-lived, however, as the failure to solve postwar problems led to the establishment of dictatorships in Poland, Hungary, Italy, and Germany.

Liberalism, particularly laissez-faire liberalism, was eclipsed by the collectivism necessary to sustain the war effort. This expanded role for government continued as postwar problems demanded state involvement in the economy. The increased power of labour unions and the expanded role of women, both caused by the wartime shortage of labour, also continued after the war. Severe damage resulting from the war demanded a high rate of taxation to finance recovery. War debts and reparations upset the international balance of payments. This was further complicated by the tariff barriers raised by the newly created states. These placed a heavy burden on Germany, which required exports to finance its reparation payments to the Allies.

The carnage caused by the war created a cultural crisis as well. In the 1920s, Paul Valery (1871–1945), a French poet, wrote:

> Everything essential in the world has been affected by the war, or more exactly by the circumstances of the war. Attrition has undermined something deeper than the renewable parts of man. You know of the great upset in the general economy, the policies of states and the very lives of individuals: distress, uncertainty, and apprehension are everywhere. *The mind itself has not been exempt from all this damage*. The mind is in fact stricken; it grieves in men of intellect, and looks sadly upon itself.
>
> From Eugen Weber (ed.), *Paths to the Present: Aspects of European Thought from Romanticism to Existentialism* (New York: Dodd, Mead and Co., 1960), p. 167.

The disillusionment evident at the turn of the century in the literature of Thomas Mann (1875–1955) and the paintings of Edvard Munch (1863–1944), Gustav Klint (1862–1918), and Oskar Kokoschka (1886–1980) became the general trend. Optimism and faith in progress was replaced with cynicism and a general belief in the decline of Western civilization.

RETROSPECTIVE

The global crisis that originated in Europe in the late nineteenth century exploded in 1914 into the bloodiest war in history. After four long years of conflict, however, many of the major issues remained unresolved.

Nationalism was reinforced with the emergence of the concept of "self-determination of nations and peoples" enshrined in the Treaty of Versailles. While Germany was stripped of its colonial possessions, the empires of the victorious Allies emerged larger and more powerful than ever. German demilitarization only increased popular resentment toward that country's neighbours. The arms race that characterized the early years of the century would re-emerge during the 1930s.

Finally, the failure of the League of Nations to establish a workable system of collective security meant that sooner or later individual nation-states would revert back to bilateral agreements and new alliances would emerge. The period of global crisis was not over yet.

JOHN A. HOBSON: Imperialism, A Study (1902)

The first full-scale economic explanation of imperialism was Imperialism, A Study *by John A. Hobson, originally published in 1902. Hobson called finance capitalism the "taproot" of imperialism and believed that the economic benefits from imperialism far outweighed the costs involved for everyone but the investor. This seminal work greatly influenced subsequent Marxist studies on imperialism, the most influential of which was Lenin's* Imperialism, the Highest Stage of Capitalism *(1917).*

From John A. Hobson, *Imperialism, A Study* (London, 1902), preface to the 1938 edition.

Aggressive Imperialism, which costs the taxpayer so dear, which is of so little value to the manufacturer and trader, which is fraught with such grave incalculable peril to the citizen, is a source of great gain to the investor who cannot find at home the profitable uses he seeks for his capital and insists that his Government should help him to be profitable and secure investments abroad.

If, contemplating the enormous expenditure on armaments, the ruinous wars, the diplomatic audacity or knavery by which modern Governments seek to extend their territorial power, we put the plain, practical question, *Cui bono?* the first and most obvious answer is, the investor.

The annual income Great Britain derives from commissions on her whole foreign and colonial trade, import and export, was estimated by Sir R. Giffen at 18 000 000 for 1899 taken at 2 ½ percent, upon a turnover of 800 000 000. This is the whole that we are entitled to regard as profits on external trade. Considerable as this sum is, it cannot serve to yield an economic motive-power adequate to explain the dominance which business considerations exercise over our imperial policy. Only when we set beside it some 90 000 000 or 100 000 000, representing pure profit upon investments, do we understand whence the economic impulse to Imperialism is derived.

Investors who have put their money in foreign lands, upon terms which take full account of the risks connected with the political conditions of the country, desire to use the resources of their Government to minimise these risks, and so to enhance the capital value and the interest of their private investments. The investing and speculative classes in general have also desired that Great Britain should take other foreign areas under her flag in order to secure new areas for profitable investments and speculation.

If the special interest of the investor is liable to clash with the public interest and to induce a wrecking policy, still more dangerous is the special interest of the financier, the general dealer in investments. In large measure the rank and file of the investors are, both for business and for politics, the cat's paw of the great financial houses, who use stocks and shares not so much as investments to yield them interest, but as material for speculation in the money market. In handling large masses of stocks and shares, in floating companies, in manipulating fluctuations of values, the magnates of the Bourse find their gain. These great businesses—banking, broking, bill discounting, loan floating, company promoting—form the central ganglion of international capitalism. United by the strongest bonds of organisation, always in closest and quickest touch with one another, situated in the very heart of the business capital of every State, controlled, so far as Europe is concerned, chiefly by men of a single and peculiar race, who have behind them many centuries of financial experience, they are in a unique position to manipulate the policy of nations. No great quick direction of capital is possible save by their consent and through their agency. Does any one seriously suppose that a great war could be undertaken by any European State, or a great State loan subscribed, if the house of Rothschild and its connexions set their face against it? . . .

The wealth of these houses, the scale of their operations, and their cosmopolitan organisation make them the prime determinants of imperial policy. They have the largest definite stake in the business of Imperialism, and the amplest means of forcing their will upon the policy of nations.

In view of the part which the non-economic factors of patriotism, adventure, military enterprise, political ambition, and philanthropy play in imperial expansion, it may appear that to impute to financiers so much power is to take a too narrow view of history. And it is true that the motor-power of Imperialism is not chiefly financial: finance is rather the governor of the imperial engine, directing the energy and determining its work: it does not constitute the fuel of the engine, nor does it directly generate the power. Finance manipulates the patriotic forces which politicians, soldiers, philanthropists, and traders generate; the enthusiasm for expansion which issues from these sources, though strong and genuine, is irregular and blind; the financial interest has those qualities of concentration and clear-sighted calculation which are needed to set Imperialism to work. An ambitious statesman, a frontier soldier, an overzealous missionary, a pushing trader, may suggest or even initiate a step of imperial expansion, may assist in educating public opinion to the urgent need of some fresh advance, but the final determination rests with the financial power. The direct influence exercised by great financial houses in "high politics" is supported by the control which they exercise over the body of public opinion through the Press, which, in every "civilised" country, is becoming more and more their obedient instrument. . . . Add to this the natural sympathy with a sensational policy which a cheap Press always manifests, and it becomes evident that the Press has been strongly biased towards Imperialism, and has lent itself with great facility to the suggestion of financial or political Imperialists who have desired to work up patriotism for some new piece of expansion.

Such is the array of distinctively economic forces making for Imperialism, a large loose group of trades and professions seeking profitable business and lucrative employment from the expansion of military and civil services, and from the expenditure on military operations, the opening up of new tracts of territory and trade with the same, and the provision of new capital which these operations require, all these finding their central guiding and directing force in the power of the general financier.

The play of these forces does not openly appear. They are essentially parasites upon patriotism, and they adapt themselves to its protecting colours. In the mouth of their representatives are noble phrases, expressive of their desire to extend the area of civilisation, to establish good government, promote Christianity, extirpate slavery, and elevate the lower races. Some of the business men who hold such language may entertain a genuine, though usually a vague, desire to accomplish these ends, but they are primarily engaged in business, and they are not unaware of the utility of the more unselfish forces in furthering their ends. Their true attitude of mind was expressed by Mr. Rhodes in his famous description of "Her Majesty's Flag" as "the greatest commercial asset in the world." . . .

---

1. Summarize Hobson's arguments against imperialism.
2. What arguments could be used to counter Hobson's thesis?
3. Stage a debate on imperialism between John A. Hobson and an imperialist.

NORMAN ANGELL:
The Great Illusion (1910)

In 1910, British economist Ralph Norman Angell Lane (writing under the name Norman Angell) published his analysis of the relationship between military power and national success. A pacifist, Lane argued that any war, even a successful one, was a futile method of achieving worthwhile national goals. Lane continued to work for international peace and was awarded the Nobel Prize for Peace in 1933.

From Norman Angell, *The Great Illusion* (New York and London: G.P. Putnam's Sons, 1913.)

What are the fundamental motives that explain the present rivalry of armaments in Europe, notably the Anglo-German? Each nation pleads the need for defence; but this implies that someone is likely to attack, and has therefore a presumed interest in so doing. What are the motives which each State thus fears its neighbours may obey?

They are based on the universal assumption that a nation, in order to find outlets for expanding population and increasing industry, or simply to ensure the best conditions possible for its people, is necessarily pushed to territorial expansion and the exercise of political force against others. . . . It is assumed that a nation's relative prosperity is broadly determined by its political power; that nations being competing units, advantage in the last resort goes to the possessor of preponderant military force, the weaker goes to the wall, as in the other forms of the struggle for life.

The author challenges this whole doctrine. He attempts to show that it belongs to a stage of development out of which we have passed; that the commerce and industry of a people no longer depend upon the expansion of its political frontiers; that a nation's political and economic frontiers do not now necessarily coincide; that military power is socially and economically futile, and can have no relation to the prosperity of the people exercising it; that it is impossible for one nation to seize by force the wealth or trade of another—to enrich itself by subjugating, or imposing its will by force on another; that, in short, war, even when victorious, can no longer achieve those aims for which people strive. . . .

The fight for ideals can no longer take the form of fight between nations, because the lines of division on moral questions are within the nations themselves and intersect the political frontiers. There is no State which is completely Catholic or Protestant, or liberal or autocratic, or aristocratic or democratic, or socialist or individualist; the moral and spiritual struggles of the modern world go on between citizens of the same State in unconscious intellectual cooperation with corresponding groups in other states, not between the public powers of rival States. . . .

War has no longer the justification that it makes for the survival of the fittest; it involves the survival of the less fit. The idea that the struggle between nations is a part of the evolutionary law of man's advance involves a profound misreading of the biological analogy.

The warlike nations do not inherit the earth; they represent the decaying human element. . . .

Are we, in blind obedience to primitive instincts and old prejudices, enslaved by the old catchwords and that curious indolence which makes the revision of old ideas unpleasant, to duplicate indefinitely on the political and economic side a condition from which we have liberated ourselves on the religious side? Are we to continue to struggle, as so many good men struggled in the first dozen centuries of Christendom—spilling oceans of blood, wasting mountains of treasure—to achieve what is at bottom a logical absurdity, to accomplish something which, when accomplished, can avail us nothing, and which, if it could avail us anything, would condemn the nations of the world to never-ending bloodshed and the constant defeat of all those aims which men, in their sober hours, know to be alone worthy of sustained endeavor?

---

1. Outline Lane's view of the justification for imperialism used by nations.

2. In what way does the author relate this argument to social Darwinism?

3. Why do you think Lane's ideas, which were published in eleven countries and translated into fifteen different languages, had so little impact on the leaders of his time?

THE OUTBREAK OF WAR

The following documents trace the development of the crisis that set off the First World War. The first excerpt is taken from a 1911 publication of the Narodna Odbrana, a secret society also known as "the Black Hand," which aimed to work for freedom from Austria and union with Serbia; the assassin of Archduke Ferdinand, Gavrillo Princip, was a member of this group. The excerpt reflects the Serbians' depth of feeling against the Austrians.

From the Narodna Odbrana (Belgrade 1911), in Louis L. Snyder (ed.), *Historic Documents of World War I* (Princeton, NJ: Van Nostrand Co., Inc., 1958), pp. 46–47.

The annexation [of Bosnia and Herzegovina] was only one of the blows which the enemies of Serbia have aimed at this land. Many blows preceded it, and many will follow it. Work and preparation are necessary so that a new attack may not find Serbia equally unprepared. . . .

A new blow, like that of the annexation, must be met by a new Serbia, in which every Serbian, from child to greybeard, is a rifleman.

The old Turks of the South gradually disappear and only a part of our people suffer under their rule. But new Turks come from the North, more feared and dangerous than the old; stronger in civilization and more advanced economically, our northern enemies come against us. They want to take our freedom and our language from us and to crush us. We can already feel the presages of the struggle which approaches from that quarter. The Serbian people are faced by the question "to be or not to be?"

The Narodna Odbrana does not doubt that in the fight against the enemies with whom we stand face to face, our people will provide a succession of heroes. . . .

[We] proclaim to the people that Austria is our first and greatest enemy. Just as once the Turks attacked us from the south, so Austria attacks us today from the north. If the Narodna Odbrana preaches the necessity of fighting Austria, she preaches a sacred truth of our national position.

Borijove Jevtic, one of the leaders of the Narodna Odbrana, was arrested along with Princip for the assassination of Franz Ferdinand. Ten years later he recalled the emotions of the period.

From *New York World*, 29 June 1924.

A tiny clipping from a newspaper, mailed without comment from a secret band of terrorists in Zagreb, capital of Croatia, to their comrades in Belgrade, was the torch which set the world afire with war in 1914. That bit of paper wrecked old, proud empires. It gave birth to new, free nations. I was one of the members of the terrorist band in Belgrade which received it.

The little clipping declared that the Austrian Archduke Francis Ferdinand would visit Sarajevo, the capital of Bosnia, June 28, to direct army manoeuvres in the neighbouring mountains. . . .

As we read that clipping in Belgrade we knew what we would do to Francis Ferdinand. We would kill him to show Austria there yet lived within its borders defiance of its rule. We would kill him to bring once more to the boiling point the fighting spirit of the revolutionaries and pave the way for revolt.

Our decision was taken almost immediately. Death to the tyrant!

The Austrian ultimatum of 23 July demanded the surrender of Serbian autonomy to the empire. This first excerpt contains a statement which the Austrian Empire demanded that the Serbian government issue publicly.

The Royal Serbian Government condemns the propaganda directed against Austria-Hungary, that is to say, the whole body of the efforts whose ultimate object it is to separate from the Austro-Hungarian Monarchy territories that belong to it, and it most sincerely regrets the dreadful consequences of these criminal transactions. . . .

The Royal Government, which disapproves and repels every idea and every attempt to interfere in the destinies of the population of whatever portion of Austria-Hungary, regards it as its duty . . . [to] proceed with the utmost rigor against any persons who shall become guilty of any such activities.

In response to the ultimatum, Serbia capitulated on almost every point. This excerpt captures the tone of the Serbian reply.

The Royal Government . . . is convinced that its reply will dissipate any misunderstanding which threatens to destroy the friendly and neighbourly relations between the Austrian monarchy and the kingdom of Serbia. . . .

The Royal Serbian Government binds itself without delay to eliminate from the public instruction in Serbia anything which might further the propaganda directed against Austria-Hungary . . . [and] declares that it is willing to accept every cooperation which does not run counter to international law and criminal law, as well as to the friendly and neighbourly relations.

German authorities were relieved by the conciliatory nature of the Serbian response. In this first excerpt, German chancellor Bethmann-Hollweg outlined the British view that it was Russian pressure that was keeping Serbia in line. Bethmann-Hollweg had just been presented with a proposal for mediation by British secretary of state for foreign affairs, Sir Edward Grey.

According to the British . . . it appeared from the reply that Serbia had agreed to the Austrian demands to an extent such as he [Grey] would never have believed possible; except in one point, the participation of Austrian officials in the judicial investigation, Serbia had actually agreed to everything that had been demanded of her. It was plain that this compliance of Serbia's was to be attributed solely to the pressure exerted from Petersburg.

Should Austria fail to be satisfied with this reply, in other words, should this reply not be accepted in Vienna as a foundation for the peaceful negotiations, or should Austria even proceed to the occupation of Belgrade, which lay quite defenseless before her, it would then be absolutely evident that Austria was only seeking an excuse for crushing Serbia.

[Hollweg commented that] by refusing every proposition for mediation, we should be held responsible for the conflagration by the whole world, and be set forth as the original instigators of the war. That would also make our position impossible in our own country, where we must appear as having been forced into the war. Our situation is all the more difficult, inasmuch as Serbia has apparently yielded to a very great degree.

In this excerpt, Kaiser Wilhelm gives his impression of the Serbian response.

After reading the Serbian reply, which I received this morning, I am convinced that on the whole the wishes of the Danube Monarchy have been acceded to. The few reservations that Serbia makes in regard to individual points could, according to my opinion, be settled by negotiation. But it contains the announcement orbi et urbi of a capitulation of the most humiliating kind, and as a result, every cause for war falls to the ground. . . .

Excerpts from B. Tierney, *et al* (eds.), *Great Issues in Western Civilization*, Vol. 2 (New York: Random House, 1976) pp. 449–450, 455–456, 461–462.

I propose that we say to Austria: Serbia has been forced to retreat in a very humiliating manner, and we offer our congratulations. Naturally, as a result, EVERY CAUSE FOR WAR HAS VANISHED. . . . I am ready to mediate for Peace with Austria. . . . This I will do in my own way, and as sparingly of Austria's NATIONALISTIC FEELING, and of the HONOUR OF HER ARMS as possible.

In spite of Wilhelm's attempts to mediate and subsequent attempts to persuade Russia to halt its mobilization, Franz Joseph was convinced that he had Germany's backing if he chose to go to war. This belief was based on a telegram sent to Vienna by Bethmann-Hollweg early in July reflecting the kaiser's support of Austria. The Austrians considered the telegram to be a "blank cheque" to be used in the punishment of Serbia.

His Majesty sends his thanks to the Emperor Francis Joseph for his letter and would soon answer it personally. In the meantime His Majesty desires to say that he is not blind to the danger which threatens Austria-Hungary and thus the Triple Alliance as a result of the Russian and Serbian Pan-Slavic agitation. . . .

The Emperor Francis Joseph may . . . rest assured that His Majesty will faithfully stand by Austria-Hungary, as is required by the obligations of his alliance and of his ancient friendship.

From M. Monteglas and W. Schucking (eds.), *Outbreak of the European War: Documents Collected by Karl Kautsky* (New York: Carnegie Endowment for International Peace, 1924), pp. 273–274.

---

1. Trace the evolution of the crisis in the Balkans. Outline the role played by the forces of nationalism, imperialism, militarism, and the alliance system to transform the assassination of one individual into a world war.

2. Following the war, the Commission on War Guilt found Germany responsible for the outbreak of the conflict. Based upon the documents presented here, defend or refute their findings.

3. Compare the goals, rhetoric, and methods of the Narodna Odbrana with those of a modern terrorist organization. Create and defend a thesis about terrorism based upon your findings.

POLITICAL RESPONSES TO WAR (1914)

On 28 July 1914, the government of Austria-Hungary declared war on Serbia. Within one week Russia, Germany, France, and Britain had followed suit. Each of the governments issued statements to explain their actions and to arouse popular support for the war effort.

From Frank Alfred Golder, *Documents of Russian History, 1914–1917* (New York: The Century Co., 1927), pp. 29–30.

Manifesto of Czar Nicholas II, 2 August 1914

By the Grace of God, We, Nicholas II, Emperor and Autocrat of all Russia, Czar of Poland, Grand Duke of Finland, etc., etc., etc., proclaim to all Our loyal subjects:

Following her historical traditions, Russia, united in faith and blood with the Slav nations, has never regarded their fate with indifference. The unanimous fraternal sentiments of the Russian people for the Slavs have been aroused to special intensity in the past few days, when Austria-Hungary presented to Serbia demands which she foresaw would be unacceptable to a sovereign State.

Having disregarded the conciliatory and peaceable reply of the Serbian Government, and having declined Russia's well-intentioned mediation, Austria hastened to launch an armed attack in a bombardment of unprotected Belgrad.

Compelled, by the force of circumstances thus created, to adopt the necessary measures of precaution, We commanded that the army and the navy be put on a war footing, but, at the same time, holding the blood and the treasure of Our subjects dear, We made every effort to obtain a peaceable issue of the negotiations that had been started.

In the midst of friendly communications, Austria's Ally, Germany, contrary to Our trust in century-old relations of neighborliness, and paying no heed to Our assurances that the measures We had adopted implied no hostile aims whatever, insisted upon their immediate abandonment, and, meeting with a rejection of this demand, suddenly declared war on Russia.

We have now to intercede not only for a related country, unjustly attacked, but also to safeguard the honor, dignity, and integrity of Russia, and her position among the Great Powers. We firmly believe that all Our loyal subjects will rally self-sacrificingly and with one accord to the defense of the Russian soil.

At this hour of threatening danger, let domestic strife be forgotten. Let the union between the Tsar and His people be stronger than ever, and let Russia, rising like one man, repel the insolent assault of the enemy.

With a profound faith in the justice of Our cause, and trusting humbly in Almighty Providence, We invoke prayerfully the Divine blessing for Holy Russia and Our valiant troops. . . .

From Ralph Haswell Lutz, *Fall of the German Empire, 1914–1918* (Stanford, CA: Stanford University Press, 1932), pp. 8–9.

Emperor William's Speech from the Throne, 4 August 1914

Honored gentlemen, at a time of such importance I have assembled the elected representatives of the German people about me. For nearly half a century we have been allowed to follow the ways of peace. The attempts to attribute to Germany warlike intentions and to hedge in her position in the world have often sorely tried the patience of my people. Undeterred, my Government has pursued the development of our moral, spiritual, and economic strength as its highest aim, with all frankness, even under provocative circumstances. The world has been witness that during the last years, under all pressure and confusion, we have stood in the first rank in saving the nations of Europe from a war between the great powers.

The most serious dangers to which the events in the Balkans had given rise seemed to have been overcome—then suddenly an abyss was opened through the murder of my friend the Archduke Franz Ferdinand. My lofty ally, the Emperor and King Franz Josef, was forced to take up arms to defend the security of his empire against dangerous machinations from a neighboring state. The Russian Empire stepped in to hinder the allied monarchy from following out her just interests. Not only does our duty as ally call us to the side of Austria-Hungary, but it is our great task to protect our own position and the old community of culture between the two Empires against the attack of hostile forces. . . .

The present situation is the result of an ill will which has been active for many years against the power and the prosperity of the German Empire.

No lust of conquest drives us on; we are inspired by the unalterable will to protect the place in which God has set us for ourselves and all coming generations. From the documents which have been submitted to you, you will see how my Government, and especially my Chancellor, have endeavored even to the last moment to stave off the inevitable. In a defensive war that has been forced upon us, with a clear conscience and a clean hand we take up the sword. . . .

From Assemble, *Annales de la Chambre des Deputies*, 1914, sess. ord. et. ext., II, 907–910, translated by George H. Knoles and Rixford K. Synder, *Readings in Western Civilization* (Chicago, IL: J.B. Lippincott Co., 1954), pp. 749–751.

Message of President Poincare to the Chamber of Deputies, 4 August 1914

Gentlemen of the Chamber of Deputies, France has become the object of a brutal and premeditated aggression which is an insolent defiance of international law. Before a declaration of war was addressed to us, before even the German ambassador had asked for his passport, our territory was invaded. . . .

For more than forty years the French, in a sincere love of peace, have stifled the desire for legitimate reparation. They have given to the world the example of a great nation which, definitively resurrected from defeat by strength of will, by patience and work, has used its renewed and revived force only in the interest of progress and for the good of humanity.

Since the Austrian crisis opened up a situation threatening to the whole of Europe, France has set herself to follow and to recommend everywhere a policy of prudence, wisdom, and moderation. No one can charge her with an act, with a gesture, with a word which has not been peaceful and conciliating. In this hour of the first combats, she has the right to credit herself with the fact that she made supreme efforts up until the last moment to avoid this war which has just broken out and for which Germany will bear before history the crushing responsibility. . . .

In the war which has begun, France will have on her side that right whose eternal moral force no people, no individual can defy with impunity. She will be heroically defended by her sons whose sacred unity before the enemy nothing can break and who are today joined in the same indignation against the aggressor and in the same patriotic faith. She is faithfully seconded by Russia, her ally; she is supported by the loyal friendship of England.

Already from all parts of the civilized world come to her expressions of sympathy and good wishes. Because she represents again today before the universe liberty, justice, and reason.

Haut les coeurs et vive la France!

From Great Britain, *The Parliamentary Debates*, 5th series, Commons, 1914, LXV, cols 2078–2079.

Statement by Prime Minister Asquith in the House of Commons, 6 August 1914

. . . I am entitled to say, and I do so on behalf of this country—I speak not for a party, I speak for the country as a whole—that we made every effort any Government could possibly make for peace. But this war has been forced upon us. What is it we are fighting for? Everyone knows, and no one knows better than the Government, the terrible, incalculable suffering, economic, social, personal and political, which war, and especially a war between the Great Powers of the world, must entail. There is no man amongst us sitting upon this bench in these trying days—more trying perhaps than any body of statesmen for a hundred years have had to pass through—there is not a man amongst us who has not, during the whole of that time, had clearly before his vision the almost unequalled suffering which war, even in a just cause, must bring about, not only to the peoples who are for the moment living in this country and in other countries of the world, but to posterity and to the whole prospects of European civilisation. Every step we took we took with that vision before our eyes, and with a sense of responsibility which it is impossible to describe. . . .

If I am asked what we are fighting for I reply in two sentences. In the first place, to fulfil a solemn international obligation, an obligation which, it it had been entered into between private persons in the ordinary concerns of life, would have been regarded as an obligation not only of law but of honour, which no self-respecting man could possibly have repudiated. I say, secondly, we are fighting to vindicate the principle which, in these days when force, material force, sometimes seems to be the dominant influence and factor in the development of mankind, we are fighting to vindicate the principle that small nationalities are not to be crushed, in defiance of international good faith, by the arbitrary will of a strong and overmatering Power.

I do not believe that any nation ever entered into a great controversy—and this is one of the greatest history will ever know—with a clearer conscience and a stronger conviction that it is fighting, not for aggression, not for the maintenance even of its own selfish interest, but that it is fighting in defence of principles the maintenance of which is vital to the civilisation of the world. With a full conviction, not only of the wisdom and justice, but of the obligations which lay upon us to challenge this great issue, we are entering into the struggle. . . .

---

1. Summarize each statement in three sentences.

2. Develop a chart outlining the reasons given for each country's declaration of war.

3. Choose one of the statements and write a pair of editorials, one prowar, one antiwar, commenting on the speech.

THE PEACE:
The Treaty of Versailles (1919)

Woodrow Wilson had idealistic aims for the peace conference. Unfortunately, much of his earlier vision was lost in the final negotiations.

In the first of two excerpts Wilson is speaking prior to the entry of the United States into the conflict. Frustrated in his attempts to bring the belligerents to the table, Wilson outlined his vision to the United States Senate in January 1917.

From Newton Baker, *Why We Went to War* (New York: Harper and Brothers, 1936), pp. 167–173.

It must be a peace without victory. . . . Victory would mean a peace forced upon the loser, a victor's terms imposed upon the vanquished. It would be accepted in humiliation, under duress, at an intolerable sacrifice, and would leave a sting, a resentment, a bitter memory upon which terms of peace would rest, not permanently, but only as upon quicksand. Only a peace between equals can last. . . .

The equality of nations upon which peace must be founded if it is to last must be an equality of rights; the guarantees exchanged must neither recognize nor imply a difference between big nations and small, between those that are powerful and those that are weak. Right must be based upon the common strength, not upon the individual strength, of the nations upon whose concert peace will depend.

The realities of the actual negotiations were depicted in the letters of Walter Simons. A member of the German delegation to Versailles in 1919, Simons wrote his impressions home to his wife.

From A. Luckau, "The German Delegation at the Paris Peace Conference," *The Paris Peace Conference: History and Documents* (New York: Columbia University Press, 1941), pp. 118–121.

The treaty which our enemies have laid before us, in so far as the French dictated it, a monument of pathological fear and pathological hatred; and in so far as the Anglo-Saxons dictated it, it is the work of a capitalistic policy of the cleverest and most brutal kind. Its shamelessness does not lie in treading down a brave opponent, but in the fact that from beginning to end all these humiliating conditions are made to look like a just punishment, while in truth there is in them neither shame, nor any respect for the conception of justice.

The Guilt Clause included in the Treaty of Versailles was immediately rejected by the Weimar Republic. In his work The Case for the Central Powers: An Impeachment of the Versailles Verdict, *German negotiator Count Max Montgelas states the German position.*

From B. Tierney *et al* (eds.), *Great Issues in Western Civilization*, Vol. 2 (New York: Random House, 1976), pp. 432–436.

Germany pursued no aim either in Europe or elsewhere which could only be achieved by means of war.

Austria-Hungary's only aim was to maintain the status quo. Her first intention of rectifying her frontiers at Serbia's expense was immediately abandoned at Germany's insistance. . . .

France aimed at recovering Alsace-Lorraine, and many leading French politicians also hoped to annex the Saar basin, whilst Russia aspired to possession of Constantinople and the Straits, both powers knowing well that these aims could not be achieved without a European war.

THE LITERARY RESPONSE TO WAR

The First World War was a shattering experience for an entire generation of Europeans. A great deal of bitterness was revealed in works written about the war, both during the conflict and after its end. Disillusionment was not confined to one side, however. All participants felt the same sense of loss of innocence and betrayal of trust. The loss of almost an entire generation of young men meant that the older generation continued to dominate political life in the immediate postwar years. For the survivors, the closed ranks of this power elite led them to discount the system entirely. As a result, rejection of traditional values became the norm for writers and artists in the 1920s.

German troops await battle in the trenches.

German author Erich Maria Remarque was in the infantry during the First World War. In this excerpt from All Quiet on the Western Front, *one of the most widely read antiwar novels of the period, he describes life in the trenches. Remarque left his native Germany to live in the United States just prior to the outbreak of the Second World War.*

All Quiet on the Western Front by Erich Maria Remarque. "Im Westen Nichts Neues," copyright 1928 by Ullstein A.G.; Copyright renewed © 1956 by Erich Maria Remarque; "All Quiet on the Western Front," copyright 1929, 1930 by Little, Brown and Company; Copyright renewed © 1957, 1958 by Erich Maria Remarque.

All Quiet on the Western Front (1928)

We wake up in the middle of the night. The earth booms. Heavy fire is falling on us. We crouch into corners. We distinguish shells of every calibre.

Each man lays hold of his things and looks again every minute to reassure himself that they are still there. The dug-out heaves, the night roars and flashes. We look at each other in the momentary flashes of light, and with pale faces and pressed lips shake our heads.

Each man is aware of the heavy shells tearing down the parapet, rooting up the embankment and demolishing the upper layers of concrete. When a shell lands in the trench we note the hollow, furious blast is like a blow from the paw of a raging beast of prey. Already by morning a few of the recruits are green and vomiting. They are too inexperienced.

Slowly the grey light trickles into the post and pales the flashes of the shells. Morning is come. The explosion of mines mingles with the gunfire. That is the most dementing convulsion of all. The whole region where they go up becomes one grave. . . .

We see men living with their skulls blown open; we see soldiers run with their two feet cut off, they stagger on their splintered stumps into the next shell-hole; a lance-corporal crawls a mile and a half on his hands dragging his smashed knee after him; another goes to the dressing-station and over his clasped hands bulge his intestines; we see men without mouths, without jaws, without faces; we find one man who has held the artery of his arm in his teeth for two hours in order not to bleed to death. The sun goes down, night comes, the shells whine, life is at an end.

Still the little piece of convulsed earth in which we lie is held. We have yielded no more than a few hundred yards of it as a prize to the enemy. But on every yard lies a dead man.

Some of the most powerful literary responses to the First World War were expressed in poetry. British poet Wilfred Owen and American poet Carl Sandburg captured the distaste with which most Europeans and North Americans regarded the conflict.

Wilfred Owen, "Dulce Et Decorum Est," in John Silkin (ed.), *The Penguin Book of First World War Poetry*, second edition (Harmondsworth, UK: Penguin Books, 1981), pp. 182–183.

"Dulce Et Decorum Est" (1920)

Bent double, like old beggars under sacks,
Knock-kneed, coughing like hags, we cursed through sludge,
Till on the haunting flares we turned our backs,
And towards our distant rest began to trudge.
Men marched asleep. Many had lost their boots
But limped on, blood-shod. All went lame; all blind;
Drunk with fatigue; deaf even to the hoots
Of gas shells dropping softly behind.

Gas! GAS! Quick boys!-An ecstasy of fumbling,
Fitting the clumsy helmets just in time;
But someone still was yelling out and stumbling,
And flound'ring like a man in fire or lime . . .

Dim, through the misty panes and thick green light,
As under a green sea, I see him drowning.

In all my dreams, before my helpless sight,
He plunges at me, guttering, choking, drowning.

If in some smothering dreams you too could pace
Behind the wagon that we flung him in,
And watch the white eyes writhing in his face,
His hanging face, like a devil's sick of sin;
If you could hear, at every jolt, the blood
Come gargling from the froth-corrupted lungs,
Obscene as cancer, bitter as the cud
Of vile, incurable sores on innocent tongues,—
My friend, you would not tell with such high zest
To children ardent for some desperate glory,
That old Lie: Dulce et decorum est
Pro patria mori.*

*It is sweet and proper to die for one's country.

"Grass" (1918)

"Grass" from *Cornhuskers* by Carl Sandburg, copyright 1918 by Holt, Rinehart and Winston, Inc. and renewed 1946 by Carl Sandburg, reprinted by permission of Harcourt Brace Jovanovich, Inc.

Pile the bodies high at Austerlitz and Waterloo.
Shovel them under and let me work—
I am the grass; I cover all.

And pile them high at Gettysburg
And pile them high at Ypres and Verdun.

Shovel them under and let me work.
Two years, ten years, and passengers ask the conductor:

What place is this?
Where are we now?

I am the grass.
Let me work.

---

1. Erich Maria Remarque's novel provides an excellent insight into the German attitude toward the First World War. Working with a group, conduct a book seminar on *All Quiet on the Western Front*. Each member of the group should read the book plus one other book written about the period (for example, Aleksandr Solzhenitsyn's *August 1914* or Barbara Tuchman's *The Guns of August*.) Make notes and prepare discussion-generating questions on each book, then meet with your group to discuss your findings.

2. Compare the views of war expressed by Owen and Sandburg. In what ways do their statements reflect the observations made by Remarque?

AT THE FRONT (1914–1918)

The following two letters illustrate the wide range of emotions that recruits, in this case Germans, went through at the beginning of the war. Both men died before the end of 1914.

From Phillip Witkop, *German Students' War Letters*, edited and translated by A.F. Wedd (London: Methuen, 1929), pp. 1–4, 17–20.

Leipzig, August 7th, 1914

Every soldier must, to start with, be as I was a week ago, oppressed by the first mental picture of horrors which are no longer mere possibilities. . . . I personally have thought out my position as if I had already done with this world—as if I were certain of not coming home again; and that gives me peace and security. Dear Father, good Mother, beloved Brothers and Sisters, please, please don't think me cruel for saying this, but it would be a good thing if already you too would, with brave hearts and firm self-control, get accustomed to the idea that you will not see me or any of my brothers again. Then if bad news does come, you will be able to receive it much more calmly. But if we all do come back, then we can accept that joy as an unexpected and all the more gracious and glorious gift of God. . . .

[The] night when England's declaration of war was announced in the barracks . . . none of us got to sleep till three o'clock in the morning, we were so full of excitement, fury, and enthusiasm. It is a joy to go to the Front with such comrades. We are bound to be victorious! Nothing else is possible in the face of such determination to win. My dear ones, be proud that you live in such times and in such a nation, and that you too have the privilege of sending several of those you love into this glorious struggle.

Freiburg, August 1st, 1914

. . . If there is mobilization now, I must join up, and I would rather do so here, where there would be a chance of going to the Front quite soon, than in Travemunde, Hamburg or Bahrenfeld, where we should probably be used only to defend the Kiel Canal. And I can't think of anything more hateful than to be forced to sit at home doing nothing when there is war and fighting out there.

You must not imagine that I write this in a fit of war-fever, on the contrary, I am quite calm and am absolutely unable to share the enthusiasm with which some people here are longing to go to war. I can't yet believe that that will happen. It seems to me impossible, and I feel sure that things will go no further than mobilization. But if it does start then you will understand that I can't stop anywhere here. I know too that you are a dear, good, sensible little Mother, and would not wish that your sons should show cowardice in the face of great danger and stay prudently behind.

. . . why I should have volunteered for the war? Of course it was not from any enthusiasm for war in general, nor because I thought it would be a fine thing to kill a great many people or otherwise distinguish myself. On the contrary, I think that war is a very, very evil thing, and I believe that even in this case it might have been averted by a more skilful diplomacy. But, now that it has been declared, I think it is a matter of course that one should feel oneself so much a member of the nation that one must unite one's fate as closely as possible with that of the whole. . . . What counts is always the readiness to make a sacrifice, not the object for which the sacrifice is made.

This war seems to me, from all that I have heard, to be something so horrible, inhuman, mad, obsolete, and in every way depraving, that I have firmly resolved, if I do come back, to do everything in my power to prevent such a thing from ever happening again. . . .

The fighting at Verdun and the Somme was among the most fierce of the war. Both sides suffered tremendous losses. The following letter by a French machine-gun sergeant describes the defense of Hill 304.

From General Richard Thoumin, *The First World War*, edited and translated by Martin Kieffer, (New York: G.P. Putnam's Sons, 1963), p. 233.

The pounding was continuous and terrifying. We had never experienced its like during the whole campaign. The earth around us quaked, and we were lifted and tossed about. Shells of all calibres kept raining on our sector. The trench no longer existed, it had been filled with earth. We were crouching in shell-holes, where the mud thrown up by each new explosion covered us more and more. The air was unbreathable. Our blinded, wounded, crawling and shouting soldiers kept falling on top of us and died while splashing us with their blood. It really was a living hell. How could one ever survive such moments? We were deafened, dizzy, and sick at heart. It is hard to imagine the torture we endured, our parched throats burned, we were thirsty, and the bombardment seemed endless. . . . Suddenly, the enemy artillery lengthened its fire, and almost at once someone shouted: "The Boches are coming!" As if by magic, all of us, still exhausted only a moment ago, immediately faced the enemy, rifles in hand, for a true infantryman never drops his weapon.

The Russian army was the most ill prepared of all the combatants. Yet despite chronic ammunition shortages and lack of equipment, the Russian army played a key role in the Allied effort. The following letter by a Russian general describes the contributions of the Russian war effort on the Eastern Front during March 1916.

From General Richard Thoumin, *The First World War*, edited and translated by Martin Kieffer, (New York: G.P. Putnam's Sons, 1963), pp. 240–241.

My recollection of all the painful details concerning our offensive is still very vivid. When, at the end of March, operations began, there was a light frost. After a short artillery bombardment, the Russian troops moved forward. Although they ran into a heavy enemy barrage and sustained enormous losses, they reached the enemy lines and broke the front. At that moment, however, an entirely unexpected thaw changed the country into one vast marshland, in which it became impossible to bring in supplies or move the artillery ahead. Still, the Russian troops, soaked to the skin and without any warm food for two days, accomplished their duty faithfully. The Germans, once they had recovered from their surprise, brought up reinforcements and their artillery caused havoc in our ranks. Many of our casualties, even the lightly wounded, could not be carried from the battlefield.

Two or three days later, the thaw was followed by a sudden cold, and a violent and icy wind began blowing. All over the ice-coated battlefield, great numbers of wounded men died from the cold. The still able-bodied men made a supreme effort to keep holding their rifles in their numbed hands. One could only admire the poor fellows' courage and patience. . . .

The result of these operations was not decisive, and even mediocre in importance. Still, the Germans were compelled to reinforce their front with several divisions withdrawn from France during the most critical days of the battle at Verdun. Our losses were very high, numbering some two hundred and fifty thousand men.

The slaughter in the trenches weighed heavily on the troops and by the third year of the war morale was low. The following letter by a French non-commissioned officer describes the demoralization in the 128th Infantry regiment during the Second Battle of the Aisne.

From General Richard Thoumin, *The First World War*, edited and translated by Martin Kieffer, (New York: G.P. Putnam's Sons, 1963), pp. 395–396.

. . . Morale in our regiment was high when it crossed the Aisne on April 16th, 1917, as part of the group that was to exploit the expected success. . . . Even after the bad news from our initial attack, the regiment was still confident when it moved into the fire-line on April 29th. Its situation was definitely unfavorable, but it trusted its officers and, as usual, was not afraid of the difficulties that lay ahead. In the early morning of May 6th, at the appointed hour, our men were full of dash when they launched their assault. They partially reached their objective, at least in the area where our artillery had opened a gap in the enemy's defense zone. This was very little, as no less than sixteen gaps had been expected, but the observations made by the Colonel and the battalion commanders had not been taken into account, at the higher echelons. . . . The 2nd Battalion ran into an intact barbed wire network and into the fire of the German machine guns, which our artillery had not been able to neutralize. . . . The regiment was relieved on May 15th, and the position it had conquered was lost. Our men were deeply disappointed. . . . The regiment went into rest billets in the village of Prouilly. . . . There, the men began to think about the insufficient support from our artillery. . . . They realized that their sacrifices had been useless, perhaps even needless, and isolated, since the other arms had not properly supported them. There remained one hope, however: that of the much needed and prolonged rest which the general had promised our regiment as a reward for its uninterrupted efforts in a fortnight's fighting. The men would also be able to resume going on furlough.

But on May 20th the regiment was ordered back into the fireline. Gone was the hope for a good rest, gone the hopes for leaves. The atmosphere became intense.

VEHICLES OF WAR:
Airplanes and Tanks

At first, aircraft were used only to observe troop movements. But once they became armed with machine guns, spectacular aerial "dogfights" occurred. One of the most colourful "aces" of the war was the German pilot Baron Manfred von Richthofen, the "Red Baron." The following excerpt from von Richthofen's diary describes a double victory obtained by him and his brother, Lothar von Richthofen.

From General Richard Thoumin, *The First World War*, edited and translated by Martin Kieffer, (New York: G.P. Putnam's Sons, 1963), p. 465.

We flew along the front. My brother was next to me, in front of the others. Suddenly I noticed two hostile artillery fliers approaching our front in the most impertinent and provocative manner. I waved to my brother and he understood my meaning. We flew side by side increasing our speed. Each of us felt certain that he was superior to the enemy. It was a great thing that we could absolutely rely on one another and that was the principal thing. One has to know one's flying partner.

My brother was the first to approach his enemy. He attacked the first and I took care of the second. At the last moment I quickly looked round in order to feel sure that there was no third aeroplane about. We were alone and could see eye to eye. Soon I had got on the favourable side of my opponent. A short spell of quick firing and the enemy machine went to pieces. I never had a more rapid success.

While I was still looking where my enemy's fragments were falling, I noticed my brother. He was scarcely five hundred yards away from me and was still fighting his opponent.

I had time to study the struggle and must say that I myself could not have done any better than he did. He had rushed his man and both were turning around one another. Suddenly the enemy machine reared. That is a certain indication of a hit. Probably the pilot was shot in the head. The machine fell and the planes of the enemy apparatus went to pieces. They fell quite close to my victim. I flew toward my brother and we congratulated one another by waving. We were highly satisfied with our performance and flew off. It is a splendid thing when one can fly together with one's brother and do so well.

The following letter by L.G. Morrison, a member of a British tank, describes the effect tanks had at the front.

From General Richard Thoumin, *The First World War*, edited and translated by Martin Kieffer, (New York: G.P. Putnam's Sons, 1963), pp. 493–496.

Four hundred tanks in line of battle. Good going, firm ground, wheel to wheel, and blazing, brilliant weather. . . .

Bang! Clang! Blatter! No words can describe it. Just the whole world heaves, rocks, tumbles, turns upside-down, ricochets; and runs off at a tangent. We can see, hear and feel nothing. . . . Millions of lights flash and stab and crisscross . . . and the darkness, which was greying, is suffused with the densest smoke-barrage in history. How in the hell is anyone to see through that?

The driver is on his seat, his hand on the clutch. The handle is rotated by four burly gunners; she snorts, coughs, stutters, and catches. . . . Soon she is humming low and sweet. I depress the pedal, and she roars . . . magnificently, like the great man-eater she is. Each man at his appointed post, six-pounder gunner to his shoulder-piece, Hotchkiss gunner along his sights . . . naked to the waist, pistol at his belt, steel-lace visors over the straining, bloodshot eyes.

Off we go again, up the opposite slope, on to an upland, wheatfield. A communication trench runs back through the field, and we amble alongside of it. The enemy are really on the run now, fast as their legs will carry them, and our machine-guns are firing at a thousand yards and over. We open the fanlights, as the only danger is long-distance-stuff, and that is spasmodic. . . . Now we are nearing the enemy artillery. Shell after shell roots itself in the ground ahead and kicks up a volcano of dirt. We change over to a zig-zag course, the better to dodge the strafing. Hullo! A shell ploughs the field in front of us, another bursts behind, one out to the right, a fourth to the left. Ranging over open sights! Then some "Jerry" field-piece must be near us. But I'm hanged if I can see anything. A bare field, with a haycock in the corner, a wood in the meadows beyond, and an old belfry just showing above the tops of the trees. Still, that haycock looks suspicious. "Too damned innocent altogether," is Mr. Allan's comment. Would they leave fodder like that—and undamaged, too? "Shoot up that haystack, Alf." "Right-o!" Target! The very first shell lands plump in the haystack, and half a dozen Germans scuttle out of it like rats. Quick! give'em a can of beans now. Oh! good shooting! Now, the belfry, Alf. One, two, three—and the old tower topples in a cloud of brick-dust. . . .

But the heat is infernal. Every bit of the bus [tank] is sizzling. The sun blazes on, the engine roars, the din is terrific, the sweat drips off us, a damp stain spreads through our shorts. More of us have recourse to the smelling-salts. It is midday now—eight hours' running. But our destination is just ahead—the hamlet of Bayonvillers. We reach it to find it deserted—an empty shell, and cracked at that. . . .

Here we halted, shut off the engine to cool it, swung open the sponson doors, and chucked out the dixie, a pannikin of half-cooked rice, bread and corned beef. . . . Occasional shells fell at long intervals, buildings clattered, a rider galloped by, aeroplanes zoomed in the blue overhead. But the sun shone peacefully, the smoke from the wood fire drifted lazily upward, and we munched and champed like boys at a picnic. It didn't seem so bad after all.

---

1. Assume that you are a member of one of the families of the men who wrote these letters and memoirs. Write a letter to the participant which includes news from the homefront as well as your reactions to the experience he has outlined.

ANALYSIS AND APPLICATION

1. *The outbreak of the First World War was not the result of a single cause; rather, it came about as a result of the interplay of complex international forces.*

Account for this statement with reference to the impact of nationalism, imperialism, militarism, and the alliance system on European society.

2. Debate the following resolution: *The values of Western civilization were sacrificed on the altar of war between 1914 and 1918.*

3. *The Treaty of Versailles did not end the First World War; it began the Second.*

Defend or refute this statement based on the terms and outcomes of the Treaty of Versailles.

4. Assume you are a participant in the First World War. (NOTE: This does not have to be in a combatant's role.) Write a biographical sketch establishing your background, then make a series of diary entries covering the following:
(a) your reasons for enlisting;
(b) your first experience at the front;
(c) your feelings about the sustained war effort and your role in it;
(d) your feelings about the armistice.

5. Examine the relationship between the causes and consequences of the First World War.

6. (a) Find out about the propaganda used by both sides during the war. Explain why this propaganda was effective.
(b) Create your own war propaganda for the First World War. You might want to create a video/newsreel, posters, newspaper editorials, etc.

7. As a direct result of their contribution to the war effort, Britain, Germany, and Austria extended voting rights to women after the First World War. Find out more about the roles of women played during the war. Present arguments to support the decision to give women voting rights based on their wartime contributions.

This great military display marked the end of the Nazi Congress at Nuremburg as soldiers marched past Hitler.

PART FOUR

The Challenge to Western Values, 1918 to 1945

The destruction of traditional Western values and the social order by the First World War left a vacuum after 1918. Into the gap left by the collapse of the old order came new social, political, and artistic standards. The values of Western liberal democracy, rejected in Russia, soon found themselves challenged in Italy, Spain, and Germany as well. As Europe struggled first with reconstruction in the 1920s and then with the Depression in the 1930s, it seemed that the Enlightenment tradition was no longer able to meet the changing needs of society.

What emerged were societies based not upon the individual rights and freedoms advocated by Locke, but on the need for strong, stable government as seen by Hobbes. In Russia, Marx's economic ideas were applied by an authoritarian regime that, while it avoided the depths of the economic depression experienced in the rest of the Western world, did so at the price of human rights. On the political right, the fascist regimes of Italy, Spain, and especially Nazi Germany viewed the state as a corporation and its citizens as expendable employees. In such a system, the needs of the individual were subordinated to the demands of the state. The result was the suppression of opposition, the imprisonment of dissidents, and the persecution and eventual murder of Jews.

By the early 1940s, this extremism threatened to overrun all of Western civilization. Those Western nations that still embraced democratic traditions resisted the rapid expansion of fascism. Through six years of global war, they eventually destroyed the regimes where fascism had taken control. As a result, for the second time in a generation, Western society had been drained of its physical and human resources. This time the eventual result would be the loss of its colonial empire around the globe.

The arts too recognized this new search for values. Dubbed the "age of anxiety," artists, writers, and film-makers sought to explore new dimensions in their work. Technology had brought new materials into use and these, combined with a rejection of the styles and techniques of the prewar generation, resulted in a radical departure in style and subject matter.

The period from 1918 to 1945 saw modern Western civilization face its greatest challenge. The basic values of the Enlightenment tradition and conventional views of society and of human progress were rejected by many; in their place there emerged a dark alternative. With the dawning of the atomic age in 1945, many members of Western society wondered whether there was any future at all.

	POLITICS	PHILOSOPHY/LEARNING	ART	SCIENCE/TECHNOLOGY
1918	1918 World War I ends 1919 Treaty of Versailles	1919 Keynes, *The Economic Consequences of the Peace*	1918 Blasco-Ibanez, *The Four Horsemen of the Apocalypse* Matisse, *Odalisques*	1918 Planck, Noble Prize for quantum theory
1920	1920 League of Nations formed U.S. Senate rejects the Treaty of Versailles End of Russian civil war 1921 German reparations set at $33 250 million 1922 Mussolini becomes prime minister of Italy 1923 Hitler's Beer Hall Putsch fails 1924 Dawes Plan reduces German reparations 1926 Germany admitted to League of Nations 1928 Kellogg-Briand Pact signed 1929 Young Plan further reduces German reparations U.S. stock market crash	1923 Freud, *The Ego and the Id* Webb, *The Decay of Capitalist Civilization* 1924 Hitler, *Mein Kampf* 1926 Keynes, *The End of Laissez-Faire* 1928 Jung, *Relationships Between the Ego and the Unconscious*	1920 Holst, *The Planets* Kafka, *A Country Doctor* 1921 Lawrence, *Women in Love* Shaw, *Heartbreak House* 1922 Eliot, *The Wasteland* Hesse, *Siddhartha* Klee, *The Twittering Machine* 1923 Bartok, *Dance Suite* Picasso, *Women* Kandinsky, *Circles in the Circle* 1924 Marinetti, *Futurism and Fascism* Miro, *Catalan Landscape* 1925 Kafka, *The Trial* (posth.) 1927 *The Jazz Singer*, first talking film 1928 Lawrence, *Lady Chatterley's Lover* Chagall, *Wedding* 1929 Remarque, *All Quiet on the Western Front*	1920 Rorschach inkblot test 1921 Morgan's chromosome theory 1922 Best and Banting discover insulin 1924 First use of insecticides 1925 First television transmission 1928 Colour TV demonstrated Fleming discovers penicillin 1929 Einstein, unified field theory
1930	1930 Last Allied troops leave the Saar 1931 Japan invades Manchuria 1933 Hitler becomes chancellor Germany and Japan withdraw from the League of Nations 1934 Hitler becomes führer 1935 Nazis repudiate the Treaty of Versailles Mussolini invades Abyssinia 1936 Germany reoccupies the Rhineland Spanish Civil War begins	1930 Keynes, *Treatise on Money* Freud, *Civilization and Its Discontents* 1933 Jung, *Modern Man in Search of a Soul* Trotsky, *History of the Russian Revolution* 1934 Einstein, *My Philosophy* 1936 Keynes, *General Theory of Employment, Interest and Money*	1930 Wood, *American Gothic* Auden, *Poems* 1931 Dali, *Persistence of Memory* 1932 Huxley, *Brave New World* 1933 Giacometti, *The Palace at Four a.m.* Matisse, *The Dance* 1934 Hindemith, *Mathis der Mahler* 1935 Eliot, *Murder in the Cathedral* 1936 Chaplin, *Modern Times* Mitchell, *Gone with the Wind*	1932 Chadwik discovers the neutron 1934 Fermi splits uranium nuclei

	POLITICS	PHILOSOPHY/LEARNING	ART	SCIENCE/TECHNOLOGY
1937	1937 Japan invades China U.S. Neutrality Act signed Rome-Berlin Axis Italy withdraws from the League of Nations 1938 Germany annexes Austria Munich Agreement Germany occupies Sudetenland 1939 Germany occupies remainder of Czechoslovakia Nazi-Soviet pact Germany invades Poland Beginning of World War II	1938 Dewey, *Logic: The Theory of Inquiry*	1937 Orwell, *The Road to Wigan Pier* Picasso, *Guernica* 1938 Wright, Taliesin West 1939 Joyce, *Finnegan's Wake* Selznick, *Gone with the Wind* (film)	1937 First jet engine 1939 Hahn and Stresseman recognize nuclear fission
1940	1940 Germany occupies Western Europe Battle of Britain begins 1941 Germany invades the U.S.S.R. U.S. enters WWII after the bombing of Pearl Harbor 1942 Highpoint of Axis advances in the Pacific, Africa, and the Soviet Union 1943 Germany defeated in Russia Allies drive Germans out of North Africa Allied invasion of Italy Italy surrenders unconditionally 1944 Allied invasion of Europe U.S. troops land in the Philippines 1945 Mussolini killed by partisans Hitler commits suicide Allied victory in Europe Atomic bombs dropped on Hiroshima and Nagasaki Allied victory in the Pacific	1940 Keynes, *How to Pay for the War* 1942 Fromm, *The Fear of Freedom* 1943 Sartre, *Being and Nothingness* 1945 Curtis, *World War: Its Cause and Cure*	1940 Chaplin, *The Great Dictator* Stravinsky, Symphony in C 1941 Welles, *Citizen Kane* Shostakovich, Symphony No. 7 1942 Camus, *L'Étranger* Bracque, *Patience* 1943 Sinclair, *Dragon's Teeth* Frost, *A Witness Tree* Schonberg, *Ode to Napoleon* 1944 Williams, *The Glass Menagerie* Sartre, *No Exit* 1945 Wright, Guggenheim Museum	1940 First electron microscope 1941 Beginning of the Manhattan Project 1941 Fermi splits the atom 1943 Discovery of streptomycin 1944 Quinine synthesized 1945 Detonation of the first atomic bomb in New Mexico

The Global Search for Norms

ALTERNATIVES TO THE ENLIGHTENMENT TRADITION: COMMUNISM AND FASCISM

In retrospect, it is clear that the Peace of Paris provided merely a breathing space within an ongoing conflict. The terms of the Treaty of Versailles had created a shaky, unstable Europe out of the Great Power balance of the century before. The Hapsburg, Hohenzollern, and Romanov dynasties had disappeared, and in their places a series of new nation-states had emerged. For the most part these new nations tended to be politically and economically fragile democracies led by inexperienced governments. In most of Europe, democratic governments struggled with immediate postwar problems and, after a short period of relative prosperity in the mid and late 1920s, were stunned by the severity of the Great Depression of the 1930s. In many cases, these challenges overpowered the newly created democracies and by 1938 many of them had been replaced by dictators and authoritarian governments. The most powerful of these antidemocratic regimes were the communist government of the Soviet Union and the fascist states of Italy and Germany. Under both these systems, the liberal democratic values of the Enlightenment tradition were rejected in favour of paternalistic state control. In the countries dominated by these regimes, the rights of the individual as advocated by Locke would be sacrificed in favour of the social security championed by Hobbes.

Background to Revolution

During the first half of the nineteenth century, the Russian people had suffered under the reactionary and oppressive rule of Czar Nicholas I (1796–1855). Coming to power on the heels of a failed revolt by liberal army officers (the Decembrist Revolt, 1825) Nicholas spent the next thirty years earning the title "the Iron Czar." Although he was able to maintain political control through the use of secret police, during his reign the gap between the aristocracy and the peasantry widened considerably. During this period alone there were over 500 peasant revolts. Clearly something had to be done.

When Nicholas died in 1855, his successor, Alexander II (1818–1881), implemented major reforms, including the elimination of serfdom. Unlike the abolition of the feudal system during the French Revolution, however, this did not mean a complete turnover of ownership. Instead, feudal estates were divided in half. One half was given to the traditional owner; the other half was divided among the members of the village commune (*mir*). This was not a gift. The mir had to repay the government over the next forty-nine years at 6 percent interest. Nevertheless, the reforms of 1861 were a major step forward for the Russian people. At least now the end of serfdom was in sight. On the other hand, because only one-half of each old estate could be farmed by the mir, the land could no longer support the peasantry. The result was a large-scale migration to the cities. This creation of an urban proletariat did not happen quite the same way as it had in the West. Forced off the land, people did not find factory jobs waiting for them in the cities. Unlike Western Europe, Russia had not industrialized.

At the same time as he was attempting to introduce internal reforms, Alexander was faced with external problems. Local revolts in Poland in 1863 took almost a year to subdue. The czar grew increasingly oppressive. Finally, in 1881, Alexander was assassinated by revolutionaries. His successor, Alexander III (1845–1894), initiated an even greater crackdown on dissent. Upon his death in 1894, Nicholas II (1868–1918) took the throne. Although he was intelligent and compassionate, he would prove to be the last of the czars.

Revolutionary Thought in Russia

Various intellectual challenges to czarism emerged in the nineteenth century. Based upon the idealization of the peasantry by such writers as Leo Tolstoy (1828–1910), teachers known as *narodniks* traveled around the countryside attempting to enlighten the people politically. Their efforts, and those of the *nihilists* who wanted to destroy the existing order, were undermined by the clergy, who encouraged the peasantry to maintain their loyalty to the czar. Political tracts, such as "What to Do?" published in 1863 by Tkachev (1844–1885), helped to develop the tactics of revolution for the overthrow of the government. During the same period, such secret societies as "Land and Freedom" (1877) and "The Will of the People" (1879) distributed propaganda and organized campaigns of sabotage and assassination.

In 1898, the Social Democratic Workers' party was formed. In 1903, it split into two factions, the *Mensheviks* (minority), who wanted to wait for the natural evolution of capitalism and the emergence of the proletariat as in classical Marxist theory, and the *Bolsheviks* (majority), who called for a dictatorship of the proletariat to be spearheaded by a small elite who would then bring agrarian Russia into the industrial age.

In 1904, Russia went to war with Japan. The Western world was shocked when Japan easily defeated Russia. The czar's popularity was further undermined when, on 22 January 1905—"Bloody Sunday"—troops fired on a peaceful march. This action temporarily united the forces of opposition against the czar. The demonstrations, riots, strikes, and acts of terrorism which followed forced Nicholas II to agree to the creation of a parliament, or *Duma*, and a constitution was drawn up. The next decade saw the introduction of some liberal reforms, but for the most part the Duma found itself powerless to counteract the aristocratic advisors who surrounded the czar. Like Louis XVI over a century earlier, Nicholas was well meaning and may have eventually emerged as a constitutional monarch. However, like his predecessor, events would not afford him the opportunity for slow change. When war broke out in 1914, it spelled the end of the Romanov dynasty in Russia.

The Russian Revolution

The patriotism with which the Russian people had entered the First World War had faded by 1917. The strains of war had revealed the shortcomings of the czarist regime. Corruption and inefficiency sapped the strength of the war effort. Dissatisfaction among the troops was so high that officers hesitated to take their own troops into battle for fear that they would turn on them and shoot them. Finally, in March of 1917, Russian soldiers refused to fire on striking workers in Petrograd. The Russian Revolution had begun.

In the face of the combined opposition of the workers, the peasants, and the army to his continued rule, Nicholas II abdicated on 15 March 1917. A provisional government headed by a prominent aristocrat, Prince Lvov (1861–1925), was formed. The government proclaimed an extension of civil liberties, released political prisoners, removed a ban on political exiles, and made plans for an election. But under pressure from the Allies, the new government continued the war effort by organizing a new offensive. This shifted public opinion away from the new government toward the Bolsheviks.

The Bolsheviks Seize Power

The Bolsheviks were a relatively small party (according to Lenin there were 240 000 Bolsheviks in 1917) and only one of the many parties that wanted to overthrow the czar. The Bolsheviks played a minor role in the March Revolution. Their most prominent members, Vladimir Ilich Lenin (1870–1924) and Leon Trotsky (1879–1940), had been out of the country at the time, while Joseph Stalin (1879–1953) had been away from the capital in Siberia. When Lenin returned to Russia from Switzerland, he found the Bolsheviks supporting the provisional government. In his April Theses he outlined why he felt this was a mistake, demanding instead that "all power to the Soviets" (workers' councils) should be the policy of the Bolsheviks. (See readings.)

The slogan "Peace, Land, and Bread" offered something to the worker, the peasant, and the soldier and drew support away from the provisional government. A premature uprising in July forced Lenin and other Bolshevik leaders underground. But when an attempt by the right-wing general L.G. Kornilov weakened the provisional government, Lenin took advantage of the opportunity. On the night of November 6th, the Bolsheviks seized power almost as easily as the provisional government had overthrown the czar in March.

Under the leadership of Lenin, chairperson of the new Soviet of People's Commissars, and Trotsky, commissar for foreign affairs, the Communists announced the dictatorship of the proletariat and called for world revolution. Their first priority, however, was to end the war. Given their inability to continue to fight, the Bolshevik government was forced to sign a disastrous peace treaty with Germany in 1917. By its terms, Russia surrendered all of its European territory; Poland, Finland, Lithuania, and Latvia were declared independent; and the Ukraine became an independent republic under German occupation. Thus Russia lost approximately 25 percent of its population and arable land as well as most of its coal reserves and heavy industry. In addition, the country also agreed to pay a war indemnity of 6 billion gold marks and to grant Germany most-favoured nation status in Russian markets.

Although the final defeat of the Germans by the Allies abrogated the harsher terms of the treaty, the immediate effects were not what the Bolsheviks had anticipated. Believing that Russia had paid too high a price for peace, some patriotic socialists abandoned the Bolsheviks and joined the civil war that had broken out against communist rule. The food shortage, which was already acute, was made worse by the loss of the rich agricultural lands of the Ukraine. But the Treaty of Brest-Litovsk allowed the Bolsheviks to channel their reserves to the civil war and bought them time to consolidate their power.

The Consolidation of Power

Lenin began a policy of "war communism" almost immediately after seizing power. All methods of production and distribution came under government ownership; all foreign and domestic debts were repudiated; troops seized crops and supplies from farmers. The *Cheka* (Commission for the Struggle with Counter-Revolution, Sabotage, and Speculation) ruthlessly liquidated internal enemies, while the new Red Army, under Trotsky, waged a war against the "white army" (the combined antirevolutionary forces). Included in this group opposing the revolution were such disparate groups as former czarist generals wishing to reinstate the monarchy; Japanese troops hoping for territorial gains in the east; and Canadian and American troops who, instead of being sent home at the end of the First World War, had been committed to this other conflict in an attempt to "restore" democracy. Lacking common aims and co-ordination, the white forces were eventually defeated by Trotsky's armies. The civil war finally ended in 1920 with the white invaders being expelled from the country, but war communism and the civil war had taken their toll.

The Bolsheviks had tried to move too far too fast. The peasants resisted collectivization and hoarded their food. Party members could not manage the factories. As a result, by 1920 industrial production was only 60 percent of prewar levels. The transportation system broke down because of the lack of skilled workers and replacement parts. Foreign trade dried up as the Allied nations boycotted communist Russia. By 1921, Lenin was forced into a partial retreat.

The New Economic Policy (NEP) reintroduced elements of private enterprise into the economy. Peasants were allowed to sell part of their produce on the open market; varying wage levels were introduced as an incentive to higher production; and private ownership of small factories was permitted. The state retained control of transportation, heavy industry, banking, and most mining operations. This "partial return to capitalism" was necessary, said Lenin, if Bolshevism was to survive.

The NEP proved an economic success. Foreign trade was revived and production rose above prewar levels. The centralization of industry was later accentuated under Stalin's Five-Year Plans following the death of Lenin in 1924.

Stalin and Trotsky

The struggle for control of the Communist party began in 1922 after Lenin suffered a stroke. Partially paralysed, Lenin played a decreasing role in the party's affairs. His death in January 1924 left no clear successor. The two contenders, Stalin and Trotsky, differed fundamentally over the role to be played by the Communist party.

Trotsky favoured world revolution, arguing that communism could not exist as a single state surrounded by capitalism. Stalin argued that the Communist party should consolidate the revolution in Russia first and not depend on similar revolutions abroad. In 1927, the Communist party adopted the policy of "Socialism in One Country." Stalin had won. Trotsky was exiled, but he continued to oppose

Iosif Vissarionovich Dzhugashvili took the name of Joseph Stalin while a young revolutionary.

Stalin and to preach world revolution until he was murdered by a Stalinist agent in Mexico in 1940.

By 1929, Stalin was firmly in control of the Communist party. Throughout the 1930s he ruthlessly eliminated all of his opponents, real or imaginary, in a series of political purges that reached to the highest levels of the party and the Red Army. Under Stalin, members of the intelligentsia, artists, and scientists were jailed or exiled, or else they simply disappeared. Although a new constitution adopted in 1936 guaranteed civil rights and provided for elected assemblies, Stalin exercised dictatorial control.

Stalin's economic policy was centred around a series of *five-year plans*. In order to industrialize more quickly, he set short-term goals for the expansion of heavy industry. Within ten years iron and steel production increased by 400 percent and coal production by 350 percent. Although the single-minded concentration on heavy industry created hardships, Stalinist industrialization worked. This lesson would not be lost on the developing nations of the world after the Second World War.

In agriculture, Stalin set out to eliminate private enterprise. Through propaganda he stimulated hatred against small independent farmers, and by grouping together small farms into government-run "collectives" he managed to consolidate about 70 percent of the farmland in the Soviet Union by 1934.

Under Stalin, one-party rule became one-person rule, but this aspect of the "new" Russia was not readily evident in the West. From an economic perspective, the Soviet Union clearly did not suffer from the extremes of the depression of the 1930s. Because the postwar boom had not really taken hold in their tightly controlled economy, the depths of depression were not felt there either. This image of equilibrium in an unstable world made the Soviet model a popular alternative for many citizens in the Western democracies.

The Fascist State

The First World War had been a testing ground for the ideas of nineteenth-century Europe. Some, like the concepts of hereditary monarchy and aristocratic privilege, had died a violent death. Economic values had been called into question, and even democratic governments had been accused of secrecy and manipulation in dealing with their own citizens.

Many members of Western society saw democratic government as essentially weak. They claimed that elected lead-

THE TRIAL OF EVGENIA GINZBURG

It is estimated that Stalin arrested approximately 8 million Russians during the 1930s. Thousands were executed, but most were sent to forced labour camps. The following passage describes the seven-minute "trial" of Evgenia Ginzburg, a university professor unjustly charged with committing acts of espionage and terrorism. She served eighteen years in labour camps and prisons and was not released until after Stalin's death.

Now my hour had come. The military tribunal of the Supreme Court—three officers and a secretary—sat facing me across the table; I stood before them, flanked by two guards . . .

"You have read the charge sheet?" the chairman asked in a voice of unutterable boredom. "You plead guilty? No! But the evidence shows . . . Thumbing through the thick file, he muttered: "Here's witness Kozlov, for instance. . . ."

"Not Kozlov—Kozlova a woman. and a despicable woman at that."

"Kozlova, yes. And there's Dyachenko."

"Dyakanov . . ."

"Yes. Well they both state . . ."

But what it was they stated the judge was too pressed for time to say. Breaking off, he asked me:

"Any questions you wish to ask the court?"

"Yes I do. I am accused under section 8 of Article 58. This is a charge of terrorism. Will you please name the political leader on whose life you believe I made an attempt?"

Taken aback by the preposterous form of my question, the judges said nothing. They looked in reproachful silence at the tiresomely inquisitive woman who was holding up their work. At last, the grey-haired one mumbled:

"Don't you know that Comrade Kirov was killed in Leningrad?"

"Yes. But it wasn't I who killed him, it was someone called Nikolayev. And I've never been in Leningrad in my life. Isn't that what is known as an alibi?

"Are you a lawyer or something?" snapped the judge. "No, I'm a teacher." "Then don't split hairs. All right, you've never been to Leningrad. But he was killed by people who shared your ideas, so you share the moral and criminal responsibility."

"The court will withdraw for consultation," grunted the chairman and all the performers of the ritual stood up and wearily stretched their limbs.

I looked at the clock again. They couldn't even have had time for a cigarette: within two minutes they were back in their seats, the chairman with a large sheet of paper in his hand. It was good thick paper covered with a closely typed and neatly laid out text. The typing must have taken at least twenty minutes. This was the verdict . . .

" . . . To ten years maximum isolation in prison, with loss of civil rights for five years . . . "

Ten years! The air grew light and warm. Ten years! That meant Life!

From E. Ginzburg, *Into the Whirlwind*, in John Robottom, *Russia in Change 1870–1945* (New York: Longman, Inc., 1984), pp. 82–83.

ers were merely the "lowest common denominator" of society and that, as Socrates had pointed out, most politicians were not concerned with effective government or social and economic planning but merely with getting elected. They looked for an alternative to the weakness of democracy. As one contemporary political leader stated:

Never more than at the present moment have the nations felt such a thirst for authority, for a direction, for order. If every century has its own peculiar doctrine, there are a thousand indications that Fascism is that of the present century.

From Benito Mussolini, *The Encyclopedia Italiana*, Vol. XIV.

The speaker was Benito Mussolini (1883–1945). Within five years of the end of the First World War, he would have the opportunity to put his philosophy into practice.

Fascism in Italy

Italy was particularly weakened by the First World War. Although on the side of the victors, its sacrifices (600 000 dead) were not recognized by the Peace of Paris. It was a high price to pay to regain the territory of *Italia Irredenta* (Istria, Trieste, and Trentino). Italian nationalists had hoped that the peace treaty would establish Italian control over the Adriatic by extending its influence into the Balkans. This was not to be the case, however. Italy was largely ignored in the division of territory. Fiume, the former Hungarian port, was made part of Yugoslavia by the Treaty of Versailles. This became the symbol of the "mutilated peace."

Domestically Italy was in chaos. Soldiers returning home found mass unemployment, rising inflation, and food shortages. Strikes paralysed industry and essential public services. In agricultural areas peasants seized land, while in industrial areas workers took over factories. The parliamentary government seemed powerless to control the increasing disorder. The country was ripe for revolution.

It was in this setting that Benito Mussolini came to power. A former socialist who was expelled from the party in 1914, Mussolini enlisted the support of dissatisfied ex-soldiers, frightened small property owners, and disappointed nationalists to save Italy from Bolshevism. *Fascio di combattimento* (a semimilitary group known as the "Blackshirts") attacked communist meetings and broke up socialist headquarters. By 1921, Blackshirts ruled entire areas of the country and the *Partito Nazionale Fascista* (the Fascist party's name was derived from the Latin *fasces*, a symbol of authority in ancient Rome) held twenty-five seats in the Chamber of Deputies. In October 1922, the Fascist Party Congress at Naples proclaimed a "March on Rome." Fifty thousand fascists occupied the capital, parading in the streets. The king, Victor Emmanuel III (1869–1947), refused to proclaim martial law and instead gave in to Mussolini's threats of violence. Mussolini was invited to form a ministry and on October 30th he was appointed prime minister.

The Consolidation of Power

Mussolini defined fascism as a rejection of the ideas of both liberal democracy and Marxism. (See readings.) For the fascist, the good of the state far outweighed the good of the individual. Where liberalism "denies the State in the interests of the particular individual," fascism "reaffirms the State as the only true expression of the individual." Rather than the state protecting the rights of the individual, Mussolini believed the individual had a duty to defend the state. "Fascism," said the Italian leader, "does not believe in either the possibility or utility of universal peace. It . . . rejects the pacificism which masks surrender and cowardice."

THE FASCIST DECALOGUE (1934)

The following "ten commandments" illustrate the basic tenets of fascist dogma.

1. Know that the Fascist, and in particular the soldier, must not believe in perpetual peace.

2. Days of imprisonment are always deserved.

3. The nation serves even as a sentinel over a can of petrol.

4. A companion must be a brother, first because he lives with you, and secondly because he thinks like you.

5. The rifle and cartridge belt, and the rest, are confided to you not to rust in leisure, but to be preserved in war.

6. Do not ever say "The Government will pay . . . " because it is *you* who pay; and the Government is that which you willed to have, and for which you put on a uniform.

7. Discipline is the soul of armies; without it there are no soldiers, only confusion and defeat.

8. Mussolini is always right.

9. For a volunteer there are no extenuating circumstances when he is disobedient.

10. One thing must be dear to you above all: the life of the Duce.

From Daniel D. McGarry and Clarence L. Hohl, Jr. (eds.), *Sources of Western Civilization*, Vol. 2 (Boston: Houghton, Mifflin Co., 1963), p. 398.

Over the course of the next two years, *Il Duce* (the leader) transformed Italy's parliamentary democracy into a dictatorship. Parliament was not abolished, but rigged elections in 1924 gave the Fascist party an overwhelming majority. After this, Mussolini became the sole head of government and was given the authority to legislate by decree. The role of the Chamber of Deputies became limited to automatic ratification. Declaring "everything in the state, nothing against the state, nothing outside the state," Mussolini crushed all opposition. Opponents were jailed or killed. Civil rights were suspended and all methods of communication were censored. Once in control, the Fascists moved to improve the domestic situation.

A major cornerstone of Fascist policy was the regulation of the national economy. Under the Fascists, strikes and lockouts were outlawed and wages, hours, and working conditions were regulated. Employment was increased through an extensive program of public works. High tariffs and foreign trade agreements improved the industrial sector, while land reclamation projects expanded agricultural output and increased jobs. By stabilizing the currency, refunding foreign debts, and drastically revising the system of taxation and finance, Mussolini encouraged foreigners to invest capital in Italy.

The last possible area of opposition within Italy was silenced in 1929. Since 1870, the Roman Catholic church had refused to recognize the Kingdom of Italy in protest against the loss of the papal states during the period of unification. Mussolini succeeded in ending this split between church and state with the Lateran Accord. Under the terms of this agreement, the pope recognized the authority of the state; in return, the state recognized the sovereignty of Vatican City and Catholicism became the state religion. By 1930, Mussolini had consolidated Fascist control at home and began to turn his attention abroad. Fervent nationalism, imperialism, and militarism were tenets in the fascist credo. Mussolini dreamed of making Italy a Great Power. To make the Mediterranean an Italian lake (*Mare Nostrum*—"Our Sea") he had already acquired control of the Dodecanese Islands in the Aegean Sea (1923); Fiume, the symbol of the weakness of democracy at the Versailles conference, became Italian (1924); and Albania first became a protectorate of Italy (1927) and was eventually occupied in 1939. In order to extend the colonial empire, Italian troops invaded and conquered Abyssinia (Ethiopia) in 1935–1936 despite sanctions imposed by the League of Nations.

On the surface, at least, Mussolini and the Fascists were achieving their dream. In reality, by 1939 Mussolini's desire to play a leading role in European foreign affairs had placed Italy in a precarious position. The fascist motto—"*Credere, Obbedire, Combattere*" ("Believe, Obey, Fight")—was soon to be tested in the Second World War.

Il Duce *(Mussolini) and* Der Führer *(Hitler) established close ties in the 1930s. After his fall from power in Italy in 1943, Mussolini was set up in a puppet government by the Germans.*

Fascism in Germany

The Hohenzollern dynasty and the twenty-five princes of the German states were overthrown in the last desperate days of the First World War. In their place, a republican government was formed. The Weimar Republic, named for the town in which its constitution was formulated, was based on a system of proportional representation. Hailed at the time as a "perfect" system of democracy, it ensured that political parties would gain seats in the *Reichstag* (parliament) on the basis of the percentage of the popular vote each earned. Although this was a fair system, no party ever won more than 50 percent of the popular vote and in so doing a majority of the seats. Minority and coalition governments were the norm during the fifteen years following the end of the war.

From the beginning the Weimar Republic faced serious problems: the humiliation of defeat, the crippling terms of the Treaty of Versailles, a worthless currency, and economic dislocation. Reparation payments and runaway inflation brought the economy close to collapse in 1923. By November of that year, it took 42 hundred million German marks to buy one United States dollar. Prices rose so quickly that an item that cost 100 marks one day cost 1 million marks the next. By the end of the year, barter had replaced the money economy in many parts of the country, and vast numbers of individuals on fixed salaries and pensions lost everything. For many members of the middle class it was a time of crisis. Economic stability would eventually prove more important than political freedom.

Stabilization of the currency and regulation of the reparation payments under the Dawes Plan of 1924 and the Young Plan of 1929 combined with American loans to ease the economic distress. But not before most of the German middle class was reduced to poverty. Political instability created by the ineffectiveness of coalition governments to cope with these problems shifted public sentiment toward extreme conservatism. As the Depression set in in 1929, anti-government feelings reached new heights. It was the ideal opportunity for Adolf Hitler.

Hitler's March to Power

Adolf Hitler (1889–1945) grew up in the small Austrian town of Braunau near the German border. Rejected by the Fine Arts Academy in Vienna, the young Hitler spent some time in that city earning a living by sketching and selling obscene postcards. While in Vienna, Hitler picked up two ideas that were to guide his future thinking. The first was the concept of "pan-Germanism." During this period, Austria was in command of a large and diverse empire. Many Austrians, including Hitler, felt that all non-Germans should be excluded from the empire and that the "pure" Austria should be united with Germany in a new *reich*. The second idea was that of anti-Semitism. Prewar Vienna was characterized by an economic and cultural elite. Many of its members were Jewish. As a result, there were strong anti-Jewish sentiments among the lower-class Viennese. Hitler agreed with their views. In his ideal world there would be a unified German state, free of "impure" races.

Hitler joined the German army in the First World War. A dispatch runner, he was twice decorated for bravery. At the end of the war he went to work for army intelligence in Munich. His job was to infiltrate and monitor radical political groups. One such group was the small, obscure German Workers' party, a remnant of the once powerful Pan-Germanic Fatherland party. Hitler recognized it as a potential vehicle for his ideas. He resigned from the army and, by 1921, he was the leader of the new National Socialist German Workers' party—the Nazis.

The Beer Hall Putsch

In 1923, encouraged by the economic disorder that plagued the Weimar Republic, Hitler and the Nazis attempted a coup against the Bavarian government. On the evening of 8 November 1923, about 3000 Germans were meeting in one of the largest beer halls in Munich. The hall was surrounded by Hitler and 600 of his storm troopers. Once inside the Nazi leader called for a national revolution. Joining Hitler in his crusade were flying ace Herman Goering, anti-Semitic agitator Julius Streicher, and war hero General Ludendorff. The next morning Nazi storm troopers, parading their swastika flags and banners, marched toward the Marienplatz in the centre of Munich. At the Odeonplatz they were met by a contingent of police, whom Hitler ordered to surrender. Instead they opened fire. Within minutes sixteen Nazis were dead and the rest had scattered. Hitler fled into the hills. Two days later he was arrested and tried for treason. However, he used his trial as a forum. He summarized his view of events in his final speech at his trial:

> I aimed from the first to. . .become the destroyer of Marxism. . . . The army that we are building grows from day to day, from hour to hour.

> . . .Gentlemen, not you will be the ones to deliver the verdict over us, but that verdict will be given by the eternal judgment of history, which will speak out against the accusation that has been made against us. . . .
>
> That court will judge us . . . as Germans [who] wanted only the best for their people and Fatherland, who fought and were willing to die. You might just as well find us guilty a thousand times, but the goddess of the eternal court of history will smile and tear up the motions of the state's attorney and the judgment of this court: for she finds us not guilty.
>
> From "Hitler's Final Speech at his Trial for Treason, March 27, 1924," in Louis L. Snyder, *The Weimar Republic*, (Princeton, NJ: Van Nostrand and Co., 1966), pp. 164–165.

Far from being seen as a traitor, Hitler was held up by conservatives as a national hero. The court was so sympathetic to the conspirators that Hitler was sentenced to only five years for his crime. He was paroled after nine months.

Mein Kampf

While in prison Hitler began writing *Mein Kampf* (literally *My Struggle*). (See readings.) In it, he outlined his view of history, of Germany's needs, and of the future. Dismissed at the time as confused nonsense, it would be described later by author William Shirer as "the Bible of a new barbarism."

In *Mein Kampf* Hitler denounced the Versailles Treaty and demanded the return of German colonies. He attacked the Jews in Germany as "aliens" and called for the restriction of citizens' rights to "Aryans." Economic prosperity was promised through the nationalization of industries and land reform. He called for a highly centralized government to rearm Germany and create an invincible army. But until the Depression reversed their fortunes, Hitler and the Nazi party attracted only the maladjusted, the dissatisfied, and the disgruntled. In 1929, Hitler's brilliant oratory and propaganda (along with the harassment of opponents by the *Sturmabteilung*, or *S.A.*) was able to win only twelve seats in the 577-seat Reichstag.

The depression of the 1930s was to prove a blessing for the Nazi party. Businesses were collapsing at an alarming rate and unemployment reached 6 million. Growing support for the Communist party convinced some German capitalists to turn to the Nazis as the lesser of two evils. In the election of 1930, Nazi support increased to 107 seats, making it the second largest party in the Reichstag. In 1932, the Nazis

Election posters in Berlin in 1933 urged Germans to vote for the joint ticket of Hindenburg and Hitler.

received over 37 percent of the popular vote and doubled their seats to control a third of the Reichstag. Now no ministry could be formed without Nazi support. On 30 January 1933, the aging president, Paul von Hindenburg (1847–1934), appointed Hitler chancellor.

A new election was called for March 1933. In February, however, a fire destroyed the Reichstag. Hitler used the subsequent trial of a Dutch citizen who set the fire to indict Communist party leaders and discredit the communists. Decrees were issued outlawing the Communist party and establishing police rule. But although they controlled the radio and newspapers, the Nazis (in alliance with the Nationalists) were able to secure only a bare majority. However, it was enough for the newly elected Reichstag to push through a law giving Hitler dictatorial powers. The Weimar Republic had come to an end. The Third Reich—the Reich to last 1000 years—had begun.

The Consolidation of Power

In less than two years Hitler had established a totalitarian state. All opposing political parties were outlawed. The civil liberties guaranteed by the Weimar constitution were abrogated. All opposition was ruthlessly crushed. Secret police—the *Gestapo*—arrested all those who opposed the regime. A "blood purge" removed dissidents from within the Nazi party. In 1934, after the death of von Hindenburg, Hitler was appointed president. As president and chancellor, *Der Führer* had absolute power.

Nearly every phase of national life was brought under Nazi control. The Nazi philosophy was taught in schools and in the Hitler Youth groups. The minister of propaganda, Joseph Goebbels (1897–1945), co-ordinated all cultural activities and controlled the press and radio. Henceforth it was required that all cultural activities glorify *Der Führer* and spread racial prejudice against and hatred for all enemies of the Third Reich. In 1935, the Nuremburg Laws were introduced in which Jews were denied German citizenship and were ruthlessly eliminated from German economic life.

Production, prices, banking, and foreign trade were all brought under Nazi control. Trade unions were abolished and workers were forced to join the Nazi-controlled German Labour Front. Compulsory military service and an extensive program of public works solved the unemployment problem. Remilitarization was financed by forced loans from banks and insurance companies. Imports were restricted, foreign exchange was controlled, and the payment of foreign debts was suspended. Under these measures the German economy began to improve. By 1937, the dismissal of women from industry, the elimination of Jews and other "undesirables" from employment, and the revival of compulsory military service actually created a labour shortage. It seemed that the Nazi program was working.

Hitler watched a parade of Nazi troops in Breslau, Germany, in 1937.

The Spread of Fascism

The apparent success of the fascist movement in Italy and Germany led to its growth in popularity outside of those countries. In England, the British Union of Fascists was founded in 1932. Its leader, Oswald Mosley (1896–1980), was originally a member of the Labour government. His proposal in 1930 to ease the depression through stimulating trade, creating an industrial strategy, and using public funds to encourage economic growth was rejected by the cabinet and he resigned to form his own party. At its peak in 1934,

Mosley's party attracted over 10 000 supporters to a rally. In spite of its appeal to the disaffected in Britain, however, Mosley's fascists remained a splinter group. In 1936, he renamed the party the National Socialists. His slogan "If you love your country you are a National—if you love her people you are a Socialist—Be a National Socialist" had little effect on a nation well grounded in the liberal democratic tradition.

France had flirted with different fascist groups during the 1920s. In 1933, the *Francistes* were founded on the German national socialist model. Although the Francistes and the French Popular party garnered some support, it would not be until the defeat of France in the spring of 1940 that fascism would emerge as a potent force in that country.

One of the most successful fascist parties in Europe was in Spain. During the 1920s and early 1930s, political extremism had been rife in that country. By the mid–1930s, Spain was ruled as a socialist republic, but in 1936 a coalition of monarchists, conservatives, clergy, and military, called the *Falange*, revolted against the republic. Led by General Francisco Franco (1892–1975), the *Nationalists*, as they were called, captured city after city. The dividing lines were clear. On one side was Spanish democracy; socialist and divided, it nonetheless represented the will of a majority of the people. On the other side were the fascists. Well armed and organized, they represented the traditional ruling class in the country.

Both Hitler and Mussolini rallied to Franco's side, using the Spanish Civil War to test out new equipment and tactics. The governments of the democracies, on the other hand, stayed neutral, although thousands of volunteers flocked to support the republic. It was not enough. By May 1939, Franco had won. He became *El Caudillo*, the leader of a fascist state.

Impact of Fascism

Fascism, some historians have said, was less a philosophy than a feeling. To many of its supporters, the actual ideas behind their beliefs remained unclear. For many Europeans, the socialist state where everyone had equal opportunities and rights was not much different from a fascist state where everyone had equal duties and obligations.

In retrospect, we can see the dark side of fascism: the racism, the violence, the suppression of dissent. At the time, however, fascism did not appear that way. In 1933, Germany had 6 million workers unemployed. By 1938, when most of the Western world was still struggling with the depression, German unemployment had dropped to 300 000. Fascism seemed to be the answer for a world looking for easy solutions to its problems.

The democracies most keenly felt the intellectual challenge of fascism. In countries with limited democratic traditions, such as Italy, Germany, and Spain, governments fell under the pressure of dedicated fascist movements. In countries where the Enlightenment tradition was stronger, it would take armed invasion to impose fascism on unwilling peoples.

The League of Nations and the Search for World Peace

The last of U.S. president Woodrow Wilson's Fourteen Points stated: "A general association of nations must be formed under special covenants for the purpose of affording mutual guarantees of political independence and territorial integrity to great and small nations alike." The end of the First World War brought with it a desire for peace. It was hoped that the League of Nations would usher in a new era in international relations, an era in which the league would provide a forum for the peaceful settlement of disputes between nations. As a result, the Covenant of the League of Nations was included in the peace treaties with Germany, Austria, Hungary, and Bulgaria. Signatories to these treaties automatically became members of the league.

The structure of the League of Nations consisted of the Assembly, the Council, the Secretariat, the World Court, and various commissions. The assembly met at least once a year and included members from each of the member states; each state had one vote regardless of size and influence. All decisions of the assembly required a unanimous vote. The council consisted of four permanent members (France, England, Italy, and Japan; initially the United States was a permanent member of the council but it never took its seat) and four nonpermanent members (this was later increased to six and then to nine). The council investigated acts of aggression and carried out the recommendations of the assembly. The secretariat published reports, conducted research, and carried on correspondence. The World Court heard cases on international disputes. Various committees, such as the International Health Organization and the International Labour Organization, helped the league to achieve its social and economic goals. One of the greatest successes of the league was its work with refugees.

The Treaty of Versailles had redrawn the map of Europe.

Poland, Czechoslovakia, Lithuania, Estonia, Latvia, and Yugoslavia were created. The Austro-Hungarian Empire was broken up. Revolution in Russia and the redrawing of boundaries set millions of people moving. The number of refugees reached such proportions that international action was initiated.

In 1921, Dr. Fridtjof Nansen (1861–1930) was appointed the league's special commissioner for refugees. In the 1920s, Nansen's principal concerns were the 1.5 million Russians displaced by the Bolshevik Revolution and the homeless Armenians and Greeks who fled Turkey after the breakup of the Ottoman Empire. Nansen was responsible for creating the "Nansen Passport," a travel document which provided displaced people with some official status. However, the problems of refugees remained acute as the long tradition of asylum began to break down and finally collapsed completely during the depression of the 1930s.

The league was successful in solving a number of disputes between smaller nations in the 1920s. These included disputes between Finland and Sweden, Germany and Poland, Yugoslavia and Albania, Greece and Italy, Greece and Bulgaria, and Iraq and Turkey. In the 1930s, however, the league was unable to solve the problems among the larger powers.

The League of Nations lacked executive power and did not have the force of authority to achieve its goals; it was essentially an open forum for international discussion. From the beginning it had problems with membership, and three of the five Great Powers—Germany, Russia, and the United States—were not members. Although both Germany and Russia subsequently joined the league, the United States never did. The lack of a means of enforcement, economic and political rivalries, and problems over membership resulted in the league's failure to achieve its ultimate goal—the prevention of war and the preservation of peace.

The Road to War

Although Hitler talked of peace he began to prepare for war. Questioning why Germany alone should be disarmed, he withdrew from the league's Disarmament Conference and from the league itself in 1933 when the military restrictions imposed by the Treaty of Versailles were not lifted. In 1935, Hitler announced Germany would rearm and he reintroduced conscription. An Anglo-German naval treaty of the same year permitted a German navy up to 35 percent as large as Britain's. In 1936, German troops moved into the Rhineland.

All of these actions were against the Treaty of Versailles and contrary to the growing support for disarmament and world peace. Rather than risk war, Britain and France adopted a policy of *appeasement* toward Germany. In 1938, Hitler occupied Austria without effective opposition and then turned his attention toward repatriating the 3 million Germans living in Czechoslovakia.

Hitler was convinced that Britain and France would once again acquiesce when he demanded that Czechoslovakia surrender German-speaking Sudetenland to Germany. When Czechoslovakia refused, Hitler became more aggressive. To avoid open conflict a compromise was reached at Munich in 1938. British prime minister Neville Chamberlain (1869–1940), French premier Edouard Daladier (1884–1970), Mussolini, and Hitler—in the absence of the Czechs—signed an agreement surrendering the Sudetenland to Germany in return for Hitler's promise that this would be his last act of territorial expansion. Chamberlain's "peace in our time" lasted until March 1939 when the rest of Czechoslovakia was surrendered to Hitler. When Hitler's quest for *lebensraum* (living space) was turned toward Poland, both Britain and France belatedly realized that conciliation was no longer possible. The German attack on Poland came on 1 September 1939. Britain and France declared war on Germany on September 3rd.

THE SECOND WORLD WAR, 1939 TO 1945

Causes of the War

In general, the same factors that brought about the First World War—nationalism, imperialism, militarism, and international alliances—also caused the Second World War. The Peace of Paris had not solved the problems that in 1914 had led to "the war to end all wars." In fact, during the twenty-year period between 1919 and 1939 these problems had simply intensified.

Germany, Italy, and Japan all resented their treatment by the Allies after the First World War. In Germany, Hitler used the Treaty of Versailles as a propaganda tool and a cornerstone in his election campaigns. Although on the victorious side, the territorial desires of both Italy and Japan went unanswered by the Peace of Paris. The German desire for *lebensraum*, the Italian dream of *mare nostrum*, and the Japanese doctrine of "Asia for the Asiatics" were all fueled by militant nationalists. The economic nationalism that resulted in high tariffs and strangled trade during the Depression merely heightened national chauvinism.

The imperialistic goals of the Axis Powers made conflict inevitable. Japan's conquest of Manchuria (1931) and attack on China (1937), Italy's conquest of Abyssinia (1936), and Germany's annexation of Austria (1936), Sudetenland (1938), and Czechoslovakia (1939) illustrated the lack of unity between Britain and France and showed the weakness of the League of Nations. If the league condemned the actions of an aggressor nation, as in the case of Japan's seizure of Manchuria, or instituted sanctions against an aggressor, as in the case of Italy's invasion of Abyssinia, the aggressor merely withdrew from the league.

The failure of the league to reduce armaments led to an arms buildup in the 1930s that further added to international tensions, and as tensions increased countries sought allies. The Anti-Cominterm Pact between Germany and Japan (1936) and the Rome-Berlin Axis (1936) became the Rome-Berlin-Tokyo Axis in 1939. The success of fascist expansion led to an alliance between Britain and France in 1938. The British guarantee of Polish independence was a threat to Hitler's plans for Poland and led to the Nazi-Soviet Non-aggression Pact in August 1939. When Hitler marched into Poland on 1 September 1939, the guarantees made to Poland by Britain and France led to the Second World War.

Victorious German troops roamed the devastated streets of Warsaw in September 1939.

The European Theatre, 1939 to 1942

Initially the Second World War was restricted to Europe. Britain and France watched helplessly as the German *blitzkrieg* (lightning war) conquered Poland in four weeks. Under the secret terms of the Nazi-Soviet pact, the Russians seized eastern Poland and occupied the Baltic states of Latvia, Lithuania, and Estonia. During the winter of 1939–1940, the French watched the Germans from the Maginot Line. But as the *sitzkreig*, or "phony war" as it was sometimes called, occurred in the West, Russia invaded Finland. In the spring of 1940, Hitler turned his *blitzkrieg* toward the West.

In April, Hitler launched an offensive against Scandinavia. Denmark fell in one day, Norway in six weeks. In May, Hitler attacked the "neutral" nations. Holland fell in five days. British and French support did not prevent Luxembourg and Belgium from following two weeks later, and France fell shortly after that. Only the evacuation at Dunkirk saved the British forces from destruction. The Battle of Europe was over. The Battle of Britain was about to begin.

Operation Sea Lion was the German plan for the invasion of Great Britain. A necessary prelude was the destruction of Britain's air defences. The Battle of Britain began 8 August 1940 when the German *luftwaffe* began to bomb British ports and airfields. Radar, and the skill, courage, and daring of the British Spitfire and Hurricane pilots, won the air battle. By September, Operation Sea Lion was postponed, never to be revived. Hitler decided to turn his attention elsewhere.

In North Africa, the German *Afrika Korps*, under the brilliant leadership of General Erwin Rommel, the "Desert Fox" (1891–1944), drove the British back to the Egyptian border. In eastern Europe, German forces invaded Bulgaria, Yugoslavia, and Greece. In 1941, despite the nonaggression pact with the Soviet Union, Hitler invaded that country.

In June 1941, the Nazi *blitzkrieg* began a campaign that overran eastern Poland and the former Baltic provinces of Lithuania, Latvia, and Estonia and drove the Red Army back to the gates of Moscow. By the end of the year, Hitler's armed forces controlled 1 300 000 km^2 of Soviet territory. But winter came early in 1941 and the ill-equipped German army had to halt its advance. The oil-rich Caucus region was conquered and Stalingrad was threatened when the offensive resumed in the spring of 1942. But the Germans had lost the advantage. The Soviet factories beyond the Ural Mountains were resupplying the Red Army and the stubborn resistance of Stalingrad sapped the strength of the *wehrmacht*. In the interim, the United States openly joined the ranks of the Allies.

The Second World War
in Europe and Africa, 1942–1945
FINLAND
NORWAY
SOVIET UNION
SWEDEN
Baltic
Sea
ESTONIA
LATVIA
LITH.
GREAT
BRITAIN
IRELAND
North Sea
DENMARK
Moscow
NETH.
Berlin
Warsaw
POLAND
Stalingrad
Atlantic Ocean
BEL.
Normandy
Paris
LUX.
GERMANY
CZECHOSLOVAKIA
FRANCE
Vienna
HUNGARY
SWITZ.
AUSTRIA
ROMANIA
Milan
VICHY
FRANCE
PORTUGAL
SPAIN
Adriatic Sea
YUGOSLAVIA
Black Sea
ITALY
BULGARIA
Rome
ALBANIA
TURKEY
GREECE
Algiers
Casablanca
SICILY
Tunis
SYRIA
ALGERIA
MOROCCO
TUNISIA
Mediterranean Sea
LEBANON
IRAQ
Tripoli
PALESTINE
TRANS-
JORDAN
El Alamein
SAUDI ARABIA
LIBYA
EGYPT
1942
1943
1944
1945
Allied advances
Greatest extent of
Axis control, 1942
Axis nations
Allied nations
Neutral nations
0
500 km

The United States Enters the War

Technically, the United States had been neutral. But Franklin Delano Roosevelt (1882–1945), the American president, had prepared the U.S. for possible involvement since the onset of the conflict. In 1939, the Neutrality Laws were revised to permit belligerents to purchase war materials as long as they paid cash and transported the goods in their own ships. This "cash-and-carry" law provided much needed assistance to Britain, particularly after the loss of all heavy equipment during the evacuation at Dunkirk. In 1940, the U.S. adopted peace-time conscription for the first time in its history. In the same year, fifty aging destroyers were given to Britain in return for naval bases along the Atlantic coast. The Neutrality Laws were further revised in 1941 to permit the U.S. government to lend or lease war materials to any nation whose defense was considered necessary to the safety of the U.S. Naval patrols were extended in the Atlantic to protect lend-lease materials. When the U.S. sent troops to occupy Iceland and Greenland in 1941, the country was at war in everything but name. Certainly its role as a neutral nation was seriously in question.

Although all these preparations were directed toward assisting the Allies (particularly Britain) in Europe, the U.S. entered the Second World War as a result of a surprise attack in the Pacific. On 7 December 1941, a massive Japanese carrier-based force devastated the naval base at Hawaii's Pearl Harbor in a sunrise attack. The U.S. immediately declared war on Japan, and Britain followed suit. When Japan's Axis partners declared war on the U.S., and the U.S. declared war on Germany and Italy, the European and Pacific theatres were linked and every major power was involved in the conflict.

The U.S.S. Arizona *was destroyed after the Japanese attack on Pearl Harbor on 7 December 1941, which brought the United States into the war.*

The Turning of the Tide, 1942 to 1943

At the beginning of 1942, the Axis forces seemed on the verge of world domination. But by the beginning of 1943 a decisive reversal had begun. In Russia, the Red Army launched counter-offensives along the entire front. In January 1943, the German Sixth Army, comprising 300 000 soldiers, was encircled and destroyed at Stalingrad. In Africa, Rommel's drive into Egypt was stopped at El Alamein, only 112 km from Alexandria. A counter-offensive launched in October 1942 reached Tripoli by January 1943. Meanwhile, Anglo-American amphibious landings in Morocco and Algeria harassed the Germans in western Africa. By mid-1943, the Allies were masters of the African continent.

In June 1943, the Allies invaded Sicily, and by September they were on the Italian mainland. Mussolini was forced out of office and the new government surrendered to the Allies in September. However, the German army still occupied much of southern Italy and stubborn resistance prevented the Allies from reaching Naples until October; Rome was not liberated until June 1944. By this time, the focus was on France.

The Collapse of Germany, 1944 to 1945

Since 1942, Stalin had been pressing for a "second front" in the west to relieve the pressure on the Soviet army in the east. Called "Operation Overlord," preparations for this new offensive began in 1942 and culminated on 6 June 1944 on the beaches of Normandy with the greatest amphibious landing in history. By August, the Allies had won the Battle of Normandy; France was liberated within seven weeks of the Allied landing. A last desperate attempt by the Germans at the Battle of the Bulge was overwhelmed and the Allies were free to continue their drive into Germany.

Early in 1945, the Russians conquered Poland. Now Germany was caught in a great pincer movement. The Russians were driving toward Berlin from the east; the other Allied forces were approaching the city from the west. In April, the Russian and Allied forces met at Torgau; Germany was now split in two. The Russians marched into Berlin in May. Hitler committed suicide. German resistance collapsed and the nation surrendered unconditionally on 7 May 1945.

Planning for Peace

The Allies had been planning for peace throughout the war. As early as 1941, even before the U.S. entered the war, Roosevelt and Churchill had signed a joint statement "on which they base[d] their hopes for a better future for the world." This Atlantic Charter was signed by twenty-six representatives of other nations early in 1942 and is considered by many to be the beginning of the United Nations. (See readings.)

The plans for a permanent system for world security were advanced in October 1943 when the foreign ministers of the Soviet Union, Great Britain, and the United States pledged their governments to form an international organization for world peace. The first draft of the U.N. charter was written at Dumbarton Oaks in 1944. The final draft was signed by fifty nations at the San Francisco Conference of 1945. But other Allied conferences were not as successful.

In 1943, American president Roosevelt, British prime minister Winston Churchill (1874–1965), and Chinese Nationalist leader Chiang Kai-shek (1887–1975) met in Cairo, where they established a policy of unconditional surrender for Japan. The first meeting between Churchill, Roosevelt, and Stalin—the "Big Three"—took place at Teheran later that year, where they confirmed a policy of unconditional surrender for Germany and Italy as well. Although the principal focus of the Teheran meeting was to plan the second front, cracks in Allied co-operation began to appear over differences in the plans for a postwar world. These divisions became readily apparent at the Yalta Conference of 1945.

The major problems at Yalta were the plans for eastern Europe. (See readings.) At the time of the conference, Russia controlled Poland and much of eastern Europe. As a result, and in return for promises concerning "the restoration of sovereign rights and self-government" in eastern Europe, Stalin was granted a number of concessions. Polish borders were fixed, giving eastern Poland to Russia; Poland was compensated by land acquired from Germany. By pledging to enter the war in the Pacific soon after hostilities in Europe were over, Stalin acquired the Kurile Islands and rights in Manchuria, which had been lost during the Russo-Japanese War (1905).

The next conference between the Big Three was held under considerably different circumstances. The war in Europe was over. FDR was dead and Harry Truman (1884–1972) was the new U.S. president. Great Britain was represented by Clement Attlee (1883–1967). Stalin continued to push Soviet demands as the Allies attempted to implement the Yalta agreements concerning Germany.

At Yalta, the Allies had agreed to divide Germany into four zones to be occupied by the United States, the Soviet Union,

Britain, and France. The capital, Berlin, although located 180 km within the Soviet zone, was to be similarly divided. An Allied Commission was to be established to act as the government of Germany during joint occupation. At Potsdam, the Allies further agreed to administer the four zones as a single economic unit. (See readings.) But the agreements for joint occupation, reparations, and the German economy were soon to be derailed as suspicions between the Allies increased. Meanwhile, the war in the Pacific continued.

The Big Three—Churchill, Roosevelt, and Stalin—gathered on the patio of Livadia Palace at the Yalta Conference in 1945.

The Defeat of Japan

Within weeks of the attack on Pearl Harbor the Japanese had seized Singapore, the Philippines, Malaysia, and the Dutch East Indies. The Japanese "Greater East Asia Co-Prosperity Sphere" threatened Australia and India. However, naval defeats at Midway Island and the Coral Sea halted further Japanese expansion and the U.S. launched a campaign of "island hopping" that gradually recaptured Japanese conquests.

In 1942, a beachhead was established in the Solomon Islands. By the end of 1943, New Guinea had been recaptured. The Gilbert, Marshall, and Mariana islands provided bases for the long-range bombing of Japan. In 1944, the

Caroline Islands and Guam were reconquered and the naval defeat at Leyt Gulf crippled the Japanese fleet, paving the way for the reconquering of the Philippines. In 1945, the capture of the Philippines and Okinawa placed the United States forces only 560 km away from the Japanese home islands. With the collapse of Italy and Germany, Japan stood alone.

When the Japanese ignored an Allied call to surrender, issued from Potsdam in July, Truman decided to use the atomic bomb. This devastating new weapon had been secretly developed in the United States by a joint British, American, and Canadian team. On 6 August 1945, the first atomic bomb was dropped on Hiroshima. When there was no response from the Japanese, a second, more powerful, bomb was dropped on Nagasaki. U.S. figures estimated the number of dead between 66 000 and 78 000 for Hiroshima and 39 000 for Nagasaki; Japanese sources cited over 240 000 dead for both Hiroshima and Nagasaki. (Neither of these figures takes into account the number of miscarriages and premature births that occurred in the first eight months following the blast nor the number of deaths due to abnormal incidences of cancer among the survivors.)

The Japanese surrendered unconditionally on August 14th. Formal papers were signed on September 2nd, V-J Day, aboard the U.S.S. *Missouri*. The Second World War was over.

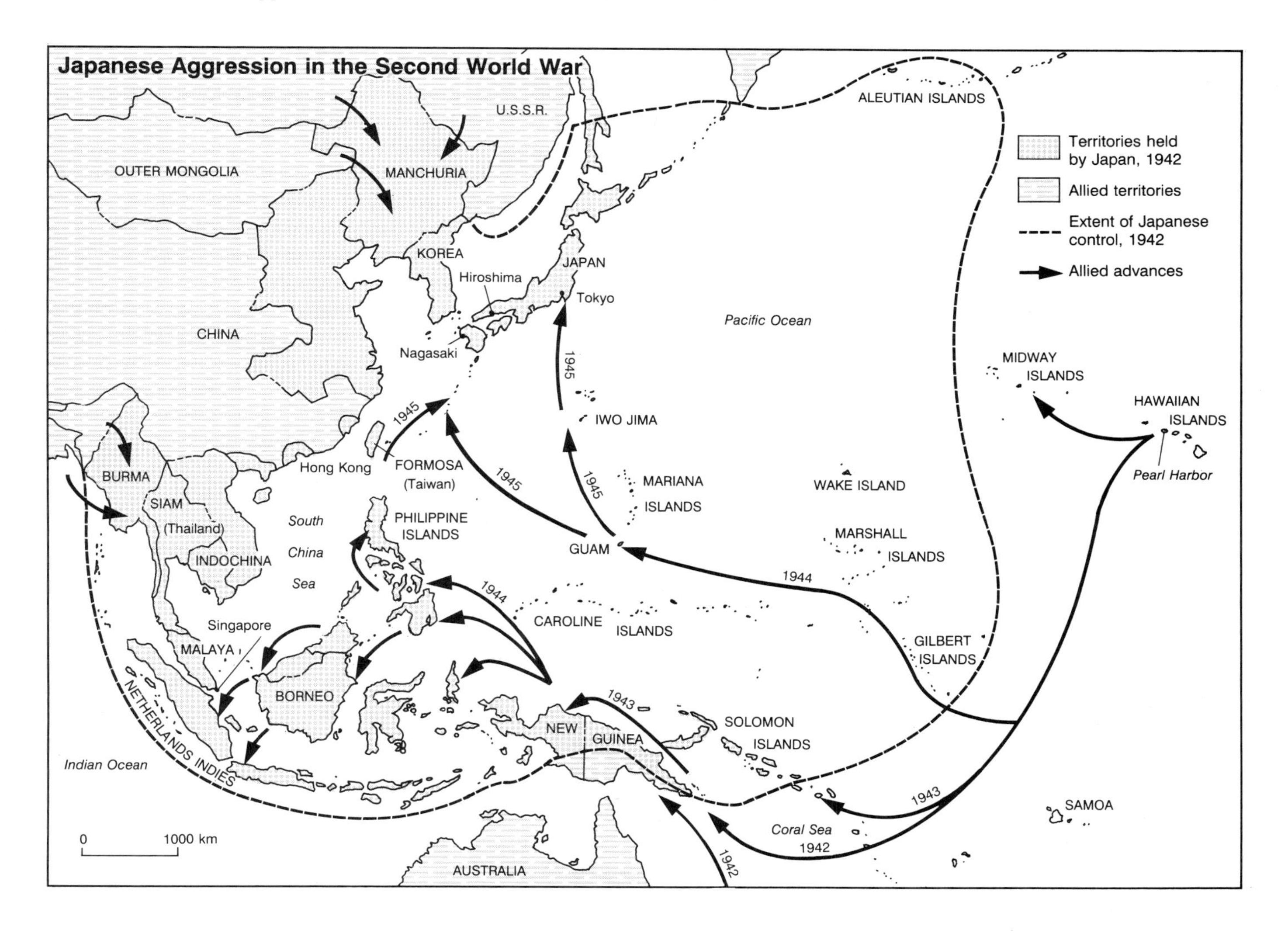

HIROSHIMA: AN EYEWITNESS ACCOUNT

In the following passage, Michihiko Hachiya describes the first minutes of the aftermath of the detonation of the atomic bomb, 6 August 1945.

The hour was early; the morning still, warm and beautiful. Shimmering leaves, reflecting sunlight from a cloudless sky, made a pleasant contrast with shadows in my garden as I gazed absently through wide-flung doors opening to the south.

Clad in vest and pants, I was sprawled on the living-room floor exhausted because I had just spent a sleepless night on duty as an air-raid warden in my hospital.

Suddenly, a strong flash of light startled me—and then another. So well does one recall little things that I remember vividly how a stone lantern in the garden became brilliantly lit and I debated whether this light was caused by a magnesium flare or sparks from a passing train.

Garden shadows disappeared. The view where a moment before all had been so bright and sunny was now dark and hazy. Through swirling dust I could barely discern a wooden column that had supported one corner of my house. It was leaning crazily and the roof sagged dangerously.

Moving instinctively, I tried to escape, but rubble and fallen timbers barred the way. By picking my way cautiously I managed to reach the roka [passage] and stepped down into my garden. A profound weakness overcame me, so I stopped to regain my strength. To my surprise I discovered that I was completely naked. How odd. Where were my vest and pants?

What had happened?

All over the right side of my body I was cut and bleeding. A large splinter was protruding from a mangled wound in my thigh, and something warm trickled into my mouth. My cheek was torn, I discovered, as I felt it gingerly, with the lower lip laid wide open. Embedded in my neck was a sizeable fragment of glass which I matter-of-factly dislodged . . .

"We'll be all right," (I told my wife). "Only let's get out of here as fast as we can."

She nodded, and I motioned for her to follow me.

The shortest path to the street lay through the house next door, so through the house we went—running, stumbling, falling, and then running again until in the headlong flight we tripped over something and fell sprawling into the street. Getting to my feet, I discovered that I had tripped over a man's head.

"Excuse me! Excuse me, please," I cried hysterically.

There was no answer. The man was dead. The head had belonged to a young officer whose body was crushed beneath a massive gate. . . .

From *Hiroshima Diary* by Michihiko Hachiya. Translated by Dr. Warner Wells.

The aftermath of the atomic bomb dropped at Hiroshima was total destruction.

THE RESULTS OF THE SECOND WORLD WAR

The Second World War had a devastating impact upon Western civilization. The long and bitter struggle had reduced Germany and Japan to rubble. Britain was physically and economically exhausted and France and the rest of Europe were suffering from unprecedented socio-economic problems. The collapse of Europe allowed the United States and the Soviet Union to increase their influence in Europe and the rest of the world. Conflicting social and political philosophies would soon lead these two new superpowers into bitter ideological conflict.

Nationalism emerged as a potent political force in Africa and Asia after the Second World War. European colonies on these continents demanded independence from their weakened masters and as a result a process of decolonization began in the late 1940s. Between 1947 and 1962 almost every European colony gained independence. This was only one reflection of the loss of power Europe had suffered in international affairs.

The human costs of the war were staggering. Both civilian and military dead surpassed the carnage of the First World War. The Soviet Union alone lost 7.5 million military personnel and 15 million civilians. Aerial bombing, mass executions, and the extermination of 6 million Jews in the

THE FINAL SOLUTION

In the following excerpt, Jack Eisner, a survivor of the Treblinka death camp, describes an incident that happened when Jewish prisoners from Warsaw arrived at the camp.

My eyes followed the line. The woman and her newly adopted child were now only moments away from the decision of life or death. They climbed the wooden barks steps. The SS doctor pulled away the raincoat. Silence for a moment, as he sized up the child and the woman.

"She can walk. Can't she?"

The woman nodded.

"Put her down then. Los!"

An SS aide stepped forward and pulled the girl from the woman.

"Here. Here's where you go." The white-clad SS officer pointed to the barracks entrance only a few feet away.

The little girl began to cry loudly and sat down.

"You can either go with her or not," the SS officer barked at the woman. "But schnell. Make up your mind."

In an instant, the sadistic bastard had transferred the choice of life or death from himself to the woman. She could abandon the child and save herself, or she could accompany the child.

The woman's conflict was so apparent, it was heartbreaking. She moved slowly toward the girl, and death; then quickly away to the left, for life. She hesitated, then once again walked back to the girl. Her hair was in wild disarray. Her mouth was clenched. Her conscience was tearing her apart.

The SS doctor quickly tired of his sport. He ordered his aide to shove both the woman and the child into the barracks. The storm trooper grabbed the hesitating woman's arm and pushed her forward. She fell over the little girl's body.

"Move. Los!"

Suddenly a screaming young woman ran wildly up the steps. It was the child's real mother. She pushed the storm trooper aside and threw herself on the crying little girl. She kissed her face, arm and head. She comforted her. She covered the child's body with her own.

Even the SS men stared in wonder for a moment. But not for long. In a violent reaction, the storm trooper she had pushed levelled his machine gun and pulled the trigger, bringing the entire episode to an abrupt end. The mother, the child and the middle-aged woman were grotesquely sprawled in their own blood only a few feet from the barracks entrance.

From Jack Eisner, *The Survivor*, in Colin C. Bayne-Jardine *The Second World War and Its Aftermath* (New York: Longman, 1987).

AUSCHWITZ

The following passage describes a visit to Auschwitz by a judge and jury of a war crimes trial held in the 1960s.

The court moves along. Here is a cellar, Penal Barracks 11. A great deal had been heard about it in the Frankfurt courtroom. Witnesses testify and with tear-choked voices have fainted from the violence of their recollections, have come to again and continued to testify. It is dark and damp in the cellar. The crowd peers into the dungeon, barely three by three yards wide, with a tiny hatch. Here, 40 people were stuffed together without food. They struggled for air, screamed, starved to death and suffocated. . . . Their crimes recorded meticulously:

> Prisoner 64 166 admitted May, 1943; he allowed a tool to drop to the ground, the handle bent.
>
> Prisoner 42 658 admitted March 14, 1943; he had tried to obtain a second bowl of soup.
>
> Prisoner 64 495 admitted June 5, 1943; he had relieved himself on the job.

At the main gate, below the cast iron band with the inscription, 'Arbeit Macht Frei' [work brings freedom] small talk cuts into the general silence. . . . The court is in a hurry. Now it stands in front of the 'Black Wall.' Some 20 000 people were murdered here. Naked, running in double-time, they came out of the penal bunkers to the right. Kapos flung them against the wall. A single shot in the nape of the neck. The blood flowed into the gutter.

Judge Hotz gives the sign for everyone to depart. The inspection is at an end. The court returns to the base camp, Auschwitz I. Here, the Polish government has converted some former prison barracks into a museum. The barracks are heated now, there are curtains strung over windows blocked by rusty bars, even doormats at the entrance. . . . And yet it is here that the sober, matter-of-fact façade of the jurors suddenly disintegrates. The Judge bursts into tears. He stands with his staff before the remains of the murdered; whole rooms filled with children's shoes, spectacles, crutches, prayer books, valises, men's suits, dresses, dentures. Thousands of toothbrushes, mountains upon mountains of women's hair, cut prior to the gassing, some still in sacks labelled for shipping to a firm in Bavaria that manufactured insulating material for submarines.

From Amos Elon, *Journey through a Haunted Land*, translated by M. Roloff (London: Andre Deutsch Ltd.).

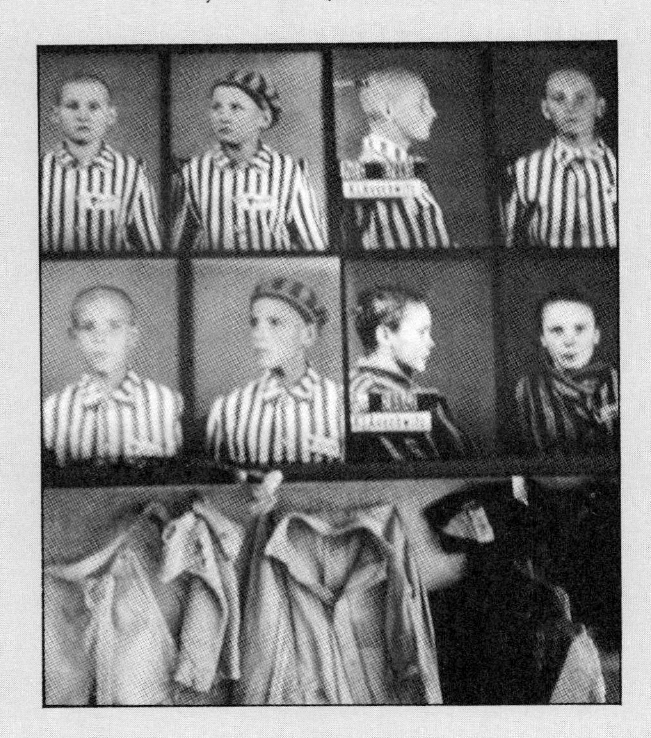

More than 2 million Jews, Gypsies, and Soviet prisoners-of-war were murdered at Auschwitz between 1941 and 1944. They are remembered at the camp today.

Holocaust meant that for the first time in modern history the number of civilians dead outnumbered the number of military dead. Only the newly formed United Nations prevented famine among the postwar refugees.

The physical costs of the war reached astronomical proportions. Entire cities were reduced to ashes and rubble. Factories and transportation systems were destroyed or crippled. Millions of tonnes of military hardware and naval equipment were destroyed. The military cost alone was estimated to exceed 1 trillion dollars. Europe was reduced to bankruptcy. Only massive economic aid provided the means for the survival of democracy in Western Europe.

The Holocaust

The full extent of Nazi barbarism began to be revealed in 1944 as the Red Army liberated concentration camps in Eastern Europe. It proved to be the worst example of deliberate inhumanity in the history of the human race.

Hitler's anti-Semitism was clearly revealed in *Mein Kampf*. In 1935, after he had consolidated his power, he institutionalized anti-Semitism in the *Nuremberger Rassengesetze* (Nuremberg Racial Laws), which were designed to "secure for the German nation for all time the purity of its blood." Systematic harassment and persecution resulted in the large-scale emigration of German Jews. The remainder were arrested and sent to concentration camps.

Concentration camps began almost as soon as Hitler became chancellor. Initially they were intended to hold political dissidents, but increasingly they became part of Hitler's plan to rid Germany of its Jewish citizens.

A shift in Nazi policy began when Germany conquered Poland (which had the largest prewar Jewish population in Europe) and invaded the Soviet Union. This left Germany in control of a large, unwanted Jewish population. On 20 January 1942, the Wansee Conference, convened by Reinhard Heydrich (1904–1942) and Adolf Eichmann (1906–1962), met and prepared the plan for the "Final Solution"—the systematic extermination of the Jewish race. After this conference, concentration camps were built on a much larger scale until there were thirty large camps and hundreds of smaller ones. Some of these camps were designed specifically for extermination. The largest—Auschwitz—was responsible for the murder of more than 2 million people, most of them Jews, between 1941 and 1944.

All of the major extermination camps—Mardanek, Auschwitz, Treblinka, and Mauthausen—were in Eastern Europe. Jews from Western Europe were transported to these camps by rail. In the camps, those who were not starved, beaten, or worked to death were shot or gassed. (See readings.) By 1945, 6 million Jews had been murdered.

The Nuremberg Trials

The extent of Nazi brutality led to the Nuremberg Trials in 1945–1946. An international military tribunal established by the United States, the Soviet Union, Britain, and France tried twenty-four Nazi leaders for crimes against humanity. Twelve were sentenced to death, including Hermann Goering (1893–1946), the head of the German air force. The rest received prison sentences. Additional trials were held at Nuremberg by a U.S. military tribunal. German judges and civilians were among the 185 Nazis tried. Twenty-four people received the death sentence. The process of ridding defeated Germany of the Nazis was continued by the new German officials, who tried 600 000 German citizens. Similiar trials were conducted in Tokyo for Japanese war crimes.

RETROSPECTIVE

The years from 1917 to 1945 saw dramatic challenges to the Enlightenment tradition, as well as the physical destruction of much of Europe. Unable to recover from the political and economic devastation caused by the First World War, the European world was plunged into a second and even more deadly conflict.

In 1917, the Bolsheviks successfully seized power from a provisional government that had been established after the abdication of the czar. Lenin and Stalin attempted to create a Marxist state out of the backward empire of the czars. While experiencing limited economic success, the new Soviet regime suppressed dissent and rejected many of the liberal democratic values of the Enlightenment tradition. The closed and oppressive "dictatorship of the proletariat" would eliminate all challenges to its authority for the next seventy years.

In response to this challenge, in Italy and then Germany, right-wing fascists seized power. Mussolini and Hitler established totalitarian corporate states and forged aggressive foreign policies. Initially Great Britain and France adopted a policy of appeasement toward fascist aggression until Germany invaded Poland in September 1939. Then they took action. For the next six years, the governments of the West, in alliance with the Soviet Union, gradually destroyed the fascist empire. To a great extent, the success of the allies was a product of the global success of Western civilization. To liberate a wartorn Britain, the Soviet Union turned to the products of European imperialism, in particular the United States and Canada, to provide the economic and military power to tip the balance in their favour.

The era between the wars saw intellectual and military challenges to the Enlightenment tradition. From the ashes of the conflict, a new Europe would eventually emerge. The half-century after 1945 would see Western civilization attempt to redefine itself and its role in world affairs.

VLADIMIR LENIN:
What Is to Be Done? (1902)

Lenin fundamentally disagreed with the philosophy of the Social Democratic party (the Russian Marxists). In 1903, he split the party and formed the Bolsheviks (the majority) along the lines he had laid out in What Is to Be Done?

From the *Collected Works of V.I. Lenin*, Vol. 5, (Moscow: Progress Publishers, 1964), pp. 234–235.

Without revolutionary theory there can be no revolutionary movement. This idea cannot be insisted upon too strongly at a time when the fashionable preaching of opportunism goes hand and hand with an infatuation for the narrowest forms of practical activity. Yet, for Russian Social-Democrats the importance of theory is enhanced by three other circumstances, which are often forgotten: first, by the fact that our Party is only in process of formation, its features are only just becoming defined, and it has as yet far from settled accounts with the other trends of revolutionary thought that threaten to divert the movement from the correct path. . . .

Secondly, the Social-Democratic movement is in its very essence an international movement. This means, not only that we must combat national chauvinism, but that an incipient movement in a young country can be successful only if it makes use of the experiences of other countries. In order to make use of these experiences it is not enough merely to be acquainted with them, or simply to copy out the latest resolutions. What is required is the ability to treat these experiences critically and to test them independently. He who realises how enormously the modern working-class movement has grown and branched out will understand what a reserve of theoretical forces and political (as well as revolutionary) experience is required to carry out this task.

Thirdly, the national tasks of Russian Social-Democracy are such as have never confronted any other socialist party in the world. We shall have occasion further on to deal with the political and organisational duties which the task of emancipating the whole people from the yoke of autocracy imposes upon us. At this point, we wish to state only that the *role of vanguard fighter can be fulfilled only by a party that is guided by the most advanced theory*. . . .

We have said that there *could not have been* Social-Democratic consciousness among the workers. It would have to be brought to them from without. The history of all countries shows that the working class, exclusively by its own effort, is able to develop only trade-union consciousness, i.e., the conviction that it is necessary to combine in unions, fight the employers, and strive to compel the government to pass necessary labour legislation, etc. The theory of socialism, however, grew out of the philosophic, historical, and economic theories elaborated by educated representatives of the propertied classes, by intellectuals. By their social status, the founders of modern scientific socialism, Marx and Engels, themselves belonged to the bourgeois intelligentsia. In the very same way, in Russia, the theoretical doctrine of Social-Democracy arose altogether independently of the spontaneous growth of the working-class movement; it arose as a natural and inevitable outcome of the development of thought among the revolutionary socialist intelligentsia. . . .

. . . I assert: (1) that no revolutionary movement can endure without a stable organisation of leaders maintaining continuity; (2) that the broader the popular mass drawn spontaneously into the struggle, which forms the basis of the movement and participates in it, the more urgent the need for such an organisation, and the more solid this organisation must be (for it is much easier for all sorts of demagogues to side-track the more backward sections of the masses); (3) that such an organisation must consist chiefly of people professionally engaged in revolutionary activity; (4) that in an autocratic state, the more we *confine* the membership of such an organisation to people who are professionally engaged in revolutionary activity and who have been professionally trained in the art of combating the political police, the more difficult will it be to unearth the organisation; and (5) the *greater* will be the number of people from the working class and from the other social classes who will be able to join the movement and perform active work in it. . . .

Social-Democracy leads the struggle of the working class, not only for better terms for the sale of labour-power, but for the abolition of the social system that compels the propertyless to sell themselves to the rich. Social-Democracy represents the working class, not in its relation to a given group of employers alone, but in its relation to all classes of modern society and to the state as an organised political force. Hence, it follows that not only must Social-Democrats not confine themselves exclusively to the economic struggle, but that they must not allow the organisation of economic exposures to become the predominant part of their activities. We must take up actively the political education of the working class and the development of its political consciousness. . . .

. . . We can never give a mass organisation that degree of secrecy without which there can be no question of persistent and continuous struggle against the government. To concentrate all secret functions in the hands of as small a number of professional revolutionaries as possible does not mean that the latter will "do the thinking for all" and that the rank and file will not take an active part in the *movement*. On the contrary, the membership will promote increasing numbers of the professional revolutionaries from its ranks; for it will know that it is not enough for a few students and for a few working men waging the economic struggle to gather in order to form a "committee," but that it takes years to train oneself to be a professional revolutionary. . . . Centralisation of the most secret functions in an organisation of revolutionaries will not diminish, but rather increase the extent and enhance the quality of the activity of a large number of other organisations, that are intended for a broad public and are therefore as loose and as non-secret as possible, such as workers' trade unions; workers' self-education circles and circles for reading illegal literature; and socialist, as well as democratic, circles among *all* other sections of the population; etc., etc. We must have such circles, trade unions, and organisations everywhere in *as large a number as possible* and with the widest variety of functions. . . .

. . . The only serious organisational principle for the active workers of our movement should be the strictest secrecy, the strictest selection of members, and the training of professional revolutionaries. Given these qualities, something even more than "democratism" would be guaranteed to us, namely, complete, comradely, mutual confidence among revolutionaries. . . . They have a lively sense of their *responsibility*, knowing as they do from experience that an organisation of real revolutionaries will stop at nothing to rid itself of an unworthy member. . . .

. . . Our worst sin with regard to organisation consists in the fact that *by our primitiveness we have lowered the prestige of revolutionaries in Russia*. A person who is flabby and shaky on questions of theory, who has a narrow outlook, who pleads the spontaneity of the masses as an excuse for his own sluggishness, who resembles a trade-union secretary more than a spokesman of the people, who is unable to conceive of a broad and bold plan that would command the respect even of opponents, and who is inexperienced and clumsy in his own professional art—the art of combating the political police—such a man is not revolutionary, but a wretched amateur! . . .

The Russian proletariat will have to . . . fight a monster compared with which an anti-socialist law in a constitutional country seems but a dwarf. History has not confronted us with an immediate task which is the *most revolutionary* of all the *immediate* tasks confronting the proletariat of any country. The fulfilment of this task, the destruction of the most powerful bulwark, not only of European, but (it may now be said) of Asiatic reaction, would make the Russian proletariat the vanguard of the international revolutionary proletariat. And we have the right to count upon acquiring this honourable title, already earned by our predecessors, the revolutionaries of the seventies. If we succeed in inspiring our movement, which is a thousand times broader and deeper, with the same devoted determination and vigour.

---

1. Outline the reasons Lenin gives for establishing revolutionary theory.
2. Why must revolutionary theory originate outside of the working class?
3. Outline Lenin's revolutionary theory. What evidence does he give to support his position?

VLADIMIR LENIN:
April Theses (1917)

When Lenin returned to Russia after the March Revolution, he found the Bolsheviks supporting the provisional government. The April Theses *demanded that the Bolsheviks abandon the "bourgeois revolution" and strive for the "proletarian revolution."*

From V.I. Lenin, "April Theses," in Bernard Issacs (ed.), *Collected Works* (38 vols.; Moscow: Progress Publishers, 1964), XXIV, pp. 21–26.

1) In our attitude towards the war, which under the new government of Lvov and Co. unquestionably remains on Russia's part a predatory imperialist war owing to the capitalist nature of that government, not the slightest concession to "revolutionary defencism" is permissible.

The class-conscious proletariat can give its consent to a revolutionary war, which would really justify revolutionary defencism, only on condition: (a) that the power pass to the proletariat and the poorest sections of the peasants aligned with the proletariat; (b) that all annexations be renounced in deed and not in word; (c) that a complete break be effected in actual fact with all capitalist interests. . . .

The widespread campaign for this view must be organized in the army at the front. . . .

2) The specific feature of the present situation in Russia is that the country is *passing* from the first stage of the revolution—which, owing to the insufficient

Lenin became a revolutionary after his brother was executed in 1887 for allegedly plotting to kill the czar.

class-consciousness and organisation of the proletariat, placed power in the hands of the bourgeoisie—to its *second* stage, which must place power in the hands of the proletariat and the poorest sections of the peasants. . . .

This peculiar situation demands of us an ability to adapt ourselves to the *special* conditions of Party work among unprecedented large masses of proletarians who have just awakened to political life.

3) No support for the Provisional Government; . . .

4) Recognition of the fact that in most of the Soviets of Workers' Deputies our Party is a minority . . .

The masses must be made to see that the Soviets of Workers' Deputies are the *only possible* form of revolutionary government, and that therefore our task is, as long as *this* government yields to the influence of the bourgeoisie, to present a patient, systematic, and persistent *explanation* of the errors of their tactics, an explanation especially adapted to the practical needs of the masses.

As long as we are in the minority we carry on the work of criticising and exposing errors and at the same time we preach the necessity of transferring the entire state power to the Soviets of Workers' Deputies, so that the people may overcome their mistakes by experience.

5) Not a parliamentary republic . . . but a republic of Soviets of Workers', Agricultural Labourers' and Peasants' Deputies throughout the country, from top to bottom.

6) The weight of emphasis in the agrarian programme to be shifted to the Soviets of Agricultural Labourers' Deputies.

Confiscation of all landed estates.

Nationalisation of *all* lands in the country . . .

7) The amalgamation of all banks in the country into a single national bank, and the institution of control over it by the Soviet of Workers' Deputies.

8) It is not our *immediate* task to "introduce" socialism, but only to bring social production and the distribution of products at once under the *control* of the Soviets of Workers' Deputies.

9) Party tasks:

(a) Immediate convocation of a Party congress;

(b) Alteration of the Party Programme, mainly

(i) On the question of imperialism and the imperialist war;

(ii) On our attitude towards the state and *our* demand for a "commune state";

(iii) Amendment of our out-of-date minimum programme.

(c) Change of the Party's name [from "Social-Democrat" to Communist].

10) A new International.

We must take the initiative in creating a revolutionary International, and International against the *social-chauvinists* and against the "Centre". . . .

---

1. Briefly outline Lenin's proposal.

2. In what ways do Lenin's plans violate orthodox Marxist doctrine?

3. Do the *April Theses* alter Lenin's theories outlined in *What Is to Be Done*?? If so, how?

ALEKSANDR KERENSKY: "Bolsheviks Hated Me" (1967)

Kerensky became the prime minister of Russia under the provisional government. The following interview reflects his views on the Bolshevik victory.

Q: Mr. Kerensky, who organized the Russian Revolution in March of 1917?
A: That revolution was never organized. It was spontaneous. You see, Russia had suffered defeats in World War I. We were not like our allies, Britain and France, who, across open oceans, received support from Canada, the United States, South Africa, India, Australia, New Zealand—food and arms, also troops from such places in the British Empire as Canada, Australia, South Africa, New Zealand, India. We had nothing. We were blockaded.

Food riots broke out in Petrograd [now Leningrad]. Disorder spread quickly and in March Czar Nicholas II abdicated.

Q: Then a Provisional Government was set up—
A: Yes. It was a moderate Government that hoped to preserve the monarchy by changing the person on the throne.

You see, Nicholas II hated even the word "constitution." He dreamed all his life of pushing Russia back to the absolutistic rule that prevailed in the seventeenth century.

Q: Do you mean that Czarist Russia had advanced beyond that kind of rule?
A: Oh, yes. There were two significant periods:

One was in the middle of the nineteenth century, during the regime of Alexander II. That was the time of Dostoyevsky and Tolstoy and other great Russian writers—and it was also the time of the development of railroads and the economy, generally.

The second period of advance began in 1895, when Count Witte—he was not Count Witte then, but only Serge Witte—developed industry by new methods and, at the same time, supported all progressive development in agriculture and science.

Also, there was the development of political ideas. To think of Russia as having been an absolutely undeveloped industrial country is ignorant. The war of 1914, of course, affected the whole economic system, as transportation links between various productive regions were weakened, but the country had already been developing for years.

Q: It was not, then, the Communists who began Russia's industrial development?
A: No.
Q: Did Lenin, Stalin or Trotsky—among Bolshevik leaders—participate in the February revolution?
A: No. Lenin was in Switzerland, Trotsky was in New York, Stalin was in Siberia.

I joined the Provisional Government as Minister of Justice and later became Minister of War. Then I became head of the Government in July of 1917.

Q: Was that after the Bolsheviks had made their first attempt to seize power?
A: Yes. That attempt, fomented by Lenin, was smashed and, in actuality, it had the effect of making the Provisional Government more stable.
Q: Did your Government intend to continue the war against Germany?
A: Of course. From the beginning of the war, I had urged the Russian people to accept a common fight against a common enemy.

When the war started, I was a member of the Duma—the Russian Parliament. In a speech on July 26, 1914, I called upon our armies to "fight and to defend Russia until the end, and, after victory, to liberate inside Russia."

Q: Did your Government get much help from America or your European allies?
A: As I have said, Russia was blockaded. Because of internal political reasons, America, under President Wilson, could not give Russia the support that it gave the European Allies—no money, no material support, no arms. We had a very difficult situation. We received some support privately from industry in America, but it came through England, and we paid what we could for this.

If I had received one-tenth of the support which Stalin received from the United States during World War II, my Government would have survived, the course of history would have been changed, and the second World War would not have occurred.

That is what I think—absolutely.

Q: Do you mean that something could have prevented the Bolshevik Revolution that overthrew your Government in October of 1917?
A: The Bolshevik Revolution could have been prevented if it had been possible to stop the support and tremendous sums of money that Lenin was receiving from Germany.

Lenin returned to Russia from Switzerland in April, 1917. He traveled through Germany. After the unsuccessful Bolshevik uprising in July, 1917, he went into hiding—first in Petrograd, then in a hut near the Finnish border, and finally inside Finland.

Late in September, he moved to the Finnish Town of Vyborg, near the Russian border. In October, he returned to Petrograd in disguise and issued his call for seizure of power by the Bolsheviks.

Q: Had he been getting help from Germany all that time?
A: The relations between Lenin and Berlin began at the end of 1915. It is all recounted in documents that were in the secret archives of the German Ministry of Foreign Affairs. Those documents became the property of the British Government after the second World War.

It is a very interesting story. The master of the German organization with which Lenin dealt with was a man who called himself Parvus—real name, Dr. Helfand. He was behind Lenin and all his movements.

Together with the German ambassador to Denmark, Count Brockdorff-Rantzau, they prepared a so-called master plan for the dislocation of Russia. The plan included support of the Bolsheviks, because the Bolsheviks were for the transformation of "imperial international war" into class wars in all belligerent countries.

Q: Hasn't it been said that the Bolshevik Revolution succeeded because the Russian people were increasingly drawn to the "no war" program promised by Lenin?
A: Lenin was absolutely not a peace-loving man. He was not for international killing—he preferred class war, in which the people of a country kill their own citizens.

When he was in Switzerland, he wrote that the class war would come not in Russia—where, he said, the Russian proletariat was "too young and too weak to organize and conduct the proletarian revolution"—but that "the real social proletarian revolution will be organized by industrial countries like Germany, England, the United States."

Q: What kind of support was Lenin getting from the Germans?
A: From Germany, Lenin received 40 million gold marks for the purpose of overthrowing the democratic Government of Russia. Another 40 million gold marks was earmarked for stabilization of Lenin's Government in Moscow. It amounted, in sum, to 80 million gold marks.
Q: Was this money smuggled into Russia?
A: Yes. It was very easy to organize the transfer. The Bolsheviks received the money through banks, notes, and other devices. Much of it went from Germany through a bank in Stockholm to the Siberian Bank in Russia.
Q: Did you know about it?
A: No, no. It was a German state secret.

After the unsuccessful Bolshevik revolt in the summer of 1917 we knew, however, that Lenin was a traitor and organizer of the revolt, which was timed to coincide with a counteroffensive operation of the German Army.

After that revolt failed and Lenin fled, a search was made of the house in which he had been staying in Petrograd. This was the house of Kshesinskaia, a former prima ballerina, which the Bolsheviks had seized for their headquarters. In that house were found some very important documents relating to Lenin's activities—the relations with the Siberian Bank and the organization of the Bolshevik revolt.

"Bolsheviks Hated Me"—
Q: Did Lenin use some of the money to finance propaganda against your Government?
A: Yes. The propaganda published and circulated by the Bolsheviks was aimed at me. It was based on the idea that Kerensky was prepared to betray all the results of the March democratic revolution to save the capitalist regime in Russia. The Bolsheviks hated me intensely.
Q: You said earlier that if your Government had survived there would not have been a second World War. Why do you believe that?
A: Because the second war was a result of the dislocation of the old balance of power. And, secondly, because after the Treaty of Versailles, Europe again was divided into two irreconcilable camps.

If Russia had continued to be democratic and strong, the balance of power would not have been changed—the situation in which Hitler was able to start World War II would not have come about.
Q: Was there anything that you could have done that you did not do to save democracy in Russia? Were there mistakes that you now can see, with the benefit of hindsight?
A: In the past 50 years, I have thought about this many times. I made a mistake in my handling of the Kornilov "mutiny."

It may have been that the Kornilov affair was a fatal event.
Q: What was the Kornilov affair?
A: Gen. Lavr Georgievich Kornilov was a hero in the eyes of many Russians. He was made supreme commander of the Russian armed forces in July, 1917, by me.

There were fears that he might organize a counter-revolution and set up a military dictatorship. He sent a cavalry corps to Petrograd in what appeared to be—to some in the Provisional Government—a step toward establishment of a new and "stronger" government. I dismissed Kornilov from his position as supreme commander. Upon the insistence of General Alexeyev, I assumed the task of commander in chief of the armed forces.

The Cossack vanguard commanded by General Krymov advanced on Petrograd and was stopped near Luga, not far from the capital, in the first night of the Kornilov revolt. Kornilov surrendered peacefully and was put in jail with other officers suspected of plotting a counterrevolution.

Out of the Kornilov affair evolved a change of psychology among the soldiers and the Petrograd workers and the leaders of the Socialist parties. The Government was weakened by a loss of confidence.

Q: What happened to Kornilov?

A: He escaped from arrest on the first day of the Bolshevik revolt and, after the Bolshevik Revolution, he took command of the White Army fighting the Red forces in Southern Russia. He was killed by a bomb that hit his office while he was working in April, 1918.

Q: What happened to you after the Provisional Government was overthrown?

A: I went underground in Russia at first, then I made my way abroad. . . .

---

1. Outline the reasons Kerensky gives for the success of (a) the March Revolution and (b) the Bolshevik victory.

2. In your opinion, what were the reasons for the success of each of these events?

BENITO MUSSOLINI:
Fascism (1932)

The political philosophy of fascism was outlined in an article that appeared in Enciclopedia Italiana *in 1932. It was signed by Mussolini and thereby attained the status of an official statement of fascist doctrine.*

From *Enciclopedia Italiana*, Vol. XIV, in Norman Sheffe and William E. Fisher (eds.), *A Sourcebook for Modern History* (Toronto: McGraw-Hill, 1964), pp. 133–135.

Anti-individualistic, the Fascist conception is for the State; it is for the individual only in so far as he coincides with the State, . . . It is opposed to the classic Liberalism which arose out of the need of reaction against absolutism, . . .

Liberalism denied the State in the interests of the particular individual; Fascism reaffirms the State as the only true expression of the individual.

. . . It is for the only kind of liberty that is serious—the liberty of the State and of the individual in the State. Because, for the Fascist, all is comprised in the State and nothing spiritual or human exists—much less has any value—outside the State. . . .

Fascism above all does not believe either in the possibility or utility of universal peace. It therefore rejects the pacifism which masks surrender and cowardice. War alone brings all human energies to their highest tensions and sets a seal of nobility on the peoples who have the virtue to face it. . . . A doctrine which has its starting-point at the prejudicial postulate or peace is therefore extraneous to Fascism.

In the same way all international creations . . . are also extraneous to the spirit of Fascism—even if such international creations are accepted for whatever utility they may have in any determined political situation.

Through this conception of life Fascism becomes the emphatic negation of that doctrine which constituted the basis of the so-called scientific Socialism or

Marxism: the doctrine of historical materialism, according to which the story of human civilisation is to be explained only by the conflict of interests between the various social groups and by the change of the means and instruments of production.

That the economic vicissitudes . . . suffice to explain human history, excluding other factors from it, is absurd: . . .

Fascism having denied historical materialism, by which men are only puppets in history, . . . it also denies the immutable and irreparable class warfare, which is the natural filiation of such an economistic conception of history: and it denies above all that class warfare is the preponderating agent of social transformation. . . .

. . . Fascism opens a breach on the whole complex of the democratic ideologies, and repudiates them in their theoretic premises as well as in their practical application or instrumentation. Fascism denies that numbers by the mere fact of being numbers, can direct human society; . . . it affirms also the fertilising, beneficient and unassailable inequality of men, who cannot be levelled through an extrinsic and mechanical process such as universal suffrage. . . .

As regards the Liberal doctrines, the attitude of Fascism is one of absolute opposition both in the political and in the economical field . . . Liberalism signifies the individual . . . Fascism signifies the State. But the Fascist State is unique of its kind and is an original creation. It is not reactionary but revolutionary. . . . The Fascist State organises the nation, but leaves a sufficient margin afterward to the individual; it has limited the useless or harmful liberties and has preserved the essential ones. The one to judge in this respect is not the individual but the State. . . .

The Fascist State is a will expressing power and empire. The Roman tradition here becomes an idea of force. . . . For Fascism, the tendency to empire, that is to say the expansion of nations, is a manifestation of vitality, its contrary . . . is a sign of decadence. Peoples who rise, or who suddenly flourish again, are imperialistic; peoples who die are peoples who abdicate. Fascism . . . most adequately represents . . . the state of mind of a people like the Italian people, which is rising again after many centuries of abandonment and of foreign servitude.

But empire requires discipline, the coordination of forces, duty and sacrifice. This explains the many phases of the practical action of the regime. . . .

Never more than at the present moment have the nations felt such a thirst for an authority, for a direction, for order. If every country has its own peculiar doctrine, there are a thousand indications that Fascism is that of the present century. . . .

Fascism has now attained in the world a universality over all doctrines. Being realised, it represents an epoch in the histroy of the human mind.

---

1. Briefly outline the elements of fascist doctrine.

2. What reasons does Mussolini give for the development of fascism in Italy?

3. In what ways is fascism antagonistic to world peace and international order?

ADOLF HITLER:
Mein Kampf (1924)

Hitler wrote Mein Kampf *while in Lansberg Prison serving his sentence for the failed attempt to overthrow the Bavarian government. This excerpt outlines his views on race.*

From Adolf Hitler, *Mein Kampf.* Translated by Ralph Manheim. (London: Hutchinson).

The Primacy of Race

No more than Nature desires the mating of weaker with stronger individuals, even less does she desire the blending of a higher with a lower race, since, if she did, her whole work of higher breeding, over perhaps hundreds of thousands of years, might be ruined with one blow.

Historical experience offers countless proofs of this. It shows with terrifying clarity that in every mingling of Aryan blood with that of lower peoples the result was the end of the cultured people. North America, whose population consists in by far the largest part of Germanic elements who mixed but little with the lower colored peoples, shows a different humanity and culture from Central and South America, where the predominantly Latin immigrants often mixed with the aborigines on a large scale. By this one example, we can clearly and distinctly recognize the effect of racial mixture. The Germanic inhabitant of the American continent, who has remained racially pure and unmixed, rose to be master of the continent; he will remain the master as long as he does not fall a victim to defilement of the blood.

The result of all racial crossing is therefore in brief always the following:

(a) Lowering of the level of the higher race;

(b) Physical and intellectual regression and hence the beginning of slowly but surely progressing sickness.

To bring about such a development is, then, nothing else but to sin against the will of the eternal creator. . . .

Everything we admire on this earth today—science and art, technology and inventions—is only the creative product of a few peoples and originally perhaps of *one* race. On them depends the existence of this whole culture. If they perish, the beauty of this earth will sink into the grave with them. . . .

All great cultures of the past perished only because the originally creative race died our from blood poisoning.

The ultimate cause of such a decline was their forgetting that all culture depends on men and not conversely; hence that to preserve a certain culture the man who creates it must be preserved. This preservation is bound up with the rigid law of necessity and the right to victory of the best and stronger in this world. . . .

If we were to divide mankind into three groups, the founders of culture, the bearers of culture, the destroyers of culture, only the Aryan could be considered as the representative of the first group. From him originate the foundations and walls of all human creation. . . .

Blood mixture and the resultant drop in the racial level is the sole cause of the dying out of old cultures; for men do not perish as a result of lost wars, but by the loss of that force of resistance which is contained only in pure blood.

All who are not of good race in this world are chaff. . . .

A state which in this age of racial poisoning dedicates itself to the care of its best racial elements must some day become lord of the earth.

[Anti-Semitism]

The mightiest counterpart to the Aryan is represented by the Jews. . . .

. . . The Jewish people, despite all apparent intellectual qualities, is without any true culture, and especially without any culture of its own. For what sham culture the Jew today possesses is the property of other peoples, and for the most part it is ruined in his hands.

In judging the Jewish people's attitude on the question of human culture, the most essential characteristic we must always bear in mind is that there has never been a Jewish art and accordingly there is none today either; that above all the two queens of all the arts, architecture and music, owe nothing original to the Jews. What they do accomplish in the field of art is either patchwork or intellectual theft. Thus, the Jew lacks those qualities which distinguish the races that are creative and hence culturally blessed. . . .

On this first and greatest lie, that the Jews are not a race but a religion, more and more lies are based in necessary consequence. Among them is the lie with regard to the language of the Jew. For him it is not a means for expressing his thoughts, but a means for concealing them. When he speaks French, he thinks Jewish, and while he turns out German verses, in his life he only expresses the nature of his nationality. As long as the Jew has not become the master of the other peoples, he must speak their languages whether he likes it or not, but as soon as they became his slaves, they would all have to learn a universal language. . . .

With satanic joy in his face, the blackhaired Jewish youth lurks in wait for the unsuspecting girl whom he defiles with his blood, thus stealing her from her people. With every means he tries to destroy the racial foundations of the people he has set out to subjugate. . . .

For a racially pure people which is conscious of its blood can never be enslaved by the Jew. In this world he will forever be master over bastards and bastards alone.

And so he tries systematically to lower the racial level by continuous poisoning of individuals.

And in politics he begins to replace the idea of democracy by the dictatorship of the proletariat.

In the organized mass of Marxism he has found the weapon which lets him dispense with democracy and in its stead allows him to subjugate and govern the peoples with a dictatorial and brutal fist.

He works systematically for revolutionization in a twofold sense: economic and political.

Around peoples who offer too violent a resistance to attack from within he weaves a net of enemies, thanks to his international influence, incites them to war, and finally, if necessary, plants the flag of revolution on the very battlefields.

In economics he undermines the states until the social enterprises which have become unprofitable are taken from the state and subjected to his financial control.

In the political field he refuses the state the means for its self-preservation, destroys the foundations of all national self-maintenance and defense, destroys faith in the leadership, scoffs at its history and past, and drags everything that is truly great into the gutter.

Culturally he contaminates art, literature, the theater, makes a mockery of natural feeling, overthrows all concepts of beauty and sublimity, of the noble and the good, and instead drags men down into the sphere of his own base nature.

Religion is ridiculed, ethics and morality represented as outmoded, until the last props of a nation in its struggle for existence in this world have fallen. . . .

The Jewish train of thought in all this is clear. The Bolshevization of Germany—that is . . . to make possible the sweating of the German working class under the yoke of Jewish world finance [which] is conceived only as a preliminary to the further extension of this Jewish tendency of world conquest. As often in history, Germany is the great pivot in the mighty struggle. If our people and our state become the victim of these bloodthirsty and avaricious Jewish tyrants of nations, the whole earth will sink into the snares of this octopus; if Germany frees herself from this embrace, this greatest of dangers to nations may be regarded as broken for the whole world. . . .

---

1. What evidence does Hitler use to support his racial theories?

2. Compare Hitler's views on Aryans and Jews.

THE ATLANTIC CHARTER (1941)

The Atlantic Charter was a declaration of common aims by the United States and Great Britain. Eventually it became the basis of Allied war goals.

From the *Congressional Record*, LXXXVII, 77th Congress, Ist Session, (Washington, D.C., 1941), p. 7217.

The President of the United States of America and the Prime Minister, Mr. Churchill, representing His Majesty's Government in the United Kingdom, being met together, deem it right to make known certain common principles in the national policies of their respective countries on which they base their hopes for a better future for the world.

FIRST, their countries seek no aggrandizement, territorial or other;

SECOND, they desire to see no territorial changes that do not accord with the freely expressed wishes of the peoples concerned;

THIRD, they respect the right of all peoples to choose the form of government, under which they will live; and they wish to see sovereign rights and self-government restored to those who have been forcibly deprived of them;

FOURTH, they will endeavor, with due respect for their existing obligations, to further the enjoyment by all States, great or small, victor or vanquished, of access, on equal terms, to the trade and to the raw materials of the world which are needed for their economic prosperity;

FIFTH, they desire to bring about the fullest collaboration between all nations in the economic field with the object of securing, for all, improved labor standards, economic adjustment and social security;

SIXTH, after the final destruction of the Nazi tyranny, they hope to see established a peace which will afford all nations the means of dwelling in safety within their own boundaries, and which will afford assurance that all the men in all the lands may live out their lives in freedom from fear and want;

SEVENTH, such a peace should enable all men to traverse the high seas and oceans without hindrance;

EIGHTH, they believe that all of the nations of the world, for realistic as well as spiritual reasons, must come to the abandonment of the use of force. Since no future peace can be maintained if land, sea or air armaments continue to be employed by nations which threaten, or may threaten, aggression outside of their frontiers, they believe, pending the establishment of a wider and permanent system of general security, that the disarmament of such nations is essential. They will likewise aid and encourage all other practicable measures which will lighten for peace-loving peoples the crushing burden of armaments.

FRANKLIN D. ROOSEVELT
WINSTON S. CHURCHILL

---

1. The Atlantic Charter was made at a time when the United States was not formally at war.
(a) What elements of the document indicate that the U.S. is not neutral?
(b) Does the document commit the U.S. to any immediate action?

2. What effect would this document have in (a) Britain, (b) the United States, and (c) Germany?

THE YALTA AGREEMENTS (1945)

The Yalta Conference attempted to solve several postwar problems. The protocol below was signed by Stalin, Roosevelt, and Churchill on 11 February 1945.

From the United States Department of State, Press Release No. 239 (Washington, D.C.: 24 March 1947).

Protocol of the Proceedings of the Crimea Conference

The Crimea Conference of the Heads of the Governments of the United States of America, the United Kingdom, and the Union of Soviet Socialist Republics, which took place from February 4th to 11th, came to the following conclusions:

I. World Organisation

It was decided:

(1) that a United Nations Conference on the proposed world organisation should be summoned for Wednesday, 25th April, 1945, and should be held in the United States of America.

(2) the Nations to be invited to this Conference should be:

(a) the United Nations as they existed on the 8th February, 1945; and

(b) such of the Associated Nations as have declared war on the common enemy by 1st March, 1945. (For this purpose by the term "Associated Nations" was meant the eight Associated Nations and Turkey.) When the Conference on World Organisation is held, the delegates of the United Kingdom and United States of America will support a proposal to admit to original membership two Soviet Socialist Republics, i.e., the Ukraine and White Russia.

(3) that the United States Government on behalf of the Three Powers should consult the Government of China and the French Provisional Government in regard to decisions taken at the present Conference concerning the proposed World Organisation. . . .

II. Declaration on Liberated Europe

The following declaration has been approved:

"The Premier of the Union of Soviet Socialist Republics, the Prime Minister of the United Kingdom, and the President of the United States of America . . . jointly declare their mutual agreement to concert during the temporary period of instability in liberated Europe the policies of their three governments in assisting the peoples of the former Axis satellite states of Europe to solve by democratic means their pressing political and economic problems.

"The establishment of order in Europe and the rebuilding of national economic life must be achieved by processes which will enable the liberated peoples to destroy the last vestiges of Nazism and Fascism and to create democratic institutions of their own choice. This is a principle of the Atlantic Charter—the right of all peoples to choose the form of government under which they will live—the restoration of sovereign rights and self-government to those peoples who have been forcibly deprived of them by the aggressor nations.

"To foster the conditions in which the liberated peoples may exercise these rights, the three governments will jointly assist the people in any European liberated state or former Axis satellite state in Europe where in their judgment conditions require (a) to establish conditions of internal peace; (b) to carry out emergency measures for the relief of distressed peoples; (c) to form interim governmental authorities broadly representative of all democratic elements in the population and pledged to the earliest possible establishment through free elections of governments responsive to the will of the people; and (d) to facilitate where necessary the holding of such elections.

"The three governments will consult the other United Nations and provisional authorities or other governments in Europe when matters of direct interest to them are under consideration.

"When, in the opinion of the three governments, conditions in any European liberated state or any former Axis satellite state in Europe make such action necessary, they will immediately consult together on the measures necessary to discharge the joint responsibilites set forth in this declaration.

"By this declaration we reaffirm our faith in the principles of the Atlantic Charter, our pledge in the Declaration by the United Nations, and our determination to build in cooperation with other peace-loving nations world order under law, dedicated to peace, security, freedom and general well-being of all mankind.

"In issuing this declaration the Three Powers express the hope that the Provisional Government of the French Republic may be associated with them in the procedure suggested."

III. Dismemberment of Germany

It was agreed that Article 12 (a) of the Surrender Terms for Germany should be amended to read as follows:

"The United Kingdom, the United States of America, and the Union of Soviet Socialist Republics shall possess supreme authority with respect to Germany. In the exercise of such authority they will take such steps, including the complete disarmament, demilitarization, and dismemberment of Germany as they deem requisite for future peace and security."

IV. Zone of Occupation for the French and Control Council for Germany

It was agreed that a zone in Germany, to be occupied by the French Forces, should be allocated to France. This zone would be formed out of the British and American zones and its extent would be settled by the British and Americans in consultation with the French Provisional Government.

It was also agreed that the French Provisional Government should be invited to become a member of the Allied Control Council for Germany.

VII. Poland

The following Declaration on Poland was agreed by the Conference:

"A new situation has been created in Poland as a result of her complete liberation by the Red Army. This calls for the establishment of a Polish Provisional Government which can be more broadly based than was possible before the recent liberation of the Western part of Poland. The Provisional Government which is now functioning in Poland should therefore be organized on a broader democratic basis with the inclusion of democratic leaders from Poland itself and from Poles abroad. This new Government should then be called the Polish Provisional Government of National Unity.

"... This Polish Provisional Government of National Unity shall be pledged to the holding of free and unfettered elections as soon as possible on the basis of universal suffrage and secret ballot. In these elections all democratic and anti-Nazi parties shall have the right to take part and to put forward candidates.

"The three Heads of Government consider that the Eastern frontier of Poland should follow the Curzon Line with digressions from it in some regions of five to eight kilometres in favour of Poland. They recognise that Poland must receive substantial accessions of territory in the North and West. They feel that the opinion of the new Polish Provisional Government of National Unity should be sought in due course on the extent of these accessions and that the final delimitation of the Western frontier of Poland should thereafter await the peace conference."

XIII. Meeting of the Three Foreign Secretaries

The Conference agreed that permanent machinery should be set up for consultation between the three Foreign Secretaries; they should meet as often as necessary, probably about every three of four months.

These meetings will be held in rotation in the three capitals, the first meeting being held in London.

E. R. STETTINIUS, JR.;
M. MOLOTOV;
ANTHONY EDEN

Agreement Regarding Japan

The leaders of the three Great Powers—the Soviet Union, the United States of America, and Great Britain—have agreed that two or three months after Germany has surrendered and the war in Europe has terminated, the Soviet Union shall enter into the war against Japan on the side of the Allies on condition that:

1. The status quo in Outer Mongolia (The Mongolian People's Republic) shall be preserved;

2. The former rights of Russia violated by the treacherous attack of Japan in 1904 shall be restored, viz.: (a) the southern part of Sakhalin, as well as all the islands adjacent to it, shall be returned to the Soviet Union, (b) the commercial port of Dairen shall be internationalized, the pre-eminent interests of the Soviet-Union in this port being safeguarded and the lease of Port Arthur as a naval base of the U.S.S.R. restored, (c) the Chinese-Eastern Railroad and the South-Manchurian Railroad which provides an outlet to Dairen shall be jointly operated

by the establishment of a joint Soviet-Chinese Company, it being understood that the pre-eminent interests of the Soviet Union shall be safeguarded and that China shall retain full sovereignty in Manchuria;

3. The Kuril islands shall be handed over to the Soviet Union.

It is understood, that the agreement concerning Outer Mongolia and the ports and railroads referred to above will require concurrence of Generalissimo Chiang Kai-shek. The President will take measures in order to obtain this concurrence on advice from Marshal Stalin.

The Heads of the three Great Powers have agreed that these claims of the Soviet Union shall be unquestionably fulfilled after Japan has been defeated.

For its part the Soviet Union expresses its readiness to conclude with the National Government of China a pact of friendship and alliance between the U.S.S.R. and China in order to render assistance to China with its armed forces for the purpose of liberating China from the Japanese yoke.

February 11, 1945

JOSEPH V. STALIN;
FRANKLIN D. ROOSEVELT;
WINSTON S. CHURCHILL

---

1. Roosevelt made a number of concessions at Yalta because he believed that Russian military support in the Far East was necessary.
- (a) Outline the concessions.
- (b) Why were these concessions unnecessary?

2. Why were the French included in the agreements about Germany?

3. In what ways did Russia violate the agreements made about Eastern Europe?

THE POTSDAM DECLARATION (1945)

The following excerpts from the Potsdam Declaration put the Yalta agreements regarding Germany into operation.

From the United States Department of State, *Bulletin*, XIII. No. 319 (Washington, D.C.: 5 August 1945), pp. 154–156.

The Allied Armies are in occupation of the whole of Germany and the German people have begun to atone for the terrible crimes committed under the leadership of those whom in the hour of their success, they openly approved and blindly obeyed.

Agreement has been reached at this conference on the political and economic principles of a co-ordinated Allied policy toward defeated Germany during the period of Allied control.

The purpose of this agreement is to carry out the Crimea [Yalta] Declaration on Germany. German militarism and Nazism will be extirpated and the Allies will take in agreement together, now and in the future, the other measures necessary to assure that Germany never again will threaten her neighbors or the peace of the world.

It is not the intention of the Allies to destroy or enslave the German people. It is the intention of the Allies that the German people be given the opportunity to prepare for the eventual reconstruction of their life on a democratic and peaceful basis. If their own efforts are steadily directed to this end, it will be possible for them in due course to take their place among the free and peaceful peoples of the world.

The text of the agreement is as follows:

1. In accordance with the agreement on control machinery in Germany, supreme authority in Germany is exercised on instructions from their respective governments, by the Commanders-in-Chief of the armed forces of the United States of America, the United Kingdom, the Union of Soviet Socialist Republics, and the French Republic, each in his own zone of occupation, and also jointly, in matters affecting Germany as a whole, in their capacity as members of the Control Council.

2. So far as practicable, there shall be uniformity of treatment of the German population throughout Germany.

3. The purpose of the occupation of Germany by which the Control Council shall be guided are:

(i) The complete disarmament and demilitarization of Germany and the elimination or control of all German industry that could be used for military production. . . .

(ii) To convince the German people that they have suffered a total military defeat and that they cannot escape responsibility for what they have brought upon themselves, since their own ruthless warfare and the fanatical Nazi resistance have destroyed German economy and made chaos and suffering inevitable.

(iii) To destroy the National Socialist Party and its affiliated and supervised organizations, to dissolve all Nazi institutions, to ensure that they are not revived in any form, and to prevent all Nazi and militarist activity propaganda.

(iv) To prepare for the eventual reconstruction of German political life on a democratic basis and for eventual peaceful cooperation in international life by Germany.

4. All Nazi laws which provided the basis of the Hitler regime or established discrimination on grounds of race, creed, or political opinion shall be abolished. No such discrimination, whether legal, administrative or otherwise, shall be tolerated.

5. War criminals and those who have participated in planning or carrying out Nazi enterprises involving or resulting in atrocities or war crimes shall be arrested and brought to judgment. Nazi leaders, influential Nazi supporters and high officials of Nazi organizations and institutions and any other persons dangerous to the occupation or its objectives shall be arrested and interned.

6. All members of the Nazi party who have been more than nominal participants in its activities and all other persons hostile to allied purposes shall be removed from public and semi-public office, and from positions of responsibility in important private undertakings. Such persons shall be replaced by persons who, by their political and moral qualities, are deemed capable of assisting in developing genuine democratic institutions in Germany.

7. German education shall be so controlled as completely to eliminate Nazi militarist doctrines and to make possible the successful development of democratic ideas.

8. The judicial system will be reorganized in accordance with the principles of democracy, of justice under law, and of equal rights for all citizens without distinction of race, nationality or religion.

9. The administration of affairs in Germany should be directed towards the decentralization of the political structure and the development of local responsibility. . . .

10. Subject to the necessity for maintaining military security, freedom of speech, press and religion shall be permitted, and religious institutions shall be respected. Subject likewise to the maintenance of military security, the formation of free trade unions shall be permitted.

---

1. (a) List the responsibilities of the Allies outlined in the Potsdam agreements.
(b) In what ways did the U.S.S.R. violate the Potsdam agreements?

2. Do you think the principles that guided the occupation of Germany were fair? Why or why not?

LIFE IN THE CAMPS

Y. Pfeffer, a survivor of the Mjdanek concentration camp in Poland, describes the treatment of Jews by their captors.

From Yehuda Bauer, *History of the Holocaust* (New York: Franklin Watts, 1982).

You get up at 3 a.m. You have to dress quickly, and make the "bed" so that it looks like a matchbox. For the slightest irregularity in bed-making the punishment was 25 lashes, after which it was impossible to lie or sit for a whole month.

Everyone had to leave the barracks immediately. Outside it is still dark—or else the moon is shining. People are trembling because of lack of sleep and the cold. In order to warm up a bit, groups of ten to twenty people stand together, back to back so as to rub against each other.

There was what was called a washroom, where everyone in the camp was supposed to wash—there were only a few faucets—and we were 4 500 people in that section (no. 3). Of course there was neither soap nor towel or even a handkerchief, so that washing was theoretical rather than practical. . . . In one day, a person there came a lowly person indeed.

At 5 a.m. we used to get half a litre of black, bitter coffee. That was all we got for what was called "breakfast." At 6 a.m.—a headcount (*Appell* in German). We all had to stand at attention, in fives, according to the barracks, of which there were 22 in each section. We stood there until the SS men had satisfied their game-playing instincts by "humorous" orders to take off and put on caps. Then they received their report, and counted us. After the headcount—work.

We went in groups—some to build railway tracks or a road, some to the quarries to carry stones or coal, some to take out manure, or for potato-digging, latrine-cleaning, barracks—or sewer—repairs. All this took place inside the camp enclosure. During work the SS men beat up the prisoners mercilessly, inhumanly and for no reason.

They were like wild beasts and, having found their victim, ordered him to present his backside, and beat him with a stick or a whip, usually until the stick broke.

The victim screamed only after the first blows, afterwards he fell unconscious and the SS man then kicked at the ribs, the face, at the most sensitive parts of a man's body, and then, finally convinced that the victim was at the end of his strength, he ordered another Jew to pour one pail of water after the other over the beaten person until he woke and got up.

A favorite sport of the SS men was to make a "boxing sack" out of a Jew. This was done in the following way: Two Jews were stood up, one being forced to hold the other by the collar, and an SS man trained giving him a knock-out. Of course, after the first blow, the poor victim was likely to fall, and this was prevented by the other Jew holding him up. After the fat, Hitlerite murderer had "trained" in this way for 15 minutes, and only after the poor victim was completely shattered, covered in blood, his teeth knocked out, his nose broken, his eyes hit, they released him and ordered a doctor to treat his wounds. That was their way of taking care and being generous.

Another customary SS habit was to kick a Jew with a heavy boot. The Jew was forced to stand to attention, and all the while the SS man kicked him until he broke some bones. People who stood near enough to such a victim, often heard the breaking of bones. The pain was so terrible that people, having undergone the treatment, died in agony.

Apart from the SS men there were other expert hangmen. These were the so-called Capos. The name was an abbreviation for "barracks police." The Capos were German criminals who were also camp inmates. However, although they belonged to "us," they were privileged. They had a special, better barracks of their own, they had better food, better, almost normal clothes, they wore special red or green riding pants, high leather boots, and fulfilled the functions of camp guards. They were worse even than the SS men. One of them, older than the others and the worst murderer of them all, when he descended on a victim, would not revive him after with water but would choke him to death. Once, this murderer caught a boy of 13 (in the presence of his father) and hit his head so that the poor child died instantly. This "camp elder" later boasted in front of his peers, with a smile on his beast's face and with pride, that he managed to kill a Jew with one blow.

In each section stood a gallows. For being late for the head count, or similar crimes, the "camp elder" hanged the offenders.

Work was actually unproductive, and its purpose was exhaustion and torture.

At 12 noon there was a break for a meal. Standing in line, we received half a litre of soup each. Usually it was cabbage soup, or some other watery liquid, without fats, tasteless. That was lunch. It was eaten—in all weather—under the open sky, never in the barracks. No spoons were allowed, though wooden spoons lay one each bunk—probably for show, for Red Cross committees. One had to drink the soup out of the bowl and lick it like a dog.

From 1 p.m. till 6 p.m. there was work again. I must emphasize that if we were lucky we got a 12 o'clock meal. There were "days of punishment"—when lunch was given together with the evening meal, and it was cold and sour, so that our stomach was empty for a whole day.

Afternoon work was the same: blows, and blows again. Until 6 p.m.

At 6 there was the evening headcount. Again we were forced to stand at attention. Counting, receiving the report. Usually we were left standing at attention for an hour or two, while some prisoners were called up for "punishment parade"—they were those who in the Germans' eyes had transgressed in some way during the day, or had not been punctilious in their performance. They were stripped naked publicly, laid out on specially constructed benches, and whipped with 25 or 50 lashes.

The brutal beating and the heart-rending cries—all this the prisoners had to watch and hear.

---

1. What evidence is there that extermination of the Jewish race was not the sole intent of the Final Solution?

2. What lessons can the Holocaust teach us about Western civilization?

ANALYSIS AND APPLICATION

1. Compare and contrast the political and economic philosophies of Marx and Lenin.

2. *All are equal, but some are more equal than others.*
Examine the validity of George Orwell's satire of Stalin's dictatorship in his antitotalitarian fable *Animal Farm* (1945).

3. Compare and contrast the techniques used by Mussolini, Hitler, and Stalin to gain and consolidate power.

4. Examine the architecture of Germany, Italy, and the Soviet Union during this period as three-dimensional propaganda.

5. Trace the antecedents of Hitler's "master race" philosophy in nineteenth-century German literature.

6. Create an editorial cartoon that illustrates the policy of appeasement.

7. Trace the steps by which the U.S. prepared itself for eventual entry into the Second World War.

8. Compare the principles of the Atlantic Charter, signed by Churchill and Roosevelt in 1941, with those of Wilson's Fourteen Points in the First World War.

9. Defend or refute this statement: *A world war might have been averted in 1914; twenty-five years later the catastrophe was inevitable.*

10. Organize a book seminar on the Holocaust. Each member of the group should read a different account and make notes. In addition, each seminar participant should prepare a series of five to ten thought-provoking questions to encourage discussion. Organize the seminar so that each person has a chance to lead the discussion and share some important insights from the book he or she read.

CHAPTER ELEVEN

The Age of Anxiety: Intellectual and Cultural Trends

ART AND SOCIETY

Between 1918 and 1945, Western civilization attempted to jettison the cultural baggage of the previous century. The nineteenth century had been bound to the past; the long-held beliefs and values of that era had died on the battlefields of the First World War as four years of destruction and carnage shook people's faith in tradition. Perhaps the French poet Paul Valéry (1871–1945) expressed the feeling of uncertainty and anxiety best when he said, "Almost all the affairs of men remain in a terrible uncertainty. We think of what has disappeared, and we are almost destroyed by what has been destroyed; we do not know what will be born, and we fear the future. . . ." Some people began to question whether Western civilization would survive. Gilbert Murray wrote in the 1930s, "There is something wrong. There is a loss of confidence, a loss of faith, an omnipresent haunting fear. People speak as they never spoke in the Victorian days of the possible collapse of civilization." The political and economic crises of the 1920s and 1930s added to the sense of uncertainty. It was, in the words of the poet W.H. Auden (1907–1973), an "age of anxiety."

Building on the radical changes of the early twentieth century, art in the interwar period reflected an abandonment of traditional styles in favour of a more expressive means of communicating ideas and emotions. Modern psychological and sociological ideas influenced artists as they tried to create something more "modern." This desire to create something new was one of the reasons for the concentration on style rather than content in the avant-garde art of the period. Although this trend was evident before the First World War, it was not until the postwar period that it gained widespread recognition.

Painting

There is no question that the modern period in painting began with the work of Paul Cézanne (1839–1906) and his successors of the impressionist, post-impressionist, and expressionist schools. In their desire to see the world objectively, these artists broke the rules that had previously dictated artistic standards. Without these constraints, artists were able to explore a wide range of new directions. A multiplicity of styles—fauvism, expressionism, cubism, and futurism—erupted between the wars as artists searched for a new means of expression. This experimentation accelerated the pace of change in Western art. The most notable new styles were dadaism and surrealism.

Dadaism

The dada movement was the most radical and rebellious example of the break with tradition. (See readings.) After four years of the destruction and violence of the First World War, dada reflected postwar disillusionment. The term *dada* is French for a child's hobby horse and was chosen at random from the dictionary by a group of rebellious artists and writers. The dadaists glorified the irrational and the absurd and expressed disgust with and ridicule of civilization.

In March 1917, the Galerie Dada opened in Zurich. It was

supported by an international group of expatriate artists who had come to live in that neutral city. The movement attempted to throw off the "dead weight" of all traditions, social and artistic, rather than to create a new style in art. One of the leaders of the movement was the German Richard Hulsenbeck (1892–1974). In 1920, he wrote a history of dada in which he said:

> The Cabaret Voltaire group [Dada] were all artists in the sense that they were keenly sensitive to newly developed artistic possibilities. . . . [They were] convinced of the necessity of combatting naturalist conception in any form. Tristan Tzara, the romantic internationalist, whose propagandistic zeal we have to thank for the enormous growth of Dada, brought with him from Romania an unlimited literary facility. In that period, as we danced, sang, recited night after night in the Cabaret Voltaire, abstract art was for us tantamount to absolute honor. Naturalism was a psychological penetration of the motives of the bourgeois, in whom we saw our mortal enemy. . . . In this sense, Dada was to give a truth a new impetus, Dada was to be a rallying point for abstract energies and a lasting slingshot for the great international artistic movements.
>
> From *A Concise History of Modern Painting* by Herbert Read. Copyright © 1975 Thames and Hudson. Reprinted by permission of the publisher.

Dadaists deliberately tried to outrage the art community by creating revised versions of classic paintings, such as Marcel Duchamp's (1887–1968) painting of the Mona Lisa with a moustache. They also made collages using the trash of Western civilization and publicly destroyed their own art or asked the audience to destroy it for them. Artists who participated in this movement included Duchamp, Hans Arp (1887–1966), Francis Picabia (1879–1953), and Georg Grosz (1893–1959).

To a great extent, dadaists did not really know what they wanted, only what they were against. When international dada fairs were held in Cologne and Berlin in 1920, the exhibition was closed by the police. Revolutionary and nihilist in character, by the 1920s dada had become more of a revolutionary social protest than an art movement. By 1922, the dadaists had been absorbed by the surrealists. Although it would be largely forgotten over the next two decades, the dada movement had given life and momentum to a new era in modern art.

Surrealism

The successor to dada, *surrealism*, explored the irrational and the subconscious mind. (See readings.) Freudian psychology was particularly influential among surrealist artists. André Breton (1896–1966), the French poet, essayist, and critic who wrote the first surrealist manifesto (1924), stated that "surrealism is based on the belief in the superior reality of certain forms of previously neglected association, in the omnipotence of dream, in the disinterested play of thought." Breton was the intellectual leader of the movement. Originally associated with dada, Breton broke away in 1922 after recognizing its lack of constructive focus. By 1929, the author had published his second *Manifesto of Surrealism* and had dedicated his publication *La Révolution Surréalist* and the surrealistic movement in general to the cause of communism.

In an attempt to tap the unconscious mind, surrealists developed "automatic painting" where the artists recreated whatever came into their minds. The Freudian symbolism of surrealist imagery is suggested in Max Ernst's (1891–1976) *Oedipus Rex* (1922) and René Magritte's (1898–1967) *The Rape* (1934). Painters such as Salvador Dali (1904–1989) and Joan Miro (1893–1983) took recognizable scenes and objects out of context and placed them in new configurations, as they might be in dreams. Dali's *Persistence of Memory* (1931) is a good example. (See colour plate.) Meret Oppenheim's (1913-) fur-lined teacup, *Object* (1936), is a classic example of the attempt to transform the familiar into the strange, another surrealist goal.

In the final analysis, surrealism cannot be simply examined in terms of its expression in the visual arts. Poetic in nature, the surrealist movement was to a great extent the heir to the values of romanticism. As Breton wrote in his 1924 Manifesto:

> Only the word freedom still exalts me. Among the many disgraces we inherit, we should do well to recognize that the *greatest freedom* of spirit is left to us. We ought not to misuse it. To reduce the imagination to slavery, even when it might lead to what one crudely calls happiness, is to evade whatever one finds, in the depths of the self, of supreme justice. Imagination alone tells me *what can be*, and that is enough to lift for a little the terrible interdict—enough also to allow me to abandon myself to this freedom without fear of self-deception."
>
> From James Johl, *Europe Since 1870: An International History*, (New York: Harper and Row, 1973), p. 308.

HITLER ON ART

Book burnings, censorship, anti-Semitism, and attacks on "decadent" art resulted in a mass exodus of talent from Germany after the Nazis assumed power. The following excerpt, from a speech inaugurating the "Great Exhibition of German Art" in Munich in 1937, illustrates Hitler's views on art.

When, four years ago, the solemn ceremony of laying the cornerstone for this building took place, we were all conscious of the fact that not only the stone for a new building must be laid but the foundation for a new and true German art. At stake was our chance to provoke a turning-point in the development of the total German cultural output. . . .

Germany's collapse and general decline had been—as we know—not only economic or political, but probably even to a much greater extent, cultural. Moreover, this process could not be explained exclusively on the grounds of the lost war. Such catastrophes have very often afflicted peoples and states, only to provide an impetus to their purification and give rise to an inner elevation.

However, that flood of slime and ordure which the year 1918 belched forth into our lives was not a product of the lost war, but was only freed in its rush to the surface by that calamity. Through the defeat, an already thoroughly diseased body experienced the total impact of its inner decomposition. Now, after the collapse of the social, economic, and cultural patterns which continued to function in appearance only, the baseness already underlying them for a long time, triumphed, and indeed this was so in all strata of our life. . . .

Until the moment when National-Socialism took power, there existed in Germany a so-called "modern art," that is, to be sure, almost every year another one, as the very meaning of this word indicates. National-Socialist Germany, however, wants again a "German Art," and this art shall and will be of eternal value. . . .

Art can in no way be a fashion. As little as the character and the blood of our people will change, so much will art have to lose its mortal character and replace it with worthy images expressing the life-course of our people in the steadily unfolding growth of its creations. Cubism, Dadaism, Futurism, Impressionism, etc., have nothing to do with our German people. For these concepts are neither old nor modern, but are only the artifactitious stammerings of men to whom God has denied the grace of a truly artistic talent, and in its place has awarded them the gift of jabbering or deception. I will therefore confess now, in this very hour, that I have come to the final inalterable decision to clean house, just as I have done in the domain of political confusion, and from now on rid the German art life of its phrase-mongering.

"Works of art" which cannot be understood in themselves but, for the justification of their existence, need those bombastic instructions for their use, finally reaching that intimidated soul, who is patiently willing to accept such stupid or impertinent nonsense—these works of art from now on will no longer find their way to the German people.

From Herschel B. Chipp (ed.), *Theories of Modern Art* (Berkley: University of California Press, 1968), pp. 474–476, 479.

Three events had a profound influence on the arts during the interwar period: (1) the Russian Revolution; (2) the political convulsions that took place immediately following Germany's defeat in the First World War and the subsequent rise and victory of the National Socialist party; and (3) the depression of the 1930s. Large-scale government intervention into the art community under totalitarian governments in Germany and the Soviet Union and under government auspices in the United States during the Depression forced art in a direction it would not have otherwise taken. In general, this art continued the renaissance tradition and avoided the avant-garde. This emphasized the split between the avant-garde and the masses.

"German art," as dictated by the Nazis, social realism in the Soviet Union, and art commissioned by the Works Project Administration (W.P.A.) during the Depression in the

United States all used art, particularly visual art, as a means of communicating with the masses. Unlike avant-garde art, this art concentrated on content rather than style. Much of it was political in its orientation. This is particularly true in Germany, where so-called "decadent" art was removed from public display. However, the political orientation of art was not new; in fact, a great deal of avant-garde art was politically oriented. What *was* new, however, was the degree of government involvement in art, either through commissions or restrictions, and the subsequent influence that accompanied this involvement.

Meret Oppenheim's Object *(1936) was a classic example of the surrealist technique of "the disturbing object."*

The political upheavals in Russia, and later in Germany, resulted in an exodus of artists from these countries. Many avant-garde artists fled the Soviet Union and took up residence in Paris, making that city the centre of modernism in the interwar period. The Nazi party's attack on art it labeled "Bolshevist," "Marxist," "Jewish," or "Degenerate" led to a mass exodus of German talent to the United States and is one of the reasons for the supremacy of the United States in avant-garde art after the Second World War.

Women Artists

The interwar period also saw a dramatic increase in the number of female visual artists. The access to education in general, and art training in particular, which was evident in the late nineteenth and early twentieth centuries bore fruit during this period. Other elements of discrimination—social, political, economic and psychological—were no longer fully operative. However, lack of commissions and discrimination forced many female artists toward the avant-garde, where the emphasis on "newness" placed women on equal footing with men.

Some prominent female artists included Käthe Kollwitz (1867–1945), whose expressionist works reflected her socialist political beliefs. The Russian avant-garde artists Natalia Goncharova (1881–1962), Lyubov Popova (1889–1924), and

Georgia O'Keeffe's paintings, such as Stables *(1932), illustrated a precise and disciplined line.*

Sonia Terk-Delaunay (1885–1979) were dedicated to abstraction. Meret Oppenheim (1913-), Remedios Varo (1913–1963), and Dorothea Tanning (1910-) were accomplished artists in the surrealist tradition. One of the best American painters of the period was Georgia O'Keeffe (1887–1986), who was not affiliated with any major school. She used magnification as a form of abstraction and her formalized representations of architectural subjects were highly regarded in the 1920s. Her later works often involved studies of particular objects. Some of her better known works include *Black Iris*, *Lake George Bains* (1926) and *Stables* (1932).

Architecture

In the twentieth century, urban living, electricity, and standards of sanitation changed the way architects designed buildings, while new materials, such as steel, glass, and reinforced concrete, created new possibilities in building design. *Functionalism* dominated new architecture; buildings were designed to fit the purpose for which they were intended. Ornamentation was shunned and simplicity and clarity of line became the order of the day.

The Bauhaus School

Although functionalism had its roots in the nineteenth century, it was not until Walter Gropius (1883–1969) founded the Bauhaus school of architecture at Weimer, Germany, in 1919 that the principles of functionalism gained widespread acceptance. The Bauhaus movement was a centre of controversy in Germany. As with the surrealist movement, advanced thought in architecture was associated with revolutionary political ideas. The Bauhaus movement was often the target of right-wing attacks and, after Hitler came to power in 1933, it was closed down and many of its leading members forced into exile. Their influence contributed to the development of an international style of architecture throughout the Western world. Its basic philosophy was to create, in the words of Gropius, "a clear organic architecture, whose inner logic will be radiant and naked, unencumbered by lying façades and trickeries; we want an architecture adapted to our world of machines, radios, and fast motor cars, an architecture whose function is clearly recognizable in the relation of its forms." The Bauhaus philosophy attempted to create a unified vision (*gestaltung*), which encompassed building construction, decoration, furniture, fittings, painting, and sculpture through an interdisciplinary school of design.

During the same period, the prolific ideas and experiments of Le Corbusier (1887–1969) in France were creating unique designs and transforming entire urban landscapes. Frank Lloyd Wright (1869–1959) in the United States was using mechanical methods and materials to create open planning and free-flowing space. Both of these innovative architects helped to spread the international style.

The influence of the Bauhaus on North American architecture is perhaps best illustrated by the work of architects George Howe (1886–1955) and William Lescaze

Bauhaus at Dessau, Germany, was designed by Walter Gropius in 1926.

(1896–1969). They entered into partnership in 1929 to design a new "skyscraper" for the Philadelphia Saving Fund Society (known as the PSFS). The PSFS building soon became an outstanding expression of the international style and is considered one of the best-displayed skyscrapers of the pre-Second World War era. (See plates.)

Art Deco

Art deco emerged as a popular style at the same time that the PSFS building was being designed. Art deco was less serious than other modern architectural movements; it attempted to bring an element of fantasy into the cityscape. Technically, art deco gave rise to the use of new materials, such as aluminum and stainless steel, and to the revival and new applications of glass. Aside from its obviously visual appeal, art deco owes much of its clean, sleek image to the straight edge and compass. As a result, the movement saw what its proponents believed to be a perfect marriage of the ornamental with the modern.

The entrance of the New York Trust Company in New York City was designed in the art deco style.

Sculpture

The trend in sculpture, like architecture, was toward an international style. National differences gradually disappeared as the ideas of cubism and futurism led to experimentation in sculpture.

Constantin Brancusi

The first sculptor to completely abandon tradition was Constantin Brancusi (1876–1957). Brancusi was interested in simplicity of form and primitivism, influences which are still evident in the sculpture of today. One of the twentieth century's foremost sculptors, Henry Moore (1898–1986), said of Brancusi:

> Since Gothic, European sculpture has become overgrown with moss, weeds—all sorts of surface excrescences which completely concealed shape. It has been Brancusi's special mission to get rid of this overgrowth, and to make us once more shape-conscious. To do this he has had to concentrate on very simple direct shapes, to keep his sculpture, as it were, one-cylindered, to refine and polish a single shape to a degree almost too precious. Brancusi's work apart from its individual value has been of great historical importance in the development of contemporary sculpture.
>
> From *Praeger Encyclopedia of Art*, Vol. 4, (New York: Praeger Publishers, 1971), p. 1408.

Alexander Calder

Other sculptors, such as Alexander Calder (1898–1976), attempted complete abstraction that approached surrealism through the use of mobiles and stabiles. Calder's work escaped traditional forms and illustrates his early training as an engineer. Some of the works are monumental, such as the mobile on the grounds of the UNESCO headquarters in Paris, yet they move at the touch of a finger or in the slightest wind. Most of Calder's works are black. They achieve their effect through their shape, their thickness, and their movement.

Literature

The end of the First World War freed minds as well as people. The destruction of traditional values and social structures left a vacuum that welcomed the emergence of new ideas and forms of artistic expression. However, if the end of the old era brought hope and excitement to the visual arts, it brought disillusionment to the literary world.

The sense of alienation evident in painting was also common to the poetry, drama, and novels of the interwar period. Many novels attacked materialism and greed, moral rigidity and hypocrisy, and the spiritual emptiness of modern society. Sinclair Lewis's (1885–1951) novel *Babbit* (1922) satirized the shallowness of American society. Other novelists examined the relationship between the individual and society. For example, Hermann Hesse's (1877–1962) *Der Steppenwolf* (1927) examined the conflict between the bourgeois world and an outsider while Franz Kafka's (1883–1924) *The Trial* (1925) tells of a man arrested for an unknown crime. Some novels expressed the restlessness of the period; Thomas Mann's (1875–1955) *The Magic Mountain* (1924), for example, was a search for values in Western civilization.

The Anti-utopian Writers

During the interwar period, a series of anti-utopian works presented nightmarish fantasies about life in the future. The vision of the machine freeing humans in the novels of H.G. Wells was replaced by the vision of humans being enslaved by machines. The first of these works, Karl Capek's (1890–1938) play *R.U.R.* (an acronym standing for Rossums' Universal Robots; 1938) dramatized a world taken over by machines and gave the English language the word "robot." Aldous Huxley's (1894–1963) *Brave New World* (1932) depicted a twenty-fifth century where technology controlled art and personal relations. George Orwell's (1903–1950) *Nineteen Eighty-Four* (1949) depicted a totalitarian state that relied on language, technology, and psychological terror to force submission to Big Brother. The central image of this popular novel is summed up in the riveting image supplied by the chief of the Thought Police: "If you want a picture of the future, imagine a boot stamping on a human face—forever."

Ernest Hemingway

Numerous novels, like Ernest Hemingway's (1898–1961) *A Farewell to Arms* (1929), expressed disillusionment with postwar society. Hemingway was part of a group of American expatriates living in Paris in the 1920s. He popularized the term "Lost Generation" in reference both to the millions of individuals who had lost their lives in the First World War and to those who had survived and wandered "lost," without purpose. His novel *The Sun Also Rises* (1926) established him as the spokesperson for this group. He followed this with *A Farewell to Arms* in 1929.

Paris became the focal point for the Lost Generation. *A Moveable Feast* (published posthumously in 1964), is Hemingway's memoirs about life in the city during this period. He depicts a group disillusioned and dissolute with life.

Ernest Hemingway lived in Paris during the interwar years.

Gertrude Stein

Hemingway was just one of the writers and artists who frequented 27, rue de Fluerus, Paris, the residence of Gertrude Stein (1874–1946). During the interwar period Stein's residence became a focus for avant-garde writers and artists. Numerous painters, including Henri Matisse (1869–1954) and Pablo Picasso (1881–1973), as well as American expatriate writers Ezra Pound (1885–1972) and Hemingway, frequented her salon. Stein's memoirs, *The Autobiography of Alice B. Toklas* (1933), contain fascinating accounts of this period in Paris.

Stein experimented with language, punctuation, and form in her writing. She is credited with the first attempt to transcribe "natural conversation"—that is, speech as it occurs in everyday life—into American literature. Her unique style influenced many American writers, particularly Sherwood Anderson (1876–1941) and Hemingway. She outlined her therories in *How to Write* (1931) and *Lectures in America* (1935). Her most important works include the novelettes *Three Lives* (1909) and the opera libretto *Four Saints in Three Acts* (1934).

Gertrude Stein's Paris residence was a meeting place for many of the leading writers and artists in the 1920s.

F. Scott Fitzgerald

F. Scott Fitzgerald (1896–1940) established himself as a chronicler of the Jazz Age. All of his major novels—*The Beautiful and the Damned* (1922), *The Great Gatsby* (1925), and *Tender Is the Night* (1934)—record the life of the lost generation. During most of the 1920s, Fitzgerald lived in Europe, mingling with wealthy society and other American expatriates. However, in the 1930s he was plagued by his wife Zelda's growing insanity and his own battles with alcoholism. He wrote nothing of consequence after he became an alcoholic in the mid–1930s and was forced to become a scriptwriter in Hollywood to pay for his mounting debts. He left an unfinished novel, *The Last Tycoon*, when he died in 1940 of a heart attack.

Marcel Proust

One of the most striking developments in the novel was the stream-of-consciousness technique, which incorporated some of Freud's concepts—persistence of memory and the formation of personality, for instance—to explore the human pysche in the past, present, and future simultaneously. The most notable works were Marcel Proust's *Remembrance of Things Past* (1919), Virginia Woolf's *Jacob's Room* (1922), and James Joyce's *Ulysses* (1922).

Marcel Proust's (1871–1922) masterpiece *Remembrance of Things Past* is a seven-part novel published between 1913 and 1927. The novel is semiautobiographical and analyses French society at the turn of the century. Suffering from asthma and nervous disorders, Proust isolated himself in a cork-lined room on the Boulevard Haussmann in Paris, where he began writing his epic work. Unable to find a publisher, Proust's first volume, *Swann's Way*, was published at his own expense. In poor health, Proust rushed to complete the seven volumes, but he did not live to see the last three volumes published. The influence of Proust's style is evident in such works as André Gide's (1869–1951) *The Counterfeiters* (1926) and Virginia Woolf's *The Waves* (1931.)

James Joyce

The Irish novelist, short story writer, and poet James Joyce (1882–1941) is regarded as one of the greatest literary talents of the twentieth century. He is noted for his technical innovations to the novel, such as stream-of-consciousness, and his development of a unique language for *Finnegan's Wake* (1939). This novel took seventeen years to write and describes the thought processes of the sleeping pub owner,

Humphrey Chimpden Earwicker. The invented words, puns, and network of allusions make this one of the most complex novels in the English language. Joyce's other works include *A Portrait of the Artist as a Young Man* (1916), a semi-autobiographical novel dealing with his Jesuit schooling, and *Ulysses* (1922), which describes the thoughts and impressions of a series of characters through the course of a single day.

Virginia Woolf
Virginia Woolf (1882–1941) was one of the forerunners of modernism in the novel. Along with Joyce, she pioneered the stream-of-consciousness technique. Her novels are noted as much for their poetry and symbolism as for their psychological examination of the characters. Woolf suffered from bouts of mental disturbances throughout most of her creative life. It was partly as therapy that she and her husband Leonard established the Hogarth Press, which published the early works of Katherine Mansfield (1888–1923), E.M. Forster (1879–1970), and T.S. Eliot (1888–1936). Among Woolf's better known works are *Mrs. Dalloway* (1925), *To the Lighthouse* (1927), and *The Waves* (1931).

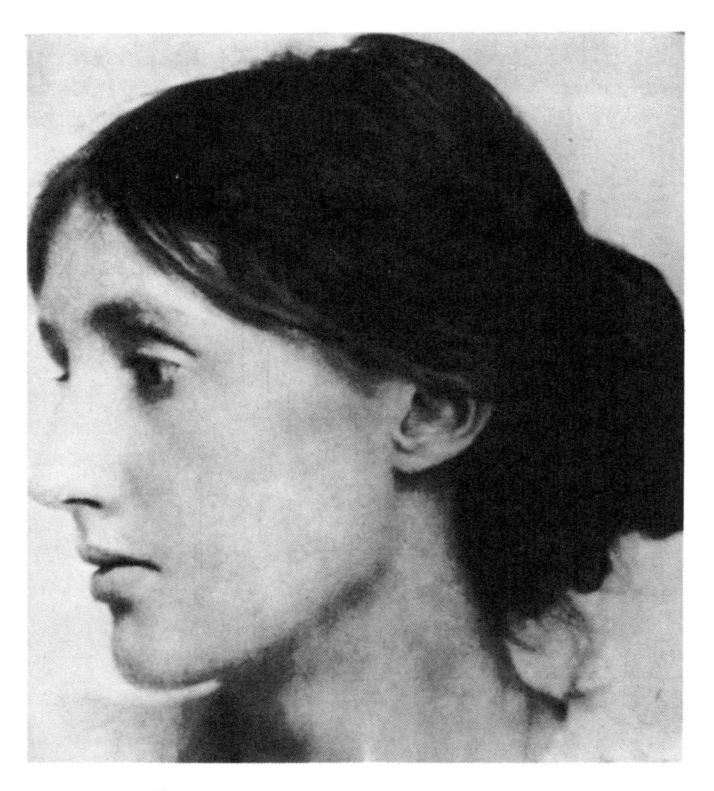

Virginia Woolf made a significant contribution to the technical development of the modern novel.

Thomas Mann
One of the most widely read authors of the period was Thomas Mann (1875–1955), who won the Nobel Prize for Literature in 1929 for his work *The Magic Mountain* (1924). This complex novel traces the personal development of a young German engineer, Hans Castorp, during his seven-year stay in a tuberculosis sanatorium at Davos in the Swiss Alps. Mann was fascinated by youth and age, health and illness. These themes are explored through the heroes and antiheroes who inhabit the sanatorium and personify every aspect of Western civilization. Castrop's search for self-realization thereby becomes an allegory for the search for values in Western civilization. Mann's other works included *Buddenbrooks* (1901), a novel about the decline of a German merchant family over four generations, and *Doktor Faustus* (1947), the story of a man who renounces normal life to devote himself exclusively to music. Mann fled Germany in 1933 and was active in anti-fascist movements, first in Europe and later in America, where he took up residence in 1938.

Franz Kafka
Franz Kafka (1883–1924), from Prague, published only a small proportion of his work during his lifetime. All of his major works—*America* (1911–1914), *The Trial* (1914–1915), and *The Castle* (1922)—were left unfinished when he died of tuberculosis in a sanatorium in Vienna in 1924. He left the manuscripts to his best friend, Max Brod. Luckily, Brod ignored the instructions to destroy the novels and instead edited and published them. Kafka's novels are characterized by fear, guilt, and foreboding for the future. His protagonists often lead a routine, middle-class life which is suddenly turned into one of anxiety and horror when punishments seem disproportionate to the perceived crime. The bewilderment and confusion of his major characters make Kafka's novels powerful statements about the age of anxiety.

D.H. Lawrence
D(avid) H(erbert) Lawrence (1885–1930) was one of the most controversial authors of the period. His most famous novel, *Lady Chatterley's Lover* (1928)—the story of a gentlewoman who falls in love with the gamekeeper on her husband's estate—was banned by British and American censors. The book was not published in its entirety in the United

States until 1959, and it was only after a sensational court case in 1960 that it was published in England. All of Lawrence's major novels deal with the relationships between men and women and the complications that arise in these relationships because of sexual and other taboos. Lawrence was highly critical of the self-deception and hypocrisy he saw in the world around him. His other works include *Sons and Lovers* (1913) and *Women in Love* (1921).

T.S. Eliot

The most influential poet in the English-speaking world was T.S. Eliot (1888–1965). (See readings.) Like many poets, Eliot rejected fixed poetic meters and rhyme schemes. His poem *The Waste Land* (1922) expressed the despair, dreariness, and desolation of the period through a series of word pictures so complex that footnotes were required to explain the allusions. After the publication of *La Jeune Parque* in 1917, Paul Valéry (1871–1945) had a similar influence in France, as did the German Stefan George (1868–1933) around whom formed "*der kreis um Stefan George*" (the George Circle).

W.H. Auden

Other prominent poets included the Englishman W(ystan) H(ugh) Auden (1907–1973). Auden, like many other intellectuals of the 1930s, supported the loyalist cause in the Spanish Civil War. His experiences as an ambulance driver provided the material for the poem "Spain, 1937." His dislike for war was also reflected in his poem "Sept., 1939" written on the eve of the Second World War. The poem concludes with the line "we must love one another or die." One of his best poems, "In Memory of W.B. Yeats" (1939), is a tribute to a poet who influenced him greatly.

William Butler Yeats

The Irishman William Butler Yeats (1869–1939) advocated the fulfilment of his country's national aspirations. As a leader of the new Irish nationalist school he encouraged other Irish writers to base their themes on the country's landscape and legends. Yeats received the Nobel Prize for Literature in 1923. Among his most memorable poems are "Easter, 1916" and "Sailing to Byzantium."

Frederico Garcia Lorca

Frederico Garcia Lorca (1898–1936) was a poet and dramatist as well as an accomplished musician and amateur painter. His greatest poems, such as "Lament for Ignacio Mejias" (1935), which was inspired by the goring and subsequent death of a bullfighter, and his famous dramatic tragedy *Blood Wedding* (1933), which relates the story of a bride killed by her husband, illustrate his preoccupation with the theme of death. He was arrested and shot without the benefit of a trial in 1936 by Falangists shortly after the outbreak of the Spanish Civil War. He is considered by critics to be the greatest Spanish poet of the twentieth century.

George Bernard Shaw

Drama was dominated by the work of George Bernard Shaw (1856–1959) in England and Eugene O'Neil (1888–1953) in the United States. Although most of Shaw's greatest works, such as *Man and Superman* (1903) and *Pygmalion* (1912), were written before the First World War, his later works continued to attack conventional morality and thought. In *Back to Methuselah* (1921), Shaw illustrates his belief in the perfectability of humanity as he traces the evolution of humankind from the days of Adam and Eve to the year 31 920 A.D. Shaw was awarded the Nobel Prize for Literature in 1925.

Eugene O'Neill

Eugene O'Neill is considered by many to be the greatest American playwright. His first major production, *Beyond the Horizon* (1920), won him the Pulitzer Prize; he was awarded the Nobel Prize for Literature in 1936. O'Neill used many different styles and experimented with different techniques. For example, *The Hairy Ape* (1922) uses expressionist techniques, while *Strange Interlude* (1928) uses "interior monologues" (the dramatic equivalent of stream-of-consciousness) to reveal the inner workings of the characters' minds. His play *Long Day's Journey into Night* (1939–1941) is one of the greatest plays ever written in the United States.

Luigi Pirandello

The most innovative playwright during this period was Italy's Luigi Pirandello (1867–1936). Pirandello challenged traditional conventions and greatly influenced European drama. His play *Six Characters in Search of an Author* (1921) presented two sets of players on the stage simultaneously, each presenting two versions of the same story, leaving the audience to draw its own conclusions. His work expressed his philosophy of uncertainty and disillusionment. Other plays include *Henry IV* (1922) and *As You Desire Me* (1930).

Music

The music of the old masters was still the most popular and traditional harmonies remained the basis of popular composition in the first half of the twentieth century. National differences continued to prevail and the folk tradition was still a major source of inspiration for many works, particularly those of Bela Bartok (1881–1945). But like the rest of the arts, there was experimentation in music, particularly among young composers.

Expressionism in music was best represented by the German composer Arnold Schoenberg (1874–1951), who invented the twelve-tone scale, a system of composition treating all twelve notes of the scale as equals rather than as tied to a common key. Other composers who experimented with atonality included Anton von Webern (1883–1945) and Alban Berg (1885–1935). Berg's opera *Wozzeck* (1920), which was based on the unfinished play of the same name by Georg Buchner (1813–1837), is one of the greatest masterpieces of modern opera and one of the best examples of atonal music.

Louis Armstrong rehearsed a trumpet duet with Roy Eldridge for the Esquire All-American Jazz Concert.

In contrast to Schoenberg and his followers is the work of the German composer Paul Hindemith (1895–1963) and the Russians Igor Stravinsky (1882–1971), Sergei Prokofiev (1891–1953), and Dimitri Shostakovich (1906–1975). Although some of these composers started as members of the avant-garde—Stravinsky's, *The Rite of Spring* (1915) actually caused a riot when it was first performed—they settled into a more traditional approach that stressed simplification and restraint in the emotional content of the music. The neoclassical music of these composers represented the dominant trend until after the Second World War.

Jazz

For many Europeans, it was not the work of the classical composers that interested them, but an imported phenomenon from the United States: *jazz*. Jazz originated in the southern states in the 1890s, most notably in New Orleans in Louisiana. Combining African and European folk music, popular songs, and American vaudeville, it could be alternatively spiritual, hot, or blues in focus.

The first identifiable jazz style was ragtime, which was performed by solo pianists such as the noted composer-player Scott Joplin (1868–1917). The jazz craze spread to New York and Chicago in the 1920s. There it gained international recognition as a unique musical style native to the United States. The classical jazz period, from 1918 until 1930, evolved as musicians such as composer-pianist Ferdinand "Jelly Roll" Morton (1885–1941) adapted ragtime for the jazz band. Jelly Roll and trumpeter Louis Armstrong (1898–1971) were the leading forces in jazz during this period.

Jazz bands became increasingly larger throughout the 1920s. This led to the more commercialized swing bands in the 1930s, which emphasized prearranged orchestration. Edward Kennedy "Duke" Ellington (1899–1974) was the creative genius of the swing band. Between 1930 and the early 1940s, however, jazz became "watered down" as dance bands across the continent began to include jazz and ragtime tunes in their repertoires. This led to a revolt by some virtuoso players, who created a new movement, *bebop*, or bop, which marked the return to smaller groups playing complex melodies. The leaders of this movement included trumpeter John Birks "Dizzy" Gillespie (1917-) and alto saxophonist Charlie "Bird" Parker (1920–1955).

By the 1920s, great female vocalists had emerged in jazz. One was Bessie Smith (1900–1937), who lived the life she sang about. She has been described as a "big, handsome, raucous, drunken and infinitely sad woman [who] liked to sing her blues slow." When she took the stage her ability commanded the attention of everyone in the room. Ella Fitzgerald (1918-) and Sarah Vaughan (1924–1990) continued the tradition of greatness after Smith's tragic death in a car accident.

The unmistakable influence of jazz can also be found in the history of modern classical music. Claude Debussy (1862–1918) wrote jazz style piano pieces, such as *Golliwog's Cakewalk* (1909) and *Minstrels* (1910). Maurice Ravel's (1875–1937) *The Child and the Enchantments* (1925) and Igor Stravinsky's (1882–1971) *Piano Rag-Music* (1919) also bear the unmistakable influence of jazz. Kurt Weill (1900–1950), one of the best-known German composers of music for the theatre, used jazz elements in his music for *The Threepenny Opera* (1928). Jazz also reintroduced the element of improvisation into modern music. Improvisation, an essential element of jazz and a key element in the jam session, was a common feature of musical performances in the eighteenth century, but was abandoned during the classical period.

Popular Culture

As with music, many of the trends in the arts did not permeate beyond the intellectuals. In general, people preferred jazz to modern music, newspapers and magazines to literature, and more traditional painting and sculpture to modern art. But above all else, the masses preferred radio and motion pictures.

Radio

Although experimental radio broadcasts began around 1910, it was not until the 1920s that commercial broadcasting became viable. The growth of radio in the United States was astounding. The first commercial radio station went on the air in August 1920. In 1922, the year of the first World Series broadcast, $60 million worth of equipment was sold. By 1925, yearly sales had topped $430 million, and by the end of the decade they had doubled again. The increase in Europe showed a similiar trend; by 1939, 25 percent of all households in Britain and Germany had radios. As the listening public expanded, radio became the major source of family entertainment. The popularity of radio made it a propaganda tool of immense proportions. Adolf Hitler, Winston Churchill, and Franklin Delano Roosevelt all made particu-

THE CABINET OF DR. CALIGARI

European cinema was far more experimental than North American film in the 1920s. The Cabinet of Dr. Caligari *was the most avant-garde film to reach North American shores. The following review describes the reaction of the critics.*

Opinions about *The Cabinet of Dr. Caligari*, at the Capitol this week, will probably be sharply divided—and that's the first thing that recommends the picture, for, although individuality so pronounced that it breeds active disagreement does not necessarily denote peculiar excellence, it is bound to have a strong appeal for habitual motion-picture spectators depressed by stock stuff.

The most conspicuous individual characteristic of the photoplay is that it is cubistic, or expressionistic. Its settings bear a somewhat closer resemblance to reality than, say, the famous *Nude Descending a Staircase*, but they are sufficiently unlike anything ever done on the screen before to belong to a separate scenic species. A house, for instance, is recognized as a house, but with its leaning, trapezoidal walls, its triangular doors, and its bizarre floor patterns, it does not look like any house anybody ever lived in—likewise the irregular alleyways between inclined buildings, the crazy corridors and the erratic roofs.

Doubtless these expressionistic scenes are full of meaning for the specialist in the form of art they represent, but the uninitiated, though they will now and then get a definite suggestion from some touch here or there, and enjoy it, are not asked to understand cubism, for the settings are the background, or rather an inseparable part, of a fantastic story of murder and madness such as Edgar Allan Poe might have written. This story is coherent, logical, a genuine and legitimate thriller, and after one has followed it through several scenes the weird settings seem to be of its substance and no longer call disturbing attention to themselves.

From "The Screen," *The New York Times*, 4 April 1921.

larly good use of this medium to spread their message to national audiences.

Motion Pictures

Motion picture technology was developed in the late nineteenth century. The first motion picture was publicly exhibited in Paris in 1895. By 1900, film had become a popular attraction in arcades, music halls, and vaudeville theatres. By the First World War, feature-length films, such as D.W. Griffith's *Birth of a Nation* (1914–1915), were produced. During the war, most European studios either closed down or concentrated on propaganda films. This created a huge demand for American feature films and resulted in U.S. domination of the medium throughout the silent film era. After the war, the European film industry recovered and created some notable masterpieces.

The 1920s was the golden age of German film. The most notable films of this period were *The Cabinet of Dr. Caligari* (1919), *Nosferatu* (1922), and *Metropolis* (1926). *The Cabinet of Dr. Caligari*, considered a masterpiece of expressionist film, portrayed the absurdity of authority. It had many of the features of the expressionist movement: identity confusion, inability to distinguish reality from the imaginary, the use of dramatic contrast, affected acting, and unrealistic makeup. *Nosferatu* was another expressionist film that received international acclaim. Unfortunately, the movie was a thinly disguised version of Bram Stoker's (1847–1912) novel Dracula (1897). The filmmakers were sued for copyright violation and the court's decision ordered all prints destroyed. *Metropolis*, directed by Fritz Lang (1890–1976), offered a chilling version of life in the twenty-first century. Lang, a former architect, used crowd scenes to create effects one critic described as "not far short of miraculous." Despite his Jewish background, he was offered the job of official film director of the Third Reich in 1933 by Joseph Goebbels (1897–1945). He declined the offer and emigrated to France and later the United States.

France became the centre for experimentation in film with a series of dadaist, cubist, and abstract films from Man Ray (1890–1976), Marcel Duchamp (1887–1968) and Fernand Léger (1881–1955). Perhaps the most significant of these was the surrealist film *An Andalusian Dog* (1928) by Salvador Dali (1904–1989) and Luis Bunuel (1900–1983). The film contained a series of deliberately shocking images, beginning with a man slitting a woman's eyeball with a razor blade, and was one of the first films to examine the role of the mind.

In the Soviet Union, Sergei Eisenstein (1898–1948) developed the use of montage in *The Armoured Cruiser Potemkin* (1925). William A. Barrett described the effect of this technique in a vivid 1926 review of the film that describes the central scene of the movie: the massacre of a crowd by Imperial troops during the abortive revolt of 1905.

> High on the steps, descending slowly in long, even lines, suddenly appear the soldiers in their white, immaculate tunics, splendid tall fellows, loading their rifles as they come. Every now and then the lines stop, fire, reload, descend again—nothing hurried, still nothing staged. And the steps below them, swept by that cold, casual rifle fire! A terror-stricken, bullet-stricken multitude, shorn in breath of all enthusiasm, all revolutionary fire, resubmitting to the old tyranny—a mob, stumbling, falling, dodging, lying flat, rising again, pitching, huddling still, dwindling, fleeing down those terrible, unescapable, everlasting steps, pursued grotesquely, almost humorously, by a bumping baby carriage bearing its unwitting infant, which has broken away from its mother's dying grasp. Most of this has been done with a swift, flickering assortment and throwing together of little pieces of pictures, a face here, a slipping body there, a flopping arm or leg, a pair of eye-glasses, a bit of torn clothing, a shuddering group or a convulsive body, as if the camera were dancing down the steps in that dance of death—as if the newsreel camera man were running madly, stumbling and falling himself at times, but ever busy with his crank.
>
> From George C. Pratt, *Spellbound in Darkness: A History of the Silent Film* (Greenwich, CT: New York Graphic Society, Ltd., 1973), pp. 511–512.

Eisenstein fell out of favour with the Soviet government when his next major film, *Ten Days that Shook the World* (1928), portrayed Trotsky, who had been exiled, as a hero. He was forced to reshoot much of the film to eliminate the offending images, rewriting Soviet history in the process.

In spite of its stature as a serious artistic medium, however, it was as popular art that film had its greatest success. Commercial film-making, based in Hollywood, gave birth to a generation of international superstars such as Mary Pickford (1893–1979), Rudolph Valentino (1895–1926), and Charlie Chaplin (1899–1977). With the advent of "talkies" in 1929, film tended to take on a more national flavour based upon language.

In Germany, there was a final flourish of creativity before freedom of expression was strangled by the Nazis. *The Blue Angel* (1930), which introduced Marlene Dietrich (1901-) to North American film audiences, was typical of what Hitler called "decadent art." Under the Nazis, propaganda films, such as Leni Riefenstahl's (1902-) record of the 1934 Party Congress at Nuremburg, *The Triumph of the Will* (1935) and *Olympia* (1938), a Nazi version of the 1936 Berlin Olympics, were the norm. In Britain and France, however, cinema was not subject to government control.

The 1930s saw a number of innovative French films. Two of the best were the antiwar film *Grand Illusion* (1937) and a satire of prewar French society, *The Rules of the Game* (1939) by Jean Renoir (1894–1979), son of the impressionist painter Pierre Auguste Renoir. In Great Britain, the brilliant director Alfred Hitchcock (1899–1980) made several popular films, including *The Man Who Knew too Much* (1934) and *The Thirty-Nine Steps* (1935) before leaving England in 1939 to pursue his career in Hollywood.

In the United States, musicals and gangster films were the order of the day. The master of the 1930s musical was Busby Berkley (1895–1976). His elaborate production numbers—one scene in *The Gold Diggers of 1933* had 100 blondes playing 100 white pianos—made him the king of extravagance. The gangster film became immensely popular after the success of *Little Caesar* (1931). But by 1934, the National League of Decency had pressured Hollywood into moving away from this genre because it felt that gangster films were corrupting American youth. Hollywood then turned to family films, with child stars such as Shirley Temple (1929-) and Mickey Rooney (1922-). Later Walt Disney's (1901–1966) first feature-length cartoon, *Snow White and the Seven Dwarfs* (1937), set attendance records and won an Academy Award. The decade climaxed with *Gone with the Wind*, which appropriately premiered in Atlanta, Georgia, on 15 December 1939.

Not all of Hollywood's output was escapist froth, however. In 1941, three superb films captured the audience's attention. The film version of John Steinbeck's novel, *The Grapes of Wrath*, won critical acclaim; *Casablanca* is perhaps the most memorable example of films Hollywood turned out in support of the Allied war effort and Orson Wells's (1915–1985) *Citizen Kane*, with its complex structure and technical brilliance, is considered the greatest American film ever produced.

SCIENCE

The first half of the twentieth century saw a series of scientific breakthroughs. Although many discoveries followed along paths already established in the nineteenth century, others, such as Planck's quantum theory and Einstein's theory of relativity, challenged long-held scientific beliefs. The arbitrary divisions between the sciences began to break down and science became more interdisciplinary as discoveries in one branch led to discoveries in another. This was particularly true in physics, which dominated all other sciences in the first half of the twentieth century.

Physics

The revolution in physics began in the 1890s when Wilhelm Roentgen (1845–1923) discovered X-rays. Since Roentgen did not know the nature of the radiation he had discovered, he called it an X-ray, X being the mathematical symbol for an unknown. The first object X-rayed was a human hand. The discovery was soon used to diagnose disease and detect objects in the human body. For his achievement, Roentgen was awarded the first Nobel Prize for Physics in 1901. In the interim, Henri Becquerel (1852–1908) discovered that certain uranium compounds emitted radiation similiar to X-rays after exposure to light. Becquerel's 1896 discovery led to a new field of research—radioactivity.

Before the turn of the century, Marie Curie (1867–1934), assisted by her husband Pierre (1859–1906), discovered two new elements, polonium and radium, that were more radioactive than uranium. These discoveries sparked considerable interest and research in the scientific community. The work of Joseph John Thomson (1856–1940), Ernst Rutherford (1871–1937), Niels Bohr (1885–1962), and Erwin Schrodinger (1887–1961) led to greater understanding of the structure of the atom. Meanwhile, Max Planck's (1858–1947) quantum theory, for which he won the Nobel Prize in 1918, and Albert Einstein's (1879–1955) theory of relativity provided greater understanding of the energy of the atom.

The Quantum Theory

Planck, writing in 1900, described his experimental observations, which had shown that atoms did not give off heat and light energy at a consistent rate at all temperatures. He surmised that such energy must be released in bundles or packets. Planck called such a packet a "quantum" from the Latin "how much." Individual atoms therefore become quite unpredictable in their characteristics. This *quantum theory*, which was a direct blow to Newtonian physics, was so revolutionary that it was not accepted in the world of physics for many years. In fact, it was only when physicists like Albert Einstein (1879–1955) and Niels Bohr (1885–1962) applied the quantum theory to their own work that it was accepted. Einstein won the Nobel Prize in 1921 for the photoelectric effect that applied the quantum theory, while Bohr won the prize in 1922 for using the quantum theory to explain the internal structure of the atom.

The Theory of Relativity

Five years after Planck published his paper on the quantum theory, Albert Einstein published his theory that motion, position, and time were all relative to the position of the observer. According to his *theory of relativity* there were no absolutes, but only relative observations depending upon position. Consider a star burning 100 000 light years away from the earth. When we observe its light through a telescope, we can pass judgment on its brightness and position as we see them. However, because it has taken so long for that light to reach us, the reality of that star, as observed from a spacecraft orbiting it, would be radically different. Which is real? To Einstein, reality depended upon the observer. His observations had a great impact upon a society used to dealing with stability and permanence in the natural world.

Nuclear Fission

In 1934, Enrico Fermi (1901–1954) split the nucleus of the uranium atom. However, this was not recognized as nuclear fission until 1939, when Otto Hahn (1879–1968) and Fritz Strassaman (1902-) conducted a similar experiment. In the same year, Fermi discovered that it was possible to create a chain reaction. Einstein's theory of mass and energy ($E=MC^2$) predicted this would release a huge amount of energy. This led him to inform United States president Franklin Roosevelt of the destructive possibilities of nuclear energy. Roosevelt moved quickly to fund nuclear research in 1940. In 1942, this was escalated into the creation of a research group called the Manhattan Project that would change the course of the world.

Led by J. Robert Oppenheimer (1904–1967), the Manhattan Project was a braintrust of scientists entrusted with the mission of creating the world's first atomic bomb. Their work culminated in 1945 with the creation of three bombs. The first was used for testing at Los Alamos in the New

Mexico desert on July 16th. The remaining two bombs had a much deadlier purpose: to defeat the Japanese in the Second World War. To this end, one atomic bomb was dropped on Hiroshima on 6 August 1945 and another on Nagasaki on 9 August 1945. The death and destruction were unprecedented. Science had produced a devastating weapon that dwarfed all previous weapons. Within a few years the atom bomb itself would be dwarfed by the even more powerful fusion, or hydrogen, bomb.

Chemistry, Biology, and Medical Science

The rediscovery of the work of Gregor Mendel (1822–1884) in 1900 laid the foundation for genetics, the science of heredity. Subsequent research by Thomas Hunt Morgan (1866–1945), who developed the gene theory, and Herman J. Muller (1890–1967), who discovered that mutations could be induced through human intervention, undermined Darwin's principle of natural selection. Subsequent discoveries in genetics provided insights into the nature of inherited

"THE WAR IS WON, BUT THE PEACE IS NOT."

When J. Robert Oppenheimer witnessed the first nuclear explosion, he quoted from the Bhagavadgita*: "I am become death, the destroyer of worlds." This feeling was common among many of the scientists of the Manhattan Project. In the following excerpt from an address delivered to the Fifth Nobel Anniversary Dinner at the Hotel Astor in New York, 10 December 1945, Albert Einstein expressed the concern felt by the physicists who had created the atomic bomb.*

Physicists find themselves in a position not unlike that of Alfred Nobel. Alfred Nobel invented the most powerful explosive ever known up to his time, a means of destruction par excellence. In order to atone for this, in order to relieve his human conscience, he instituted his awards for the promotion of peace and for achievements of peace. Today, the physicists who participated in forging the most formidable and dangerous weapon of all times are harassed by an equal feeling of responsibility, not to say guilt. And we cannot desist from warning, and warning again, we cannot and should not slacken in our efforts to make the nations of the world, and especially their governments, aware of the unspeakable disaster they are certain to provoke unless they change their attitude toward each other and toward the task of shaping the future. We helped in creating this new weapon in order to prevent the enemies of mankind from achieving it ahead of us, which, given the mentality of the Nazis, would have meant inconceivable destruction and the enslavement of the rest of the world. We delivered this weapon into the hands of the American and the British people as trustees of the whole of mankind, as fighters for peace and liberty. But so far we fail to see any guarantee of peace, we do not see any guarantee of the freedoms that were promised to the nations in the Atlantic Charter. The war is won, but the peace is not. . . .

The picture of our postwar world is not bright. So far as we, the physicists, are concerned, we are no politicians and it has never been our wish to meddle in politics. But we know a few things that the politicians do not know. And we feel the duty to speak up and to remind those responsible that there is no escape into easy comforts, there is no distance ahead for proceeding little by little and delaying the necessary changes into an indefinite future, there is no time left for petty bargaining. The situation calls for a courageous effort, for a radical change in our whole attitude, in the entire political concept. May the spirit that prompted Alfred Nobel to create his great institution, the spirit of trust and confidence, of generosity and brotherhood among men, prevail in the minds of those upon whose decisions our destiny rests. Otherwise, human civilization will be doomed.

From Albert Einstein, *Ideas and Opinions*, edited by Carl Seelig, translated and revised by Sonja Bargmann (New York: Bonanza Books, 1954), pp. 115–117.

disease. This was particularly true when further research discovered the master genetic key, dioxyribonucleic acid (DNA) in 1953.

Early in the twentieth century, biochemists made important discoveries into the nature of hormones and vitamins. The pharmaceutical industry exploded with the discovery of antitoxins, antibiotics, and the development of chemotherapy, the treatment of disease by drugs.

The development of antitoxins began in the 1890s when the German bacteriologist, Emil Adolf von Behring (1854–1917), discovered a means of building immunity to tetanus. By the interwar period, diphtheria and tetanus were almost completely eliminated. Yellow fever was added to this list when the microbiologist Max Theiler (1899–1972) developed a vaccine against the disease in 1937. Some diseases, however, resist antitoxins. For these, antibiotics were necessary.

Antibiotics fight disease by inhibiting the growth of bacteria. Their ability to fight diseases such as pneumonia, spinal meningitis, and typhoid fever led to the label "wonder drug." Antibiotics are produced naturally by moulds and bacteria or are synthesized. Initially they were produced in limited quantities in laboratories, but with the advent of the Second World War large-scale production was developed.

Antibiotics were introduced with the accidental discovery of penicillin in 1928 by the Scottish bacteriologist Alexander Fleming (1881–1955). Fleming noticed that a mould that had grown on an uncovered culture had killed the surrounding bacteria. When he isolated the mould he had discovered *penicillum notatum*. Unfortunately, the clinical use of penicillin did not occur until the 1940s when the drug was produced in quantity. In 1932, the first of a growing number of sulfa drugs, Prontosil, was discovered by the German biochemist Gerhard Domagk (1895–1964). Domagk first used the drug on his own daughter to prevent her death from streptococcal infection after other treatments had failed. The discovery of streptomycin in 1940 by the microbiologist Selman Abraham Waksman (1888–1973) was useful in treating bacteria that had resisted treatment by penicillin.

One of the main reasons for the tremendous strides in medicine in the twentieth century was the speed with which the research of biochemists and microbiologists was applied to clinical practice. This was particularly true with research into nutrition and the identification of basic vitamins. Although the connection between diet and health had been made in the eighteenth century when the Scottish physician James Lind (1716–1794) discovered that scurvy could be cured by adding lemons and oranges to the diet, it was not until the twentieth century that the systematic study of nutrition began in earnest. During the 1920s and 1930s, the biochemist Elmer Verner McCollum (1879–1967) isolated vitamins A, B, C, and D and Herbert McLean Evans (1882–1971) isolated vitamin E. This represented a remarkable decade of research and had a profound impact on eradicating diseases such as rickets, pellegra, and beriberi, which were caused by diet deficiencies. The synthetic production of vitamins that began when Tadeus Reichstein (1897-) synthesized vitamin C in 1933, and the hunger and want during the Depression that focused public attention on diet led to the rapid exploitation of these discoveries.

Medical research provided other important breakthroughs in the interwar period. The Canadians Frederick Grant Banting (1891–1941) and Charles Herbert Best (1899–1978) provided a means to control, but not cure, diabetes when they successfully extracted insulin from the pancreas of dogs in 1921. In 1925, the English chemist Robert Robinson (1886–1975) synthesized morphine, a painkiller which was to provide relief to the hundreds of thousands of wounded in the Second World War. Karl Landsteiner (1868–1943) won the Nobel Prize for Medicine in 1930 for identifying the major blood groups: A, B, AB, and O. This discovery made blood transfusions safe and greatly improved a patient's chances of surviving surgery.

Similiar developments occurred in the area of medical apparatus. The electroencephalograph (EEG) assisted the diagnosis of brain tumours and epilepsy. Radioisotopes discovered in atomic research eventually helped trace the course of diseases through the body. A means of mechanical respiration—the iron lung—enabled patients suffering from respiratory paralysis to breathe. This saved many lives, particularly during the polio epidemic in the United States in the 1950s. Alexis Carrell (1873–1944), the Nobel prize-winning scientist, working with Charles Lindbergh (1902–1974), developed a chamber that could keep vital organs alive outside of the body. This "artificial heart" was first used in cardiac surgery in 1935.

Science, Technology, and the Second World War

The need to treat wartime casualties and to maintain a fit fighting force led to several breakthroughs during the war.

Penicillin was not available for large-scale clinical use until the treatment of casualties in the war forced the development of new production techniques. The high incidence of malaria among fighting troops in the Pacific led to the development of the insecticide dichlorodiphenyltrichoroethane (DDT), the herbicide 2,4-dichlorophenoxyacetic acid (2,4-D), and the development of a process to synthesize the antimalarial drug quinine. Until American chemists Robert Burns Woodward (1917–1979) and William von Eggers Deoring (1917-) discovered this process, quinine could be obtained only from cinchona bark and was available in limited quantities.

Just as the development of aircraft and the automobile had been accelerated by the First World War, the Second World War hastened the development of jet aircraft and liquid-fueled rockets. German scientists led the field in both of these areas, developing the Messerschmitt ME 262, the first fully operational turbojet aircraft, and the V–2 rocket. Both of these developments were exploited in the postwar period. The need to co-ordinate aerial defence led to research in the field of computers, which led to the development of a new industry. Similiarly, nuclear research provided a means of generating electrical power.

One trend that emerged during the war was the union of science and technology. Prior to the Second World War, almost all scientific research was conducted by university professors, while the practical application of science to everyday life—technology—was the concern of technicians and engineers. During the war this isolation of the two fields broke down in such megaprojects as the development of radar and the harnessing of nuclear energy and the subsequent development of the atomic bomb. This trend continued in the postwar period when the union of research and technology produced new industries such as computers and consumer electronics.

Another trend that grew out of the megaprojects was the movement toward "big science." The isolated scientist gave way to the research team where each member was a specialist in a narrowly defined field. The poorly equipped laboratory was replaced by large-scale research facilities. In the United States, although some of these facilities were connected with large corporations, they were increasingly maintained through government financing or were part of the military-industrial complex conducting research for military purposes.

THE SOCIAL SCIENCES

Psychoanalysis

An important change in medical science was in the attitude toward and treatment of mental illness. By the nineteenth century, the days of imprisoning the mentally ill had gradually disappeared and the scientific study of insanity had begun. At the turn of the century, the work of Sigmund Freud (1856–1939) revolutionized the way of looking at the human mind through a system of treatment called *psychoanalysis*.

Freud believed that the key to understanding human behaviour lay in understanding the unconscious mind—the *id*. The *id* was driven by aggressive and pleasure-seeking desires; these in turn were controlled by the *ego* (the rationalizing mind) and the *superego* (ingrained moral values). The key to understanding the *id*, and therefore human behaviour, lay in understanding the messages from the unconscious mind free of the controlling influence of the *ego* and the *superego*.

One method used by Freud to understand the unconscious mind was *free association*—that is, saying what immediately comes to mind in response to a prompt. Another was *dream analysis*. By listening to the patient, the psychiatrist could decipher his or her unconscious motivation and when he or she began to accept unconscious thoughts and feelings then they had started on the road to recovery.

Although Freudian theory represented the new trend in psychology, psychoanalysis was not popular in France and was restricted primarily to the German- and English-speaking worlds. Nevertheless, Freud's influence spread far beyond the field of psychiatry into the arts, education, and the social sciences. Among Freud's most influential works were *The Interpretation of Dreams* (1900), *Beyond the Pleasure Principle* (1920), and *The Ego and the Id* (1923).

Freud's theories represented the mainstream in psychology but they did not go unquestioned. Notable challenges came from Alfred Adler (1870–1937) and Carl G. Jung (1875–1961). Adler was the founder of the school of *individual psychology*, which examined the individual's role in the group and stressed a reaction to the inferiority complex rather than Freud's sexual motivation. Jung founded the school of *analytical psychology* and stressed the will to live rather than sex as the motivating factor in human behaviour. It was Jung who coined the terms *introvert* and *extrovert*. In the laboratory,

John B. Watson (1878–1958) laid the foundations for the study of behaviouralism and Ivan Petrovich Pavlov (1849–1936) made important discoveries in conditioning. These findings had sociological implications as the research techniques of psychology were applied to society by sociologists such as Max Weber (1864–1920).

Economic Theory

The theories of John Maynard Keynes (1883–1946) revolutionized economics. Keynes's rise to popularity began with his criticism of the Treaty of Versailles in *The Economic Consequences of the Peace* (1919). He believed that the treaty had created a Carthaginian peace (a peace so severe that it would destroy the defeated country) and warned the peacemakers that it would create "such strains in the European structure and letting loose such human and spiritual forces as, pushing beyond frontiers and races, will overwhelm not only you and your 'guarantees' but your institutions, and the existing order of your society." The problems related to the economic aspects of the treaty, particularly over reparations, confirmed his economic insight.

The basic elements of Keynes's economic theory were introduced in his major work, *The General Theory of Employment, Interest and Money*, published in 1936 at the depth of the Depression. Keynes stressed *macroeconomics* (the analysis of the economy as a whole), particularly the causes and results of changes in spending and income. He believed that government manipulation of interest rates, monetary supply, public investment, and public works during the depression phase of a business cycle would stimulate spending and create investment. This theory was welcomed with open arms in the United States, where it seemed to justify the newly expanded role played by the federal government. Keynes's theories gained more widespread acceptance in Europe after the Second World War, when increased government involvement in the economy was necessary to coordinate recovery efforts.

The Study of History

This period saw several discoveries that began to uncover the path of human evolution. In 1924, Raymond Dart (1893–1988) discovered the Taung Baby, the first example of *Australopithecus Africanus*—the southern (Australo) ape (pithecus) from Africa. This discovery moved the evolutionary timetable back 3 million years. A second type of australopithecine, *Australopithecus Robustus*, was discovered by Robert Broom (1866–1951) in 1938. The Steinheim skull, found in 1933, and the Swanscombe skull, found in 1935, placed Neanderthal beings on an evolutionary offshoot that led to extinction rather than along the direct line of descent to

THE PILTDOWN FOSSIL HOAX

In 1912, an amateur scientist, Charles Dawson, reported finding parts of a skull and jawbone in a gravel pit near Piltdown Common in Sussex, England. Sir Kenneth Clark, the most prominent British anthropologist of the day, reconstructed the skull and pronounced it authentic. He named the find *Eoanthropus dawsoni* (Dawson's dawn fossil) after the man who had found it. Sir Arthur Smith Woodward of the British Museum also vouched for its authenticity.

But the Piltdown fossil conflicted with the fossil record. Previous finds indicated that prehistoric humans had a smaller brain than modern humans. The Piltdown fossil had a brain capacity similiar to modern humans despite being several hundred thousand years old. The jaw of the Piltdown fossil was very apelike, except for its molars, which had flat grinding surfaces similiar to those of modern humans. A human skull and an apelike jaw—was this the missing link between modern humans and the apes? The controversy raged on for forty years.

In 1953, the Piltdown fossil was revealed to be a deliberate hoax. Fragments of a modern skull (radiocarbon tests dated the skull at 1230 A.D.) and the jaw of an ape, altered by filing the molars, had been "seeded" into the gravel pit along with several extinct mammal fossils. In the absence of reliable dating techniques, it was the authentic mammal fossils which were used to authenticate the Piltdown fossil. The desire for the find to be real allowed cursory examination to overcome careful scientific study. Who perpetrated the fraud? Despite two exhaustive studies—J.S. Weiner's, *The Piltdown Forgery* (1955) and Ronald Miller's, *The Piltdown Men* (1972)—absolute blame cannot be established. The likely candidate, Charles Dawson, died before the hoax was revealed.

modern humans, as had long been believed. Many researchers, however, continued to dispute these findings and it was not until the work of the Leakey family (Louis [1903–1972], Mary [1913-], and Richard [1944-]), and Don Johanson (1943-) in the 1960s and 1970s that many of these early findings were confirmed.

Historians appeared to be preoccupied with theories of decline between 1918 and 1945. Oswald Spengler's (1880–1936) *The Decline of the West* became a bestseller after its publication in 1918. Spengler proposed that civilization was subject to natural laws and so experienced a cycle of youth, maturity, and old age. As the title suggested, Spengler's views of the postwar West were not optimistic. He believed that Western civilization was already in its old age and that the cycle was about to be completed.

Arnold Toynbee (1889–1975) also believed that Western civilization had passed its prime and was experiencing "a time of troubles." Toynbee analysed the courses of different civilizations and developed his theories in a multivolume work entitled *A Study of History*, written between 1934 and 1954. Unlike Spengler, however, Toynbee believed that Western civilization could be revitalized through a return to ethical and moral values and a renewal of Western creativity.

It was Toynbee who observed that historical study had to be divided into intelligible units. It was pointless, he claimed, to study the history of a single nation or, on the other hand, to consider humanity as a whole. For Toynbee, humanity was divided into certain regional/cultural groupings or societies. His study was of one such society, Western civilization. In one section of his work, Toynbee criticizes Spengler's attempt to compare the vitality of one civilization with another.

> Some recent Western writers, more particularly Spengler, have pursued this subject of the 'characters' of the different civilizations to a point at which sober diagnosis passes over into arbitrary fantasy. . . .
>
> We [Toynbee and the reader] have compared our civilizations to rock-climbers, and on the showing of this simile the several climbers, though they are certainly separate individuals, are all engaged on an identical enterprise. They are all attempting to scale the face of the same cliff from the same starting-point on a ledge below towards the same goal on a ledge above. The underlying unity is apparent here; and it appears again if we vary our simile and think of the growths of civilizations in terms of the Parable of the Sower. The seeds sown are separate seeds, and each seed has its own destiny. Yet the seeds are all of one kind; they are all sown by one Sower in the hope of obtaining one harvest.
>
> From Arnold J. Toynbee, *A Study of History* (London: Oxford University Press, 1946), pp. 242–243.

Philosophy and Religion in the Age of Anxiety

It is not suprising that in this period of insecurity and anxiety many people turned to religion. Despite the influence of Freud, who believed that religion was an illusion, atheism no longer attracted many converts. In fact, the opposite was true as more and more people became reacquainted with Christianity. This led to a modest religious revival. However, over the long-term the influence and popularity of the Church continued its downward trend. This was especially true in the Soviet Union, where the Orthodox church gradually succumbed to communist pressure and the spread of communism post–1945 led to the disestablishment of churches in Eastern Europe.

The conflict between religion and natural science that had grown wider as a result of the discoveries of the nineteenth century remained unresolved in the twentieth century. But the rapid scientific advances did not heighten this conflict. Churches, in particular the Protestant church, began to reassess their religious thought so that their doctrine did not contradict science.

Two radically different philosophical schools dominated the first half of the twentieth century. *Existentialism* was the abstract one of the two; *logical positivism* (or logical empiricism, as it was sometimes called) was more analytical.

One of the foundations of logical positivism was Ludwig Wittgenstein's (1889–1951) *Essay on Logical Philosophy* (1922). Wittgenstein rejected most of the concerns of traditional philosophy, insisting that only that which could be verified through mathematical or symbolic logic was worth discussing. For Wittgenstein, philosophy was based on the principle of verification: "To understand a proposition means to know what is the case if it is true." This principle radically restricted the domain of philosophical discourse and might explain why it was not popular on the European continent, although it became the mainstream of British and American philosophy. In Europe, the dominant philosophy was existentialism.

Existentialist philosophers rejected the objectivity of the scientist. For them, only the subjective consciousness of the individual was worth studying. Although the philosophy of personal existence can be traced to the work of the Danish philosopher Sören Kierkegaard (1813–1855), twentieth-century existentialism can be attributed to the work of the German philosopher Martin Heidegger (1889–1976) and his student Jean-Paul Sartre (1905–1980). Sartre's *Being and Nothingness* (1943), written while a prisoner of the Germans during the Second World War, was responsible for awakening public interest in existentialism after the war. (See readings.)

Existentialists asked certain fundamental questions, "Is there anything of which we can be certain?," or what Heidegger called the basic question of metaphysics, "Why is there something rather than nothing?" At a time of political collapse and social and economic uncertainty, the bleak outlook of existentialism was attractive to many Europeans. (Also see chapter 15.)

RETROSPECTIVE

Many of the intellectual and cultural trends associated with the Lost Generation—increasing pessimism and doubt about Western civilization; the application of modern psychological and sociological approaches to painting, literature, poetry, architecture, sculpture, and music; and the rejection of tradition, rules, and inhibitions—were all evident before the First World War. The effect of the war was to accelerate the spread of these ideas among the intellectual community.

One of the most striking trends in the 1918 to 1945 period was the apparent separation of the elite from the masses. People were far more familiar with Chaplin, Pickford, and Valentino than they were with Kafka, Joyce, and Eliot. The discovery of King Tut's tomb in 1922 and Lindberg's solo transatlantic flight generated far more interest than the discovery of insulin and the publication of Heidegger's *Being and Time*, which occurred in the same years. The popularity of fads, crazes, popular songs, sports heroes, and the other paraphernalia of developing modern mass culture appeared to confirm Ortega's thesis about the collapse of civilized traditions. However, there had always been a gap between the intellectual and the masses. The spread of literacy as a result of education, an increase in disposable income, and greater leisure time coincided with the development of radio and the motion picture. The result was a qualitative change in popular culture. Increasingly, culture was international and, as the United States assumed a more dominant role in world affairs, increasingly American influenced.

The increased liberalization in the arts contrasted sharply with the decline in liberalism in politics and economics. Intellectual and cultural trends were blunted by censorship and repression in fascist and communist countries and the preparation for, and participation in, the Second World War. As a result, the experimentation in the arts did not produce a new consensus in taste between 1918 and 1945 and the trends evident in the intellectual community did not penetrate popular culture until after the Second World War.

THE DEVELOPMENT OF MODERN ART

Dadaism and surrealism are two of the artistic trends that developed after the First World War. Tristan Tzara attempted to define dadaism in a Dada Manifesto *written in 1918.*

From Arthur Haberman, *The Modern Age: Ideas in Western Civilization* (Toronto: Gage Educational Publishing Co., 1987), p. 335.

Every product of disgust apt to become a negation of the family, is *dada*; protest with the fists of all of one's being in destructive action: DADA; knowledge of all the means up to now rejected by the sex chaste with facile compromise and manners: DADA; abolition of logic, dance of the impotents of creation: DADA; of all hierarchy and social equation set up for the values by our valets: DADA; every object, all the objects, the sentiments and the obscurities, the phantoms and the precise clash of parallel lines, are means in our struggle: DADA; abolition of memory: DADA; abolition of archaeology: DADA; abolition of prophets: DADA; abolition of the future: DADA; absolute undisputable belief in every god that is the immediate product of spontaneity: DADA; elegant and unprejudiced leap from one harmony to the other sphere; trajectory of a word cast like an emphatic record cry; respect of all individualities in their monetary folly: serious, timorous, timid, ardent, forceful, decisive, enthusiastic; stripping one's church of all heavy and useless accessories; spitting out like a luminous cascade the unkindly or loving thought, or pampering it—with the lively satisfaction of knowing that it doesn't matter either way—with the same intensity in the thicket, unblemished by insects for the wellborn blood, and gilded by bodies of archangels, of one's soul. Liberty: DADA DADA DADA, shriek of the shriveled colors, blending of the contraries and of all the contradictions, the grotesqueries, the inconsistencies: LIFE.

André Breton (1896–1966) defined surrealism in a Manifesto of Surrealism *in 1924.*

From André Breton, *Manifestos of Surrealism* (Ann Arbor: University of Michigan Press, 1972), p. 26.

SURREALISM, *n.* Psychic automatism in its pure state, by which one proposes to express—verbally, by means of the written word, or in any other manner—the actual functioning of thought. Dictated by thought, in the absence of any control exercised by reason, exempt from any aesthetic or moral concern.
ENCYCLOPEDIA. *Philosophy.* Surrealism is based on the belief in the superior reality of certain forms of previously neglected associations, in the omnipotence of dream, in the disinterested play of thought. It tends to ruin once and for all the other psychic mechanisms and to substitute itself for them in solving all the principal problems of life. . . .

---

1. Outline the similarities and differences between dadaism and surrealism.

2. How do dada and surrealist painters differ from the impressionists?

T.S. ELIOT: "The Hollow Men" (1925)

T.S. Eliot was one of the most influential poets writing in the English language in the first half of the twentieth century. "The Hollow Men," like his poem "The Waste Land" (1922), represents a pessimistic view of Western civilization.

* A saying used by children on Guy Fawkes night.
From Desmond Pacey (ed.), *Our Literary Heritage* (Toronto: McGraw-Hill Ryerson Ltd., 1967, 1982), pp. 466–467.

The Hollow Men

*A penny for the old guy**

I

We are the hollow men
We are the stuffed men
Leaning together
Headpiece filled with straw. Alas!
Our dried voices, when
We whisper together
Are quiet and meaningless
As wind in dry grass
Or rats' feet over broken glass
In our dry cellar.

Shape without form, shade without color,
Paralyzed force, gesture without motion;

Those who have crossed
With direct eyes, to death's other Kingdom
Remember us—if at all—not as lost
Violent souls, but only
As the hollow men
The stuffed men.

II

Eyes I dare not meet in dreams
In death's dream kingdom
These do not appear:
There, the eyes are
Sunlight on a broken column
There, is a tree swinging
And voices are
In the wind's singing
More distant and more solemn
Than a fading star.

Let me be no nearer
In death's dream kingdom
Let me also wear
Such deliberate disguises
Rat's skin, crowskin, crossed staves
In a field
Behaving as the wind behaves
No nearer—

Not that final meeting
In the twilight kingdom.

III

This is the dead land
This is cactus land
Here the stone images
Are raised, here they receive
The supplication of a dead man's hand
Under the twinkle of a fading star.

Is it like this
In death's other kingdom
Walking alone
At the hour when we are
Trembling with tenderness
Lips that would kiss
Form prayers to broken stone.

IV

The eyes are not here
There are no eyes here
In this valley of dying stars
In this hollow valley
This broken jaw of our lost kingdoms

In this last of meeting places
We grope together
And avoid speech
Gathered on this beach of the tumid river

Sightless, unless
The eyes reappear
As the perpetual star
Multifoliate rose
Of death's twilight kingdom
The hope only
Of empty men.

V

Here we go round the prickly pear
Prickly pear prickly pear
Here we go round the prickly pear
At five o'clock in the morning.

Between the idea
And the reality
Between the motion
And the act
Falls the Shadow

For Thine is the Kingdom

Between the conception
And the creation
Between the emotion
And the response
Falls the Shadow

Life is very long

Between the desire
And the spasm
Between the potency
And the existence
Between the essence
And the descent
Falls the Shadow

For Thine is the Kingdom

For Thine is
Life is
For Thine is the

This is the way the world ends
This is the way the world ends
This is the way the world ends
Not with a bang but a whimper.

---

1. What is the intent of Eliot's imagery?

2. In what ways does the poem represent what other intellectuals felt about life in the 1920s?

FRANZ KAFKA:
The Trial (1937)

Only a fraction of Kafka's (1883–1924) work was published during his lifetime. His most famous novels The Trial, The Castle, *and* America, *were all published posthumously. In* The Trial, *the solitary central character finds himself under arrest by some mysterious and overwhelming power and cannot discover the nature of the charge against him.*

On the evening before K.'s thirty-first birthday—it was about nine o'clock, the time when a hush falls on the streets—two men came to his lodging. In frock coats, pallid and plump, with top hats that were apparently irremovable. After some exchange of formalities regarding precedence at the front door, they repeated the same ceremony more elaborately before K.'s door. Without having been informed of their visit, K. was sitting also dressed in black in an armchair near the door, slowly pulling on a pair of new gloves that fitted tightly over the fingers, looking as if he were expecting guests. He stood up at once and scrutinized the gentlemen with curiosity. "So you are meant for me?" he asked. The gentlemen bowed, each indicating the other with the hand that held the top hat. K. admitted to himself that he had been expecting different visitors. He went to the window and took another look at the dark street. Nearly all the windows at the other side of the street were also in darkness; in many of them the curtains were drawn. At one lighted tenement window some babies were playing behind bars, reaching with their little hands toward each other although not able to move themselves from the spot. "Tenth-rate old actors they send for me," said K. to himself, glancing round again to confirm the impression. "They want to finish me off cheaply." He turned abruptly toward the men and asked: "What theater are you playing at?" "Theater?" said one, the corners of his mouth twitching as he looked for advice to the other, who acted as if he were a dumb man struggling to overcome a stubborn disability. "They're not prepared to answer questions," said K. to himself and went to fetch his hat.

While still on the stairs the two of them tried to take K. by the arms, and he said: "Wait till we're in the street, I'm not an invalid." But just outside the street door they fastened on him in a fashion he had never before experienced. They kept their shoulders close behind his and instead of crooking their elbows, wound their arms round his at full length, holding his hands in a methodical, practiced, irresistible grip. K. walked rigidly between them, the three of them were interlocked in a unity which would have brought all three down together had one of them been knocked over. It was a unity such as can hardly be formed except by lifeless matter.

Under the street lamps K. attempted time and time again, difficult though it was at such very close quarters, to see his companions more clearly than had been possible in the dusk of his room. "Perhaps they are tenors," he thought, as he studied their fat double chins. He was repelled by the painful cleanliness of their faces. One could literally see that the cleansing hand had been at work in the corners of the eyes, rubbing the upper lip, scrubbing out the furrows at the chin.

When that occurred to K. he halted, and in consequence the others halted too; they stood on the verge of an open, deserted square adorned with flower beds. "Why did they send you, of all people!" he said; it was more a cry than a question. The gentlemen obviously had no answer to make, they stood waiting with their free arms hanging, like sickroom attendants waiting while their patient takes a rest. "I won't go any farther," said K. experimentally. No answer was needed to that. It was sufficient that the two men did not loosen their grip and tried to propel K.

from the spot; but he resisted them. "I shan't need my strength much longer, I'll expend all the strength I have," he thought. Into his mind came a recollection of flies struggling away from the flypaper till their little legs were torn off. "The gentlemen won't find it easy."

And then before them Fraulein Burstner appeared, mounting a small flight of steps leading into the square from a low-lying side-street. It was not quite certain that it was she, but the resemblance was close enough. Whether it were really Fraulein Burstner or not, however, did not matter to K.; the important thing was that he suddenly realized the futility of resistance. There would be nothing heroic in it were he to resist, to make difficulties for his companions, to snatch at the last appearance of life by struggling. He set himself in motion, and the relief his warders felt was transmitted to some extent even to himself. They suffered him now to lead the way, and he followed the direction taken by the girl ahead of him, not that he wanted to overtake her or to keep her in sight as long as possible, but only that he might not forget the lesson she had brought into his mind. "The only thing I can do now," he told himself, and the regular correspondence between his steps and the steps of the other two confirmed his thought,the only thing for me to go on doing is to keep my intelligence calm and analytical to the end. I always wanted to snatch at the world with twenty hands, and not for a very laudable motive, either. That was wrong, and am I to show now that not even a year's trial has taught me anything? Am I to leave this world as a man who has no common sense? Are people to say of me after I am gone that at the beginning of my case I wanted to finish it, and at the end of it I wanted to begin it again? I don't want that to be said. I am grateful for the fact that these half-dumb, senseless creatures have been sent to accompany me on this journey, and that I have been left to say to myself all that is needed."

Fraulein Burstner meanwhile had gone round the bend into a side-street, but by this time K. could do without her and submitted himself to the guidance of his escort. In complete harmony all three now made their way across a bridge in the moonlight, the two men readily yielded to K.'s slightest movement, and when he turned slightly toward the parapet they turned, too, in a solid front. The water, glittering and trembling in the moonlight, divided on either side of a small island, on which the foliage of trees and bushes rose in thick masses, as if bunched together. Beneath the trees ran gravel paths, now invisible, with convenient benches on which K. had stretched himself at ease many a summer. "I didn't mean to stop," he said to his companions, shamed by their obliging compliance. Behind K.'s back the one seemed to reproach the other gently for the mistaken stop they had made, and then all three went on again.

They passed through several steeply rising streets, in which policemen stood or patrolled at intervals; sometimes a good way off, sometimes quite near. One with a bushy mustache, his hand on the hilt of his saber, came up as of set purpose close to the not quite harmless-looking group. The two gentlemen halted, the policeman seemed to be already opening his mouth, but K. forcibly pulled his companions forward. He kept looking round cautiously to see if the policeman were following; as soon as he had put a corner between himself and the policeman he started to run, and his two companions, scant of breath as they were, had to run beside him.

So they came quickly out of the town, which at this point merged almost without transition into the open fields. A small stone quarry, deserted and desolate, lay quite near to a still completely urban house. Here the two men came to a standstill, whether because this place had been their goal from the very beginning or because they were too exhausted to go farther. Now they loosened their hold of K., who stood waiting dumbly, took off the top hats and wiped the sweat from their brows with pocket handkerchiefs, meanwhile surveying the quarry. The moon shone down on everything with that simplicity and serenity which no other light possesses.

After an exchange of courteous formalities regarding which of them was to take precedence in the next task—these emissaries seemed to have been given no specfic assignments in the charge laid jointly upon them—one of them came up to K. and removed his coat, his waistcoat, and finally his shirt. K. shivered involuntarily, whereupon the man gave him a light, reassuring pat on the back. Then he folded the clothes carefully together, as if they were likely to be used again at some time, although perhaps not immediately. Not to leave K. standing motionless, exposed to the night breeze, which was rather chilly, he took him by the arm and walked him up and down a little, while his partner investigated the quarry to find a suitable spot. When he had found it he beckoned, and K.'s companion led him over there. It was a spot near the cliffside where a loose boulder was lying. The two of them laid K. down on the ground, propped him against the boulder, and settled his head upon it. But in spite of the pains they took and all the willingness K. showed, his posture remained contorted and unnatural-looking. So one of the men begged the other to let him dispose K. all by himself, yet even that did not improve matters. Finally they left K. in a position which was not even the best of the positions they had already tried out. Then one of them opened his frock coat and out of a sheath that hung from a belt girt round his waistcoat drew a long, thin, double-edged butcher's knife, held it up, and tested the cutting edges in the moonlight. Once more the odious courtesies began, the first handed the knife across K. to the second, who handed it across K. back again to the first. K. now perceived clearly that he was supposed to seize the knife himself, as it traveled from hand to hand above him, and plunge it into his own breast. But he did not do so, he merely turned his head, which was still free to move, and gazed around him. He could not completely rise to the occasion, he could not relieve the officials of all their tasks; the responsibility for this last failure of his lay with him who had not left him the remnant of strength necessary for the deed. His glance fell on the top story of the house adjoining the quarry. With a flicker as of a light going up, the casements of a window there suddenly flew open; a human figure, faint and insubstantial at that distance and that height, leaned abruptly far forward and stretched both arms still farther. Who was it? A friend? A good man? Someone who sympathized? Someone who wanted to help? Was it one person only? Or was it mankind? Was help at hand? Were there arguments in his favour that had been overlooked? Of course there must be. Logic is doubtless unshakable, but it cannot withstand a man who wants to go on living. Where was the Judge whom he had never seen? Where was the High Court, to which he had never penetrated? He raised his hands and spread out all his fingers.

But the hands of one of the partners were already at K.'s throat, while the other thrust the knife deep into his heart and turned it there twice. With failing eyes K. could still see the two of them immediately before him, cheek leaning against cheek, watching the final act. "Like a dog!" he said; it was as if the shame of it must outlive him.

---

1. (a) What is the theme of *The Trial*?
(b) How does Kafka establish the theme?

2. Is *The Trial* an existentialist novel? Why or why not?

JOSÉ ORTEGA Y GASSET: The Revolt of the Masses (1929)

Ortega was a Spanish philosopher who sought to establish the ultimate reality. His Revolt of the Masses, *in which he argued that an intellectual minority must direct the masses or else chaos would result, gained him worldwide attention.*

No one knows towards what centre human things are going to gravitate in the near future, and hence the life of the world has become scandalously provisional. Everything that to-day is done in public and private—even in one's inner conscience—is provisional, the only exception being certain portions of certain sciences. He will be a wise man who puts no trust in all that is proclaimed, upheld, essayed, and lauded at the present day. All that will disappear as quickly as it came. All of it, from the mania for physical sports (the mania, not the sport themselves) to political violence; from "new art" to sun-baths at idiotic fashionable watering-places. Nothing of all that has any roots; it is all pure invention, in the bad sense of the word, which makes it equivalent to fickle caprice. It is not a creation based on the solid substratum of life; it is not a genuine impulse or need. In a word, from the point of view of life it is false. . . .

The European cannot live unless embarked upon some great unifying enterprise. When this is lacking, he becomes degraded, grows slack, his soul is paralysed. We have a commencement of this before our eyes to-day. The groups which up to to-day have been known as nations arrived about a century ago at their highest point of expansion. Nothing more can be done with them except lead them to a higher evolution. They are now mere past accumulating all around Europe, weighing it down, imprisoning it. With more vital freedom than ever, we feel that we cannot breathe the air within our nations, because it is a confined air. What was before a nation open to all winds of heaven, has turned into something provincial, an enclosed space.

Everyone sees the need of a new principle of life. But as always happens in similiar crises—some people attempt to save the situation by an artifical intensification of the very principle which has led to decay. This is the meaning of the "nationalist" outburst of recent years. And, I repeat, things have always gone that way. The last flare, the longest; the last sigh, the deepest. On the very eve of their disappearance there is an intensification of frontiers—military and economic.

But all these nationalisms are so many blind alleys. Try to project one into the future and see what happens. There is no outlet that way. Nationalism is always an effort in a direction opposite to that of the principle which creates nations. The former is exclusive in tendency, the latter inclusive. In periods of consolidation, nationalism has a positive value, and is a lofty standard. But in Europe everything is more than consolidated, and nationalism is nothing but a mania, a pretext to escape the necessity of inventing something new, some great enterprise. Its primitive methods of action and the type of men it exalts reveal abundantly that it is the opposite of historical creation.

Only the determination to construct a great nation from the group of peoples of the Continent would give new life to the pulse of Europe. She would start to believe in herself again, and automatically to make demands on, to discipline, herself. But the situation is much more difficult than is generally realised. The years are passing and there is the risk that the European will grow accustomed to the lower tone of the existence he is at present living, will get used neither to rule others nor to rule himself. In such a case, all his virtues and higher capacities would vanish into air.

. . . Europe has been left without a moral code. It is not that the mass-man has thrown over an antiquated one in exchange for a new one, but that at the centre of his scheme of life there is precisely the aspiration to live without conforming to any moral code. Do not believe a word you hear from the young when they talk about the "new morality." I absolutely deny that there exists to-day in any corner of the Continent a group inspired by a new *ethos* which shows signs of being a moral code. When people talk of the "new morality" they are merely committing a new immorality and looking for a way of introducing contraband goods. Hence it would be a piece of ingenuousness to accuse the man of to-day of his lack of moral code. The accusation would leave him cold, or rather, would flatter him. Immoralism has become commonplace, and anybody and everybody boasts of practising it. . . .

It will not do, then, to dignify the actual crisis by presenting it as the conflict between two moralities, two civilisations, one in decay, the other at its dawn. The mass-man is simply without morality, which is always, in essence, a sentiment of submission to something, a consciousness of service and obligation. But perhaps it is a mistake to say "simply." For it is not merely a question of this type of creature doing without morality. No, we must not make his task too easy. Morality cannot be eliminated without more ado. What, by a word lacking even in grammar, is called *amorality* is a thing that does not exist. If you are unwilling to submit to any norm, you have, *nolens volens*, to submit to the norm of denying all morality, and that is not amoral, but immoral. How has it been possible to believe in the amorality of life? Doubtless, because all modern culture and civilisation tend to that conviction. Europe is now reaping the painful results of her spiritual conduct. She has adopted blindly a culture which is magnificent, but has no roots.

---

1. (a) Why does Ortega believe that European civilization is bankrupt?
(b) What does he believe is the solution to the problem?

2. (a) What is Ortega's evaluation of nationalism in the twentieth century?
(b) What events lend credence to his evaluation?

3. In your opinion, what would Ortega think about the recent trends in European economic and political affairs? Defend your answer.

SIGMUND FREUD:
Civilization and its Discontents (1930)

In Civilization and Its Discontents, *Freud extended his theories about psychoanalysis from the individual to civilization itself. The impact of his work went beyond medicine and psychotherapy; it also profoundly influenced literature, religion, and education.*

From *The Standard Edition of the Complete Psychological Works of Sigmund Freud*, translated by James Strachey, Vol. XXI (London: The Hogarth Press, 1961), pp. 141–145.

The analogy between the process of civilization and the path of individual development may be extended in an important respect. It can be asserted that the community, too, evolves a super-ego under whose influence cultural development proceeds. It would be a tempting task for anyone who has a knowledge of human civilizations to follow out this analogy in detail. I will confine myself to bringing forward a few striking points. The super-ego of an epoch of civilization has an origin similar to that of an individual. It is based on the impression left behind by the personalities of great leaders—men of overwhelming force of mind or men in whom one of the human impulsions has found its strongest and purest, and therefore often its most one-sided, expression. In many instances the analogy goes still further, in that during their lifetime these figures were—often enough, even if not always—mocked and maltreated by others and even despatched in a cruel fashion. In the same way, indeed, the primal father did not attain divinity until long after he had met his death by violence. The most arresting example of this fateful conjunction is to be seen in the figure of Jesus Christ—if, indeed, that figure is not part of mythology, which called it into being from an obscure memory of that primal event. Another point of agreement between the cultural and the individual super-ego is that the former, just like the latter, sets up strict ideal demands, disobedience to which is visited with "fear of conscience." Here, indeed, we come across the remarkable circumstance that the mental processes concerned are actually more familiar to us and more accessible to consciousness as they are seen in the group than they can be in the individual man. In him, when tension arises, it is only the aggressiveness of the super-ego which, in the form of reproaches, makes itself noisily heard; its actual demands often remain unconscious in the background. If we bring them to conscious knowledge, we find that they coincide with the precepts of the prevailing cultural super-ego. At this point the two processes, that of the cultural development of the group and that of the cultural development of the individual, are, as it were, always interlocked. For that reason some of the manifestations and properties of the super-ego can be more easily detected in its behaviour in the cultural community than in the separate individual.

The cultural super-ego has developed its ideal and set up demands. Among the latter, those which deal with the relations of human beings to one another comprised under the heading of ethics. People have at all times set the greatest value on ethics, as though they expected that it in particular would produce especially important results. And it does in fact deal with a subject which can easily be recognized as the sorest spot in every civilization. Ethics is thus to be regarded as a therapeutic attempt—as an endeavour to achieve, by means of a command of the super-ego, something which has so far not been achieved by means of any other cultural activities. As we already know, the problem before us is how to get rid of the greatest hindrance to civilization—namely, the constitutional inclination of human beings to be aggressive towards one another; and for that reason we are especially interested in what is probably the most recent of the cultural commands of the super-ego, the commandment to love one's neighbour as oneself. In our research into, and therapy of, a neurosis, we are led to make two reproaches against the super-ego of the individual. In the severity of its commands and prohibitions it troubles itself too little with the happiness of the ego, in that it takes insufficient account of the resistances against obeying them—of the instinctual strength of the id (in the first place), and of the difficulties presented by the real external environment (in the second). Consequently we are often obliged, for therapeutic purposes, to oppose the super-ego, and we endeavour to lower its demands. Exactly the same objections can be made against the ethical demands of the cultural super-ego. It, too, does not trouble itself enough about the facts of the mental constitution of human beings. It issues a command and does not ask whether it is possible for people to obey it. On the contrary, it assumes that a man's ego is psychologically capable of doing anything that is required of it, that his ego has unlimited mastery over his id. This is a mistake; and even in what are known as normal people the id cannot be controlled beyond certain limits. If more is demanded of a man, a revolt will be produced in him or a neurosis, or he will be made unhappy. The commandment, "Love thy neighbour as thyself," is the strongest defence against human aggressiveness and an excellent example of the unpsychological proceedings of the cultural super-ego. The commandment is impossible to fulfill; such an enormous inflation of love can only lower its value, not get rid of the difficulty. Civilization pays no attention to all this; it merely admonishes us that the harder it is to obey the precept the more meritorious it is to do so. . . .

. . . It is very far from my intention to express an opinion upon the value of human civilization. I have endeavoured to guard myself against the enthusiastic prejudice which holds that our civilization is the most precious thing that we possess or could acquire and that its path will necessarily lead to heights of unimagined perfection. . . . My impartiality is made all the easier to me by my knowing very little about all these things. One thing only do I know for certain and that is that man's judgements of value follow directly his wishes for happiness—that, accordingly, they are an attempt to support his illusions with arguments. . . .

The fateful question for the human species seems to me to be whether and to what extent their cultural development will succeed in mastering the disturbance of their communal by the human instinct of aggression and self-destruction. It may be that in this respect precisely the present time deserves a special interest. Men have gained control over the forces of nature to such an extent that with their help they would have no difficulty in exterminating one another to the last man. They know this, and hence comes a large part of their current unrest, their unhappiness and their mood of anxiety. And now it is to be expected that the other of the two 'Heavenly Powers,' eternal Eros, will make an effort to assert himself in the struggle with his equally immortal adversary. But who can foresee with what success and with what result? . . .

---

1. What analogies does Freud draw between the individual and the community super-egos?

2. According to Freud, what is the greatest hindrance to civilization? Why?

3. In your opinion, to what extent is Freud's thought a manifestation of the cultural super-ego of the period?

JEAN-PAUL SARTRE: Being and Nothingness (1943)

Sartre was one of the major existentialist philosophers of the era. He believed that there is no God and no human nature, and that therefore the individual is totally free and entirely responsible for his/her life. He expressed these beliefs in Being and Nothingness.

From Jean-Paul Sartre, *Being and Nothingness*, translated by Hazel E. Barnes (New York: Washington Square Press, 1969), pp. 707–711.

Although the considerations which are about to follow are of interest primarily to the ethicist, it may nevertheless be worthwhile after these descriptions and arguments to return to the freedom of the for-itself and to try to understand what the fact of this freedom represents for human destiny.

The essential consequence of our earlier remarks is that man being condemned to be free carries the weight of the whole world on his shoulders; he is responsible for the world and for himself as a way of being. We are taking the word "responsibility" in its ordinary sense as "consciousness (of) being the incontestable author of an event or of an object." In this sense the responsibility of the for-itself is overwhelming since he is the one whom it happens that *there is* a world; since he is also the one who makes himself be, then whatever may be the situation in which he finds himself, the for-itself must wholly assume this situation with its peculiar coefficient of adversity, even though it be insupportable. He must assume the situation with the proud consciousness of being the author of it, for the very worst disadvantages or the worst threats which can endanger my person have meaning only in and through my project; and it is on the ground of the engagement which I am that they appear. It is therefore senseless to think of complaining since nothing foreign has decided what we feel, what we live, or what we are.

Furthermore this absolute responsibility is not resignation; it is simply the logical requirement of the consequences of our freedom. What happens to me happens through me, and can neither affect myself with it nor revolt against it nor resign myself to it. Moreover everything which happens to me is *mine*. By this we must understand first of all that I am always equal to what happens to me *qua* man, for what happens to a man through other men and through himself can be only human. The most terrible situations of war, the worst tortures do not create a non-human state of things; there is no non-human situation. It is only through fear, flight, and recourse to magical types of conduct that I shall decide on the non-human, but this decision is human, and I shall carry the entire responsibility for it. But in addition the situation is *mine* because it is the image of my free choice of myself, and everything which it presents to me is *mine* in that this represents me and symbolizes me. It is not I who decide the coefficient of adversity in things and even their unpredictability by deciding myself?

Thus there are no *accidents* in a life; a community event which suddenly bursts forth and involves me in it does not come from the outside. If I am mobilized in a war, this war is *my* war; it is in my image and I deserve it. I deserve it first because I could always get out of it by suicide or by desertion; these ultimate possibilities are those which must always be present for us when there is a question of envisaging a situation. For the lack of getting out of it, I have *chosen* it. . . .

But in addition the war is *mine* because by the sole fact that it arises in a situation which I cause to be and that I can discover it there only by engaging myself for or against it, I can no longer distinguish at the present the choice which I make of myself from the choice which I make of the war. To live this war is to choose myself through it and to choose it through my choice of myself. There can be no question of considering it as "four years of vacation" or as a "repreive," as a "recess," the essential part of my responsibilities being elsewhere in my married,

Jean-Paul Sartre declined to accept the Nobel Prize for Literature in 1964.

family, or professional life. In this war which I have chosen I choose myself from day to day, and I make it mine by making myself. If it is going to be four empty years, then it is I who bear the responsibility for this.

Finally, as we pointed out earlier, each person is an absolute choice of self from the standpoint of a world of knowledges and of techniques which this choice both assumes and illumines; each person is an absolute upsurge at an absolute date and is perfectly unthinkable at another date. It is therefore a waste of time to ask what I should have been if this war had not broken out, for I have chosen myself as one of the possible meanings of the epoch which imperceptibly led to war. I am not distinct from this same epoch; I could not be transported to another epoch without contradiction. Thus *I am* this war which restricts and limits and makes comprehensible the period which preceded it. . . .

. . . Someone will say, "I did not ask to be born." This is a naive way of throwing greater emphasis on our facticity. I am responsible for everything, in fact, except for my very responsibility, for I am not the foundation of my being. Therefore everything takes place as if I were compelled to be responsible. I am *abandoned* in the world, not in the sense that I might remain abandoned and passive in a hostile universe like a board floating on the water, but rather in the sense that I find myself suddenly alone and without help, engaged in a world for which I bear the whole responsibility without being able, whatever I do, to tear myself away from this responsibility for an instant. For I am responsible for my very desire of fleeing responsibilities. To make myself passive in the world, to refuse to act upon things and upon Others is still to choose myself, and suicide is one mode among others of being-in-the-world. Yet I find an absolute responsibility for the fact of my facticity (here the fact of my birth) is directly inapprehensible and even inconceivable, for this fact of my birth never appears as a brute fact but always across a projective reconstruction of my for-itself. I am ashamed of being born or I am astonished at it or I rejoice over it, or in attempting to get rid of my life I affirm that I live and I assume this life as bad. Thus in a certain sense I *choose* being born. . . .

Under these conditions since every event in the world can be revealed to me only as an *opportunity* (an opportunity made use of, lacked, neglected, etc.), or better yet since everything which happens to us can be considered as a *chance* (i.e., can appear to us only as a way of realizing this being which is in question in our being) and since others as transcendences-transcended are themselves only *opportunities* and *chances*, the responsibility of the for-itself extends to the entire world as a peopled-world. It is precisely thus that the for-itself apprehends itself in anguish; that is, as a being which is neither the foundation of its own being nor the Other's being not of the in-itselfs which form the world, but a being which is compelled to decide the meaning of being—within it and everywhere outside of it. The one who realizes in anguish his condition as *being* thrown into a responsibility which extends to his very abandonment has no longer either remorse or regret or excuse; he is no longer anything but a freedom which perfectly reveals itself and whose being resides in this very revelation. But as we pointed out at the beginning of this work, most of the time we flee anguish in bad faith.

---

1. According to Sartre, why are there no accidents in life?

ARTHUR KOESTLER: The God That Failed (1942)

Arthur Koestler was one of many intellectuals who became communists during the 1930s. His story is, in many respects, representative of a generation who believed they were witnessing the collapse of Western civilization and the democratic tradition. He joined the Communist party in 1931 but formally denounced the U.S.S.R. in 1939 at the time of the Russo-German Nonaggression Pact. The following excerpt is from an essay Koestler contributed to The God That Failed.

From Richard Crossman (ed.), *The God That Failed*. Reprinted by permission of the Peters Fraser & Dunlop Group Ltd.

I became converted because I was ripe for it and lived in a disintegrating society thirsting for faith. But the day when I was given my Party card was merely the climax of a development which had started long before I had read about the drowned pigs or heard the names of Marx and Lenin. Its roots reach back into childhood; and though each of us, comrades of the Pink Decade, had individual roots with different twists in them, we are products of, by and large, the same generation and cultural climate. It is this unity underlying diversity which makes me hope that my story is worth telling.

I was born in 1905 in Budapest; we lived there till 1919, when we moved to Vienna. Until the First World War we were comfortably off, a typical Continental middle-class family: my father was the Hungarian representative of some old-established British and German textile manufacturers. In September, 1914, this form of existence, like so many others, came to an abrupt end; my father never found his feet again. He embarked on a number of ventures which became the more fantastic the more he lost self-confidence in a changed world. He opened a factory for radioactive soap; he backed several crank-inventions (everlasting electric bulbs, self-heating bed bricks and the like); and finally lost the remains of his capital in the Austrian inflation of the early 'twenties. I left home at twenty-one, and from the day became the only financial support of my parents.

At the age of nine, when our middle-class idly collapsed, I had suddenly become conscious of the economic Facts of Life. As an only child, I continued to be pampered by my parents; but, well aware of the family crisis, and torn by pity for my father, who was of a generous and somewhat childlike disposition, I suffered a pang of guilt whenever they bought me books or toys. This continued later on, when every suit I bought for myself meant so much less to send home. Simultaneously, I developed a strong dislike of the obviously rich; not because they could afford to buy things (envy plays a much smaller part in social conflict than is generally assumed) but because they were able to do so without a guilty conscience. Thus I projected a personal predicament onto the structure of society at large.

It was certainly a tortuous way of acquiring a social conscience. But precisely because of the intimate nature of the conflict, the faith which grew out of it became an equally intimate part of my self. It did not, for some years, crystallize into a political creed; at first it took the form of a mawkishly sentimental attitude. Every contact with people poorer than myself was unbearable—the boy at school who had no gloves and red chilblains on his fingers, the former traveling salesman of my father's reduced to cadging occasional meals—all of them were additions to the load of guilt on my back. The analyst would have no difficulty in showing that the roots of his guilt-complex go deeper than the crisis in our household budget; but if he were to dig even deeper, piercing through the individual millions of particular variations on the same theme—"Woe, for they chant to the sound of harps and anoint themselves, but are not grieved for the affliction of the people."

Thus sensitized by a personal conflict, I was ripe for the shock of learning that wheat was burned, fruit artificially spoiled and pigs were drowned in the depression years to keep prices up and enable fat capitalists to chant to the sound of harps, while Europe trembled under the torn boots of hunger-marchers and my father hid his frayed cuffs under the table. The frayed cuffs and drowned pigs blended into one emotional explosion, as the fuse of the archetype was touched off. We sang the "Internationale," but the words might as well have been the older ones: "Woe to the shepherds who feed themselves, but feed not their flocks."

In other respects, too, the story is more typical than it seems. A considerable portion of the middle classes in central Europe was, like ourselves, ruined by the inflation of the 'twenties. It was the beginning of Europe's decline. This disintegration of the middle strata of society started the fatal process of polarization which continues to this day. The pauperized bourgeois became rebels of the Right or Left; Schickelgruber and Djugashwili shared about equally the benefits of the social migration. Those who refused to admit that they had become declasse, who clung to the empty shell of gentility, joined the Nazis and found comfort in blaming their fate on Versailles and the Jews. Many did not even have the consolation; they lived on pointlessly, like a great black swarm of tired winterflies crawling over the dim windows of Europe, members of a class displaced by history.

The other half turned Left, thus confirming the prophecy of the "Communist Manifesto":

> Entire sections of the ruling classes
> are . . . precipitated into the proletariat,
> or are at least threatened in their
> conditions of existence. They . . . supply
> the proletariat with fresh elements of
> enlightenment and progress.

That "fresh element of enlightenment," I discovered to my delight, was I. As long as I had been nearly starving, I had regarded myself as a temporarily displaced offspring of the bourgeoisie. In 1931, when at last I had achieved a comfortable income, I found that it was time to join the ranks of the proletariat. But the irony of this sequence only occurred to me in restrospect.

> The bourgeois family will vanish as a
> matter of course with the vanishing of
> Capital. . . . The bourgeois claptrap about
> the family and education, about the
> haloed correlation of parent and child,
> becomes all the more disgusting the more,
> by the action of modern industry, all
> family ties among the proletarians are
> torn asunder. . . .

Thus the "Communist Manifesto." Every page of Marx, and even more of Engels, brought a new revelation, and an intellectual delight which I had only experienced once before, at my first contact with Freud. Torn from its context, the above passage sounds ridiculous; as part of a closed system which made social philosophy fall into a lucid and comprehensive pattern, the demonstration of the historical relativity of institutions and ideals—of family, class, patriotism, bourgeois morality, sexual taboos—had the intoxicating effect of a sudden liberation from the rusty chains with which a pre–1914 middle-class childhood had cluttered one's mind. Today, when Marxist philosophy has degenerated into a Byzantine cult and virtually every single tenet of the Marxist program has become twisted round into its opposite, it is difficult to recapture that mood of emotional fervor and intellectual bliss.

I was ripe to be converted, as a result of my personal case-history; thousands of other members of the intelligentsia and the middle classes of my generation were ripe for it, by virtue of other personal case-histories; but, however much these differed from case to case, they had a common denominator: the rapid disintegration of moral values, of the pre–1914 pattern of life in postwar Europe, and the simultaneous lure of the new revelation which had come from the East.

I joined the Party (which to this day remains "the" Party for all of us who once belonged to it) in 1931, at the beginning of that short-lived period of optimism, of that abortive spiritual renaissance, later known as the Pink Decade. The stars of that treacherous dawn were Barbusse, Romain Rolland, Gide and Malraux in France; Piscator, Becher, Renn, Brecht, Eisler, Saghers in Germany; Auden, Isherwood, Spender in England; Dos Passos, Upton Sinclair, Steinbeck in the United States. (Of course, not all of them were members of the Communist Party.) The cultural atmosphere was saturated with Progressive Writer's congresses, experimental theaters, committees for peace and against Fascism, societies for cultural relations with the USSR, Russian films and avant-garde magazines. It looked indeed as if the Western world, convulsed by the aftermath of war, scourged by inflation, depression, unemployment and the absence of a faith to live for, was at last going to

> Clear from the head the massive of impressive rubbish;
> Rally the lost and trembling forces of the will,
> Gather them up and let them loose upon the earth,
> Till they construct at last a human justice.
>
> —Auden

The new star of Bethlehem had risen in the East; and for a modest sum, Intourist was prepared to allow you a short and well-focused glimpse of the Promised Land.

I lived at that time in Berlin. For the last five years, I had been working for the Ullstein chain of newspapers—first as a foreign correspondent in Palestine and the Middle East, then in Paris. Finally, in 1930, I joined the editorial staff in the Berlin "House." For a better understanding of what follows, a few words have to be said about the House of Ullstein, symbol of the Weimar Republic.

Ullstein's was a kind of super-trust; the largest organization of its kind in Europe, and probably in the world. They published four daily papers in Berlin alone, among these the venerable *Vossische Zeitung*, founded in the eighteenth century, and the *B.Z. am Mittag*, an evening paper with a record circulation and a record speed in getting the news out. Apart from these, Ullstein's published more than a dozen weekly and monthly periodicals, ran their own news service, their own travel agency, etc., and were one of the leading book publishers. The firm was owned by the brothers Ullstein—they were five, like the original Rothschild brothers, and like them also, they were Jews. Their policy was liberal and democratic, and in cultural matters progressive to the point of avant-gardism. They were antimilitaristic, antichauvinistic, and it was largely due to their influence on public opinion that the policy of Franco-German rapprochement of the Briand-Stresemann era became a vogue among the progressive part of the German people. The firm of Ullstein was not only a political power in Germany, it was at the same time the embodiment of everything progressive and cosmopolitan in the Weimar Republic. . . .

My transfer from the Paris office to the Berlin house was due to an article I wrote on the occasion of the award of the Nobel prize for Physics to the Prince de Broglie. My bosses decided that I had a knack for popularizing science . . . and offered me the job of Science Editor of the *Vossische* and adviser on matters scientific to the rest of the Ullstein publications. I arrived in Berlin on the fateful day of September 14, 1930—the day of the Reichstag Election in which the National Socialist Party, in one mighty leap, increased the number of its deputies from 4 to 107. The Communists had also registered important gains; the democratic parties of the Center were crushed. It was the beginning of the end of Weimar; the situation was epitomized in the title of Knickerbocker's bestseller: *Germany,—Fascist or Soviet?* Obviously there was no "third alternative."

. . . With one-third of its wage-earners unemployed, Germany lived in a state of latent civil war, and if one wasn't prepared to be swept along as a passive victim by the approaching hurricane it became imperative to take sides. Stresemann's party was dead. The Socialists pursued a policy of opportunistic compromise. Even by a process of pure elimination, the Communists, with the mighty Soviet Union behind them, seemed the only force capable of resisting the onrush of the primitive horde with its swastika totem. But it was not by a process of elimination that I became a Communist. Tired of electrons and wave-mechanics, I began for the first time to read Marx, Engels and Lenin in earnest. By the time I had finished with *Feuerbach* and *State and Revolution*, something had clicked in my brain which shook me like a mental explosion. To say that one had "seen the light" is a poor description of the mental rapture which only the convert knows (regardless of what faith he has been converted to). The new light seems to pour from all directions across the skull; the whole universe falls into pattern like the stray pieces of a jigsaw puzzle assembled by magic at one stroke. There is now an answer to every question, doubts and conflicts are a matter of the tortured past—a past already remote, when one had lived in dismal ignorance in the tasteless, colorless world of those who *don't know*. Nothing henceforth can disturb the convert's inner peace and serenity—except the occasional fear of losing faith again, losing thereby what alone makes life worth living, and falling back into the outer darkness, where there is wailing and gnashing of teeth. This may explain how Communists, with eyes to see and brains to think with, can still act in subjective *bona fides*, anno Domini 1949. At all times and in all creeds only a minority has been capable of courting excommunication and committing emotional harakiri in the name of an abstract truth.

---

1. Summarize the reasons Koestler became a communist.

2. What insights does Koestler's essay provide into the age of anxiety?

BERTRAND RUSSELL:
The Scientific Outlook (1931)

British philosopher Bertrand Russell was involved in many of the social and political issues of the day. He was imprisoned during the First World War for his support of conscientious objectors. He was a confirmed pacifist and supported the policy of appeasement adopted by the British and French toward Germany. The following essay illustrates Russell's belief in a growing menace from the field of science. In his later years, Russell became an active opponent of the manufacturing of atomic weapons and was the first president for the Campaign for Nuclear Disarmament that was launched in 1958.

From Bertrand Russell, *The Scientific Outlook* (New York: W.W. Norton and Co., 1962).

The impulse towards scientific construction is admirable when it does not thwart any of the major impulses that give value to human life, but when it is allowed to forbid all outlet to everything but itself it becomes a form of cruel tyranny. There is, I think, a real danger lest the world should become subject to a tyranny of this sort, and it is on this account that I have not shrunk from depicting the darker features of the world that scientific manipulation unchecked might wish to create.

Science in the course of the few centuries of its history has undergone an internal development which appears to be not yet completed. One may sum up this development as the passage from contemplation to manipulation. The love of knowledge to which the growth of science is due is itself the product of a twofold impulse. We may seek knowledge of an object because we love the object or because we wish to have power over it. The former impulse leads to the kind of knowledge that is contemplative, the latter to the kind that is practical. In the development of science the power impulse has increasingly prevailed over the love impulse. The power impulse is embodied in industrialism and in governmental technique. It is embodied also in the philosophies known as pragmatism and instrumentalism. Each of these philosophies holds, broadly speaking, that our beliefs about any object are true in so far as they enable us to manipulate it with advantage to ourselves. This is what may be called a governmental view of truth. Of truth so conceived science offers us a great deal; indeed there seems no limit to its possible triumphs. To the man who wishes to change his environment science offers astonishingly powerful tools, and if knowledge consists in the power to produce intended changes, then science gives knowledge in abundance.

But the desire for knowledge has another form, belonging to an entirely different set of emotions. The mystic, the lover, and the poet are also seekers after knowledge—not perhaps very successful seekers, but none the less worthy of respect on that account. In all forms of love we wish to have knowledge of what is loved, not for purposes of power, but for the ecstasy of contemplation. "In knowledge of God standeth our eternal life," but not because knowledge of God gives us power over Him. Wherever there is ecstasy or joy or delight derived from an object there is the desire to know that object—to know it not in the manipulative fashion that consists in turning it into something else, but to know it in the fashion of the beatific vision, because in itself and for itself it sheds happiness upon the lover. In sex love as in other forms of love the impulse to this kind of knowledge exists, unless the love is purely physical or practical. This may indeed be made the touchstone of any love that is valuable. Love which has value contains an impulse towards that kind of knowledge out of which the mystic union springs.

Science in its beginnings was due to men who were in love with the world. They perceived the beauty of the stars and the sea, of the winds and the mountains. Because they loved them their thoughts dwelt upon them, and they wished to understand them more intimately than a mere outward contemplation made possible. "The world," said Heraclitus, "is an ever-living fire, with measures kindling and measures going out." Heraclitus and the other Ionian philosophers, from whom came the first impulse to scientific knowledge, felt the strange beauty of the world almost like a madness in the blood. They were men of Titanic passionate intellect, and from the intensity of their intellectual passion the whole movement of the modern world has sprung. But step by step, as science has developed, the impulse of love which gave it birth has been increasingly thwarted, while the impulse of power, which was at first a mere camp-follower, has gradually usurped command in virtue of its unforeseen success. The lover of nature has been baffled, the tyrant over nature has been rewarded. As physics has developed, it has deprived us step by step of what we thought we knew concerning the intimate nature of the physical world. Colour and sound, light and shade, form and texture, belong no longer to that external nature that the Ionians sought as the bride of their devotion. All these things have been transferred from the beloved to the lover, and the beloved has become a skeleton of rattling bones, cold and dreadful, but perhaps a mere phantasm. The poor physicists, appalled at the desert that their formulae have revealed, call upon God to give them comfort, but God must share the ghostliness of His creation, and the answer that the physicists think they hear to their cry is only the frightened beating of their own hearts. Disappointed as the lover of nature, the man of science is becoming its tyrant. What matters it, says the practical man, whether the outer world exists or is a dream, provided I can make it behave as I wish? Thus science has more and more substituted power-knowledge for love-knowledge, and as this substitution becomes completed science tends more and more to become sadistic. The scientific society of the future as we have been imagining it is one in which the power impulse has completely overwhelmed the impulse of love, and this is the psychological source of the cruelties which it is in danger of exhibiting.

Science, which began as the pursuit of truth, is becoming incompatible with veracity, since complete veracity tends more and more to complete scientific scepticism. When science is considered contemplatively, not practically, we find that what we believe, we believe owing to animal faith, and it is only our disbeliefs that are due to science. When, on the other hand, science is considered as a technique for the transformation of ourselves and our environment, it is found to give us a power quite independent of its metaphysical validity. But we can only wield this power by ceasing to ask ourselves metaphysical questions as to the nature of reality. Yet these questions are the evidence of a lover's attitude towards the world. Thus it is only in so far as we renounce the world as its lovers that we can conquer it as its technicians. But this division in the soul is fatal to what is best in man. As soon as the failure of science considered as metaphysics is realized, the power conferred by science as a technique is only obtainable by something analogous to the worship of Satan, that is to say, by the renunciation of love.

This is the fundamental reason why the prospect of a scientific society must be viewed with apprehension. The scientific society in its pure form, which is what we have been trying to depict, is incompatible with the pursuit of truth, with love, with art, with spontaneous delight, with every ideal that men have hitherto cherished, with the sole exception of ascetic renunciation. It is not knowledge that is the source of these dangers. Knowledge is good and ignorance is evil: to this principle the lover of the world can admit no exception. Nor is it power in and for itself that is the source of danger. What is dangerous is power wielded for the sake of power, not power wielded for the sake of genuine good. The leaders of the modern world are drunk with power: the fact that they can do something that no one previously thought it possible to do is to them a sufficient reason for doing it. Power is not one of the ends of life, but merely a means to other ends, and until men remember the ends that power should subserve, science will not do what it might to minister to the good life. But what then are the ends of life, the reader will say. I do not think that one man has a right to legislate for another on this matter. For each individual the ends of life are those things which he deeply desires, and which if they existed would give him peace. Or, if it be thought that peace is too much to ask this side of the grave, let us say that the end of life should give delight or joy or ecstasy. In the conscious desires of the man who seeks power for its own there is something dusty: when he has it he wants only more power, and does not find rest in contemplation of what he has. The lover, the poet and the mystic find a fuller satisfaction than the seeker after power can ever know, since they can rest in the object of their love, whereas the seeker after power must be perpetually engaged in some fresh manipulation if he is not to suffer from a sense of emptiness. I think therefore that the satisfactions of the lover, using that word in its broadest sense, exceed the satisfactions of the tyrant, and deserve a higher place among the ends of life. When I come to die I shall not feel that I have lived in vain. I have seen the earth turn red at evening, the dew sparkling in the morning, and the snow shining under a frosty sun; I have smelt rain after drought, and have heard the stormy Atlantic beat upon the granite shores of Cornwall. Science may bestow these and other joys upon more people than could otherwise enjoy them. If so, its power will be wisely used. But when it takes out of life the moments to which life owes its value, science will not deserve admiration, however cleverly and however elaborately it may lead men along the road to despair. The sphere of values lies outside science, except in so far as science consists in the pursuit of knowledge. Science as the pursuit of power must not obtrude upon the sphere of values, and scientific technique, if it is to enrich human life, must not outweigh the ends which it should serve.

The number of men who determine the character of an age is small. Columbus, Luther and Charles V dominated the sixteenth century; Galileo and Descartes governed the seventeenth. The important men in the age that is just ended are Edison, Rockefeller, Lenin, and Sun Yat-sen. With the exception of Sun Yat-sen these were men devoid of culture, contemptuous of the past, self-confident and ruthless. Traditional wisdom had no place in their thoughts and feelings; mechanism and organisation were what interested them. A different education might have made all these men quite different. Edison might in his youth have acquired a knowledge of history and poetry and art; Rockefeller might have been taught how he had been anticipated by Croesus and Crassus; Lenin, instead of having hatred implanted in him by the execution of his brother during his student days, might have made himself acquainted with the rise of Islam and the development of Puritanism from piety to plutocracy. By means of such an education some little leaven of doubt might have entered the souls of these great men. Given a little doubt their achievement would perhaps have been less in volume, but much greater in value.

Our world has a heritage of culture and beauty, but unfortunately we have been handing on this heritage only to the less active and important members of each generation. The government of the world, by which I do not mean its ministerial posts but its key positions of power, has been allowed to fall into the hands of men ignorant of the past, without tenderness towards what is traditional, without understanding what they are destroying. There is no essential reason why this should be the case. To prevent it is an educational problem, and not a very difficult one. Men in the past were often parochial in space, but the dominant men of our age are parochial in time. They feel for the past a contempt that it does not deserve, and for the present a respect that it deserves still less. The copy book maxims if a former age have become outworn, but a new set of copy book maxims is required. First among these I should put: "It is better to do a little good than much harm." To give content to this maxim it would of course be necessary to instil some sense of what is good. Few men in the present day, for example, can be induced to believe that there is no inherent excellence in rapid locomotion. To climb from Hell to Heaven is good, though it be a slow, a laborious process; to fall from Heaven to Hell is bad, even though it be done with the speed of Milton's Satan. Nor can it be said that a mere increase in the production of material commodities is in itself a thing of great value. To prevent extreme poverty is important, but to add to the possessions of those who already have too much is a worthless waste of effort. To prevent crime may be necessary, but to invent new crimes in order that the police may show skill in preventing them is less admirable. The new powers that science has given to man can only be wielded safely by those who, whether through the study of history or through their own experience of life, have acquired some reverence for human feelings and some tenderness towards the emotions that give colour to the daily existence of men and women. I do not mean to deny that scientific technique may in time build an artifical world in every way preferable to that in which men have hitherto lived, but I do say that if this is to be done it must be done tentatively and with a realization that the purpose of government is not merely to afford pleasure to those who govern, but to make life tolerable for those who are governed. Scientific technique must no longer be allowed to form the whole culture of the holders of power, and it must become an essential part of men's ethical outlook to realize that the will alone cannot make a good life. Knowing and feeling are equally essential ingredients both in the life of the individual and in that of the community. Knowledge, if it is wide and intimate, brings with it a realization of distant times and places, an awareness that the individual is not omnipotent or all-important, and a perspective in which values are seen more clearly than by those to whom a distant view is impossible. Even more important than knowledge is the life of the emotions. A world without delight and without affection is a world destitute of value. These things the scientific manipulator must remember and if he does his manipulation may be wholly beneficial. All that is needed is that men should not be so intoxicated by new power as to forget the truths that were familiar to every previous generation. Not all wisdom is new, nor is all folly out of date.

Man has been disciplined hitherto by his subjection to nature. Having emancipated himself from this subjection, he is showing something of the defects of a slave-turned-master. A new moral outlook is called for in which submission to the powers of nature is replaced by respect for what is best in man. It is where this respect is lacking that scientific technique is dangerous. So long as it is present, science, having delivered man from bondage to nature, can proceed to deliver him from bondage to the slavish part of himself. The dangers exist, but they are not inevitable, and hope for the future is at least as rational as fear.

---

1. (a) Summarize Russell's thesis.
(b) What evidence does Russell use to support his thesis?
(c) Do you agree or disagree with Russell? Why?

2. What arguments could a scientist use to counter Russell's thesis?

3. Have events since 1931 confirmed or denied Russell's point of view?

ANALYSIS AND APPLICATION

1. Choose an artist of the surrealist period and analyse his or her use of Freudian symbolism.

2. Choose a novel that expresses the alienation experienced during this era. Read the book and write a book report explaining how the writer has expressed his or her attitude toward the age of anxiety.

3. Examine the philosophy of existentialism in the drama of this period.

4. Write a review of the Paris premiere of Igor Stravinsky's *The Rite of Spring*.

5. Research the Nazi use of propaganda during this period. Choose an example to present to the class and explain how it served the Nazis' purposes.

6. Prepare a time chart highlighting the major innovations, both artistic and technological, in the film industry.

7. Debate the following: *Governments are justified in censoring the arts if it is in the national interest.*

8. The postwar era saw changing social attitudes, including those toward women. Divide into three groups to research the changing role of women in (a) Europe, (b) the Soviet Union, and (c) North America. Discuss your findings with the class.

9. Examine how the U.S. government applied Keynesian economics during the Depression.

10. Create an editorial cartoon that responds to the "Piltdown Man Hoax."

PART FIVE

The Modern World, 1945 to the Present

In 1900, Western Europe dominated the world politically and economically. At the end of the Second World War, however, in response to his own question, "What is Europe now?" Winston Churchill replied: "It is a rubble heap, a charnel house, a breeding-ground of pestilence and hate." Through two devastating and self-destructive world wars Europe had forfeited its position of leadership to two new superpowers, the United States and the Soviet Union. Problems over different visions of the postwar world led to political and economic rivalry between the two superpowers. It was a conflict made all the more deadly by the development of the atomic, and eventually the nuclear, bomb.

The postwar period was a time of economic adjustment for all countries. During the 1960s and 1970s, the world economy experienced significant change and the trend toward a global economy was accelerated as international trade increased. Most of the industrialized, non-communist world enjoyed a period of sustained growth. However, the drastic increase in oil prices and the temporary oil embargo in 1973 slowed economic growth. The resulting inflation and unemployment created a recession in most industrialized countries that lasted into the 1980s.

This slowdown resulted in substantial re-evaluation of economic policies in most industrialized nations in the 1980s. The Soviet Union introduced *perestroika* and Eastern European countries moved away from centrally planned economies toward market socialism or free market economies. At the same time, Western Europe dropped economic barriers to create a more fully integrated international economy. Outside of Europe, Canada and the United States entered into a bilateral free trade agreement, and Japan continued to shift away from heavy industry toward high-tech manufacturing as it became the world's leading creditor nation.

As the Western world moved toward a political and economic accommodation by the early 1980s, conflicts and economic hardships still afflicted much of the developing world. Political unrest and war characterized the Middle East. Famine crippled parts of sub-Saharan Africa. Human rights violations victimized blacks in southern Africa and political dissidents in China and Latin America.

As science and technology developed exponentially during the period, new technologies and increased affluence had a profound impact upon the arts and social values of the West. By 1990, a new and distinct character to Western culture had emerged.

	POLITICS	PHILOSOPHY/LEARNING	ART	SCIENCE/TECHNOLOGY
1945	1945 Yalta Conference UN charter signed World War II ends 1946 Churchill's "Iron Curtain" speech Nuremberg Trials 1947 Marshall Plan announced Truman Doctrine Cominform established India becomes independent 1948 Marshall Plan begins State of Israel created Berlin airlift 1949 China falls to the communists NATO established South Africa initiates policy of apartheid German Democratic Republic and German Federal Republic created	1945 Curtis, *World War: Its Cause and Cure* 1946 Benedict, *The Chrysanthemum and the Sword* 1947 Cole, *The Intelligent Man's Guide to the Post-War World* Discovery of the Dead Sea Scrolls 1948 Sartre, *Existentialism and Humanism* Mead, *Male and Female: A Study of the Sexes in a Changing World* 1949 Schweitzer, *Hospital in the Jungle* Beauvoir, *The Second Sex*	1945 Orwell, *Animal Farm* Wright, Guggenheim Museum 1946 O'Neill, *The Iceman Cometh* Hersey, *Hiroshima* 1947 Camus, *The Plague* Mann, *Doktor Faustus* Auden, *The Age of Anxiety* 1948 Pollock, *Composition No. 1* Moore, *Family Group* Schonberg, *Survivor from Warsaw* 1949 Orwell, *Nineteen-Eighty Four* Miller, *Death of a Salesman*	1945 U.S. explodes first atomic bomb 1946 ENIAC—first large electronic computer 1947 Transistor invented First atomic pile at Harwell, England 1948 Long-playing record invented First transatlantic flight by jet Kinsey, *Sexual Behaviour in the American Male* 1949 U.S.S.R. tests its first atomic bomb
1950	1950 Korean War begins 1952 Turkey and Greece join NATO 1953 Death of Stalin Korean war ends Riots in East Germany 1954 U.S. involvement in Vietnam begins Revolt against British rule in Kenya 1955 Warsaw Pact established West Germany joins NATO 1956 De-Stalinization process begins Khruschev's "Peaceful Co-existence" speech Hungarian revolt Suez Crisis 1957 European Economic Community created by the Treaty of Rome Eisenhower Doctrine 1959 Castro takes over Cuba	1950 Mead, *Social Anthropology* 1951 y Gasset, *Man as Utopist Creature* 1952 Piltdown human revealed as a hoax Linear B deciphered 1953 Skinner, *Science and Human Behaviour* 1955 Paton, *The Modern Predicament* 1956 Toynbee, *A Historian's Approach to Religion* Churchill, *A History of the English-Speaking Peoples* 1958 Galbraith, *The Affluent Society* 1959 Wright, *The Causes of World War III*	1950 Hersey, *The Wall* 1951 Wouk, *The Caine Mutiny* Dali, *Christ of St. John on the Cross* 1952 Hemingway, *The Old Man and the Sea* Beckett, *Waiting for Godot* 1954 Golding, *The Lord of the Flies* Copeland, *The Tender Land* 1955 Dali, *The Lord's Supper* Johns, *Flag above White with Collage* Brecht, *The Life of Galileo* 1956 Utzon, Sydney Opera House 1957 Kerouac, *On the Road* Corbusier, Tokyo Museum of Art 1958 Pasternak, *Dr. Zhivago* Garsse, *The Tin Drum* 1959 Berg, *Wozzeck* Miro murals for UNESCO building	1951 Electric power generated from atomic energy 1952 Great Britain tests its first atomic bomb U.S. tests first hydrogen bomb First nuclear accident, Chalk River, Canada 1953 U.S.S.R. explodes hydrogen bomb 1954 First solar battery CERN (European Centre for Nuclear Research) established First atomic submarine, *Nautilus* 1955 Sanger determines molecular structure of insulin 1956 Transatlantic cable telephone service begins FORTRAN becomes the first computer programming language 1957 U.S.S.R. launches *Sputnik* 1958 U.S. launches *Explorer I*

	POLITICS	PHILOSOPHY/LEARNING	ART	SCIENCE/TECHNOLOGY
1950				1959 U.S.S.R.'s *Luna III* photographs the moon St. Lawrence Seaway opens
1960	1960 Belgian Congo becomes independent U-2 incident Cyprus becomes independent 1961 Berlin Wall erected Bay of Pigs fiasco 1962 Cuban Missile Crisis U.S. observers sent to Vietnam Algeria gains independence Burundi, Uganda, Tanganyika, Jamaica, Trinidad, and West Samoa gain independence 1963 Nuclear Test Ban Treaty "Hotline" established between U.S. and U.S.S.R. U.S. sends financial aid to Vietnam Kenya gains independence 1964 Escalation of Vietnam War Khruschev replaced by Kosygin and Brezhnev Tonkin Gulf Resolution Malawi, Zambia, and Tanzania gain independence 1965 Rhodesia gains independence 1966 Guyana gains independence 1967 Arab-Israeli Six-Day War Cultural Revolution begins in China Botswana and Lesotho gain independence 1968 Czechoslovakian revolt brutally suppressed Tet offensive in Vietnam My Lai massacre in Vietnam 1969 First U.S. troops withdrawn from Vietnam	1960 Ayer, *Logical Positivism* 1962 Carson, *Silent Spring* 1965 Born, *On the Responsibility of Scientists* Hawkins, *Stonehenge Decoded* 1966 Cameron, *Witness* Ardrey, *The Territorial Imperative* 1968 Pope Paul VI, *Humanae Vitae* 1969 Dubos, *So Human an Animal*	1960 Bolt, *A Man for All Seasons* 1961 Albee, *The American Dream* Steinbeck, *The Winter of Our Discontent* 1962 Solzhenitsyn, *A Day in the Life of Ivan Denisovich* Albee, *Who's Afraid of Virginia Woolf?* 1963 Ionesco, *Exit the King* Lichtenstein, *Whaam!* 1964 Picasso, *The Painter and His Model* 1965 Nader, *Unsafe at Any Speed* 1966 Abu Simball moved to avoid waters from the Aswan Dam 1967 Zuffre, *Hiroshima* Zeidler, Ontario Place 1968 *2001: A Space Odyssey* Wolfe, *The Electric Kool-Aid Acid Test* 1969 Woodstock Atwood, *The Edible Woman*	1960 First weather satellite 1961 Yuri Gagarin first astronaut-controlled orbital flight 1962 Telestar communication satellite *Mariner 2* reaches Venus 1963 First use of an artificial heart during an operation Audio cassette introduced 1964 Aswan Dam completed Green Revolution introduced 1965 Aleksei Leonov first person to walk in space Soft contact lens introduced BASIC computer language introduced 1966 *Luna IX* (U.S.S.R.) makes soft landing on the moon 1967 Synthetic DNA produced First partially successful heart transplant 1968 First supertankers introduced First use of radar for weather predictions 1969 First astronaut-controlled lunar landing

	POLITICS	PHILOSOPHY/LEARNING	ART	SCIENCE/TECHNOLOGY
1970	1970 End of Biafran civil war U.S. troops enter Cambodia 1971 People's Republic of China joins UN 1972 U.S. re-establishes relations with Communist China Marcos becomes leader of the Philippines Great Britain assumes direct rule of Northern Ireland 1973 End of U.S. involvement in Vietnam OPEC oil boycott Arab-Israeli War Great Britain joins the Common Market 1974 Worldwide inflation, economic growth in industrialized nations approaches zero Turkey invades Cyprus Portugal grants independence to its African colonies 1975 U.S. leaves Cambodia 1976 North and South Vietnam reunited Mao Zedong dies 1977 Amnesty International receives Noble Prize for Peace 1978 Israel-Egypt Camp David Accord 1979 Soviet invasion of Afghanistan Khomeini assumes control of Iran	1970 Roszak, *The Making of a Counter-Culture* Deutsch, *Between Philosophy and History* 1973 Fitzgerald, *Fire in the Lake* 1975 W. and A. Durant, *The Age of Napoleon* 1976 Arlen, *Passage of Ararat* 1978 Arendt, *The Life of the Mind* (posthumous)	1970 Snow, *Last Things* 1971 Solzhenitsyn, *August 1914* 1972 Shostakovich, *Symphony #15* Thompson, *Fear and Loathing in Los Angeles* 1973 Britten, *Death in Venice* 1974 Solzhenitsyn, *The Gulag Archipelago: 1918–1956* 1975 Albee, Seascape 1976 Bellow, *Humboldt's Gift* Haley, *Roots* 1977 Lucas, *Star Wars* Findlay, *The Wars* Zeidler, Toronto Eaton's Centre *Roots*, TV mini-series 1978 *Holocaust,* TV mini-series	1970 First synthetic gene Boeing 747, first jumbo jet introduced 1971 U.S.S.R. soft lands probe on Mars Intel introduces the first microprocessor 1972 First computerized axial tomography (CAT scan) imager 1974 Discovery of "Lucy" (Australopithecus afarensis) 1975 *Apollo-Soyez* Test Project 1976 Freon danger to ozone layer identified Concorde becomes the first supersonic airliner with regular service 1977 U.S. space shuttle program begins Apple II computer introduced 1978 First test-tube baby 1979 Nuclear accident at Three Mile Island *Gossamer Albatross*, first human-powered aircraft to cross the English Channel
1980	1980 Solidarity occupies Gdansk shipyard War between Iraq and Iran 1981 Martial law in Poland; Solidarity leaders arrested	1981 Johanson and White, *Lucy: The Beginnings of Humankind*		1981 Introduction of IBM personal computer AIDS (Acquired Immune Deficiency syndrome) recognized by U.S. Centers for Disease Control

POLITICS	PHILOSOPHY/LEARNING	ART	SCIENCE/TECHNOLOGY
1982 U.S. national debt exceeds $1 trillion Falklands War Israel returns Sinai Peninsula to Egypt Israel invades Lebanon		1982 Erickson, Roy Thompson Hall	1982 Introduction of the compact disc First IBM clone introduced
1983 High unemployment in the West U.S. invasion of Grenada			
1984 Indira Ghandi assassinated	1984 Tuchman, *The March of Folly*		1984 AIDS identified as a virus
1985 Gorbachev announces *perestroika* and *glasnost*	1985 Postman, *Amusing Ourselves to Death*	1985 Live Aid concert	1985 Announcement of a hole in the ozone layer over the Antarctic
1986 Aquino becomes president of the Philippines U.S. bombs Tripoli, Libya Iran-*contra* affair		1986 Tyler, *The Accidental Tourist* Zeidler, Canada Place, Expo '86, Vancouver	1986 Space shuttle *Challenger* explodes Nuclear accident at Chernobyl British scientist confirms greenhouse effect
1987 Single European Act			
1988 Protests in Poland and Hungary lead to reforms U.S. destroys Iranian airliner	1988 Duncan, *Mass Media and Popular Culture* Kennedy, *The Rise and Fall of the Great Powers*	1988 Erickson, Canadian embassy, Washington, D.C. Atwood, *Cat's Eye*	1988 Shroud of Turin revealed as a fake The human-powered *Daedules 88* flies from Crete to Santorini
1989 Solidarity forms opposition in Polish parliament Popular unrest and reforms in most of Eastern Europe Berlin Wall dismantled		1989 Salman Rushdie sentenced in absentia by Khomeini to execution for his novel *Satanic Verses*	
1990 East and West Germany reunited			

CHAPTER TWELVE

The Politics of the Western World

FROM COLD WAR TO DÉTENTE TO GLASNOST

Within two years after the end of the Second World War, a new war had begun—the Cold War. To many, the Cold War represented the ultimate philosophical conflict between the two ideologies that were the legacies of Western civilization. On the one side were nations such as the United States, Great Britain, France, and Canada, looking to re-establish Europe's liberal-democratic traditions and to expand these on a global scale. On the other side was the Soviet Union and its adherence to the European traditions of authoritarianism and paternalistic state control. In more practical terms, however, the Cold War was about global power politics between the two new superpowers to determine which one would reign supreme in the postwar world.

The roots of the Cold War can be traced to the Yalta Conference in February 1945. The conference was a tripartite meeting among the principal allies of the Second World War—Great Britain, the Soviet Union, and the United States. By 1945, a combination of "Lend-Lease" (the practice of lending military equipment manufactured in the United States for use by the Soviet army) and mass conscription had given the Soviet Union the most powerful military force in the world. As the Soviet and American armies converged at the centre of a devastated Europe, it was the Soviets who would use their role as liberators more effectively to obtain their political objectives.

Stalin's main goal was a simple one: he wanted a guarantee that the Soviet Union would not be exposed to further invasions from the West. To accomplish this, he demanded the creation of a Soviet sphere of influence in Eastern Europe. This would include the right to become involved in the internal politics of those countries to prevent the emergence of hostile governments on the border of the U.S.S.R. Most of all, Stalin feared a resurgent Germany.

For Churchill and Great Britain, the future looked bleak in 1945. The nation was bankrupt and exhausted from six years of war. In addition, the ease with which the Japanese had conquered British positions in the Pacific exposed the vulnerability of the entire empire. For Churchill, the Yalta Conference offered a chance to gain allied support in reasserting Britain's global position. In addition, the British people had gone to war to restore democracy in Europe. Now half of the continent found itself freed from Hitler, but controlled by another authoritarian regime.

The United States was still actively fighting a two-theatre war in February 1945. Roosevelt could see that Germany would soon be defeated and so came to Yalta looking for increased Soviet support against Japan. In addition, Roosevelt, like Wilson in 1919, advocated the creation of an international organization that would prevent such a global conflict from ever erupting again. Agreement on the creation of the United Nations would prove to be the American president's last major foreign policy initiative before his death in April 1945.

Under the Yalta protocol, each nation partly achieved its goals. The British received American promises of support in re-establishing order in those parts of their empire occupied by Japan; the Soviets were given the right to assist liberated countries to establish "acceptable" governments and economic systems (in actual fact, it allowed the creation of an Eastern European buffer zone under Soviet control); the British and Americans were promised Soviet aid against Japan; and the Soviets agreed to become full participants in the new United Nations.

The greatest area of contention at Yalta was Germany. Stalin, Roosevelt, and Churchill all wanted a say in the country's future. They finally agreed to divide Germany into separate zones of occupation. Along with France, each would control one sector. This temporary division would minimize problems among the occupying forces and would establish the mechanism for military administration and the division of reparation payments. It would not be until the 1990s that this "temporary" division would finally end. (See pages 385 to 388 and readings.)

The European Schism

It soon became apparent that the Soviet army of occupation had no intention of allowing the nations of Eastern Europe to decide their own political futures. By the fall of 1945, they had canceled planned democratic elections in Poland and were tightening control in Czechoslovakia and their sector of Germany. The problem was intensified by the rapid process of Western demilitarization in Europe. At the end of the Second World War, the American armed forces had numbered 12 million. By 1947, they were reduced to 1.4 million worldwide. By contrast, the Soviet armed forces, which had totaled 12 million in 1945, had been cut to 4 million, with almost all of these stationed in Eastern Europe.

The growing distrust between East and West had intensified by 1946. On March 5th, Churchill described the Soviet occupation as placing "an iron curtain . . . across the continent" of Europe. (See readings.) Soviet leaders responded by pointing out that Britain had control of a global empire with troops on four continents. In addition, Stalin asserted that Britain and the United States were following Hitler's ideas and were now attempting world domination by the "English" race. This, he claimed, was "a call to war against the Soviet Union."

Harry S. Truman (1884–1972) had become president of the United States upon the death of Roosevelt in 1945. He authorized military support and over $400 million in economic aid to support pro-democracy forces in Greece and Turkey. Under this policy, known as the Truman Doctrine, the United States pledged itself to "support free peoples" who were resisting "armed minorities" and "outside pressures." This doctrine would soon become the centrepiece of American foreign policy in the Cold War years.

Introducing the Truman Doctrine in Greece was largely experimental, however, and was not really a realistic application of the policy. Its geographic position in the Mediterranean favoured the navally superior West. In addition, during 1944 and 1945 Stalin had encouraged the Greek Communist party to co-operate with its non-communist counterparts. Stalin had wanted to thwart the position of Yugoslavia's communist leader Marshall Tito (1892–1980), who had forced the German army out of his country before it was "liberated" by the Soviet Union and who now maintained independence from Soviet control. Because the Tito government was actively supporting the Greek Communist party, Stalin refused to come to their aid. As a result, the communists' ability to resist the Truman Doctrine was weakened. Thus the conditions in Greece were right for the successful intervention of the United States. In practical terms, the Truman Doctrine resulted in $400 million in American economic aid going to the region as well as the military support necessary to overcome the communist opposition.

Over the next three years, American financial and military commitments expanded. By 1947, the U.S. had realized the importance of European economic recovery. The only solution was for the United States to bankroll such a recovery, and so in 1947 the European Recovery Plan (also known as the Marshall Plan) was born. It was based on three assumptions:

(1) that the Soviet division of Europe was unacceptable and therefore aid would be offered to every European nation, whether communist or non-communist;

(2) that communism's appeal was largely economic, and so the elimination of poverty would stop its growth; and,

(3) that the conflicts of the twentieth century had been the result of economic competition, so the creation of an international economy would break down the national rivalries that had led to two world wars.

The Soviet Union rejected the American offer of aid, objecting to two of the plan's provisions. The first was that the borrowing governments had to allow American lenders to examine their books, analyse their economic policies, and control their spending. As a rival great power, the Soviets could not allow this embarrassing infringement on their sovereignty. The second provision was that the bulk of the money lent had to be used to buy American goods. Stalin denounced the plan as thinly disguised capitalist imperialism and accused Truman of "political pressure by means of dollars."

The Western European response to the Marshall Plan was swift. A joint proposal by seventeen nations requested $22 billion over a four-year period. The U.S. Congress approved $17 billion, although only about $12 billion was actually spent. The influx of capital from the Marshall Plan managed to avert the economic collapse of Western Europe. Grants were issued for articles of immediate consumption, such as food and fuel; purchases of capital equipment were financed through loans. Within four years production was twice that of prewar levels and Europe had entered a period of economic boom.

The Berlin Crisis and the Formation of NATO

When Germany was divided at Yalta it was agreed that Berlin, which was in the Soviet sector, would be subject to four-power occupation as well. (See map.) Isolated from the other Western zones, the former capital was particularly vulnerable to Soviet pressures. In 1947, Britain, France, and the United States initiated currency reforms in their sectors. Included in this decision was the cancellation of any further reparation payments by the Western part of Germany to the Soviet Union. With that leak plugged, the three Western powers proceeded to supply their sectors with large amounts of aid to speed up the rebuilding process. It was only a matter of time before the Soviets retaliated.

Berlin was to be the Soviet target. The economic isolation of the city began as sporadic interference with supply routes, but soon it escalated to a full-scale blockade. On 24 July 1948, the Soviets cut all road and rail access to West Berlin. Over 2 million people in the Allied zones of the city were being held hostage over 150 km inside the Soviet zone.

The U.S. and Royal air forces responded with an immense airlift. For the next eleven months all of the city's supplies were flown into Tempelhof, Gatow, and Tegel airfields from Allied bases in the West. At the height of the airlift, transport planes were landing at a rate of one per minute.

In the face of the West's tremendous efforts to keep West Berlin functioning, the Soviets lifted the blockade on 12 May 1949. Their plan had been to divide the Allies, but instead their aggression focused attention on the vulnerability of Western Europe to Soviet attack. The reality of the Soviet threat prompted Western leaders to commit their nations to a mutual defence pact in Europe. The result was the North Atlantic Treaty, which decreed that an attack on any one member nation would be considered an attack on all members. (See readings.) It was signed in April 1949 by the United States, Canada, Britain, France, Belgium, the Netherlands, Luxembourg, Denmark, Norway, Portugal, Italy, and Iceland. Turkey and Greece joined in 1952, the Federal Republic of (West) Germany in 1955, and Spain in 1982. (Germany remained a member after unification in 1990.)

North Americans clearly saw the North Atlantic Treaty Organization (NATO) in terms of the defence of Western values. U.S. president Truman committed the support of his country in an address to Congress in which he said: "I am sure that the determination of the free countries of Europe to protect themselves will be matched by an equal determination on our part to help them do so." These sentiments were echoed by Canadian prime minister Mackenzie King (1874–1950). Pledging Canadian support for the preservation of liberal democracy, King stated that if any nations were to form "a league of free people . . . there could be no doubt on the part of anyone as to our being in." Since then NATO has remained the primary focus of Canadian and American defence policies in Europe.

From the beginning, NATO was highly outnumbered by the Soviets in terms of conventional forces on the continent, with 14 divisions to their 175. To a great extent, NATO policy-makers relied heavily on the American "atomic umbrella" to protect them, believing that the Soviets would not dare launch a conventional attack for fear of an atomic reprisal. This sense of security came to an abrupt end in July 1949, however, when the Soviet Union exploded its first atomic device. The American response was swift. In addition to stepping up work on the development of a hydrogen bomb, they radically increased the number of troops in Europe.

As Cold War tensions heightened in the late 1940s, the superpower conflict began to spread outside of Europe as well. Nineteenth-century imperialism had expanded Western interests to include all parts of the world. As a result, the Cold War soon spread to other global theatres.

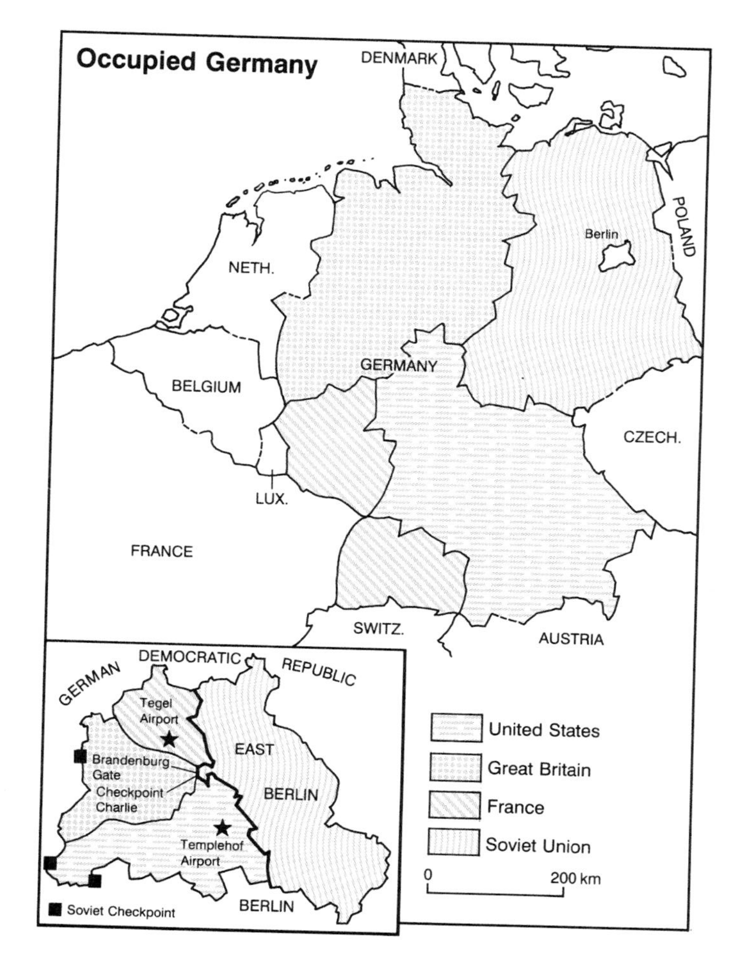

The United Nations and the Cold War

The preamble to the charter of the United Nations identifies the four principal aims of the international organization as:

• "to save succeeding generations from the scourge of war . . . "

• "to reaffirm faith in fundamental human rights, in the dignity and worth of the human person, in the equal rights of men and women and of nations large and small . . ."

• "to establish conditions under which justice and respect . . . for international law can be maintained, and"

• "to promote social progress and better standards of life in larger freedom."

This mandate for the protection of human rights and freedoms would put the world organization on the front lines in the ideological battle between the Eastern and Western blocs in the late 1940s.

The first major crisis facing the UN was the plight of the millions of refugees displaced by the Second World War. In 1943, two years before the forming and signing of the charter, the first United Nations agency was formed. The United Nations Relief and Rehabilitation Administration (UNRRA) was the result of an agreement among the forty-four main Allied nations at war with Germany and Japan. Its mandate was to provide supplies and help in repatriation of homeless individuals liberated by the Allied armies. By the end of 1945, over 3 million refugees had been returned home.

Of the almost 2 million refugees remaining in camps at the end of the war, over 650 000 were still under UNRRA control by the middle of 1947. Virtually all of these people were Eastern Europeans who had refused to return to nations now under Soviet control. Soviet officials accused the American commanders in charge of the refugee camps of attempting "to poison the souls and minds of these unfortunate men so as to thwart them in their natural aspirations and their legitimate desire to their native country." Compounding the refugee problem were the millions of ethnic Germans who had been expelled from countries previously occupied by the Nazis. Added to these were the millions of German citizens who had fled in the face of the Soviet advance in 1944–1945 and were now homeless in the Western zones of occupation. They had no desire to live in the Soviet zone. By November 1945, there were 2.5 to 3 million German refugees under Allied control, while a further 2 million remained in the Soviet zone.

In the final analysis, however, it was not UNRRA that solved the German refugee crisis. Always considered a stopgap measure, it provided support until the Marshall Plan came into effect. Eventually, an economically prosperous West Germany was able to absorb over 8 million German-speaking refugees.

UNRRA was succeeded in 1947 by the International Refugee Organization (IRO). This agency reflected a broad compromise between the Eastern and Western power blocs at the United Nations. Although the IRO had the same powers and resources as UNRRA, it was not tainted, in Soviet eyes, by the former agency's refusal to repatriate Eastern Europeans against their will. Included in their mandate were victims of the Nazi and other fascist regimes; Spanish republicans and other prewar exiles; and wartime deportees, prisoners, and forced labourers. Excluded were war criminals, traitors, collaborators, and all Germans. Eventually the IRO found homes for over 1 million people. Of these, the majority emigrated from Europe. The United States received 329 000, Australia 182 000, Israel 132 000, and Canada 123 000.

By the end of the 1940s, the IRO, combined with the economic aid of the Marshall Plan, had brought the refugee problem in Europe under control. The fundamental right of individuals living in camps to determine their own fate had been settled by their ability to leave the continent rather than return to the oppressive regimes of Eastern Europe. But while this worked in Europe, it would be of little use in the international refugee crisis to come. (See chapter 13.)

The primary goal of the United Nations was the preservation of world peace. Theoretically, there were three sanctions it could employ against aggressor nations. The first was a moral sanction or condemnation of a country's actions. This could be followed by economic sanctions, such as trade embargoes or blockades. Finally the UN could impose military sanctions and intervene with armed forces. Since its inception, the United Nations has imposed all of these sanctions, with mixed results.

Korea

The first real test of the military option came in Korea. Korea had been liberated from the Japanese at the end of the Second World War. As part of the peace agreement in 1945, the Soviet army occupied the northern half of the peninsula while the Americans remained in control of the south. The original plan had been to reunify the nation under a common political system. However, when it became apparent that a new government of a united Korea would likely be pro-Western, the Soviets blocked all attempts at reunification. As a result, two Koreas emerged: the Soviet-backed Korean Peoples' Republic in the north and the American-supported Republic of Korea in the south. To guard against any attempt by the Soviets to reunite the country by force, the United Nations guaranteed the territorial integrity of South Korea and the occupying powers withdrew. In spite of this precaution, however, in June 1950 the army of North Korea invaded the south in an attempt to forcibly reunite the country. The United Nations honoured its commitment and undertook a military defence of the south. Although the mainstay of the UN forces was the United States and the North Korean army was supported by the Peoples' Republic of China, over seventeen other nations, including Canada, were involved.

The first year of the war saw rapid movement. Between June and August 1950, the North Korean army had pushed the South Korean defenders back to a small perimeter position near Pusan. In September of that year, the UN forces, led by American general Douglas MacArthur (1880–1964), launched a surprise invasion at Inchon hundreds of kilometres behind enemy lines. Caught off guard, the North Koreans were routed and forced back deep into their own territory. By November, it appeared that the UN forces might occupy the entire peninsula. At that point the Peoples' Republic of China launched a counterattack against the UN troops. Forced back to a point near the 38th parallel, the UN forces dug in and stopped the northern advance. For the next three years the war remained static and the conflict eventually ended in a stalemate. On the positive side, it increased the credibility of the United Nations. As with the refugee crisis in Europe, the international organization had shown that it was willing to act according to its avowed aims and principles. During the next decade it would be tested again in a series of international crises.

The Cold War at its Peak

The foreign policies of the Western nations in the 1950s tended to follow the lead of the United States. The architect of American strategy was secretary of state John Foster Dulles (1888–1959), who believed that "the ability to get to the verge without getting into the war is the necessary art. . . . If you are scared to go to the brink you are lost." Dulles's theory of "brinkmanship" would dominate Western foreign policy until the end of the decade.

The 1950s marked the peak of Cold War propaganda. In the West, broadcasts by Radio Free Europe and the Voice of America, encouraging revolt against Soviet control, were beamed to Eastern Europe. The broadcasts led many anti-communists in the East to believe that the United States would come to their aid in a crisis. However, as events would later prove, this was not to be the case.

Dulles believed that peace could be maintained only through a demonstration of military might and readiness. He encouraged President Dwight Eisenhower (1890–1969) to begin an immediate buildup of the United States' nuclear arsenal. For their part, the Soviets were trying to catch up to the Americans. They had exploded their first hydrogen bomb in 1953, three years after the Americans had developed theirs, but they were still far behind the United States in the devel-

OFFICIAL ANNOUNCEMENT OF STALIN'S DEATH, 6 MARCH 1953

Few leaders have had the impact on world affairs that Joseph Stalin had. Although the brutality of Stalin's rule would later be exposed and denounced by the Soviet bureaucracy, during his lifetime positive feelings about the dictator were manipulated through the use of propaganda. The following official announcement of Stalin's death illustrates how the Soviet people were encouraged to revere their leader.

Dear comrades and friends: The Central Committee of the Communist party of the Soviet Union, the U.S.S.R. Council of Ministers and the Presidium of the U.S.S.R. Supreme Soviet announce with profound sorrow to the party and all workers of the Soviet Union that on the 5th of March . . . after a grave illness, the Chairman of the U.S.S.R. Council of Ministers and the Secretary of the Central Committee of the Communist party of the Soviet Union, Joseph Vissarionovitch Stalin, died.

The heart of the comrade and inspired continuer of Lenin's will, the wise leader and teacher of the Communist Party of the Soviet people—Joseph Vissarionovitch Stalin—has stopped beating.

Stalin's name is boundlessly dear to our party, to the Soviet people, to the workers of the world.

Together with Lenin, Comrade Stalin created the mighty party of Communists, reared and forged that party.

Together with Lenin, Comrade Stalin was the inspirer and leader of the great October Socialist Revolution, founder of the world's first Socialist state.

Continuing Lenin's immortal cause, Comrade Stalin led the Soviet people to a world-historic victory of Socialism in our land.

Comrade Stalin's death—the man who devoted all his life to the unselfish service of the Communist cause—is a tremendous loss to the party, to the workers of the Soviet Union and to the whole world.

Comrade Stalin armed the party and all the people with a great and lucid program of building communism in the U.S.S.R.

The news of Comrade Stalin's death will bring profound pain to the hearts of the workers, the collective farmers, the intelligentsia, and all the workers of our Motherland, to the hearts of millions of workers in all countries of the world. . . .

The immortal name of Stalin will live forever in the heart of the Soviet people and all progressive mankind.

Long live the great and all-conquering teachings of Marx, Engels, Lenin and Stalin!

Long live our mighty Socialist Motherland!

Long live our heroic Soviet people!

Long live the great Communist party of the Soviet Union!

From *The New York Times*, 6 March 1953.

opment of an effective nuclear arsenal. For the next four years the Americans would remain untouchable.

There were, however, some signs in the mid–1950s that both sides might be interested in a thaw in the Cold War. Stalin had died in 1953. During the five years before his death, the dictator had become even more tyrannical than he had been before. Intellectuals who had shown enthusiasm for Western ways of thinking during the wartime alliance were removed from their academic posts or imprisoned. The works of artists and writers were controlled and censored. Criticism of the government was suppressed. Soviet author Alexander Solzhenitsyn (1918-) depicted the inner workings of Stalin's mind during this period in *The First Circle* (1968). In this excerpt, the Soviet leader is thinking about himself in the third person.

> How many successful trials Stalin had conducted, how many enemies he had compelled to abase themselves and confess to any despicable crime—yet he had failed in Kostov's case! A disgrace throughout the world! What

black resourcefulness, to deceive the experienced interrogators, to crawl at their feet—and then in the public session, in the presence of foreign correspondents, to repudiate everything! What had become of decency? And the Party conscience? And proletarian solidarity? All right die, but die so that you're some use to us!

. . . A carefree country can sleep, but not its Father.

In early 1953, it appeared that a new series of purges might be being planned by the aging leader. There were rumours that he suspected a "doctor's plot" to have been responsible for the death of Andrei Zhdanov (1883–1948), head of the Agitation and Propaganda Directorate, five years earlier. He named nine well-known physicians as those involved in the plot, but before he could act on his suspicions he died suddenly of a heart attack.

To avoid renewing Stalin's "cult of personality" in another form, the Soviet government replaced the dictator with a form of collective leadership, with Georgi Malenkov (1902-) as chair of the Council of Ministers. Within four years, however, this collective leadership had collapsed. Moving into the power vacuum was one member of the council, Nikita Khrushchev (1894–1971). He portrayed a new image of the Soviet Union as a friend to the developing world rather than as a military aggressor. He condemned Western colonialism and offered "democratic socialism" as an alternative. At first it seemed that Khrushchev was serious in his attempts to change the direction of Soviet policy. At the Twentieth Party Congress in 1956, he denounced the atrocities of the Stalinist period. At the same time, he spearheaded such Soviet foreign policy initiatives as the signing of the Austrian State Treaty ending the postwar occupation of that country and establishing it as an independent, neutral state and establishing new friendly relations with Tito in Yugoslavia.

In 1955, Albania, Bulgaria, Czechoslovakia, East Germany, Hungary, Poland, Romania, and the Soviet Union signed the Warsaw Pact. Created in response to the admission of

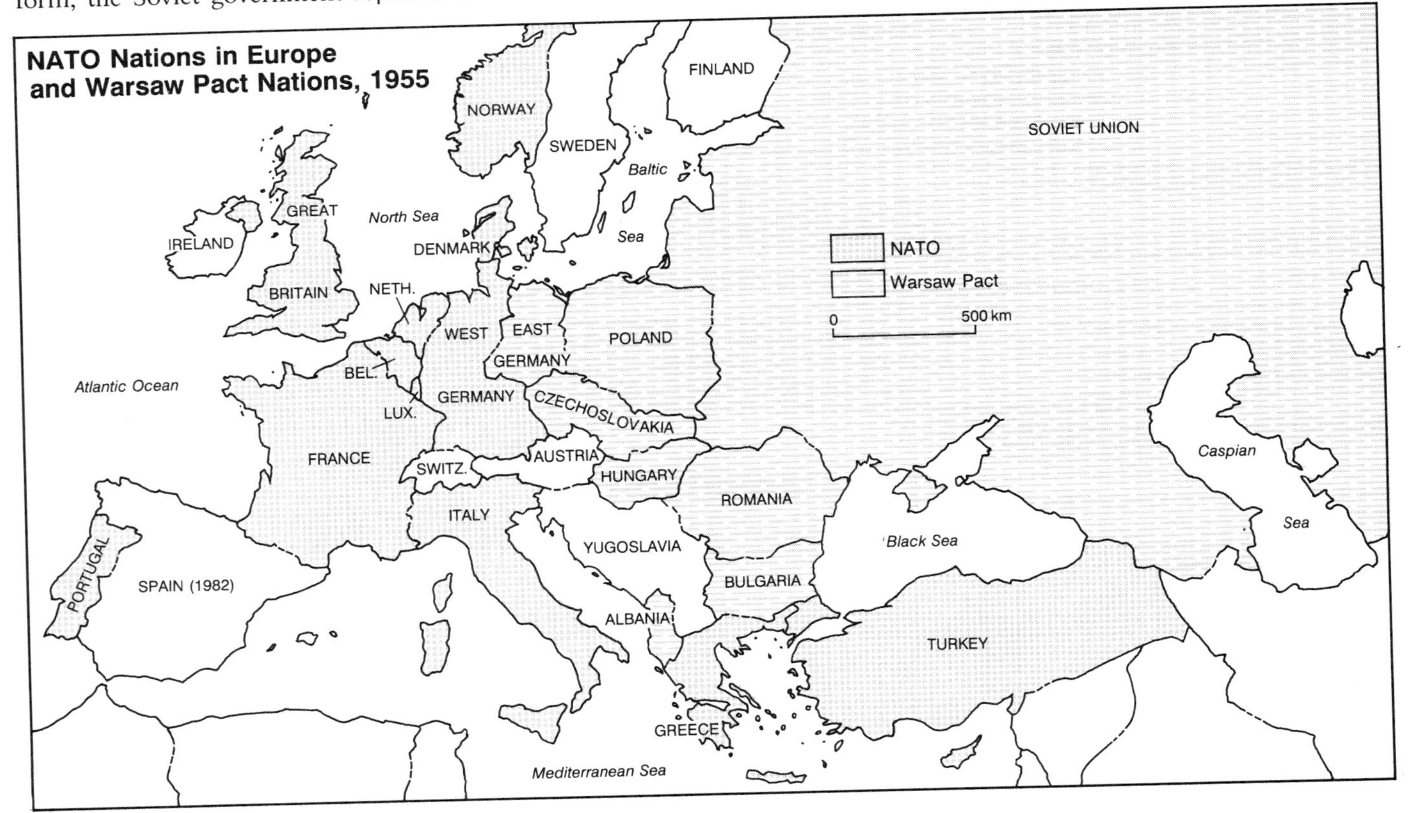

West Germany into NATO, the alliance required automatic mutual assistance in the event of a military attack against a member nation and appeared to give the nations of Eastern Europe equality with the Soviet Union in matters of defence. In reality, however, the Warsaw Pact merely confirmed the Soviet right to station troops throughout the region and left all major military decisions to the Soviet high command.

KHRUSHCHEV DENOUNCES STALIN

Khrushchev attempted to solidify his own power by distancing himself from the man who had been his mentor during his rise to prominence. At the Twentieth Congress of the Communist party in 1956, Khrushchev stunned the delegates with his stinging denunciation of his predecessor.

Stalin acted not through persuasion, explanation, and patient co-operation with people but by imposing his concepts and demanding absolute submission to his opinion. Whoever opposed this concept or tried to prove his viewpoint and the correctness of his position was doomed to removal from the leading collective and to subsequent moral and physical annihilation. . . .

Stalin originated the concept "enemy of the people." . . . This concept . . . actually eliminated the possibility of any kind of ideological fight or the making of one's views known on this or that issue, even those of a practical character. In the main, and in actuality, the only proof of guilt used, against all norms of current legal science, was the "confession" of the accused himself; and, as subsequent probing proved, "confessions" were acquired through physical pressures against the accused.

This led to glaring violations of revolutionary legality, and to the fact that many entirely innocent persons, who in the past had defended the party line, became victims. . . .

Comrades! In order not to repeat [the] errors of the past, the Central Committee has declared itself resolutely against the cult of the individual. We consider that Stalin was excessively [praised].

From *The New York Times*, 5 June 1956.

Revolution in Europe

The Western objective during the 1950s was the containment of communism. As long as the Soviet system could be prevented from expanding, it was likely to collapse from within. Early signs gave some credence to the theory. In 1953, East German workers revolted against the shortages caused by Soviet economic control. Although the crisis became so severe that the East German government had to call in Soviet tanks to crush the uprising, the West did nothing to intervene.

Three years later, Poland showed signs of liberalizing its government. The Soviet Union moved troops to the Polish border, but waited to see what events would take place next. This reluctance to take aggressive action encouraged nationalists in Hungary, who took to the streets demanding the establishment of a Western-style democratic government. Anxious to avoid a general revolt in Eastern Europe, the Soviet Union moved quickly. On 4 November 1956, Soviet troops entered Budapest and suppressed the uprising. (See readings.) Calls for Western aid had fallen on deaf ears. For a generation that had seen the Western allies stand by while Hitler had swept across the region fifteen years earlier, it may have appeared that history was repeating itself.

In an attempt to ease the tensions of the Cold War, Eisenhower and Khrushchev established superpower summit meetings in the mid–1950s. These face-to-face discussions softened tensions between the two leaders and paved the way for further negotiations. This policy was continued by Eisenhower's successor, John F. Kennedy (1917–1963). However, the Kennedy-Khrushchev relationship broke down quickly. After an initial summit in Vienna in 1961, the two leaders squared off over the issue of Berlin. The Soviets demanded a Western withdrawal from the city so that it might be reunified as the capital of the German Democratic Republic (East Germany). The United States responded by increasing troop strength in its sector of the city. Tensions mounted. During the summer of 1961, over 30 000 people escaped from the Eastern zone through the Western sectors. Having seen over 2 million citizens escape since the end of the blockade in 1949, the Soviets decided to stop the flow. Suddenly, on August 13th, West Berlin was cordoned off from the rest of East Germany. A 40 km barricade of stone and barbed wire was built up around the Western sectors. For the Soviets, however, it was a mixed victory. While the Berlin Wall stopped the flow of refugees to the West, it also preserved the territorial integrity of West Berlin. For the

In the early stages of building the Berlin Wall, ground floors of buildings were bricked up to create barriers. Here East German police tried to prevent the escape of a woman while West German police and firefighters tried to help her.

next twenty-eight years it would remain a base of Western democracy in the centre of communist Europe.

The End of the Cold War, 1965 to 1990

The first real thaws in the Cold War came with a change in leadership in the Soviet Union. Khrushchev's hold on power had been severely shaken by miscalculations in Berlin and later in Cuba. As a result, on 15 October 1964, he was overthrown by a more conservative faction within the Politburo. His successor, Alexei Kosygin (1904–1980), made greater use of the direct contact with the U.S. president via a telephone hotline between Washington and Moscow which had been established in September 1963. The two nations demonstrated its strategic importance during the Six Day War in 1967. (See chapter 13.) Egyptian president Gamal Abdel Nasser (1918–1970) closed the Gulf of Aqaba to Israeli shipping. In retaliation, Israel launched a series of preemptive military strikes, capturing large sections of territory, including the Egyptian Sinai Peninsula. With Moscow backing Egypt and Washington supporting Israel, the conflict could have escalated into a superpower confrontation. However, American president Lyndon Johnson (1903–1973) and Soviet premier Kosygin used the hotline to assure one another that their countries had no interest in becoming actively involved in the conflict. Thus the lines of communication were kept open and the situation remained tense but under control.

In June 1967, Johnson met with Kosygin in Glassboro, New Jersey, to discuss ways of limiting the spread of nuclear weapons. Two months later, both countries submitted identical proposals for the nonproliferation of nuclear arms to the United Nations Disarmament Conference in Geneva. This was the first time since the detonation of the atomic bomb over Hiroshima that the Soviet Union and the United States had agreed on any policy regarding nuclear weapons and it demonstrated their common concern that the arms race had begun to escalate out of control.

Détente in the Brezhnev Era

Relations between the two superpowers were dominated from 1969 until 1982—and through four American presidencies—by the policies of Soviet premier Leonid Brezhnev (1906–1982). While acting as Khrushchev's deputy, Brezhnev gained control of the party machine and became first secretary in 1964. In this role he shared power with Kosygin, and with the latter's retirement in 1969 Brezhnev emerged as the undisputed leader of the Politburo, assuming the combined roles of premier and party secretary. Brezhnev believed that a socialist state had an obligation to intervene in the affairs of another socialist state if the continuance of socialism was threatened. This doctrine was applied brutally in Czechoslovakia in 1968. In the spring and summer of that year, the communist Czech government, led by Alexander Dubcek

(1921-), attempted to liberalize their regime. After months of progress, however, the "Prague Spring" was cut short as Warsaw Pact troops, under Brezhnev's direction, invaded and overthrew the government. (See readings.)

Brezhnev's first American counterpart, Richard Nixon (1913-), recognized the dangers in a highly polarized world and tried to establish reasonable relations with the communist bloc. His first significant move came in February 1972 when he paid a state visit to the People's Republic of China. Within a year both nations had moved toward improved diplomatic and trade relations. Formal recognition of the People's Republic, however, did not come until 1979.

While Soviet leader Leonid Brezhnev maintained a hard line policy with the U.S.S.R.'s communist satellite countries, he pursued a policy of détente with the West. Here he talked with U.S. president Richard Nixon during Nixon's state visit to the Soviet Union in 1974.

Three months after Nixon visited China, the U.S. and the U.S.S.R. reached a new agreement on Strategic Arms Limitations. SALT I set ceilings on Intercontinental Ballistic Missiles (ICBMs) and Submarine-Launched Ballistic Missiles (SLBMs) for the five-year period from 1972 to 1977. Although it was a start, SALT I left several nuclear issues unanswered. First, it dealt only with the number of missiles or launch vehicles, not with the number of warheads. By the mid–1970s, the United States had large numbers of Multiple Independently Targeted Reentry Vehicles (MIRVs). These single missiles were capable of delivering a shower of nuclear devices. A second problem was the Antiballistic Missile system (ABM). The ABM system was intended as a defensive shield to destroy incoming enemy missiles. A forerunner of the "Star Wars" of the 1980s, the ABMs upset the theory of mutual deterrence. The final issue was that of intermediate-range missiles, such as those both NATO and the Warsaw Pact were developing in Europe. These "battlefield" weapons were of particular concern to the European members of the two alliances on whose home territory they would be used. But although the SALT agreements did not address all of these problems, they did lay the groundwork for a new era of consultation and negotiation. Called *détente,* it seemed to mark the end of the Cold War.

Since the 1950s, the Soviet leadership had been calling for a European Security Conference to lessen the military tensions in Central Europe. Western leaders had always rejected this proposal, claiming that a reduction in military arms and troops had to precede any such discussions. As a result, when Brezhnev agreed to open arms reduction talks with the Americans in 1972, he did so under the proviso that the West agree to a European Security Conference.

The conference began in Helsinki in January 1973. For the next year and eight months negotiators worked out an agreement. The Helsinki Accords were signed by U.S. president Gerald Ford (1913-) in August 1975. The boundaries established at the end of the Second World War were finally recognized and guarantees were provided for basic human rights in Europe. Critics claimed that Ford had sold out to the Soviets. In reality, however, the Americans had simply recognized the political facts in Europe in return for concessions in the area of human rights. The political security given to the Soviet Union by the Helsinki Accords also gave future Soviet leadership the flexibility to open up even further over the next fifteen years.

Afghanistan

The Soviet invasion of Afghanistan in December 1979 brought the era of détente to an end. American president Jimmy Carter (1924-) responded to the Soviet aggression with a high technology and grain embargo against the Soviet Union. As a further measure, the United States and fifty-seven other countries, including Canada, boycotted the 1980 Olympics in Moscow. Not surprisingly, the Soviet Union and most of the Warsaw Pact nations (except Romania) responded in kind to the Los Angeles Olympics four years later.

Critics of Carter's anti-Soviet policies called them token

gestures that did little to deter the Soviets while succeeding in hurting small sectors of the American economy. Among these groups were the farmers who were affected by the grain embargo. Feeling victimized by Carter's policies, the farm vote swung to his Republican opponent, Ronald Reagan (1911-), in 1980. Reagan stressed the need for an expanded military force and an enlarged nuclear arsenal to combat the Soviet menace. (In later speeches he would refer to the Soviet Union as an "evil empire.") More than any other factor, the election of Ronald Reagan seemed to mark the death of détente.

Political Instability

At the same time, the Soviets were experiencing a period of internal instability. Brezhnev, who had dominated the country for two decades, died in 1982. His successor, Yuri Andropov (1914–1984), died soon after taking office, as did Constantin Chernenko (1911–1985), who followed him into power. Soviet foreign policy drifted uncertainly. It was in this vacuum that the Reagan administration announced the beginnings of a new Strategic Defense Initiative (SDI), popularly known as "Star Wars." SDI was supposed to protect North America with a defensive screen of satellite-mounted laser and particle beam weapons. Theoretically, incoming nuclear missiles would be identified and detonated "harmlessly" long before they reached their targets. In reality, however, in spite of the predictions of a ten-year development program and the expenditure of over $70 billion, the technology for Star Wars simply did not exist. Nevertheless, SDI became a central bargaining point in nuclear negotiations.

The Geneva Conference

In November 1985, Reagan and the new Soviet premier Mikhail Gorbachev (1931-) met in Geneva, Switzerland. It was the first time an American president and a Soviet premier had held a summit since Carter and Brezhnev had met in 1979. For two days the leaders talked, negotiated, and socialized. Their final comuniqué announced some significant gains, including agreements to move toward a 50 percent reduction in long-range weapons; to outlaw chemical weapons and destroy all existing stockpiles; and to expand the membership of the nuclear nonproliferation treaty. Most notable, however, was the agreement to disagree on Star Wars; the Soviets rejected SDI as they felt it eliminated the deterrence factor that prevented nuclear war. In other areas, the leaders discussed human rights and agreed to resume the cultural exchanges that had been suspended since the Soviet invasion of Afghanistan.

The success of the Geneva Conference gave Reagan the confidence to deal more aggressively with Gorbachev. In the spring of 1986, he announced that the United States was going to resume nuclear testing and predicted that the arms limits of SALT II, which had been voluntarily observed by both sides since 1979, would soon be exceeded. In spite of this rhetoric, however, by July Reagan seemed to be moving closer to a serious resumption of negotiations with the Soviets. For the Americans, such a decision was not based simply on altruistic ideals. By the mid–1980s, the United States was a great power in decline. Although still the most powerful nation in the world, economically it was being outperformed by Japan and Korea in the Pacific Rim and by the growing economic might of the European Community. (See pages 383 to 384.) Faced with a staggering deficit, the Reagan administration had to find ways of scaling down its Cold War commitments.

Soviet leader Mikhail Gorbachev and U.S. president Ronald Reagan talked during the opening ceremonies of Gorbachev's state visit to the United States in 1987.

Restructuring the Soviet Union

For the Soviet Union in the 1980s, there was increasing impetus toward compromise with the West. One of the primary reasons for this change in attitude was a rapidly worsening economic situation.

To a great extent, Soviet economic problems were rooted in the Second World War. During the conflict, the Soviet Union suffered 20 million casualties, half of them civilians. Western Russia, Belorussia, and the Ukraine had been ravaged by the Germans. Over 1700 cities and towns had been destroyed, including Stalingrad, Minsk, and Kiev. In their desperate retreat from the advancing Red Army, the Germans destroyed over 62 000 km of railway track.

After the war, Stalin followed his traditional path of five-year plans. The first postwar plan in 1946 continued the wartime emphasis on heavy industry—iron, steel, coke, and coal production. To speed up recovery, the U.S.S.R. removed capital equipment from Eastern Europe, particularly from Germany. Agriculture continued to be backward and unproductive because of a lack of investment in machinery, buildings, fertilizer, transportation, and storage facilities. The extent of the problems in agriculture were revealed in 1946 when drought produced widespread famine.

After Stalin's death in 1953, a policy of de-Stalinization was carried out in economics as well as politics. Khrushchev initiated a series of reforms intended to increase agricultural production. These policies included offering higher returns to farmers and bringing new land into production. Initially the reforms were successful, but they did not solve the basic problems in the agricultural sector. By 1963, crop failures required the importation of 12 million tonnes of wheat. The failure of Khrushchev's economic plans became increasingly apparent and was responsible in part for his ouster from the leadership in 1964.

One of the reasons that agriculture was the weakest sector in the Soviet economy was the continued emphasis successive Soviet leaders had placed on heavy industry—the backbone of the military establishment. Under Brezhnev, the agricultural sector remained a problem because once again he concentrated on the industrial sector. In an attempt to increase industrial production, Brezhnev allowed some of the "profits" put into socio-cultural funds, production funds, and incentive funds. These funds increased workers' salaries substantially; the resulting economic recovery lasted from 1967 until the early 1970s. However, the reforms did not solve the problems of labour inefficiency, low productivity, and wasted raw materials. Under Brezhnev and his successor Andropov, there was a decline in the quantity and quality of industrial development. This was particularly true in the crucial high-tech/electronics industry. Although heavy industry showed growth, agriculture, light industry, and the production of consumer goods actually declined. As a result, industrial growth began to slow. The death of Andropov in 1984 resulted in a struggle for power between Gorbachev, who advocated a radical restructuring of the Soviet economy, and Chernenko, a member of the old guard. Chernenko won that struggle, but his death in 1985 brought Gorbachev to power.

Since the late 1970s, the Soviet Union had been increasing its military spending at the rate of 10 percent a year. At the same time, the Soviet economy was experiencing only 1 percent in real growth. The result was increasing pressure on the domestic economy and the threat of internal unrest. In addition, Soviet nuclear inferiority had always been balanced by an overwhelming superiority in conventional arms. But as a result of a declining birth rate and the reluctance of trained soldiers to re-enlist after fighting in the unpopular war in Afghanistan, it was becoming more difficult for the Politburo to maintain the quality of its armed forces. To combat these problems, Gorbachev announced major economic reforms in the *Principle Directions of the Economic and Social Development of the U.S.S.R. for the Years 1986 to 1990 and for the Period up to 2000*. These included greater research and development in science and technology, the reorganization of investment policies, and better economic management. Gorbachev also called for the greater use of chemicals, increased mechanization, and the planting of new crops to improve the agricultural sector.

Perestroika

A new watchword was coined, *perestroika* (meaning restructuring), which called for the democratization of the Soviet government and economy. The result was the first open elections since the revolution in 1917. Observers of the Congress of People's Deputies (two-thirds of whose members were freely elected) in the spring and early summer of 1989 were astounded at the openness of debate and the depth of political passion.

At the same time, the Soviet government formally denounced the Hitler-Stalin nonaggression pact of 1939. As part of this pronouncement, the Soviet Union admitted that its 1940 invasions of Latvia, Lithuania, and Estonia were illegal. This gave rise to nationalist sentiments in these Baltic republics, which now had a legitimate claim that the Soviet Union had no right of occupation. During the first half of 1990, all three republics passed resolutions of independence from the Soviet empire. In Lithuania, the nationalist Sajudis party formed a government and declared itself an independent state. Gorbachev responded with a show of military strength, occupying key communications and government buildings, and with an economic embargo. As Lithuania struggled to adjust, Latvia and Estonia also declared independence. By the summer of 1990, it had become clear that it would take force to keep the Baltic republics in the Soviet Union.

In spite of his efforts, however, by 1990 Gorbachev's *perestroika* appeared to be failing. His reforms had run head-on into entrenched attitudes and structures which had been in place for decades. Outright mistakes, such as emphasis on industrial investment instead of consumer goods, and uncertainty about the type of system to be created—democratic socialism, a free-market economy, or a more efficient command economy—also slowed reform. Foreign trade, which could have increased the number of available consumer goods, had been hindered by a currency that was not easily converted. As a result, economic growth was approaching zero in 1990.

In foreign policy, Gorbachev called for *glasnost*, or openness, and a new era of peaceful co-existence. The result was the first major agreement to reduce the number of missiles based in each country. As the ante was lowered on global nuclear conflict, the stage was also set for the reduction of intermediate-range missiles and conventional forces in Europe. In a speech to the United Nations in December 1988, Gorbachev stated: "The use or threat of force no longer can or must be an instrument of foreign policy. . . . All of us, and primarily the stronger of us, must exercise self-restraint and totally rule out any outward-oriented use of force. . . . It is now quite clear that building up military power makes no country omnipotent. What is more, one-sided reliance on military power ultimately weakens other components of national security." (See readings.) This statement was coupled with a sweeping proposal to reduce the size of the Soviet armed forces by over 500 000 troops and to withdraw large numbers of troops and weapons from Eastern Europe. Addressing the NATO heads of state in Brussels in June 1989, American president George Bush (1924-) responded favourably to the Soviet proposals, calling for sweeping arms cuts and an accelerated timeline that would see major reductions by 1992.

If military expenditures can be reduced, *perestroika* has a chance. If not, East-West relations may be in jeopardy. The fate of *glasnost* appears to be tied to Gorbachev, and Gorbachev's fate is tied to *perestroika*. If *perestroika* fails, *glasnost* fails, and the thaw in East-West relations that has accompanied *perestroika* could be reversed.

A sign of the changing times: Soviet artist Stanislav Kapilov hung a portrait of Czar Nicholas II on the Arbat pedestrian mall in Moscow in 1988. Only a few years earlier, Kapilov would have been arrested for such action.

The New Europe

One contemporary commentator observed in the spring of 1945, "At the moment when military operations ceased in Europe, the continent offered a spectacle of desolation." For most Europeans, 1945 was the end of one nightmare and the beginning of another. Their cities were destroyed, their factories were in ruins, their farms were unproductive, and their political, social, and economic norms had been swept away.

Recovery in the West was uneven until the introduction of the Marshall Plan. The plan forced the integration of the European economy. Nations began to specialize and customs

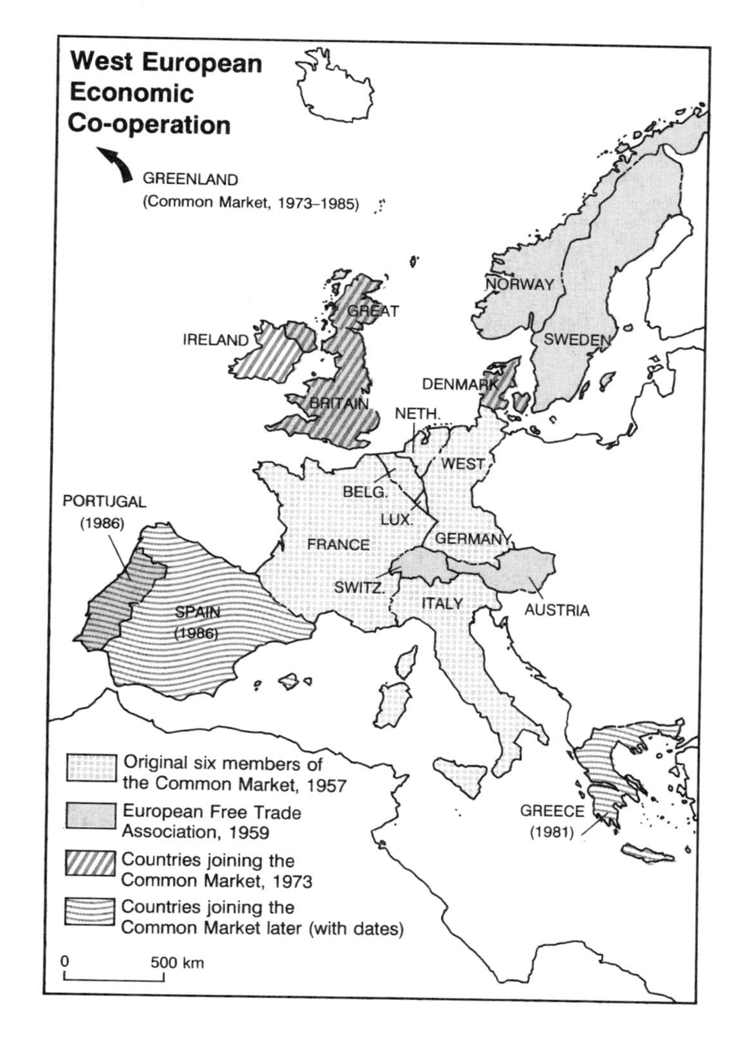

barriers slowly disappeared. Following a successful experiment in the coal and steel industries, the Treaty of Rome created the European Economic Community (EEC) in 1957. Within five years, trade among the members (France, West Germany, Italy, Belgium, Luxembourg, and the Netherlands) had increased by 73 percent and industrial production had gone up by over 30 percent. Britain led the development of another trading bloc. The "outer seven"—Britain, Denmark, Norway, Sweden, Austria, Portugal, and Switzerland—united under the European Free Trade Association. The EFTA had looser ties than the EEC, but it brought most of the industrial West into some form of common market. Eventually Great Britain, Denmark, and Ireland joined the EEC (1973), as did Greece (1981) and Spain and Portugal (1986).

Although the economic integration initiated by the Treaty of Rome was to be accomplished within a twelve-year period, the removal of internal tariffs and the erection of a common external tariff took place in 1968, two years ahead of schedule. A common agricultural policy protected farmers against foreign competition through a system of subsidies. But the development of common economic policies proved to be difficult in other areas, such as the elimination of migration restrictions on labour. Even today, a common currency has yet to be established. Despite these problems, however, the EEC proved to be a great success and Europe enjoyed an uninterrupted economic boom into the 1970s.

Europe in 1992

In the 1970s, international pressures, such as the oil crisis, resulted in the erection of a variety of non-tariff barriers by individual members of the EEC. In the 1980s, restrictions on capital movement, transport regulations, value added taxes, and government purchase policies gradually resulted in economic stagnation. Meetings to improve the situation resulted in the Single European Act, which came into effect 1 July 1987. The act is intended to complete the liberalization of trade begun by the Treaty of Rome by creating "an area without internal frontiers in which the freedom of movement of goods, persons, services, and capital is ensured." To accomplish this, all economic borders, whether physical or bureaucratic, will be eliminated by 1992. A single Eurocurrency will be established and a central bank will coordinate the monetary policies of member states.

Although a united Europe will require adjustments by all members, the EEC estimates that expanding intra-European trade could result in a 5 to 7 percent increase in gross domestic product over a five-year period. As a single market of 320 million consumers, the EEC has equal or greater potential in wealth, technological skills, and human resources than either the United States or the Soviet Union.

Many observers saw the entry of Britain, Denmark, and Ireland into the EEC as the first step toward a truly unified United States of Europe. Today the political, military, and economic structures are already in place. The European Parliament, with its 517 democratically elected members from across the continent, provides the political forum. Founded in 1952, the European Parliament predates the Common Market. Current membership, however, is restricted to members of the EEC. Based in Strasbourg, the parliament boasts its own bureaucracy of over 12 000 "Eurocrats." Currently, once the parliament approves a mandate, it is ratified by the twelve-member Council of Ministers and then submitted to the governments of the member nations for internal approval. In addition, an integrated defence system is provided for all EEC nations (except Ireland) through NATO.

On the other side of the ledger, however, are centuries of animosity and nationalism. These feelings will not disappear easily. Difficulties of language, immigration, economic disparity, and historical suspicion pose obstacles to a unified Europe. But, with the largest share of trade in the world, the EEC has an opportunity to take its place alongside the United States, the Soviet Union, and the growing economic giants of the Pacific Rim. It is only a matter of political will. (See readings.)

THE AWAKENING OF EASTERN EUROPE

Post–1945

Eastern Europe suffered considerable damage during the Second World War. This, coupled with prewar problems such as the lack of skilled labour, low standards of living, and a general lack of education, created severe economic problems in many countries. Most of the economies of Eastern Europe were agricultural with little heavy industry. Almost immediately, Eastern Europe was drawn under Soviet economic influence through co-ordination of their economies in the Soviet five-year plans.

Collective farms were introduced in agriculture; industry was nationalized and an emphasis on heavy industry was begun. Since only Poland and Czechoslovakia were industrialized before the war, this created significant social change. People started moving to the cities, creating overcrowding and often unsanitary conditions. While significant industrial growth was created, standards of living remained low and consumer goods were in short supply.

In 1947, the Soviets tried to consolidate their economic and political control over Eastern Europe through the Communist Information Bureau (Cominform). This ran into trouble almost immediately when Yugoslavia refused to participate and followed its own economic path in the form of a "socialist market economy." Competition and supply and demand determined production quotas, and management (which included the workers in the decision-making process) had greater freedom in buying and selling.

In the 1950s, the Soviets appeared to loosen their grip on Eastern Europe and reforms were introduced in Hungary, Czechoslovakia, and Poland. But in Hungary reforms took on political overtones and Soviet tanks stopped the program in 1956.

After 1956, the Soviet Union moved away from direct economic integration of the Eastern European economies with the Soviet economy. Instead, Khrushchev attempted to co-ordinate economic growth through specialization, the division of labour, and co-operative economic planning. Henceforth raw materials would be supplied by the Soviet Union, Bulgaria, and Romania; East Germany, Czechoslovakia, Poland, and the Soviet Union would convert these raw materials into finished products and then sell them back to their suppliers. However, Romania realized that this would actually increase Eastern Europe's economic dependence on the Soviet Union by preventing them from industrializing. The country was able to resist further integration into the Soviet economy and instead adopted its own policy of industrialization.

Change in the Sixties

By the 1960s, economic growth had slowed down in Eastern Europe. Collectivization in agriculture was creating a stagnant economy; production was unable to keep up with a growing population. Faced with increasing unrest over the lack of consumer goods and a failure to make any significant improvements in standards of living, some Eastern European countries began to move away from a centralized economy.

In Czechoslovakia, the government announced plans to determine production goals based on market factors and to increase trade with the West. However, the Soviets were not prepared to have their satellite nations move too far out of their orbit. In 1968 when Warsaw Pact troops launched an invasion of Czechoslovakia, the economic reform movement was crushed. The emphasis on central planning was renewed and the Eastern European focus on trade was maintained.

With the memory of 1956, Hungary was more circumspect in its reforms. It attempted to combine communist politics with a mixed economy similar to the Yugoslavian model. The move toward market socialism had almost immediate results. There was an improvement in the quality of goods and a higher growth rate. Agriculture in Hungary outperformed that in all of the other countries in Eastern Europe. But by 1989 the state still controlled 85 percent of the economy and Hungary was burdened with the highest per capita debt in Eastern Europe. These problems, plus *stagflation*—the simultaneous presence of inflation and high unemployment—led to demands for an immediate move to a market economy. Such a move, however, will require drastic measures and could lead to further social unrest.

A New Era

Soviet leader Mikhail Gorbachev ushered in a new era in Eastern Europe in the late 1980s. The policies of *perestroika* and *glasnost* opened up not only the Soviet Union but its satellite states as well. Although the communist states of Yugoslavia and Romania had always followed somewhat different paths, in the other Eastern European countries there had been little tolerance for anything other than strict Soviet doctrine. In 1989, however, a number of remarkable changes took place.

Poland

The winds of change blew first over Poland. Discontent in that country had been growing for years. Following a series of economic setbacks in the 1970s, Polish workers in the shipyards of the port city of Gdansk organized against the government in August 1980. Led by Lech Walesa (1943-), the Solidarity Trade Union demanded full recognition from the government. As Solidarity grew in importance and popularity, its leadership began to make even greater demands on the government, calling for free elections and democratic reforms. As a result, the government finally cracked down and proclaimed martial law in December 1981. Solidarity was outlawed and its leaders were jailed.

During the 1980s, the union continued to operate underground and, as economic conditions worsened, Solidarity's strength grew. By 1989, the nation had reached a crisis. With food shortages, high unemployment, and a foreign debt ranging from between $39 and $47 billion, it was clear that the government could no longer deal with the problem. So it declared that a coalition of political forces was necessary

Solidarity supporters welcomed U.S. president George Bush on his 1989 visit to Gdansk, Poland.

to lead Poland out of its economic crisis. As a result, open elections were held in the spring of 1989. The results shocked even government opponents. Although a number of seats had been guaranteed to the Communist party, Solidarity and its supporters won virtually all of the others. As a result, by the summer a Solidarity-led coalition controlled 264 of the 460 seats in the National Assembly. On August 18th, Polish president and Communist party leader Wojciech Jaruzelski asked Solidarity member and Roman Catholic intellectual Tadeusz Mazowjecki to become prime minister of Poland. (Walesa had earlier turned down the post.) For the first time since the late 1940s, a non-communist party would form the government of an Eastern European nation. Members of the Polish Communist party appealed to Gorbachev for support. The Soviet response was only that there should be communist participation in the government. It was a signal to the rest of the Soviet bloc to be flexible in the changing times.

Hungary

One of the first states to liberalize was Hungary. Renaming itself the Hungarian Socialist party, the Communist party attempted to retain power in free elections in March and April of 1990 by riding the crest of the reform movement. The strategy did not work. It was ousted from power and replaced with a coalition of democratic parties dedicated to the reintroduction of a free market economy.

Czechoslovakia

Czech officials, too, found that the new openness of the Soviet regime had left them behind. Protests marking the twenty-first anniversary of the 1968 invasion were suppressed by Czech authorities in August 1989, but as Alexander Dubcek's former foreign minister noted: "Civil courage is growing, and people seeing what happens in other parts of Eastern Europe are being encouraged to demand democracy, to revive the spirit of the 'Prague Spring.'" (See readings.) In early December 1989, the first Czech cabinet since 1948 to be formed without a communist majority was sworn in. Three weeks later, playwright Vaclav Havel (1938-), nine months earlier a prisoner of the former regime, was sworn in as president.

Romania

Anti-communist revolution took its most violent turn in Romania. Dictator Nicolae Ceauşescu (1918–1989) brought in the army to suppress a mass pro-democracy demonstration in the city of Timisoara in December 1989. The bloody crackdown killed at least 1000 unarmed civilians and overnight turned the entire nation against him. Within a week, Ceauşescu was in prison. On Christmas Day, the former dictator faced a military tribunal. Accused of genocide and plundering more than $1 billion from the treasury, the court took only two hours to find him guilty. He and his wife were then immediately executed by firing squad.

In the months that followed, sporadic uprisings continued to protest the slow pace of change in the country. However, in spite of a wave of anti-government protest in May, which called for the purging of all former members of the Communist party from positions of power, when elections were held on May 20th former communist Ion Iliescu (1930-) won 85 percent of the popular vote for president. In addition, his National Salvation Front party, a coalition which includes many former communists, won two-thirds of the seats in the country's new two-chamber parliament. The increased violence, especially directed against ethnic Hungarians living in the country, had convinced the electorate to vote for the stability of experience and the promise of gradual change. In spite of this convincing victory and Iliescu's promise to transform Romania into a "Swedish-style" social democracy, Romania's reform movement still appears to be the most fragile of the former communist satellites.

Germany

Given the new mood sweeping Europe, it is hardly surprising that these radical changes should have spread to the heart of the Cold War, divided Germany. With the opening of borders between Hungary, Czechoslovakia, and the West during the summer of 1989, the East German government witnessed a mass migration of its citizens. As the exodus mounted, so did internal protest as citizens demanded access to the economic benefits and political freedoms found in the West. Finally, in November 1989, the government relented. In an act of desperation, the borders were opened. The Berlin Wall, for almost thirty years a symbol of repression, was breached and dismantled. Wire services around the world showed German youth, East and West, sitting atop the hated barrier. Initially interested in establishing some form of peaceful co-existence between the two Germanies, by the winter of 1990 politicians on both sides of the border were talking about reunification. Even Gorbachev, who months earlier had called the prospect "unthinkable," was now saying that reunification was inevitable. In March, free elections were held in the German Democratic Republic for the first time since 1932. The vote resulted in a massive victory for the Alliance for Germany (a party affiliated with West German chancellor Helmut Kohl's [1930-] Christian Democratic Union). Its main campaign promise was to act quickly to reunify the two German states.

By the summer of 1990, the decision to reunite had been made and both sides had begun the process of transition. In July, currency reform took place as the GDR mark disappeared to be replaced by the West German deutschemark. Under the agreement, East German citizens were given a one to one exchange on their first 4000 marks and one West German mark for two East German marks on the remainder. Prior to the exchange, most East Germans went on a shopping spree, emptying shops with the last of their soon-to-be-worthless currency. That same month Gorbachev, after meeting with Kohl, announced that the Soviet Union had no objection to a reunified Germany remaining as a member of NATO. With the last major obstacle to reunification removed, the process was established for holding a national election in early December and the declaration of a reunified Germany by the end of the year. The pace of reunification was accelerated in the fall of 1990 and by October 3rd the two Germanies were officially reunited. Not all Europeans are pleased about a reunified Germany, however. Many are concerned that nationalist factors that contributed to the First and Second World Wars may resurface. Jewish leaders, as well as politicians in France, Britain, and the Soviet Union, have expressed concern about a resurgent and potentially expansionist Germany.

Most observers agree, however, that the real strength of a united Germany is an economic one. The second largest European nation in area (after France), a united Germany boasts the fourth largest gross domestic product in the world (after the United States, the Soviet Union, and Japan), with total exports equivalent to that of France and Britain combined. It also has the third largest capital city on the continent and the largest population of any European nation outside of the Soviet Union.

Germans used any tools at their disposal to knock down the Berlin Wall in 1989.

The Enlightenment Tradition

The events of 1989 and 1990 marked a victory for the Enlightenment tradition. After almost fifty years of authoritarian rule, the nations of Eastern Europe were finally able to break free and re-embrace the ideas of liberal democracy. For the first time in over half a century, almost all Europeans were free to discuss important issues such as human rights, political preferences, and economic theories. Most observers predict that by the end of the century, the economic, political, and military co-operation that characterizes the Western nations will expand to encompass the continent and that a new resurgent Europe will emerge as a great power in its own right, based not on nationalist but internationalist principles.

SEARCHING FOR VALUES: THE TRIUMPH OF THE ENLIGHTENMENT TRADITION

The charter of the United Nations committed that organization "to reaffirm faith in fundamental human rights, in the dignity and worth of the human person, in the equal right of men and women and of nations large and small." These basic principles were to set the tone for an era. Yet these values of modern Western civilization have not always been applied by Western societies. The colonizing nations, in their treatment of their overseas subjects, frequently denied people their fundamental human rights. (See chapter 13.) As we have seen, the Soviet Union and its Eastern European satellites have only recently allowed their citizens to reaffirm their adherence to the Enlightenment tradition. It has been generally argued, however, that the domestic policies of the West—that is, Western Europe and North America—have maintained the ideas of the Enlightenment tradition. But this in fact has not been the case. Fundamental human values, rights, and freedoms have not always been equitably applied by these nations to their own citizens. Prior to the Second World War, certain injustices were tolerated to the point where, for many people, they had become an unquestioned fact of life. As a result racial and linguistic minorities, women, and the economically disadvantaged have found themselves second-class citizens in their own countries.

The Individual and the Community: The Human Rights Challenge

The European Experience

The horrors of the Holocaust were still clearly etched in the European mind when, in 1948, the United Nations adopted the Universal Declaration of Human Rights. Among its proclamations were that "all human beings are born free and equal in dignity and rights . . . ; no one shall be subjected to arbitrary arrest, detention or exile . . . ; [and] everyone has the right to freedom of thought, conscience, and religion . . .; everyone has the right to freedom of opinion and expression."

This was clearly not the case in Eastern Europe in the decades following the end of the Second World War. In addition to the excesses of dictators such as Stalin and Ceauşescu and such obvious interventions as those seen in Hungary in 1956 and Czechoslovakia in 1968, most Eastern European nations maintained a stranglehold on dissent by controlling the media, education, and emigration. In his monumental work *The Gulag Archipelago*, published in 1973, Soviet dissident writer Alexander Solzhenitsyn (1918-) chronicled the treatment of political prisoners under Stalin. During the 1950s and 1960s, Solzhenitsyn and other human rights activists used the United Nations declaration to pressure governments to honour the human rights of their citizens. In spite of such protests, however, repressive regimes continued their practices.

By the late 1970s, two events seemed to give some hope to the activists' cause. In 1975, both the Soviet Union and the United States signed the Helsinki Accord, which guaranteed such basic human rights as the reunification of families, the easing of travel restrictions, and the encouragement of cultural exchanges. The following year the United Nations published a series of human rights covenants which laid out basic rights in the areas of working conditions, trade unionism, social security, and health. Over forty-five nations, including Canada, have signed the covenants, although the Soviet Union has so far refused to do so.

In spite of obvious violations of the UN charter and the subsequent *Universal Declaration of Human Rights*, the United Nations did nothing to interfere in the policies of its member nations. As a result, independent watchdog groups appeared. One such organization was Amnesty International (1962), which issues a report each year on the global state of human rights. In addition, it orchestrates mass appeals for the release of political prisoners, pressures democratic governments to take economic and political actions against nations that violate human rights, and stages protests and demonstrations against human rights abuses. In 1977, Amnesty International was awarded the Nobel Prize for Peace. In spite of these efforts, however, in the late 1980s four out of five people in the world still lived without basic human rights.

In the Soviet Union, the Helsinki Rights Group was founded in 1976. In spite of the frequent persecution and imprisonment of its members, who included Soviet physicist Andrei Sakharov (1921–1990), the group continued to publicize Soviet violations of human rights throughout the seventies and eighties.

Racial Discrimination in the United States

Throughout the twentieth century, the United States had considered itself the leader of the great egalitarian democracies. Yet during this same period it was U.S. policy to provide racially segregated facilities for black and white citizens. This concept of "separate but equal" access to goods and services kept the races apart in almost all aspects of life. There were "white only" restaurants, parks, public washrooms, and beaches. There were separate railway cars and waiting rooms for blacks, and white and black patients visited different doctors and stayed in separate hospitals. Theoretically, each group was provided with equal facilities, but in fact there was no equality in such a system. Invariably the quality of the services reserved for blacks was inferior to that reserved for whites. Nowhere was this more evident than in the education system.

In the nation's universities it was economically impossible to provide separate but equal facilities. The provision of scientific equipment, library resources, and even entire faculties at black institutions could not even begin to meet the standards of the white universities. Blacks were thereby forced to receive inferior standards of education. Black lawyers systematically challenged the concept of separate but equal in the courts. Gradually the academic community relented and by the early 1950s universities and colleges began to integrate.

The next target was the public school system. In May 1954, the United States Supreme Court gave the unanimous opinion in *Brown vs the Board of Education of Topeka* that the concept of "separate but equal has no place" in the field of public education. Segregation of school children on the basis of race "generates a feeling of inferiority as to their status in the community that may affect their hearts and minds in a way unlikely ever to be undone." This required that segregation be ended not immediately but at least with "all deliberate speed."

For some states, however, "all deliberate speed" meant "as slowly as possible." As a result, although some progress was made, by the mid-sixties only 1 percent of all black students attended integrated schools in the southern United States.

Following the passage of the second Civil Rights Bill (1964) under Johnson, federal officials were able to place greater legal pressure on school districts to integrate. For many cities, integration meant bussing. As blacks tended to live in different parts of the city from whites, in order to integrate schools black and white students had to be transported to other neighbourhoods. This confused the issue by allowing anti-integration forces to argue their case on non-racist grounds. Protestors emphasized their concern for children and the need to allow all students to attend their neighbourhood schools. Given the demographics of neighbourhoods, this meant de facto segregation. It was an even more critical problem because the schools located in white middle-class neighbourhoods tended to be better equipped, better staffed, and more modern than their black inner city counterparts. Finally, many American cities circumvented the problem through the creation of "magnet" schools. Certain schools were given designations as centres for specialized programs, such as science, performing arts, and enrichment. Students were then encouraged to attend the school that best matched their interests and talents. This integration by self-selection was an effective method of voluntary integration.

During the late 1950s and early 1960s protests were held all over the south. Students joined Dr. Martin Luther King Jr.'s (1929–1968) example of nonviolent protest and staged a series of sit-ins at all-white cafes, theatres, shops, bars, and beaches. At the same time, King and his supporters worked to ensure that all eligible black voters were registered to vote.

King had emerged during the Montgomery Bus Boycott as an effective and committed leader of the civil rights movement. While imprisoned after one demonstration, King wrote "Letter from Birmingham Jail." A powerful document, it clearly outlined his case against the status quo. (See readings.) In addition, King captured national attention at the head of a massive march on Washington in the summer of 1963. Addressing over 200 000 blacks and whites, he declared:

I say to you today, my friends, that in spite of the difficulties and frustrations of the moment I still have a dream. It is a dream deeply rooted in the American dream.

I have a dream that one day this nation will rise up and live out the true meaning of its creed: "We hold these truths to be self-evident; that all men are created equal."

I have a dream that one day on the red hills of Georgia the sons of former slaves and the sons of former slaveholders will be able to sit down together at the table of brotherhood. . . .

I have a dream that my four little children will one day live in a nation where they will not be judged by the colour of their skin but by the content of their character.

THE MONTGOMERY BUS BOYCOTT

It was below freezing on 1 December 1955 when black seamstress Rosa Parks (1914-) boarded a bus in Montgomery, Alabama, to return home after a day's work. The bus was filled to its thirty-six-seat capacity with twenty-two blacks and fourteen whites. When more white passengers boarded, the driver asked a row of blacks to leave their seats and stand at the back of the bus. Some complied, but Parks, a former assistant with the NAACP, refused. The bus driver immediately arrested her and summoned two police officers to take her to jail.

Parks was charged with violating Alabama's bus segregation law. The arrest triggered a call to action by Montgomery's black leaders. A one-day bus boycott was organized for the day of Park's court case to protest the charges and the treatment of blacks in general on the city's public transportation system. Fliers were distributed and public meetings were held to rally the black community. On Monday, 5 December 1955, the majority of blacks in Montgomery refused to board the buses.

The protest had little effect on Parks's court case, however. Parks was declared guilty and fined $10 plus $4 in court costs. But the conviction enabled the black community to challenge the segregation laws on appeal all the way to the U.S. Supreme Court.

Black leaders decided to continue their boycott. The Montgomery Improvement Association was formed under the leadership of Dr. Martin Luther King, Jr., to organize the protest. The MIA established a list of demands, which included seating on a first-come, first-served basis and black bus drivers for predominantly black routes. They organized a transportation committee to figure out ways to get 17 500 blacks to and from work and a finance committee to raise funds for legal fees and transportation. The executive committee met with city executives to discuss their demands, but Montgomery officials were not prepared to change the status quo. The boycott continued.

In the meantime, four black women filed a suit in the U.S. District Court challenging Alabama's transportation laws. On 4 June 1956, the court announced its decision: two to one declaring segregation to be unconstitutional. The case then went to the U.S. Supreme Court. On 13 November 1956, after almost a year of boycotts and court battles, the Supreme Court affirmed the decision of the U.S. District Court that Alabama's state and local laws requiring segregation on buses were unconstitutional.

The boycott in Montgomery was over. In a speech to an overflowing crowd gathered to mark the end of the segregated bus system, King said, "We came to see that, in the long run, it is more honourable to walk in dignity than ride in humiliation. So in a quiet, dignified manner, we decided to substitute tired feet for tired souls, and walk the streets of Montgomery until the sagging walls of injustice had been crushed." But it was only one hard-fought victory in the long battle against racial discrimination in the South. There would be many more to come.

Five years later, that dream was ended by an assassin's bullet. On 4 April 1968, King was shot and killed in Memphis, Tennessee. On his gravestone were the words with which he finished his Washington speech: "Free at last, free at last, thank God almighty I'm free at last."

King and his supporters had made substantial gains but for many blacks change did not come quickly enough. In the late 1960s there was an upsurge in racial unrest. Rioting in Watts, a black neighbourhood in Los Angeles, in 1965 saw thirty-five people killed. The next summer violence erupted in Chicago, and in 1967 twenty-six people were killed and over 1200 wounded in riots in Newark, New Jersey. The violence came to a peak soon after as Detroit exploded with rioting. In that city, forty-three people were killed and over 4000 fires were set, causing millions of dollars worth of damages. In spite of a new generation of black leadership that was calling for increased violence, however, soon after these incidents the attention of blacks and whites turned to ending the war in Vietnam instead. As a result, the slow process of change continued as before. It would take at least another decade before animosities reflected in the protesting and rioting would give way to co-operative achievement. By the late 1980s, Democrat Jesse Jackson (1941-) was able to run a strong campaign for that party's presidential nomination, and many cities and states were led by black mayors and governors.

Dr. Martin Luther King and 5000 demonstrators marched from Selma to Montgomery to demonstrate for civil rights in 1965.

Challenges to the Individual and the Community: The Western Experience

The Refugee Challenge

As a result of human rights violations in Soviet-occupied Eastern Europe, a flood of refugees escaped to the West. Following the suppression of the Hungarian Revolution in October 1956, over 200 000 Hungarians (2 percent of the population) fled the country. The vast majority of these, over 180 000, arrived in Austria, where they were helped to find new homes by the United Nations High Commissioner for Refugees. Eventually, half of these people left Europe, with over 35 000 resettling in the United States and almost 23 000 in Canada. At the same time, the decade from 1951 until the building of the Berlin Wall saw over 3.5 million East Germans leave for the Federal Republic in the West.

Even as the borders were tightened against the exodus, certain groups were encouraged to leave. In 1967, Poland expelled most of the 30 000 Jews living there and between 1970 and 1985 close to 300 000 Jews were allowed to emigrate from the Soviet Union. On occasion, changing internal conditions sparked a mass movement. For example, over 200 000 Poles who were out of the country when martial law was proclaimed in 1981 chose to remain in the West.

For the most part, these European refugees found safe haven among their neighbours. In 1951, the European Convention of Human Rights prohibited aliens from being deported back to a country where they would be subject to persecution. This was strengthened by the 1967 protocol that protected aliens who might find their basic human rights violated in their country of origin.

The European refugee problem was not limited to Cold War persecutions, however. By the late 1950s, more and more European repatriates began returning from newly independent colonies. These groups included over 250 000 Dutch citizens from Indonesia, 90 000 Belgians from the Congo, and over 1 million French immigrants from Indochina and Algeria. For the most part, these people had never set foot in Europe before. They were the children of generations of colonial emigrés and in the postwar period they were returning to Europe to demand their birthright. Most European countries responded positively at first, but the economic slowdown of the 1970s resulted in a tightening of regulations that slowed the influx to a trickle. By 1980, only France and Switzerland still maintained an admirable record in absorbing these refugees.

At the same time, the influx of non-White refugees led to growing problems of discrimination and racial unrest. In Britain, France, and Belgium, racial tensions heightened significantly as increasing unemployment in the 1980s led to growing resentment of the more than 10 million foreign workers holding jobs on the continent. Prior to this, racial equality had been a minor concern in a predominantly white Europe. In the late 1980s, however, race riots in England and racism among the political right wing in France were giving European leaders cause for concern.

West Germany faces another problem at the beginning of the 1990s. For decades, foreign "guest workers" have filled many of the jobs unwanted by German citizens. It is predicted that reunification will result in the laying off of large numbers of East German workers as government-run industries close down. These surplus workers will likely displace the guest workers throughout the country. Lacking the rights of citizens, workers from Italy, Yugoslavia, and Turkey will be forced to return home with their German-speaking and educated children to look for work in their native, economically depressed countries. This reverse refugee crisis could be a major issue of the 1990s.

The Terrorist Challenge

In early December 1989, one of West German chancellor Helmut Kohl's chief economic advisors was assassinated in a bomb blast that destroyed his car. The assassins claimed to be members of the terrorist Red Army Faction. This is only one of the more recent incidents of terrorism to strike Western society.

Terrorists tend to use random acts of violence to unsettle their opponents and to attract media attention to their cause. The postwar period has seen two distinct brands of terrorism emerge to challenge the liberal democratic values of the Enlightenment tradition. In the decolonizing world, terrorist groups tend to attack the symbols of foreign support for what they consider to be oppressive regimes. Too weak to launch full-scale offensives, these groups use kidnappings, bombings, and murder to draw attention to their cause. Within Western society, disaffected social and political groups use terrorist tactics to destabilize society in an attempt to bring about change. Although such individuals see themselves as revolutionaries, most Western leaders see them the way former Canadian prime minister Pierre Trudeau (1919-) did, as "bandits."

Diplomats, military leaders, and government officials have long been subject to terrorist attacks. Earlier in the 1980s, a bomb aimed at American service personnel destroyed a West Berlin nightclub; sixty-three American hostages were taken and held for over a year after Iranian students seized their embassy in Tehran in 1979; in October 1970, a Quebec cabinet minister was killed and a British trade commissioner held hostage by two cells of the Front de Libération du Québec (FLQ); eleven Israeli athletes were killed by Palestinian Black September terrorists in an attack at the 1972 Munich Olympics; and the Grand Hotel in Brighton was destroyed by a 1984 Irish Republican Army (IRA) attack against key members of the British government who were meeting there at the time.

Groups such as Ireland's IRA, West Germany's Bäader-Meinhoff Gang, Canada's FLQ, Italy's Red Brigade, and France's Action Directe have conducted campaigns of random violence against the state and its citizens. Over the past twenty years such groups have taken the lives of over 7000 people. In 1985 alone, terrorist attacks against power stations, oil and water pipelines, and communication transmission lines numbered over 350. As international tensions eased between the superpowers toward the end of the 1980s, there seemed to be no lessening of terrorist activity.

Western society is particularly vulnerable to terrorist attack. The open nature of the Western democratic process means that political leaders are easy targets for determined assassins. In the past thirty years, successful and unsuccessful attacks have been made against such international figures as American presidents John Kennedy (1917–1963), Gerald Ford (1913-) and Ronald Reagan (1911-); British prime minister Margaret Thatcher (1925-); Norwegian president Olaf Palme (1927–1986); Indian prime minister Indira Gandhi (1918–1981); Pope John Paul II (1920-); and Egyptian president Anwar al-Sadat (1918–1981).

Another vulnerability is the Western belief in the worth of the individual and the value of life. This has led terrorist groups to kidnap and hold hostage several Americans, British, French, and Italians in the hope that these Western governments will give into their demands in order to save the hostages' lives. Often, however, the kidnappers' demands are so far-reaching that it is impossible for Western governments to negotiate their release.

The Women's Movement

Perhaps the greatest revolution in the twentieth century has been in the status of women in Western society. After winning suffrage in the early decades of the century (see chapter 7), women began to pursue higher levels of education and to enter into fields traditionally reserved for men. This trend continued until the Great Depression, when the number of women seeking university degrees declined as money became scarce. However, the number of women who were employed outside the home continued to increase, although at a slower pace than during the previous decade.

During the Second World War, the role of women expanded to meet the demands of the war effort. Women volunteered to join the army, performing such services as nursing, driving ambulances, and operating telegraph systems. Their contribution to the military freed men for combat. On the home front, women played an important part working in the war industries in such nontraditional trades as welding and rivetting. However, whatever steps toward equality that were obtained during the war lasted only as long as the hostilities. The attitude of the government and in fact of the public in general was that women were only doing their patriotic duty. Once the men returned from overseas, women were expected to resume their places in the home. To that end, government-subsidized daycare facilities were closed down and married women were let go from their jobs to make room for the returning soldiers. After six years of war, society began to return to traditional values. This, of course, meant a return to traditional family life, with the man as breadwinner and the woman as wife, mother, and homemaker.

The Beginnings of the Women's Rights Movement

In 1949, French existentialist writer Simone de Beauvoir (1908–1986) sounded the first rallying cry for the modern women's movement. *The Second Sex* called for the abolition of "the slavery of half of humanity, together with the whole system of hypocrisy that it implies." De Beauvoir wanted to free women from their dependence on men. She rejected traditional roles for women and caused a storm of protest when she declared that "given that one can hardly tell women that washing up saucepans is their divine mission, they are told that bringing up children is their divine mission." For de Beauvoir, motherhood had become a trap that prevented many women from pursuing significant careers outside of the home.

Building on the ideas of de Beauvoir, women looked to establish greater equality for themselves during the postwar era. Low birth rates during the Depression and the impact of war on the male working population created a labour shortage during the 1950s that women workers moved to fill. Underpaid and usually under-challenged in their jobs, these women and their counterparts who continued to work in the home began to demand fairer treatment from a male-dominated society.

In the 1960s, the introduction of the birth control pill also helped to liberate women from traditional roles. Women were suddenly able to control the timing and the number of their pregnancies, which gave them the ability to chart their future, a future that increasingly included higher education and career goals.

The United States

The women's movement began to gain focus in 1963 with the publication of Betty Friedan's (1921-) *The Feminine Mystique*, in which she explained how women had given up power to men and were little better than prisoners in their own society. Friedan argued that "women can affect society as well as be affected by it and in the end a woman has the power to choose." Her book sparked a wealth of other feminist works, among them Germaine Greer's (1939-) *The Female Eunuch* and Kate Millet's (1934-) *Sexual Politics*.

In 1966, Friedan founded the National Organization of Women (NOW), a group whose focus was to redress the sexual inequalities in society. Its statement of purpose reflected the liberal principles of John Stuart Mill's *The Subjection of Women*:

> NOW is dedicated to the proposition that women, first and foremost, are human beings, who like all other people in our society, must have the chance to develop their fullest human potential. We believe that women can achieve such equality only by accepting to the full the challenges and responsibilities they share with all other people in our society, as part of the decision-making mainstream of American political, economic and social life.
>
> From Josephine Donovan, *Feminist Theory: The Intellectual Traditions of American Feminism* (New York: Frederick Ungar Publishing Co., 1985), p. 25.

Women marched in Ottawa in 1983 demanding better jobs and equality with men.

NOW's aims were revolutionary for the day, including equal pay for work of equal value, affirmative action in hiring, and universal daycare. Its "bill of rights" for women demanded legal statutes that would ensure women's equality within society.

In 1972, an Equal Rights Amendment to the Constitution was introduced to entrench women's rights. The amendment had to be passed by the legislature of two-thirds of the fifty states. A fierce battle erupted, however, between pro and anti ERA forces. Ultimately ERA proponents lost the battle when they fell one state short of the required number and the amendment died on the ratification deadline date in June 1982.

Women made significant gains in terms of equality in the workplace; increasing numbers of women chose to work outside the home and many women launched successful careers in traditional male fields. But progress in other areas has been limited. With the defeat of the ERA, equal rights are still not guaranteed in law. The federal government provides little in the way of public funding for daycare centres and affirmative action programs have been opposed on the grounds that they establish a quota system. And while many women have embarked on careers in professions and trades formerly reserved for men, by 1990 two-thirds of all employed women were still working in traditionally female office and service jobs.

Canada

In Canada, Laura Sabia spearheaded the women's movement. In 1966, she organized the Committee on Equality for Women, which lobbied the federal government to establish a royal commission to investigate the status of women in Canadian society. In 1967, the Royal Commission on the Status of Women was established "to inquire and report upon the status of women in Canada, and to recommend what steps might be taken by the Federal Government to ensure for women equal opportunities with men in all aspects of Canadian society."

The commission conducted special studies and held public hearings across the country. It broadened its mandate to include areas under provincial jurisdiction, such as education, family law, and health. In 1970, the *Report of the Royal Commission on the Status of Women* outlined four principles:

> (1) women should be free to choose whether or not to take employment outside their homes;
> (2) the care of children is a responsibility to be shared by the mother, the father, and society;
> (3) society has a responsibility for women because of pregnancy and childbirth, and special treatment related to maternity will always be necessary; and
> (4) in certain areas women will for an interim period require special treatment to overcome the adverse effects of discriminatory practices.

From the *Report of the Royal Commission on the Status of Women in Canada* (Ottawa: Information Canada, 1970), p. xii.

The establishment of the royal commission marked the first success in the second wave of Canadian feminism. Following publication of the report, the National Action Committee on the Status of Women (NAC) was formed from the earlier Committee on Equality for Women to ensure that the government acted on the commission's recommendations. Women's groups sprang up around the country to pressure provincial governments to heed the report. Gradually, some changes were made. Divorce and family laws were changed to reflect women's equal contribution to the family; unemployment insurance was granted for women on maternity leave; abortion laws were modified to allow termination of pregnancy under certain conditions; and affirmative action programs were introduced to promote the hiring of women in the workplace. However, other recommendations, such as pensions and paid vacations for housewives and equal pay for work of equal value, have yet to be implemented. (In 1990, Ontario enacted North America's first equal pay for work of equal value legislation, beginning with the public sector; the plan will gradually be implemented in the private sector.)

Canadian women's rights were formally guaranteed in 1982 in the Charter of Rights and Freedoms, which stated that "Every individual is equal before and under the law and has the right to the equal protection and equal benefit of the law without discrimination and, in particular, without discrimination based on race, national or ethnic origin, colour, religion, sex, age, or mental or physical disability."

One of the most tragic events in the history of the women's movement in Canada occurred in December 1989. A twenty-five-year-old man named Marc Lepine entered the University of Montreal's École Polytechnique brandishing a semi-automatic rifle and proclaiming to hate feminists. He then shot twenty-seven female engineering students, killing fourteen of them. The event polarized opinion in Canada. Many people saw Lepine as a symbol of the depths of antiwomen

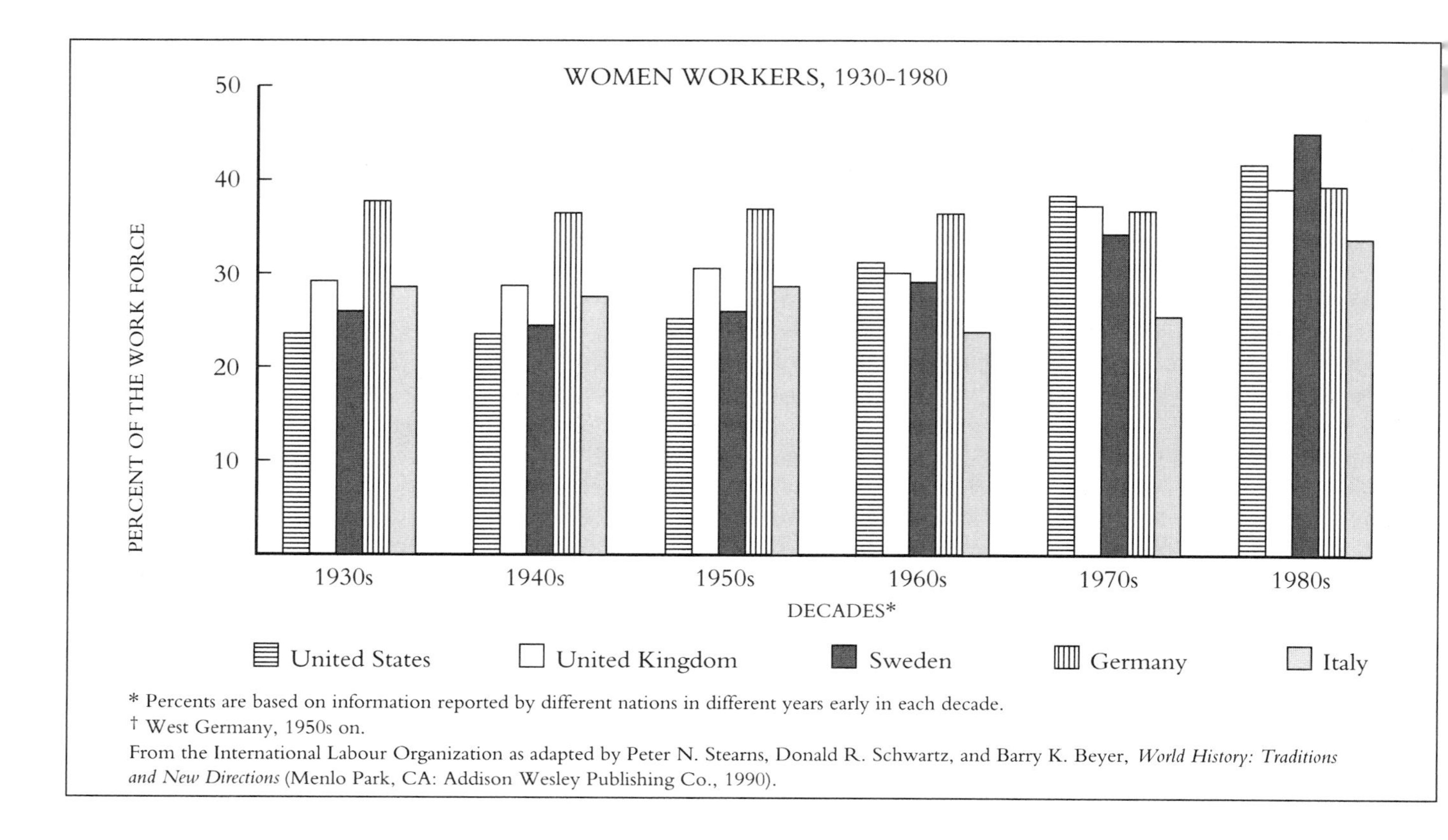

* Percents are based on information reported by different nations in different years early in each decade.
† West Germany, 1950s on.
From the International Labour Organization as adapted by Peter N. Stearns, Donald R. Schwartz, and Barry K. Beyer, *World History: Traditions and New Directions* (Menlo Park, CA: Addison Wesley Publishing Co., 1990).

sentiment in the country and extreme feminists refused to share memorial services for the victims with men. Other people saw Lepine as a single, crazed individual and resented the implication that he represented a significant portion of the male population. In either event, the incident was graphic proof that there are still extremist elements in society that reject the principles of equality and tolerance inherent in the Western tradition.

Progress in Other Countries

The progress made by women's rights groups in the Western world varies from country to country. In some countries, such as Sweden, women have made significant gains, both in terms of government legislation and in changing male attitudes. In Britain, however, the progressive trends of the 1970s have actually been reversed as the government has actively discouraged mothers from returning to work. In other countries, like the Soviet Union, where equality is guaranteed in the communist ideology, the harsh conditions of life make such a guarantee seem meaningless.

Women in the West, however, still fare much better than their counterparts in the non-Western world. Although some of these countries have been influenced by the women's movement, most do not have the resources to provide additional help for working mothers. In developing countries, women must work for their very survival and their days are long and gruelling. In addition, it is often even more difficult to change traditional male attitudes about the roles of the sexes. Ironically, however, it is in developing countries where women have had the greatest success in being elected as heads of government. The first woman leader in the world was Sirimavo Bandaranlike (1916-), who became prime minister of Ceylon (now Sri Lanka) in 1960. Other women to follow in her footsteps include Indira Gandhi (1917–1984) in India; Golda Meir (1898–1978) in Israel; Corazon Aquino (1933-) in the Philippines; and Benazir Bhutto (1953-) in Pakistan. By comparison, only Margaret Thatcher in Great Britain has led a nation of the Western world.

THE STATUS OF WOMEN IN SELECTED WESTERN COUNTRIES

	SOVIET UNION	SWEDEN	BRITAIN	CANADA	UNITED STATES
Number of Working Women	• 93% of women work or study full time; Soviet Women's Committee lobbying for the right to stay home	• 86% of women with children under 7 and 93% with children between 11 and 16 work outside the home	• 25% of mothers with children under 5 work; government discourages mothers from working; only 50% of professional women with children work	• 62% of women with children under 16 work	• 65% of women with children under 18 work
Women in the Workforce	• women hold few management jobs; 95% of jobs in public education are held by women but only 50% of the school directors are women	• although strides have been made toward equality, women still get the lower paid jobs with fewer opportunities, although this is often by choice to spend more time at home	• number of working mothers declining	• 30% of women are clerical workers; 27% are in sales and service	• 66% of women still employed in traditional female fields of office work and service industries
Maternity Benefits	• 3 years maternity leave; paid full salary for 2 months before and 2 months after birth, then paid partial salary until child is 1 1/2; job guaranteed	• 15 months parental leave can be divided between either parent; 90% of salary is paid; right to work a 6-hour day at reduced pay until child is 8	• only EEC country not to give women automatic right to keep jobs after maternity leave—woman must hold job for 2 years first; women who meet this requirement entitled to 90% of salary for 6 weeks and partial payment for 12 more weeks	• may collect unemployment insurance up to 60% of wages for 25 weeks	• employers do not have to offer maternity leave; women can utilize an employer's disability plan for leave of 6 weeks to 3 months, with payment in accordance with terms of the plan
Daycare	• provided as part of benefit package, by government, or through co-operative; affordable daycare in high demand	• government subsidizes 90% of daycare funding as well as leisure centres for children up to 12	• poorest child care facilities in Europe; only 2% of children under 2 are in publicly funded daycare; private babysitters expensive	• need for licensed daycare; promised government funding yet to materialize	• no federal funding for daycare facilities, although some state and municipal governments provide subsidies
Women at Home	• men rarely help with domestic chores, especially caring for children; women must line up 2 hours each day for food and spend 3 hours each day doing housework	• women do 40 hours of housework per week compared with men's 10; men fairly enlightened about chores they perform, which include cooking, shopping, and babysitting	• housework the exclusive responsibility of working-class mothers but is shared in higher income families; father rarely involved in childcare	• women spend 90–100 hours per week on jobs inside and outside the home; men willing to help but not to accept responsibility—act under the direction of women	• number of hours women devote to housework has dropped 8 hours per week since 1965; but women who work outside the home still work full-time equivalent on domestic duties

Based on "From Toronto to Tokyo," in *Homemakers*, April 1990, pp. 77–96.

Minority Rights: The Canadian Experience

The issue of cultural imperialism which had been prevalent throughout modern Western civilization continued through the latter part of the twentieth century. In Canada, the debate over the ratification of the Meech Lake Accord in June 1990 revealed different views of the relationships among the three founding cultures. Following the referendum campaign in Quebec in 1980, the federal government of Pierre Trudeau (1919-) made a commitment to patriate the Canadian constitution and entrench a Charter of Rights within its framework. The subsequent agreement, which protected minority language rights in Canada, was ratified by the federal government and the nine English-speaking provinces. When it became law in 1982, the Parti Québécois government of Quebec agreed to follow the agreement without signing it. Changes in government in the mid–1980s led to a new round of constitutional talks. The Meech Lake Accord (1987), signed by Prime Minister Brian Mulroney (1939-) and Quebec Premier Robert Bourassa (1933-), recognized "that the existence of French-speaking Canadians, centred in Quebec but also present elsewhere in Canada, and English-speaking Canadians, concentrated outside Quebec but also present in Quebec, constitutes a fundamental characteristic of Canada; and the recognition that Quebec constitutes within Canada a distinct society."

For the next three years, Meech Lake became the focal point of debate across the country. Central to the issue was the fact that the accord could not be changed in any way. As a result, many interest groups, including women and Native peoples, complained that it was "a bad deal, made behind closed doors, by ten white men afraid to ask the country for advice." Other critics pointed to the fact that the need for unanimity to amend the accord in the future might preclude important political changes, such as the admission of new provinces or senate reform. Finally, changes in provincial governments resulted in three provinces—Manitoba, New Brunswick, and Newfoundland—rescinding their support and demanding changes. Meanwhile, the government of Quebec proclaimed that a rejection of Meech Lake would mean a rejection of Quebec. After around-the-clock, last-minute bargaining, New Brunswick's concerns were satisfied and the eleven governments agreed to approve the accord if it could be passed by the legislatures of Newfoundland and Manitoba prior to the deadline of 23 June 1990.

In Manitoba, it was Native Canadians who rose up against the accord. Forgotten in the negotiations, representatives of Canada's third founding culture moved to block ratification. Elijah Harper, a Native Canadian member of the Manitoba legislature, carried out a one-person fillibuster to block approval of the accord. For Native Canadians, the issue was fundamental. For decades they had been attempting to entrench recognition of Native culture in the constitution, without success. The president of the 30 000 member Inuit Tapirisat of Canada stated: "Many claim that Quebec has been humiliated. They have not begun to understand the meaning of the word. We have had to live with it for 300 years."

As George Erasmus, national chief of the Assembly of First Nations, observed: "The distinct society perpetuates a myth. Canada was not born when the English and French cultures joined. It was born when the treaties were signed with the First Nations. We allowed people from Europe to come here and settle peacefully."

With Manitoba at an impasse, the Newfoundland legislature did not even vote on the issue. The Meech Lake Accord was dead.

For Canadians, the debate represented several principles that were fundamental to the values of Western civilization. It considered the role of language and culture as a facet of nationalism. As Europe begins to soften national boundaries and focus on common concerns rather than differences, it would seem that Canadians are still wrestling with basic concepts of nation-building. Much of the debate around the accord centred on the "breaking up of the nation." Both sides of the political debate used nineteenth-century concepts of nationalism as they applied to the Canadian and Quebec nations. The result, as in any conflict of opposing national sentiments, was discord rather than unity.

The second issue inherent in the accord was the nature of the liberal democratic process. In the late twentieth century, many significant decisions in democratic states are made through secret deals or summits. The desire for free and open debate is often shrouded in secrecy for the sake of national or international security. The result is a form of paternalistic government that asks the electorate to give it unquestioning trust for four or five years at a time.

The final issue is the legacy of imperialism. Native Canadians have yet to be granted the rights considered to be fundamental to Western society. Legal agreements between Native groups and the government were systematically broken, alliances and treaties unilaterally abrogated, and land arbitrarily confiscated.

Meech Lake is a Canadian issue, but its ramifications are global for Western civilization. To what extent are the rights reflected in Enlightenment values extended to all members of our society? To what extent have the citizens of Western democracies relinquished their political rights in return for an occasional ballot? In a pluralistic society, are the rights of distinct cultural groups afforded the same protection as the rights of the individual? The answers to these questions will provide a window on the future of Western civilization in the twenty-first century.

RETROSPECTIVE

The half century since the outbreak of the Second World War has seen the destruction of the old European world order and its replacement with a new set of global relationships. The Enlightenment tradition, long suppressed in Eastern Europe, had re-emerged by 1990 to become the basis of the social and political systems of most nations on the continent.

During the era of the Cold War, the world seemed irrevocably split into two bipolar camps led by the superpower victors of 1945. Over the past fifteen years, however, this great power leadership has declined, to be replaced with a multipolar world. In many respects, the economic and political power balance of the year 2000 will resemble its predecessor 500 years earlier as the decolonized world rises up to challenge the supremacy of Western civilization.

An important aspect of the development of Western civilization in the past half-century has been the growing concern over human rights. Legal, political, social, and economic equality for women and men of all races and nations has become a driving force in Western society. To a great extent, the postwar era has finally seen Western values internalized and applied to ourselves.

STALIN AND CHURCHILL:
Rhetoric of the Early Cold War (1945–1946)

Soviet premier Nikita Khrushchev, rising in the ranks of the Communist party in 1945, was in a position to observe the approach that Stalin took toward his former allies as soon as the war was over. In this excerpt from his unauthorized memoirs, Khrushchev relates his predecessor's attempt to rewrite the history of the conflict.

From *Khrushchev Remembers*, translated and edited by Strobe Talbott.

Stalin had formed good relations with Eisenhower and even better ones with Roosevelt. . . . Stalin always stressed Eisenhower's decency, generosity, and chivalry in his dealings with his allies. Stalin said that if it hadn't been for Eisenhower, we wouldn't have succeeded in capturing Berlin. The Americans could have been there first. . . . Stalin appealed to Eisenhower in a letter to hold back his armies; Stalin told Eisenhower that according to his agreement with Roosevelt and in view of the amount of blood our people had shed, our troops deserved to enter Berlin before the Western Allies. Eisenhower then held his troops back and halted their offensive, thus allowing our troops to take Berlin. . . .

The Potsdam decision was a compromise based on the distribution of power among the Allies at the end of the war. . . . Berlin and Vienna were each divided into four sectors. We received one sector, and the Western powers, England, America, and France—received the other three. This says something about the distribution of power at the end of the war. . . .

We must give credit to the Allies for their contribution to the common cause of defeating Hitlerite Germany. . . . The people and the Party of the Soviet Union must be properly informed about the contribution of the Allies to the common cause and to the Soviet Union itself. If the past isn't analyzed objectively, the building of the future will be based upon illusions and primitive patriotism instead of proven facts. Unfortunately our historical works about World War II have perpetrated an illusion. They have been written out of a false sense of pride and out of a fear to tell the truth about our Allies' contribution all because Stalin himself held an incorrect, unrealistic position. He knew the truth, but he admitted it only to himself in the toilet. He considered it too shameful and humiliating for our country to admit publicly.

Perhaps no single statement signaled the start of the Cold War as much as Winston Churchill's speech in Fulton, Missouri, in March 1946. Churchill, although by now a private citizen, still carried the weight of a wartime leader. Endorsed by Truman, his speech was a call for an Anglo-American alliance to negotiate in strength with the Soviet Union. It was, however, his imagery that captured the popular imagination.

A shadow has fallen upon the scene so lately lighted up by the Allied victory. From Stettin, in the Baltic, to Trieste, in the Adriatic, an Iron Curtain has descended across the Continent. Behind that line lie all the capitals of the ancient states of Central and Eastern Europe. Warsaw, Berlin, Prague, Vienna, Budapest, Belgrade, and Sofia, all . . . lie in what I must call the Soviet sphere. . . . Police governments are prevailing. . . . In front of the Iron Curtain . . . and through the world, Communist fifth columns are established and work in complete unity and absolute obedience to the directions they receive from the Communist centre. . . .

Last time I saw it all coming and cried aloud to my fellow countrymen and to the world, but no one paid any attention. Up until the year 1933 or even 1935, Germany might have been saved . . . and we might all have been spared the miseries Hitler let loose upon mankind. . . . We must surely not let that happen again.

1. (a) Write a first-person critique of one of these excerpts. You may either choose to take the viewpoint of Winston Churchill and comment on Stalin's view as outlined by Khrushchev or play the role of Khrushchev or Stalin and critique Churchill's view of events.
(b) Once you have completed your critique, stage a debate with one of your classmates who has chosen the other point of view.

THE MARSHALL PLAN (1947)

When the United States unveiled the European Recovery Plan in November 1947, it was viewed with concern by the Soviet Union. North America alone had emerged economically stronger as a result of the war. The Soviet sphere of influence, maintained by military occupation and meagre financial support, was threatened with destruction by the infusion of vast sums of American capital. Eventually sixteen Western nations accepted money under the Marshall Plan. Although there were strings attached, there is no question that American aid hastened the economic recovery of Western Europe. This excerpt is from a speech given by secretary of state George Marshall at Harvard University the previous June.

From the Senate Committee on Foreign Relations, *A Decade of American Foreign Policy* (Washington, 1950).

This community before the was accounted for nearly one-half of the world's trade. They owned nearly two-thirds of the world's shipping. Their industrial production in terms of the basic commodities of coal, steel, and chemicals was before the war slightly greater than that of the United States. Their economy was highly integrated, each part depending upon the efficient working of the others.

The Committee of European Economic Co-operation, meeting in Paris, produced a recovery program extending over 4 years. . . . It is a program of construction, production and recovery. It menaces no one. It is designed specifically to bring an end in the shortest possible time the dependence of these countries upon aid from the United States. We wish to see them self-supporting. . . .

The automatic success of the program cannot be guaranteed. The imponderables are many. The risks are real. They are, however, risks which have been carefully calculated, and I believe the chances of success are good. There is convincing evidence that the peoples of western Europe want to preserve their free society and the heritage we share with them. To make that choice conclusive they need our assistance. . . .

We must not fail to meet this inspiring challenge. We must not permit the free community of Europe to be extinguished. . . .

Whether we like it or not, we find ourselves, our Nation, in a world position of vast responsibility. We can act for our own good by acting for the world's good.

1. What rationale does Marshall use to justify rebuilding the economy of Europe?

2. What role does he outline for American involvement in world affairs?

3. Soviet foreign minister Molotov called the Marshall Plan the "Truman Doctrine with dollars." To what extent would you agree with his analysis?

NATO:
Collective Security in Western Europe (1949)

The Berlin blockade convinced many North Americans of the need to maintain a Western military presence in Europe to counter the Soviet "threat." Even prior to the events of June 1948, however, many political leaders were calling for the creation of a "collective security league." On 4 April 1949, the twelve original members of the North Atlantic Treaty Organization signed the charter formally creating the alliance.

This first excerpt is taken from the text of the treaty. In it, the signatories outlined the depth of their political commitments.

From Norman Sheffe and William Fisher, *A Sourcebook for Modern History* (Toronto: McGraw-Hill, 1964), pp. 177–179.

The parties to this treaty . . . are determined to safeguard the freedom, common heritage, and civilization of their peoples, founded on the principles of democracy, individual liberty, and the rule of law.

They seek to promote stability and well-being in the North Atlantic area.

They are resolved to unite their efforts for collective defense and for the preservation of peace and security. . . .

The parties will contribute toward the further development of peaceful and friendly international relations by strengthening their free institutions . . . and by promoting conditions of stability and well-being. . . .

The parties agree that an armed attack against one or more of them in Europe or North America shall be considered an attack against them all; and consequently they agree that, if such an armed attack occurs, each of them, in exercise of the right of individual or collective self-defence . . . will assist the party or parties so attacked by taking forthwith, individually and in concert with the other parties, such action as it deems necessary, including the use of armed force, to restore and maintain the security of the North Atlantic area.

Louis St. Laurent, prime minister of Canada, outlined the rationale for Canadian involvement in NATO during the House debate on the ratification of the treaty.

From Canada, Parliament, *Debates of the House of Commons* (Ottawa: 1949).

The fear of subversive communism allied to Soviet might is in fact the mainspring of the development leading up to this North Atlantic security pact. . . .

The treaty, if signed, will bring together in alliance against war the free nations of the North Atlantic community which share a common heritage, a common civilization, a common belief in the purposes and principles of the charter of the United Nations and a common desire to live in peace with all peoples and all governments.

This treaty is far more than an old-fashioned military alliance. It is based on the common belief of the North Atlantic nations in the values and virtues of our Christian civilization. It is based on our common determination to strengthen our free institutions and to promote conditions of stability and well-being. It is based on the belief that we have in our collective manpower, in our collective natural resources, in our collective industrial potential and industrial know-how, that which would make us a very formidable enemy for any possible aggressor to attack.

---

1. Outline the philosophy behind the formation of the NATO alliance. How are these ideas reflected in the speech by St. Laurent?

2. How does St. Laurent describe the two forces vying for control in Europe? Comment on his argument for the creation of a collective security league.

3. To what extent has the basic premise for NATO's existence changed in the past forty years?

IMRE NAGY:
The Hungarian Revolution (1956)

The decision by the Soviet Union and its satellite states in Eastern Europe to undergo perestroika *and introduce* glasnost *in the late 1980s and early 1990s marked a radical departure from past practices. Two previous attempts by Eastern European governments to liberalize their regimes, in Hungary (1956) and Czechoslovakia (1968), were met with strong resistance by the Soviets.*

In 1956, the Hungarian people overthrew the communist regime that had held power since the end of the Second World War. The West, embroiled in the Suez Crisis, did not come to the aid of the Hungarians, though, and the revolution was crushed by the Soviet armed forces. In the first of two excerpts, premier Imre Nagy (1895–1958) outlines the goals of the revolution.

The second excerpt is from a public speech by Nagy as the Soviets moved to overthrow his government.

From Norman Sheffe and William Fisher, *A Sourcebook for Modern History* (Toronto: McGraw-Hill, 1964), pp. 179–181.

People of Hungary: The Hungarian National Government, imbued with profound responsibility towards the Hungarian people and history, and giving expression to the undivided will of the Hungarian millions, declares the neutrality of the Hungarian People's Republic. The Hungarian people, on the basis of independence and equality and in accordance with the spirit of the UN Charter, wishes to live in true friendship wih its neighbours, the Soviet Union and all the peoples of the world. . . .

It is indeed true that our people are as united in this decision as perhaps never before in their history. Working millions of Hungary: protect and strengthen—with revolutionary determination, sacrificial work and the consolidation of order—our country, free, independent, democratic and neutral Hungary.

This fight is the fight for freedom by the Hungarian people against the Russian intervention . . . the whole world will see how the Russian armed forces, contrary to all treaties and conventions, are crushing the resistance of the Hungarian people. . . .

I ask that . . . the revolutionary leaders . . . turn to all the peoples of the world for help and explain that today it is Hungary and tomorrow, or the day after tomorrow, it will be the turn of other countries because the imperialism of Moscow does not know borders, and is only playing for time.

PRAGUE SPRING (1968)

In the spring and early summer of 1968, the communist government of Czechoslovakia, led by Alexander Dubcek, attempted to liberalize their regime. After months of progress, however, Czechoslovakia's Warsaw Pact neighbours stepped in and put an end to the experiment. These excerpts chronicle the rise and fall of the Dubcek regime.

16 March 1968

In Warsaw they are rioting in the streets; in Prague they are talking their heads off. Action speaks louder than words, but in Eastern Europe right now it looks as if it is the talking that could have the really momentous consequences. . . .

Mr. Brezhnev and Mr. Kosygin . . . may find it difficult to grasp that Mr. Dubcek is embarking on a very important experiment. He is trying to demonstrate that the communist system can be made to work in a human and efficient way in a modern industrial state. His experiment may easily fail; the clock may be put back, or the communist system may vanish from Czechoslovakia altogether. But if he or his successors succeed, one day the Russians will be thanking the Czechs.

20 April 1968

A ghost is haunting the bureaucratic leaders of eastern Europe. It is the ghost of change.

The Russians and their friends are worried about three things. The first is the way the Czech economic reform is moving. . . .

The Russians' second worry is about Czech foreign policy. If the Czechs continue to push ahead along their own road to socialism, the changes they are making are bound to have a bearing on their conduct in the councils of world communism. It might even lead in the end to a realignment of their foreign policy. . . .

The real Czech heresy is political. It is the open debate in Prague that has sent a shiver down the spine of established party rulers throughout eastern Europe. It is not pleasant to admit that you are frightened of freedom.

1 June 1968

Freedom of speech, in the press, on radio and television and at public meetings, has been welcomed with such gusto that things would have to go very badly wrong for the gains to be lost.

20 July 1968

For some years it has been widely assumed that the Russians would never again do to another east European people what they did to the Hungarians 12 years ago. That assumption is now beginning to look too easy. The Russian troops who entered Czechoslovakia more than a month ago for Warsaw Pact manoeuvres are taking an unconscionable time to go away again. . . .

10 August 1968

The prospect that is haunting eastern Europe today is not really that of counter-revolution, but of counter-evolution. Peaceful change, if it comes, will have to come by consent of the communist parties.

At five o'clock on the morning of 21 August 1968, the armies of the Soviet Union, Poland, East Germany, Hungary, and Bulgaria invaded Czechoslovakia. The Czech government denounced the action as "contrary not only to the fundamental principles of relations between socialist states but also as a violation of the norms of international law."

24 August 1968

The extraordinary popular defiance which had marked the first day of the Russian aggression appeared to be undiminished on Thursday, though the Russians had finally silenced the television stations which . . . had broadcast to the world pictures of Soviet tanks surrounded and defied by unarmed demonstrators. Two tanks at least had been set on fire. Some were chalked with swastikas and slogans denouncing the occupation troops as fascists. . . .

The men in the Kremlin are frightened of change, especially within their own borders. But by stamping on it in Czechoslovakia, they may be making radical political change inevitable in their own country—not now, not probably for many years, but some time.

---

1. Large numbers of Hungarians and Czechs fled their homelands in 1956 and 1968 and came to Canada.

(a) Identify one such person in your local community and arrange to interview him or her to obtain some first-person insight into events. If possible, secure permission to audiotape or videotape the interview.

Or

(b) Create a diary account that might have been written by a Czech student of your age during the spring and summer of 1968. Try to express the emotions you think this person might have felt.

PAUL KENNEDY:
The Twilight of the Cold War (1988)

Historian Paul Kennedy's book The Rise and Fall of the Great Powers *became required reading in government circles in Washington and Moscow in the late 1980s. In his monumental study, Kennedy examined patterns in international power and the rise to prominence of various nation-states. In his analysis, the author sees both the Soviet Union and the United States as powers in decline. In this excerpt, he introduces one possible outcome of this situation.*

It is worth bearing in mind the Soviet Union's difficulties when one turns to analyse the present and the future circumstances of the United States, because of two important distinctions. The first is that while it can be argued that the American share of world power has been declining relatively faster than Russia's over the past few decades, its problems are probably nowhere near as great as those of its Soviet rival. Moreover, its absolute strength (especially in industrial and technological fields) is still much larger than that of the U.S.S.R. The second is that the very unstructured, laissez-faire nature of American society . . . probably gives it a better chance of readjusting to changing circumstances than a rigid and dirigiste power would have. But that in turn depends upon the existence of a national leadership which can understand the larger processes at work in the world today, and is aware of both the strong and weak points of the U.S. position as it seeks to adjust to the changing global environment.

1. Apply Kennedy's thesis to events in the Soviet Union and Eastern Europe during the period 1988 to 1990.

MIKHAIL GORBACHEV:
Address to the United Nations (1988)

On 7 December 1988, Soviet premier Mikhail Gorbachev addressed the General Assembly of the United Nations. He called for an end to the arms race and international conflict.

The world in which we live today is radically different from what it was at the beginning or even in the middle of this century. And it continues to change. . . .

The use or threat of force no longer can or must be an instrument of foreign policy. . . . All of us, and primarily the stronger of us, must exercise self-restraint and totally rule out any outward-oriented use of force. . . . It is now quite clear that building up military power makes no country omnipotent. What is more, one-sided reliance on military power ultimately weakens other components of national security.

It is also quite clear to us that the principle of freedom of choice is mandatory. Its nonrecognition is fraught with extremely grave consequences for world peace. Denying that right to the peoples under whatever pretext or rhetorical guise means jeapordizing even the fragile balance that has been attained. Freedom of choice is a universal principle that should allow no exceptions. . . .

We are not abandoning our convictions, our philosophy or traditions, nor do we urge anyone to abandon theirs. But neither do we have any intention to be hemmed in by our values. That would result in intellectual impoverishment, for it would mean rejecting a powerful source of development—the exchange of everything original that each nation has independently created. We are, of course, far from claiming to be in possession of the ultimate truth.

1. Summarize Gorbachev's remarks. Using specific examples, apply them to past and current Soviet foreign policy actions.

2. Assume that you are the American president, the Canadian prime minister, or the leader of another Western nation. Write a response to Gorbachev's remarks that you would have delivered to the General Assembly the following day.

PAUL KENNEDY: The New Europe (1988)

Historian Paul Kennedy's study The Rise and Fall of the Great Powers *provides a sweeping view of the changes in Europe over the past five centuries. In this excerpt, he assesses Western Europe's future prospects.*

Europe's "problems" are, of course, more than those considered here: they include ageing populations and ageing industries, ethnic discontent in the inner cities, the gap between the prosperous north and poorer south and the political/linguistic tensions in Belgium, Ulster, and northern Spain. . . .

As it is, if one considers Europe—as represented by the EEC—as a power-political unit in the global system, the most important issues it faces are clearly those discussed above: how to evolve a common defence policy for the coming century which will be viable even in what may be an era of significant change in the international power balances; and how to remain competitive against the very formidable economic challenges posed by new technology and new commercial competitors. In the case of [other] . . . regions and societies . . . it is possible to suggest what changes are likely to occur: . . . that Japan and China will probably see their status in the world enhanced, and that the U.S.S.R. and even the United States will see theirs eroded. But Europe remains an enigma. If the European Community can really act together, it may well improve its position in the world, both militarily and economically. If it does not—which, given human nature, is the more plausible outcome—its relative decline seems destined to continue.

1. Monitor the press for one month and clip any articles pertaining to the EEC, European Parliament, or NATO. Identify the key issues, trends, and personalities.

2. From your news clippings and additional research, write your own thesis about the future prospects for Europe.

ADAM MICHNIK: The Awakening of Eastern Europe (1989)

In 1985, Adam Michnik, one of the leaders of the then underground Solidarity movement, wrote this analysis of the situation in Poland.

Long-lived dictatorships engender their own characteristic subculture and peculiar normalcy. They create a type of man unused to freedom and truth, ignorant of dignity and autonomy. Rebels are only a tiny minority in such dictatorships. . . .

We live in truly interesting times. We witness the barren twilight of the old world of totalitarian dictatorship. We, the people of Solidarity, have been put to a difficult trial. But even if it becomes an ordeal by fire, fire purifies and cleans what it cannot consume. . . .

Sooner or later . . . we shall leave the prisons and come out of the underground onto the bright square of freedom. But what will we be like then?

I am not afraid of what they will do to us, but of what they can make us into. For people who were outlaws for a long time feed on their own traumas and emotions which, in turn, strangle their reason and ability to recognize reality. Even the best people can be demoralized by years of persecution and the shock of regaining their lost stature. I pray that we do not return like ghosts who hate the world, cannot understand it, and are unable to live in it. I pray we do not change from prisoners to prison guards.

1. In August 1989, Michnik's prediction came true and Solidarity found itself in a position of power in Poland. To what extent was the Solidarity leadership able to escape the trap of the former prisoner?

MARTIN LUTHER KING: Letter from Birmingham Jail (1963)

Perhaps no single document expressed the principles of the nonviolent protest of the black civil rights movement than the "Letter from Birmingham Jail" by Martin Luther King. Written while King was in jail after being arrested for demonstrating in Birmingham, Alabama, the letter is directed to those who were critical of his nonviolent approach.

April 16, 1963
My dear fellow Clergymen:

While confined here in the Birmingham city jail, I came across your recent statement calling my present activities "unwise and untimely." Seldom do I pause to answer criticism of my work and ideas. . . . But since I feel that you are men of genuine good will and that your criticisms are sincerely set forth, I want to try to answer your statement in what I hope will be patient and reasonable terms. . . .

You deplore the demonstrations taking place in Birmingham. But your statement, I am sorry to say, fails to express a similar concern for the conditions that brought about the demonstrations. I am sure that none of you would want to rest content with the superficial kind of social analysis that deals merely with effects and does not grapple with underlying causes. It is unfortunate that demonstrations are taking place in Birmingham, but it is even more unfortunate that the city's white power structure left the Negro community with no alternative.

In any nonviolent campaign there are four basic steps: collection of the facts to determine whether injustices exist; negotiation; self-purification; and direct action. We have gone through these steps in Birmingham. There can be no gainsaying the fact that racial injustice engulfs this community. Birmingham is probably the most thoroughly segregated city in the United States. Its ugly record of brutality is widely known. Negroes have experienced grossly unjust treatment in the courts. There have been more unsolved bombings of Negro homes and churches in Birmingham than in any other city in the nation. These are the hard, brutal facts of the case. On the basis of these conditions, Negro leaders sought to negotiate with the city fathers. But the latter consistently refused to engage in good-faith negotiation. . . .

You may well ask: "Why direct action? Why sit-ins, marches and so forth? Isn't negotiation a better path?" You are quite right in calling for negotiation. Indeed, this is the very purpose of direct action. Nonviolent direct action seeks to create such a crisis and foster such a tension that a community which has constantly refused to negotiate is forced to confront the issue. It seeks so to dramatize the issue that it can no longer be ignored. My citing the creation of tension as part of the work of the nonviolent-resister may sound rather shocking. But I must confess that I am not afraid of the word "tension." I have earnestly opposed violent tension, but there is a type of constructive, nonviolent tension which is necessary for growth. Just as Socrates felt that it was necessary to create a tension in the mind so that individuals could rise from the bondage of myths and half-truths to the unfettered realm of creative analysis and objective appraisal, so must we see the need for nonviolent gadflies to create the kind of tension in society that will help men rise from the dark depths of prejudice and racism to the majestic heights of understanding and brotherhood.

The purpose of our direct-action program is to create a situation so crisis-packed that it will inevitably open the door to negotiation. I therefore concur with you in your call for negotiation. Too long has our beloved Southland been bogged down in a tragic effort to live in monologue rather than dialogue. . . .

I have tried to stand between these two forces, saying that we need emulate neither the "do-nothingism" of the complacent nor the hatred and despair of the black nationalist. For there is the more excellent way of love and nonviolent protest. I am grateful to God that, through the influence of the Negro church, the way of nonviolence became an integral part of our struggle.

If this philosophy had not emerged, by now many streets of the South would, I am convinced, be flowing with blood. And I am further convinced that if our white brothers dismiss as "rabble-rousers" and "outside agitators" those of us who employ nonviolent direct action, and if they refuse to support our nonviolent efforts, millions of Negroes will, out of frustration and despair, seek solace and security in black-nationalist ideologies—a development that would inevitably lead to a frightening racial nightmare.

Oppressed people cannot remain oppressed forever.

---

1. Outline King's description of a nonviolent campaign and the reasons for it.

2. To what extent do King's tactics reflect the values of the Enlightenment tradition?

3. Compare King's methods with those used by antiwar, Native, and feminist activists in North America in the 1970s and 1980s.

GLORIA STEINEM: Women in the 1980s (1982)

Gloria Steinem was an important feminist spokesperson during the 1970s and 1980s. Through her magazine Ms., *Steinem had a great impact on raising the awareness of both women and men to some of the fundamental issues of the feminist movement. The following is an excerpt from a lecture given at the University of Manitoba in 1982. In it, Steinem talks about the "second wave" of feminism of the 1980s.*

From Joan Turner and Lois Emery (eds.), *Perspectives for Women in the 1980s* (Winnipeg: The University of Manitoba Press, 1983), pp. 14–17. Reprinted with the permission of the University of Manitoba Press.

We come together tonight at a stage in history, and that stage of history is the "second wave" of feminism, or what we view in these young countries of North America as the second wave. I keep on my wall in the office a radical feminist poem from the second century A.D. to remind myself that the process of overthrowing or humanizing the caste system based on sex and race is a very long process. Nevertheless, there was a first wave within our families' memories. That was the great suffragist and abolitionist wave. . . . The earlier wave lasted 100 to 150 years, depending on how you measure it. We are about fifteen years into this one; we probably have a long time to go. . . .

The first stage of this second wave was primarily one of consciousness raising. It was a stage that received national and international recognition, because of the courage that women had and gave each other to speak out and tell the truth about our lives. For the first time in the United States, the public opinion polls now indicate majority support for all the basic issues raised by the women's movement. . . .

There are . . . two consequences which flow from this majority approval. The first is the necessity of a second stage to create the structural changes which will make these new possibilities real for most people. And structural change, or institutional change, takes much longer and is more difficult than the consciousness raising and value change which must precede it.

The second consequence is that we now have a growing right wing authoritarian backlash against the movement for equality of the sexes and races. There are many who believe that their lifestyle, necessitating as it does the right to dictate to other folks, is in danger. . . .

This backlash, though small, is very forceful and very painful. . . .

I suppose what has happened is that we have begun to redefine politics. We have finally come to understand that the term politics refers not only to what happens in our electoral systems, but is any power relationship in our daily lives. Any time one group is habitually dominant over another group, or one person over another person—not because of talent or experience but because of birth group, whether of sex or race or class, or all three—that is politics, that is a power relationship. It is from those power relationships that our more conventional politics spring. So, yes, it is political that women have two jobs and men have one. If women are working outside the home, they still have to take care of children in the home. That is unfair, and that is politics.

---

1. Outline some of the accomplishments of what Steinem refers to as the first wave of feminism.

2. What does the author identify as the two consequences of consciousness raising? From your own experience, cite examples to defend her point of view.

3. Debate the following statement: *Women tend to be conservative when they are young but the oppressions of their life invariably radicalize them.*

MARLENE PIERRE-AGGAMAWAY: Native Women and the State (1982)

In the ongoing debate between Native leaders and governments in North America, one group appears to have been ignored. Native women suffer a double set of persecutions, both as Native people and as women. In this address, Marlene Pierre-Aggamaway confronts the issue of activism for Canadian women of Native descent.

From Joan Turner and Lois Emery (eds.), *Perspectives for Women in the 1980s* (Winnipeg: The University of Manitoba Press, 1983), pp. 66–72. Reprinted with the permission of the University of Manitoba Press.

When I became involved in the native women's movement and in the general Native movement fifteen years ago, I, like others, believed that anything I could imagine vividly and that I desired ardently—like equality and justice for Native people in this country—would come about. I believed in this so much that I worked every moment of my life for it. I slept it; I ate it; I greeted every obstacle with optimism; I believed that all those things that I was fighting for must come to pass. After fifteen years, from my own perspective, very little has happened. . . .

Our native leadership continues to deny the legal rights of Native women. And, much to our dismay, our own women have become entangled in this legal dilemma. What better way is there to destroy a people than to take away the rights of women? . . .

In "Indian country," it is the women who pass on the ways in which we are to arrange ourselves as families, the ways in which we arrange ourselves in our communities. Passing on the ways was always our responsibility. In clan societies, in a matriarchal society, it was also the women who selected the leadership. But one of the sad facts about the condition of Native women today is that, although we have the responsibility to pass on that which makes up the Indian system, we ourselves do not know our heritage. Anthropologists may know more about us than we know ourselves. Some of us do not know our language; we do not know our culture nor do we understand how it can be lost.

We have not begun to address these basic issues in our own world and yet we are expected to respond rationally to a government that has created these problems for us. We have to say "Well, this is how it should be," when we have not been able to put the whole story together and believe in it. We, as Native women, have also to contend with the attitude of almost all of the Indian leadership in the country: our place is at home. We are supposed to be ten paces behind men, not beside men or in front of men or wherever we want to be. . . .

About two years ago, recognizing that we seemed always to be reacting to the government rather than planning a good future for our children, we decided that we had to become more political and much more organized in the ways we presented ourselves to the government and the people. . . .

Some of us are telling our Indian leaders that they are not our leaders: Indian leadership comes only when leaders have demonstrated to us their capabilities to make wise decisions and to speak to every need, not only to their own need. That is a form of power, to be able to say, "You cannot be my leader. I will not let you be my leader. I want to choose someone who will speak for the majority of Native people in this country." I still believe that the majority of Native people in this country have not yet spoken about their ideals and beliefs . . .

I believe, however, that Native women are moving ahead. Their sensitivity to the family, to who they are, convinces me that we are going to win this battle of aboriginal rights. . . .

Culture and economy are inseparable. Many people today have come to accept culture as being the music, dress and language of a people. . . . But cultures are inconceivable without an economic base. . . .

One of the alarming aspects of the loss of a culture is that, in the absence of processes which meet a people's needs, social disintegration takes place. That is why acculturation can be associated with alcoholism, suicide, family disintegration and all other social ills for which the federal government has programs. This is a model of colonialism: first, one creates the problem through the destruction of the Native economy and then one offers welfare programs as a remedy. . . .

Many people are looking to the Canadian government for assistance with their economic problems, but people cannot invoke native sovereignty in one breath and demand that Canada enact its trust responsibility in the next.

---

1. What case does the author make for a reconsideration of Native leadership?

2. To what extent do her beliefs and assumptions present a counterpoint to the beliefs and assumptions that characterize the Enlightenment tradition?

3. Research the rights of Native women. To what extent has the situation changed since 1982?

ANALYSIS AND APPLICATION

1. Trace the record of the United Nations in dealing with European refugees. From further research, determine the extent to which the experience of agencies such as UNRRA and IRO aided refugee efforts on other continents.

2. Create a timeline of the Cold War. Colour code your line to highlight the hot and cold periods of the relationship. Based upon your findings, create a thesis that explains the relationship between personal leadership and international tension during the period.

3. Select one Eastern European nation or Soviet republic and chronicle its political and social history for the past five years. Profile the nation selected in a three-minute radio news report. Use appropriate sound effects, interviews, and archival voice-overs where appropriate.

4. Recent news reports indicate that anti-Semitism is on the rise in Eastern Europe. Discuss whether the loosening of Soviet control in the region is a factor in this resurgence.

5. Write an obituary for Leonid Brezhnev or Ronald Reagan. Set the tone of your obituary as if it were appearing in one of the following: (a) the *Globe and Mail*, (b) *Rolling Stone*, or (c) *Pravda*.

6. Write a review of Yuri Afanasyev's editorial from the viewpoint of either Mikhail Gorbachev or Vaclav Havel.

7. Martin Luther King patterned his nonviolent demonstrations after those of India's Mahatma Gandhi. Create an imaginary conversation between the two men in which they discuss their philosophy and why they believe it will be affective in winning racial equality.

8. In chart form, trace the acquisition of political, social, and legal rights by Canadian women. To what extent has the progress been uneven? Is it complete? What remains to be done?

9. Write an editorial defending the actions of one of the following players in the drama surrounding the Meech Lake Accord: (a) Elijah Harper, (b) Clyde Wells, or (c) Robert Bourassa.

10. In the summer of 1990, the Mohawk people occupied the town of Oka in protest over plans to turn land within disputed Native territory into a golf course. Use newspaper and magazine clippings from the time to write the script for a docudrama about the events at Oka.

CHAPTER THIRTEEN

The Individual and the Community: Decolonization and the West

DECOLONIZATION AND THE EMERGENCE OF THE DEVELOPING WORLD

Since 1945 the global political and economic realities have undergone radical changes. The bipolar world dominated by the two superpowers that emerged after the Second World War has gradually evolved into a decentralized and complex system. To understand this process, it is important to examine not only issues such as the Cold War and the revitalization of Europe, but also the decolonization and emergence of the developing world as modern Western civilization has gradually expanded to take on greater global dimensions.

The Second World War broke down the controls of the old colonial system. As a result, the imperial powers were unable to resist the powerful movements for national independence in the colonies. The struggle in these nations was not only for national self-determination, however. It was also a battle for human rights and equality. Europeans, still trying to deal with the horrors of the Holocaust, found themselves charged with racism. The rising tide of nationalism first surfaced in India and the Middle East, then in Indo-China, and finally in Africa.

Some historians have called the end of the Second World War "the end of history." This is an accurate assessment in that it was the end of imperial history. During the nineteenth century, Europeans had taken colonial rule as a right and duty. By 1945, however, this self-confidence had vanished and the political will to dominate the rest of the world had disappeared with it.

India

The independence of the Indian subcontinent from Great Britain appeared inevitable in 1945. During the 1930s, Britain had introduced a measure of self-government to the region; continuing pressure by Indian leaders had resulted in a commitment by the new Labour government elected in Britain in 1945 to grant independence to India with all possible speed.

The leader of India's drive for independence was Mohandes K. Gandhi (1869–1948), who preached the tactics of nonviolence and civil disobedience. Known as the Mahatma ("Great Souled"), Gandhi's *Satyagraha* campaigns of non-cooperation began in the 1920s and continued to frustrate Britain and ultimately make it more amenable to negotiation.

During the first *Satyagraha* campaign in 1920–1922 Gandhi was arrested and sentenced to six years in prison. On his second campaign in 1930, Gandhi led thousands on a 332 km protest march. This action received more positive results, however. The Delhi Pact between Gandhi and British authorities in 1931 called for a series of conferences on the issue of Indian independence. The outcome of the talks was the Government of India Act (1935). It gave limited representative government but still left ultimate power in the hands of the British viceroy. During the Second World War, Gandhi, supported by Jawaharlal Nehru (1889–1964), staged a third *Satyagraha*. British spokesperson Sir Stafford

MAHATMA GANDHI: Satyagraha

Gandhi believed that freedom could not be taken by force. His method of creating change was called Satyagraha, *meaning "soul force." This included all forms of nonviolent opposition to British rule of India, including strikes and refusal to pay taxes. This developed into a general campaign of civil disobedience. Gandhi describes* Satyagraha *here.*

The term *Satyagraha* . . . means holding on to truth. Hence truth-force. I have also called it Love-force. In the application of *Satyagraha* I discovered in the earliest stages that pursuit of truth did not admit of violence being inflicted on one's opponent; but he must be weaned from error by patience and sympathy. . . . And patience means self-suffering. So the doctrine came to mean vindication of truth not by infliction of suffering on the opponent, but on one's self.

Carried out on its utmost limit, this force is independent . . . of physical force or violence. Indeed, violence is the negation of this great spiritual force, which can only be cultivated or wielded by those who will entirely eschew violence. It is a force that may be used by individuals as well as by communities. It may be used as well in political as in domestic affairs. Its universal applicability is a demonstration of its permanence and invincibility. It can be used alike by men, women, and children. It is totally untrue to say that it is a force to be used only by the weak so long as they are not capable of meeting violence by violence. It is impossible for those who consider themselves to be weak to apply this force. Only those who realise that there is something in man which is superior to the brute nature in him, and that the latter always yields to it, can effectively be *Satyagrahis*. This force is to violence, and therefore to all tyranny, all injustice, what light is to darkness. In politics, its use is based upon the immutable maxim that Government of the people is possible only so long as they consent either consciously or unconsciously to be governed.

From M.K. Gandhi, *Satyagraha in Gandhi's Own Words*, in Louis L. Snyder (ed.), *The Imperialism Reader: Documents and Readings on Modern Expansionism* (Princeton, NJ: Van Nostrand Co., Inc., 1962), pp. 417–418.

Mahatma Gandhi acknowledged the cheers of his supporters following his release from Yeravada jail in 1931.

Cripps (1889–1952) offered to grant dominion status at the end of the Second World War. Gandhi's advice to the British was simple: "Quit India!" Finally, the India Independence Act was proclaimed in 1947. What emerged was two independent parliamentary states, one Hindu (India) and the other Muslim (Pakistan). Severe crises followed as vast numbers of the population moved from one nation to the other. In the tension-filled atmosphere, members of religious minorities were brutally beaten or killed. One of the victims of the violent forces unleashed by independence was Gandhi himself. He was assassinated in 1948. Nehru, who became the first prime minster after independence, was eventually able to quell the violence and India was established as the world's most populous democracy.

Algeria

Other nations would not throw off their colonial bonds as peacefully as the Indians had. Frantz Fanon (1925–1961), in his book *The Wretched of the Earth* (1961), called upon the developing nations to take arms against their white oppressors.

> Decolonization, which sets out to change the order of the world, is, obviously, a program of complete disorder. . . .
>
> The naked truth of decolonization evokes for us the searing bullets and bloodstained knives which emanate from it. For if the last shall be first, this will only come to pass after a murderous and decisive struggle between the two protagonists. That affirmed intention to place the last at the head of things, and to make them climb a pace (too quickly, some say) the well-known steps which characterize an organized society, can only triumph if we use all means to turn the scale, including, of course, that of violence.
>
>

Fanon said that native people were merely possessions under colonial rule. He rejected European values, saying "it is a question of the Third World starting a new history of Man, a history which will have regard to the sometimes prodigious theses which Europe has put forward, but will also not forget Europe's crimes." (See readings.)

Fanon, a black citizen of the French empire, witnessed the process of decolonization firsthand in Algeria. Unlike the British in India, France would not part with its colonial possessions without a fight. Although forced out of Indo-China in the 1950s (see page 414), the French held on tenaciously to their colonies in North Africa.

France first colonized Algeria in 1830 and in 1871 the territory was annexed as an overseas department of France. This was followed by large-scale emigration to the colony by French *colons* in the late nineteenth century. By the 1950s, one out of every nine Algerians was of European French origin. These people were concentrated in the cities along the prime coastal areas and in the agricultural hinterlands that surrounded them, while the Arab Muslim majority was forced to occupy the less hospitable interior regions. By 1954, the hostilities that had resulted from this inequitable situation had reached the point of civil war. Both groups considered Algeria to be their homeland, but they viewed the country and its future differently. The Arab majority, who were relegated to second-class political and economic status, wanted independence. The *colon* minority wanted to remain a part of France. The Algerians' demands led to a terrorist revolt initiated by the Nationalist Liberation Front.

Both sides were supported by outside forces, the Algerian nationalists by Egypt and the French *colons* by the army and political right in France. The conflict raged on until 1959 when French president Charles de Gaulle (1890–1970) granted the Algerians the right to self-determination. Two years later, this decision was put to the people of France in a referendum and was ratified by a 75 percent majority. The attitude of many Europeans toward colonial independence was simple: independence was the lesser of two evils. The alternative was to allow colonial subjects to become full citizens. This concept was abhorrent to the underlying racial prejudices of many Europeans, as is evident in a statement made by a member of the French National Assembly that "the Republic must not be prostituted by allowing the Algerian people to become part of it." This attitude reflects the racism that characterized Western attitudes toward the non-white world during this period.

Although violent and hard-fought, Algerian independence was won within a relatively short time. By contrast, the French colony of Indo-China would fight for almost thirty years to throw off first its European master and then that master's American successor.

Vietnam

At the end of the Second World War, France regained control of its colonies in Indo-China (Cambodia, Laos, and Vietnam) from defeated Japan. Throughout the war, Vietnamese nationalist forces under Ho Chi Minh (1890–1969) had fought against the Japanese invaders. Now they turned their fight against the French. By the early 1950s, after several years of internal struggle, the French were ready to pull out. The United States, however, did not want the French to leave Indo-China to the communist Ho Chi Minh and his Vietminh supporters, fearing that a communist victory would have a "domino" effect—that is, that it would set off a chain reaction of other communist revolutions. To prevent this, the United States provided financial backing to the French defence forces. But this was not enough to enable the French to overcome the Vietminh. By 1954, France was ready to negotiate with the communists.

A peace conference was convened in Geneva in April 1954. No sooner had the two sides begun negotiations when they received news of an overwhelming victory by the Vietminh at the French stronghold of Dien Bien Phu. The Vietnamese town, near the border with Laos, had been occupied by the French in 1953 to cut supply lines to the Vietminh. Now the French at Dien Bien Phu had been surrounded and defeated by the Vietminh. Twenty thousand French troops had surrendered. The peace agreement signed in July granted independence to Cambodia and Laos and divided Vietnam in half. North of the 17th parallel, the Vietminh would be free to establish their own government. South of the 17th parallel, the emperor, Bao Dai (1913-), would continue to rule.

This new division of power did not last long, however. Within a year, Bao Dai had been overthrown and a new authoritarian republic had been established under the leadership of Ngo Dinh Diem (1901–1963). His government was immediately recognized by the United States, which began to send in military advisors to help build up his defences. The Geneva Conference had proposed that general elections be held to reunify the country. But knowing that in a popular vote Ho Chi Minh would win easily, Diem refused. It was an exact reversal of the situation in Korea seven years earlier. This time, however, the United States, in following its policy of containment, backed a dictator instead of a popular regime.

U.S. marines waded through a rice paddy near Hoa My, South Vietnam, June 1965. Moments later they were ambushed by Viet Cong snipers.

American Intervention

American interference in Vietnam was opposed by many nations in the developing world. They saw it as a return to the old imperialist order which they were struggling to bring to an end. There was little outcry from America's Western allies, however. Human rights issues during this period still tended to focus on white Europeans rather than non-white colonial peoples. Dissent at home and condemnation from allies was still more than a decade away.

The American commitment to prevent the fall of South Vietnam to communist rule cost little more than money in the 1950s. Military advisors were sent to assist the South Vietnamese army, but there were no troops involved in the actual conflict. In the 1960s, however, communist activity in South Vietnam increased. The United States responded with greater financial support and an increase in the number of American military personnel, from 3200 in 1961 to 16 000 by late 1963. However, these personnel were still not combat troops. Even with so many people involved, only 120 Americans had been killed.

In spite of American support, however, the 150 000 strong Army of the Republic of Vietnam (ARVN) was unable to deal with the 15 000 communist Vietcong guerrillas. Part of the problem was the unpopularity of the Diem regime. Although originally supported by the U.S., corruption, favouritism of Roman Catholics over the Buddhist majority, and military setbacks created growing opposition. Finally, an American-backed coup overthrew and killed the dictator in early November 1963.

Escalation of the War

For the next two years American involvement remained at the same level. However, in February 1965, the United States launched "Operation Rolling Thunder," which called for sustained American bombing of North Vietnam. In March, American combat troops arrived in Vietnam for the first time. Beginning with 5000 marines, American military involvement escalated rapidly. By the end of the year, there were 185 000 American troops in the field and within two more years there were over half a million military personnel in the war-torn country. But in spite of this radical influx of American combat support, the war was far from over. The Vietcong refused to collapse under U.S. military might.

The war continued to escalate. By the middle of 1967, the United States had dropped more explosives on North Vietnam than had been dropped on Germany during the entire Second World War. And yet the South seemed no closer to victory. And the costs of U.S. involvement were staggering. By 1968, the war had a price tag of $25 billion a year, 25 000 Americans had been killed, and Vietnamese military and civilian losses were catastrophic.

Finally, in 1968, newly elected United States president Richard Nixon (1913–) moved to end American involvement in the conflict. The first step was the process of "Vietnamization." Nixon wanted to turn back the clock to the early years of the conflict when the United States was fulfilling only a supporting role. The second step was "Peace with Honour." Nixon wanted to find a way to pull out of the war without either side appearing to have lost or without the United States appearing to have deserted its allies in the region.

On 27 January 1973, a peace agreement was reached, calling for an immediate cease-fire and the complete withdrawal of American troops and advisors within sixty days. Within two months all American prisoners of war had been freed. In spite of the agreement, fighting continued between the South Vietnamese and the communists. Two years after the American withdrawal, a well-planned invasion from the North swept through South Vietnam. Saigon, which fell on 30 April 1975, was renamed Ho Chi Minh City and the country was finally unified under the name the Socialist Republic of Vietnam. Fifty-six thousand Americans and over 1 million Vietnamese had died in the twenty-year conflict, yet in the final analysis, the years of battle had only delayed the inevitable. (See readings.)

The Impact of the War on the West

Vietnam was the first war to be broadcast nightly into the living rooms of Western society. As Americans and their allies became aware of the mass destruction and death in Indo-China, a storm of protest erupted against further involvement; there were antiwar protest marches and demonstrations. The 1968 Democratic convention in Chicago was disrupted by antiwar protestors and helped lead to the defeat of the Democratic candidate Hubert Humphrey (1911–1978) and the election of Richard Nixon as president of the United States.

Many Americans looked for strong government action to quell dissent, while others pointed to such right-wing reaction as proof that the war was taking its toll on the Western values of free speech and association. Several unsettling incidents illustrated the extent to which the war had undermined Enlightenment traditions in the democratic West. In two instances, peaceful antiwar demonstrations had taken a tragic turn. On 5 May 1970 at Kent State University in Ohio, the National Guard opened fire on a protest demonstration, killing four students and wounding nine others. A similar incident at Mississippi's Jackson State University claimed two more lives.

In 1970, it was revealed that American troops had massacred over 100 men, women, and children in the Vietnamese village of My Lai in 1968. Fourteen officers were charged with concealing information from the military. William Calley, the lieutenant in charge of the mission, was convicted in November and sentenced to life in prison.

Western foreign policy became afflicted with the "Vietnam syndrome" during the 1970s. Afraid to become embroiled in another such costly struggle, most Western powers withdrew from some of their global commitments. The perception that the United States had become militarily weakened by the Vietnam experience would make the country more vulnerable to terrorist attack throughout the decade.

The end of the war also coincided with a turndown in the American economy. By the mid–1970s, the U.S. economy was suffering from *stagflation*. Economic growth was slow, but unemployment and inflation were at staggering highs. This was caused in part by the energy crisis created by the oil embargo by the Organization of Petroleum Exporting Countries (OPEC) in 1973. But the embargo alone was not the only source of blame. Declining productivity, balance of payment deficits, and Nixon's monetary policy vacillations also contributed to the worsening economic situation. Attempts to solve these problems by both the Ford and Carter administrations only increased unemployment. By 1980, the U.S. was entering a recession.

The Impact of the War on Vietnam

April 1990 marked the fifteenth anniversary of the end of the fighting in Vietnam. Politically divided by the decades of war, the unified nation still remained economically split. The industrial and commercial base developed by the French and the Americans in the south has resulted in that part of the nation remaining about thirty-five years ahead of the north in development. The government in Hanoi moved in the late 1980s to develop a mixed economy with fewer government controls. Moderately successful, this program saw the annual rate of inflation drop from a high of 700 percent to below 50 percent. In spite of attempts at reform, however, Vietnam still suffered from a lack of foreign capital.

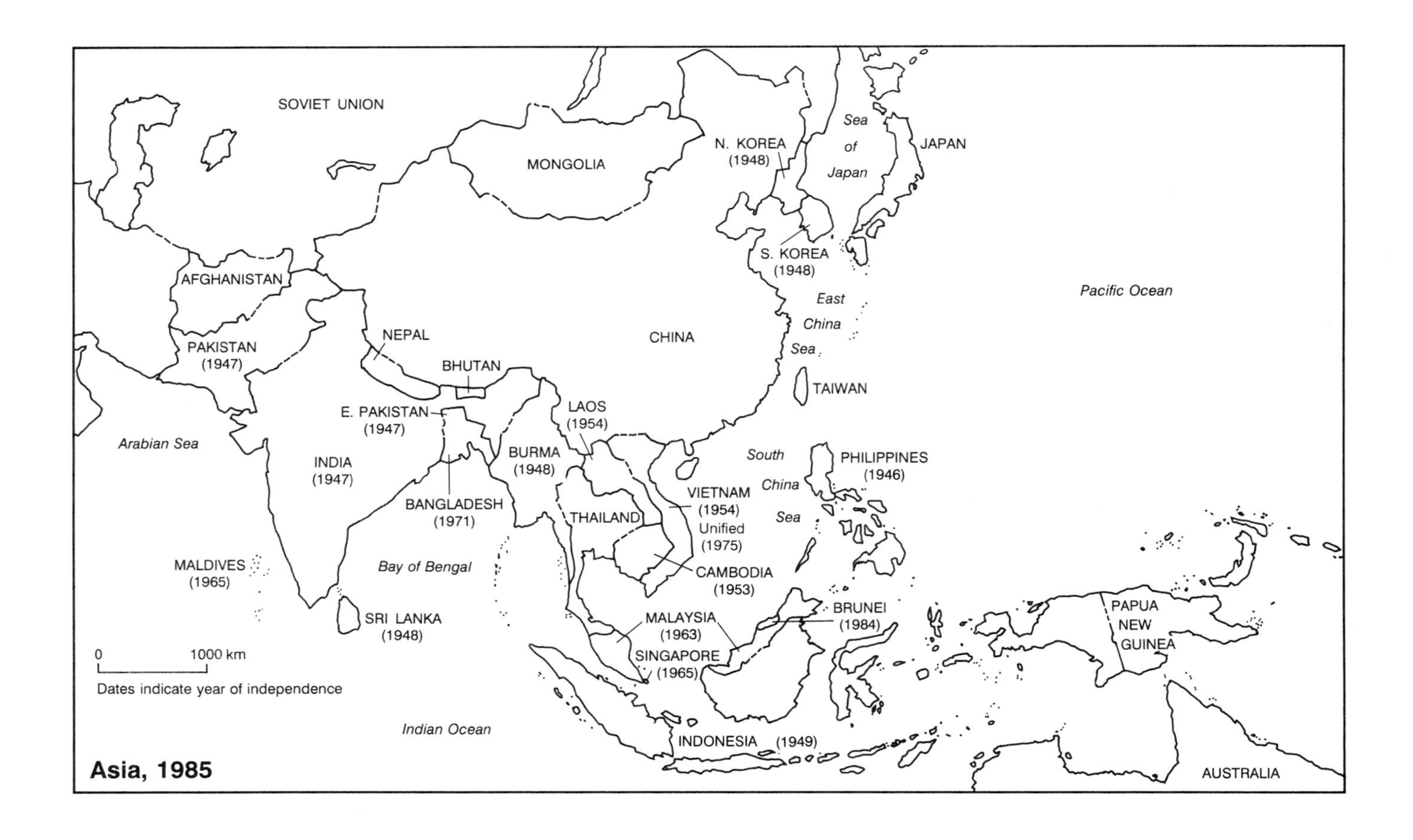

Asia, 1985

With the disappearance of Soviet foreign aid under *glasnost*, Hanoi had to turn to China for economic support. The resulting $2 billion loan was given on the condition that there would be no Eastern European-style democratic reforms instituted on China's southern border.

In spite of such external pressures, the Vietnamese government has been working to improve living conditions for the average citizen. As one Hanoi resident commented in the spring of 1990: "I remember when Ho Chi Minh declared independence. We all liked it. Now the government is calling for reform. I like that too. It's the direction the whole world is moving in, isn't it?*

*From *Time*, 30 April 1990, p. 30.

THE SOVIET UNION IN AFGHANISTAN

The United States was not the only superpower to become embroiled in an unwinnable conflict in the developing world. Afghanistan, an independent monarchy since 1921, had maintained a neutral position in central Asia during the 1950s and 1960s. A military coup in 1973 deposed the king, however. The subsequent government remained unstable, and increasingly the Soviet Union made its influence felt. In 1978, a series of coups resulted in a pro-Soviet regime led by the once-exiled rebel Babrak Karmal, who had been brought in by the Soviet Union. Between December 1979 and the spring of 1980, over 100 000 Soviet troops entered Afghanistan to support the Karmal government. They faced a Muslim fundamentalist resistance, backed by covert military assistance from the West.

The West responded to the Soviet invasion by condemning the action and boycotting the 1980 Summer Olympics in Moscow; they also placed an embargo on grain shipments to the Soviet Union. These actions, however, had little impact. The war in Afghanistan continued for another ten years, with Afghan rebels conducting a guerrilla campaign against the Soviet forces. Increasingly unpopular at home, financially draining, and monopolizing some of their best personnel, the Soviets finally withdrew their forces. By the fall of 1989, the Afghan resistance had taken the capital city of Kabul. Over the next six months, their forces continued to isolate and undermine the Karmal regime, waiting for its inevitable collapse. Afghanistan had turned out to be the Soviet Union's Vietnam.

REVOLUTIONARY CHINA, 1949 TO 1990

At the end of the Second World War, two groups struggled for control of liberated China. The Kuomintang, or Nationalist faction, was led by Chiang Kai-shek (1887–1975) and backed by the United States. They faced the far more popular Mao Zedong (1893–1976) and his communist supporters. By 1949, the communists were in control of the country. The Nationalists retreated to the island of Formosa (now called Taiwan), where they continued to claim to be the legitimate government of China.

The new People's Republic of China made positive economic advances during the 1950s and early 1960s as a result of successful reforms in agriculture and greater emphasis on postsecondary education. However, this process came to an abrupt halt in 1966. Fearing that he was losing control of the revolution, Mao initiated the Cultural Revolution. He wanted to renew China's revolutionary fervour and rid the country of its ancient ideas and customs. Much of the nation's intellectual leadership was purged and progress in education was curtailed as students were sent back to the land in an effort to promote equality between the peasants and the proletariat. The infamous Red Guard policed any violations of Mao's revolutionary agenda. For more than two years China was convulsed by the Cultural Revolution. It would take almost a decade to regain the lost ground.

By 1968, Mao was once again in complete control of the revolutionary agenda. During the late 1960s and early 1970s, the militancy of the Cultural Revolution waned and the situation in China began to normalize. Also in the early 1970s, the People's Republic of China began to re-establish contacts with the West. Under the leadership of Premier Zhou Enlai (1898–1976), efforts resumed to restructure the economy of the country with a focus on industrialization.

A new generation of leadership took control after Mao's death in 1976. By 1980, power rested in the hands of Deng Xiaoping (1904-). Deng initiated a quiet program of pragmatic reform. Throughout the 1980s, China once again experienced a significant increase in agricultural output and, as Deng opened his country up to the West, China began to step up the pace of industrialization. The result was an increase in per capita income of over 132 percent between 1978 and 1987. At the same time, the government allowed the introduction of Western consumer goods.

Rising expectations eventually led to a crisis in the spring of 1989. Coinciding with a visit in May by Soviet premier

Mikhail Gorbachev, whose policies of *glasnost* allowed for flexibility in the communist system, 3000 Chinese students staged a hunger strike in Beijing's Tiananmen Square. They were demanding greater democracy and prosperity. The protestors were soon joined by over 1 million citizens from all walks of life. The world watched on television as the Chinese people occupied the square in defiance of all orders to disperse and against all threats of armed intervention. For several weeks the standoff continued as the government hesitated to attack the peaceful demonstration. Finally, on Sunday morning, June 4th, the troops moved in, beating and shooting protestors in the square. Between 500 and 2500 people were killed. Within hours the square had been cleared. The propaganda campaign began almost immediately. As dissident leaders were rounded up, Chinese television announced the government's victory over counter-revolutionary forces. The actual events and details of the massacre were quickly suppressed. Throughout the summer of 1989, all evidence of the government's actions was systematically eliminated.

Although Deng was a reformer, the Chinese students had tried to move too far, too fast. By the first anniversary of the massacre, it appeared that the Chinese government had been able to keep a lid on dissent. However, the real impact of events in Tiananmen Square may not be realized for years to come. (See readings.)

Students rallied during a pro-democracy march in Beijing on 4 May 1989, just one month before the Chinese military killed between 500 and 2500 people in Tiananmen Square.

"JUST LIKE US"

During the 1980s, China opened up to the West in an attempt to modernize and keep pace with technological developments. But along with technology, China also imported Western culture.

The first thing that people who had visited China in 1970s noticed when they returned in the early 1980s was the fashions. The sea of green and blue unisex Mao suits, which once stamped China as the world's largest anthill, had become a kaleidoscope of brightly colored skirts and blouses for women, and jeans and T-shirts with Western logos for the men. The fashions were not always, or even often, very well coordinated, but they represented a freedom of personal expression that had been denied for years.

The people's minds were also opened by foreign radio broadcasts. . . . China's rulers had sanctioned listening to these mouthpieces of the bourgeoisie so that people could improve their English. That they did, but they also learned about rock 'n' roll, love and sex, and the struggle for democracy waged by people in such nearby countries as South Korea and the Philippines. . . .

Western visitors found this ferment intoxicating. China experts extolled it. The world watched in fascination as a country that had long shrouded itself in mystery appeared to be opening up . . . and propelling itself into the 20th century. Coca-Cola came to China, along with Cadillac luxury cars, Kentucky Fried Chicken, the rock group Wham! and those ageless 1960s surfer-rock stars, Jan and Dean. It seemed that the Chinese were on the verge of becoming, as Western visitors would marvel, "just like us." In fact, most of these changes were restricted to urban China. The vast majority of the country's 900 million peasants were untouched by the trappings of Western pop culture. But it was the urban population about which the leadership worried, and worry they did.

WESTERN IDEALS VS WESTERN PRACTICES: THE LATIN AMERICAN EXPERIENCE

During the era of the Cold War, the United States trumpeted the traditional liberal/democratic values of Western civilization. In theory, they offered an alternative to the repressive nature of the Soviet system. In practice, however, European ideals were more rhetorical than real. No region illustrated this better than Latin America.

Although most of Central and South America had been independent for more than a century, at the end of the Second World War the area still exhibited many of the characteristics of colonial dependency. Economically dependent upon the United States as their principal market and investor and dominated by conservative political oligarchies and dictators, the Latin American nations suffered from a variety of problems. The postwar years saw a population explosion, from 132 million in 1945 to 303 million in 1975. Most nations had agrarian economies, with little industrialization. As a result, although resource rich, virtually all Latin American countries were net importers of manufactured goods. In addition, years of neglect and political corruption had resulted in widespread poverty and a low standard of living. Often sharing the blame with the national governments for these conditions were American companies who reaped huge profits based on low salaries and favourable deals with co-operative local officials. The result was a tarnished reputation for the United States among a rising class of nationalists and reformers in the developing world.

The United States had initiated the creation of the Organization of American States (OAS) in 1947. Intended to foster co-operation and security, it seemed to indicate a willingness on the part of the U.S. to enter into an equal partnership with other American nations. (Canada, which had declined membership in this and all other American defence groups except NATO, finally joined the OAS in 1990.) However, many nations, including Canada, regarded the organization as a tool for legitimatizing American policy in Latin America—the Monroe Doctrine of the nineteenth century under a new guise.

Guatemala

The first evidence of American domination of the OAS came in 1954. Guatemala, under the leadership of President Jacabo Arbenz Guzman, had expropriated 100 000 ha of land belonging to the American-owned United Fruit Company and had redistributed it to the peasants. Officials of the United Fruit Company lobbied in Washington against the Guatemalan government. Working with the CIA, they organized and armed Guatemalan exiles living in Honduras for a possible invasion. At the same time, the U.S. government imposed an arms embargo on Guatemala. Guzman responded by ordering light arms from Czechoslovakia.

To the American administration, this was proof of Guatemala's communist sympathies, and so the U.S. continued to arm and support antigovernment exiles. Supplied with planes and other military hardware and backed by the governments of Honduras and Nicaragua, in 1954 these Guatamalan *contras* successfully invaded their homeland and overthrew the government. The new government, led by Col. Carlos Castillo Armas, instituted a policy of brutal repression and, to the delight of the United Fruit Company, Castillo Armas immediately revoked the land reform program. The invasion and overthrow of the government paralleled the North Korean invasion of the south in 1950. However, this time when the United Nations moved to intervene, the United States vetoed use of economic or military sanctions. The problem would be dealt with by the OAS. It was a strategy that would be applied with less success in Cuba in the early 1960s and in Nicaragua itself in the late 1980s.

American leadership continued to support dictatorial regimes throughout Latin America. Consequently many reformers saw the United States as the main obstacle to change. Like many European powers in the nineteenth century, U.S. foreign policy was not based upon the Enlightenment values of individual freedom and self-determination, but on economic motives. Resentment against the United States mounted in these countries and soon led to violence. On a good will tour of South America in 1958, vice-president Richard Nixon was mobbed and his car pelted with eggs and rocks.

Cuba

A successful revolution in Cuba in 1958 against the corrupt dictatorship of Fulgencio Batista (1901–1973) brought a new regime to power. The new Cuban government, led by Fidel Castro (1927–), looked to both the superpowers for support.

Castro had a genuine desire to reform Cuban society. Although his struggle against Batista had been supported by the American government, the United States was not ready for the reality of Castro in power. Castro announced a radical program of land reform in which considerable American-owned property was confiscated to be redeveloped as collective farms. In order to calm fears in the United States, the Cuban leader visited Washington in April 1959. Convinced that the Americans now understood his plan, Castro returned to Cuba to continue the revolution. Former government officials were executed. Many more fled into exile in the United States, where they agitated against the new government.

Castro wanted to diversify Cuba's export trade to reduce its dependency on the United States. As one step toward this goal, in February 1960 Cuba signed a trade agreement with the Soviet Union. This was followed in June by the nationalization of British and American oil refineries. The United States retaliated by reducing Cuban sugar imports in July and instituting a complete trade embargo in October.

American leaders were convinced that Castro and his economic advisor, Che Guevara (1928–1967), planned to export communist revolution throughout Latin America. On 3 January 1961, the United States cut off diplomatic relations with its island neighbour. Seventeen days later, John F. Kennedy (1917–1963) was sworn in as president of the United States. But even as he called for a "new alliance for progress" in Latin America, plans were afoot to oust Castro from power. (See readings.)

The Bay of Pigs

In 1960, under the presidency of Dwight Eisenhower (1890–1969), the United States Central Intelligence Agency (CIA) had been planning the overthrow of the Cuban government. At a secret base in Guatemala, anti-Castro Cuban exiles had been training for an invasion. Military analysts estimated that with American air support the operation would be successful. Once he became president, Kennedy was informed of the plan, which he approved. On April 17th, a force of 1500 soldiers invaded Cuba near the Bay of Pigs. The invasion was a fiasco, however. Cuba had been prepared and when significant American air support was withdrawn at the last minute, the invaders had little chance of success. Within seventy-two hours the conflict was over. Twelve hundred members of the invading force had been captured and the reputations of both Kennedy and the United States had been seriously tarnished.

The Cuban Missile Crisis

Over the next eighteen months, the Soviets took advantage of the closer ties with Cuba that had resulted from the Bay of Pigs invasion. Soon another crisis was brewing. On 22 October 1962, Kennedy appeared on national television to announce that U–2 spy planes over Cuba had indicated that the Soviets were building missile bases on the island. Faced with a possible nuclear threat in the United States' own backyard, Kennedy quickly set up a naval blockade, or *quarantine*, around Cuba. Mobilizing the armed forces, the U.S. president notified Soviet president Nikita Khrushchev that either the Soviets cease shipping weapons to Cuba and dismantle the bases already there or there would be war. After two days of hesitation, the Soviet Union agreed to withdraw. Soviet ships on their way to Cuba were redirected to Africa and Khrushchev cabled Kennedy that he would "remove those weapons from Cuba which you regard as offensive." To save face, he demanded an American pledge that they would not invade the island. Kennedy agreed. The Cuban Missile Crisis had passed. (See readings.)

The events of the early 1960s encouraged Cuba to pursue its own course in development in isolation, for the most part, from the rest of the hemisphere. During the next thirty years, the Cuban government continued to follow traditional Marxist-Leninist economic theories. By the early 1990s, however, Castro and his aging leadership found themselves out of step with the liberal forces sweeping the rest of the communist world.

Soviet premier Nikita Khrushchev and U.S. president John Kennedy met in Vienna in 1961.

Grenada

Following the two Cuban crises, the United States limited its involvement in Latin American affairs to covert operations by organizations such as the CIA. Although blamed for the military coup that overthrew democratically elected Marxist president Salvador Allende (1908–1973) of Chile in 1973, no overt actions were taken in the region until the Reagan era.

During the Reagan and Bush administrations, the United States reverted to military intervention as a means of enforcing their foreign policy objectives on their weaker neighbours. In October 1983, the United States launched a surprise invasion of the island of Grenada. Claiming that the Soviets and Cubans were building an advance base for communist aggression in the Caribbean basin, over 5000 troops landed and within three days had subdued local resistance. Although the "advance base" turned out to be an airstrip designed to receive large commercial tourist planes, the American government claimed an unconditional victory for the operation. The American action was supported by other political leaders in the region. Canada, however, was not even informed prior to the invasion. The Reagan administration knew that the government of Pierre Trudeau (1919-) would oppose the U.S. plan and so decided not to consult them.

Panama

United States president George Bush (1924-) took similar action to overthrow Panamanian leader Manuel Noriega (1934-) in December 1989. In a surprise invasion, American forces overthrew the dictator's government and eventually took Noriega back to the United States to face drug-trafficking charges. Noriega and his Panama Defence Force had prevented democratically elected president Guillermo Endara from assuming office. Now the new leader quickly established control. As in Grenada, the action by the United States was popular locally, but faced widespread criticism abroad. In early January 1990, the United Nations General Assembly adopted a resolution that called the Panamanian invasion a "flagrant violation of international law."

Nicaragua

The most notorious demonstration of the Western double standard on the rights of local self-determination took place not in Grenada or Panama, but in Nicaragua. A popular revolution in 1979 had replaced the U.S.-backed dictator

Anastasio Somoza (1925–1980) with the left-wing Sandinista government led by Daniel Ortega (1945-). The American government saw the new regime as a danger to neighbouring El Salvador and Honduras and introduced a policy of full-scale military aid to those countries. At the same time, the Reagan administration gradually increased military and financial support of the *contras*, a force of about 15 000 anti-government rebels operating out of the countryside. In 1984, the CIA mined Nicaragua's harbours, a move which brought condemnation by both congressional and international leaders. By mid–1986, many of the *contras* had been forced to flee back over the Honduran border in an attempt to hide from Sandinista forces.

At home, Reagan's Latin American policies raised the haunting spectre of Vietnam. Similar rhetoric about the domino theory, the defense of democracy, and national security resurfaced. But Congress remained unconvinced. Restricted in their bid to Congress for funding for the *contras*, members of the Reagan White House looked for other methods of providing aid to their anti-communist allies. The administration authorized the sale of arms to the hostile regime of the Ayatollah Khomeini (1900–1989) in Iran. Because the sale of arms to Iran was illegal under American law, the operation was carried out in secrecy. Reagan later claimed that the action was part of a strategy to normalize relations between the two countries and that the weapons were part of an "arms for hostages" deal designed to free American hostages being held in the Middle East.

There was, however, another agenda. Under the direction of presidential advisor Lieutenant-Colonel Oliver North (1943-), profits from the arms sales were siphoned off and earmarked for delivery to the *contras*. In nationally televised congressional hearings into what became known as the Iran-Contra Affair, North testified that in order to defend democracy in Nicaragua he had found it necessary to subvert the democratic process in his own country.

In 1988, the Sandinista government finally reached a cease-fire agreement with the *contras*. Since 1985, an American economic embargo, combined with massive aid to the *contras*, had seriously weakened the Sandinista regime; Nicaragua's GNP had dropped by 40 percent and inflation had reached 1700 percent. In addition, more than 30 000 people had been killed in the civil war and over 500 000 more had fled the country.

In the spring of 1990, Ortega finally agreed to free elections. After a hard-fought campaign, the Sandinistas were defeated by Violeta Barrios de Chamorro (1930-) and her National Opposition Union, a coalition of fourteen opposition parties. The Sandinistas agreed to turn over power to the victors and to disband their army, with the understanding that the *contra* forces would do the same. Unfortunately, by the summer of 1990, the *contras* had refused to co-operate with the new government and it appeared that the United States might have to take action against its former agents.

The End of Decolonization

By the beginning of the 1990s, it appeared that the period of decolonization was coming to an end in Latin America. The United States was finally willing to accept its neighbours as independent equals. (See readings.) With the exception of Panama, the U.S. government entered the decade professing a new arms-length relationship with the rest of the hemisphere. To a great extent, the American public, rejecting the interventionism of the previous decade, have encouraged this change in direction.

The Falkland Crisis

The 1980s also marked the end of an era for another Western colonial power in Latin America. In 1982, Great Britain and Argentina came to an impasse in their negotiations over the Falkland Islands in the south Atlantic, 400 km off the Argentine coast. Although Britain had administered and occupied the islands since the nineteenth century, Argentina claimed sovereignty; Britain, on the other hand, wanted to protect the interests of the small British population living there. Further complicating the issue was the fact that the islands sat on the edge of a potentially oil-rich continental shelf.

After talks between the two countries broke down, Argentina invaded the islands on April 2nd. The British government responded by dispatching a naval task force to the South Atlantic. Although one ship was lost to French-designed EXOCET missiles, the British navy was able to blockade the islands and force Argentine troops occupying the capital of Port Stanley to surrender on June 14th. The British resumed their control of the islands, but the issue of sovereignty has yet to be resolved. Although the war lasted less than three months, for the British it was a reminder of the grander days of empire. For the developing countries, it was a bitter reminder of the same thing.

REVOLUTION IN THE PHILIPPINES

The Philippines became fully independent in 1946. During the late 1940s and early 1950s, the communist-dominated Hukbalahap movement launched guerrilla attacks against the government. By the mid–1950s, the insurgency had been put down, but the government had come to be dominated by right-wing factions.

Ferdinand Marcos

In 1965, Ferdinand Marcos (1917–1989) was elected president. He promised to clean up the corruption which had been characteristic of his predecessors and to introduce economic reforms. However, Marcos proved to be as corrupt as any of the leaders who had gone before him. He increased his personal power and control to the point of dictatorship. Growing unrest with his rule in the early 1970s resulted in Marcos declaring martial law and suspending the constitution.

Marcos's main political opponent, Senator Benigno Aquino (1933–1983), was imprisoned for eight years until a personal appeal from American president Jimmy Carter (1924-) secured his release into exile in 1980. When Aquino returned to the Philippines in 1983, he was assassinated. Eventually the assassination was linked to the Marcos regime and dissatisfaction with his rule led to the rapid growth of political opposition by the mid–1980s.

In February 1986, Marcos called an election to silence critics of his authoritarian rule. Instead of the victory he expected, however, he was soundly defeated by political newcomer Corazon Aquino (1933-). Widow of the assassinated opposition leader, Cory Aquino led a popular front opposition that proclaimed "people power" rather than "Marcos power." Marcos refused to accept the verdict of the electorate, but was unable to hold on to power as people took to the streets and the army proclaimed its allegiance to the newly elected president. Marcos fled to the United States, where he died in 1989.

Throughout the years of Marcos's rule, successive American administrations supported his dictatorship regime. This typified a major inconsistency in American foreign policy during the postwar era. As with many Western democracies, the United States was willing to overlook violations of liberal democratic traditions if it meant maintaining its own military security and containing communism. In the case of the Philippines, the U.S. wanted to maintain its naval and airforce bases on the islands. Marcos supported American military presence in the region, and so in turn the United States supported Marcos. It was not until the outcome was inevitable that the U.S. government encourged Marcos to step aside and let the rightfully elected government of Aquino take the reins of government.

The country that Aquino was left to run was a deeply divided one. From the start she faced challenges from both the right and the left. The New People's Army, a group of communist insurgents, had been growing in strength since its foundation in the late 1960s. The destabilization caused by communist attacks has resulted in attempted coups from the right to reassert authoritarian control. The failure of the Aquino government to meet either of these challenges could very well mean the end of liberal democratic rule in the Philippines.

Philippine president Ferdinand Marcos and U.S. president Ronald Reagan were hung in effigy after a mock trial found them guilty of crimes against the Filipino people.

CORAZON AQUINO AND PEOPLE POWER

When Corazon Aquino became president of the Philippines in 1986, few could believe how a politically inexperienced homemaker had overthrown a powerful dictator like Ferdinand Marcos. Yet Aquino and her "people power" movement had done just that.

After the assassination of her husband Benigno, Marcos's foremost political opponent, Corazon Aquino became the unlikely leader of a popular movement to restore democracy in the Philippines. Although Aquino had been well educated in the United States, her personal involvement in politics had been limited to a supporting role to her husband. Now, as the grieving widow of a martyr, the people began to rally around her. When Marcos announced he would hold free elections in 1986, Aquino emerged as the challenger for his presidency.

Everywhere that Aquino went, crowds numbering in the tens of thousands gathered, chanting "Co-ry! Co-ry! Co-ry!" Although she clearly lacked great oratorical skills, and in fact was considered lacklustre in her speaking style, she captured the collective imagination of the Philippine people.

Her biggest detractor, of course, was Marcos, who employed various tactics to discredit her. But Aquino was prepared. When Marcos took her to task for her lack of experience, she quickly replied, "I concede that I cannot match Mr. Marcos when it comes to experience. I admit that I have no experience in cheating, stealing, lying, or assassinating political opponents."

As Aquino campaigned throughout the Philippines, it was clear that her support was strong and growing. Fearful that his opponent would win the popular vote, Marcos rigged the election and had the National Assembly declare him the winner. Aquino quickly responded with a call for massive civil disobedience and a boycott of all companies that were owned by Marcos supporters.

As the standoff between Aquino and Marcos continued, violence erupted between the opposing factions. As Marcos fortified himself in Malacañang Palace against an anticipated coup, the people in the streets faced the tanks of those soldiers still loyal to Marcos. Aquino's "people power" movement formed human barricades to block the tanks' way. Women and girls presented flowers to the soldiers. Unsettled by the peaceful defiance, the soldiers turned their tanks away.

On February 25th, Aquino took a revolutionary oath of office, which stated, "Sovereignty resides in the people and all government authority emanates from them. On the basis of the people's mandate clearly manifested last February 7, I and Salvador H. Laurel are taking power in the name and by the will of the Filipino people as president and vice-president, respectively." An hour later, Marcos was also sworn in as president in his own inaugural ceremony. By then, however, his hours in the Philippines were numbered. That night he fled the country to a life of exile in Hawaii. It was a glorious victory for Corazon Aquino and "people power."

An Aquino supporter pleaded to pro-Marcos troops not to fire their weapons during a rock-throwing skirmish in February 1986.

DECOLONIZATION IN SUB-SAHARAN AFRICA

The end of the Second World War saw an increased commitment by the European colonial powers to independence for their African colonies. British prime minister Harold Macmillan (1894–1986), after spending a month on the African continent in 1960, commented: "The most striking of all the impressions I have formed since I left London a month ago is of the strength of this African national consciousness. In different places it may take different forms. But it is happening everywhere. The wind of change is blowing through the continent."

The Belgian Congo

One example of this change was in the Belgian Congo. Increasingly violent riots during the late 1950s had led Belgium to relinquish control of its colony in 1960. Elections were held in May of that year and in June the Congo became independent. For the next five years the new nation was rocked by civil war. Intervention by the United Nations, and eventually by Belgium and the United States, brought some measure of stability. With the accession of General Joseph Mobutu (1930-) to the presidency in 1965, the country entered a period of prosperity. As part of the process of phasing out European influences and re-establishing its African roots, the Congo was renamed Zaïre in 1971. Unfortunately, border conflicts with Angola throughout the 1970s and 1980s have prevented Zaïre from reaching its full economic potential.

Rhodesia

The former British colony of Southern Rhodesia presented other problems. Granted internal self-government in the 1920s, in 1961 Rhodesia moved to disenfranchise its black majority. British objections eventually led to Rhodesia's unilateral declaration of independence in 1965. Over the next thirteen years, more than 6000 Rhodesians, white and black, were killed in civil unrest. Finally, British negotiators were able to reach a settlement, which saw the gradual transfer of power to the black majority. By the late 1980s, the new black nation of Zimbabwe had established itself as an African economic and social success story.

Angola

The former Portugese colony of Angola provided a base for a Soviet incursion into the southern part of the continent in 1975–1976. During that period the Soviet Union transported over 20 000 Cuban troops into the region to support the Marxist Popular Movement for the Liberation of Angola (MPLA) in its fight against its Western-backed counterpart, the National Union for the Total Independence of Angola (UNITA). The Vietnam experience caused the United States to back away from its commitments and eventually the MPLA took power. By the early 1980s, however, the Soviets found that, like most European colonizers, they were no longer welcome in the region. Nevertheless, the Reagan administration continued to provide money for the anti-Marxist factions. In December 1988, Angola, Cuba, and South Africa signed agreements calling for Cuban withdrawal from Angola and South African withdrawal from Namibia. In June 1989, the Angolan government and UNITA agreed to a truce.

South Africa

Perhaps the most enduring and distressing legacy of the colonial era is the Republic of South Africa. Since its independence from Britain in 1910, the government of South Africa has pursued a policy of *apartheid,* or separate development for whites, blacks, and coloured people. At the end of the Second World War, South Africa became a charter member of the United Nations, but Afrikaner opposition prevented the government from signing the Universal Declaration of Human Rights. In 1948, the Afrikaner Nationalist Party gained power under Daniel Malan (1874–1954). The new government soon began to legislate apartheid. After 1948, voting rights were restricted to whites only. Increasingly, other rights were withdrawn from the black majority. A campaign of passive resistance was initiated in 1952 by the African National Congress (ANC). At a national convention in 1955, the ANC proclaimed its Freedom Charter, which called for equality for all South Africans regardless of colour.

Throughout the decade, white resistance to black demands grew and eventually led to violence. In 1960, police fired on demonstrators in the black town of Sharpville, killing or wounding more than 250 people. In a series of riots in 1976, more than 600 people were killed by South African security forces. Increasingly, opposition to the regime came to be based outside the country in the so-called "front-line" states. By the early 1980s, the South African government was launching military strikes in Mozambique and Angola against the bases of the South West Africa People's Organization

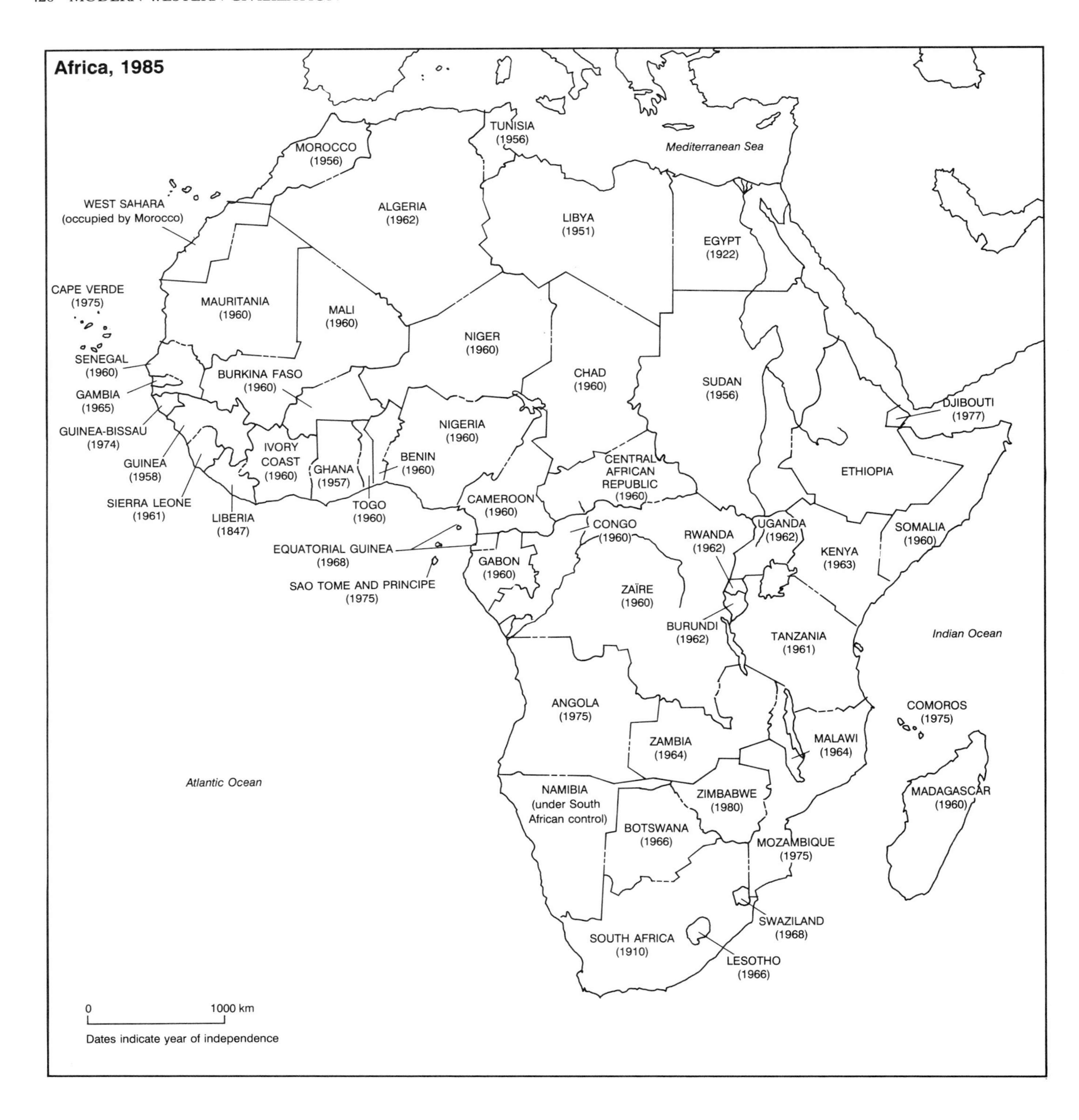
Africa, 1985
TUNISIA (1956)
Mediterranean Sea
MOROCCO (1956)
WEST SAHARA (occupied by Morocco)
ALGERIA (1962)
LIBYA (1951)
EGYPT (1922)
CAPE VERDE (1975)
MAURITANIA (1960)
MALI (1960)
NIGER (1960)
SENEGAL (1960)
BURKINA FASO (1960)
CHAD (1960)
SUDAN (1956)
GAMBIA (1965)
DJIBOUTI (1977)
GUINEA-BISSAU (1974)
NIGERIA (1960)
IVORY COAST (1960)
BENIN (1960)
GUINEA (1958)
GHANA (1957)
CENTRAL AFRICAN REPUBLIC (1960)
ETHIOPIA
SIERRA LEONE (1961)
TOGO (1960)
CAMEROON (1960)
LIBERIA (1847)
CONGO (1960)
UGANDA (1962)
SOMALIA (1960)
RWANDA (1962)
EQUATORIAL GUINEA (1968)
KENYA (1963)
GABON (1960)
SAO TOME AND PRINCIPE (1975)
ZAÏRE (1960)
BURUNDI (1962)
TANZANIA (1961)
Indian Ocean
COMOROS (1975)
ANGOLA (1975)
ZAMBIA (1964)
MALAWI (1964)
Atlantic Ocean
NAMIBIA (under South African control)
ZIMBABWE (1980)
MADAGASCAR (1960)
BOTSWANA (1966)
MOZAMBIQUE (1975)
SWAZILAND (1968)
SOUTH AFRICA (1910)
LESOTHO (1966)
0
1000 km
Dates indicate year of independence

(SWAPO). In 1986, they launched simultaneous attacks on Zimbabwe, Botswana, and Zambia to destroy ANC strongholds in those countries.

Since the mid–1980s, the South African government has declared a continual state of emergency. Until late 1989, this led to a crackdown on dissent and on the media, both foreign and domestic.

Prominent figures such as the ANC deputy leader Nelson Mandela (1918-), jailed from 1962 until 1990, and Nobel Peace Prize winner Bishop Desmond Tutu (1931-), have called for continued strong economic sanctions against their homeland. But Western response has been mixed. Calls for the divestment of interests in South African companies by Western investors has been met with charges that the lower standard of living that would result would only hurt the black majority. Britain continually refused to support Commonwealth initiatives extending sanctions during the 1980s. Canada and the United States have adopted a policy of providing moral leadership and calling for voluntary sanctions and some observers claim that recent concessions made by the South African government are proof that Western policy has had an impact.

The first concrete indication of reform in South Africa came with the resignation of long-time president P.W. Botha (1916-) in August 1989. His successor, F.W. de Klerk, pledged to open talks with Zambian president Kenneth Kaunda (1924-). Zambia hosts the outlawed ANC and therefore has been a constant target for South Africa's Security Forces. De Klerk, whose white Afrikaner minority represents only 7 percent of South Africa's population, has pledged to break "the cycle of conflict, tension, and isolation" that has crippled his country. The question is whether or not his government will have the political will to respond to the needs of the nation's 28 million blacks and remove such obstacles to equality as the Group Areas Act, which defines where people can live by the colour of their skin; the Population Registration Act, which legally defines people according to race; and the Separate Amenities Act, which limits access to public facilities by colour.

Some positive gestures toward reform were made in late 1989. A number of political prisoners were freed, and the ban on peaceful antigovernment protests was lifted. These actions were followed by the dramatic release of Nelson Mandela in February 1990 after twenty-seven years of imprisonment. (See readings.)

The campaign for Mandela's release, spearheaded by his

Nelson Mandela, deputy leader of the African National Congress, was jailed by the South African government from 1962 to 1990 and became a powerful symbol of the fight against apartheid.

activist wife, Winnie (Nomzamo) Mandela (1936-), gained international support in the 1980s. World interest was so captivated by the Mandela case that his release was carried live on television worldwide. Prime Minister Mulroney extended greetings to a "free Nelson Mandela on behalf of the Canadian people" and February 12th was proclaimed "Nelson Mandela Day" in Toronto.

NELSON MANDELA

The release from prison of Nelson Mandela on 11 February 1990 marked the end of an epic personal struggle and the beginning of a new age for South Africa. Mandela was the son of a chieftain and studied law in Johannesburg. In 1952, he joined the ANC and traveled widely throughout the 1950s promoting the idea of a free, democratic, and multiracial state in South Africa. Mandela went underground when the ANC was banned in 1961 but was arrested in 1962 and jailed for five years. Before that sentence had expired, he was charged again and, after a six-month trial in which he defended himself brilliantly, he was sentenced to life imprisonment under the Suppression of Communism Act. In prison, Mandela remained a symbol of resistance to the white-only regime.

In his trial in 1964 Mandella stated:

> I have fought against white domination and I have fought against black domination. I have cherished the ideal of a democratic and free society in which all persons live together in harmony and with equal opportunity. It is an ideal which I hope to live for and to achieve. But if needs be, it is an ideal for which I am prepared to die.

At a meeting of the leaders of the front-line states in Lusaka, Zambia, in March, Mandela was named deputy president of the African National Congress. At that meeting, he declared that the ANC had three preconditions to opening talks with the white government: the lifting of the state of emergency; the release of all political prisoners; and the free return of all ANC exiles now living outside of South Africa.

The spring of 1990 saw increasing violence within the black community as rival groups struggled to gain a leadership role in the expected transition to black majority rule. Both Nelson Mandela, representing the ANC, and the more conservative *Inkatha* organization, called for an end to the bloodshed and the over 3000 deaths of the previous two-and-a-half years.

With the prospect of a civil war looming, Mandela and de Klerk met in mid-May. Their final communiqué committed the government to the release of remaining political prisoners, the return of political exiles without risk of arrest, and the lifting of the state of emergency. For its part the ANC gave some assurances that it would suspend its guerrilla activities and stop pressing foreign governments to maintain or increase economic sanctions against South Africa. It was the first time that representatives of the government had sat down to negotiate with the ANC since its formation in 1912.

THE LEGACY OF DECOLONIZATION IN THE MIDDLE EAST

In 1947, the United Nations approved a plan for the partition of the British mandate in Palestine that would allow for the creation of a new Jewish state (Israel) and an Arab Palestinian homeland. With the withdrawal of British troops in May 1948, however, Israel's neighbours, Egypt, Syria, Lebanon, and Iraq, launched an attack to destroy the new nation. But the results were the opposite of what they hoped to achieve. Israeli forces not only withstood the invaders, but ended up occupying all of Palestine. Arab Palestinians, who had been advised by their Arab League neighbours to leave their homes during the fighting, found themselves homeless refugees.

The Suez Crisis

Following the conflict, an uneasy peace descended on the region. Border incidents between Israel and Egypt were common in the early 1950s. But matters reached crisis proportion in 1956. In that year, the Egyptian president, Gamal Abdel Nasser (1918–1970), was negotiating loans from Britain and the United States to build a huge dam across the Nile River near Aswan. At the same time, Egypt was also buying arms from Czechoslovakia. American secretary of state John Foster Dulles warned Nasser that if Egypt's arms deal with the Czechs was not canceled, the United States might cut off its financial aid for the dam. Nasser responded that if the

Americans would not finance the dam, then he would turn to the Soviet Union for support.

Furious with Nasser's response, the Americans withdrew their loan. Nasser nationalized the Suez Canal (which was owned by Britain and France) and declared that he would use the tolls collected for the use of the canal to pay for the dam. Nasser's move, which was directed at the three Western powers, struck a blow at Israel as well. Israel depended on the Suez Canal for its shipments of oil and did not want that lifeline in enemy hands. In a move prearranged with London and Paris, Israel attacked Egypt in the Sinai Peninsula. British and French paratroops landed to protect "their" canal, while the Soviets backed Egypt. The possibility of a major war loomed on the horizon.

Popular sentiment in the United States condemned Britain and France, believing their actions to be imperialistic and unfair to the Egyptians. Not all Canadians agreed, however. Prime minister Louis St. Laurent's (1882–1973) reference to France and Britain as the "supermen of Europe" who had yet to recognize that their day was over sparked a national outcry. Meanwhile, the UN was paralysed. Both Britain and France threatened to use their Security Council vetoes if any action was proposed against them. The United States was caught in the middle. It could not support the actions of its allies, yet it was U.S. policy that had initiated the crisis in the first place.

Finally, the United Nations stepped in. Spearheaded by the work of Canadian representative Lester B. Pearson (1897–1972), the UN proposed an immediate cease-fire. To keep the peace, an international army was sent to occupy the

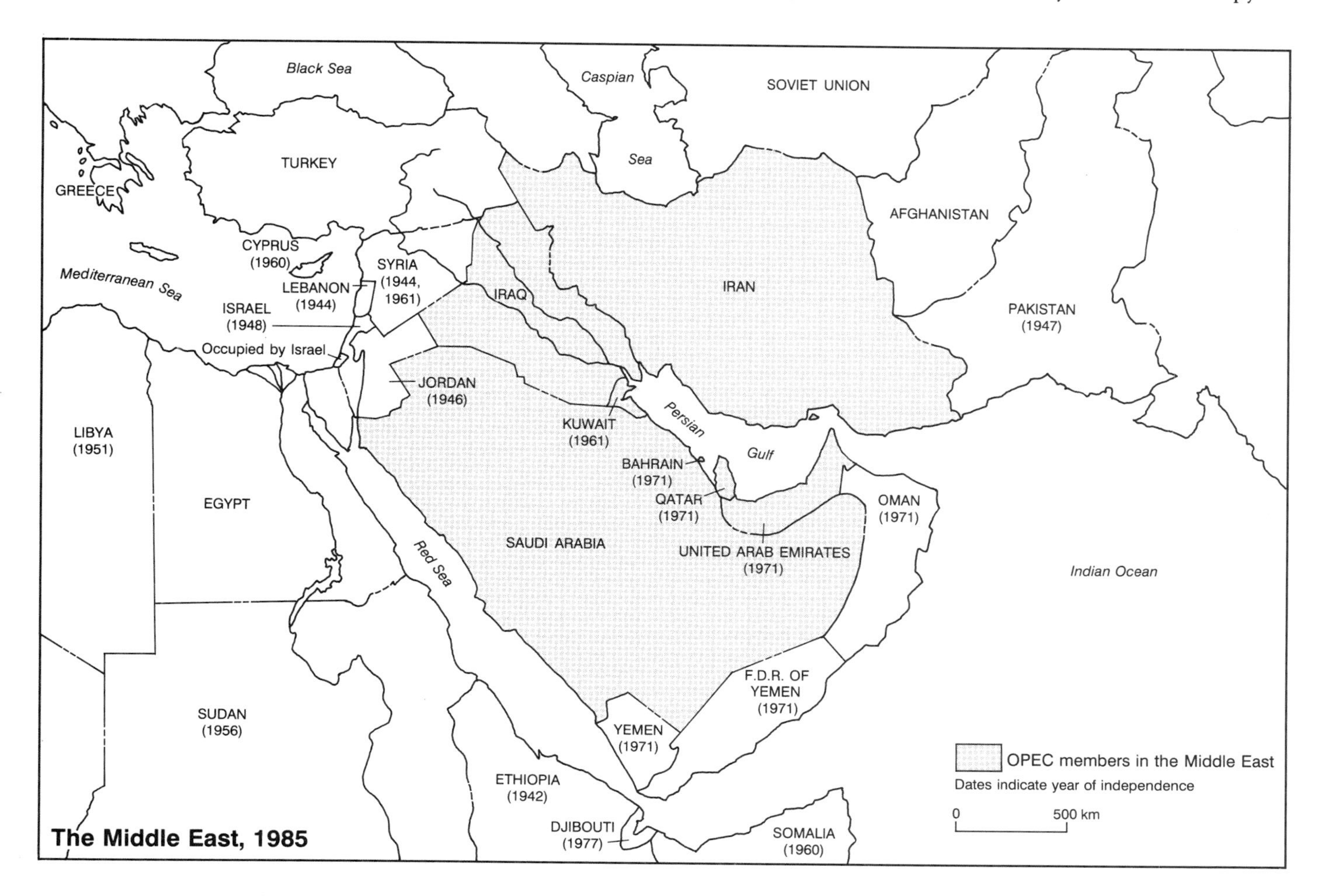

The Middle East, 1985

region. The United Nations Emergency Force (UNEF) was to become a principal arm of UN action in the future. As this provided an opportunity for Britain and France to withdraw their troops without jeapordizing the canal, they readily agreed.

While Pearson received the Nobel Prize for Peace in 1957 for his efforts in the Middle East, he was condemned by some Canadians, who feared that by refusing to back Britain he was turning Canada into a satellite of the United States. Most Canadians, however, believed that the crisis established Canada as a "middle power" that could act as a buffer between the superpowers and other countries of the world. This opinion was reinforced when Canadian troops formed an integral part of the first peacekeeping force in Egypt. Since then, Canadians have performed peacekeeping duties in the Sinai, on the Golan Heights, and in Cyprus, and have offered their services in such diverse places as Vietnam, Namibia, Haiti, and Central America.

Arab-Israeli Conflicts

In early 1967, Nasser called for the withdrawal of the UN peacekeeping forces from the Middle East. After the UN complied, Egypt initiated a blockade of Israel by closing the Straits of Tiran to Israeli shipping, thereby cutting off Israel's access to the Red Sea. Israel responded with a pre-emptive strike against Egypt and Syria on June 5th. The Six-Day War that ensued saw Israel destroy its neighbours' military forces and seize the buffer zones of the Golan Heights from Syria and the Sinai Peninsula from Egypt.

Over the next five years, Egypt and Israel faced each other across the Sinai. The Suez Canal was blocked and Western Europe was forced to develop supertankers capable of traveling around the southern tip of Africa in order to maintain the flow of their critical oil supplies. Finally, in October 1973, Egyptian president Anwar al-Sadat (1918–1981) launched a surprise attack on the Jewish religious holiday of Yom Kippur. After initial Arab successes, the better-equipped Israelis began to get the upper hand. Finally the United Nations intervened and arranged a cease-fire. After two years of tense negotiations, Egypt and Israel agreed to a settlement in the Sinai. For Sadat, the outcome was a political victory at home. Although Egypt had lost the war, it had at least partially won the peace. This would prove valuable in future negotiations.

During the height of the crisis American forces airlifted supplies to Israel. In retaliation, the Organization of Petroleum Exporting Countries (OPEC), led by Middle East Arab oil-producing nations, launched an oil embargo against the U.S. Recognizing their economic power, the OPEC nations also quadrupled the price of oil over the next two years. For many developing nations this economic clout was a revelation. The industrial West depended heavily on raw materials from the developing world. The possibility of similar actions by other nations might cause the Western countries to be more equitable in future dealings.

Egyptian gains in the war had given Sadat the flexibility to open negotiations with Israeli prime minister Menachem Begin (1913–1987) in 1977. After early negotiations failed, American president Jimmy Carter offered to act as a mediator. For twelve days in September 1978, the three leaders met behind closed doors at the American presidential retreat of Camp David. Finally, they emerged with a new "Framework for Peace in the Middle East." Under its terms, Israel was to withdraw from occupied Egyptian territory and further discussions were to be held to settle border disputes with Jordan and the question of resettlement of Palestinian refugees. The final treaty was signed in March 1979. Israel completed its withdrawal from the Sinai Peninsula in April 1982.

Over the next decade, the ongoing crisis in the Middle East focused on Lebanon and the demands of the Palestine Liberation Organization (PLO) for the creation of an Arab Palestinian homeland. As Israel began to depend more and more on the use of force to suppress the Palestinians, public opinion continued to demand that a solution be found.

NEUTRALISM AND THE DEVELOPING WORLD

The new rulers of the former European colonies were faced with the question of which side to support in the era of the Cold War. Although some were drawn into regional alliances, most rejected a role in this struggle between the superpowers, preferring to remain nonaligned.

During the 1950s and 1960s, the nonaligned movement was divided into two camps. Nations such as India attempted to occupy the middle ground between the two superpowers. Indian prime minister Jawaharlal Nehru stressed the values of pacifism and attempted to remain neutral in international disputes. Other nonaligned nations, such as Egypt, had their own agendas. They often used the support of one or the other superpowers to gain their own objectives, but they were also willing to switch sides when it was in their best interests to do so. For the most part, however, the rhetoric of the Cold War had little meaning in the developing world. Whether it was socialist values, democratic principles, Soviet weaponry, or American capital, most developing nations simply used the most effective tools at hand to help them in their development. (See readings.)

JAPAN

Economic Recovery

At the end of the Second World War almost all of the major cities of Japan were severely damaged from American bombing raids and over 8 million people were dead or injured. The economy was at a standstill. Yet by 1968, Japan had the second largest GNP in the non-communist world, surpassed only by the United States. The rapid recovery of Japan, like that of West Germany, was one of the economic miracles of the postwar era.

Japan's recovery was based on a number of factors. The lack of large-scale reparations, the de-emphasis on military spending, and $2 billion in direct American aid were obvious spurs to economic recovery. But long-term economic growth was based on other factors.

Prior to the Second World War, the Japanese economy was dominated by a number of large *zaibatsu*—giant financial trusts. The nine largest of these were liquidated after the war and their securities purchased by the public. This had three important results: it broadened the base of the Japanese economy; it increased competition; and it freed individual enterprises and managers from a conservative elite and allowed them to expand and develop. Development concentrated on new technologies (largely imported from the U.S.) that allowed the Japanese to increase production. New technology was particularly important in the steel, shipbuilding, electronics, household appliance, and automotive industries. Capital for this expansion was supplied largely through people's savings and was therefore not a drain on industry or the government. The government's primary role in economics was to project trends and formulate programs.

The United States' interest in Japan's recovery and Japan's desire for economic collaboration with the U.S. were also major factors in Japanese recovery. With increased tensions between East and West in Europe and the fall of China to the communists, the U.S. wanted to maintain political and economic stability in Japan and to prevent the spread of communism in the East. To that end they became involved first in the Korean War and then in the Vietnam War. These military commitments poured billions of dollars into heavy industries in Japan, particularly the steel industry, and enabled their rapid expansion. In addition, the extension of the U.S. defence umbrella over Japan allowed that country to limit its military expenditures and divert the funds into more productive areas of the economy.

The liberalization of trade after the war enabled Japan to increase its foreign trade throughout the 1950s and 1960s at an annual rate of almost 6 percent. At the same time, the internal Japanese market was almost exclusively the domain of Japanese industry. As the population rose and standards of living increased, the domestic market became a major factor in the growth of Japanese industry.

The oil crisis of the 1970s revealed one of the major weaknesses of Japan's economy—its lack of natural resources. Japan imports almost 80 percent of its raw materials and all of its oil. The oil crisis created spiraling inflation and made Tokyo the most expensive city in the world in which to live.

In the late 1970s and throughout the 1980s, Japan has been shifting away from heavy industrial manufacturing toward high-tech industries. It is predicted that by the twenty-first century, Japan will either lead or be second in robotics, computers, and telecommunications, while maintaining similar positions in the more traditional automobile and shipbuilding industries.

Japan's success is forcing economists to re-evaluate traditional ideas about industrial development. Unlike most industrialized countries, Japan lacks raw materials. Factors such as a commitment to quality and education, a social ethos of hard work and loyalty, protection of the domestic market, financing from the private sector, and little military spending are credited as the reasons for Japan's success. Although the Japanese experience is not directly transferable to any other country, it could provide lessons for countries in the developing world.

THREE WORLDS OR ONE?

The division of countries into three "worlds" occurred in the 1950s during the Cold War. Initially the divisions were made along political lines. The First World contained the liberal, capitalist countries of the Western Bloc—Western

Europe, the United States, Canada, New Zealand, and Australia. The Second World comprised the countries of the Communist Bloc—the Soviet Union and Eastern Europe. The Third World contained all the countries that did not belong to either the First or Second worlds.

Most of the countries of the Third World had been European colonies. Although the legacy of imperialism is not entirely negative (colonial powers did build transportation infrastructures and supplied Western technology), the benefits received by the colonial powers greatly exceeded those received by the colonies. Colonies had primarily been sources of raw materials and markets for finished manufactured goods. This dependency retarded economic development even after independence.

Today the Third World is still in a position of dependency and its burden of debt is staggering. In 1988, the Organization for Economic Co-operation and Development listed the outstanding debt of developing nations as $1.2 trillion (U.S.). Because many Third World countries still rely heavily on single agricultural crops or raw material exports (commodities that fluctuate greatly on the world market and therefore provide unstable sources of income), they are unable to pay the interest on their debt, let alone the principal.

The recession in the developed world in 1981–1982 illustrated clearly the interdependence of the global economy and the fate of the developing countries if action is not taken. The substantial drop in raw material prices on the world market resulted in a lack of income. This in turn forced many developing countries to default on their debts, which placed the international financial system in jeopardy.

The 1980 report of the Independent Commission on International Development Issues, entitled *North-South: A Program of Survival* (popularly called the Brandt Report after the commission's leader, Willy Brandt [1913-], former chancellor of West Germany) pointed out that the economies of the world were interrelated and that the future prosperity of the developed countries relies on the development of the Third World. But the recommendations of the report were largely ignored by the developed world, primarily because of a lack of political will to achieve change. In 1987, *Our Common Future*, the report of the World Commission on Environment and Development, pointed out that the environmental crisis, the development crisis, and the energy crisis were in fact interlocking crises that required a "global agenda for change." (See chapter 14.) Preventing the collapse of the economies of the developing countries is the challenge of the 1990s.

RETROSPECTIVE

The decades since the end of the Second World War have seen a re-examination of the relationship between the individual and the community. In the European world, conflicting philosophies faced each other through the tense era of the Cold War. In the former European colonies, new nations have emerged and old cultures have reasserted themselves. These societies have created many interesting alternatives to Western civilization. Other areas reflect an interesting blend of Western values and local traditions, for as modern Western civilization has spread, it has also grown and diversified.

The 1980s also saw a growing concern over basic human rights for the citizens of the developing world. Repressive regimes in the Philippines, Zimbabwe, Chile, and Panama were replaced with democratically elected governments. The opening of formal talks between the white minority government of South Africa and the African National Congress seemed to indicate a liberalizing trend there. On the other hand, the most populous nation in the world, China, ended the 1980s with a massacre of pro-democracy students and workers and marked the anniversary of that event with continued opposition to all "counterrevolutionary" movements.

In the final analysis, human rights in the developing world continue to be tied to economic prosperity. In sub-Saharan Africa and southeast Asia, with their poverty, famine, and economic stagnation, most people are too preoccupied with the realities of day-to-day survival to have time for political protest and change. The challenge for Western civilization in the 1990s will be to support these nations as they build a solid economic base and obtain political equality.

FRANTZ FANON:
The Wretched of the Earth (1961)

Frantz Fanon was a psychiatrist assigned to a hospital in Algeria during the French-Algerian conflict. Born in the French colony of Martinique, Fanon expressed the anger of many black nationalists. Fanon believed that black Africans had been made to feel that their values were inferior to those of Western civilization. He claimed that African society had been decapitated by European colonizers and that the cream of African society had been brainwashed to see themselves as white Europeans, denying their own heritage. In this first excerpt, he makes the case for a rejection of European values.

Europe has done what she set out to do and on the whole she has done it well; let us stop blaming her, but let us say to her firmly that she should not make such a song and dance about it. We have no more to fear; so let us stop envying her.

The Third World today faces Europe like a colossal mass whose aim should be to try to resolve the problems to which Europe has not been able to find the answers. . . .

It is a question of the Third World starting a new history of Man, a history which will have regard to the sometimes prodigious theses which Europe has put forward, but which will not forget Europe's crimes. . . .

So, comrades, let us not pay tribute to Europe by creating states, institutions, and societies which draw their inspiration from her.

Humanity is waiting for something from us other than such an imitation, which would be almost an obscene caricature.

If we want to turn Africa into a new Europe, and America into a new Europe, then let us leave the destiny of our countries to Europeans. They will know how to do it better than the most gifted among us.

But if we want humanity to advance a step further, if we want to bring it up to a different level than that which Europe has shown it, then we must invent and we must make discoveries.

If we wish to live up to our peoples' expectations, we must seek the response elsewhere than in Europe.

The existentialist Jean-Paul Sartre wrote the introduction to Fanon's book. He echoes, in emotional terms, many of Fanon's arguments.

Our worthiest souls contain racial prejudice.

They would do well to read Fanon; for he shows clearly that this irrepressible violence is neither sound and fury, nor is the resurrection of savage instincts, nor even the effect of resentment: it is man recreating himself. I think we understood the truth at one time, but we have forgotten it—that no gentleness can efface the marks of violence; only violence itself can destroy them. The native cures himself of colonial neurosis by thrusting out the settler through force of arms. . . .

Once begun it is a war that gives no quarter. You may fear or be feared; that is to say, abandon yourself to the disassociations of a sham existence or conquer your birthright of unity. When the peasant takes a gun in his hands, the old myths grow dim and the prohibitions are one by one forgotten. The rebel's weapon is the proof of his humanity. To shoot down a European is . . . to destroy an oppressor and the man he oppresses at the same time: there remain a dead man, and a free man; the survivor, for the first time, feels a national soil under his foot.

---

1. Account for Fanon's rejection of European methods and values. To what extent is this attitude explained in Sartre's view of the need for liberation?

2. Compare Fanon and Sartre's analysis with the justification given by Rudyard Kipling in "The White Man's Burden."

3. To what extent have Fanon's predictions come true in the period from 1960 to 1990?

HO CHI MINH: Vietnam Declaration of Independence (1945)

After the Japanese withdrawal from Vietnam in August 1945, the way was clear for the creation of an independent Vietnamese state. Ho Chi Minh was a revolutionary communist. Born Nguyen Tat Thanh, during the 1920s and 1930s he agitated against French colonial rule in Indochina, and after attempting an uprising in 1940 he was forced to flee to China. In 1943, he returned to Vietnam. Taking the alias Ho Chi Minh (Ho means the Seeker of Light), he led the resistance against the Japanese occupation. In September 1945, he proclaimed the creation of the Democratic Republic of Vietnam and on 2 September read this declaration to cheering crowds in Hanoi's Ba Dinh Square.

From Marvin E. Gettleman, *et al*, *Vietnam and America: A Documentary History*, (New York: Grove Press, 1985), pp. 40–42.

"All men are created equal. They are endowed by their Creator with certain inalienable rights; among these are Life, Liberty, and the pursuit of happiness."

This immortal statement was made in the Declaration of Independence of the United States of America in 1776. In a broader sense, this means: All the people on the earth are equal from birth, all the peoples have a right to live, to be happy and free.

The Declaration of the French Revolution made in 1791 on the Rights of Man and the Citizen also states: "All men are born free and with equal rights, and must always remain free and have equal rights."

Those are undeniable truths.

Nevertheless, for more than eighty years, the French imperialists, abusing the standard of Liberty, Equality, and Fraternity, have violated our Fatherland and oppressed our fellow-citizens. They have acted contrary to the ideals of humanity and justice.

In the field of politics, they have deprived our people of every democratic liberty.

They have enforced inhuman laws. . . .

They have built more prisons than schools. . . .

They have fettered public opinion. . . .

They have robbed us of our rice fields, our mines, our forests, and our raw materials. . . .

Notwithstanding all of this, our fellow-citizens have always manifested toward the French a tolerant and humane attitude. . . .

From the autumn of 1940, our country had in fact ceased to be a French colony and had become a Japanese possession.

After the Japanese surrendered to the Allies, our whole people rose to regain our national sovereignty and to found the Democratic Republic of Vietnam.

The truth is that we have wrested our independence from the Japanese and not from the French. . . .

Our people have broken the chains which for nearly a century have fettered them and have won independence for the Fatherland. . . .

We are convinced that the Allied nations which at Tehran and San Francisco have acknowledged the principles of self-determination and equality of nations will not refuse to acknowledge the independence of Vietnam. . . .

For these reasons, we, members of the Provisional Government of the Democratic Republic of Vietnam, solemnly declare to the world that Vietnam has the right to be a free and independent country—and in fact is so already. The entire Vietnamese people are determined to mobilize all their physical and mental strength, to sacrifice their lives and property in order to safeguard their independence and liberty.

---

1. Account for Ho Chi Minh's optimistic outlook in 1945.

HO CHI MINH:
The Last Testament (1969)

Ho led the Viet Minh in their resistance to continued French colonial rule from 1945 to 1954. In 1954 he became president of North Vietnam and from 1963 on provided support to Viet Cong rebels in the south. A few months before he died, the Vietnamese leader published a "last testament" to his people. In it, he looked forward to the final defeat of the imperialists. In honour of this spiritual parent of a united, independent Vietnam, the old capital of South Vietnam, Saigon, was renamed Ho Chi Minh City in 1975.

From Marvin E. Gettleman, *et al*, *Vietnam and America: A Documentary History*, (New York: Grove Press, 1985), pp. 439–441.

Our people's struggle against U.S. aggression, for national salvation, may have to go through even more difficulties and sacrifices, but we are bound to win total victory.

That is a certainty. . . .

In the plains as in the mountain areas [our people] have for ages endured hardships, feudal and colonial oppression and exploitation; they have moreover experienced many years of war. . . .

Whatever difficulties and hardships may be ahead, our people are sure of total triumph. The U.S. imperialists shall have to quit. Our Fatherland shall be reunited. Our compatriots in the North and in the South shall be reunited under the same roof. We, a small nation, will have earned the unique honour of defeating, through a heroic struggle, two big imperialisms—the French and the American—and making a worthy contribution to the national liberation movement.

1. Contrast Ho Chi Minh's ideals in 1945 with the realities of the Vietnam experience.

2. How have Ho Chi Minh's views changed as a result of twenty-five years of war?

MAO ZEDONG:
Imperialism and All Reactionaries Are Paper Tigers (1946, 1958)

Mao Zedong led the communist forces during the Chinese civil war in the late 1940s. After ten years as president of the new People's Republic of China, he relinquished the post in 1959. Within six years Mao, rejecting the more conservative path chosen by his successors, launched the Cultural Revolution to reassert his power and radicalize the revolution. During this period of upheaval, millions of Chinese citizens could be seen carrying and quoting from Mao Zedong's "Little Red Book." In this excerpt, Mao comments on imperialism.

All reactionaries are paper tigers. In appearance, the reactionaries are terrifying, but in reality they are not so powerful. From a long-term point of view, it is not the reactionaries but the people who are really powerful. . . . Imperialists and all reactionaries have a dual—they are real tigers and paper tigers at the same time. In past history, before they won state power and for some time afterwards, the slave-owning class, the feudal landlord class and the bourgeoisie were vigorous, revolutionary and progressive; they were real tigers. But with lapse of time, because their opposites, the slave class, the peasant class and the proletariat—grew in strength step by step, struggled against them more and more fiercely, these ruling classes changed step by step into the reverse, changed into reactionaries, changed into backward people, changed into paper tigers. . . .

To destroy the rule of imperialism, feudalism and bureaucrat-capitalism in China took the Chinese people more than a hundred years and cost them tens of millions of lives before the victory in 1949. Look! Were these not living tigers. Iron tigers, real tigers? But in the end they changed into paper tigers, dead tigers, bean-curd tigers. These are historical facts.

1. How does Mao depict the difference between real and paper tigers?

2. Apply Mao's analogy to the government's reaction to the protest in Tiananmen Square in 1989.

THE BEIJING SPRING (1989)

The student fast and mass protest in Tiananmen Square in May and June 1989 seemed to herald a new age of openness in the People's Republic of China. The government's brutal response and relentless propaganda campaign, however, attempted to rewrite history. In this excerpt a reporter from Time *profiles one of the student leaders.*

From Ted Gup, "Portrait of a 'Hooligan'," *Time*, 26 June 1989.

Wuer Kaixi. 21. A Uighur with wavy black hair, big round eyes, high cheekbones. Shown last week on Chinese television on secret videotape from a Beijing hotel that falsely suggested he was eating when he was on a hunger strike in Tiananmen Square. Wanted by the Chinese government. His crime: he was a leader of the prodemocracy movement. . . .

China's hard-liners have vilified Wuer and other student protesters as counter-revolutionaries. But those who have known Wuer for years say he never sought to overthrow the government and that he one day hoped to join the Communist Party. During the protests, he told reporters his aim was to "form a nationwide citizens' organization, like the Polish Solidarity," able to deal "openly and directly" with the government. . . .

He was born . . . in Beijing on Feb. 17, 1968 . . . in the midst of the Cultural Revolution, when an aging Mao Zedong fomented social unrest in the name of class struggle. A family portrait shows Wuer, age 1, holding up a copy of Mao's Little Red Book. . . . When thousands of China's intellectuals were forced out of the cities to work with the peasants in the countryside, Wuer's father went willingly. . . .

Wuer . . . spent most of his boyhood and school years in Beijing in an apartment adorned by a portrait of Mao put there by his father. . . .

[Wuer's] political views grew out of his own experiences, not Western influence; he never went abroad, but his voracious reading exposed him to all sorts of modern concepts, Chinese and foreign. "He believed," said a friend, "the Chinese expression that the leaders should serve the people."

1. Research the current status of the student leaders of the pro-democracy movement. Assess the impact of their actions upon Chinese government policies.

JOHN F. KENNEDY: The Alliance for Progress (1961)

Faced with growing anti-Americanism in Latin America, newly elected president John F. Kennedy called for a new "Alliance for Progress" to improve the quality of life in Latin America. All the American states (with the exception of Cuba) met in Uruguay in August 1961 to improve economic co-operation. They pledged to help one another resist the spread of communism in the hemisphere. Kennedy and his successor

At the dawn of freedom throughout this hemisphere . . . Bolivar spoke of his desire to see the Americas fashioned into the greatest region in the world, "greatest," he said, "not so much by virtue of her area or her wealth, as by her freedom and her glory."

Never, in the long history of our hemisphere, has this dream been nearer to fulfillment, and never has it been in greater danger. . . .

Throughout Latin America—a continent rich in resources and in the spiritual and cultural achievements of its people—millions of men and women suffer the daily degradations of hunger and poverty. They lack decent shelter or protection from disease. Their children are deprived of the education or the jobs which are the gateway to a better life. And each day the problems grow more urgent. . . .

Therefore I have called on all the people of the hemisphere to join in a new Alliance for Progress . . . a vast cooperative effort, unparalleled in magnitude and

Lyndon Johnson used the Alliance for Progress as a diplomatic weapon against Cuba in the early 1960s.

From Henry Steele Commager, *Documents of American History* (7th ed.), (New York: Appleton-Century-Crofts, 1963), pp. 693–699.

nobility of purpose, to satisfy the basic needs of the American people for homes, work and land, health and schools.

---

1. Summarize Kennedy's analysis of the current situation in Latin America. To what extent had the United States contributed to this?

2. Assess American policy toward Latin America between 1961 and 1990. Comment on the contention that the policy of the United States in Latin America actually proved to be the opposite of the values outlined in Kennedy's "Alliance for Progress."

GAMAL ABDEL NASSER: Egypt's Liberation (1955)

Gamal Abdel Nasser was a key figure in the Free Officers Movement in the 1940s. Anti-British, republican, and fiercely nationalistic, the movement helped to spark the abdication of King Farouk in 1952. Nasser became minister of the interior and deputy to the president. In 1954, he became president. Three years after the proclamation of the republic, Nasser discussed his nation's role in world affairs.

From Gamal Abdel Nasser, *Egypt's Liberation: The Philosophy of the Revolution*, (Washington, D.C.: Public Affairs Press, 1955), pp. 83–90, 98, 102–114.

The age of isolation is gone. . . .

We cannot look at the map of the world without seeing our own place upon it, and that our role is dictated by that place.

Can we fail to see that there is an Arab circle surrounding us—that this circle is a part of us, and we are a part of it, our history being extricably part of its history?

. . . It is not without significance that our country is situated west of Asia, in contiguity with the Arab states whose existence our own is interwoven. It is not without significance, too, that our country lies in northeast Africa, overlooking the Dark Continent, wherein rages a most tumultuous struggle between the white colonizers and black inhabitants for control of its unlimited resources. . . . So far as I can recall, the first glimmers of Arab awareness began to steal into my consciousness when I was a student in secondary school. I used to go out on a general strike with my comrades every year on the second of December to protest the Balfour Declaration which Britain had made on behalf of the Jews, giving them a national home in Palestine, thus tyrannously wresting it from its rightful owners. . . .

Let me go back, now, to what I was saying—that imperialism is the great force that is imposing a murderous, invisible seige upon the whole region. . . .

When all these truths had impressed themselves upon me, I began to realize the need for a common struggle. . . . The Dark Continent is now the scene of a strange and excited turbulence: the white man, representing various European nations, is again trying to re-divide the map of Africa. We shall not, in any circumstance, be able to stand idly by in the face of what is going on, in the false belief that it will not affect or concern us.

I will continue to dream of . . . an enlightened African consciousness . . . sharing with others from all over the world the work of advancing the welfare of the peoples of this continent.

---

1. (a) How does Nasser view Egypt's role in Africa?
(b) To what extent did leaders such as Nasser see themselves as a new generation of "friendly" imperialists?

JAWAHARLAL NEHRU:
Independence and After (1946–1949)

In the late 1940s, India's prime minister, Jawaharlal Nehru, outlined his view of the role of emerging nations in maintaining world peace. Nehru had become India's first prime minister after independence and held the post until his death. He was one of the principal proponents of the nonaligned movement which saw itself as a buffer between the superpowers.

From Jawaharal Nehru, *Independence and After. A Collection of the More Important Speeches of Jawaharlal Nehru from September 1946 to May 1949*, (New Delhi: Government of India, 1949), pp. 4–6, 8, 12–14.

One of the major questions of the day is the readjustment of the relations between Asia and Europe. When we talk of Asia, remember that India, not because of any ambition of hers, but because of the force of circumstances, because of geography, because of history and because of so many other things inevitably has to play a very important part in Asia. . . . One of the major questions of the day is the readjustment of the relations between Asia and Europe. In the past, especially by virtue of her economic and political domination, the West ignored Asia, or at any rate did not give her the weight that was due to her. Asia was really given a back seat and one unfortunate result of it was that even the statesmen did not recognize the changes that were taking place. There is, I believe, a considerable recognition of these changes now, but it is not enough yet. . . . In each country of Asia—underdeveloped countries more or less—the main problem is the problem of food, of clothing, of education, of health. We are concerned with these problems. We are not directly concerned with problems of power politics. Some of us, in our minds, may perhaps think of that.

Europe, on the other hand, is also concerned with these problems, no doubt, in the devastated regions. Europe has a legacy of conflicts of power, and of problems which come from the possession of power. The have the fear of losing that power and the fear of some one else getting greater power and attacking one country or the other. So that the European approach is a legacy of the past conflicts of Europe.

I do not mean to say that we in Asia are in any way superior, ethically or morally, to the people of Europe. In some ways, I imagine that we are worse. There is, however, a legacy of conflict in Europe. In Asia, at the present moment at least, there is no such legacy. . . .

We might note that the world progressively tends to become one—one in peace, and it is likely to be one, in a sense of war. No man can say that any country can remain apart when there is a major conflagration. But still one can direct one's policy towards avoiding this conflict and being entangled in it.

1. Why does Nehru feel that Asian nations such as India could play a major role in providing international leadership for world peace?

2. Write a dialogue between Nehru and Nasser. Have the two leaders discuss the topic: *The role of developing nations in providing international leadership.*

NIKITA KHRUSHCHEV:
Cuba (1962)

Following the Cuban revolution and the Bay of Pigs fiasco, the United States saw Cuba as an advance base for a Soviet takeover of Latin America and the Caribbean

Flouting generally accepted standards of international relations, the United States reactionary forces have been doing everything from the first day of the victory of the Cuban revolution to overthrow Cuba's revolutionary Government and to restore their domination there. They broke off diplomatic relations with Cuba, were and are conducting subversive activity, established an economic blockade of Cuba. . . . This is an inhuman policy—a desire to starve a whole nation.

. . . Revolutionary Cuba was compelled to take all measures to strengthen her *basin. In October 1962, the world was pushed to the brink of nuclear war over the Missile Crisis. After the fact, a number of conflicting views emerged. In December 1962, Soviet premier Nikita Khrushchev outlined his country's position.*

From *The Worker Supplement*, 23 December, 1962, in Robert A. Divine (ed.), *The Cuban Missile Crisis*, (Chicago: Quadrangle Books, 1971), pp. 106–112.

defense. The Soviet Union helped her to build a strong army standing guard over the achievements of the Cuban people. . . .

What were the aims behind this decision? Naturally, neither we nor our Cuban friends had in mind that this small number of IRBMs, sent to Cuba, would be used for an attack on the United States or any other country.

Our aim was to defend Cuba. We saw how the American imperialists were sharpening their knives, threatening Cuba with a massed attack. We could not remain impartial observers in the face of this bandit-like policy, which is contrary to all standards of relations between states and the United Nations Charter.

In response to Khrushchev's statement, Kennedy made the following remarks on a nationwide television interview.

From *Public Papers of the Presidents: Kennedy, 1962*, (Washington, D.C., 1963).

I think in that speech this week [Khrushchev] showed his awareness of the nuclear age, But of course, the Cuban effort has made it more difficult for us to carry out any successful negotiations, because this was an effort to materially change the balance of power, it was done in secret, steps were taken really to deceive us by every means they could, and they were planning in November to open to the world the fact that they had these missiles so close to the United States; not that they were intending to fire them, because if they were going to get into a nuclear struggle, they have their own missiles in the Soviet Union. But it would have changed the balance of power. . . .

The real problem is the Soviet desire to expand their power and influence. . . .

I think that anybody who looks at the fatality lists on atomic weapons, and realizes that the Communists have a completely twisted view of the United States, and that we don't comprehend them, that is what makes life in the sixties hazardous. . . .

---

1. Kennedy and Khrushchev faced each other at the height of the Cold War. With a friend, create a two-person debate on the Cuban Missile Crisis. One of you should prepare a position paper from the standpoint of Khrushchev and the other from Kennedy's perspective.

Deliver your papers to each other and then take time to refute your opponent. After you have argued the issues, step out of role and discuss the nature of the Cold War as exemplified by these two leaders.

NELSON MANDELA:
The Struggle Must Go On (1990)

The release from prison of Nelson Mandela on 11 February 1990 marked the end of an epic personal struggle and the beginning of a new age for South Africa. That evening Mandela spoke to a crowd of over 50 000 people in Cape Town in his first public appearance in over twenty-seven years. This is an excerpt from his address.

Friends, comrades and fellow South Africans! I greet you all in the name of peace, democracy and freedom for all . . .

Today the majority of South Africans, black and white, recognize that apartheid has no future.

It has to be ended by our own decisive mass action in order to build peace and security. The mass campaign of defiance and other actions of our organization and people can only culminate in the establishment of democracy.

The apartheid destruction on our subcontinent is incalculable. The fabric of family life of millions of my people has been shattered. Millions are homeless and unemployed. Our economy lies in ruins and our people are embroiled in political strife. . . .

From *The Toronto Star*, 12 February 1990.

The factor which necessitated the armed struggle still exists today. We have no option but to continue . . .

Mr. de Klerk has gone further than any other Nationalist president in taking real steps to normalize the situation. However, there are further steps . . . that have to be made before negotiations on the basic demands of our people can begin . . .

Negotiations on the dismantling of apartheid will have to address the overwhelming demand of our people for a democratic non-racial and unitary South Africa. There must be an end to white monopoly on political power, and a fundamental restructuring of our political and economic systems to ensure that the inequalities of apartheid are addressed and our society thoroughly democratized . . .

Our struggle has reached a decisive moment. We call on our people to seize this moment, so that the process toward democracy is rapid and uninterrupted . . .

We call on our white compatriots to join us in the shaping of a new South Africa. The freedom movement is a political home for you too. . . .

Our march to freedom is irreversible. We must not allow fear to stand in our way.

---

1. Summarize Mandela's basic goals.

2. Comment on Mandela's call for a unified multiracial state in South Africa. Write a letter to Mandela offering your support or raising your concerns with the practicality of his vision.

3. Trace the role Nelson Mandela has played in the anti-apartheid movement since his release in February 1990.

ANALYSIS AND APPLICATION

1. Reread the quotation by Frantz Fanon at the beginning of this chapter. Write a defence of Fanon's call to arms based upon your understanding of the history of Western imperialism in Africa.

2. Select three African nations that were formerly colonies of three different European nations.
(a) Compare the processes by which these three nations regained their independence.
(b) Based upon your findings, create a thesis with regard to the decolonization process in Africa.

3. *The war in Vietnam is a modern example of the destructive impact of overseas imperialism both on the oppressor and the oppressed.*
Account for this statement with specific reference to the American experience in Vietnam.

4. Create a visual essay, using newspaper and magazine clippings, illustrating the rise and fall of the pro-democracy movement in China in the spring of 1989.

5. Divide into groups of two. Stage a two-person debate between Ronald Reagan and Daniel Ortega. Resolved: *The United States has the right to intervene in the internal politics of any nation in the Western Hemisphere.*

6. Write an editorial for *Pravda* critiquing Kennedy's statements and actions during the Cuban Missile Crisis.

7. In a group, create a new constitution for a democratic South Africa. Be certain to include a democratic system of government, a charter of rights, and a proposal for redress and compensation.

8. Write your own profile of one of the following: Winnie Mandela; Indira Gandhi; Golda Meir; Eva Peron.

CHAPTER FOURTEEN

Science and Technology

DEVELOPMENTS SINCE 1945

The world has seemed to become smaller in the postwar world. Today highways and railways link communities across the nation. Commercial jetliners link countries in all parts of the world. Telecommunications transmit messages around the globe via satellite. Telephone networks provide a link between individuals around the world. Television and radio signals bounce off satellites to provide up-to-the-minute accounts of events anywhere in the world.

In the last twenty years alone, we have progressed from landing the first person on the moon to launching space shuttle flights so frequently that few of us watch the televised takeoffs and landings anymore. Medicine treats diseases and injuries that were fatal only decades ago. Chemistry has developed to the point that over 90 percent of the drugs we use today were not even available thirty years ago. The spread of science has been so explosive that 90 percent of all the scientists in history were still alive in the 1960s. The development of the computer has led to advances in automation, miniaturization, and robotics, all of which have changed the way many of us work.

Our scientific and technological achievements have not been without a price, however. Our ability to control and alter the physical world has caused serious environmental problems. In the 1990s, we now realize that it is our responsibility to safeguard our planet from the destructive forces of our own making.

SCIENCE

Physics

Following the explosion of the world's first atomic bombs in 1945, research into thermonuclear weapons continued. By 1954, the U.S. was ready to test its first hydrogen bomb at Bikini Atoll. The bomb proved to have an explosive force 1000 times greater than the bomb dropped on Hiroshima. Today the nuclear club includes the United States, the Soviet Union, Britain, France, China, Brazil, Israel, and India. Other countries capable of producing nuclear weapons, such as Japan, West Germany, and Canada, have chosen not to do so. Despite the overwhelming power of the hydrogen bomb, nuclear testing (almost all of which is conducted underground since the Limited Nuclear Test Ban Treaty of 1963) continues.

The spread of the technological capabilities required to develop nuclear weapons led to the Treaty on the Nonproliferation of Nuclear Weapons (1968). This UN treaty, which was intended to halt the spread of nuclear weapons, went into effect without the signatures of, among others, France, China, India, and Israel.

Research into the nature of the atom accounted for a bewildering list of subatomic particles, such as leptrons and quarks, which led to the development of a new Standard Model of the atom. Today, physicists believe that all matter is made up of only four particles: the two quarks—that is, the protons and neutrons which make up the nucleus of the atom; electrons which orbit the nucleus; and neutrinos which are given off during atomic reactions. These particles are acted upon by four forces: the strong nuclear force which binds the nucleus together; the weak nuclear force which triggers radioactive decay; electromagnetism; and gravity. Bosons transmit these forces between different particles.

These discoveries have resulted from research conducted in particle accelerators, machines that accelerate small amounts of matter to speeds almost that of light and then smash them together in an attempt to discover the building blocks of nature. The largest of these, the 27 km ring-shaped electron-positron collider (LEP), is at CERN, the European Organization for Nuclear Research. The competition to make new discoveries has prompted the U.S. to build an even larger particle collider near Waxahachie, Texas. The 87 km supercollider will cost over $7 billion and is expected to be completed in the year 2000.

Many advances in physics have been invaluable to other sciences. James Watson (1928-) and Francis Crick (1916-) used a technique developed by physicists—X-ray crystallography—to discover the molecular structure of DNA (deoxyribonucleic acid), the substance that is the basis of heredity; they shared the Nobel Prize in Physiology and Medicine in 1962 with Maurice Wilkins (1916-), who had initially discovered the structure of DNA was a helix. By-products of nuclear research, such as the radioactive isotopes Cobalt–60 used as a source of radiation in the treatment of cancer and plutonium–238 used as an electrical source for cardiac pacemakers, are invaluable in medicine. Physicists discovered the transistor, which revolutionized communications and the computer industry, and the laser, which is used in communications, industry, and medicine. Current research into superconductors, materials which lose resistance to the flow of electric current when cooled below a certain temperature, may have applications as diverse as transmitting electricity and faster data retrieval in computers.

Chemistry

As in physics, research in chemistry was stimulated by the Second World War. The demand for explosives, medicines, and synthetic replacements for scarce raw materials such as rubber greatly expanded industrial chemistry. After the war, the chemical industry continued to develop a wide range of products for consumer and industrial use.

Applied chemistry has developed fertilizers, pesticides, and herbicides for the agricultural industry; plastics, antifreeze, gasoline additives, and synthetic rubber and fabrics for the automobile industry; and additives, preservatives, and colouring agents for the food industry. And the list goes on for just about all industries in modern Western society. In fact, there are few products that do not bear the stamp of the chemical industry and the rate of innovations has been staggering. Over 50 percent of consumer products and 90 percent of medicines did not exist thirty years ago.

Unfortunately, however, industrial chemistry has also been the source of considerable damage to the environment. We have come to realize, albeit belatedly, that the benefits of applied chemistry have a hidden cost which ultimately may be too high for this planet to bear. (See Science, Technology, and the Environment on pages 458 to 465.)

Biology

Studies in genetics continued to dominate biology in the postwar period. The structure of the key genetic material—deoxyribonucleic acids, or DNA as it is commonly called—was discovered by Watson and Crick in 1953. Since then molecular biologists have synthesized genes in the laboratory and transferred them into the DNA of living organisms. In the early 1970s, biologists produced insulin outside of the human body by transferring the gene responsible for the production of insulin into bacteria. This became the first recombinant-DNA drug to be approved for human use by the U.S. Food and Drug Administration.

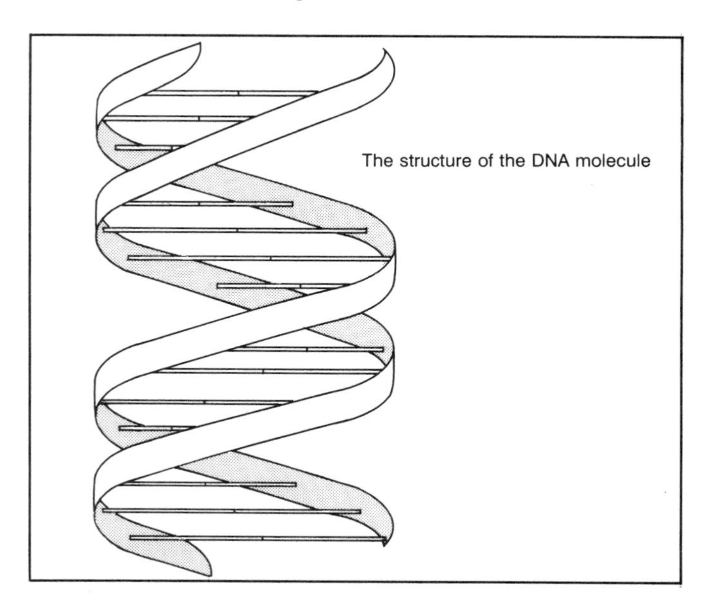
The structure of the DNA molecule

The next step in DNA research is mapping the twenty-three pairs of chromosomes in a human cell. Watson, co-discoverer of DNA and the new director of the U.S. segment of the International Human Genome Project, explains the significance of the research:

> As we analyze the information hidden within the chemical composition of every gene in the human body, the role of medicine will shift from treatment to prevention. For instance, genetic analysis of a newborn may be used to screen for a wide range of genetic disorders. Wherever a defect is found, the child may be protected from illness by the proper diet or by avoiding environmental hazards. Mapping the human genome will also give doctors the tools to test adults for vulnerability to certain diseases before symptoms appear. And eventually drugs may be developed to correct deficiencies within genes that cause genetic errors, and perhaps defective genes may someday be replaced by healthy ones.
>
> From James D. Watson, "First Word," *OMNI Magazine*, June 1990, p. 6.

Genetic Engineering

There are many moral and ethical questions associated with the manipulation of DNA in human beings. It is already possible to test a fetus to determine genetic disorders. Will this lead to more abortions? When it becomes possible to genetically erase a disorder, should gene therapy be used to "improve" the fetus? Should adults be tested to determine their predisposition to fatal or disabling diseases? If so, will the information be available to insurance companies who could then raise the individual's insurance premiums? The questions go on and on.

And while genetic engineering may be used to improve lives, there is also the possibility of this science being used for evil purposes. Genetic engineering raises the spectre of past abuses of genetics, such as the eugenics programs in Great Britain and the United States in the 1920s that attempted to improve the human race through selective breeding. Criminals, the mentally retarded, and the insane were prevented from breeding and laws were introduced to prevent interracial marriages. The best known eugenics program was the Nazis' attempt to achieve racial purity through the mass extermination of Jews. As scientific discoveries become more advanced, the possibility of science being used to control the reproduction of the human race increases. Watson suggests that "we can prevent . . . atrocities from recurring if scientists, doctors and society at large refuse to cede control of genetic discoveries to those who would misuse them." Huxley's nightmare vision of the future in *Brave New World* serves as a warning of what can happen if genetic discoveries are misused.

GENETIC FINGERPRINTING

Each cell in the human body has the same unique DNA imprint. This makes DNA fingerprints valuable tools in legal cases.

Genetic fingerprints are prepared in the following manner: (1) a blood sample is taken; (2) white blood cells containing DNA are extracted; (3) the cells are burst open, releasing the DNA strands; (4) restriction enzymes cut the DNA strands into fragments; (5) electrophoresis aligns the DNA pieces by size—the longest pieces at one end, the shortest pieces at the other—on a sheet of gel; (6) the DNA pattern is transferred to a nylon sheet; (7) the sheet is exposed to radioactively tagged probes which identify the DNA; (8) the sheet is further exposed to X-rays, which results in black bands where the probes stuck; (9) the resulting DNA print results in a pattern of black bands in a white column; (10) the DNA print is compared to the blood, hair, skin, or semen sample obtained at the scene of the crime.*

The technique of DNA fingerprinting was first used in Britain in 1987 to solve the rape-murder of two fifteen-year-old girls. Over 1000 men had their DNA tested. The tests cleared one man who had been under suspicion and led to the arrest of another, who was subsequently found guilty. One year later the test was used in the U.S. to find a man named Tommie Lee Andrews guilty of sexual battery. Andrews was found guilty despite a supposedly airtight alibi backed by his girlfriend and her sister. The jury believed that the .00000001 percent (one in ten billion) chance that the DNA print could belong to someone else did not establish a reasonable doubt and found him guilty.

*Adapted from Ricki Lewis,"DNA Fingerprints: Witness for the Prosecution," in *Discover*, June 1988, pp. 48–49.

ALDOUS HUXLEY:
Brave New World

In the foreword to the 1946 edition of Brave New World *(1932), Huxley wrote: "[in the novel the] standardization of the human product has been pushed to fantastic, though not perhaps impossible, extremes. Technically and ideologically we are still a long way from bottled babies. . . ." Today science has the capability to produce bottled babies, although ethical and moral considerations have prevented it from occurring. The following selection from the novel outlines the biological process used to produce genetic standardization in Huxley's vision of the future.*

"I shall begin at the beginning," said the D.H.C., and the more zealous students recorded his intention in their note-books: *Begin at the beginning.* "These," he waved his hand, "are the incubators." And opening an insulated door he showed them racks upon racks of numbered test-tubes. "The week's supply of ova. Kept," he explained, "at blood heat; whereas the male gametes," and here he opened another door, "they have to be kept at thirty-five instead of thirty-seven. Full blood heat sterilizes." Rams wrapped in thermogene beget no lambs.

Still leaning against the incubators he gave them, while the pencils scurried illegibly across the pages, a brief description of the modern fertilizing process; spoke first, of course, of its surgical introduction—"the operation undergone voluntarily for the good of Society, not to mention the fact that it carries a bonus amounting to six months' salary"; continued with some account of the technique for preserving the excised ovary alive and actively developing; passed on to a consideration of optimum temperature, salinity, viscosity; referred to the liquor in which the detached and ripened eggs were kept; and, leading his charges to the work tables, actually showed them how this liquor was drawn off from the test-tubes; how it was let out drop by drop on to the specially warmed slides of the microscopes; how the eggs which it contained were inspected for abnormalities, counted, and transferred to a porous receptacle; how (and he now took them to watch the operation) this receptacle was immersed in a warm bouillon containing free-swimming spermatozoa—at a minimum concentration of one hundred thousand per cubic centimetre, he insisted; and how, after ten minutes, the container was lifted out of the liquor and its contents re-examined, how, if any of the eggs remained unfertilized, it was again immersed, and, if necessary, yet again; how the fertilized ova went back to the incubators; where the Alphas and Betas remained until definitely bottled; while the Gammas, Deltas, and Epsilons were brought out again, after only thirty-six hours, to undergo Bokanovsky's Process.

"Bokanovsky's Process," repeated the Director, and the students underlined the words in their little note-books.

One egg, one embryo, one adult—normality. But a bokanovskified egg will bud, will proliferate, will divide. From eight to ninety-six bud, and every bud will grow into a perfectly formed embryo, and every embryo into a full-sized adult. Making ninety-six human beings grow where only one grew before. Progress.

"Essentially," the D.H.C. concluded, "bokanovskification consists of a series of arrests of development. We check the normal growth and, paradoxically enough, the egg responds by budding."

Responds by budding. The pencils were busy.

He pointed. On a very slowly moving band a rackful of test-tubes was entering a large metal box, another rackful was emerging. Machinery faintly purred. It took eight minutes for the tubes to go through, he told them. Eight minutes of hard X-rays being about as much as an egg can stand. A few died; of the rest, the least susceptible divided into two; most put out four buds; some eight; all were returned to the incubators, where the buds began to develop; then, after two days, were suddenly chilled, chilled and checked. Two, four, eight, the buds in their turn budded; and having budded were dosed almost to death with alcohol; consequently burgeoned again and having budded—bud out of bud out of bud—were thereafter—further arrest being generally fatal—left to develop in peace. By which time the original egg was in a fair way to becoming anything from eight to ninety-six embryos—a prodigious improvement, you will agree, on nature. Identical twins—but not in piddling twos and threes as in the old viviparous days, when an egg would sometimes accidentally divide; actually by dozens, by scores at a time.

"Scores" the Director repeated and flung out his arms, as though he were distributing largesse. "Scores."

But one of the students was fool enough to ask where the advantage lay.

"My good boy!" The Director wheeled sharply round on him. "Can't you see? Can't you see? He raised a hand; his expression was solemn. "Bokanovsky's Process is one of the major instruments of social stability!"

Major instruments of social stability.

Standard men and women; in uniform batches. The whole of a small factory staffed with the products of a single bokanovskified egg.

"Ninety-six identical twins working ninety-six identical machines!" The voice was almost tremulous with enthusiasm. "You really know where you are. For the first time in history." He quoted the planetary motto. "Community, Identity, Stability." Grand words. If we could bokanovskify indefinitely the whole problem would be solved. . . .

From Aldous Huxley, *Brave New World* (London: Chatto and Windus). Reprinted with permission of Random Century Group and Mrs. Laura Huxley.

Medicine

Today the medical profession can perform feats that would have been considered miracles only a generation ago. Some diseases, such as smallpox, have been virtually eliminated. A polio vaccine has prevented another epidemic, such as the one that broke out in the United States in the 1950s, from occurring again. Babies are now regularly inoculated against numerous childhood diseases, such as measles, which once killed thousands. But not all drugs have proven to be safe. Although carefully tested and approved by governments, the sedative thalidomide, taken by women in the early stages of pregnancy during the late 1950s, was found to cause severe limb deformities in babies. The drug was banned, but not before thousands of children were afflicted with what was a preventable disability.

Medical Machines

Medicine today has become very high tech. Sophisticated machines, such as the electroencephalograph (EEC) and the electrocardiograph (EEG), monitor brain and heart activity. Computerized tomography (CT), positron emission tomography (PET), and nuclear magnetic resonance (NMR) reveal soft-tissue organs and their functions and greatly assist in the diagnosis and treatment of disease and injury, often eliminating the need for exploratory surgery. In some cases conventional surgery has been replaced by medical lasers. These are particularly effective for delicate eye surgery because they can be aimed and fired with pinpoint accuracy using computers.

Pacemakers, coronary bypasses, and heart transplants have dramatically cut the death rate from heart attacks, one of the highest causes of death in the developed world. The first step toward these new developments was the heart-lung machine (1952), which can temporarily perform the functions of the heart and lungs to allow surgeons time to perform surgery. Electronic devices called pacemakers can be placed on the heart to strengthen or regulate the beat. Although the first pacemakers were bulky and had to be carried outside the body, by 1957 their size had been reduced to the point where they could be surgically implanted. An artificial heart pump which fulfilled the requirements of the human heart was first used in 1966 and prolonged the patient's life for five days. In 1967, Dr. Christiaan Barnard (1922-) performed the first human heart transplant in Cape Town, South Africa; his patient lived eighteen days. The following year another heart-transplant patient lived seventy-four days. The world's first totally artificial heart was implanted in 1969. Made out of plastic and metal, this device was intended as a temporary measure until a heart transplant donor could be found. Since then, research has continued on mechanical replacements for the human heart. The most successful replacement so far, the Jarvik 7, prolonged a man's life for an additional 112 days in 1982.

The Challenge of AIDS

AIDS, a disease not even identified until 1981, is today one of the largest challenges facing the medical profession. The World Health Organization estimates that as of 1989 over 700 000 people had developed AIDS worldwide. And as many as 6 to 8 million had contracted the virus that causes AIDS. HIV–1, the human immunodeficiency virus, is spread almost exclusively by infected blood or sperm. Sufferers of AIDS do not die from the virus but from pneumonia, infections, and cancers that develop after the virus destroys the immune system. To date there is no known cure, although some drugs, such as Zidovudine (AZT), have been found to slow the spread of the disease.

The Moral and Ethical Questions

A number of modern medical advances have raised moral and ethical questions. For instance, the widespread use of oral contraceptives since the 1960s has met with opposition from some religions and the birth of the first test-tube baby in the 1970s has raised questions about tampering with human life.

The debate over whether prolonging life by mechanical means is in fact prolonging death has raised the question of euthanasia. Today scientific and technological advances have made it possible to extend life almost indefinitely. It is the quality of life that comes into question. Some people feel that life-support systems for persons in an irreversible coma or for those who are terminally ill is inhumane and serves little purpose. This side of the debate argues that such individuals have the right to decide whether they want to continue living under such circumstances. There is considerable support in the medical community for this argument. Many

THE SOCIAL DIMENSIONS OF AIDS

Acquired Immune Deficiency Syndrome (AIDS) was not identified until 1981. Subsequent research has revealed that the disease is spread by a virus, HIV–1, in infected blood and semen. AIDS is lethal; there is no known cure. It is the twentieth-century equivalent of the plague. The following article, by Harvey V. Finberg, dean of the Harvard School of Public Health, outlines some of the social implications of AIDS.

The AIDS epidemic exposes hidden vulnerabilities in the human condition that are both biological and social. AIDS prompts courageous and generous acts, and it provokes meanspirited and irrational responses. AIDS throws new light on traditional questions of value, compels a fresh look at the performance of the institutions we depend on and brings society to a crossroads for collective action that may, with the passage of years, mark a key measure of our time.

In the seven years since AIDS was recognized, the epidemic has touched on almost all aspects of society. Its reach extends to every social institution, from families, schools and communities to businesses, courts of law, the military and Federal, state and local governments. It has also had a profound impact on the way science, medicine and public health are practised in the world.

Through its association with sex, blood, drugs and death, AIDS evokes basic human fears and inhibitions. In her book *Illness as Metaphor* Susan Sontag writes: "Although the way in which disease mystifies is set against a backdrop of new expectations, the disease itself . . . arouses thoroughly old-fashioned kinds of dread. Any disease that is treated as a mystery and acutely enough feared will be felt morally, if not literally, contagious. . . . Contact with someone afflicted with a disease regarded as a mysterious malevolency inevitably feels like a trespass; worse, like the violation of a taboo."

Although she was reflecting on cancer, Sontag's words are even more appropriate for AIDS, a condition that is literally as well as morally contagious. The contagion is compounded by the stigma attached to the behaviors most prominently associated with HIV infection in the U.S.: homosexual intercourse and intravenous drug use. Knowledge of HIV and its mode of spread, convincing as it is to scientists and epidemiologists, is not powerful enough to fully dissolve the public sense of mystery and old-fashioned dread. The protective garb needlessly donned by workers transporting a person with AIDS is reminiscent of the costume worn by physicians treating plague victims in eighteenth-century France. People known to be infected with HIV have lost jobs, homes and friends. Children with AIDS have been denied access to public schools and in 1987 a major air carrier temporarily refused to transport patients with AIDS. People with AIDS have been denied transportation to the grave, as some funeral directors have refused to handle their corpses.

AIDS is a modern affliction. The AIDS epidemic was fomented by changes in social mores and lifestyle that are unique to the latter part of the twentieth century; urbanization in Africa, gay consciousness and liberation in the U.S., development of technologies for the preservation and shipment of blood-clotting factors for hemophiliacs, and modern air travel. Unlike some other infectious diseases, the AIDS virus is carried and transmitted by the human host; there is no apparent insect or other animal vector and the virus has no special climatic requirements. Because AIDS spreads directly from one person to another, the disease is—at least potentially—a universal problem. It is the one contemporary disease that is keenly felt as an urgent problem in both industrialized and less developed countries.

HIV is insidious. It corrupts vital body fluids, turning blood and semen from sources of life into instruments of death. The virus insinuates itself into the genetic material of selected cells, where it may remain quiescent for prolonged periods of time. When it is active, the virus gradually undermines the body's immune system, eventually rendering it vulnerable to opportunistic infections. During the latency period, which may average eight years or longer, the patient feels perfectly well yet is capable of transmitting the virus to others. HIV infection remains at the present time incurable, a pointed reminder of humanity's thrall to the tyranny of nature. . . .

Our world has been made a different place by the human immunodeficiency virus. More profoundly, our society is being shaped by our response to the epidemic. Will AIDS enhance understanding and tolerance of different sexual orientations, or will it harden traditional norms of acceptable and deviant sexual behavior? Will AIDS be perceived as a universal threat to all humanity, or will it be regarded as a problem of the underclass, the poor and uneducated, and the minorities? Will AIDS heighten the tension between moralistic and pragmatic approaches to behavior and health, or can solutions be found that are both effective and morally acceptable? Will AIDS evoke the selfless dedication of physicians, nurses and other health professionals, or will caregivers shun AIDS patients and seek other ways to practise their craft? How we choose to answer such questions, and the society we thus shape, is up to us.

From Harvey V. Finberg, "The Social Dimensions of AIDS."

physicians feel that they should provide comfort and relief while the patient awaits death rather than artificially prolonging that person's life. This form of passive euthanasia has led to the development of a living will that indicates the patient's desire not to be kept alive by artificial means if they become terminally ill. Opponents of euthanasia argue that passive euthanasia can lead to active euthanasia—that is, taking definite means to end someone's life—which is considered a serious crime in most parts of the world. This side of the debate stresses that the sanctity of human life does not depend on its quality or its cost and that it should be sustained under all circumstances.

Perhaps the greatest debate in medical ethics has been the question of abortion. The debate surrounding abortion centres on the competing rights of the mother and the unborn child. Pro-life supporters argue for the rights of the fetus and claim that there is no rational basis for distinguishing between a fetus and a newborn infant; both are helpless, but only one is protected by law. Pro-choice supporters argue for the rights of the woman to have control of her own body. They claim that in the early stages of pregnancy, the fetus exhibits few human characteristics and is therefore outside of the law.

Today, abortion is legal in all but one (Ireland) of the twelve countries that make up the European Community. France has even introduced an abortion pill—RU 486—which is taken in a physician's office. In both Canada and the United States abortion is legal under certain circumstances.

The debate over abortion has been most volatile in the U.S., where all states legalized abortion after the Supreme Court declared barriers to abortion unconstitutional in the case of *Roe v. Wade* (1973). Since then, massive demonstrations, both pro-choice and pro-life, have been held in the nation's capital. Literature, videos, banners, placards, and T-shirts scream pro-life or pro-choice slogans. Pro-life and pro-choice supporters confront each other outside abortion clinics. The fervour of the debate illustrates how deeply entrenched are opposing opinions about individual rights in Western civilization.

Despite these and other controversies, there is little doubt that medical advances have been beneficial to humankind. In the developed world, the average life span has increased by almost thirty years in this century. Western medical technology has been used to increase life expectancy in the developing world as well. As science and technology continue to advance, so too will the benefits to humanity and the controversies that arise among us.

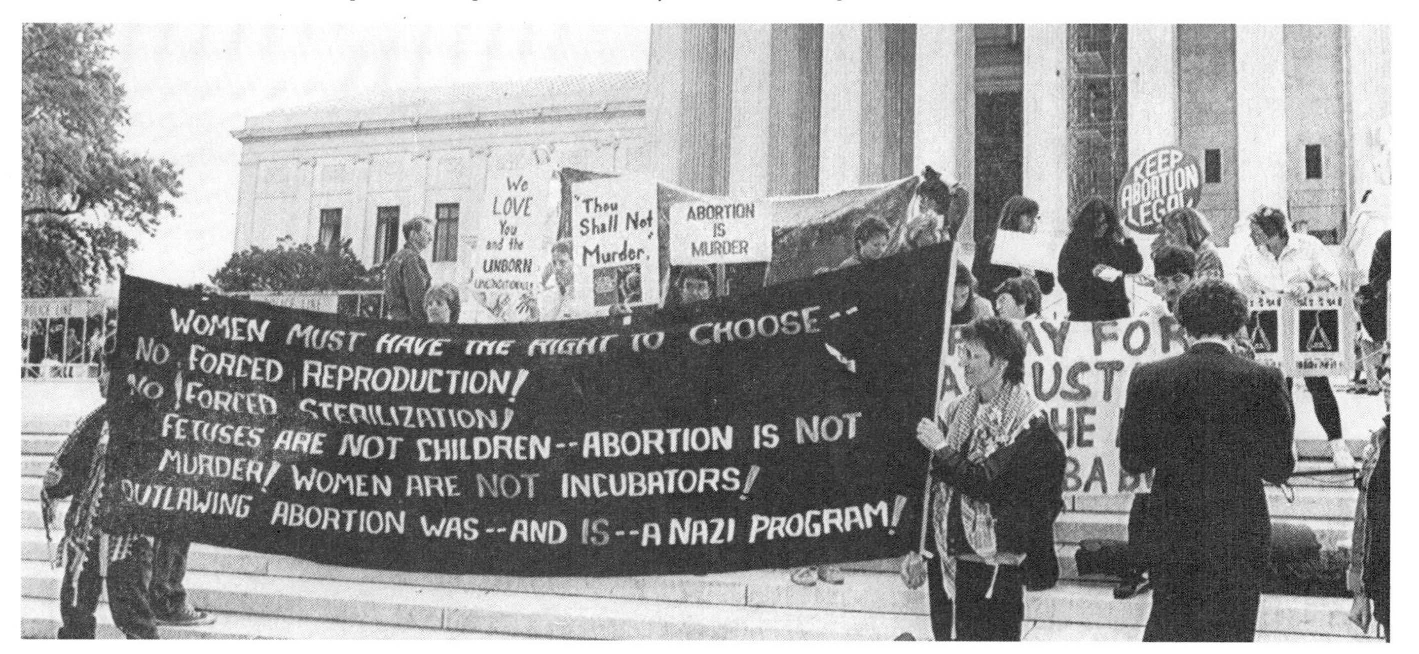

Pro-choice and pro-life activists demonstrated outside the U.S. Supreme Court in April 1989.

The Space Age

The space race was inaugurated on 4 October 1957 with the launching of the Soviet satellite *Sputnik*, which circled the earth for several months. This technological achievement indicated that the Soviets were more advanced than the West. The demonstrated capability of a rocket which could reach anywhere in the U.S. led to massive budget expenditures to close the missile gap. The National Aeronautics and Space Administration (NASA) was created and charged with the responsibility of catching the Soviets in the space race. Each Soviet success was exploited for its full propaganda value. National prestige and defense spurred the U.S. effort.

Both the U.S. and the U.S.S.R. wanted to be the first nation to send astronauts into space. Again, however, it was the Soviets who launched the first astronaut-controlled space flight when on 12 April 1961 Yuri Alekseyevich Gagarin (1934–1968) completed a single orbit around the earth nine months before John Glenn's (1921-) orbital flight for the United States. Between June 16 and 19, 1963, the Soviet Union sent a woman into space, Valentina Vladimirovna Tereshkova (1937-) aboard *Vostok 6*. But it was the U.S. *Apollo* program that landed the first human on the moon when Neil Armstrong (1930-) took his historic walk on 16 July 1969.

In 1975, the United States and the Soviet Union launched a co-operative space mission, the *Apollo-Soyez* Test Project, to establish the feasibility of docking two dissimiliar craft in space and the possibility of rescue missions of each other's spacecraft. By then, however, the superpowers had been joined in the space fraternity by France (1965), Australia (1967), Japan (1970), the People's Republic of China (1970), and Great Britain (1970). Most of these launches were of communication or weather satellites. Other countries, such as India, relied on Soviet launch vehicles for their satellites, while countries such as Canada used American launch rockets. Since the late 1970s, the European Space Agency (ESA) has been a major competitor of the United States in the launching of European satellites.

In the 1980s, the U.S. space program focused on the development of the space shuttle, a reusable launch vehicle designed to launch, recover, and repair satellites. When the *Challenger* shuttle exploded just seventy-five seconds after liftoff on 28 January 1986, killing all seven crew members including a civilian schoolteacher, the program was put on hold while the causes of the accident were investigated. As a result, the U.S. did not send astronauts into space for the next three years. The Soviet program, on the other hand, which had concentrated on space station development since the early 1970s, continued uninterrupted throughout the decade.

Buzz Aldrin posed beside the U.S. flag during the Apollo 11 *moon landing in July 1969.*

The Benefits of Space Exploration

Although military reasons were the prime motivation for the space race, the space program has provided a number of benefits to humankind. Communications satellites link the global village. Weather satellites make it possible to provide more accurate forecasts as well as track hurricanes at sea, thereby providing early warnings to threatened population centres. Resource satellites have been used to monitor urban development and track air and water pollution as well as to locate valuable resources. Navigation satellites have greatly assisted rescues on land, sea, and air by making it possible to pinpoint an exact location on earth.

Space probes such as the U.S. *Mariner* and *Viking* missions to Mars and Venus and the *Voyager* missions to Jupiter, Saturn, Uranus, and Neptune have provided us with new information about our solar system. The ESA Giotti probe and Japan's Planet-A probe intersected with Halley's comet and sent back information that scientists are still analysing. Orbiting observatories are able to "see" invisible wavelengths, such as X-ray, gamma, ultraviolet, and infrared, that are blocked out by the earth's atmosphere. The Hubble Space Telescope, launched by the U.S. space shuttle program in the spring of 1990, was intended to provide a vantage point from which astronomers could see ten times farther and more clearly than ever before. Unfortunately, a problem with the mirrors used in the telescope has meant that astronomers will be unable to receive these pictures until a shuttle is sent to repair the damage.

ASTRONAUT-CONTROLLED SPACE FLIGHTS

NAME	NATION	YEAR	SIGNIFICANCE
Vostok 1	U.S.S.R.	1961	First astronaut-controlled flight
Mercury/ Redstone 3	U.S.	1961	First U.S. flight
Vostok 2	U.S.S.R.	1962	First flight exceeding 24 hours
Vostok 6	U.S.S.R.	1963	First woman in space
Voskhod 2	U.S.S.R.	1965	First extravehicular activity
Gemini 8	U.S.	1966	First docking of two orbiting spacecraft
Apollo 8	U.S.	1968	First astronaut-controlled orbit of the moon
Apollo 11	U.S.	1969	First landing of a human being on the moon
Soyuz 10	U.S.S.R.	1971	Docks with Salyut 1, the first space station
Appollo/Soyuz Test Project	U.S./ U.S.S.R.	1975	First co-operative space mission
Columbia	U.S.	1981	First shuttle flight
Mir	U.S.S.R.	1986	First permanently inhabited space station

Compiled from Bernard Grun, *The Timetables of History* (New York: Touchstone Books, 1982) and Alexander Hellmans and Bryan Bunch, *The Timetables of Science* (New York: Simon and Schuster, 1988).

SOME SPACE FIRSTS
Unmanned Satellites and Space Probes

NAME	NATION	YEAR	SIGNIFICANCE
Sputnik 1	U.S.S.R.	1957	First artificial satellite
Sputnik 2	U.S.S.R.	1957	First animal in space (a dog)
Explorer 1	U.S.	1958	First U.S. satellite; discovery of the Van Allen radiation belt
Luna 1	U.S.S.R.	1959	First space probe to achieve Earth-escape velocity
Luna 2	U.S.S.R.	1959	First spacecraft on the moon
TIROS 1	U.S.	1960	First weather satellite
Transit 1B	U.S.	1960	First navigation satellite
Echo 1	U.S.	1960	First communication satellite
Ariel 1	U.S./U.K.	1962	First international co-operative satellite
Telstar 1	U.S.	1962	First transatlantic relay of television
Mariner 2	U.S.	1962	Venus flyby
Mars 1	U.S.S.R.	1963	Mars flyby
Intelsat 1	U.S.	1965	First commercial communications satellite
Venera 3	U.S.S.R.	1965	First spacecraft to land on another planet (Venus)
A–1 Asterix	France	1965	First French satellite
Luna 9	U.S.S.R.	1966	First soft lunar landing
Osumi	Japan	1970	First Japanese satellite
China 1	China	1970	First Chinese satellite
Anik 1	Canada	1972	First domestic communications satellite
Landsat 1	U.S.	1972	First Earth-resources satellite
Venera 8	U.S.S.R.	1972	Venus landing
Mariner 10	U.S.	1973	Mercury flyby
Aryabhata	India/ U.S.S.R.	1975	First Indian satellite
Voyager 1 & 2	U.S.	1977	Jupiter, Saturn, Uranus flyby
Giotto	E.S.A.		
Veg 1 & 2	U.S.S.R.	1986	Halley's comet

Compiled from Bernard Grun, *The Timetables of History* (New York: Touchstone Books, 1982) and Alexander Hellmans and Bryan Bunch, *The Timetables of Science* (New York: Simon and Schuster, 1988).

TECHNOLOGY

The speed of technological development has been accelerating since the Industrial Revolution. By the late nineteenth century, these developments had altered daily life to the extent that one commentator noted:

> Beyond doubt, the most salient characteristic of life in this latter portion of the nineteenth century is its SPEED,—what we call its hurry, the rate at which we move, the high-pressure at which we work;—and the question to be considered is, first, whether this rapid rate is in itself good; and, next, whether it is worth the price we pay for it. . . .
>
> From W.R. Greg, "Life at High Pressure," *Contemporary Review*, XXV, (1875), p. 623.

A century later the dizzying succession of technological achievements in the postwar period prompted futurist Alvin Toffler to coin the phrase "future shock" to explain the phenomenon. In his book of the same name, Toffler wrote:

> We have in our time released a totally new social force—a stream of change so accelerated that it influences our sense of time, revolutionizes the tempo of daily life, and affects the way we "feel" the world around us. We no longer "feel" as men did in the past. And this is the ultimate difference, the distinction that separates the truly contemporary man from all others. For this acceleration lies behind the impermanence—the transience—that permeates and tinctures our consciousness, radically affecting the way we relate to other people, to things, to the entire universe of ideas, art, and values.
>
> From *Future Shock* by Alvin Toffler. Copyright © 1970 by Alvin Toffler. Reprinted by permission of Random House, Inc.

What has caused such a dizzying pace of development? More than any other factor it has been discoveries in the field of computer science.

Computers

No other industry has made advances similar to those in computers in such a short time. The first large-scale computer, the Mark I, was introduced in 1944. It was electromechanical—essentially a large (2.5 m x 15 m) adding machine. The first digital computer, the Electronic Numerical Integrator and Computer (ENIAC), was introduced in 1946. ENIAC contained 18 000 vacuum tubes and filled a room 12 m by 6 m. This digital computer worked 1000 times faster than the Mark I, performing 5000 arithmetic operations a second. The first commercially available computer was the Universal Automatic Computer (UNIVAC I) introduced in 1951.

The first generation of computers depended on bulky vacuum tubes; the second generation utilized transistors. Although the transistor was invented in 1947, it was not until solid-state circuitry was developed in the 1950s that it could be fully utilized by the computer industry. The shift from vacuum tubes to transistors became commercially viable by the end of the 1950s.

It was the third generation of computers that produced the rapid expansion of the computer industry. Integrated circuitry and the development of microprocessors made computers smaller, faster, cheaper, and more reliable. A single microprocessor chip about 9 mm^2 has the same computing power as the ENIAC, which filled an entire room. The first microprocessor was introduced by the American company Intel in 1971. By the end of the decade, the Apple II, the first fully assembled personal computer, was available to the public. It was followed in the early 1980s by the IBM

The invention of the integrated circuit, commonly called a chip, revolutionized the computer industry.

Personal Computer, which introduced the disk-operating system (DOS) that is now the industry standard.

In the 1980s, so-called fourth generation computers increased the density of microcircuitry. (Because fourth generation computers merely continued the development trend of third generation computers, some experts dispute the terminology.) This allowed the development of laptop computers. The substantial decrease in size and cost made the technological applications of microprocessors almost endless.

Today the race is on between Japan and the United States to develop the fifth generation of computers: computers with artificial intelligence. Instead of merely executing a program, fifth generation computers will be able to adapt to new situations. They will be capable of reasoning and will be able to learn. This breakthrough may not be too far in the future. There is already the "fuzzy" computer which, although it is preprogrammed, has highly flexible rules allowing it to approximate real-life decision-making. Washing machines that determine how the laundry should be washed are already on the market. Soon this technology will be available in hundreds of household appliances.

Computers have changed the pace of business. Although a computerized, global marketplace is some years in the future, Canadian, British, American, and Japanese officials are meeting to establish the ground rules for such a market. The National Association of Securities Dealers (NASDA), the second largest exchange in the U.S. and the third largest in the world, already has no trading floor; it is a completely electronic market. Once launched globally, these exchanges will allow traders to participate in world markets to a much greater extent than is currently possible. However, not all aspects of the application of computers to business have proven beneficial. The market collapse of October 1987 was caused in part by computerized "program trading"—the automatic sale of a stock or commodity at a predetermined price—which created a sell-off of stocks. This resulted in the largest drop on the New York Stock Exchange since the Great Depression. As a result, the NYSE now restricts some forms of computerized trading during volatile periods.

Computers have had a great impact on how we do things. They control traffic lights, print newspapers, prepare payrolls, and design buildings and automobiles. They will have an even greater influence on our lives when they create entirely new activities rather than merely being applied to current activities.

COMPUTER VIRUSES

On the evening of 2 November 1988, 6000 computers along the Internet computer network began to slow down or stopped functioning entirely. A computer virus had infected the nationwide network that connected 18 000 university, corporate, and military computers. The virus, designed by Robert Tappan Morris, Jr., a Cornell University graduate student, duplicated itself hundreds of times in each computer until it exceeded the memory of each machine it infected. Within hours it had crossed the country via telephone links between the computers along the network.

Morris's virus was the most sophisticated example of what is a growing problem. Fortunately, the virus that infected the Internet network did not create permanent damage. Other viruses deliberately destroy software programs, scramble data, erase files, and disable peripheral devices such as printers.

Viruses are sophisticated computer programs which typically invade a computer through borrowed computer disks and public domain software or, as in the case of Morris's virus, via electronic mail. The virus duplicates itself a number of times and attaches itself to other programs. Each time one of these programs is run, the virus program is run as well. In the worst cases, the virus has a built-in delay period before beginning to attack its host. By that time it has infected the computer's backup disks so that the process of rebuilding data files from these disks reinfects the computer.

Viruses pose a real threat to computer systems because to be effective computers must be able to communicate with each other in networks. This makes them vulnerable to attack from a virus. Although some programs have been developed to prevent viruses from attacking a computer network, none is 100 percent effective. There is always the possibility that a new virus will circumvent the program. It does not take much imagination to envision the chaos that could be created by a virus attack on computers that control the traffic lights or the telephone system!

Automation, Robotics, and Microtechnology

The history of technology has followed a path toward automation. This development was accelerated by the introduction of the assembly line, which broke down the overall job into subtasks. Today, many of these tasks are being performed by machines. For instance, in the automobile industry, computerized robots weld, paint, assemble, and inspect parts. It is expected that by 1995 over 80 percent of the automobile assembly process will be performed by robots.

Automation is also leading toward the paperless office as individual computers are linked together via computer networks. Instead of paper memos we now have electronic memos; instead of a room full of filing cabinets we now have only several computer disks. The first area to be completely automated was payroll and accounting. Automation allowed companies to eliminate paycheques and deposit salaries directly into employees' bank accounts. In industry, automation is being accomplished through the union of the computer and robotics.

The first robotics patent was awarded in Britain in 1954. Since then robots have replaced humans in some repetitive, arduous, and hazardous jobs. A study by the Robotics Institute of America broke down industrial robot usage in the United States as follows:

ACTIVITY	PERCENT
Spot welding	19
Arc welding	4
Painting	5
Finishing	0.5
Fitting	1
Loading and unloading	23.5
Die casting	14
Investment casting	2
Material handling	31

Adapted from Brian Morris, *The World of Robots* (New York: Gallery Books, 1985), p. 76.

These robots do not even vaguely resemble characters from the Star Wars movies. They are simply arms that paint, weld, or manipulate parts. The largest robot arm is the space shuttle's remote manipulator—the Canada-Arm—built by Spar Aerospace of Canada.

Sight, sound, and touch sensors allow robots to have a much wider scope of activity outside of industry. In space, robots such as Surveyor and Viking I have analysed soil and mineral samples and photographed the surface of the moon and Mars. Surveillance robots "sniff" the air and sense even the slightest temperature variations. Although domestic robots are still largely a modern myth, developments in pattern recognition and "fuzzy" logic mean that they are just around the corner.

The process of miniaturization, so vital to the development of the microchip and the microcomputer, which are the keys to automation and robotics, has created an entirely new field, *microtechnology*. Today engineers are using techniques similar to those used to make computer chips to build motors and sensors that cannot be seen by the human eye. Japan, the leader in the field of microtechnology, has committed $100 million to research in this field. A number of applications, such a microsensors in automobiles, are currently available. In the future, medical micromachinery may be able to function in the human body to perform surgery, power an artificial heart, or monitor insulin levels.

Nuclear Energy: A Failed Promise

Nuclear power plants were developed after the Second World War. The first full-scale plant was built in 1948 at Calder Hall, England. A vision of cheap energy led to the rapid development of plants in the United States and the Soviet Union. By the 1980s, there were more than 250 reactors in 22 countries, including Belgium, France, West Germany, India, Italy, Japan, the Netherlands, Spain, Sweden, Switzerland, the United Kingdom, the United States, and the Soviet Union. Canada has nineteen reactors, which by 1993 will generate 20 percent of its electricity. (Nuclear power now accounts for 60 percent of Ontario's electricity.) Atomic Energy of Canada Limited has also built twenty-seven CANDU units in Pakistan, Romania, South Korea, and Argentina.

Today nuclear plants generate approximately 20 percent of the world's electrical power. Although this is a small proportion of the world's total, it plays a more significant role in countries with a shortage of fossil fuels. Belgium, for instance, generates over 40 percent of its electricity from nuclear power and France over 45 percent.

In the 1960s, it was estimated that nuclear power plants would generate over 50 percent of the world's electricity by the year 2000. Based on current trends, however, the actual figure will likely be less than 30 percent. Why has nuclear power failed to deliver what its advocates promised?

CHERNOBYL

At approximately 1:24 a.m., 26 April 1986, Reactor #4 at the Chernobyl nuclear power plant blew apart, hurling uranium dioxide fuel and other radioactive contaminants 5 km into the air. Operators conducting a generator test had disconnected several emergency systems, including ones that would have prevented the explosion by shutting down the reactor. The result was the worst nuclear disaster in history.

Soviet officials were slow to tell the world what happened. The first indication of a problem came from Sweden, 1250 km north of Chernobyl, when monitors at a nuclear power plant indicated an unusually high level of radiation. Confirmation by the Soviets came only after Norway, Finland, and Denmark also reported high radiation levels and photographs from a U.S. satellite confirmed one of the reactors at Chernobyl had been damaged. Soviet secrecy extended even to their own people, who were told little about the accident or the extent of the danger from radiation. The residents of the town of Chernobyl, only 14 km from the plant, were not evacuated until six days after the accident.

With four working reactors and two more under construction, Chernobyl was one of the largest nuclear power stations in the Soviet Union. Until April 26th it was also one of the most reliable. After the explosion it became a living laboratory to examine nuclear decontamination techniques, medical treatment of overdoses of radioactivity, and the link between radioactivity and the incidence of cancer.

Thirty-one people died from radiation overdoses, most of them firefighters who first responded to the explosion at Reactor #4. Over 500 others living in the immediate area were hospitalized with acute radiation syndrome. It is expected that approximately 200 cancer deaths will occur among the 116 000 people who were evacuated within a 30 km radius of Chernobyl. The number of people affected by the radioactive contaminants that drifted from the Baltic Sea to the Mediterranean is the subject of fierce debate. Estimates range as high as 70 000. In addition, the cost of the cleanup could run over $350 billion.

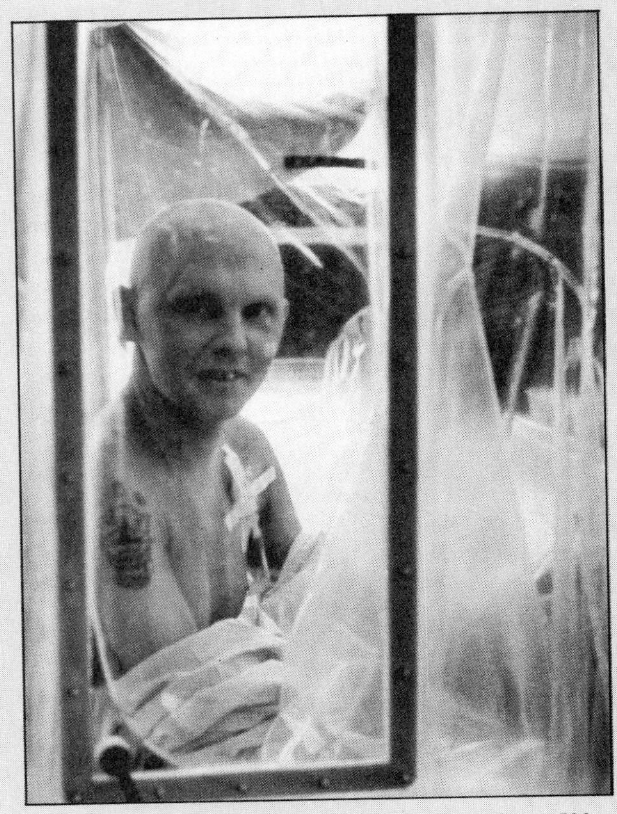

The explosion at the Chernobyl power station exposed over 500 people to the devastating effects of acute radiation syndrome.

Chernobyl was not the first nuclear accident in the Soviet Union; it was merely the first accident to be reported. Unconfirmed reports indicate that past accidents may have claimed hundreds of lives. And there are still fifteen reactors of the Chernobyl-type operating in the Soviet Union.

Although nuclear power plants have some advantages over conventional power plants—they do not burn scarce fossil fuels or pollute the air with smoke and gases—they do generate thermal pollution and radioactive waste. There are also concerns about the safety of nuclear power plants after accidents like those at Three Mile Island in the United States in 1979 and at Chernobyl in the Soviet Union in 1987. The Three Mile Island accident resulted in the cancellation of hundreds of projects, some of them already half built, in the United States. Sweden has announced its intention to phase out its nuclear program completely, and other countries have cut back on the number of nuclear developments on their soil. The future of the nuclear power industry is not positive unless the fears of nuclear catastrophe can be alleviated.

TRANSPORTATION AND COMMUNICATION

People have become much more mobile in the postwar world. The commercial development of jetliners eliminated distance as a barrier to travel and linked all parts of the world. The rapid expansion of the highway system that accompanied the surge in automobile ownership linked communities across nations. While the use of railways in North America declined, in Europe and elsewhere high-speed trains whisked people from place to place in record time. Freight transportation expanded to include not only trucks and trains but supertankers and pipelines.

Air Travel

The first commercial airlines were developed in Europe during the 1920s. Overseas flights began prior to the Second World War, but it was not until jet airliners were introduced in the 1950s that these flights became popular. The tremendous increase in air travel that resulted from nonstop flights displaced the ocean liner as the most popular means of transatlantic travel. The introduction of jumbo jets, such as the Boeing 747 in the 1970s, dramatically increased the number of passengers, while the supersonic Concorde cut flying time in half. Throughout all of these developments, air travel became more accessible and more affordable to the average consumer.

Unfortunately, the popularity of air travel has made airlines a target for terrorism. In 1985, an Air India 747 exploded over the Atlantic off the coast of Ireland as a result of a terrorist bomb. All 329 people aboard were killed. In 1989, a Pan American 747 exploded over the Scottish village of Lockerbie, killing all 258 people aboard and over 20 people on the ground. These and other incidents, plus the numerous bomb threats received daily by airlines, have resulted in strict security measures at airports around the world. It is necessary that all passengers and their baggage be checked before boarding. However, few people object to these procedures if it helps to ensure safety in the air.

Automobiles

Automobiles had become a familiar sight on the roads of Europe and North America in the interwar period. But their numbers remained relatively small until after the Second World War.

The United States was the largest manufacturer of automobiles. Over 2 million cars were sold in the U.S. in 1946, while only 5 million cars were sold in all of Western Europe in the same year; U.S. automobile production remained greater than that of the rest of the world combined for over two decades. France, West Germany, Great Britain, Italy, Sweden, and Japan all had thriving industries, but they did not cut into the American market until the 1960s. The greatest growth was in the Japanese car industry, which now ranks number two in the world.

By 1985, it was estimated that there were over 385 million cars worldwide. The sheer number of automobiles has created problems with air and noise pollution in crowded cities and with the loss of food-producing land and animal habitats through the creation of a vast network of highways in rural areas.

The energy crisis of the 1970s and the problems associated with air pollution led to a number of improvements in automobiles over the last twenty years. Cars have become smaller and improvements in carburetor performance and fuel injection have made them more fuel efficient. Catalytic converters, which promote the combustion of unburned hydrocarbons in the exhaust and exhaust-gas recirculation, have made cars less polluting. However, the benefits of increased fuel efficiency and the use of unleaded fuel and catalytic converters have been outweighed by the explosive growth of the industry. Alternate fuels, such as methanol, ethanol, propane, and natural gas, give poor performance and, in the case of propane and natural gas, have expensive conversion costs that have restricted their use. Electric-powered vehicles have limited availability and slower speeds and are slow to recharge, plus there are still the costs of the electricity, both financial and environmental, to consider. A better option to the automobile is mass transit such as railways.

Railways

Since 1945, railways in Canada and the United States have suffered from declining revenues. As a result, rail service has been eliminated in some areas. For instance, VIA passenger rail service in Canada was cut by 51 percent in January 1990. Yet in other countries railways have experienced a resurgence, thanks to a new generation of streamlined, superswift, comfortable, and ecologically friendly trains.

In Japan, the *shinkansen* (or the "bullet train" to North Americans), travels the 515 km between Tokyo and Osaka in three hours. But this is only the beginning for modern-day Japanese rail service. At Expo '86 in Vancouver, the Japanese National Railway demonstrated a new monorail train which uses magnets to keep the train 10 cm above a single track, allowing even higher speeds to be attained.

In France, a bullet-nosed train called the TGV *(Trains à Grande Vitesse)* made its debut in 1981. France will be one of the main hubs from which the major lines in a new network of European rail traffic will radiate. The $122 billion super-train network will utilize 11 000 km of improved existing track and 8000 km of new track. Speeds of 300 km are expected.

The agreement between the British and the French to build an all-rail tunnel under the English Channel will extend this European rail network. At a cost of $7 billion, the completion of the tunnel is scheduled for June 1993. Automobiles will be accommodated on specially designed flatbed carriages that will allow people to drive on and off.

The future will belong to trains that use magnetic levitation (or maglev for short), which will enable them to fly on a magnetic cushion and be propelled by magnetic waves. Maglev trains will be faster than the high-speed trains, perhaps reaching speeds of 500 km/h. (The theoretical maximum of high-speed trains is approximately 330 km.) Maglev trains are not science fiction. The German government is building the first commercial high-speed maglev line from Hamburg to Hanover, and by the late 1990s a line will carry gamblers between Los Angeles and Las Vegas in the United States.

Freight Transportation

Most long-distance domestic freight is transported by railway. But trucks have become the principal means of moving goods short and medium distances. In North America, trucks are increasingly competing with railways for the long-distance market as well. Barges, one of the earliest means of freight transport, continue to deliver cargo along the major river systems of the world. This is particularly true in Western Europe, which has a network of canals and rivers over 40 000 km long.

Pipelines are used to provide municipal services such as water, sewage, and gas. Over 2 million km of pipelines worldwide transport oil and natural gas. The world's longest pipeline carries oil from the Ural Mountains in the Soviet Union to Eastern Europe, a distance of 6120 km. Other major pipelines include the 3700 km Trans-Canada pipeline, the 1300 km Trans-Alaska pipeline, the 1200 km Trans-Arabian pipeline, and the 724 km Adriatic pipeline. The danger of a leak, particularly in highly sensitive ecological areas such as Alaska, has caused concern among environmentalists.

Internationally, most cargo is carried by ships. The removal of trade barriers after the war greatly expanded world trade and the increased demand for cargo ships of all kinds led to new developments in the merchant marine fleet. Standardized containers which could also be transported on railroad freight cars and trucks were industry-wide by the 1960s and dramatically improved the movement of goods to and from the harbour. Bulk carriers for grain, coal, and oil became increasingly large in size until the supertanker was developed.

Supertankers revolutionized the bulk carrier, particularly for transporting oil. The sheer size of these ships makes them unmanoeuvrable and prevents them from using most harbours. (One of the largest, the *Seawise Giant*, is 458 m long and has a cargo capacity of 565 000 t.) Offshore human-made islands, connected by pipeline to the shore, are necessary to enable oil supertankers to discharge their cargo. The 40 million litres of crude oil spilled into Prince William Sound in Alaska by the *Exxon Valdez* in 1989 illustrates the ecological dangers that accompany the economic benefits of the supertankers.

Communications

Until the twentieth century, almost all information was delivered via print. And almost all printing presses used a method of printing that varied very little from the one developed by Johann Gutenberg (1400–1468) in the fifteenth century. This began to change with the development of offset printing, which uses a printing plate made by a photographic technique rather than individual metal letters. This process became even more cost effective and efficient after the development of the computer. Today, text from word processors can be directly transferred to film, thereby accelerating communication and enabling books to be published in record time. The development of ink-jet printers by IBM in 1976 eliminated offset printing for some applications and made desktop publishing on computers a reality.

Communication has been aided by developments in photography. Modern single-lens reflex cameras have electronic eyes, microchip brains, and infra-red sensors to focus lenses and set shutter speeds and apertures automatically. Instant cameras, first developed by Edwin Land (1909-) in 1948, develop film inside the camera. Ultra-high speed cameras are capable of freezing action in less than a millionth of a second. Three-dimensional photography, or *holography*, is still in its infancy, but it may soon be used in movies and television.

Telecommunications have progressed from the first wireless transmission in 1901 to global transmissions via satellite. Telephone networks provide a link to people in all parts of the world. The first transatlantic telephone service was inaugurated in 1927 and used radio signals. The atmospheric interference was eliminated in 1956 with the first transatlantic cable. Telestar, the first communications satellite, was launched six years later. Today television and radio signals bounce off satellites to give us up-to-the-minute accounts of events anywhere in the world.

Television

Television has become the medium of our age. It has in large part created what Marshall McLuhan (1911–1980) called the "global village." The worldwide viewing audience has become immense. In 1985, for example, the Live-Aid concert to benefit African victims of famine reached an estimated 1.5 billion people.

In the 1930s and 1940s, the radio was the centre of home entertainment. Since the 1950s television has taken over that role. The first practical television system was demonstrated in 1929. By 1936, Britain had regular public television transmission. Germany experimented with televised broadcasts of the Berlin Olympics in the same year. U.S. broadcasts were largely experimental until after the Second World War,

Anik C *was deployed from the cargo bay of the space shuttle by the Canada Arm.*

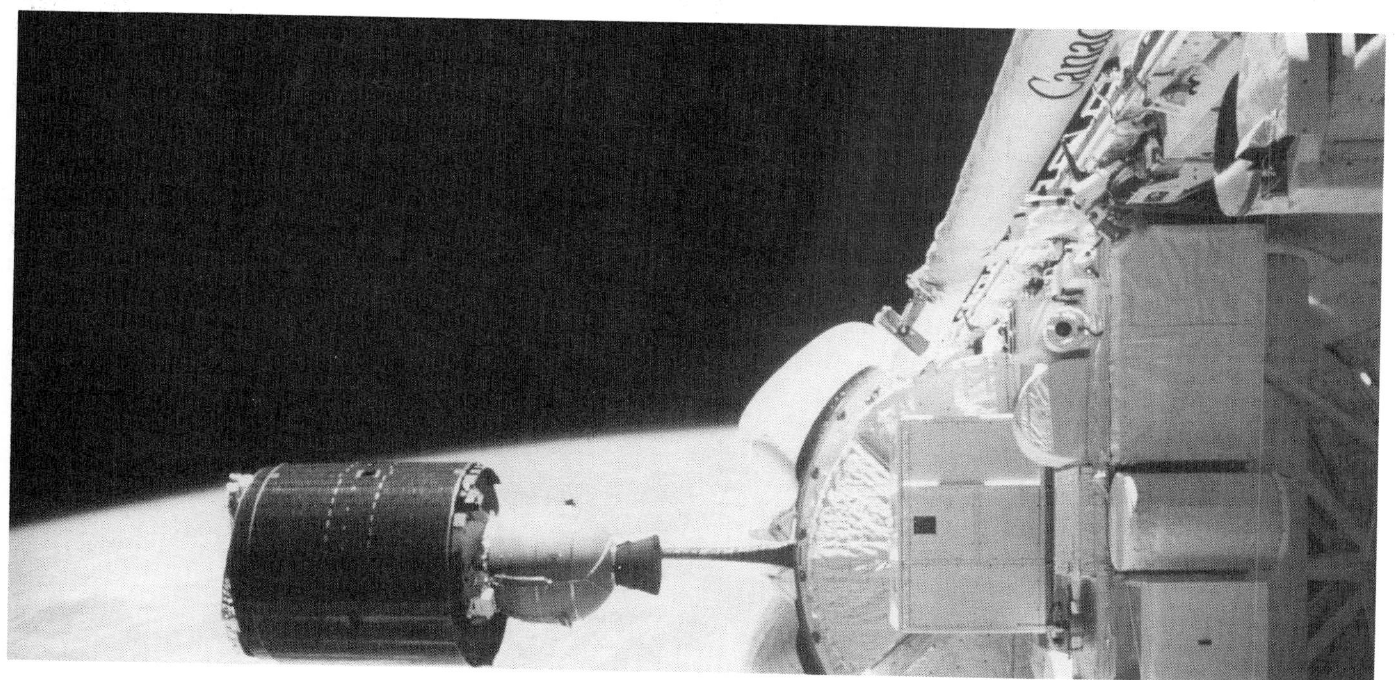

when the television boom started. Continental Europe did not initiate regular programming until the 1950s. Colour, first broadcast in 1940, became part of regular commercial broadcasting in the 1950s. Stereo broadcasts were initiated in the 1970s. Digital broadcasts that reduce the signal to a series of numbers which allows compact disc quality sound are now being developed in Germany.

In the 1980s, the television became the centrepiece of an extended home entertainment system that included a videotape recorder and/or videodisc player and video games. By the 1980s, specialty programming, such as movies, sports, music, and news, was delivered via cable systems or satellite. Interactive shopping systems using cable networks and computers are already in the experimental phase in some urban centres. As the new century approaches, there will undoubtedly be more ways in which we use television in our daily lives.

SCIENCE, TECHNOLOGY, AND THE ENVIRONMENT

Our ability to control and alter nature is a two-edged sword. Chemical fertilizers provided the means for a Green Revolution to feed the world's population, but the runoff from these fertilizers contaminated rivers and streams, causing birth defects and higher incidences of stillbirths. The use of DDT eliminated malaria-carrying mosquitoes in some tropical areas, but a reduction in death rates in areas with high birth rates contributed to overpopulation. Chlorofluorocarbons (CFCs) replaced ammonia and sulphur dioxide as a refrigeration coolant, but caused damage to the ozone layer. The burning of fossil fuels are essential to industrialization, but the by-products of this combustion contribute to the three most pressing atmospheric problems in the world today: global warming, ozone depletion, and acid rain.

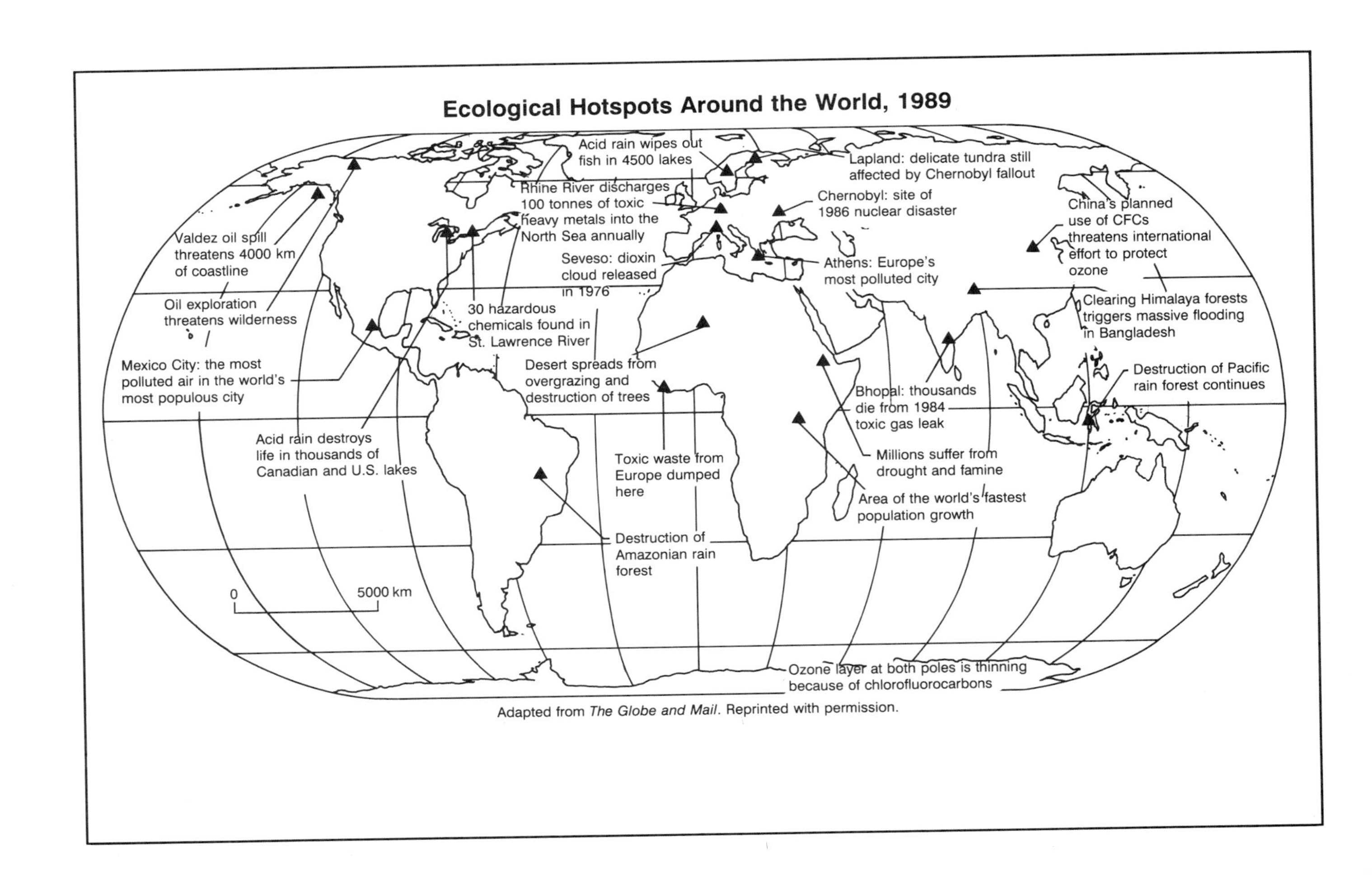

Adapted from *The Globe and Mail*. Reprinted with permission.

The Atmosphere

The Greenhouse Effect

Global warming, or the *greenhouse effect* as it is popularly called, is a recently identified environmental problem. Since the Industrial Revolution the average global surface temperature has risen 1°C. Scientists estimate that by the year 2030, the temperature could rise by as much as 4.5°C. Why is this alarming? Because a temperature rise of this significance could dramatically alter existing weather patterns and substantially change the earth's climate. Droughts in food-growing areas could lead to widespread famine. The melting of glaciers and polar icecaps could flood coastal cities, causing a mass migration of the world's population, which would further reduce arable land.

What causes the greenhouse effect? Several contributors have been identified, including CFCs and the burning of tropical rain forests. But the primary culprit is carbon dioxide, which is released by the burning of fossil fuels. The level of carbon dioxide in the atmosphere has risen over 20 percent since the Industrial Revolution. It was estimated that over 15 billion tonnes of carbon dioxide were released into the atmosphere in 1989 alone. Almost every facet of modern living—manufacturing, transportation, recreation, and entertainment—is derived from the burning of fossil fuels.

Depletion of the Ozone Layer

In 1985, British scientists discovered a hole in the ozone layer over Antarctica. Canadian scientists discovered another hole over the Arctic shortly thereafter. What caused these holes? After years of controversy, the depletion of the ozone layer has been blamed on chlorofluorocarbons. CFCs have been widely used as propellants in aerosols and as coolants in refrigerators and air conditioners; they are also used in fast-food packaging. Once in the atmosphere, CFCs destroy the ozone layer, which protects the earth from the sun's ultraviolet radiation, thereby contributing to global warming and greater incidents of skin cancer.

Although the danger of CFCs to the ozone layer was known as early as 1974, it was not until the late 1980s that anything was done. The Montreal Protocol, signed by Canada, the United States, the European Community, and over twenty other countries, was initiated in 1987. The aim of the agreement was to cut CFC production to 50 percent of 1987 levels by the year 1999. Since then, the European Commmunity has announced it will eliminate all production of CFCs before 1999, and Canada and the United States are considering following this lead. However, the most populous country in the world, China, is not a signatory to the Montreal Protocol. Refrigerators are important symbols of progress in China, and the government will not sign a document that will slow down the spread of a technology that is already common in the households of the developed world.

Acid Rain

Another environmental problem is acid rain. The raw materials of acid rain—sulphur dioxide and nitrous oxides—are released into the atmosphere whenever fossil fuels are burned. Acid rain has already killed over 40 000 lakes in Canada and the United States and is endangering thousands more. In Europe, over 4 million hectares of forest, including the famous Black Forest in Germany, are showing the effects of acid rain and may be dying.

Acid rain has been the principal environmental concern for Canadians since the early 1970s. Yet it was not until 1985 that the federal government imposed restrictions on Canadian sources of sulphur and nitrous oxides. Yet even if these sources were completely eliminated, it would not end the problem of acid rain in Canada because over 50 percent of the rain originates in the United States. It was not until 1990 that formal negotiations on a bilateral accord to reduce acid rain were announced.

Water Pollution

Over 75 percent of the earth's surface is covered by water, but only 2 percent is classified as fresh water. Increasingly, fresh-water supplies are being polluted by the by-products of population growth and industrialization.

Population growth has accelerated water pollution in a number of ways. Untreated human sewage pollutes water sources and leads to an increase in diseases such as typhoid fever, cholera, and dysentery. In the developed world, detergents and toxic chemicals in cleaning solvents combine with agricultural chemicals and fertilizer runoff to further degrade the water supply, causing higher incidences of birth defects and some types of cancer. The problem is so widespread that the World Health Organization (WHO) estimates that 80 percent of the world's diseases are caused in some way by contaminated water.

The principal source of water pollution, however, is industrial waste. Industry regularly discharges heavy metals, such as lead and mercury, and toxic chemicals, such as dioxin and polychlorinated biphenyl (PCBs), into the water system. These chemicals kill some plants and animals outright; in others they cause birth defects or total reproductive failure. Thermal pollution from industry and nuclear power plants accelerates eutrophication, which speeds the growth of oxygen-consuming algae, thereby depleting the supply of game fish. Ultimately, all of the industrial waste finds its way into the oceans.

The 40 million litres of crude oil discharged into Prince William Sound in Alaska by the *Exxon Valdez* is only the most spectacular example of the estimated 907 000 t of oil that were released into the oceans in 1989. But it was the image of oil-coated birds and sea otters and tar-smeared beaches that caught the media's attention. Over 34 000 birds and 900 sea otters died as a result of the spill and the annual salmon catch was reduced by over 40 percent. The $1 billion clean-up operation mounted by Exxon employed over 11 000 people at its peak. Despite the clean-up efforts, however, it will take decades for the area to completely recover.

Far more dangerous, however, is the long-term effect of oil's toxicity. Chemicals in the ocean build up in concentration in the higher species of the food chain and can lead to deaths in humans. For instance, methyl mercury poisoning from eating tuna with heavy concentrations of mercury resulted in 3500 known victims in Japan between 1950 and 1975. DDT has even been discovered in the fatty tissues of Antarctic penguins, evidence that contaminants are spreading even to the most remote areas of the planet.

Waste from a mine site in Elliot Lake pollutes the local river systems.

Cleaning Up Our Waterways

What is being done to resolve these problems? There have been several agreements to clean up specific areas, such as the Bonn Agreement of 1969 which focused on oil pollution in the North Sea, and the project sponsored by Switzerland, West Germany, France, and the Netherlands to clean up the Rhine River, considered to be the most polluted in Western Europe. The most ambitious clean-up project is the Regional Seas Program initiated by the United Nations Environmental Program in 1974. This program is based on the premise that no one country can solve regional pollution and that common problems require common solutions. Since the first regional plan was initiated in the Mediterranean Sea in 1975, ten other regional efforts have been implemented.

A clean-up program has also been launched for the Great Lakes. Lake Erie, the shallowest and most polluted of the lakes, was declared "dead" in the late 1960s. Nearly 1000 chemicals from factories, sewage plants, and farmers' fields were identified in water samples taken from the lake. To date, the clean-up program has cost over $8 billion. While these efforts have restored considerable aquatic life to Lake Erie, they have still not elminated all of the toxic wastes in the lake.

Pollution Probe has identified 343 "toxic hotspots" on the Great Lakes. A scheme devised by the International Joint Commission—the Canada-United States boundary water advisory body—to clean up forty-two of the most hazardous sites was adopted by Canada and the eight states that border the Great Lakes in 1985. The cost of the overall project is estimated to be in the tens of billions of dollars; the cost of cleaning up the seventeen Canadian sites, all in Ontario, is in excess of $2 billion. Unfortunately, a debate over who is responsible and who should pay could delay the program for years.

Water Pollution in Eastern Europe

The Aral Sea in the Soviet Central Asian republics of Uzbekistan and Kazakhstan is perhaps the best example of what can happen when short-term economic goals are placed before long-term environmental concerns. In 1918, the Amu Darya and Syr Darya rivers, which feed the Aral Sea, were diverted to irrigate millions of hectares of cotton. Because of the diversion of the principal sources of the sea, evaporation began to exceed inflow. As a result, in the last thirty years the Aral Sea has lost 28 500 km^2 of its surface area. The once thriving fishing industry is dead. Salt storms have killed the

SILENT SPRING

The awakening of the public toward environmental degradation was due in part to the publication of Silent Spring *(1962). In this seminal work, Rachel Carson (1907–1964) identified the long-term effects of pesticides, such as DDT, on the environment. Since the 1960s the use of DDT has been restricted in North America; however, it is still commonly used in the developing world. The warning expressed in the following excerpt, "A Fable for Tomorrow," from the first chapter of* Silent Spring, *is as appropriate in the 1990s as it was in the 1960s.*

There was once a town in the heart of America where all life seemed to live in harmony with its surroundings. The town lay in the midst of a checkerboard of prosperous farms, with fields of grain and hillsides of orchards where, in spring, white clouds of bloom drifted above the green fields. In autumn, oak and maple and birch set up a blaze of color that flamed and flickered across a backdrop of pines. Then foxes barked in the hills and deer silently crossed the fields, half hidden in the mists of the fall mornings.

Along the roads, laurel, viburnum and alder, great ferns and wildflowers delighted the traveler's eye through much of the year. Even in winter the roadsides were places of beauty, where countless birds came to feed on the berries and on the seed heads of the dried weeds rising above the snow. The countryside was, in fact, famous for the abundance and variety of its bird life, and when the flood of migrants was pouring through in spring and fall people traveled from great distances to observe them. Others came to fish the streams, which flowed clear and cold out of the hills and contained shady pools where trout lay. So it had been from the days many years ago when the first settlers raised their houses, sank their wells, and built their barns.

Then a strange blight crept over the area and everything began to change. Some evil spell had settled on the community: mysterious maladies swept the flocks of chickens; the cattle and sheep sickened and died. Everywhere was a shadow of death. The farmers spoke of much illness among their families. In the town the doctors had become more and more puzzled by new kinds of sickness appearing and unexplained deaths, not only among adults but even among children, who would be stricken suddenly while at play and die within a few hours.

There was a strange stillness. The birds, for example—where had they gone? Many people spoke of them, puzzled and disturbed. The feeding stations in the backyards were deserted. The few birds seen anywhere were moribund; they trembled violently and could not fly. It was a spring without voices. On the mornings that had once throbbed with the dawn chorus of robins, catbirds, doves, jays, wrens, and scores of other bird voices there was now no sound; only silence lay over the fields and woods and marsh.

On the farms the hens brooded, but no chicks hatched. The farmers complained that they were unable to raise any pigs—the litters were small and the young survived only a few days. The apple trees were coming into bloom but no bees droned among the blossoms, so there was no pollination and there would be no fruit.

The roadsides, once so attractive, were now lined with browned and withered vegetation as though swept by fire. These, too, were silent, deserted by all living things. Even the streams were now lifeless. Anglers no longer visited them, for all the fish had died.

In the gutters under the eaves and between the shingles of the roofs, a white granular powder still showed a few patches; some weeks before it had fallen like snow upon the roofs and the lawns, the fields and streams.

No witchcraft, no enemy action had silenced the rebirth of new life in this stricken world. The people had done it themselves.

foliage surrounding the lake for kilometres. Airborne dust has led to a sharp increase in respiratory and eye diseases. Pesticides used in the cotton fields have contaminated the drinking water and have contributed to one of the highest infant death rates in the Soviet Union. Perhaps one of the saddest features of this debacle is that scientists in the Soviet Union were aware of this ecological disaster by the early 1960s, but were prevented from speaking out or acting to solve it.

The plight of the Aral Sea was just one of the many environmental disasters revealed by the new openness behind the Iron Curtain. The single-minded concentration on economic goals in a succession of five-year plans spanning decades has created industrial pollution that the West German Institute for Economic Research estimates will cost over $200 billion to clean up. Half of Poland's rivers are so polluted they are unsuitable even for industrial use. Over 70 percent of Czechoslovakia's rivers are rated as "heavily polluted" by the government. Perhaps public pressure from the newly formed environmental groups in Eastern Europe will alter government policies that have emphasized industrialization over everything else. However, the pressure will have to be considerable. The major question is, how much attention can governments struggling for their economic survival afford to give to the environment?

The Land

The earth's population has exploded in the twentieth century. After the First World War, the population was approximately 2 billion. Advances in technology and medicine and an overall improvement in health and diet substantially reduced the death rate in developing countries during the interwar period. This, combined with high birth rates, resulted in a population explosion. It is expected that the world's population will exceed 6 billion by the turn of the century. Most of this growth will take place in the developing world, where over 90 percent of the population struggles for survival.

Desertification and Deforestation

The population explosion has significantly increased the demand for land. As urban areas encroach on prime agricultural lands, farmers have been forced to cultivate marginal areas which are often unsuitable for agriculture. Once cleared, these lands, with their poorer soils, are subject to erosion. As a result, *desertification*—the degradation of lands into barren deserts—has become a major problem in Africa, Asia, and Latin America. It is not possible to wait for the centuries needed for natural processes to replace the lost soil. Human intervention is required to rehabilitate degraded soil and to halt desertification and the related problem of *deforestation*.

The problems of deforestation and desertification are less immediate in the developed world, but they do exist. North America was once covered by forests, but very little old-growth forest exists today. What has survived is constantly threatened by the lumber industry. Overcutting and other poor forestry management practices have led to rapid deforestation throughout the Western world. Only in recent years have we started to realize the value of reforestation programs.

The loss of topsoil from wind and water erosion is also a serious problem. Poor farming practices have resulted in Canada's Prairie provinces losing more than half their organic value over the past several decades. It is estimated that the price of soil degradation in Canada could reach $44 billion by 2005 unless we improve our land management practices. Fortunately, governments are starting to take action to reclaim eroded lands by planting grasses and trees. A return to sustainable farming with organic fertilizers, biodegradable pesticides, crop diversification, and fallowing will also help to reduce the problem of land degradation.

Rain Forest Destruction

Worldwide, 11 to 15 million hectares of rain forest are lost to fire or the chain saw every year. The greatest loss is in Brazil, which accounts for one-third of all the rain forests in the world. In Brazil, 25 percent of the rain forest has been destroyed in the last twenty years for hydro-electric power sites, logging operations, cattle ranching, and farming. If the present rate of clearing continues, the South American rain forest will disappear in less than thirty years. The extent of the damage has led some to suggest it is the biggest contributor to global climatic change. Others point out the impact that deforestation has had on the Kazakhstan region in the Soviet Union. Less than thirty years after Khrushchev ordered the region's forests cleared for agriculture, the area has become a 12 million hectare dustbowl.

The loss of the rain forests is a multiple threat to humankind. Burning the forest releases large amounts of carbon dioxide into the atmosphere, contributing to the greenhouse effect. The rain forest is also a major source of recycled precipitation. If it is destroyed, it can affect the amount of moisture other areas receive, which affects their overall climate. Flooding and erosion is another result of rain forest destruction. Removing the vegetation exposes the poor soils that lie beneath and makes them vulnerable to erosion. The soils are quickly destroyed, which makes farming or attempts at regenerating plant life even more difficult. In addition, the loss of vegetation can lead to flooding in lower lying areas as there is no plant life to prevent excess water runoff.

One of the greatest threats caused by rain forest destruction is the loss of the largest reserve of the earth's plant and animal species. Some species may be native to a single square kilometre of the forest, or perhaps even to a single tree. Once the area is destroyed, these species are gone forever. At the present rate of destruction, half of all the animal species existing today will be extinct or endangered by the middle of the next century.

The rain forest may also hold the secrets to new medical cures. Many plant species have been found to cure deadly diseases. For example, the discovery of the rosy periwinkle in the Madagascar rain forest was a major breakthrough in treating some forms of leukemia in children; it reduced the death rate from the disease from 80 percent to 20 percent. It has been estimated that as many as 3000 plants may offer a cure to cancer alone. In addition, many plant species have not even been identified and so their value as medicinal agents is unknown. Perhaps by destroying the rain forest we are destroying a form of plant life that could provide the key to curing cancer or AIDS.

Brazil and other developing nations argue that Western countries cut their own forests at record pace in the past and that they are entitled to the same economic reward that their forests can bring them now. But the demand for foreign exchange to pay debts forces most developing countries to cut exotic tropical trees at a faster rate than the forest can be regenerated. Unless the West provides relief from the massive burden of foreign debt, the destruction of the rain forest will continue.

Waste Management and Recycling

The principal means of solid waste management are incineration and landfills. Both of these methods contribute to the greenhouse effect and waste the trees, minerals, energy, and human resources that were used to create the waste in the first place. In addition, people are actively starting to oppose having these waste sites in their communities and are beginning to demand other solutions.

The sheer amount of the waste is staggering. Canadians throw out 10 million tonnes of household garbage and at

This 1989 photograph showed the destruction of the rain forest to permit an open-cast mine in Ariquesnes, Brazil.

WHAT CAN WE DO TO PROTECT MOTHER EARTH?

David Suzuki is considered by many to be the Canadian environmental conscience. He appears weekly on CBC's The Nature of Things *and participated in the 1985 series* A Planet for the Taking *and the 1989 special* Amazonia. *The following article is from a science column Suzuki wrote for the* Globe and Mail.

Reports about global pollution, atmospheric degradation and destruction of the wilderness seem to assault us daily. In an atmosphere of heightened sensitivity about the urgency of acting to counteract planetary decay, we need solutions that are at once effective and profound.

There are many practical steps that can and must be taken immediately. You can be a conservationist in your daily life: recycling, using cloth instead of disposable diapers, composting kitchen leftovers. You will be amazed at the reduction in garbage. Use your power as a consumer to exert pressure by what you choose to buy. Urge stores to use only biodegradable plastics; ask supermarkets and fast food outlets to replace foam containers and other wasteful packaging. Point out the energy wasted by having doorless refrigerators and freezers in food stores. Don't buy leaded gas. Support politicians who have serious environmental platforms as well as groups working to protect the environment.

The most pressing challenge is to try to preserve as much of the remnants of untouched wilderness as possible and to impose severe restrictions on pollution. At the same time, we must keep our sights fixed on the long-term horizon.

We are in a turbulent period of change when old assumptions about growth and progress must be radically and quickly redefined. Only with a profound ecological awareness of our place in the natural world can we begin to frame effective action.

There are important perspectives from which to begin that reassessment. For example, the air, water and soil that we depend on are finite and whatever we put into them will eventually be recycled through all life forms, including us. . . . We have to learn to "think globally and act locally."

Each of us, by our actions and priorities, contributes to the fate of the earth. . . . As consumers, each of us can exert power by what we buy or don't buy. . . . We also have power as voters—that's what has made politicians take the environment seriously in the first place and now that we have their attention, we have to press for more than cosmetic action. . . .

Global economics as much as overpopulation is the cause of the enormous output of toxic products, waste and despoilation of wilderness and natural resources. The drive to maximize corporate profit subsumes all else, especially something as ephemeral as the environment, yet the "private sector" has responsibilities to the public that go beyond payment of taxes and maximizing profits for shareholders. They must define and justify "reasonable" profit.

And business cannot continue to use air, water and soil as if they are simply sources of raw materials or dumping grounds for wastes, when they are the very support system for all life on earth. The true price of a manufactured item has to encompass the extraction of material for its production, through to its final disposal, the so-called "cradle-to-grave" cost accounting.

It is only when all segments of society recognize that we cannot go on with business as usual—that we have to adopt a more holistic, ecological attitude—that we will begin to divert ourselves along a new path. Deliberately choosing to live in balance with the world that sustains us would be a true measure of progress.

least 10 million tonnes of industrial garbage every year. Every citizen in the United States throws out 2 kg of garbage everyday. But in Japan, this figure is less than 1 kg. The reason for this is a successful recycling program. Over 40 percent of Japan's solid waste is recycled. It is a lesson that Western society, particularly in North America, could well learn. North America's most successful recycling effort, Ontario's "Blue Box" program, while a step in the right direction, has reduced the total garbage volume by only 5 percent.

Recycling is not just a solution to waste management, however. It offers us the opportunity to extend the life of our dwindling resource base. The developed world, which has 20 percent of the world's population, uses 80 percent of the world's resources. This can be reduced significantly through recycling programs. How much impact can one household have by separating recyclable items from garbage? Environment Ontario lists the following benefits:

- by recycling newspaper, the average household saves 1.5 trees every year;
- by recycling glass, steel, aluminum and polyethylene terephalate (PET) soft drink bottles, the average household saves 407 kilowatt-hours of electricity and reduces sulphur dioxide and nitrogen oxide emissions by 4.7 kg;
- by recycling, the average household saves 0.3 m^3 of landfill space every year.

Multiply these figures by all the households in the developed world and the conservation of resources and the reduction of waste is substantial.

The Greening of the Western World

"Greening" is the new word in the Western vocabulary to describe concern for the environment. Publications such as *The Green Consumer's Guide* are becoming instant best-sellers as consumers seek to make intelligent choices in the marketplace. Retail merchants are scrambling to provide environmentally acceptable products. As a result, products such as CFC-pressurized aerosol cans and foam egg cartons made from CFCs have virtually disappeared from store shelves. Investors can now choose from investment groups such as Investors Summa Fund and the Environmental Investment Canadian Fund, which offer a portfolio of stocks from companies that are either environmentally friendly or have good pollution-control records.

Green consciousness has started to spread to the political arena as well. The West German Green party was the first of its kind to gain parliamentary representation in 1983. By 1989, Greens sat in the national parliaments of Austria, Australia, Belgium, Finland, West Germany, Italy, Luxembourg, Portugal, Switzerland, and Sweden. The new European parliament even has a slight left-green majority. Unfortunately, the growth of environmental parties in North America lags far behind the movement in Europe.

In the United States, environmentalists working within the established parties have forced several state and municipal governments to pass environmental laws that are much stricter than federal government regulations. In Canada, the Green party has yet to have a candidate elected to office. But as environmental awareness spreads in the 1990s, the Green party could gain strength. Even a slight increase in popular support for Green party candidates would force the established parties to adopt more and better evironmental programs. In Canada, the mounting public pressure has already forced the federal government to begin a process to establish the priorities of *The Green Plan: A National Challenge*, which intends to make Canada the most environmentally friendly country in the world by the year 2000.

RETROSPECTIVE

Science has made remarkable progress since 1945. Scientific discoveries have given us greater knowledge about our bodies and the universe. Chemistry has developed new medicines and synthetic materials. Biology has unlocked the secret of life itself with the discovery of DNA, while medical discoveries have enabled us to live longer, healthier lives.

Developments in transportation and communications have made the world a "global village." Distance is no longer a barrier, and mass media and economic interdependence have brought people from around the world into closer contact. The resulting spread of ideas from one culture to another has increased cultural homogeneity.

Technology has produced an amazing variety of appliances, devices, and gadgets to fuel the consumer society that accompanied the recovery from the Second World War. At the same time, our technological developments have caused serious damage to our natural environment by wasting resources and increasing pollution. Rising expectations worldwide can only accelerate our demand for energy, thereby accelerating the depletion of resources and pollution. Only recently have we discovered that the earth is the only planet we have. We are still learning how to care for it.

LIEBE F. CAVALIERI:
Twin Perils: Nuclear Science and Genetic Engineering (1985)

The ethical basis of scientific discoveries has been challenged since the time of Galileo. In the second half of the twentieth century, the threat from nuclear war, toxic waste, and DNA manipulation has widened the scope of the debate beyond the narrow confines of the religious community to the community at large. As the author points out, "There is only one Earth, one earthly biosphere, and we are part of it. There is no margin for error. . . ."

There is a striking similarity between nuclear science and genetic engineering. Both major scientific accomplishments confer a power on humans for which they are psychologically and morally unprepared. The physicists have already learned this, to their dismay; the biologists, not yet. Molecular biologists are still euphoric over the potential of their achievements. Indeed, Nobel laureate David Baltimore has proclaimed: "We can outdo evolution"—a signal that molecular biologists are about to translate genetic engineering into an instrument of power, much the way the physicists did when they exploited their discoveries at the beginning of the nuclear age.

The early part of this century was a golden era for physics. It was a time when physicists had become deeply submerged in finding the "truth" about the physical universe—a period of reasoned excitement that prevailed for a number of years; but it gave way to an urgent mood with the discoveries of the 1930s. There was no opportunity for the usual lapse of time between scientific discovery and its application. The discovery of nuclear fission defined the bomb. World War II and the threat of Nazi science provided an immediate rationale for physicists to tap one of nature's most powerful forces. "Truth" was converted instantaneously to power. . . .

The power to create the bomb, originally in the hands of physicists, led insidiously to a new kind of power. The military stepped in, superseding any possibility of decisionmaking by the physicists. Those who had created the technology in the first place were cast aside, left only to reflect on the inhuman consequences of their work. . . .

As nuclear physics was approaching its climax, the golden age of molecular biology was just beginning. DNA was shown to be the genetic substance in 1944; in 1953 another milestone was reached, when James Watson and Francis Crick proposed the DNA double helical structure, with its molecular basis for genetic continuity. This was the dawn of molecular genetics; a new paradigm was born.

As in the development of nuclear physics, once the elegance of the new discoveries had been felt and the intrinsic beauty of that corner of nature revealed, the enticement for further investigation and exploitation proved irresistible. Indeed, the science and its applications are so closely coupled that they are virtually one and the same. Like the discoveries in atomic physics, truth and use are hard to separate. Molecular biologists have succumbed to intellectual and emotional forces just as the physicists did, with medical and economic pretexts in place of the Nazi threat. No one heeds the trap that befell the physicists: scientists can choose and control their experiments, but once the science has escaped from the laboratory, they are no longer in control.

Already, an academic-industrial complex has been formed. More and more, the direction of university research is open to influence by commercial considerations. In the normal sequence of events, large corporations will gobble up the smaller, scientist-controlled operations as soon as they prove profitable. Nobel laureate Walter Gilbert says that the genetic engineering venture will be different from other commercial forays—scientists will be in control. Well, perhaps, for a while. It would take far more profound social changes than that to prevent the transfer of power to the corporate structure. The fascination of the endeavor, the "glitter" of genetic engineering and the "illusion of illimitable power" are again in the air; after chemistry and physics, it's now biology's turn. Few have asked with Erwin Chargaff, "Have we the right to counteract, irreversibly, the evolutionary wisdom of millions of years, in order to satisfy the ambition and the curiosity of a few scientists? . . . My generation, or perhaps the one preceding mine, has been the first to engage, under the leadership of the exact sciences, in a destructive colonial warfare against nature. The future will curse us for it."

There was an attempt not to go all the way with atomic fission. . . . And indeed it seemed at first that a similar social action would occur with recombinant DNA technology. In a spirit of humanitarian concern, when molecular biologists first perceived the impact of recombinant DNA technology, they decided to convene a conference in 1975 to seek a modus operandi. The serious and sincere discussion at the outset concerned only the immediate hazards of the research; future effects of the technology did not enter the discussion in any meaningful way. No public health experts, ecologists, ethicists, or philosophers were invited, and the questions discussed were those most intimately connected to the research projects of the molecular biologists in attendance. The discussion was, therefore, not broad-based and it revolved about the possible escape of a pathogen from the laboratory into the environment. No long-range ethical and social consequences were considered.

The ad hoc discussion at the 1975 conference served as a basis for guidelines for recombinant DNA research, first promulgated by the National Institutes of Health in 1976. Since then, the guidelines, under constant pressure from interested parties, have been relaxed to the point where they afford virtually no protection. In extricating themselves from government control, molecular biologists crossed an energy barrier and have become adept at political manipulation. The hope for meaningful public input on the ethical and moral implications of this technology had faded as the momentum of genetic engineering has grown.

With the spectre of Nazism before them, physicists felt it necessary to develop atomic weapons. Molecular biologists, in choosing to push full-speed ahead with genetic engineering, cannot so convincingly rationalize their war on Nature. In this period of unparalleled ecological stress, with so many socially important areas of inquiry unexplored, there is no overriding need to develop a technology that is pregnant with unpredictable consequences. All forms of life are vulnerable to this technology—any DNA can be connected to any other DNA; human DNA can be put into viruses and bacteria and vice versa; cancer virus DNA has already been put into bacteria, and so on. The gene pool of the Earth, the life-determinant of the future, is the experimental subject for genetic engineering. This precious, irreplaceable legacy of natural evolution is in the truest sense a one-time occurrence, and it would be naive to assume that we can manipulate it without harming ourselves. We do not have the infinite wisdom that would be required. . . .

The discoveries that energy can be released from the atomic nucleus and that DNA, the material of the cell nucleus, is the genetic stuff of life are without parallel in human experience. These twin scientific feats demand a new consciousness if human life on this planet is to continue. We have mismanaged the applications of the first discovery. Now, as the second is about to be exploited, we must not permit the biosphere, surpassing as it does our understanding, to become an experimental subject. There is only one Earth, one earthly biosphere, and we are part of it. There is no margin for error. . . .

1. What similarities does the author draw between the development of the atomic bomb and genetic engineering?

2. Discuss what responsibilities scientists have for their research and discoveries.

3. Discuss what role the public should play in determining guidelines for scientific research and its technological applications.

J. DAVID BOLTER: The Computer as a Defining Technology (1984)

Computers developed from ENIAC, a computer the size of a room, to the ubiquitous computer chip in a quarter of a century, the most rapid development of any technology in the twentieth century. In the process, the computer has become the "defining technology" of our age.

Men and women throughout history have asked how it is that they and their culture (their technology in the largest sense) transcend nature, what makes them characteristically human and not merely animal. For the Greeks, a cardinal human quality was the ability to establish the political and social order embodied in a city-state: men at their best could set collective goals, make laws, and obey them, and none of these could be achieved by animals in a state of nature. Their city-state was a feat of social technology. In the Middle Ages, the accomplishments of technology were perhaps more physical than social, but the use of inanimate sources of power, wind and water, fostered a new view of mankind versus the forces of nature. The discoveries of the Renaissance and the Industrial Revolution moved men closer to nature in some respects and separated them even more radically in others. Continued emphasis on exploring and manipulating the physical world led to a deeper appreciation of the world's resources. Yet the desire to master nature—to harness her more efficient sources of power in steam and fossil fuels and to mine her metals for synthetic purposes—grew steadily throughout this period. When Darwin showed convincingly that man was an animal like any other, he shattered once and for all the barrier that separated man from the rest of nature in the Greek and medieval chains of being. Yet nineteenth-century engineers with their railroads and still more twentieth-century physicists with their atomic bombs seemed less natural than ever before, less under the control of either nature or a personal deity and more responsible for their own misjudgments.

Continually redrawing the line that divides nature and culture, men have always been inclined to explain the former in terms of the latter, to examine the world of nature, through the lens of their own created human environment. So Greek philosophers used analogies from the crafts of pottery and woodworking to explain the creation of the universe: the stars, the planets, the earth, and its living inhabitants. In the same way, the weight-driven clock invented in the Middle Ages provided a new metaphor for both the regular movements of heavenly bodies and the beautifully intricate bodies of animals, whereas the widespread use of the steam engine in the nineteenth century brought to mind a different, more brutal aspect of the natural world. It is certainly not true that changing technology is solely responsible for mankind's changing views of nature, but clearly the technology of any age provides an attractive window through which thinkers can view both their physical and metaphysical worlds.

Technology has had this influence even upon philosophers, like Plato, who generally disdain human craftsmanship and see it as a poor reflection of a greater nonhuman reality. And even in Christian theology and poetry, the pleasures of heaven could only be described as a grand version of the tainted pleasures men know on earth, and the tortures of hell were earthly tortures intensified. Almost every sort of philosopher, theologian, or poet has needed an analogy on the human scale to clarify his or her ideas. Speaking of creation as the imposition of order upon the natural world, he or she generally assumed a creator as well, and this creator is a craftsman or technologist.

It is in this context that I propose to examine electronic technology. The computer is the contemporary analog of the clocks and steam engines of the previous six centuries, it is as important to us as the potter's wheel was to the ancient world. It is not that we cannot live without computers, but that we will be different people because we live with them. All techniques and devices have the potential to become defining technologies because all to some degree redefine our relationship to nature. In fact, only a few devices or crafts in any age deserve to be called defining technologies. In the ancient world, carpentry and masonry were about as important as spinning and pottery, and yet poets and philosophers found that latter two far more suggestive. In medieval Europe, crop rotation and the moldboard plough had a greater economic and social impact than the early clockwork mechanisms. Yet not many philosophers and theologians compared the world to a lentil bean. Certain skills and inventions have moved easily out of the agora into the Academy, out of the textile mill into the salon, or out of the industrial research park into the university classroom.

The vision of particular philosophers and poets is important to such a transference. Descartes and his followers helped to make the clock a defining technology in Western Europe. Certainly the first poet to elaborate the myth of the Fates who spin the thread of life helped to make textiles a defining technology for ancient Greece. But there must be something in the nature of the technology itself, so that its shape, its materials, its modes of operation appeal to the mind as well as to the hand of their age—for example, the pleasing rotary motion of the spindle or the autonomy and intricacy of the pendulum clock.

Such qualities combine with the social and economic importance of the device to make people think. Very often a device will take on a metaphoric significance and be compared in art and philosophy to some part of the animate or inanimate world. Plato compared the created universe to a spindle. Descartes thought of animals as clockwork mechanisms, and scientists in the nineteenth century and early twentieth century have regularly compared the universe to a heat engine that is slowly squandering its fuel. Today the computer is constantly serving as a metaphor for the human mind or brain; psychologists speak of input and output, sometimes even the hardware and software, of the brain; linguists treat human language as if it were a programming code; and everyone speaks of making computers "think."

A defining technology develops links, metaphorical or otherwise, with a culture's science, philosophy, or literature; it is always available to serve as a metaphor, example, model, or symbol. A defining technology resembles a magnifying glass, which collects and focuses seemingly disparate ideas in a culture into one bright, sometimes piercing ray. Technology does not call forth major cultural changes by itself, but it does bring ideas into a new focus by explaining or exemplifying them in new ways to larger audiences. Descartes's notion of a mechanistic world that obeyed the laws of mathematics was clear, accessible, and therefore powerful because his contemporaries lived with clocks and gears. So today electronic technology gives a more catholic appeal to a number of trends in twentieth-century thought, particularly the notions of mathematical logic, structural linguistics, and behaviourial psychology. Separately these trends were minor upheavals in the history of ideas; taken together, they become a major revision in our thinking.

---

1. Explain the phrase *defining technology*.

2. (a) Make a chart identifying the historical period and its appropriate defining technology.
(b) Discuss how appropriate the defining technology is for each period.

3. In what ways does identifying a defining technology for a historical period further our knowledge of that era?

OUR COMMON FUTURE (1983)

The World Commission on Environment and Development was established by the United Nations in 1983 to formulate "a global agenda for change." The following is an excerpt from the commission's report.

From The World Commission on Environment and Development, *Our Common Future* (Oxford: Oxford University Press, 1987), pp. 4–8. Reprinted by permission of Oxford University Press.

The Interlocking Crises

Until recently, the planet was a large world in which human activities and their effects were neatly compartmentalized within nations, within sectors (energy, agriculture, trade), and within broad areas of concern (environmental, economic, social). These compartments have begun to dissolve. This applies in particular to the various global "crises" that have seized public concern, particularly over the past decade. These are not separate crises: an environmental crisis, a development crisis, and energy crisis. They are all one.

The planet is passing through a period of dramatic growth and fundamental change. Our human world of 5 billion must make room in a finite environment for another human world. The population could stabilize at between 8 billion and 14 billion sometime next century, according to UN projections. More than 90 percent of the increase will occur in the poorest countries, and 90 percent of that growth in already bursting cities.

Economic activity has multiplied to create a $13 trillion world economy, and this could grow five- or tenfold in the coming half-century. Industrial production has grown more than fiftyfold over the past century, four-fifths of this growth since 1950. Such figures reflect and presage profound impacts upon the biosphere, as the world invests in houses, transport, farms, and industries. Much of the economic growth pulls raw material from forests, soils, seas, and waterways.

A mainspring of economic growth is new technology, and while this technology offers the potential for slowing the dangerously rapid consumption of finite resources, it also entails high risks, including new forms of pollution and the introduction to the planet of new variations of life forms that could change evolutionary pathways. Meanwhile, the industries most heavily reliant on environmental resources and most heavily polluting are growing most rapidly in the developing world, where there is both more urgency for growth and less capacity to minimize damaging side effects.

These related changes have locked the global economy and global ecology together in new ways. We have in the past been concerned about the impacts of economic growth upon the environment. We are now forced to concern ourselves with the impacts of ecological stress—degradation of soils, water regimes, atmosphere, and forests—upon our economic prospects. We have in the more recent past been forced to face up to a sharp increase in economic interdependence among nations. We are now forced to accustom ourselves to an accelerating ecological interdependence among nations. Ecology and economy are becoming ever more interwoven—locally, regionally, nationally, and globally—into a seamless net of causes and effects.

Impoverishing the local resource base can impoverish wider areas: Deforestation by highland farmers causes flooding on lowland farms; factory pollution robs local fishermen of their catch. Such grim local cycles now operate nationally and regionally. Dryland degradation sends environmental refugees in their millions across national borders. Deforestation in Latin America and Asia is causing more floods, and more destructive floods, in downhill, downstream nations. Acid precipitation and nuclear fallout have spread across the borders of Europe. Similar phenomena are emerging on a global scale, such as global warming and loss of ozone. Internationally traded hazardous chemicals entering foods are themselves internationally traded. In the next century, the environmental pressure causing population movements may increase sharply, while barriers to that movement may be even firmer than they are now.

Over the past few decades, life-threatening environmental concerns have surfaced in the developing world. Countrysides are coming under pressure from increasing numbers of farmers and the landless. Cities are filling with people, cars, and factories. Yet at the same time these developing countries must operate in a world in which the resources gap between most developing and industrial nations is widening, in which the industrial world dominates in the rule-making of some key international bodies, and in which the industrial world has already used much of the planet's ecological capital. This inequality is the planet's main "environmental" problem; it is also its main "development" problem.

International economic relationships pose a particular problem for environmental management in many developing countries. Agriculture, forestry, energy production, and mining generate at least half the gross national product of many developing countries and account for even larger shares of livelihoods and employment. Exports of natural resources remain a large factor in their economies, especially for the least developed. Most of these countries face enormous economic pressures, both international and domestic, to overexploit their environmental resource base.

The recent crisis in Africa best and most tragically illustrates the ways in which economics and ecology can interact destructively and trip into disaster. Triggered by drought, its real causes lie deeper. They are to be found in part in national policies that gave too little attention, too late, to the needs of smallholder agriculture and to the threats posed by rapidly rising populations. Their roots extend also to a global economic system that takes more out of a poor continent than it puts in. Debts that they cannot pay force African nations relying on commodity sales to overuse their fragile soils, thus turning good land to desert. Trade barriers in the wealthy nations—and in many developing ones—make it hard for Africans to sell their goods for reasonable returns, putting yet more pressure on ecological systems. Aid from donor nations has not only been inadequate in scale, but too often has reflected the priorities of the nations giving the aid, rather than the needs of the recipients. The production base of other developing world areas suffers similarly both from local failures and from the workings of international economic systems. As a consequence of the "debt crisis" of Latin America, the region's natural resources are now being used not for development but to meet financial obligations to creditors abroad. This approach to the debt problem is short-sighted from several standpoints: economic, political, and environmental. It requires relatively poor countries simultaneously to accept growing poverty while exporting growing amounts of scarce resources.

A majority of developing countries now have lower per capita incomes than when the decade began. Rising poverty and unemployment have increased pressure on environmental resources as more people have been forced to rely more directly upon them. Many governments have cut back efforts to protect the environment and to bring ecological considerations into development planning.

The deepening and widening environmental crisis presents a threat to national security—and even survival—that may be greater than well-armed, ill-disposed neighbours and unfriendly alliances. Already in parts of Latin America, Asia, the Middle East, and Africa, environmental decline is becoming a source of political unrest and international tension. The recent destruction of much of Africa's dryland agricultural production was more severe than if an invading army had pursued a scorched-earth policy. Yet most of the affected governments still spend far more to protect their people from invading armies than from the invading desert.

Globally, military expenditures total about $1 trillion a year and continue to grow. In many countries, military spending consumes such high proportion to gross national product that it itself does great damage to these societies' development efforts. Governments tend to base their approaches to "security" on traditional definitions. This is most obvious in the attempts to achieve security through the development of potentially planet-destroying nuclear weapons systems. Studies suggest that the cold and dark nuclear winter following even a limited nuclear war could destroy planet and animal ecosystems and leave any human survivors occupying a devastated planet very different from the one they inherited.

The arms race—in all parts of the world—pre-empts resources that might be used more productively to diminish the security threats created by environmental conflict and the resentments that are fuelled by widespread poverty.

Many present efforts to guard and maintain human progress, to meet human needs, and to realize human ambitions are simply unsustainable—in both the rich and poor nations. They draw too heavily, too quickly, on already overdrawn environmental resource accounts to be affordable far into the future without bankrupting those accounts. They may show profits on the balance sheets of our generation, but our children will inherit the losses. We borrow environmental capital from future generations with no intention or prospect of repaying. They may damn us for our spendthrift ways, but they can never collect on our debt to them. We act as we do because we can get away with it: future generations do not vote; they have no political or financial power; they cannot challenge our decisions.

But the results of the present profligacy are rapidly closing the options for future generations. Most of today's decision makers will be dead before the planet feels the heavier effects of acid precipitation, global warming, ozone depletion, or widespread desertification and species loss. Most of the young voters of today will still be alive. In the Commission's hearings it was the young, those who have the most to lose, who were the hardest critics of the planet's present management.

---

1. (a) What are the interlocking crises?
(b) Why does this situation exist?

2. Prepare arguments for a class discussion on how the present crises in the developing world—political, economic, social, and environmental—can be improved.

3. What responsibility does the developed world have to the developing world?

SANDY IRVINE:
The Limits of Green Consumerism (1989)

The development of a green conscience is a relatively recent phenomenon. This new sensibility is responsible for the growth of environmental awareness, increased membership in organizations such as Greenpeace, and the success of Green political parties. It is also responsible for green consumerism—shopping for environment-friendly products. The following article, originally published in The Ecologist, *outlines the limits of individual choices.*

From Sandy Irvine, "The Limits of Green Consumerism," in *Canadian Dimension* (October 1989), pp. 22–24.

. . . In terms of choice between green and ungreen consumerism, it is clear which variety anyone who cares about the future should support. Nevertheless, there are crucial limitations to the successes this approach can achieve by itself. It is not just that it is wide open to being cynically hijacked by the established interests in business and politics. Rather, it is that the construction of a better world requires a collective and political restructuring of our institutions. This in turn depends upon a clear diagnosis of what is wrong with society and what must be done to put it right.

Green Consumerism Is Still Consumerism

Responsible 'shopping around' fails to escape the logic and limitations of consumerism as a whole.

The central thrust of green consumerism is the rejection at the shopping counter of 'flawed' goods and services in favour of a more benign ones. However, in the absence of other changes, this risks merely substituting one type of hazard for another. Many green consumers, for example, advocate natural materials instead of synthetics yet, at present levels of population and living standard expectations, this amounts to a switch from the resource depletion and pollution of oil production and processing to the hazards of cotton monoculture and large-scale sheep grazing.

Green consumer guides also discuss at length products from renewable sources. It is, of course, true that those resources based on solar energy and biological systems do replenish themselves, unlike the world's once and for all endowment of minerals. However, because of the diffuse and variable nature of solar energy sources and because of the physical, ecological and moral limits to what can be taken from populations of plants and animals, renewable resources cannot underwrite present human numbers and lifestyles. They only become appropriate in the context of a greatly scaled down society—which can only come about through structural changes to society through the exercise of political power.

There is in fact a considerable literature demonstrating that scientific fixes for social and environmental problems are more likely to multiply the problems than solve them. As Paul Ehrlich and John Holdren have memorably commented, "those that believe that science will pull a technological rabbit out of the hat to save us at the last minute suffer from an inability to learn. Technological rabbits . . . usually have large appetites and abundant noxious droppings."

Sustainable Development?

Underlying the current green consumer boom is the idea that with careful housekeeping, we can somehow have our cake and eat it—that, in fact we can have growth that is sustainable. Indeed, the word 'sustainability' pops up these days in one official report after another. It is now even being used as an argument for such environmentally and socially inappropriate technologies as nuclear fusion, large-scale wind turbines, solar power 'towers,' megadams, food irradiation and recombinant genetic engineering.

However, in a finite, ecologically interconnected and entropy-bound world, belief in sustainable growth is no different to a belief in perpetual motion. Sustainable growth is a contradiction in terms. In practice, 'sustainable' production has been responsible for displacement of human communities, intolerable health hazards, much cruelty to animals, and destruction of other species in general.

'Sustainability' is too easily equated with efficiency in terms of production of this or that resource for purely human material needs and often merely private profit. The 'scientific management' of America's forests, for example, justified the replacement of old woods by uniform tree factories in which toxic spraying has threatened wildlife and humans alike. The same story is repeating itself in the destructive and cruel fish farms 'blossoming' around Scotland. It can be seen in all those National Parks which have been increasingly yoked to a new production industry—mass, organised leisure—to the detriment of the very things that they were intended to preserve. Lands belonging to local peoples and local species have often been drowned to provide 'sustainable' hydroelectricity.

Green Producers, Consumers and the Growth Economy

The most important driving force behind our environmental crisis is the sheer size of the throughput of energy and materials through the economy. Even if their produce is based on renewable resources and less polluting production processes, business' enterprises are locked into a spiral of overdevelopment that is colliding with the rhythms, tolerances and capacities of the environmental systems on which all life depends.

Not only is the total human economy overgrown, so too are its institutional components, not least business enterprises. Because of this they are able to manipulate the consumer to their advantage and frustrate attempts to make them serve the needs of local communities and local environments. The production and retailing of environment-friendly produce does not make a transnational owned factory or a chain store any more democratic or responsive. Profits are still repatriated outside the local community while local branches are first to be closed when the remote headquarters decides to cut back on its activities.

Advertising: Massaging the Message of More

The modern advertising industry provides the crucial link between mass production and mass consumption. It is big business with a vengeance, bombarding us daily with messages about every area of life. The public images of leading politicians are as carefully managed as those of toilet cleaners, and as accurate.

The very dynamic of advertising multiplies the social and ecological disruptions caused by mass industrialism. It seeks to exploit our hopes and fears by harnessing them into the purchase of this or that commodity. Modern ideas about marketing proceeded hand-in-hand with the innovations in production by Henry Ford and his kind. Both depend on discouraging self-reliance on one's own resources and judgment, and on encouraging weakness and dependence. Advertising is based upon the creating and maintenance of a state of unease and dissatisfaction. Who we are and what we own become blurred together in an unreal world of style, fashion and image.

Advertising encourages every form of waste, from unnecessary model changes to gimmicks to differentiate identical products. Its paraphernalia disfigure townscapes and landscapes. Its bottom line can only be more environmental destruction. This in turn can only become a marketing opportunity as the consequent scarcity of what many communities had at hand—open space, wildlife, clean streams—creates a chance to market what still survives or to hawk technological substitutes.

Corporate Greed and Government Regulation

Enlightened consumerism is therefore fundamentally constrained by the nature of the society in which we live. This raises questions about power and vested interests in society.

In fact, many promising initiatives have been stifled by corporate greed, government regulations, land ownership patterns, taxes and subsidies that discriminate against them. Moreover, many wasteful and polluting goods are alluringly cheap because they do not incorporate the full costs of their production, passing them on to the environment at large. Only the exercise of governmental power can remedy this. Similarly, without such protection, green consumerism will also provide a golden opportunity for the unscrupulous to cash in on public concerns. We are charged more for unsliced wholemeal bread, which has not been expensively refined, then for its sliced white imitation.

Limits To Individual Decision-Making

However, the most fundamental case for a collective approach is the way in which what is individually and what is publicly rational can diverge. Green consumersim still embodies much of the mythology of the sovereign consumer, supposedly the economic equivalent of the voter at the ballot box. Even if the green consumer has all day to go from one store to another checking prices and labels, it is still often very difficult to know which is the best buy. It is far from easy to know where products have originally come from, what has gone into them, how long they will last, etc.

More generally, the short-term disadvantages of collectively appropriate changes in lifestyle often outweigh personal benefits. For example, a household which buys expensive waterway-friendly washing powders from the socially friendly wholefood shop around the corner is out of pocket compared to its neighbours who are destroying lakes, seas, and rivers with the phosphates contained in the cheap supermarket brands. Individual acts of responsibility might make one feel good but are otherwise futile if most other people continue to behave irresponsibly.

It is not surprising therefore that many of our long-term problems are caused by the cumulative consequence of all those little decisions we make, so insignificant in themselves but so disastrous in total. The long-term price is resource depletion, pollution and environmental degradation. Any answer to these problems must start from a recognition of just how difficult it is for individuals to take account of this dynamic of collective ruin in their daily decisions, especially in the anonymous mass society of industrialism. We need social institutions that act as the custodian of the collective conscience, and must not just put out eggs in the basket of individual self-transformation.

Changing the Institutional Framework

What is necessary is not just a private, but also a collective approach in which society sets down appropriate parameters for technological choice and economic activity. Political decisions are necessary to set the outside limits within which market mechanisms can operate. . . .

We need to think in terms of the sustainable and balanced satisfaction of different kinds of present and future needs—material, psychological and spiritual—and those of other species. This is true ecological sustainablity. We would not try to satisfy the aspirations of one community, culture or generation by destroying other species. Within this framework we can begin to devise lasting ways of supplying the needs of a truly worthwhile society.

Ecological sustainability is a potent concept if set in the context of the limits to growth and the rights of both future generations and other species. If not, it will be a cloak for yet more manipulation and exploitation.

---

1. According to the author, what are the limits of green consumerism?

2. The author points out that the institutional framework of modern Western civilization must be changed to produce ecological sustainability.

(a) Discuss the steps that would be necessary to implement change of this magnitude.

(b) How could these changes be implemented in a democratic society?

ANALYSIS AND APPLICATION

1. Write a short paper on the role played by the Augustinian monk, Gregor Johann Mendel (1822–1884), in modern genetics.

2. Read Joseph Wambaugh's novel *The Blooding,* a true account of the first genetic fingerprinting case in Britain. Outline the steps involved in uncovering the identity of the murderer.

3. (a) Discuss the conflict between the rights of the community and the rights of an individual suffering from a disease such as AIDS.
   (b) Discuss the question of euthanasia for patients who are terminally ill with diseases such as cancer or AIDS.

4. Defend or refute the following statement: *In the nineteenth century it was the railroad that spurred industrial development; in the second half of the twentieth century it was the race for space.*

5. Prepare a collage to highlight the discoveries made by space probes.

6. Write a short paper outlining the benefits that society has derived from developments in the computer industry from 1945 to today.

7. Stage a two-person debate with the following resolution: *The benefits of nuclear energy outweigh the costs.*
   (a) Have each participant prepare a position paper outlining his or her point of view.
   (b) Using formal debating procedures, present the arguments, allowing time for rebuttal.

8. Discuss the ways in which communications technology has created a global village.

9. Stage a two-person debate between an environmentalist and an industrialist on the issue of economic growth vs. environmental concerns. Follow the procedures outlined in question 7.

10. Conduct a panel discussion on the issue of destroying the rain forest. Role play the various panel members; these should include aboriginal peoples, developers, environmentalists, scientists, and representatives from local, national, and international governments.
    (a) Have each participant prepare a position paper outlining his or her point of view.
    (b) The questioning of panel members by the class should be controlled by a moderator.
    (c) Prepare a paper which uses the data from the discussion to support your thesis on the issue.

11. Create an editorial cartoon depicting the interlocking crises outlined in *Our Common Future.*

CHAPTER FIFTEEN

Themes for Our Times

SEARCHING FOR VALUES

In the postwar era, Western civilization tried to define a new set of values to govern human behaviour. As we saw in chapter 11, one school of thought, *logical positivism*, had already emerged prior to the end of the war and it flourished after 1945. Logical positivists felt that recent discoveries in science and the emergence of new scientific disciplines such as psychology and sociology had taken over much of the ground formerly covered by philosophical questions and replaced it with data based upon scientific research. For logical positivists there were only two types of statements which had meaning. The first were those that were tautological—that is, merely a definition, such as "a triangle is a three-sided plane figure" in which "triangle" and "three-sided plane figure" are the same thing. The second type of meaningful statement was one that could be proven through sensory observation or experience such as "boiling water is hot." To logical positivists, all other statements were meaningless, including metaphysical discussions such as those on the nature of truth or the existence of God. The only area they believed was still open to philosophical examination was the study of science itself. Logical positivists were concerned with the nature of scientific reasoning and attempted to apply the test of logic to the conclusions reached by "pure" scientists.

Through the work of writers like Bertrand Russell (1872–1970), symbolic logic became an effective tool for the philosophical analysis of the concepts derived from research. Russell and Alfred North Whitehead (1861–1947) tried to create a new "logical language" through which scientists could express their findings. Rejecting metaphysics and superstition, logical positivists had no interest in determining appropriate moral values or beliefs. They were more interested in describing the nature of the world as a product of logical relationships and interconnections. Their realm was that of the observable and provable.

The second major challenge to the established philosophic and religious order also had its roots before 1945. But if the period between the wars had been an age of anxiety, the new age was one of experimentation and change.

Sartre and Existentialism

Jean-Paul Sartre (1905–1980) contended that individuals can be sure of nothing except their own immediate actions. In his existentialist view, there were no predetermined norms or values that humanity should follow. In such an environment, the critical act for each human was that of choice. As Sartre said in *Existentialism and Humanism* (1948): "If man . . . is not definable, it is because to begin with he is nothing. He will not be anything until later, and then he will be what he makes of himself. Thus, there is not human nature, because there is no God to have a conception of it."

Not only do the decisions we make determine who we are as individuals, they also determine what the world is like. Each decision sets off its own unique chain of events; consequently, it also closes the door on an infinite number of "futures" that reflect the ramifications of alternative choices—the "might have beens." Choice places a burden of responsibility on the individual, resulting in the continual state of anxiety that is central to existentialist thinking.

The existentialists' world view is one of subjectivity. For Sartre, the greatest human adventure was the discovery of the self. Selfhood is based upon consciousness and it is that consciousness that distinguishes humanity from the rest of nature. The individual human is called the "being-for-itself" because only humans can be aware of their own existence. All other life belongs to the realm of "being-in-itself"—that is, possessing no "capacity for reflection upon their own existence or the world they inhabit."

Consequently, for Sartre, the world only has that meaning which we subscribe to it. For instance, consider a man without money who lives in Vancouver and is in love with a woman who lives in Japan. To that man, the Pacific Ocean is an insurmountable barrier to his happiness. A wealthy woman, however, standing on the beach looking out to sea sees the Pacific in a totally different way. For someone of wealth, the ocean may be crossed and recrossed without a second thought, or perhaps she might have all that she needs within her own community. In either case, the ocean is not a barrier to her happiness; in fact, in its natural beauty it may bring her great pleasure.

What is different about these two cases? Certainly not the nature of the Pacific Ocean. What separates the cases is the meaning that each individual ascribes to that ocean. Alone it has no objective meaning; its existence as either a barrier or as a source of pleasure is based upon the subjective judgment of the observer.

The human observer, then, has the choice to interpret the world as she or he sees fit. Life, as existence, has no more meaning than the Pacific Ocean. But life as a series of conscious choices becomes meaningful. "I am not what I am," says Sartre. "I am a host of possibilities, none of which is completely realized; and I am what I am not: I am no longer the past that I was, and I am not yet the future that I will be. Completeness is always beyond my grasp."

Sartre's beliefs were expanded upon by the French author Albert Camus (1913–1960), who contended that freedom of choice was the essence of being human. For Camus and most existentialists, with the freedom to choose came the responsibility for the choices made. And responsibility for one's actions was what made individuals human.

Simone de Beauvoir (1908–1986), a lifelong associate of Sartre, based her thoughts on the liberation of women on

ALBERT CAMUS

Albert Camus was born in the French colony of Algeria in 1913. Raised in North Africa, he eventually moved to France, where he became a journalist. During the Nazi occupation, Camus became an active member of the Resistance and edited an undergound newspaper called Combat. *In addition, he began to write novels, including one of his greatest,* The Stranger *(1942). After the war Camus retired from journalism to devote more of his time to writing novels. His major works,* The Plague *(1947),* The Rebel *(1952), and* The Fall *(1956), led to his being awarded the Nobel Prize for Literature in 1957. Three years later, Camus was killed in a road accident in what the English newspaper* The Guardian *described as "a terrible blow to French literature."*

In an address to a group of French artists in 1950, Camus outlined his view of the contemporary world:

We live in a time of ideologies, of totalitarian ideologies, ideologies so sure of themselves and of their imbecile reason, and their narrow truth, that they can see the salvation of the world only in their own domination. The wish to dominate someone or something is a wish for sterility, it is to desire the silence or death of someone. . . .

There is no life without dialogue. And over most of the world today dialogue is replaced by polemics. The twentieth century is the century of polemic and insult. Among nations and individuals, and even within disciplines which were formerly disinterested, it holds the place traditionally occupied by thoughtful dialogue. . . . The mechanism of polemic . . . consists of considering the adversary as an enemy, consequently to simplify him and to refuse to see him. When I insult a man I cease to know the nature of his expression, the character of his smile. Made three-fourths blind thanks to polemics we no longer live among men, but in a world of silhouettes.

existentialist principles. (See chapter 12). In *The Second Sex* (1949), de Beauvoir contended that the traditional role of women was not biological but was based on social conditioning. ("One is not born, but rather becomes, a woman.") The postwar period saw women, who had been a vital part of the nonmilitary war effort, revert back to traditional roles within the home and family. De Beauvoir saw this in existentialist terms. She said that women must make active choices to be independent and not simply to accept the passive role of a domestic slave. All women, said de Beauvoir, had the freedom to choose "an independent existence . . . [which would] abolish the slavery of half of humanity."

RELIGION AND WESTERN SOCIETY

Christianity

The horrors of the Holocaust and of the Second World War itself called into question the enduring strength of Christian values in late twentieth century Western society. The Roman Catholic church entered a new period of reform beginning with the Second Vatican Council in 1962. Called by Pope John XXIII (1881–1963), it encouraged a movement away from the highly centralized authoritarian practices of the past. This attempt to reconcile the church with the modern world was continued by his successor, Paul VI (1897–1978), who called for efforts to fight hunger, poverty, and social injustice. This pro-active approach to social and political issues has been continued by Pope John Paul II (1920-). Although a conservative on issues such as birth control, abortion, the ordination of women, clerical celibacy, and the active participation of priests in politics, John Paul has proven to be an international activist on human rights issues. Dubbed John Paul "superstar," the pope travels around the world and does not hesitate to speak openly on local political and social issues. In spite of his personal popularity and the rapid growth of Roman Catholicism in the developing world, however, the influence of the church in Western society has continued to decline.

This change in outlook by the established church did not occur in a vacuum. Theologians such as Dietrich Bonhoeffer (1906–1945), Paul Tillich (1886–1965), and Martin Buber (1878–1965) had been calling for a reassessment of the role of organized religion since the 1940s. They stressed that new scientific insights about the nature of the universe had made traditional ideas obsolete. Rather than looking upward for salvation, they argued, humanity should look inward. (See readings.)

Televangelism

Mass media began to influence religion during the postwar era. Building upon the radio evangelism of the Depression, modern fundamentalist Christian groups began to broadcast their messages on television beginning in the 1950s. In the United States in particular, by the 1970s "televangelists" had established a sizable following as they made their weekly pitch for a return to basic Christian values. Using such techniques as faith healing and testimonials, this new generation of religious promoters raised billions of dollars from personal contributions.

Building on their popularity, leaders of this Moral Majority commanded considerable political influence as well. During the Reagan presidency in the United States, they reached their peak of power, only to see it rapidly decline as a series of scandals revealed questionable moral character and illegal financial dealings by some of the highest profile religious leaders. In spite of this setback, however, the simple message of the evangelist struck a responsive chord in many people in Western society, who continued to look for basic "truths" in a rapidly changing world.

Judaism

Christianity was not the only Western religion to experience a change during the postwar era. Western European Judaism had been devastated by the Holocaust, which had claimed the lives of 6 million Jews. Former religious centres such as Warsaw, Prague, and Vienna were decimated and few Jewish survivors returned to them after the war. Many Jews turned away from the anti-Semitism of Western civilization and emigrated to the Middle East; after centuries of persecution, they were determined to build their own homeland. The result was the creation of the independent state of Israel in 1948 after 2000 years of Jewish statelessness.

Since the end of the war, Jewish communities in Europe and North America have attempted to preserve the memory of the Holocaust, not just as a memorial to those who died but as a reminder to modern Western civilization about what atrocities and injustices can happen even in our enlightened society. Despite these efforts, however, in the early 1990s anti-Semitism seemed to be on the rise. With the political liberalization of Eastern Europe, right-wing, anti-Jewish slogans and groups have re-emerged. In East Germany, an election rally in the spring of 1990 included hundreds of young "skinheads" goose-stepping through the city of Leipzig chanting Nazi slogans. In Romania, the nation's 140 000 Jews have been accused of being in league with the regime of deposed leader Nicolae Ceauşescu. Currently Israel is negotiating for exit visas for all Eastern European Jews who wish to emigrate to the Middle East.

The revival of anti-Semitism is not limited to Eastern Europe, however. In France, Britain, Canada, and the United States, the spring of 1990 witnessed desecration of synagogues and Jewish cemetaries as neo-Nazi sentiments emerged in these countries as well.

Further cause for concern is the increase in Holocaust denial and Jewish conspiracy theories. Activists such as Ernst Zundel in Toronto and Malcolm Ross in Moncton have tried to defend their right to publish anti-Semitic materials under the freedom of speech provisions of the Canadian Charter of Rights and Freedoms.

On the positive side, however, Poland, whose prewar Jewish population of 3.5 million was virtually eliminated, has promised to improve the position of the remaining 7000 Jews in the country. The Czech government of Vaclav Havel has also made efforts to recognize its Jewish citizens by appointing Jews as ambassadors to Washington and Moscow.

New Challenges

As traditional Judeao-Christian beliefs were re-examined in the postwar decades, the massive immigration to Western Europe and North America radically changed the makeup of the religious landscape. As a result, modern Western civilization has experienced a radical increase in Islamic, Sikh, Hindu, and Buddhist populations. This new, more heterogeneous society will continue to challenge many of the traditionally held beliefs and customs of Western civilization.

THE ARTS AND SOCIETY

Rapid social changes in the second half of the twentieth century were reflected in an explosion of creativity in the arts. The new affluence of the postwar era combined with an increase in government patronage to provide a fertile environment for the expansion of the artistic community. If traditional social norms disappeared, so too did artistic conventions. If Western tradition had been challenged at the beginning of the century, by the end of the 1900s challenge and change themselves had become Western traditions.

The Visual Arts

Abstract Expressionism

With Europe still recovering from the ravages of war in the late 1940s, New York emerged as a new centre of Western culture. In painting, the undisputed leader of this "new Paris" was the American Jackson Pollock (1912–1956).

Pollock built upon many of the techniques of the surrealists. In 1944, he stated that he had been impressed by certain European painters such as Picasso and Miro because to them the source of all art was in the unconscious. Pollock attempted to free his work from the pictorial images of the surrealist movement. To him, such images came from the superficial level of the subconscious—what Freud termed the pre-conscious. His approach came to be known as *abstract expressionism*. Pollock believed that the artist had to delve deeper in order to release not an unconscious image, but an unconscious sensation. It was his goal to create "concrete pictorial sensations" free from any association with the artist's memory—in other words, to give the painting a "life of its own."

Some modern critics have claimed that abstract expressionism has more in common with the work of charlatans than that of artists—that is, that the artists are only pretending to be experts on artistic expression. For many critics the concept that the artist expresses her or himself and then the viewer appreciates that expression has little to do with the true purpose of art. They argue that the artist should create a "worldly object," independent of her or his feelings. Pollock agreed. He intended for his art to have a "life of its own," leaving it up to the viewer to react to it emotionally. But the painting itself should not express those emotions; it should merely provoke them in the same way that a beautiful sunset might create an emotional response.

Other abstract expressionist artists included the American Mark Rothko (1903–1970), whose paintings characteristically featured large bands of colour of different hues arranged parallel to one another (in sharp contrast to the frenzied energy of Pollock) and the Scot Alan Davie (1920–), whose strong ornamental style, accentuated by his interest in myths and magic, created some of the most powerful images of this century.

JACKSON POLLOCK:
The Painting Has a Life of Its Own

Abstract impressionism created considerable controversy among some critics, often not because of the paintings themselves but because of the techniques the artists employed. The following describes the methodology of Jackson Pollock.

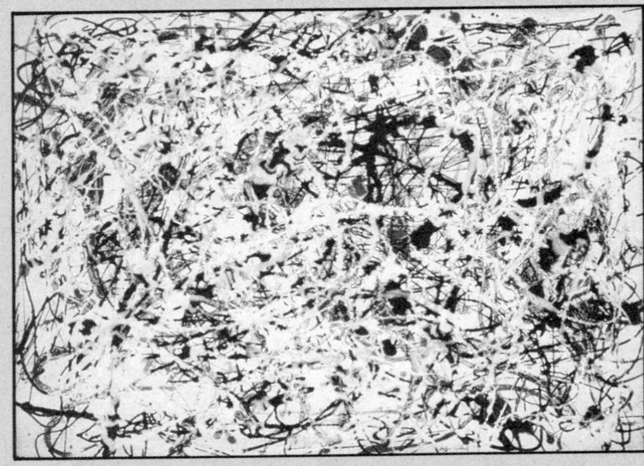

Jackson Pollock's paintings, such as Composition #1 *(1948), marked the ascension of the United States to a leading role in Western art.*

[Pollock's] method has become a legend—the unstretched canvas on the floor, the use of sticks, trowels, knives and dropping fluids, the occasional use of sand or broken glass—all these dodges have usually been interpreted as a means to automatism. But Pollock's aim, as he said, was to get in his painting, to become part of the painting, walking round it and working in all directions, like the Indian sand painters of the West. "When I am in my painting, I'm not aware of what I'm doing. It is only after a sort of 'get acquainted' period that I see what I have been about. I have no fears about making changes, destroying the image. etc., because the painting has a life of its own. I try to let it come through. It is only when I lose contact with the painting that the result is a mess. Otherwise there is pure harmony, an easy give and take, and the painting comes out well.

Pop Art

In the 1950s, the art market became established as part of the consumer culture. Unlike earlier eras in which artists were commissioned to produce specific works or painted to be included in a show, the contemporary artist creates with one eye on the marketplace. Modern art has emerged as a good investment. Corporations decorate offices and public waiting areas with expensive originals as assets rather than reproductions of past masters. As this practice grew in popularity, it began to mirror the values and norms of Western society. American artists such as Jasper Johns (1930-), Robert Rauschenberg (1925-), and Andy Warhol (1930–1987) began to incorporate graphic and photographic materials into their paintings. Johns and Rauschenberg are often mistaken as pop artists, but in actual fact they represent a synthesis of abstract expressionism and a desire to present commonplace objects as images. From their work, however, emerged the pop art movement. Pop art was a style based on the products of modern consumer society and popular culture such as soup cans, coke bottles, comics, and advertisements. Centred in London and New York, pop art was intended to reprocess popular imagery and to present a radical alternative to traditional values in the fine arts.

English painter Richard Hamilton (1922-) was known for his pop art montages of various images. In 1957 he listed the qualities of pop:

Popular (designed for a mass audience)
Transient (short-term solution)
Expendable (easily forgotten)
Low-cost
Mass-produced
Young (aimed at youth)
Witty
Sexy
Gimmicky
Glamourous
Big Business

Perhaps the most famous examples of pop art are Andy Warhol's *100 Cans* (1962), in which he depicted Campbell's Soup cans as a subject for a still life, and Roy Lichtenstein's *Whaam!* (1963), an adaptation of comic-strip techniques exploiting the bright colours and sharp images of commercial graphics.

In Europe, the pop movement was characterized by such artists as Martial Raysse (1936-) from France, Oyvind Fahlstrom (1928-) from Sweden, and Peter Phillips (1939-) from England. The English school took a different tact from its American and continental contemporaries. Peter Blake (1932-) focused on nostalgic themes and completed a pop-style illustrated version of Lewis Carroll's *Through the Looking Glass*. David Hockney (1937-) used visual puns and spread contemporary images in almost random "graffiti-esque" fashion across his canvases. Like their American counterparts, however, these artists were interested in bridging the gap between art and everyday life. In addition, artists such as Rauschenberg supported the view of composer John Cage (see page 490), who believed that if the spectator's mind could be "unfocused" from its grounding in everyday reality, she or he would become more aware of the world around them. To accomplish this "unfocusing," artists staged "hap-

Roy Lichtenstein's Whaam! *was an example of pop art's attempt to expand the parameters for viewing and understanding art.*

IS IT ART?

The National Gallery's controversial $1.8 million American painting, *Voice of Fire,* could be:

- Sold to provide money to buy Canadian paintings.
- Hung sideways to save space.
- Reproduced as a tie.

These are among a variety of suggestions the House of Commons culture and communications committee had for the gallery director Shirley Thomson yesterday. She was defending the art purchase, paid for with tax dollars.

Tory Al Horning (Okanagan-Centre) wanted to know how the painting "saves my farmers who are going broke from the devastating cares of everyday life."

Thomson said the painting's impact could be compared to the playing of great music like Bach's St. Matthew Passion.

The work by American "minimalist" Barnett Newman is a floor-to-ceiling canvas, 5.4 metres (18 feet) long by 2.4 metres (8 feet) wide, consisting of a red stripe on a blue background.

Committee chairman Felix Holtmann showed up sporting a *Voice of Fire* necktie. The Manitoba pig farmer offered no apology for a previous statement that he could have painted the same thing for a few dollars.

Thomson and gallery officials said the painting is on the "cutting edge" of art and has nearly doubled in value since it was bought in 1987.

Tory Larry Schneider of Regina suggested selling the painting and using the money to buy Canadian art.

Instead, the members voted to uphold the arm's-length relationship between the government and the gallery.

Holtmann asked whether *Voice of Fire* could be shown on its side to make it easier to display in smaller museums. "That would make it a landscape," a gallery official observed dryly.

Reprinted with permission—the Toronto Star Syndicate.

penings" to shock and surprise viewers. So respected did this practice become that one university in California actually established a chair in happenings in the 1960s.

The happenings movement in the United States gave birth to the fluxus movement internationally. Fluxus aimed to release the individual from all physical, mental, and political inhibitions. It was disruptive and anti-authoritarian and placed more emphasis on the process of creating art rather than the final product. The fluxus movement, like dadaism, saw the barriers between different facets of the arts as artificial. As a result, a fluxus festival included not only painters and sculptors, but musicians, dancers, and poets.

Many observers have felt that the art world has become so compartmentalized and specialized in the past few decades that it has lost much of its social relevance. In his assessment of the state of painting in the late twentieth century, art historian Herbert Read observed: "Painting has become a highly restricted language and interest, a specialist activity in a society rigidly divided into specialist fields, the result of positivist and materialist thinking."

The commercialization of art in the late twentieth century has led some observers to conclude that art is simply a product to be bought, displayed, and discarded when it is no longer in fashion. Art has come to be identified as a specific discipline, isolated from other aspects of Western culture. Such compartmentalization, according to Read, is a product of the French Revolution and specialization of the industrial world. As a result, art may become focused on the physical technique rather than on the spiritual motivation. Read concludes by offering this warning about isolating art from other fields of human endeavour:

> The result is modern man's alienation, his inability to relate spirit and material, or to comprehend the totality of the world. In this divided world, art still stands as an activity without predetermined confines. When this open brief is accepted negatively, it leads to the dead-ends and the triviality that have characterized much of recent art. Taken as a challenge, it could forge a new and expanded concept of art as an interdisciplinary activity, bridging fields of knowledge and linking man's polarities: his intuition and his intellect; chaos and order.

From Herbert Read, *A Concise History of Modern Painting.* (New York: Oxford University Press, 1974), p. 322–324.

Sculpture

Developments in sculpture in the postwar era have been the most inventive of the visual arts. Spurred on by the development of new media, sculpture has once again returned to the renaissance tradition of site-specific constructions and massive commissioned public works.

Canada produced several outstanding sculptors during the 1950s and 1960s. Robert Roussil (1925-) based his work on that of British sculptor Henry Moore (1898–1986). Using the basic structural qualities of his materials (cast-iron, gold, copper, stone, clay, and wood), he created distinct abstract works. Roussil usually focused on humans and birds; his work is characterized by its slender forms, curved edges, conical surfaces, holes, and rings.

New schools of sculpture have appeared since the Second World War. *Constructivism* used wood, glass, and industrial materials to express the nature of modern society; Alexander Calder (1898–1976) used this same approach in his mobiles. It was expanded during the 1960s and 1970s in "found art." Often called *assemblage* or *collage*, this form of sculpture utilized ready-made materials, found objects, and fragments. Louise Nevelson (1899–1988) created box-like enclosures, each with a carefully chosen composition of assembled objects. In such a composition, the media could range from empty boxes and cans from a supermarket shelf to steel, wire mesh, and broken machinery. Everything became part of an integrated whole. American David Smith (1906–1965) and British sculptor Anthony Caro (1924-) set new standards in their use of clean linear lines of steel in their sculpture.

The 1980s saw Western sculptors bring a new generation of materials to their art, such as neon tubing and molded fibreglass. With the increase in interest in art for public institutions, artists have begun to work in closer co-operation with architects to create sculptures to fit a specific site. This new trend is illustrated in Michael Snow's geese sculpture which flies high over the concourse in Toronto's Eaton Centre and in the gargoyle-like fans who lean precariously over the entrance to the city's Skydome. As a result, by the 1990s sculpture seemed to be reaching out to a new generation of appreciative patrons.

Henry Moore

Henry Moore was the leading British sculptor of the twentieth century. His early sculpture was widely criticized by the popular press, partially because of his practice of piercing his

HENRY MOORE: Notes on Sculpture

Appreciation of sculpture depends upon the ability to respond to form in three dimensions. That is, perhaps, why sculpture has been described as the most difficult of all arts; . . . Many more people are 'form-blind' than colour-blind. The child learning to see first distinguishes only two-dimensional shape; it cannot judge distances, depths. Later, for its personal safety and practical needs, it has to develop (partly by means of touch) the ability to judge roughly three-dimensional distances. But having satisfied the requirements of practical necessity most people go no further. Though they may attain considerable accuracy in the perception of flat form, they do not make the further intellectual and emotional effort needed to comprehend form in its full spatial existence.

This is what the sculptor must do. He must strive continually to think of and use form in its full spatial completeness. He gets the solid shape, as it were, inside his head—he thinks of it, whatever its size, as if he were holding it completely enclosed in the hollow of his hand. He mentally visualizes a complex form *from all round itself*: he knows while he looks at one side what the other side is like; he identifies himself with its centre of gravity, its mass, its weight; he realizes its volume, as the space that the shape displaces in the air.

And the sensitive observer of sculpture must also learn to feel shape simply as shape, not as description or reminiscence. He must, for example, perceive an egg as a simple single solid shape, quite apart from its significance as food, or from the literary idea that it will become a bird. And so with solids such as a shell, a nut, a plum, a pear, a tadpole, a mushroom, a mountain peak, a kidney, a carrot, a tree-trunk, a bird, a bud, a lark, a ladybird, a bullrush, a bone. From these he can go on to appreciate more complex forms or combinations of several forms.

From Henry Moore, "Notes on Sculpture" from *Sculpture and Drawing*, Vol. 1, 4th ed., edited by David Sylvester and Percy Lund, Humphries and Co. Ltd., Publisher.

figures with holes in an attempt to achieve a balance between the material and created space. It was not until the 1940s that he achieved international acclaim, partly because of the publication of an illustrated record of his work. In 1948, he won the International Prize for Sculpture at the Venice Biennale, an honour he would receive again in 1953 in São Paulo and again in 1959 in Tokyo.

Moore combined his interest in three-dimensional spatial construction with a romantic sensitivity for the material. He created a style that was recognizable as uniquely his own. Many of Moore's works were architectural sculptures (works designed to be in the open air), such as the *Reclining Figure* (1957–1958) in the forecourt of the UNESCO headquarters in Paris and *Archer* (1967) in Nathan Phillips Square at the Toronto City Hall. Moore once said, "I would rather have a piece of my sculpture put in a landscape, than in, or on the most beautiful building I know." The largest and most comprehensive public collection of Moore's work is exhibited in the Henry Moore Sculpture Centre at the Art Gallery of Ontario.

Henry Moore's The Archer *dramatically adorns Toronto's Nathan Phillips Square.*

Architecture

What little construction there was during the Second World War tended to be utilitarian and economical. By the late 1940s, however, a new generation of architects were applying the ideals of European modernism on both sides of the Atlantic.

One of the earliest proponents of the clean lines and symmetry of the modernist movement was Ludwig Mies van der Rohe (1886–1969). Escaping from Naziism in 1937, the German architect emigrated to the United States, where he found the money and artistic freedom to explore his talents. His most notable contribution to the cityscape was the reticulated skeletal building with highly polished metal and glass walls. The designs for his Lake Shore Drive Apartments in Chicago (1948–1951) acted as an inspiration to American architect Wallace Harrison, who constructed the United Nations Secretariat in New York City between 1947 and 1950. Van der Rohe's most famous building, the Seagram Building in New York (1954–1958), captured the style perfectly. In Canada, he acted as an advisor for the construction of the Toronto Dominion Centre (1964–1968).

Free-form architecture found its earliest expression in the Solomon R. Guggenheim Museum in New York City, built between 1956 and 1959. The architect was Frank Lloyd Wright (1869–1959). Cast from reinforced concrete, the Guggenheim was described by Wright as having "one floor flowing into another (more like sculpture) . . . [and] the net result of such construction is a greater repose, the atmosphere of the quiet unbroken wave."

The flags of the member states fly in front of the UN Secretariat in New York City.

Canada Place is characteristic of Eberhard Henrich Zeidler's incorporation of external structure and technological themes in his designs.

European architects, such as Viljo Revell of Finland, applied sweeping curves to constructions like the Toronto City Hall (1965), as did Canadian architect Raymond Moriyama (1929-), whose designs of the Ontario Science Centre (1969), Scarborough Civic Centre (1973), and Metropolitan Toronto Reference Library (1977) have won him international acclaim. Other internationally accomplished Canadian architects include Ron Thom (1923–1986) (Massey College, 1963; Shaw Festival Theatre, 1973); Arthur Erikson (1924-) (Simon Fraser University, 1963–1965; theme buildings for Expo '67, the Museum of Anthropology at the University of British Columbia, 1971–1977; Roy Thomson Hall, 1982; the Canadian Embassy in Washington, 1988); and Eberhard Henrich Zeidler (1926-). Zeidler was trained at the Bauhaus in Weimar, East Germany. He emigrated to Canada in 1951. His work is often characterized by external structural and technological themes such as exposed trusses and air ducts. Included among his more notable designs are Ontario Place (1967–1971), the Toronto Eaton Centre (1977), Queen's Quay Terminal (1979–1983), and Canada Place for Expo '86 in Vancouver.

The Frank Lloyd Wright design for the Guggenheim Museum seemed appropriate to house a collection of modern art.

Literature

Popular Fiction

Publishing in the postwar era has become big business. Modern novels are mass produced on low budgets. They are often written based on a standard formula, then thrown on the market and left to the whims of the reading public. The result is that about 80 percent of all novels published are financial failures. Fortunately for the publishing industry, however, it takes only five bestsellers to support every one hundred books published. As a result, the market has been saturated with second-rate publications and many good novels have been lost in the crowd.

The majority of the books published in the West have been characterized as "pulp" or popular fiction. This "new" medium contains elements of the nineteenth-century serial and the detective novel of the 1920s and 1930s. However, it does boast a wide range of genres and can claim a variety of successful authors, such as John Le Carré and Robert Ludlum (spy novels); Isaac Asimov, Arthur C. Clarke, Frederick Pohl, and Frank Herbert (science fiction); Mary Renault, James Michener, and Gore Vidal (historical fiction); and Danielle Steele and Judith Krantz (romance), to name just a few.

A New Literary Generation

The 1950s and 1960s also saw the final few publications of the greats of the previous generation. W.H. Auden published *The Age of Anxiety* (1947); Ernest Hemingway *The Old Man and the Sea* (1952); William Faulkner *A Fable* (1955); and John Steinbeck *The Winter of Our Discontent* (1961). To a great extent, however, most of these authors had already produced their best and most influential works prior to 1945. In the postwar era, their work was being eclipsed by a new generation of writers. Saul Bellow (1915-), born in Quebec, lived most of his life in the United States. His short novel *Seize the Day* (1956) is a starkly detailed story of a day in the life of Tommy Wilhelm, an out-of-work sales executive. Typical of Bellow's characters, Wilhelm is an introspective, contemplative hero "whose anger and pain are turned chiefly on himself." Bellow was one of the first of a postwar generation of Jewish writers that included Norman Mailer (1923-), Phillip Roth (1933–), and Mordecai Richler (1931-). Their work tends to be male-centred, with the protagonists characterized by an individual struggle against over-regimentation and assimilation.

Another genre of the era is the protest novel. This was first expressed in Joseph Heller's (1923-) *Catch 22* (1961). The novel outlines the events of the Second World War from the standpoint of the disillusionment of the postwar period. Heller legitimatizes the conscientious objector and has his hero, Yossarian, reject the dehumanizing bureaucracy and the living death which it represents. The social criticism in Heller's work is paralleled by that of Jack Kerouac (1922–1969) who identified the characteristics of the new postwar youth, most notably in his book *On the Road* (1957), and the black protest writer James Baldwin (1924–1987). Baldwin's *The Fire Next Time* (1963) is a stinging indictment of the treatment of blacks in the United States. For Baldwin, as for many black protest writers, future integration seemed an impossibility.

Kurt Vonnegut, Jr. (1922-) followed Heller's technical lead in his blackly humorous portrayal of the values of modern society. The hero of *Slaughterhouse 5* (1969) becomes unstuck in time and drifts in and out of different incidents in his life. As almost a dispassionate observer of his own existence, he is able to pass comment on the human condition.

A third innovation of the postwar period is the nonfiction novel. Seemingly paradoxical, the genre often results in the author putting her or himself into the action. Norman Mailer's (1923-) *Armies of the Night* (1968) is ostensibly a documentary account of the homefront during the war in Vietnam. In actual fact, however, it is an account of Mailer's own coming to terms with the conflict. Tom Wolfe takes the same tact in *The Electric Kool-Aid Acid Test* (1968), as does Hunter Thompson, in *Fear and Loathing in Los Angeles* (1972).

Several outstanding female authors have gained recognition since the Second World War. Joyce Carol Oates (1938-) has written about the struggle for liberation of working-class women. For Oates, the women's movement is a parallel to the New World experience of breaking out from old patterns and reshaping life to meet new challenges. Toni Morrison (*Sula*, 1973; *Tar Baby*, 1981) has taken Oates's theme and applied it to the struggle of black women to free themselves. Morrison's characters insist on the same personal rights as their male counterparts—sexual liberation, freedom of movement, and indifference to familial commitments. To a great extent, Morrison attempts to provide a model for black lower-class women that parallels that provided for white middle-class women by Betty Friedan. Canadian writer Margaret Atwood's (1939-) writing reflects an underlying theme of women's alienation from society. Beginning with *The Edible Woman* (1969), her work demonstrates an unerring crafting and precision of language and is characterized by a satirical, reflexive approach. Her international reputation has been secured through the publication of such works as *The Handmaid's Tale* (1985) and *Cat's Eye* (1988).

Other major authors whose work has risen to prominence during the period include Canadians Mordecai Richler (*The Apprenticeship of Duddy Kravitz*, 1959), Robertson Davies (*Fifth Business*, 1970), Margaret Laurence (*The Stone Angel*, 1964), and Timothy Findlay (*The Wars*, 1977); English authors Graeme Greene (*The Comedians*, 1966), John Fowles (*The Magus*, 1966), and George Orwell (*Nineteen Eighty-Four*, 1949); Germany's Herman Hesse (*Sidhartha*, 1951), and Gunter Grass (*The Tin Drum*, 1958); France's Albert Camus (*La Peste*, 1947), and Jean-Paul Sartre (*Black Orpheus*, 1971); Russians Boris Pasternak (*Dr. Zhivago*, 1958) and Alexander Solzhenitsyn (*One Day in the Life of Ivan Denisovitch*, 1963); and Americans Philip Roth (*Goodbye, Columbus*, 1960), John Updike (*The Centaur*, 1964), Katherine Anne Porter (*Collected Stories*, 1966), J.D. Salinger (*The Catcher in the Rye*, 1951), Anne Tyler (*The Accidental Tourist*, 1986), Norman Mailer (*The Naked and the Dead*, 1948), and John Irving (*The World According to Garp*, 1975).

Drama

Traditional theatre saw the addition of such works as *A Streetcar Named Desire* (1947) by Tennessee Williams (1911–1983), *Death of a Salesman* (1949) by Arthur Miller (1915-), *The Life of Galileo* (1955) by Bertolt Brecht (1898–1956), and *A Man for All Seasons* (1960) by Robert Bolt (1924-). Williams was highly varied in his subject matter and style. Through his plays he called into question what he referred to as the "horror of insincerity, of not meaning" that overlay social interactions in Western society. The setting of one of his most famous works, *The Glass Menagerie* (1944), is described by the author as one of those huge urban apartment buildings that are "always burning with the slow and implacable fires of human desperation." Williams's work reached an audience of millions through film, although the original power of his plays was often emasculated to make them more popular with the movie-going public.

Miller wrote tragedies, which he believed was the one road to personal enlightenment, a "condition of life . . . in which the human personality is able to flower and realize itself." In *Death of a Salesman*, he takes the pathetic Willie Loman and transforms his personal failures into a more symbolic tragedy for postwar Western society. Loman, a pseudonym for "everyman," is caught in a downward spiral of unrealized expectations. The ultimate product of consumer society, the salesperson, he is unable to reap any of its tangible benefits. His son Biff saw through his dilemma and the dilemma of Western society in general in his comments at his father's funeral: "He had the wrong dreams. All, all wrong."

Theatre of the Absurd

If the work of authors such as Williams and Miller continued the dramatic traditions of Western theatre, then existentialist thought gave birth to a new school. Called the *theatre of the absurd*, it presented the view that life was pointless, with no order to history, no pattern, and no relationship between intention and outcome. Theatre of the absurd abandoned the usual literary devices; rather than a series of scenes connected together to build a cohesive story, it provided "a pattern of images presenting man as a bewildered being in an incomprehensible universe."

The first drama of this genre was Eugene Ionesco's (1912-) *The Bald Soprano* (1950). This was followed by such works as Samuel Becket's (1906-) *Waiting for Godot* (1953) and Jean Genet's (1910–1986) *The Balcony* (1957). Edward Albee (1928-) once wrote that he was deeply offended to be told that he was "a member in good standing" of the theatre of the absurd, for he believed that the really absurd theatre was "the theatre uptown—Broadway." He claimed that theatre was a reflection of the health of society, so if television sitcoms were all that people wanted, then society was morally bankrupt. Albee critiqued Western society in general and life in the United States in particular. In his preface to the *American Dream* (1961), he wrote that his work was "an examination of the American Scene, an attack on the substitution of artificial for real values in our society, a condemnation of complacency, cruelty, emasculation, and vacuity; it is a stand against the fiction that everything in this slipping land of ours is peachy-keen."

In *A Zoo Story* (1959), Albee examines the nature of human alienation through Peter, a textbook writer who is sitting on a park bench reading, and Jerry, a passerby who engages Peter in a bizarre conversation about his trip to the zoo. The play is a struggle between Jerry's need to be noticed and Peter's desire to defend his own privacy. The play ends with Jerry's violent accidental death at the unwitting hands of

Peter. In *A Zoo Story*, Albee demonstrated the potentially tragic results of indifference and inaction and called upon people to demonstrate compassion for their fellow human beings.

Although Albee received a Pulitzer Prize in Literature for *A Delicate Balance* in 1967, most critics feel that his greatest play was *Who's Afraid of Virginia Woolf?*. The principal characters in the play are George and Martha (named after George and Martha Washington) whose failed lives reflect the bankruptcy of the American dream in the late twenthieth century. A powerful film version of the play has made this one of Albee's best known works.

Music

The music of modern Western civilization experienced the same crises that affected all facets of society in the latter half of the twentieth century. The conflicts between freedom and order, tradition and innovation, young and old, all found their place in music.

Prior to the twentieth century, music, like most fine arts, was the captive of the patron system. But with innovations such as the phonograph, film, and radio, great music suddenly became accessible to everyone regardless of wealth or class. Two examples of this new access in the years prior to the Second World War took place in the United States. In 1937, the great composer and conductor Arturo Toscanini (1867–1957) took over the leadership of the NBC Symphony. For the next seventeen years, until he stepped down at the age of eighty-seven, Toscanini drew millions of North Americans to their radios every Sunday afternoon. At almost the same time, Leopold Stokowski (1882–1977) began a two-year project with Walt Disney using the symphonic piece "The Sorcerer's Apprentice" as the basis for an animated short feature. The result was *Fantasia* (1940), one of the most revolutionary musical films ever produced.

In fact, the movies and radio were accelerating the spread of a new cultural literacy in music. The result was the growth in popularity of not only the work of classical composers, but the appearance of a new generation of modern greats, such as Americans Aaron Copeland, Roger Sessions, and Leon Kirchner and Canadians Murray Schafer and Harry Somers.

John Cage

In the postwar era, challenges to the traditional musical establishment came from many directions. French composer Edgard Varese (1883–1965) felt that sounds rather than melody, harmony, and rhythm were the essential components of music. His ideas were taken a step further by the American experimental composer John Cage (1912-). Cage is best known for his compositions for prepared piano. This preparation meant placing screws, nuts, bolts, paper, felt, thumbtacks, and paperclips between the piano's strings and on the hammers themselves. The results were remarkable. Cage's compositions produced a variety of new sounds and vibrations. This exploration of different possibilities was of far greater interest to the composer than devising a new tune or melody. In one instance, Cage staged a happening in Cambridge, Massachusetts, which he entitled *Harvard Square*. Placing a piano on a traffic island in the centre of a busy intersection, he started a stopwatch, closed the keyboard lid, and waited. Finally he opened the lid again, stood up, and took his bows, to the thunderous applause of the large crowd that had gathered to watch him. What was the performance? Cage was using the sounds of the city—traffic, street noises, and casual conversation—as his composition.

The famed avant-garde composer John Cage delivered a lecture at Harvard University in 1976.

Jazz

Jazz also continued to evolve during this period. Sometimes called the most democratic of musical forms because it allows each musician to make a spontaneous contribution, jazz has boasted some of the most outstanding musicians of the twentieth century, including Americans Louis Armstrong (1900–1971), John Birks "Dizzy" Gillespie (1917-), Charlie "Yardbird" Parker (1920–1955), vocalist Ella Fitzgerald (1918-), and Canadian Oscar Peterson.

Jazz became popular in Europe in the 1920s and 1930s. However, it was not until the late 1940s that the style became widespread in Canada, primarily through the efforts of cornetist Jimmy "Trump" Davidson (1908–1978). Today jazz is characterized as traditional or Dixieland, mainstream, improvised, or fusion. Primarily urban music, jazz is well established in major cities throughout North America and Western Europe. Clubs such as The Cellar in Vancouver, the Yardbird Suite in Edmonton, George's Spaghetti House in Toronto, and Café St. Michel in Montreal draw a regular clientele. Harbourfront in Toronto hosted Canada's first jazz festival in 1979. This was followed in 1980 by major festivals in Edmonton and Montreal. So quickly did the popularity of these events grow that by 1986 the ten-day long Festival International de Jazz de Montréal attracted over 400 000 people.

The Emergence of Rock and Roll

The real centre stage in the postwar period belonged to rock and roll. Emerging in the 1950s, rock combined black and white traditions in music, contained a rhythm and blues component, and used country and western ideas and the traditional folk ballads of protest. During the 1950s, the rock music scene was dominated by American artists such as Chuck Berry (1926-), Peggy Lee (1920-), and Elvis Presley (1935–1977).

Elvis Presley

Elvis Presley was originally a country and western performer. His first country hit was "Mystery Train" in 1954. Within two years he had released his first rock tune, "Heartbreak Hotel" (1956), which topped the American charts for eight straight weeks. It was followed the same year by "Hound Dog," "Don't Be Cruel," and "Love Me Tender." Presley occupied the number one spot for twenty-five weeks in 1956. The secret of his popularity was twofold. Presley had managed to combine many of the elements of rock music, rhythm and blues, and country and western, which gave his music a broad-based audience. And in addition to the music, there was the show. Presley had spent considerable time watching the performances of black musicians and he copied their sexually charged gyrations in his performances. So erotic were his actions that television host Ed Sullivan, under public pressure, broadcast Elvis's performances from the waist up only.

Much of Presley's early impact was due more to shock value rather than to any substantial contribution to music. At the time, he was accused of corrupting the morals of the young. It is more accurate to say, however, that Elvis Presley was a reflection of the changing values of his times rather than the cause of them. A combination of postwar affluence in North America and renewed economic stability in Europe had created a young generation that was beginning to reject many of the values of its parents.

The Beat Generation

American author Jack Kerouac called this new generation of youth the *beat generation*. The beat movement offered an alternative view of society. Rejecting traditional Western values, the beats (or beatniks) advocated voluntary poverty and communal living. They rejected political and personal commitment and called for a more introspective life complete with sexual freedom and extensive drug use. Although representing only a small percentage of society, the beats were an extreme example of the alienation that characterized the youth of the period. Initially the beats identified with the "cool jazz" of artists such as saxophonist Stan Getz (1927-). And as this counterculture grew in influence, its poetry began to form the basis for protest songs in coffee houses throughout Europe and North America. This folk music of the beat generation remained an essential part of the youth subculture through the 1960s.

The Beatles

The mid–1960s saw the "British invasion" of rock. Led by The Beatles and The Rolling Stones, rock music explored new directions. American rock and roll had started to follow a formula; by contrast, the music of The Beatles seemed fresh and original. After five years of experimentation, The Beatles emerged on the North American scene well-formed and established. Beginning their professional careers in Germany and then their native England, The Beatles added to the international flavour of modern popular music. Their lyrics called for companionship and compassion rather than

During the 1960s, Beatlemania swept the culture of the Western world. The music of The Beatles remains extremely popular today, even though the group disbanded in 1970.

the raw sex of rock and roll. Combining the talents of writers/composers John Lennon (1940–1980) and Paul McCartney (1942-), The Beatles left a legacy of compositions that have already become an integral part of modern music. A generation later, their influence still reverberates around the musical world and their style of flamboyant behaviour and gentle ballad-style rock is still in evidence in the work of such artists as Madonna, Phil Collins, Elton John, Billy Joel, and Tracy Chapman.

The more hard-driving approach of The Rolling Stones was based in another tradition of the period. Emerging about two years later than The Beatles, The Rolling Stones drew more extensively on rhythm and blues. They rejected what they saw as the homogenized style of The Beatles and those groups that imitated them and combined more discordant, rasping music with raunchy, suggestive lyrics. Their legacy still finds voice, not only in that group itself but in such aggressive musicians as Aerosmith and Mötley Crüe.

The Hippie Movement

The music of The Beatles reflected the views of the successors to the beat generation. Called "hippies" or "flower children," they supported the antiwar movement of the 1960s and 1970s. Universities became home to this counterculture. Primarily white and middle class, these students rejected the old values of power politics that had led to the war in Vietnam and the nuclear arms race. Like the beats of the previous decade, their culture included a belief in relaxed sexual morals and the liberal use of "soft" drugs. The event that came to characterize this generation was the Woodstock Music and Art Fair. Held in August 1969, Woodstock was a three-day "love in" where between 300 000 and 400 000 young people gathered to listen to music and indulge their lifestyles. Jerry Rubin was an active member of the Woodstock generation. In 1969, he summarized the sentiments of the era: "Screw work. We want to know ourselves. But of course the goal is to free oneself from American society's sick notion of work, success, reward, and status and to find and establish oneself through one's own discipline, hard work, introspection." However, in the 1970s the hippie generation began to fade. A tightening of drug laws, growing feminism, and tougher economic times made the affluent counterculture a part of history. Today Jerry Rubin is a stockbroker on Wall Street.

The Rock Concert

In many ways, Woodstock was the ultimate manifestation of another musical phenomenon, the rock concert. The mass hysteria and huge crowds first drawn by Elvis Presley and later by The Beatles has become the norm for public performances. The concert hall, now too small, has been replaced by the hockey arena or football stadium as a more appropriate venue. Aided by massive amplification equipment, giant video screens, and space-age pyrotechnics, modern performances are more "events" than actual concerts. With high-quality digital tapes and compact disc recordings, most fans listen to the music at home and attend the shows just to see their idols in action.

Musical groups used to go on tour to promote a new song or album. By the late 1980s, however, it was the concert itself that had become big business. In 1988, for example, the top-grossing concert series was performed by The Grateful Dead at Madison Square Garden in New York City. Receipts from the eight-performance series totaled $2.9 million.

Single concerts were potentially lucrative as well, and beginning in the 1980s many performers used their box-office draw to raise money for charitable causes. A concert held in Philadelphia in September 1988 to raise funds to fight for human rights worldwide, the Human Rights Now! tour featuring Bruce Springsteen, Sting, Peter Gabriel, Tracy Chapman, Youssou N'Dour, and Joan Baez, raised over $2.6

million. A second performance staged in Los Angeles two days later raised a further $1.9 million.

The greatest benefit concert ever held was a worldwide phenomenon in July 1985. Rock musician Bob Geldof co-ordinated mass concerts in Philadelphia and London to raise money for famine relief in Africa. Live Aid was broadcast to almost 2 billion people in over 150 countries and resulted in pledges totaling over $70 million. Canada's contribution was *Tears Are Not Enough* (1985), written by singer Brian Adams and Vancouver composer David Foster.

Musical Technology

Technology helped to change the face of music in the post-war period. The record album, recorded in stereo by the early 1960s, was supplanted first by the eight-track and then the cassette tape in the 1970s. By the 1980s, things had changed again. Coupled with the compact disc, the major musical innovation of the 1980s was the music video. Evolving out of early rock films, such as The Beatles' *A Hard Day's Night* (1964) and *Help* (1965), the rock video gives the performer/composer/producer an opportunity to reinforce the message of the music with powerful imagery. By the 1990s, no urban centre in North America was without a television station devoted almost exclusively to broadcasting music videos.

The Musical Legacy

Western rock and pop music has become a global phenomenon. Although some types of popular music have been short-lived or regional, the hard-driving rock of the 1950s, the ballads of the 1960s, and the black motown music of the 1960s and 1970s have formed the basis of popular music worldwide. There have also been revolutionary changes in musical technology. Today synthesizers and computers often replace backup musicians and bands. As recording technology has expanded and home stereo systems have improved, the concert hall has gradually been replaced by the living-room stereo. The result has been greater musical perfection for the performer, but the social aspects of a shared concert experience have been exchanged for the solitude of the perfect listening experience.

As with most periods in the study of Western civilization, popular music has merely reflected popular culture. The radical changes in Western music since the Second World War have been a window on the radical changes in society as well.

POPULAR CULTURE

The Westernization of Global Culture

> In a culture like ours, long accustomed to splitting and dividing all things as a means of control, it is sometimes a bit of a shock to be reminded that, in operational and practical fact, the medium is the message."
>
> Marshall McLuhan, *Understanding Media: The Extensions of Man* (New York: McGraw-Hill Book Co., 1964), p. 23.

Canadian media expert Marshall McLuhan (1911–1980) challenged traditional Western thinking when he contended that the means of communication was actually more important than the message being communicated. Building on the work of historian Harold Adams Innis (1894–1952), McLuhan pointed out that the structures of industrial society had been based on the printed page. He used the traditional classroom as an example. The teacher, he said, represented the title at the top of the page. The students and their desks, arranged in neat and equally spaced rows, were like interchangeable blocks of type. As the printed page began to lose its influence during the television revolution, the traditionally structured classroom began to disappear as well. The new structure of the education system was interactive and immediate. The classroom environment became filled with a wealth of images and technologies such as taperecorders, computers, and videocassette recorders. For McLuhan, this was no coincidence.

The culture of modern Western civilization has never been so homogeneous as it is in the late twentieth century. Students in Germany, France, and the United States all listen to the same music, watch the same movies, and wear the same fashions. With the physical destruction of Europe during the Second World War, much of that continent was rebuilt with American money in the American image. Coupled with a new technology that put this new Americanized image of Western society into every home, regional differences began to break down. By the late twentieth century, only remote pockets of Europe and North America were still isolated from the mainstream of Western culture. Even these outposts of tradition had by the early 1990s begun to construct satellite dishes to receive broadcasts from the industrialized world. For many observers, this phenomenon marked "the end of ideology" and the emergence of the affluent consumer society.

In his book *The Affluent Society* (1958), Canadian-born economist John Kenneth Galbraith (1908-) contended that the consumer-oriented society of the postwar period was ignoring the infrastructure of social support agencies that were necessary to divide prosperity more equitably. In spite of his warnings, however, the United States and other Western nations traded many basic human concerns for economic prosperity. Detractors of this value system called it anti-human, claiming that the worth of individuals was being measured not in terms of who they were but what they owned and consumed. This Americanization of global cultural values was accelerated by the extensive economic and military networks established by the United States government and American-based multinational corporations.

Increasingly, Western cultural norms have been shaped by American advertising, films, and television programs. In Japan, for instance, television is saturated with commercials—about twice as many per hour as in North America. Recognizing that one product is not much different from another, these commercials concentrate on image rather than substance. For many Japanese, American images are associated with progress and sophistication. However, this has created a growing rift between a younger generation that is increasingly Western in dress, outlook, and aspirations and an older generation that is trying to hold on to traditional practices and values.

Companies like McDonald's (pictured here in Japan) spread Western culture around the globe.

American Culture in Canada

The impact of Americanization has often been debated in Canada. Rapid urbanizaton since the end of the Second World War has meant the adoption of some American mistakes, such as the overdependence on the automobile, the disposal of garbage, and the rapid consumption of arable farmland. Facing the full impact of American cultural imperialism, Canadian governments have attempted to erect artificial barriers as a defence. Modern Canadian radio and television programming is governed by a fixed percentage of Canadian content, and even football teams are required to keep a minimum number of Canadians on their rosters. This cultural "national policy" means that Canadian taxpayers contribute ten times more per capita than their American neighbours in support of the artistic community. In spite of these controls, however, American influence in Canada has continued to grow. Between 1969 and 1979, viewership of the CBC dropped by one-third, while the number of Canadians watching American programming increased by one-quarter. By the end of that period, eight out of the top ten television programs watched by Canadians were American in origin.

Western Culture vs Native Tradition

Western cultural imperialism has met its greatest resistance from North American Native peoples. There are over 500 000 aboriginal Canadians in 1990. About 1.5 percent of the population, they represent an indigenous culture that has refused to be assimilated into the mainstream of Western society. During the nineteenth century, Native peoples in Canada were disenfranchised and relegated to reserves comprising a small fraction of their original landholdings. With traditional means of support removed, these people became increasingly dependent upon government largesse to survive. This dependence led to an erosion of traditional values and cultural pursuits, so that by the postwar period Native culture was threatened with extinction. Over the past forty years, however, conditions have changed. Demanding that the Canadian government live up to the Western ideals of self-determination and justice, Native leaders have pressed for compensation for lands taken by earlier governments. Backed by a 1973 Supreme Court decision, various Canadian federal and provincial governments have so far paid out $150 million in compensation and returned 70 000 ha of land to Native control.

Many of the traditional assumptions about the innate superiority of Western culture have come into question in the 1980s and 1990s. The environmental movement has brought worldwide attention to the damage caused by rapid industrialization and many North Americans have looked to Native peoples for leadership in devising ways to live in greater harmony with the natural world. Western societies are now taking a second look at the values of the cultures they overran.

The Carriers of Culture

Film

The Western film industry experienced a boom in the 1940s and 1950s. Closely tied to the war effort, films often carried a patriotic message to soldiers and civilians alike. After 1945, technological advances began to change the look of films. Advanced camera and sound equipment, colour photography, and eventually videotape took film out of the studio and moved it to locations around the world. As films expanded in scope and budget, so did their market. American films in particular received worldwide distribution and the Hollywood star system set up Americans as global role models.

After this boom period, however, the film industry began to decline in influence during the 1960s and 1970s. Television began to attract the loyalty of former moviegoers. By the 1980s, however, the new video technology had brought the movie theatre right into the home and the increased revenues brought a renewed vigour to the industry.

Film tended to reflect social values. *Bonnie and Clyde* (1967) and *The Godfather* (1972) helped commercialize violence. In both cases, violent criminals were romanticized and brutal killings were presented in a stylized form, such as the slow-motion riddling of Bonnie's body by machine-gun bullets. The rejection of traditional religious values was typified by the satanism of *Rosemary's Baby* (1968). In *2001: A Space Odyssey* (1968), humans triumphed over machines as the menacing computer HAL was disconnected. But in the 1986 sequel, *2010: the Year We Make Contact*, society's change in attitude toward computers was reflected as HAL was depicted as a sentient being. Film also confronted contemporary social issues such as race relations (*To Kill a Mockingbird*, 1962; *Guess Who's Coming to Dinner?*, 1967), mental illness (*One Flew Over the Cuckoo's Nest*, 1975), the war in Vietnam (*The Deer Hunter*, 1978), and divorce and child custody (*Kramer vs Kramer*, 1979).

Among the significant American films produced during the period were black comedies such as *Dr. Strangelove* (1964) and *M★A★S★H* (1970); science fiction such as *The Day the Earth Stood Still* (1955) and the *Star Wars* trilogy; and dramas such as *The Manchurian Candidate* (1960), *Taxi Driver* (1976), *Reds* (1981), and *Rainman* (1988).

Worldwide the film industry also flourished. Nations such as Czechoslovakia (*Closely Watched Trains*, *The Unbearable Lightness of Being*), France (*Jean de Florette, Manon of the Spring*), Germany (*Das Boot, The Tin Drum*), Australia *Gallipoli*), Great Britain (*Hope and Glory, Room with a View*), Greece (*Z*), and Canada (*The Apprenticeship of Duddy Kravitz*, *I've Heard the Mermaids Singing*, *The Decline and Fall of the American Empire*) all developed excellent films. Although still over-shadowed by American film-makers, other Western nations have begun to challenge American domination of the industry.

The Television Generation

Popular culture in the late twentieth century has been both shaped and transmitted by television. Many parts of the world, long isolated from the influences of Western civilization, are now linked by satellite to the full range of Western programming. Like the film industry, the United States has dominated the global television market. Some Western nations, such as Great Britain, France, and Canada, have preserved strong local industries through government ownership and regulation. Even so, the televised norms of American society are readily available worldwide.

During the 1950s, television tended to reinforce traditional stereotypes about women, the family, and society. Programs such as *Father Knows Best*, *Leave it to Beaver*, and *The Donna Reed Show* depicted the family as white, suburban, and middle class, with the father the head of the household and the mother devoted to her domestic responsibilities. The implied sexism of *The Honeymooners* and *I Love Lucy* were also accepted norms during the decade.

By the 1960s, some of television's earlier taboos began to disappear. Politics, sex, and race relations were gradually being introduced to television screens. Programs appeared that reflected many of the values of the new counterculture. *The Life and Loves of Dobie Gillis*, for instance, followed the trials and tribulations of a working class youth and his beatnik friend trying to come to grips with life. The early sixties also saw the introduction of hard-hitting news programs such as *This Hour Has Seven Days* in Canada and *That Was the Week that Was* in the United States which investigated the political and social issues of the day. In the 1970s, the children's market became a prime target for North American programmers. Shows such as *Sesame Street* and *Electric Company* provided a free educational headstart for many children. Primetime programming also began to obtain some balance. Programs such as *All in the Family*, *The Jeffersons*, and *Mary Tyler Moore* exploded many of the existing stereotypes about blacks and women and reflected the changing values of the decade.

Public and educational television also emerged in the 1970s. In the United States, the Public Broadcasting System (PBS) brought quality programming to discerning viewers, relying on public funding for their operation base rather than commercial advertising. In Canada, TVOntario emerged as an educational network designed for children and adult learners in both the schoolroom and the livingroom.

The real impact of television, however, has nothing to do with actual programming. More akin to pulp fiction than serious literature, the majority of television shows have aimed at the lowest common denominator in Western society. Burlesque, spectator sport, and the tabloid have all been brought into the home by television. Although many commentators have contended that television reflects a debasement of Western culture, to a great extent it is merely the technological updating of a facet of popular culture that already existed.

The real concerns regarding television have been social ones. Television has affected the outcome of political campaigns, shaped public opinion of major issues, and desensitized many members of Western society to extreme violence and questionable moral values. Much of this violence has appeared not only via programs such as *Miami Vice* but as part of the daily news coverage. If society became increasingly violent during the 1970s and 1980s, so too did the graphic details of violence presented under the guise of journalism. This phenomenon has been particularly characteristic of the American media. In fact, research in the 1970s showed that on any given evening, CBS TV devoted up to 78 percent of its national news broadcasts to scenes and stories depicting violence. By comparison, on the same nights, the average coverage of violent stories by CBC TV in Canada was only 38 percent.

So important has television journalism become to publicizing issues that many events are tailored to meet television deadlines. During the crisis in the Persian Gulf in 1990, both Iraqi president Sadam Hussein and his American counterpart George Bush negotiated not through diplomats but through CNN, the Cable News Network. As one critic observed, "television has become the extension of diplomacy . . . it makes you wonder sometimes what the world is coming to when leaders are depending on a television operation to keep them informed."

American educator and social critic Neil Postman commented on the all-pervasive nature of television in *Amusing Ourselves to Death: Public Discourse in the Age of Show Business* (1985). In this excerpt, he outlines his concern that image is replacing substance in modern democratic society.

> Film, records, and radio . . . are, of course, equally devoted to entertaining the culture, and their effects in altering the style of American discourse are not insignificant. But television is different because it encompasses all forms of discourse. No one goes to a movie to find out about government policy or the latest scientific advances. No one buys a record to find out about baseball scores or the weather or the latest murder. . . . But everyone goes to television for all these things and more, which is why television resonates so powerfully throughout the culture. Television is our culture's principal mode of knowing about itself. Therefore—and this is the critical point—how television stages the world becomes the model for how the world is properly to be staged. . . .
>
> In courtrooms, classrooms, operating rooms, board rooms, churches, and even airplanes, Americans no longer talk to each other, they entertain each other. They do not exchange ideas; they exchange images. . . . For the metaphor of television is not only that all the world is a stage but that the stage is located in Las Vegas, Nevada. . . .
>
> The nature of . . . discourse is changing as the demarcation line between what is show business and what is not becomes harder to see with each passing day.
>
> From Neil Postman, *Amusing Ourselves to Death: Public Discourse in the Age of Show Business* (London: William Heinemann Ltd.)

Television has become the common social denominator in the 1990s. Conversations centre around news, sports, drama, and comedy witnessed second-hand rather than experienced. The release of Nelson Mandela, the armed stand-off at Oka, Quebec, and the massing of troops in the Persian Gulf were all part of the personal experiences of Canadians in 1990 through the medium of television. Some critics have argued that television creates new social values and norms. What is more likely is that television merely reflects who we are.

RETROSPECTIVE

If life is the product of a series of personal decisions and the world is fundamentally absurd, then perhaps the values of popular culture make sense in the late twentieth century. In the 1990s, social and political change, fueled by a rapidly advancing technology, have created the global village predicted by McLuhan in the 1960s. The last decades of the century have seen a contradictory trend in Western civilization. Technology and a rising standard of living have led to a more homogeneous, mass culture. At the same time, society has come to respect the rights of the individual to a far greater extent than during any period in the past. Many of the social and artistic norms that directed and constrained individual behaviour in the past disappeared in the postwar era. The result was an explosion of creativity and experimentation unprecedented in the previous three centuries.

BERTRAND RUSSELL: What Happens and What Is Observed (1958)

Bertrand Russell first responded to Einstein's theory of relativity in 1925. In this excerpt from the 1958 revised edition of his book The ABC of Relativity, *Russell attempts to examine Einstein's theories in simple language. A brilliant philosopher and mathematician, Russell was also an educator who wanted to show the average reader the ways in which the theory of relativity had revolutionized humanity's conception of the physical world and changed the course of science.*

A certain type of superior person is fond of asserting that "everything is relative." This is, of course, nonsense, because, if everything were relative, there would be nothing for it to be relative to. However, without falling into metaphysical absurdities it is possible to maintain that everything in the physical world is relative to an observer. This view, true or not, is not that adopted by the "theory of relativity." Perhaps the name is unfortunate; certainly it has led philosophers and uneducated people into confusions. They imagine that the new theory proves everything in the physical world to be relative, whereas, on the contrary, it is wholly concerned to exclude what is relative and arrive at a statement of physical laws that shall in no way depend upon the circumstances of the observer. It is true that these circumstances have been found to have more effect upon what appears to the observer than they were formerly thought to have, but at the same time Einstein showed how to discount this effect completely. This was the source of almost everything that is surprising in his theory. . . .

The physicist, like the plain man, believes that his perceptions give him knowledge about what is really occuring in the physical world, and not about his private experiences. Professionally, he regards the physical world as "real," not merely as something which human beings dream. An eclipse of the sun, for instance, can be observed by any person who is suitably situated. . . . The physicist is persuaded that something has really happened over and above the experience of those who have looked at the sun or at photographs of it. I have emphasized this point, which might seem a trifle obvious, because some people imagine that Einstein made a difference in this respect. In fact he has made none. . . .

If there were no reality in the physical world, but only a number of dreams dreamed by different people, we should not expect to find any laws connecting the dreams of one man with another. It is the close connection between the perceptions of one man and the (roughly) simultaneous perceptions of another that makes us believe in a common external origin of the different related perceptions.

1. How does Russell contrast the difference between reality and perception?

2. Contrast the logical positivist view as expressed by Russell with that of the existentialists.

ALBERT CAMUS:
The Plague (1947)

Albert Camus won the Prix des Critiques in 1947 for his book The Plague. *Considered to be his finest work, in it he chronicles the events surrounding the plague which hit Oran in 1940. Approachable on two levels, it is first seen simply as a narrative about those terrible events. However, Camus used the plague as a symbol, in this case a symbol for the Nazi occupation of France which began that same year. In this excerpt, the author recounts the emotions unleashed on the eve of "liberation" from the quarantine imposed by the plague.*

From Albert Camus, *The Plague* (Paris: Librairie Gallimard).

Though this sudden setback of the plague was as welcome as it was unlooked for, our townsfolk were in no hurry to jubilate. While intensifying their desire to be set free, the terrible months they had lived through had taught them prudence, and they had come to count less and less on a speedy end of the epidemic. All the same, this new development was the talk of the town and people began to nurse hopes none the less heartfelt for being unavowed. . . .

All agreed that the amenities of the past couldn't be restored at once; destruction is an easier, speedier process than reconstruction. . . . No doubt the plague was not yet ended—a fact of which they were to be reminded; still in imagination they could already hear, weeks in advance, trains whistling on their ways to an outside world that had no limit, and steamers hooting as they put out from the harbour across shining seas. . . .

At last, at daybreak on a fine February morning, the ceremonial opening of the gates took place, acclaimed by the populace, the newspapers, the wireless, and official communiquées. . . .

Elaborate day and night fetes were organized, and at the same time smoke began to rise from locomotives in the station and ships were already heading for our harbour. . . .

In the streets and squares people were dancing. Within twenty-four hours the motor traffic had doubled and the ever more numerous cars were held up at every turn by merry-making crowds. . . . Tomorrow real life would begin again, with its restrictions. But for the moment people in very different walks of life were rubbing shoulders, fraternizing. The levelling-out that death's imminence had failed to accomplish was realized at last, for a few gay hours, in the rapture of escape.

. . . as he listened to the cries of joy rising from the town, Rieux remembered that such joy is always imperilled. He knew what those jubilant crowds did not know but could have learned from books: that the plague bacillus never dies or disappears for good; that it can lie dormant for years and years in furniture and linen-chests; that it bides its time in bedrooms, cellars, trunks, and bookshelves; and that perhaps the day would come when, for the bane and the enlightening of men, it roused up its rats again and sent them forth to die in a happy city.

---

1. Speculate why Camus, writing in 1947, would use the symbol of the plague to recount the events of the Nazi occupation.

2. Comment on this passage as a description of the liberation of France.

3. Respond to Camus' last paragraph. What evidence is there in the late twentieth century that his "bacillus" is still alive and well in Western society?

YEHUDI MENUHIN AND GLENN GOULD: The Concert Hall vs the Studio (1979)

Some critics have said that high technology and the recording studio have taken the heart out of music. How, they ask, can the spontaneity of the artists show through if they are allowed a series of takes before they find the sound they are looking for? This criticism of the modern musician was answered in an interview by the late Glenn Gould (1932–1982). Gould, a brilliant Canadian pianist, was challenged by the highly talented musician and writer Yehudi Menuhin to defend the use of the studio rather than performing in public. (Gould stopped performing in public in 1964.)

From Yehudi Menuhin, and Curtis W. Davis, *The Music of Man* (Toronto: Methuen, 1979), pp. 290–295.

Gould: We've had this conversation before, Yehudi, and I suspect that what inhibits you from making full use of the technology is the fact that it compels the performer to relinquish some control in favour of the listener—a state of affairs, by the way, which I happen to find both encouraging and charming, not to mention aesthetically appropriate and morally right. . . .

It matters not to me whether I am "successful" in creating a performance through one take, or whether I do it with 262 tape splices. The issue is simply not important.

Menuhin: Take The Beatles, who started out playing in public spontaneously; by the time they became accustomed to crutches which enabled them to record tracks separately and put them all together, to add notes and take them away, they could no longer play in public because the public expected something else, having become accustomed to this form of recorded creation.

Gould: In a sense, that is also what happened to me. I found I was competing with my own recordings, which nobody can do really. My recordings represent my best thoughts. . . . It seems to me that there is no greater community of spirit than that between the artist and the listener at home, communing with the music. I would even go so far as to say that the most important thing technology does is to free the listener to participate in ways that were formerly governed by the performer. It opens up options he didn't have before.

Menuhin: That still doesn't invalidate the concert hall, the experience of which is essential, and remains the standard against which everything else is judged.

Gould: Nonsense, Yehudi. It was the standard until something else came along to replace it, which is exactly what the recording did; and the recording, surely, is now the standard against which the concert must be judged.

---

1. Precis the arguments put forward by Menuhin and Gould. In your own words, build on their argument, extending it through two or three more exchanges.

2. Some people feel that the music video has combined the audio purity of the recording studio and the visual impact of the live performance. To what extent do you feel that Menuhin would be satisfied with this compromise?

3. Listen to a recording by Glenn Gould. Through an interview or discussion with an expert musician (amateur or professional) raise the issues put forward by Gould and Menuhin in the context of the performance to which you have just listened.

SYLVIA ANN HEWLITT: A LESSER LIFE (1986)

Many observers in the 1980s believed that the gains of the feminist revolution had been more illusory than real. The main instrument of popular culture—television, film, and especially music videos—still tended to portray women as second-class citizens. Much of this lower status seemed to be founded in the economic ghetto in which many women found themselves.

During the 1950s and 1960s the economic status of women in North American society began to decline. In her book A Lesser Life: The Myth of Women's Liberation in America, *Sylvia Ann Hewlitt discussed the economic restraints imposed upon women by marriage and the changing nature of society.*

From Sylvia Ann Hewlitt, *A Lesser Life: The Myth of Women's Liberation in America* (New York: William Morrow and Company, Inc., 1986).

American women suffer immense economic vulnerability. They have less economic security than their mothers did and are considerably worse off than women in other advanced countries.

Way back in the 1950s a traditional division of labor gave women a substantial degree of financial security. Maybe many were stuck in bad marriages, but the man did go out every day and earn enough to support his family. In exchange the woman ran the home and brought up the children.

Fifties women pumped an extraordinary amount of energy into the emotional and cognitive development of their children and into supporting their husband's careers. . . . It was not the era of the dual-career family but of the two-person career. The competitive pressures of the male work world created great tensions, which the wife was supposed to offset by providing elaborate emotional support. . . . A wife was meant to liberate her husband's total energy for the job. She must maintain their home as an island of tranquility, and herself act as "sounding board," "refueling station," and "wailing wall." . . . In 1956 . . . an article for the *New York Times Magazine* described the male executive as being totally dependent on his spouse: "Without a capable wife to screen his speaking and social engagements, keep track of his personal finances, run his house and take care of his children, he would have been 'lost.' . . ."

The plain truth is that modern American women, liberated or not, have little economic security as wives and mothers, or as workers. They are squeezed between traditional and modern forms of financial security to an extent which is unknown in other societies.

Our mothers sought, and the majority of them found, economic security in marriage, but that avenue no longer offers any such guarantee. Because of stagflation, higher rates of unemployment, and much higher rates of divorce, men can no longer be relied upon to be family breadwinners. . . . The escalating divorce rate is a critical factor because with divorce men generally relinquish responsibility for their wives and often for their children. Thus the breakdown of marriage massively increases the disparity between male and female incomes. . . . After divorce the standard of living of the ex-husband rises 42 percent while that of the ex-wife (and her children) falls 73 percent. . . . Partly because of this economic fallout of divorce, 77 percent of this nation's poverty is now borne by women and their children. . . .

Women in other countries have better maintained the security of their marriage and have steadily improved the material conditions of their lives . . . [while] women in this country are becoming more and more vulnerable. Despite their legendary claims to power and privilege, American women actually face a bad and deteriorating economic reality. . . .

Traditional women are not dumb Barbie dolls. They are essentially correct when they say that they are worth more in the house than outside it. A wife is still "given" more money by her husband than she herself could earn at a job. All women need to do is look around them to realize that work for wages outside the home does not effectively free women because of the undervaluation of their work.

. . . women are paid too little in the labor force. And many traditional American women are clear-sighted enough to know it.

1. Account for Hewlitt's contention that "many housewives do not buy the argument that work outside of the home makes women sexually and economically independent of men. They see that the streets are cold, and that the women on them are tired, sick, and bruised."

C.P. SNOW: The Two Cultures (1959)

C.P. Snow expressed his concern that Western civilization was becoming polarized between the scientific, technocratic culture and the more humanistic one. In this lecture Snow outlines his views.

From C.P. Snow, *The Two Cultures: and A Second Look* (Cambridge: Cambridge University Press, 1965), pp. 2, 3–4, 5, 10–11, 16.

There have been plenty of days when I have spent the working hours with scientists and then gone off at night with some literary colleagues. I mean that literally. I have had, of course, intimate friends among both scientists and writers. It was through living among these groups and much more, I think, through moving regularly from one to the other and back again that I got occupied with the problem of what, long before I put it on paper, I christened to myself as the 'two cultures.' For constantly I felt I was moving among two groups—comparable in intelligence, identical in race, not grossly different in social origin, earning about the same incomes, who had almost ceased to communicate at all, who in intellectual, moral and pyschological climate had so little in common that instead of going from Burlington House or South Kensington to Chelsea, one might have crossed an ocean. . . .

I believe the intellectual life of the whole of Western society is increasingly being split into two polar groups. When I say the intellectual life, I mean to include also a large part of our practical life, because I should be the last person to suggest the two can at the deepest level be distinguished. . . . Two polar groups: at one pole we have the literary intellectuals, who incidentally while no one was looking took to referring to themselves as 'intellectuals' as though there were no others. . . .

Literary intellectuals at one pole—at the other scientists, and as the most representative, the physical scientists. Between the two a gulf of mutual incomprehension—sometimes (particularly among the young) hostility and dislike, but most of all lack of understanding. They have a curious distorted image of each other. Their attitudes are so different that, even on the level ground of emotion, they can't find much common ground. . . .

The non-scientists have a rooted impression that the scientists are shallowly optimistic, unaware of man's condition. On the other hand, the scientists believe that the literary intellectuals are totally lacking in foresight, peculiarly unconcerned with their brother men, in a deep sense anti-intellectual, anxious to restrict both art and thought to the existential moment. And so on. . . .

This polarization is sheer loss to us all. To us as a people, and to our society. . . .

There seems then to be no place where the cultures meet. . . .

---

1. Precis Snow's characterization of the nature of the two groups.

2. To what extent are his observations, made in 1959, still valid today?

3. Interview your science teacher and/or your English teacher. To what extent do you think that the "two cultures" problem exists in your school?

HAROLD ADAMS INNIS: Empire and Communications (1950)

Canadian historian Harold Adams Innis revolutionized perceptions of the economic history of North America with the publication of The Fur Trade in Canada *in 1930. Dubbed by the* London Times *as one of Canada's "few intellectual giants," Innis expressed fear that unique national cultures such as Canada's would be swept away by the wave of popular mass culture rolling out of the United States as American cultural imperialism extended throughout the Western world. In the last few years of his life, Innis assembled collections of his views on the impact of language and the means of communication upon society.*

From H.A. Innis, *Empire and Communications*. Reprinted by permission of University of Toronto Press.

The United States, with systems of mechanized communication and organized force, has sponsored a new type of imperialism imposed on common law in which sovereignty is preserved *de jure* and used to expand imperialism *de facto*. It has been able to exploit the tendencies toward imperialism which have emerged in members of the British Commonwealth. Canada has been used as a means of penetrating the British Commonwealth. Resistance to this influence can be made effective by adherence to common-law traditions and notably to the cultural heritage of Europe. The state and the Church have lost control in large areas of Europe as a result of successive periods of occupation, and survival in the West depends on their continual subordination and on a recognition of the cultural leadership and supremacy of Europe. States are destroyed by lack of culture and so too are empires and civilizations. Mass production and standardization are the enemies of the West. The limitations of mechanization of the printed and the spoken word must be emphasized and determined efforts to recapture the vitality of the oral tradition must be made. . . .

Concentration on a medium of communication implies a bias in the cultural development of the civilization concerned either towards an emphasis on space and political organization or towards an emphasis on time and religious organization. Introduction of a second medium tends to check the bias of the first and to create conditions suited to the growth of empire. . . . In the United States the dominance of the newspaper led to large-scale development of monopolies of communication in terms of space and implied a neglect of problems of time. Regional monopolies of metropolitan newspapers have been strengthened by monopolies of press associations. The bias of paper towards an emphasis on space and its monopolies of knowledge has been checked by the development of a new medium, the radio. The results have been evident in an increasing concern with problems of time reflected in the growth of planning and the socialized state. The instability involved in dependence on the newspaper in the United States and the Western world has facilitated an appeal to force as a possible stabilizing factor. The ability to develop a system of government in which the bias of communication can be checked and an appraisal of the significance of space and time can be reached remains a problem of empire and of the Western world.

---

1. Account for Innis's contention that the concentration on one method of communication tends to bias a civilization.

2. Why does Innis state that "mass production and standardization" are enemies of the West?

3. To what extent does the viewpoint expressed by Innis reflect the rejection by many Western intellectuals of the rapid spread of American popular culture during the postwar period?

MARSHALL McLUHAN: Understanding Media (1964)

Marshall McLuhan owed much of his early thinking on communications to the work of Innis. Although many of McLuhan's observations, such as the electronic creation of a "global village" and the assertion that "the medium is the message," have become almost clichéd with overuse, the fundamental observations he made still remain valid. The following excerpt is from Understanding Media.

From Marshall McLuhan, *Understanding Media* (New York: McGraw-Hill, 1964).

In the mechanical age now receding, many actions could be taken without too much concern. Slow movement insured that the reactions were delayed for considerable periods of time. Today the action and the reaction occur almost at the same time. We actually live mythically and integrally, as it were, but we continue to think in the old, fragmented space and time patterns of the pre-electric age.

Western man acquired from the technology of literacy the power to act without reacting. The advantages of fragmenting himself in this way are seen in the case of the surgeon who would be quite helpless if he were to become humanly involved in his operation. We acquired the art of carrying out the most dangerous social operations with complete detachment. But our detachment was a posture of noninvolvement. In the electric age, when our central nervous system is technologically extended to involve us in the whole of mankind and to incorporate the whole of mankind in us, we necessarily participate, in depth, in the consequences of our every action. It is no longer possible to adopt the aloof and dissociated role of the literate Westerner.

This is the Age of Anxiety for the reason of the electric implosion that compels commitment and participation, quite regardless of any "point of view." The partial and specialized character of the viewpoint, however noble, will not serve at all in the electric age. At the information level the same upset has occurred with the substitution of the inclusive image for the mere viewpoint. If the nineteenth century was the age of the editorial chair, ours is the century of the psychiatrist's couch. . . .

The aspiration of our time for wholeness, empathy and of awareness is a natural adjunct of electrical technology. The age of mechanical industry that preceded us found vehement assertion of private outlook the natural mode of expression. Every culture and every age has its favorite model of perception and knowledge that it is inclined to prescribe to everybody and everything. The mark of our time is its revulsion against imposed patterns. We are suddenly eager to have things and people declare their beings totally. There is a deep faith to be found in this new attitude—a faith that concerns the ultimate harmony of all being. Such is the faith in which this book has been written. It explores the contours of our own extended beings in our technologies, seeking the principle of intelligibility in each of them. In the full confidence that it is possible to win an understanding of these forms that will bring them into orderly service, I have looked at them anew, accepting very little of the conventional wisdom concerning them. One can say of media as Robert Theobald has said of economic depressions: "There is one additional factor that has helped to control depressions, and that is a better understanding of their development." Examination of the origin and development of the individual extensions of man should be preceded by a look at some general aspects of the media, or extensions of man, beginning with the never-explained numbness that each extension brings about in the individual and society.

1. Write a short story illustrating McLuhan's view with regard to the impact of media upon the way in which we view the world.

MASS MEDIA AND POPULAR CULTURE (1988)

Barry Duncan, in his book Mass Media and Popular Culture, *provides a wide range of viewpoints on various facets of popular culture in Western society. This series of excerpts begins with one by the author.*

From Barry Duncan, *Mass Media and Popular Culture* (Toronto: Harcourt Brace Jovanovich, 1988), pp. 16–18.

What is popular culture? It's skateboards and Cabbage Patch Kids, *Miami Vice* and *60 Minutes*, leather jackets and acid-washed jeans, McDonald's and Burger King, teen films and Rambo, Marilyn Monroe and Madonna, Diet Coke and exercise videos, Trivial Pursuit and Barbie dolls, *People* and *Rolling Stone*, talk show hosts and TV evangelists, shopping malls and drive-in movies. . . .

Mass media and popular culture are, first and foremost, businesses. Our economy is intimately connected with the marketing of the wares of media and pop culture. For example, $6 billion were spent on advertising in Canada in 1984, and an approximate $35 billion are spent each year on advertising in the United States. . . .

By examining these ideologies in popular culture and their value messages, we take the pulse of our society or, to borrow another metaphor, take a cultural barometer reading.

Gregory Hall commented on the fast-food industry in his 1983 work Ronald Revisited.

From *Ronald Revisited* by Gregory Hall. (Bowling Green, OH: Bowling Green State University).

. . . McDonald's has become a virtual religious experience for millions of Americans. Kottak [a professor from the University of Michigan] believes that McDonald's eateries, much like churches or temples, offer uniformity in an otherwise chaotic world. He says "From the rolling hills of Georgia to the snowy plains of Minnesota, with only minor variations, the menu is located in the same place, contains the same items and has the same prices. . . . We know what we are going to see, what we are going to say, what will be said to us and what we will eat." From that first request for a Big Mac to the final "Have a nice day!", every move is ritualized much like a religious service.

But the religious experience of McDonald's goes deeper than ritual. McDonald's is the Messiah carrying the new theology into a world of chaos: the Messiah whose Golden Arches are symbols heralding the new age of Yankee fast food technology. Eateries which are the same everywhere destroy the artificial boundaries of local custom and become a unifying force, bringing together all believers in a common personhood of those who have been cured of a Big Mac attack. This applies to the people of Europe and the Orient as well as Americans, because everyone must have a chance to believe. It is understandable why Steve Barnes, head of the McDonald's International Operations, says of the European campaign, "It's corny, but I feel like a missionary over here."

In this excerpt, Noreene Janus examines the impact of international marketing in her article "Cloning the Consumer Culture: How International Marketing Sells the Western Lifestyle."

From Noreene Janus, "Cloning the Consumer Culture: How International Marketing Sells the Western Lifestyle," in *Cultural Survival Quarterly*, Vol. 7, No. 2.

The common theme of transnational culture is consumption. . . . Campaigns suggest that solutions to human problems are to be found in individual consumption, presented as an ideal outlet for mass energies . . . a socially acceptable form of action and participation which can be used to defuse potential political unrest. "Consumer democracy" is held out to the poor around the world as a substitute for political democracy. After all, as the advertising executive who transformed the U.S. Pepsi ad campaign "Join the Pepsi Generation" for use in Brazil as "Join the Pepsi Revolution" explains, most people have no other means to express their need for social change other than by changing their brands and increasing their consumption. . . .

Transnational advertising [and its creation] . . . transnational culture strive to eliminate local culture variations. . . .

Since an important characteristic of transnational culture is the speed and breadth with which it is transmitted, communications and information systems play an important role. . . . [and] television is undisputedly the key communications development of our era.

---

1. Select one corporation or product that advertises internationally. Research differences among its campaign strategies, advertising materials, slogans, etc. outside of its home market.

ANALYSIS AND APPLICATION

1. Stage a debate between Bertrand Russell and Jean-Paul Sartre on the resolution: *The future is what you make it.*

2. Write a defence of the following thesis: *Society should not practice censorship under any conditions.*

3. Interview a cross-section of age groups about their attitudes toward religion and the church. What patterns, if any, did you discover? What do your observations suggest about the attitudes of different age groups?

4. If art reflects society, what did movements such as pop art and fluxus indicate about Western civilization in the 1960s and 1970s?

5. Research the impact of McDonald's or another fast-food chain on Western society. To what extent has the exportation of the fast-food concept exported Western values?

6. Do you regard the Westernization of global culture as a positive or negative trend? Defend your answer.

7. Read a book by Margaret Atwood. In a class forum, discuss to what extent her work reflects the mainstream view of Western society in the 1980s and 1990s.

8. Choose a musician or musical group from the postwar era and write an analysis of their contribution to contemporary music.

9. Review a current film. Identify the significance of the subject in terms of Western society.

10. (a) Conduct a survey of a typical evening's programming on television. List the programs by category, such as drama, situation comedy, or news. Which types of programs predominate?
(b) Choose one of television's highest rated programs in any category. View an episode of the program and write a critique of it.

EPILOGUE

Five centuries have passed since Christopher Columbus inaugurated the new age of European global expansion. Western civilization which, with the exception of the Crusades, had remained insular and isolated for over 1000 years now began to reach out and extend its influence worldwide.

The Europe that stepped onto the world stage in 1500 was a collection of diverse kingdoms, duchies, and city-states divided by language, culture, and religion. Strangely enough, however, it was this lack of unity that was to prove to be the dynamic strength of modern Western civilization.

In our study of the past 500 years, we have witnessed radical change. The relationship between the individual and the community has evolved from that of subject in an absolutist state to one of active participant in a modern democracy. As part of this process of change, philosophers and politicians have debated the nature of the relationship between the individual and the state. We have also been introduced to a variety of systems of social organization. In France, for example, the nature of the state has evolved through several stages. The proprietary state of Louis XIV became the republican French nation. The empire of merit under Napoleon became a bourgeois constitutional monarchy. The Third French Republic became a fascist corporate state during the Second World War. And now the pluralist democracy of the postwar era seems to be evolving into a component part of a larger European national and economic community.

In economic and technological terms, Western civilization in the late twentieth century bears little resemblance to its sixteenth-century forerunner. Agrarian Europe, transformed by the Industrial Revolution, became the crucible to worldwide industrial and technological growth. If nationalism was the dividing line that separated rival imperial powers, then economics was the driving force that sent them across the seas in search of new markets, raw materials, and potential colonies for their surplus populations. Military and economic competition led to an escalation in the pace of technological development. As a result, modern Western civilization outperformed its international competitors and eventually entered a period of global domination. By the late twentieth century, however, internal pressures and a resurgence of local autonomy worldwide had resulted in the gradual withdrawal of Western society from its global role. In its place has emerged a group of regional economies interrelated through bilateral and multilateral international trade agreements.

The industrial system that drove the Western economies in the nineteenth and early twentieth centuries has gradually been replaced by a new information-oriented system based on high technology and communications. In the industrial economy of North America, the shift in recent decades has been away from industrial employment in favour of service industry jobs as technology replaces people in formerly labour-intensive fields. In the Pacific Rim, a focus on high technology has given that region a decided competitive edge over Western civilization. By the beginning of the twenty-first century, however, the globalization of the economy may eliminate many of these regional differences.

The Scientific Revolution changed the world view of early modern Europe. By the eighteenth century a "cult of science" had taken hold of Western civilization. The application of the scientific method to all facets of society in the nineteenth century and its logical positivist successors in the twentieth century have considered science and scientific advancement to be the answer to humanity's problems. However, the twentieth century has also borne witness to the dark side of scientific achievement—the mass killings of the First and Second World Wars and the development of such "advanced" means of mass destruction as poison gas, fire bombing, and atomic and nuclear weapons.

In the postwar world a gradual change in attitude has resulted in a rejection of the view that science can resolve all of our problems. Increasingly, world opinion has come to recognize that humanity has been a destructive force in its relationship with the environment. As a result, Western society has started to take into account the environmental impact of its actions. For the citizens of the twenty-first century, the challenge of the scientific community will be to arrest and reverse the destructive trends of the recent past.

Throughout these changes the arts have remained an essential component of the human condition. In the traditional artistic fields of music, drama, poetry, dance, architecture, paint, and sculpture, new techniques, materials, and philosophies have given the various periods of Western culture their own unique flavour. The modern era has seen the emergence of new art forms, such as the novel, film, video, and electronically synthesized music, all of which have added new dimensions to creative expression.

To a great extent, the last century has seen a democratization of culture. More people in Western society have become literate and the nature of literature and drama has adapted to meet the needs of this new and broader based audience. The twentieth century has also seen the emergence of a global culture. Some critics argue that this has simply taken art to its lowest common denominator, but others contend that it has provided access to sophisticated art forms and cultural events to all people regardless of their social status. What everyone would agree, however, is that Western culture has become global in its scope. The result has been a greater richness and heightened level of appreciation and awareness for members of Western civilization.

The past five centuries have seen Western civilization question and challenge many of its traditional values. A greater emphasis has been placed on the individual. Although racism and sexism still exist, great strides have been made in protecting the rights of every individual regardless of race, religion, sex, physical or mental ability, or ethnic origin. In addition, the belief in continuous human progress has been replaced with a recognition of the fragility of the human condition and an awareness of the critical state of the environment in our modern world. As barriers of doctrine, nationality, and race begin to crumble in the late twentieth century, a growing number of people are banding together in common causes that will affect our global future. If the past century has emphasized the differences among us, the next promises to focus upon our common characteristics.

In studying modern Western civilization the day-to-day realities of human existence may become obscured in the ebb and flow of historical trends and events. Perhaps the most important observation we can make is of the role of the individual in the course of history. Revolutions, economic patterns, imperialism, war, and social changes are really the stories of people. Millions, thousands, or even one individual can make a significant difference to the experience of humanity. The impact of the British navy on the history of the eighteenth and nineteenth centuries is no more significant than the impact of Beethoven or Marie Curie. Often, when we sit in judgment on past events, we forget that critical decisions were made by individuals, doing the best they could without the benefit of historical hindsight. When we apply the standards by which we judge our decision makers today to the leaders of the past, it gives us a clearer picture of the challenges they faced.

Another principal focus of any study of modern Western civilization has to be an appreciation of the cultural richness of the Western experience. If social development, values, and norms are fluid, then so too are the artistic manifestations they exhibit. A study of dates, events, and economic and political trends leaves only a barren field without the rich foliage of humanity's accomplishments.

As you complete this book on modern Western civilization, you are ready to turn the first page in the next chapter of our collective experience. The lives and accomplishments of your generation will form the basis of study for future students.

BIBLIOGRAPHY

Introduction

Bronowski, J. *The Ascent of Man*. London: British Broadcasting Corporation, 1976.

Burke, J. *The Day the Universe Changed*. London: British Broadcasting Corporation, 1985.

Janson, H.W., D.J. Janson, and J. Kerman. *A History of Art and Music*. Englewood Cliffs, NJ: Prentice-Hall, 1968.

Kennedy, P. *The Rise and Fall of the Great Powers: Economic Change and Military Conflict from 1500 to 2000*. New York: Random House, 1987.

Lang, P.H. *Music in Western Civilization*. New York: W.W. Norton and Co., 1960.

Ronan, C.A. *Science: Its History and Development Among the World's Cultures*. New York: Hamblyn, 1982.

Chapter One: Absolutism in the Age of Reason

Drake, S. ed. *Discoveries and Opinions of Galileo*. Garden City, NY: Doubleday and Co., 1957.

Grout, D.J. *A History of Western Music*. New York: W.W. Norton and Co. Inc., 1973.

Irwin, D. ed. *Winckelmann: Writings on Art*. London: Phaidon Press, 1972.

Kennedy, P. *The Rise and Fall of the Great Powers*. London: Unwin Hyman, 1988.

Ogg, D. *Europe of the Ancien Regime 1715–1783*. London: Collins, 1965.

Ranum, O. and Patricia Ranum, eds. *The Century of Louis XIV*. New York: Harper and Row, 1972.

Rowen, H. *From Absolution to Revolution 1648–1848*. New York: Macmillan, 1968.

Snyder, L. ed. *Frederick the Great*. Englewood Cliffs, NJ: Prentice-Hall, 1971.

Tuchman, B. *Practicing History*. New York: Ballantine Books, 1981.

Chapter Two: The Age of Reason: The Enlightenment to 1789

Becker, C. *The Heavenly City of the Eighteenth Century Philosophes*. New Haven, CT: Yale University Press, 1932.

Bufkozer, M. *Music in the Baroque Era*. New York: W.W. Norton and Co., 1947.

Butterfield, H. *The Origins of Modern Science*. New York: Macmillan, 1951.

Crocker, L.G., ed. *The Age of the Enlightenment*. New York: Walker, 1969.

Hall, A.R. *From Galileo to Newton, 1630–1720*. New York: Harper and Row, 1963.

Rosen, C. *The Classical Style: Haydn, Mozart, Beethoven*. New York: W.W. Norton and Co., 1972.

Smith, A.G.R. *Science and Society in the Sixteenth and Seventeenth Centuries*. New York: Harcourt Brace Jovanovich, 1972.

Chapter Three: French Revolutionary Europe to 1815

Breunig, C. *The Age of Revolution and Reaction: 1789–1950*. New York: W.W. Norton and Co., 1977.

Burke, E. *Reflections on the Revolution in France*. Harmondsworth, UK: Penguin Books, 1969.

Creal, M. *The Dynamics of Revolution: France 1789–94*. Toronto: Macmillan, 1970.

Lefebvre, G. *The Coming of the French Revolution*. Princeton: Princeton University Press, 1947.

———. *The Directory*. New York: Vintage Books, 1964.

Gershoy, L. *The Era of the French Revolution 1789–1799*. Princeton: Anvil Press, 1957.

Paine, T. *The Rights of Man*. Harmondsworth, UK: Penguin Books, 1969.

Rude, G. *Revolutionary Europe 1783–1815*. London: Collins, 1964.

Schama, S. *Citizens*. Toronto: Random House, 1989.

Wollstonecraft, M. *A Vindication of the Rights of Woman*. Ed. by Carol H. Poston. New York: W.W. Norton and Co., 1975.

Chapter Four: Nationalism in Europe, 1815 to 1880

Hobsbawm, E.J. *The Age of Revolution: 1789–1848*. New York: Times Mirror, 1962.

Kohn, H. *Nationalism: Its Meaning and History*. Princeton, NJ: Van Nostrand, 1955.

May, A.J. *The Age of Metternich, 1814–1848*. Rev. ed. New York: Holt, Rinehart, and Winston, 1963.

Pflanze, O. *Bismarck and the Development of Germany: The Period of Unification, 1815–1871*. Princeton, NJ: Princeton University Press, 1963.

Simon, W.M. *Germany in the Age of Bismarck*. London: Allen and Unwin, 1968.

Snyder, L. *The Meaning of Nationalism*. Westport, CT: Greenwood Press, 1968.

Talmon, J.L. *Romanticism and Revolt: Europe 1815–1848*. London: Thames and Hudson, 1967.

de Tocqueville, A. *Recollections*. New York: Columbia University Press, 1949.

Chapter Five: The Industrial Revolution to 1880

Ashton, T.S. *The Industrial Revolution, 1760–1830*. Oxford: Oxford University Press, 1948, 1972.

Engels, F. *The Condition of the Working Class in England*. Trans. and ed. by W.O. Henderson and W.H. Chaloner. Stanford: Stanford University Press, 1968.

Henderson, W.O. *The Industrialization of Europe, 1780–1914*. London: Thames and Hudson, 1969.

Klingender, F. *Art and the Industrial Revolution*. St. Albans, UK: Paladin, 1972.

Landes, D.S. *The Unbound Prometheus: Technological Change and Industrial Development in Western Europe from 1750 to the Present*. Cambridge, UK: Cambridge University Press, 1969.

Taylor, P. ed. *The Industrial Revolution in Britain: Triumph or Disaster*. Boston: D.C. Heath & Co., 1970.

Thompson, E.P. *The Making of the English Working Class*. New York: Vintage Books, 1966.

Chapter Six: Romanticism, 1815 to 1848

Barzun, J. *Classic, Romantic and Modern*. Boston: Little, Brown, 1961.

Clark, K. *The Romantic Rebellion*. New York: Harper and Row, 1973.

Jones, H.M. *Revolution and Romanticism*. Cambridge, MA: Belknap Press of Harvard University Press, 1974.

Longyear, R.M. *Nineteenth Century Romanticism in Music*. Englewood Cliffs, NJ: Prentice-Hall, 1969.

Peckham, M. *Romanticism, The Culture of the Nineteenth Century*. New York: G. Braziller, 1965.

Schmitt, C. *Political Romanticism*. Trans. by G. Oakes. Cambridge, MA: MIT Press, 1986.

Talmon, J.L. *Romanticism and Revolt: Europe 1815 to 1848*. London: Thames and Hudson, 1967.

Chapter Seven: Nineteenth-century Ideas and Perceptions of Reality

Barry, J. Transl. and ed. *George Sand: In Her Own Words*. Garden City, NY: Anchor Books, 1979.

Darwin, C. *The Origin of Species*, Ed. by J.W. Burrow. Harmondsworth, UK: Penguin Books, 1968.

Korey, K. *The Essential Darwin*. Toronto: Little, Brown, 1984.

Nachlin, L. ed. *Realism and Tradition in Art 1848–1900*. Englewood Cliffs, NJ: Prentice-Hall, 1966.

Schoenwald R. ed. *Nineteenth Century Thought: The Discovery of Change*. Englewood Cliffs, NJ: Prentice-Hall, 1965.

Thomson, D. *England in the Nineteenth Century*. Harmondsworth, UK: Penguin Books, 1950.

Tucker, R.C. ed. *The Marx-Engels Reader*. New York: W.W. Norton, 1978.

Weber, M. *The Methodology of the Social Sciences*. New York: The Free Press, 1949.

Chapter Eight: The Tradition Challenged: The Human Crisis, 1880 to 1918

Freud, S. *The Interpretation of Dreams*. Trans. by James Strachey. New York: Avon Books, 1965.

Van Gogh, V. *The Complete Letters of Vincent Van Gogh*. Greenwich, CT: New York: Graphic Society, 1959.

Nietzsche, F. *The Will to Power*. Trans. by W. Kaufmann and R.J. Hollingdale. New York: Vintage Books, 1968.

Read, H. *A Concise History of Modern Painting*. London: Thames and Hudson, 1974.

Schlipp, P.A. ed. *Albert Einstein: Philosopher-Scientist*. New York: Tudor Publishing, 1951.

Tuchman, B. *The Proud Tower*. New York: Macmillan, 1976.

Chapter Nine: The Tradition Challenged: The Global Crisis, 1880 to 1918

Derfler, L. *The Third French Republic, 1870–1940*. Princeton: Van Nostrand, 1966.

Granatstein, J.L. and R.D. Cuff. *War and Society in North America*. Toronto: Thomas Nelson, 1971.

Green, T. *Wilson at Versailles*. Boston: D.C. Heath and Co., 1965.

Kolko, G. *Main Currents in American Foreign Policy*. New York: Pantheon Books, 1984.

Plesur, M. *Creating an American Empire, 1869–1914*. New York: Jerome S. Ozer, 1971.

Snyder, L. *Historic Documents of World War I*. Toronto: Van Nostrand, 1958.

Solzhenitsyn, A. *August 1914*. Harmondsworth, UK: Penguin Books, 1974.

Stone, R. ed. *Wilson and the League of Nations*. New York: Holt, Rinehart and Winston, 1967.

Tuchman, B. *The Guns of August*. New York: Dell Publishing, 1962.

________. *The Zimmerman Telegram*. New York: Ballantine Books, 1966.

Chapter Ten: The Global Search for Norms

Bullock, A. *Hitler, A Study in Tyranny*. New York: Harper and Row, 1962.

Churchill, W. *The Second World War*. 6 vols. Boston: Houghton Mifflin, 1948–1954.

Clark. A. *Barbarossa: The Russian-German Conflict, 1941–1945*. New York: Morrow, 1965.

Conquest, R. *The Great Terror: Stalin's Purge of the Thirties*. New York: Macmillan, 1968.

Davidowicz, L., ed. *A Holocaust Reader*. New York: Behrman House, 1976.

________. *The War Against the Jews, 1933–1945*. New York: Holt, Rinehart and Wilson, 1975.

Frank, A. *The Diary of a Young Girl*. Trans. by B.M. Mooyaart, New York: Pocket Books, 1953.

Shirer, W. *The Rise and Fall of the Third Reich*. New York: Simon and Schuster, 1960.

Speer, A. *Inside the Third Reich: Memoirs*. Trans. by R. and C. Winston. New York: Macmillan, 1970.

Tannebaum, E.R. *The Fascist Experience: Italian Society and Culture, 1922–1945*. New York: Basic Books, 1972.

Taylor, A.J.P. *The Origins of the Second World War*. New York: Atheneum, 1966.

Wiskemann, E. *Europe of the Dictators, 1919–1945*. New York: Harper and Row, 1966.

Wolfe, B.D. *Three Who Made a Revolution: A Biographical History*. London: Thames and Hudson, 1956.

Chapter Eleven: The Age of Anxiety: Intellectual and Cultural Trends

Baumer, F. *Modern European Thought: Continuity and Change in Ideas, 1600–1950*. New York: Macmillan, 1977.

Benson, F.R. *Writers in Arms: The Literary Impact of the Spanish Civil War*. New York: New York University Press, 1967.

Booker, M. *Music in the Twentieth Century: Composers and Their Work*. Ifracombe: Stockwell, 1980.

Crossman, R. ed. *The God That Failed: Six Studies in Communism*. London: Hamish Hamilton, 1950.

Ganow, G. *Thirty Years That Shook Physics*. Garden City, NJ: Doubleday & Co., 1966.

Gay, P. *Weimar Culture*. New York: Harper & Row, 1970.

Hofmann, W. *Turning Points in Twentieth Century Art*. New York: G. Braziller, 1969.

Ortega, y Gassett, J. *The Revolt of the Masses*. New York: W.W. Norton and Co., 1932.

Schiller, G. *Early Jazz: Its Roots and Musical Development*. New York: Oxford University Press, 1968.

Chapter Twelve: The Politics of the Western World

Acheson, D. *Present at the Creation*. New York: Signet Books, 1969.

Foner, P.S. *The Voice of Black America*. New York: Simon and Schuster, 1972.

Haley, A. *The Autobiography of Malcolm X*. New York: Ballantine Books, 1964.

Kennedy, P. *The Rise and Fall of the Great Powers*. London: Unwin Hyman, 1988.

King, M.L. *Why We Can't Wait!* New York: Signet Books, 1964.

Kolko, G. *The Limits of Power: The World and United States Foreign Policy, 1945–54*. New York: Harper and Row, 1972.

Lafeber, W. *America, Russia and the Cold War*. New York: John Wiley and Sons, 1967.

Landsberg, M. *Women and Children First*. Toronto: Macmillan of Canada 1982.

Turner J. and L. Emery, eds. *Perspectives for Women in the 1980s*. Winnipeg: University of Manitoba Press, 1983.

Weisberger, B.A. *Cold War, Cold Peace*. New York: American Heritage, 1985.

Chapter Thirteen: The Individual and the Community: Decolonization and the West

Caputo, P. *Rumour of War*. New York: Holt, Rinehart and Winston, 1977.

Fitzgerald, F. *Fire in the Lake*. New York; Vintage Books, 1973.

Gettleman, M. *et al.*, *Vietnam and America: A Documentary History*. New York: Grove Press, 1985.

Morrison, D. ed. *Massacre in Beijing: China's Struggle for Democracy*. New York: Time Life Books Inc., 1989.

Searle, C. *Grenada: The Struggle Against Destabilization*. New York: Writers and Readers Publishing Inc., 1984.

Snyder, L. ed. *The Imperialism Reader: Documents and Readings on Modern Expansionism*. Princeton: Van Nostrand Co., 1962.

Stairs, D. *The Diplomacy of Constraint: Canada, the Korean War and the United States*. Toronto; University of Toronto Press, 1974.

Tuchman, B. *The March of Folly*, New York: Alfred Knopf, 1984.

Chapter Fourteen: Science and Technology

Carson, R. *Silent Spring*. Boston: Houghton Mifflin, 1987.

Edwards, G. *The Nuclear Debate: From Chalk River to Chernobyl*. Toronto: Lorimer, 1987.

Meadows, D.H., D. Meadows, J. Randeas, and W. Behrens. *The Limits of Growth: A Report for the Club of Rome's Project on the Predicament of Mankind*. 2nd ed. New York: Universe Books, 1974.

Seymour, J., and H. Giradet. *Blueprint for a Green Planet: Your Practical Guide to Restoring the World's Environment*. Englewood Cliffs, NJ: Prentice-Hall, 1987.

Toffler, A. *Future Shock*. New York: Random House, 1970.

The World Commission on Environment and Development. *Our Common Future*. Oxford: Oxford University Press, 1987.

Chapter Fifteen: Themes for Our Times

Corwin, N. *Trivializing America: The Triumph of Mediocrity*. Seacaucus, NJ: Lyle Stuart, 1988.

Duncan, B. *Mass Media and Popular Culture*. Toronto: Harcourt, Brace, Jovanovich, 1988.

Hall, J.B. and B. Ulanov. eds. *Modern Culture and the Arts*. New York: McGraw-Hill, 1967.

Leuchtenburg, W.E. *A Troubled Feast: Society Since 1945*. Boston: Little, Brown and Co., 1973.

Menuhin, Y. and C.W. Davis. *The Music of Man*. Toronto: Methuen, 1979.

Read, H. *A Concise History of Modern Painting*. New York: Oxford University Press, 1974.

Russell, B. *The ABC of Relativity*. New York: Signet Science Library, 1958.

Singer, B.D. *Communications in Canadian Society*. Don Mills, Ont.: Addison-Wesley, 1983.

Stearn, G.E. *McLuhan: Hot and Cold*. New York: Signet Books, 1967.

Wills, G. *Reagan's America*. New York: Penguin Books, 1988.

PHOTO CREDITS

page iii Reproduced by permission of the Estate of Jack Bush. Copyright 1990; **page 4** The Bettmann Archive; **page 11** The Granger Collection, New York; **page 14** The Bettmann Archive; **page 19** The Bettmann Archive; **page 20** Canapress Photo Service; **page 21 (top)** UPI/Bettmann Archive **(bottom)** Canapress Photo Service; **page 37** The Bettmann Archive; **page 38** The Granger Collection, New York; **page 44** The Bettmann Archive; **page 45** The Granger Collection, New York; **page 47** The Bettmann Archive; **page 57** James R. Christopher; **page 63** The Granger Collection, New York; **page 67** James R. Christopher; **page 68** The Granger Collection, New York; **page 71** The Granger Collection, New York; **page 72** The Granger Collection, New York; **page 96** The Granger Collection, New York; **page 102** The Bettmann Archive; **page 103** The Bettmann Archive; **page 119** Mary Evans Picture Library; **page 120** Private collection; **page 121** Bettmann/Hulton; **page 122** The Granger Collection, New York; **page 126** The Granger Collection, New York; **page 128** The Bettmann Archive; **page 144** The Bettmann Archive; **page 147 (left and right)** The Granger Collection, New York; **page 148** Foto Marburg/Art Resource, New York (192 161) C.D. Friedrich, The monk and the sea. Berlin, National Gallery; **page 149 (top)** The Bettmann Archive **(bottom)** The Granger Collection, New York; **page 150** The Bettmann Archive; **page 151 (top)** Mary Evans Picture Library **(bottom)** UPI/Bettman; **page 155** Bildarchiv Preussischer Kulturbesitz; **page 160** The Bettmann Archive; **page 164** The Granger Collection, New York; **page 169** The Granger Collection, New York; **page 175** The Bettmann Archive; **page 177** The Bettmann Archive; **page 180** The Granger Collection, New York; **page 184** The Bettmann Archive; **page 186** The Bettmann Archive; **page 187** The Bettmann Archive; **page 188** Private collection; **page 190** The Granger Collection, New York; **page 212** The Granger Collection, New York; **page 214** James R. Christopher; **page 216** Canapress Photo Service; **page 217** The Granger Collection, New York; **page 219** The Bettmann Archive; **page 221** The Granger Collection, New York; **page 231** Canapress Photo Service; **page 235** The Bettmann Archive; **page 252** Trustees of the Imperial War Museum; **page 254 (top)** Canapress Photo Service **(bottom)** Culver Pictures Inc.; **page 255** Canapress Photo Service; **page 257** Mary Evans Picture Library; **page 270** UPI/Bettman; **page 278** Canapress Photo Service; **page 285** Canapress Photo Service; **page 288** The Bettmann Archive; **page 290** The Bettmann Archive; **page 291** Canapress Photo Service; **page 294** Canapress Photo Service; **page 296** UPI/Bettmann; **page 298** The Bettmann Archive; **page 300** The Bettmann Archive; **page 302** Peter Byron/Black Star/First Light; **page 307** The Bettmann Archive; **page 327 (top)** Meret Oppenheim, Object (1936) Fur covered cup, saucer and spoon; cup 10.9 cm diameter; saucer 23.7 cm diameter; spoon 20.2 cm long; overall height 7.3 cm Collection, The Museum of Modern Art, New York. Purchase.: © Meret Oppenheim 1991/VIS*ART Copyright Inc. **(bottom)** Georgia O'Keeffe, *Stables*, 1932, oil on canvas (12 × 32 inches), accession no. 45.454 © The Detroit Institute of Arts, Gift of Robert H. Tannahil; **page 328** The Granger Collection, New York; **page 329** The Bettmann Archive; **page 330** Canapress Photo Service; **page 331** The Granger Collection, New York; **page 332** Canapress Photo Service; **page 334** UPI/Bettmann; **page 335** Canapress Photo Service; **page 378** UPI/Bettmann; **page 379** UPI/Bettmann; **page 380** Reuters/Bettmann; **page 382** Canapress Photo Service; **page 385** Reuters/Bettman; **page 387** Canapress Photo Service; **page 391** UPI/Bettmann; **page 394** Canapress Photo Service; **page 412** UPI/Bettmann; **page 414** UPI/Bettmann; **page 418** Canapress Photo Service; **page 421** Canapress Photo Service; **page 423** Reuters/Bettman; **page 424** Canapress Photo Service; **page 427** Canapress Photo Service; **page 448** Canapress Photo Service; **page 449** The Bettmann Archive; **page 451** IBM; **page 454** Dr. Robert Gale/Sygma/Publiphoto; **page 457** Telesat Canada; **page 460** Canapress Photo Service; **page 463** Reuters/Bettmann; **page 482** Superstock/Four By Five, © Jackson Pollock 1991/VIS*ART Copyright Inc.; **page 483** Tate Gallery, London/Art Resource, New York (T897) Roy Lichtenstein, Whaam! London, Tate. © Roy Lichtenstein 1991/VIS*ART Copyright Inc.; **page 486 (left)** Canapress Photo Service **(right)** United Nations Photo; **page 487 (top)** Guy Marche/Miller Comstock **(bottom)** Canapress Photo Service; **page 490** Canapress Photo Service; **page 492** Canapress Photo Service; **page 494** James R. Christopher.

INDEX